CLASSIC TEST

Classic
Testimonies Omnibus

Run Baby Run

NICKY CRUZ

The Hiding Place

CORRIE TEN BOOM

Chasing the Dragon

JACKIE PULLINGER

Hodder & Stoughton
LONDON SYDNEY AUCKLAND

This omnibus edition first published 1997

Run Baby Run first published in Great Britain 1969
by arrangement with Logos International, Plainfield,
New Jersey, USA
Copyright © Nicky Cruz and Jamie Buckingham, 1968

The Hiding Place first published in Great Britain 1972
Copyright © Corrie ten Boom and John
and Elizabeth Sherrill, 1971

Chasing the Dragon first published in Great Britain 1980
Copyright © Jackie Pullinger and Andrew Quicke, 1980
This story is fact but for obvious reasons
some names have been changed

1 3 5 7 9 10 8 6 4 2

British Library Cataloguing in Publication Data
A record for this book is available from the British Library

ISBN 0 340 67893 3

Typeset by Hewer Text Composition Services, Edinburgh
Printed and bound in Great Britain by
Cox & Wyman Ltd, Reading, Berkshire

Hodder and Stoughton Ltd
A Division of Hodder Headline PLC
338 Euston Road
London NW1 3BH

Run Baby Run

Nicky Cruz with Jamie Buckingham

a Gloria

El corazón de su marido está en ella confiado.

PROVERBIOS 31:11

Preface

When I undertook this project Catherine Marshall remarked that writing a book of this nature was like having a baby. I was going to have to live with it until it was born.

In this case, not only did I have to live with it, but so did my family and the congregation of the Tabernacle Baptist Church where I was pastoring. They suffered through every bout of morning sickness, every labour pain, and even a couple of false deliveries. But family and church both realized this book was conceived of the Holy Spirit, written with prayer and tears, and was to be published to the glory of God. The church virtually released me from all obligations until it was finished and several pitched in and helped share the typing duties.

However, it was John and Tibby Sherrill and the editors of *Guideposts* magazine who were the god-parents of the book. It was John's recommendation and confidence that initiated the project and in the end it was the Sherrills' criticism that gave us the final insight into the stark but beautiful story of the life of Nicky Cruz.

But the credit for the actual movement of the story goes to Patsy Higgins, who volunteered her services to the glory of God. She lived and breathed the manuscript as critic, editor and typist – displaying a talent for cutting and rewriting that could have come only from God.

The book itself defies one of the basic literary laws. It closes with an open end. No nice, neat wrap-up here. Every time I'd interview Nicky he'd relate some fantastic new experiences taking place in his life. But this is material for a sequel – perhaps several. Therefore, 'Run

7

Baby Run' is the story, told as accurately as possible, of the first twenty-nine years of the life of a young man whose greatest days are yet ahead.

Jamie Buckingham
Eau Gallie, Florida

Contents

Introduction

RUN BABY RUN, the story of Nicky Cruz, is remarkable. It has all the elements of tragedy, violence, and intrigue – plus the greatest of all ingredients: the power of the Gospel of Jesus Christ.

The first chapters form a dark, foreboding background for the thrilling denouement of this unusual story. So, don't despair of the somewhat gory atmosphere delineated in the first half of the story.

Nicky is a young man, and today he is making an impact upon great segments of our youth in these United States. The adult population can no longer ignore the youth with their staggering twentieth-century problems. They search for meaning. They are not enamored with our time-worn social taboos. They press for sincerity in religion, for honesty in politics, and for fairness for the underprivileged. The encouraging thing about these millions of "new folk" (who will by 1970 outnumber the adult population), they are desperately searching for answers. In my contact with hundreds of students on our university campuses, I am tremendously impressed with their quest for truth, for reality, and for honest answers. Some of the young people in our ghettos are restless for a fair deal from society, and justly so. Some of them are influenced by advocates of violence and mob rule, and are easily sucked into the vortex of rioting, burning and looting. Nicky Cruz is a glowing example that restless youth can find meaning and purpose in Christ.

In our crusades nearly half of our audiences are under the age of twenty-five. They do not come to scoff, but in a sincere search for truth and purpose, and hundreds of them respond to the call of Christ.

Run Baby Run is a thrilling story! My hope is that it

shall have a wide reading, and that those who read shall
come to know the Christ who changed the empty, restless
heart of Nicky Cruz and has made him a Christian legend
in his time.

Billy Graham

Foreword

Nicky's story is possibly the most dramatic in the history of the Pentecostal movement, but it is not unique. Nicky is only a very colorful representative of a vast number of people who, in the past few decades, have been delivered from crime, alcoholism, drug addiction, prostitution, homosexuality, and almost every type of perversion and degeneration known to man. Psychiatric care, medical treatment, and spiritual counseling had failed to affect these people, when with astounding abruptness they were set free from their bonds by the power of the Holy Spirit and led to a life of useful service and sometimes of profound prayer.

It is natural to suspect the genuineness of changes that are so radical and abrupt. But there is no theological reason to discount them. God's grace can take hold of a man in an instant and transform a sinner into a saint. "I say to you that God is able out of these stones to raise up children to Abraham" (Luke 3:8). Human effort cannot produce such changes, either in oneself or in others, because nature needs time to develop gradually; but God can do in an instant what takes man years and years.

Such conversions have occurred in the history of Christianity ever since the beginning. Zachaeus, Mary Magdalene (i.e. the penitent of Luke 7:37), the "Good Thief", St. Paul, and even St. Matthew are the beginning of a long list. However, the great number of such conversions that are taking place today in connection with what is called the "Pentecostal Movement" is, I believe, without precedent. What is the meaning of this amazing fact?

I have often wondered about this, and what comes to my mind over and over is the parable of the marriage feast (Matthew 22:1-14). When the invited guests did not show, the master told his servants, "Go out quickly into the streets and lanes of the city, and bring in here the poor, and the crippled, and the blind, and the lame" (Luke 14:21). When even that did not suffice, the servants were sent out once more, this time to the highways and hedges, with the order, "Make them come in, so that my house may be filled."

I believe that this is what we are seeing take place today. The "invited guests" at the table of the Lord, that is the "born Christians", the righteous, the law-abiding members of society, have too often proved themselves unworthy. They have "gone to Church", but they have not really partaken of the banquet provided by the King. This is why the Church, instead of being a living Body and a challenging witness, so often appears as an ineffectual pious custom.

But while the pundits discuss what new vocabulary will bring God back to life (because all they know about Him is words), and what new symbols will make the liturgy meaningful (because all they see in religion is man's part), God Himself is quietly gathering new guests for His Banquet. And He is gladly taking in those who, by human standards, are spiritually and morally poor, crippled, blind, and lame. And by the power of His Spirit, He is indeed "making" them come in, snatching them off the streets of degradation and the by-ways of perversion.

Nicky Cruz and the thousands like him are not just moving examples of the Good Shepherd's faithful love, they are also signs of the times which we had better not fail to read. They are an encouraging sign that God is acting with new power in our time, so that we should not be afraid to declare the Gospel boldly to anyone. They are also a sign of warning to anyone who feels that, because of his habits of piety, or his sacred ministry, or for any other reason whatsoever, he has an established title to a place at the banquet table. "I tell you that none of those who were invited shall taste of my supper" (Luke 14:24). For "the marriage feast indeed is ready, but those who were invited were not worthy" (Matthew 22:8).

Prof. Edward D. O'Connor, C.S.C.
University of Notre Dame

1

No One Cares

"Stop that crazy kid!" someone shouted.

The door of the Pan Am Constellation had just swung open and I darted down the steps toward the terminal at New York's Idlewild Airport. It was January 4, 1955, and the cold wind stung my cheeks and ears.

Just hours before my father had put me aboard the plane in San Juan, a rebellious, bitter fifteen-year-old Puerto Rican kid. I had been assigned to the pilot's custody and told to remain in the plane until turned over to my brother, Frank. But when the door opened I was the first one out, running wildly across the concrete apron.

Three line attendants converged on me, pinning me against the rough chain link fence beside the gate. The bitter wind whipped through my thin, tropical clothing as I tried to pull free. A gate policeman grabbed me by the arm and the attendants scurried back to their jobs. It was a game to me and I looked up at the cop and grinned.

"You crazy Puerto Rican! What the hell do you think you're doing?" he said.

My grin faded as I sensed the hatred in his voice. His fat cheeks were flushed in the biting cold and his eyes watered from the wind. He had a stub of an unlit cigar chomped in his flabby lips. Hate! I felt it surge through my body. The same hate I had felt toward my father and mother, my teachers, the cops in Puerto Rico. Hate! I tried to twist free but he held my arm in an iron-vice grip.

"Com'on, kid, let's go back to the plane." I looked up at him and spat.

"Pig!" he snarled. "Filthy Spic!" He loosened his hold

15

on my arm and tried to grab me by the back of the neck. Ducking under his arm, I slithered through the open gate that led inside the terminal.

Behind me was shouting and pounding feet. I raced down the long concourse swerving in and out of the mobs making their way to planes. Suddenly, I emerged in a large terminal room. Spotting an outside door, I darted across the floor and out into the street.

A large bus was sitting at the curb, door open, engine throbbing. People were boarding and I elbowed my way into line. The driver grabbed me by the shoulder and asked for my fare. I shrugged my shoulders and answered him in Spanish. He gruffly shoved me out of line, too busy to fool with a silly kid who could barely understand English. As he turned his attention to a woman who was fumbling with her purse, I ducked my head and squeezed behind her through the door and into the crowded bus. Glancing over my shoulder to make sure he hadn't seen me, I jostled my way to the rear and sat down next to a window.

As the bus pulled from the curb, I saw the fat gate guard and two others puff out the side door of the terminal looking in all directions. I couldn't resist knocking on the window, waving and grinning through the glass. I had made it.

Slumping down in the seat, I put my knees against the back of the seat in front of me and pressed my face against the cold dirty glass of the window.

The bus ground its way through the heavy New York traffic toward the middle of the city. Outside, there was snow and slush along the streets and sidewalks. I had always pictured snow as clean and beautiful, stretched out over acres of fairyland. But this was dingy, like dirty mush. My breath made fog on the window and I leaned back and ran my finger through it. It was a different world entirely from the one I had just left.

My mind flashed back to yesterday when I stood on the hillside in front of my home. I remembered the green grass under my feet, spotted with pastel dots of tiny wild flowers. The field sloped gently away toward the village below. I remembered the soft breeze against my cheek and the warmth of the sun against my bare bronzed back.

Puerto Rico is a beautiful land of sunshine and barefoot children. It is a land where men wear no shirts and women walk lazily in the sun. The sounds of the steel drums and strumming guitars are heard day and night. It's a land of singing, flowers, laughing children, and sparkling azure water.

But it is also a land of witchcraft and voodoo, of religious superstition and great ignorance. At night the sounds of the voodoo drums roll down from the palm-covered mountains as the witch doctors practice their trade – offering sacrifices and dancing with snakes in the light of flickering fires.

My parents were spiritualists. They made their living casting out demons and supposedly contacting dead spirits. Papa was one of the most feared men on the island. Well over six feet, his huge stooped shoulders had led the islanders to refer to him as "The Great One". He had been wounded during World War II and received a government pension. But there were seventeen boys and one girl in the family and after the war he turned to spiritualism to make a living.

Mama worked with Papa as a medium. Our house was the headquarters for all sorts of voodoo, seances, and sorcery. Hundreds of people came from all over the island to participate in seances and meditation sessions.

Our big house on top of the hill had a winding path that led to the sleepy little village of Las Piedras snuggled in the valley below. Villagers would climb the path at all hours of the day and night to come to the "Witch's House." They would try to talk to departed spirits, participate in sorcery, and ask Papa to deliver them from demons.

Papa was the director, but there were many other Puerto Rican mediums who would come and use our home for headquarters. Some would stay for weeks at a time conjuring up evil spirits and chasing out devils.

There was a long seance table in the front room around which the people sat while trying to communicate with dead spirits. Papa was well read on the subject and had a library of magic and sorcery books that was unequaled in that part of the island.

Early one morning two men brought an afflicted woman to the house. My brother, Gene, and I slipped out of bed and peeked through the door as they stretched her on the

long table. Her body was twitching and loud moans came
from her lips as the men stood at each end of the table
holding her down. Mama stood at her feet with her eyes
raised toward the ceiling chanting strange words. Papa went
to the kitchen and returned with a small black urn which
was filled with burning incense. He also had a large green
frog which he placed on the woman's quivering stomach.
Then, suspending the urn over her head with a small chain,
he sprinkled powder on her twitching body.

We stood shaking with fear as he commanded the evil
spirits to leave the woman and enter the frog. Suddenly,
the woman threw her head back and emitted a piercing
scream. The frog jumped off her stomach and smashed
itself against the doorsill. Suddenly she began to kick, and
twisting free from the grip of the men, rolled off the table
and fell heavily to the floor. She was slobbering and gnawing
her lips and tongue while blood mixed with froth drooled
from her mouth.

Eventually, she quieted down and lay very still. Papa
pronounced her cured and the men gave him money. They
picked up her unconscious form and backed out the door,
thanking Papa over and over and calling him, "The Great
Miracle Worker."

My early childhood was filled with fear and resentment.
The large family meant there was very little individual attention given to each child. I resented Papa and Mama and
was afraid of the sorcery that took place each night.

The summer before I started school Papa locked me in
the pigeon house. It was late in the evening and he had
caught me stealing money out of Mama's purse. I tried to
run but he reached out and grabbed me by the back of the
neck, "You can't run, baby. You're going to have to pay the
price for stealing."

"I hate you," I shouted.

He grabbed me off the ground, shaking me in front of him.
"I'll teach you to talk to your Papa like that," he bit out. Putting
me under his arm like a sack of grain he strode across the dark
yard to the pigeon house. I heard him fumbling with the lock
as he opened the door. "Inside," he snarled. "You can stay in
there with the birds until you learn your lesson."

He shoved me through the door and slammed it behind me, leaving me in total blackness. I heard the lock snap into place and Papa's muffled voice came through the cracks in the walls. "And no supper." I heard his footsteps fade into the distance back toward the house.

I was petrified with fear. Hammering my fists against the door, I kicked it frantically, shouting and screaming. Suddenly the shack was filled with the sound of wildly flapping wings as the frightened birds slammed against my body. I threw my hands over my face and screamed hysterically as the birds smashed against the walls and ferociously pecked at my face and neck. I collapsed to the filthy floor burying my head in my arms trying to protect my eyes and shut out the sound of the flapping wings overhead.

It seemed like an eternity before the door opened and Papa yanked me to my feet and dragged me into the yard. "Next time you'll remember not to steal and sass back when you're caught," he said harshly. "Now wash up and go to bed."

I cried myself to sleep that night, dreaming of the fluttering birds that slammed against my body.

My resentment against Papa and Mama carried over the next year when I started school. I hated all authority. Then, when I was eight years old, I turned against my parents completely. It was a hot summer afternoon and Mama and several other mediums were sitting at the big table in the living room drinking coffee. I had grown tired of playing with my brother and entered the room bouncing a small ball on the floor and catching it in my hand. One of the mediums said to Mama, "Your Nicky's a cute boy. He looks just like you. I know you must be very proud of him."

Mama looked hard at me and began to sway in her chair, rocking back and forth. Her eyes rolled back into her head until only the whites showed. She held her arms straight out in front of her across the top of the table. Her fingers stiffened and quivered as she slowly raised her arms above her head and began to speak in a sing-song tone of voice . . . "This . . . not . . . my . . . son. No, not Nicky. He never been mine. He child of greatest of all witches. Lucifer. No, not mine . . . no, not mine . . . Son of Satan, child of Devil."

I dropped the ball and it bounced across the room. I slowly backed up against the wall while Mama continued in her trance, her voice rising and falling as she chanted. "No, not mine, not mine . . . hand of Lucifer upon his life . . . finger of Satan touch his life . . . finger of Satan touch his soul . . . mark of beast on his heart . . . No, not mine . . . no, not mine."

I watched as the tears coursed down her cheeks. Suddenly, she turned at me with eyes wide and in a shrieking voice cried: "Get out, DEVIL! Get away from me. Leave me, DEVIL. Away! Away! Away!"

I was petrified with fear. I ran to my room and threw myself on my bed. The thoughts flowed through my mind like rivers churning down a narrow canyon. "Not her child . . . child of Satan . . . not love me . . . No one cares. No one cares."

Then the tears came and I began to scream and wail. The pain in my chest was unbearable and I pounded my fists against the bed until I was exhausted.

The old hate welled up inside me. Suddenly it consumed my soul, like a tidal wave over a coral reef. I hated my mother. God, how I hated her! I wanted to hurt her – to torture her – to get even. I threw open the door and ran screaming into the living room. The mediums were still there with Mama. I smashed my hands against the top of the table and screamed. I was so frustrated with hate I was stuttering and the words would not come plainly. "I-I-I . . . h-h-hate you." I pointed a quivering finger at Mama and shouted, "I-I-I . . . g-g-gonna make you pay. I gonna make you pay."

Two of my younger brothers stood curiously in the door as I pushed by them and ran out the back. Plunging down the steps, I turned and crept under the porch in the cool dark place where I had often gone to escape before. Crouching under the steps in the dry powdery dirt, I could hear the women laughing and above all the others I heard my mother's voice as it penetrated the floorboards. "See, I told you he Satan's child."

How I hated her! I wanted to destroy her but didn't know how. Pounding my fists into the dust I cried in frustration, my body shaking in convulsive sobs. "I hate you! I hate you! I hate you!" I cried. But no one heard – no one cared. In my frustration, I grabbed great handfuls of the soft dirt and furiously flung it in all directions. It settled on my face and turned to rivulets of mud as it mixed with the tears.

Eventually, the frenzy wore off and I sat silently. In the side yard, I could hear the other children playing. One of the younger boys was singing about birds and butterflies. But I felt isolated, alone. Tortured with hate and persecution, obsessed with fear, I heard the door of the pigeon house close and the heavy crunch of Papa's feet as he rounded the back corner of the house and started up the steps. Pausing, he peered into the shadows through the cracks in the wooden steps. "What you doing under there, boy?" I remained silent, hoping he wouldn't recognize me. He shrugged and went on up the steps, letting the screen door slam behind him.

No one cares, I thought.

Inside the house I could hear more laughter as my father's deep bass voice joined with the women. I knew they were still laughing at me.

The waves of hate flooded over me again. The tears coursed down my face and once more I began to scream. "I hate you, Mama! I hate you. I hate you. I hate you." My voice echoed against the emptiness under the house.

Reaching a stage of complete emotional climax I collapsed on my back in the dirt and rolled over and over, the dust covering my body. Exhausted, I closed my eyes and wept until I fell into a tortured sleep.

The sun had already sunk in the western sea when I awoke and crept out from under the porch. Sand still gritted between my teeth and my body was caked with grime. The frogs and crickets were chirping and the dew felt damp and cool against my bare feet.

Papa opened the back door and a shaft of yellow light fell on me as I stood at the foot of the steps. "Pig!" he shouted. "What you been doing under that house so long? Look at you. We don't want no pigs around here. Go clean up and come to supper."

I obeyed. But as I washed my body under the pump, I knew I would hate forever. I knew I would never love

again . . . anyone. And I knew I would never cry again
. . . never. Fear, dirt, and hate for the Son of Satan. I had
started to run.

It is the practice of many Puerto Rican families to send their
children to New York when they are old enough to take care
of themselves. Six of my older brothers already had left the
island and moved to New York. All were married and trying
to make a new life for themselves.

But I was too young to go. However, during the next five
years, my parents realized I couldn't stay in Puerto Rico
either. I had become a rebel at school. I was picking fights,
especially with the smaller children. One day I hit a small
girl on the head with a rock. I stood and stared with a warm
feeling as the blood oozed through her hair. The child was
screaming and crying while I stood laughing.

That night my father slapped my face until my mouth bled.
"Blood for blood," he shouted.

I bought a B.B. gun so I could kill birds. It wasn't enough
to kill them. I loved to mutilate their bodies. My brothers
would shy away from me because of my unusual craving for
blood.

In the eighth grade I had a fight with my shop teacher. He
was a tall, skinny man who liked to whistle at the ladies. One
day in class I called him "nigger." The room became quiet
and the other kids backed off among the shop machines,
sensing tension in the air.

The teacher walked back through the class to where I was
standing beside a lathe. "You know what, kid? You're a
phony."

I sassed him back, "Sorry, nigger. I don't mean to be a
phony."

Before I could move, he lashed out with his long skinny
arm and I felt the flesh of my lips mash against my teeth
under the savage blow. I tasted blood flowing into my mouth
and down over my chin.

I started toward him flailing both arms. He was a grown
man and I weighed less than 100 pounds, but I was filled
with hate and the blood set off the fuse. He put his hand
against my forehead and held me away with his arm while

I helplessly beat the air with my fists.

Realizing the hopelessness of the situation, I backed off. "You've had it now, nigger," I shouted. "I'm going to the police. Just wait and see." I ran out of the classroom.

He ran after me calling, "Wait. I'm sorry." But I was gone.

I didn't go to the police. Instead, I went to Papa and told him the teacher tried to kill me. He was infuriated. He marched in the house and came out with his huge pistol stuck in his belt. "Let's go, boy. I'm gonna kill myself a bully."

We headed back toward the school. I was having difficulty keeping up with Papa's long strides, half running behind him. My heart skipped as I thought of the thrill of seeing that tall teacher cringe beneath the fury of my Papa.

But the teacher wasn't in the classroom. "Wait here, boy," said Papa. "I'll talk to the principal and get to the bottom of this." I cringed, but waited.

Papa was in the principal's office a long time. When he came out, he walked rapidly toward me and yanked me up by the arm. "Alright, boy, you've got some explaining to do. Let's go home."

Once again we marched through the little village and back up the path to the house. He was pulling me behind him by my arm. "You filthy liar," he said to me in front of the house. He raised his hand to slap me but I ducked out of his reach and ran back down the path. "That's right. Run baby run!" he shouted. "You'll come home. And when you do I'm gonna lash you."

I did come home. But it was three days later. The police picked me up walking alongside a road heading back toward the inland mountains. I begged them to let me go but they returned me to my father. And he was true to his promise.

I knew I would leave again. And again. And I would run and run until I was so far away no one could ever bring me back. During the next two years, I ran away five times. Each time, the police found me and brought me home. Finally, in desperation, Papa and Mama wrote my brother, Frank, asking him if he would let me come and live with him. Frank agreed and plans were made for me to go.

The morning I left, the children lined up on the front porch.

Mama hugged me close to her bosom. There were tears in her eyes when she tried to speak, but no words came. I had no feeling for her one way or the other. Picking up my little suitcase, I sullenly turned my back and walked to the old pickup truck where Papa waited. I never looked back.

It was a forty-five-minute drive to the San Juan airport where Papa gave me my ticket and stuck a folded $10 bill in my hand. "Call Frank as soon as you reach New York," he said. "The pilot will take care of you until he comes."

He stood and looked at me for a long moment, towering over me, his shock of gray wavy hair blowing in the warm breeze. I must have seemed small and pathetic to him as I stood by the gate with my little bag in my hand. His lower lip quivered as he stuck out his hand to shake mine. Then, suddenly, he wrapped his long arms around my frail body and pulled me close to him. I heard him sob just once. "Hijo mio," (my son).

Releasing me, he said quickly, "Be a good boy, little bird." I turned and ran up the steps of the huge plane and took my seat beside a window.

Outside I could see the gaunt solitary figure of my father, "The Great One", as he stood beside the fence. He raised his hand once as if to wave but was self-conscious and turned and walked quickly back toward the old pickup.

What was it he had called me? "Little bird". I remembered that rare moment so many years before when sitting on the steps of the big porch Papa had called me that.

He sat in a rocking chair on the veranda smoking his pipe and told me about a bird that had become a legend in Puerto Rico. It had no legs and was continually on the wing. Papa looked down sadly at me, "That's you, Nicky. You're restless. Like a little bird, you'll ever be on the run." He slowly shook his head and looked up at the sky, blowing smoke toward the vines that tumbled off the porch roof.

"The bird is tiny and very light. He weighs no more than a feather and he picks the moving air currents and sleeps on the wind. He's always running. Running from hawks. Eagles. Owls. Birds of prey. He hides by keeping himself between them and the sun. If they ever get above him they can see him against the dark earth. But his little wings are transparent, like the clear water in the lagoon. As long as he stays high they can't see him. He never rests."

Papa sat back and blew a stream of blue smoke into the fresh air. "But how does he eat?" I asked.

"He eats on the wing," Papa replied. He talked slowly, like he had seen the tiny creature. "He catches insects and butter-flies. He has no legs — no feet — he is forever moving."

I was fascinated by the story. "But what about in gray weather?" I had asked him. "What happens when the sun doesn't shine? How does he escape his enemies then?"

"In gray weather, Nicky," Papa said, "he flies so high no one can see him. The only time he ever stops flying — the only time he ever stops running — the only time he comes to earth — is when he dies. For once he touches the earth, he can never run again."

Papa patted me on the bottom and shooed me away from the house. "Go now, little bird. Run and fly. Your Papa will call you when it is time to run no more."

I skipped through the grassy field flapping my arms like a bird trying to take off. But for some reason I could never seem to gain enough speed to be airborne.

The motors of the plane coughed, belched black smoke, and roared to life. At last, I was going to fly. I was on my way. . . .

The bus jerked to a stop. Outside, the bright lights and multicolored signs blinked and gleamed in the cold darkness. The man across the aisle got up to leave. I followed him out the back door. The doors swished shut behind me and the bus pulled away from the curb. I was left alone in the middle of eight million people.

I picked up a handful of dirty snow and brushed the crust off the top. There it was, sparkling white and pure. I wanted to put it to my mouth and eat it but as I watched, small dark spots began to appear on the surface. I suddenly realized the air was filled with soot from the chimneys above and the snow was taking on the appearance of cottage cheese sprinkled with black pepper.

I threw it to one side. It made little difference. I was free.

For two days I wandered through the city. I found an old coat thrown across a garbage can in a back alley. The sleeves drooped over my hands and the hem scraped the sidewalk. The buttons had been ripped off and the pockets torn open, but it kept me warm. That night I slept on the subway, curled up on one of the seats.

By the end of the second day, the excitement had worn off. I was hungry . . . and cold. On two occasions, I tried to talk to people and ask for help. The first man simply ignored me. He walked by like I wasn't there. The second man pushed me back against the wall, "Beat it, Spic. Don't put your greasy hands on me." I was afraid. I kept trying to keep the panic from bubbling up from my stomach into my throat.

That evening I walked the streets again. The long overcoat dragging the sidewalk, my little suitcase clutched in my hand. People would move around me and look back but no one seemed to care. They just looked and walked on.

That night I spent the $10 Papa had given me. I stopped in a little restaurant and ordered a hot dog by pointing at a picture of one that hung over the greasy counter. I gobbled it up and pointed that I wanted another. The man at the counter shook his head and held out his hand. I reached in my pocket and pulled out the wadded up bill. Wiping his hands on a towel, he opened it up, stretched it a couple of times, and then slipped it in the pocket of his dirty apron. He then brought me another hot dog and a bowl of chili. When I finished, I looked for him but he had disappeared into the kitchen. I picked up my bag and went back into the cold street. I'd had my first experience with American enterprise. And how was I to know that American hot dogs didn't cost $5 each?

Moving on down the street I stopped in front of a church. A heavy iron gate had been pulled across the front doors and it was fastened with a chain and padlock. I stood in front of the gray stone building, looking up at the steeple which pointed toward the heavens. The cold stone walls and dark stained glass windows huddled for protection behind the iron fence. The statue of a man with a kind face and sad eyes peered through the locked gate. His arms were outstretched and covered with snow. But he was locked in. And I was locked out.

I shuffled on down the street . . . moving . . . moving.

The panic was creeping back. It was almost midnight and I was shaking not only from the cold but from fear. I kept hoping someone would stop and ask if they could help me. I don't know what I would have said if someone had offered to help. But I was lonely. And afraid. And lost.

The hurrying crowd moved on and left me. I never knew a person could be lonely in the midst of a million people. To me, loneliness was being lost in the woods or on a desert island. But this was the worst of all loneliness. I saw fancy-dressed people coming home from the theater . . . old men selling newspapers and fruit from little all-night stands . . . policemen patrolling in pairs . . . sidewalks full of busy people. But as I looked in their faces they, too, seemed full of loneliness. No one was laughing. No one was smiling. All were in a hurry.

I sat down on the curb and opened my little suitcase. There, tucked inside, was a folded piece of paper with Frank's phone number in Mama's handwriting. Suddenly I felt something poking me from behind. It was an old shaggy dog, nosing at the huge overcoat draped around my thin frame. I put my arm around his neck and pulled him close to me. He licked my cheeks as I buried my head in his mangy hair.

I don't know how long I sat there trembling and stroking the dog. But when I looked up I saw the feet and legs of two uniformed policemen. Their rubber overshoes were wet and dirty. The mangy cur sensed danger and darted away into an alley.

One of the cops poked me in the shoulder with his night stick. "What'cha doing sittin' here in the middle of the night?" he demanded. His face seemed a hundred miles above me. Laboriously I tried to explain in my broken English that I was lost.

One of them muttered something to the other and walked off. The one who remained knelt beside me on the dirty sidewalk. "Can I help you, kid?"

I nodded and shoved the slip of paper with Frank's name and phone number at him. "Brother," I said.

He shook his head as he looked at the scrawled writing. "Is this where you live, kid?"

I didn't know how to answer and just said, "Brother." He nodded and pulled me to my feet and we made our way to a phone booth behind a newsstand. Fishing in his pocket he found a coin and dialed the number. When Frank's sleepy voice answered he handed the phone to me. In less than an hour I was safe in Frank's apartment.

The hot soup at Frank's tasted good and the clean bed was nice. The next morning Frank told me I was to stay with him and they would take care of me and get me in school. But something inside me told me I'd never stay. I had begun to run, and nothing would stop me now.

2

Blackboard Jungle

I stayed with Frank two months learning how to handle the English language. But I wasn't happy and the tensions from within were driving me away.

Frank enrolled me in the tenth grade the first week. The school was almost entirely Negro and Puerto Rican. It was run more like a reformatory than a public school. The teachers and administrators spent more of their time trying to maintain discipline than they did teaching. It was a wild place of fights, immorality, and a constant battle against those who had authority.

Every high school in Brooklyn had at least two or three gangs represented. These gangs were made up of boys and girls who lived in certain neighborhoods. Sometimes the gangs were enemies which invariably caused fights when they were thrown together in school classrooms.

This was a new experience for me. Every day in school there would be a fight in the halls or in one of the classrooms. I would cower against the wall, afraid some of the bigger kids would pick on me. After school, there would always be a fight in the school yard, and someone would be left bleeding.

Frank used to caution me not to walk the streets at night. "The gangs, Nicky! The gangs will murder you. They run like packs of wolves at night. They'll kill anyone who is a stranger on the streets."

He warned me to come straight home from school each afternoon and stay in the apartment away from the gangs.

I soon learned that the gangs weren't the only ones I should fear. There were also the "little people." These were the nine and ten year olds who roamed the streets during the afternoons and early evenings or played in front of their slum apartments.

I got my first experience with the little people walking home from school that first week. A gang of about ten kids, ranging in age from eight to ten, came charging out of a side door and ran into me on the sidewalk.

"Hey, you kids. Watch what you're doing."

One of the kids whirled and said, "Go to hell!"

Another crept up behind me and knelt down and before I knew it, I was sprawled on the sidewalk on my back. I tried to get up but one of the kids grabbed hold of my foot and began to pull. They were shouting and laughing all the time.

I lost my temper and swung at the nearest one, knocking him to the sidewalk. Just then, I heard a woman screaming. I looked up and she was leaning out a window about two floors up. "Get away from my boy, you stinking Spic, or I'll kill you."

At the moment there was nothing I wanted more than to get away from her boy. But now the others were coming at me. One threw a coke bottle at me. It hit the sidewalk beside my shoulder and the glass showered over my face.

The woman was screaming louder, "Leave my kids alone! Help! Help! He's killing my baby."

Suddenly, another woman appeared out of a doorway with a broom in her hand. She was a fat woman, waddling as she ran, and had the meanest look on her face I'd ever seen. She waded into the gang of boys with the broom held high over her head. I tried to roll away from her but she smashed the broom against my back. I turned over and she hit me again on top of the head. She was screaming and I was suddenly aware that several other women were leaning out of their windows screaming and calling for the police. The fat woman hit me a third time before I could get to my feet and start to run. Behind me I heard her call out, "If you ever come around here again picking on our boys, we'll kill you."

The next afternoon I came home from school a different way.

A week later I had my first run-in with a "gang." I had taken my time coming home from school and was loitering around in a park looking at a man who had a talking parrot. I was dancing around him, laughing and talking to the bird when the man suddenly lost interest, held his parrot against his chest and turned to leave. I looked up and about fifteen boys were standing behind me in a semi-circle. These weren't "little people." They were "big people." Most of them bigger than me.

They quickly formed a circle around me and one of the boys said, "Hey, kid, what you laughing at?"

I pointed to the man with the parrot who was now hurrying out of the park. "Man, I was laughing at that crazy bird."

"Yeah, you live around here?" the mean looking boy asked in return.

I sensed that something was wrong and began to stammer a little. "I-I live with my brother down the street."

"You mean just because you live down the street you think you can come into our park and laugh like a hyena? Huh? That what you think? Don't you know this is Bishop turf? Man, we don't allow no strangers in our turf. And especially be-boppers who laugh like hyenas."

I glanced around and saw they meant business. Before I could answer, the mean looking kid pulled a knife out of his pocket and with a flick of a button it opened, revealing a gleaming seven-inch blade.

"You know what I'm gonna do?" he said. "I'm gonna cut your throat and let you bleed like the animal you sound like."

"Hey, m-m-man," I stammered. "What's wrong with you? How come you want to cut me?"

"Because I don't like your looks, that's why," he said. He jabbed the knife toward my stomach and started to move in on me.

Another member of the gang, a tall, colored boy, spoke up. "Aw, come on, Big Daddy. Leave him be. This kid just got in from Puerto Rico. He don't even know what's going on."

The mean boy backed off, still sneering. "Okay, but one of these days he'll find out what's going on. And he better keep off Bishop turf."

They turned and walked away. I hurried to the apartment and spent the rest of the afternoon thinking.

The next day at school some of the kids had heard about the incident in the park. I found out that the mean kid with the knife was named Roberto. That afternoon during physical ed class we were playing baseball. Roberto deliberately knocked me down. The other kids all began to shout, "Fight him, Nicky. Jump him. Show him he's not so tough if he doesn't have a knife. Come on, Nicky, we'll back you up. Hit him!"

I got up and brushed myself off. "Okay," I said, "let's see how good you are with your fists."

We squared off and the other kids all formed a big circle around us. I could hear shouts of "Fight! Fight!" and knew the crowd was growing bigger.

Roberto grinned because I had taken a traditional boxing stance, with my hands up in front of my face. He slumped down and awkwardly put his hands up too. It was obvious he was unaccustomed to fighting this way. I danced toward him and before he could move, hit him with a left jab. Blood squirted from his nose and he backed up, looking surprised. I moved toward him.

Suddenly, he put his head down and charged into me, knocking me backwards to the ground. I tried to get up but he kicked me with his pointed shoes. I rolled over and he jumped on my back and pulled my head back, deliberately jamming his fingers into my eyes.

I kept thinking the other kids would join in and help me out, but they just stood there and yelled.

I didn't know how to fight this way. All my fights had been following boxing rules. But I sensed that this boy would kill me if I didn't do something. So, I reached up and pulled his hand down out of my eyes, grabbing his finger with my teeth. He howled with pain and rolled off my back.

I jumped to my feet and took my boxing stance again. He slowly got off the ground holding his injured hand. I danced toward him and hit him with two left jabs on the side of the face. It hurt him and I moved in to hit him again when he reached out and grabbed me by the waist, pinning my arms to my side. Using his head like a battering ram, he hit me time and time again in the face with his forehead. It felt like he was hitting me with a sledge hammer.

My nose was bleeding and I couldn't see from the pain. He finally turned me loose and hit me twice with his fists until I collapsed in the dirt of the school playground. I felt him kick me once before a teacher arrived and pulled him away from me.

That night I went home and Frank screamed at me. "They're going to kill you, Nicky. I told you to keep away from the gangs. They'll kill you." My face was badly hurt and it felt like my nose was broken. But I knew from now on, no one would take advantage of me any more. I could fight just as dirty as they could – and even more. And the next time, I'd be ready.

The next time came several weeks later. School was out and I was walking down the hallway toward the door. I was aware that some kids were following me. I glanced over my shoulder. Behind me were five Negro boys and a girl. I knew there had been some pretty mean fights between the Puerto Rican kids and the Negro kids. I began walking faster but sensed they had speeded up also.

Going through the outside door, I started down a concrete passageway that led to the street. The colored kids caught up with me and one of them, a big boy, slammed me up against the wall. I dropped my books and another of the kids kicked them down the concrete sidewalk and into a little gutter filled with dirty water.

I looked around but there was no one I could call for help. "What you doing in this turf, baby?" the big boy asked. "Don't you know this is our turf?"

"Man, this high school turf. This turf don't belong to no gangs," I said.

"Don't get smart with me, kid, I don't like you." He put his hand against my chest and pinned me back against the wall. Just then I heard a "click" and realized it was the sound of the switchblade knife.

Nearly all the teenage boys carried knives. They preferred to carry the "switchblade." The knife is operated on a spring. When a small switch button on the side of the knife is pressed, a strong spring is released and the blade flips open and locks in place.

The big boy held the knife against my chest, picking at the buttons of my shirt with the needle sharp point.

"Tell you what I'm gonna do, smart boy," he said. "You're new in this school and we make all new kids buy protection from us. It's a pretty good deal. You pay us twenty-five cents a day and we make sure no one hurts you."

One of the other boys gave a crazy snicker and said, "Yeah, man, like we makes sure we don't hurt you either."

The other kids all laughed.

I said, "Yeah? And what's to prove that even if I give you twenty-five cents a day you won't take advantage of me anyway?"

"No proof, wise guy. You just give it to us anyway. If you don't, you get killed," he answered.

"Okay, man. You better kill me now, then. Because if you don't, I'll be back later and kill every one of you." I could tell the others were a little scared. The big boy with the knife against my chest thought I was right-handed. Therefore, he didn't expect me to grab him with my left hand. I twisted his hand away from my chest and spun him around and bent the hand behind his back.

He dropped the knife and I scooped it up off the ground. It felt good in my hand. I put it against the side of his throat, pressing it just hard enough to indent the skin without puncturing it.

I pushed his face against the wall with the knife at the side of his neck just under his ear. The girl began to scream, afraid I was going to kill him.

I turned to her and said, "Hey, baby. I know you. I know where you live. Tonight I'm gonna come to your place and kill you. How you like that?"

She screamed louder and grabbed hold of one of the other boys and began to pull him away. "Run! Run!" she screamed. "This guy's crazy. Run!"

They ran, including the big boy who had been pinned against the wall. I let him go, knowing they could have killed me if they had tried.

I walked on down the sidewalk to where my books were lying in the water. I picked them up and shook them off. I still had the knife in my hand. I stood still for a long time, opening and shutting the blade. It was the first switchblade I'd ever held. I liked the feel of it. I slipped it in the pocket of my jacket and started home. From now on, I thought, they better think twice before they try to tangle with Nicky.

The word soon got out that I was to be feared. That made me fair bait for anyone who wanted to fight. I soon realized it was just a matter of time until something drastic happened. But I was prepared – regardless of what it was.

The final explosion came after I had been in school two months. The teacher had just called the class to order and was calling the roll. A Negro boy was late to class. He came swinging in, wiggling his hips and laughing. There was a pretty little Puerto Rican girl sitting on the back row. He bent over and kissed her on the side of the neck.

She jerked away from him and sat back upright in her desk. He reached around and kissed her on the mouth, at the same time putting his hand on her breast. She jumped up from her seat and began to scream.

The other boys in the class were laughing and shouting, "Go, man, go."

I glanced at the teacher. She started down the aisle but a big boy stood up in front of her and said, "Now, Teach, you wouldn't wanna spoil a little fun would you?" The teacher glanced up at the boy who was taller than she. She retreated back toward her desk while the class howled in delight.

By this time, the boy had the girl pinned against the wall and was running his hands all over her body while he tried to kiss her mouth. She was screaming and pushing him away from her.

Finally, he gave up and flopped down in his seat. "No sense in fighting for it," he announced to the class, "I'll get her tonight and she'll be glad to give it to me when I finish."

I heard the teacher clear her throat and begin again with the roll call.

Something snapped inside of me. I got up from my desk and walked around to the back of the room. The girl had taken her seat and was sitting there sobbing while the teacher called the roll.

I walked up behind the boy who was now sitting at his desk picking his fingernails. I reached over and picked up a heavy wooden chair that was sitting at the rear of the aisle. "Hey, look baby, I have something for you."

As he turned to look back, I brought the heavy chair down on top of his head. He collapsed in his seat, blood pouring from a deep cut in his head.

The teacher ran out of the room and returned in a moment with the principal. He grabbed me by the arm and pulled me down the hall to his office. I sat there while he called an ambulance and made arrangements for someone to take care of the hurt boy.

Then he turned to me. After telling me that all he had heard for the last two months was the trouble I had been in, he asked me for an explanation of what went on in the classroom. I told him exactly what happened. I told him the boy was taking advantage of the Puerto Rican girl and that the teacher hadn't done anything to stop it, so I stood up for her.

As I talked, I could see his face beginning to flush. Finally, he stood up and said, "Well, I've had all I'm going to take of these fights. You kids come in here and think you can act the same way you act out on the streets. I think it's about time I made an example and maybe we can have some respect for authority around here. I'm not going to sit here day after day and listen to you kids try to lie your way out of killing each other. I'm going to call the police."

I was on my feet. "Mister, those police will put me in jail."

"I hope so," said the principal. "At least the rest of these monsters around here will learn to respect some authority for a change if they do."

"You call the police," I said, backing up against the door shaking with fear and rage, "and when I get out of jail, I'll be back. And one day, I'll catch you alone and I'll kill you."

I was gritting my teeth as I talked.

The principal blanched. His face turned white and he thought for a moment. "All right, Cruz. I'll let you off this time. But I don't ever want to see you around this school again. I don't care where you go, go to hell as far as I care, but don't you ever let me see your face around here again. I want you to leave here running and don't stop until you're out of my sight. Understand?"

I understood. I left . . . running.

3

On My Own

A life motivated by hate and fear has no room for anyone but self. I hated everyone, including Frank. He represented authority. And when he began to object to my being out of school and staying out late at night, I made up my mind to leave.

"Nicky," he said, "New York is a jungle. The people who live here live by the law of the jungle. Only the tough survive. You really haven't seen what it's like, Nicky. I've been here five years and I know. This place is crawling with prostitutes, junkies, winos and killers. Those guys out there, they'll kill you. And no one will even know you're dead until some junkie stumbles over your rotting body under a pile of trash."

Frank was right. But I couldn't stay here. He was insisting I go back to school and I knew I'd have to make it on my own.

"Nicky, I can't force you to go back to school. But if you don't you're lost."

"But the principal kicked me out. He said for me never to come back."

"I don't care. You're going back if you live here. You've got to go to school someplace."

"If you think I'm going back," I spit back, "then you're crazy. And if you try to make me, I'll kill you."

"Nicky, you're my brother. That's crazy talk. Mama and Papa told me to look out after you. I'm not going to have you talk like that. Either you go to school or you get out. Go ahead, run if you want. But you'll be back because you don't have no place to go. But if you stay, you're going to school, and that's final."

That was Friday morning before Frank went to work. That afternoon I left a note on the kitchen table telling him some friends had invited me to come stay with them for a week. I had no friends, but I couldn't stay at Frank's any longer.

That night I wandered into the Bedford-Stuyvesant section of Brooklyn to look for a place to stay. I walked up to a group of young teenagers hanging around a street corner. "Any you guys know where I can find a room?"

One of the young kids turned and looked at me, puffing at his cigarette. "Yeah," he said, jerking his thumb over his shoulder in the direction of Brooklyn Technical High School. "My old man's the super at those apartments across the street. Talk to him and he'll find you a place. That's him sitting there on the steps playing cards with those other guys. He's the one that's drunk." The other kids all laughed.

The apartment the boy had reference to was on Ft. Greene Place, in the heart of one of the world's largest housing projects. More than thirty thousand people lived in the towering buildings, most of them Negro and Puerto Rican. The Ft. Greene Project runs from Park Avenue to Lafayette Avenue, surrounding Washington Park.

I walked over to the group of men and asked the superintendent if he had a room to rent. He looked up from his cards and grunted, "Yeah. I got one. Why?"

I hesitated and stammered, "Well, because I need a place to stay."

"You got fifteen bucks?" he said, spitting tobacco juice at my feet.

"Well, no, not right now, but . . . "

"Then, I ain't got no room," he said, and turned back to his cards. The other men didn't even look up.

"But I can get the money," I argued.

"Look kid, when you can show me fifteen bucks in advance the room is yours. I don't care how you get it. Rob some old lady for all I care. But until you got the money get your nose out of here, you're buggin' me."

I walked back toward Lafayette past Papa John's, Harry's Meat House, Paradise Bar, Shery's, The Esquire, Valhal Bar, and Lincoln's Rendezvous. Pausing beside the last

one I stepped into an alley trying to figure out how to raise
the money.

I knew that if I tried to rob someone and got caught, I'd
go to jail. But I was desperate. I'd told Frank I wouldn't be
back for a week. A room was going to cost money and I
didn't have a penny. It was almost 10 p.m. and the winter
wind was freezing cold. I shrank back into the shadows of
the alley and saw people passing by on the sidewalk. I pulled
the switchblade out of my pocket and pressed the button.
The blade snapped open with a soft click. I pressed the tip
against the palm of my hand. My hand was shaking as I tried
to imagine just how I would perform the robbery. Would it
be best to pull them into the alley? Should I go ahead and
stab them or just scare them? What if they yelled? . . .

My thoughts were interrupted by two people talking at the
entrance of the alley. An old wino had stopped a young man
in his late teens who was carrying a huge sack of groceries.
The old man was begging him for a dime to buy a cup of
coffee. I listened as the young man tried to get away – telling
the wino he didn't have any money.

The thought ran through my mind that the old man probably had a pocket full of money he had begged and stolen.
He wouldn't dare scream for help if I robbed him. As soon
as the boy left I'd pull him into the alley and take it from
him.

The young man was putting his grocery sack on the sidewalk. He fished in his pocket until he found a coin. The old
man mumbled and shuffled away.

"Damn," I thought to myself. "Now what will I do?"

Just then the boy tipped over his sack of groceries. A
couple of apples rolled onto the sidewalk. He bent to pick
them up and I pulled him into the alley and smashed him
up against the wall. Both of us were scared to death but I
had the advantage of surprise. He was petrified with fear as
I held my knife in front of his face.

"I don't want to hurt you, but I need money. I'm desperate. Give it to me. Now! Quick! All you got before I kill
you."

My hand was shaking so badly I was afraid I'd drop the
knife.

"Please. Please. Take it all. Don't kill me," the boy pleaded. He pulled out his billfold and tried to hand it to me. He dropped it and I kicked it down the alley. "Take off," I said. "Run, man, run! And if you stop running for two blocks, you're a dead man."

He looked at me, eyes wide with horror, and started to run. He tripped over his groceries and sprawled on the pavement at the mouth of the alley. Scrambling to his feet, he tripped again as he half crawled, half ran down the sidewalk. As soon as he turned the corner, I grabbed the wallet and sprinted down the alley. Emerging in the darkness on De Kalb, I vaulted the chain link fence surrounding the park and ran through the high grass into the trees. Squatting behind an embankment, I paused to catch my breath and let my pounding heart settle down. Opening the wallet I counted out $19. It felt good to hold the bills in my hand. I tossed the wallet into the high grass and counted the money again before I folded it and put it in my pocket.

Not bad, I thought. The gangs are killing hobos for less than a dollar and I get nineteen on my first try. This isn't going to be so bad after all.

But my confidence didn't remove all my fear, and I stayed hidden in the high grass until after midnight. By then it was too late to get the room and I walked back to the spot where I had committed the robbery. Someone had already picked up all the spilled groceries with the exception of a crushed box of crackers. I picked up the box and shook it as the crumbs fell out on the pavement. I relived the experience in my mind and grinned. I should have cut him, just to find out what it felt like, I thought. Next time I will.

I walked to the subway entrance by Papa John's and boarded the first train that came along. I spent the night on the subway and early the next morning I was back on Ft. Greene Place to rent the room.

The super walked with me up three flights of stairs. The room opened out over the street facing Brooklyn Tech. It was small with cracks in the ceiling. The super told me there was a public bathroom on the second floor and that I could adjust the heat by turning the handle on the steel radiator. He handed me the key and told me the rent was due every

Saturday a week in advance. The door closed behind him and I heard him clomping down the steps.

I turned and looked at the room. There were two single beds, a chair, a small table, a wash basin on the wall and a small closet. Walking to the window, I peered into the street below. The early morning traffic was moving with a steady hum on Lafayette at the end of the block. Across the street, Brooklyn Tech towered into the sky. It ran the length of the block and shut out any view I might have had. But it made little difference. I was on my own.

Later that morning I made my first tour through the neighborhood. Coming down the steps of the slum apartment I saw a young man stagger out from under the stairwell. His face was blanched white and his eyes sunk deep in their sockets. His filthy, tattered jacket hung half off one shoulder and his pants were unzipped where he had urinated behind the radiator. I couldn't tell whether he was drunk or high on dope. I stood on the landing and watched him as he reeled through the door and onto the outside steps. He bent over the side of the steps and heaved and retched as he threw up on the sidewalk below. A gang of little people burst out a side door on the first floor and ran into the street completely oblivious of his presence. The man finished gagging and slumped on the top step, looking blankly at the street.

I walked past him and down the steps. Overhead I heard a window open and looked up just in time to duck a barrage of garbage thrown from the third floor to the sidewalk below. Next door one of the little people was squatting in the shadows under the steps, using an abandoned basement entrance for a latrine. I shuddered but told myself I could get accustomed to it.

Behind the apartment building was an open lot, waist high with weeds and scraggly bushes. A few scrawny trees poked their naked branches toward the gray sky. Spring had begun but the trees seemed almost reluctant to put forth new buds and face another summer in the ghetto. I kicked an empty beer can – the trashy lot was covered with them. Old cardboard boxes, newspapers, and rotting boards were strewn in the high weeds. A broken down wire fence stretched across the lot to another apartment building that opened on St. Edward Street. Looking back at my building I could see some of the first floor windows boarded shut or closed in with sheets of galvanized tin to keep out the cold wind. Two apartments down, I could see the round faces of little Negro children with their noses pressed against a filthy window pane watching me as I kicked through the rubbish. They reminded me of small animals in a cage yearning for freedom and yet afraid to venture out for fear of being hurt or killed. Part of the window had been broken out and replaced with sheets of waterstained cardboard. I could count five frightened faces. There were probably five more in the small three room apartment.

I walked back around toward the front of the building. The basement apartment under No. 54 was vacant. The iron gate hung loose on its hinges. I kicked it open and started in. The smell of urine, body excretions, wine, smoke and grease was more than I could stand and I backed out gagging. At least I had a room on the third floor.

I started down the sidewalk. The whores on the street were a pathetic sight. The white girls worked the right side of the street and occupied apartments down the block from me. The colored girls worked the opposite side of the street and lived near the subway entrance. All the girls were addicts. They were standing around in leotards and dirty coats. Some were yawning because they were sick or because they needed a "wake up," an early morning shot of heroin to get them going.

After two months I still wasn't accustomed to New York. Back in Puerto Rico I had seen pictures of the Statue of Liberty and the United Nations building. But here, in the ghetto, as far as the eye could see there was nothing but apartments, filled with human flesh. Each window symbolized a family, cramped into tiny living quarters, eking out a miserable existence. I thought of the zoo in San Juan with the pacing bears and chattering monkeys behind bars. They wallow in their own filth. They eat stale meat or wilted lettuce. They fight among themselves and the only time they get together is when they are attacking an intruder. Animals aren't meant to live this way, with only a painted jungle scene on the rear of the cage to remind them of what they're supposed to be. And neither are people. But here, in the ghettos, they do.

I paused on the curb at the corner of Myrtle Avenue, waiting for the light to change. Overhead an elevated train roared and clattered by, showering those below with a fine coat of soot and grime. The streets were covered with a slushy mixture of snow, dirt, and salt which the people waded through as the light changed.

Behind the apartments the clothes lines hung from one dingy balcony or fire escape to another. The blue shirts and khaki pants flopped in the freezing wind. Underclothes that used to be white were now a dirty gray from constant exposure to the filth-filled air.

It was Saturday morning and the storekeepers were pulling the heavy iron grates away from their store fronts. For blocks and blocks not a single store was without a mesh grate or iron bars to protect it from the roving gangs at night.

But it was the apartments that depressed me most. There were evidences of feeble attempts of the occupants to reach up from the concrete jungle and brick canyons for some essence of identity. But it was a hopeless reach. Like a man sinking in quicksand who gropes with stretching fingers for a weed on the edge of the quagmire, grasping desperately as he is sucked under with the weed in his clenched fist.

A dirty red clay flowerpot sat behind a soot covered window pane. A scraggly geranium drooped limply against the glass.

Occasionally, one of the apartments would have brightly painted steps, or perhaps a window sill would be painted so it stood out in stark relief against the drab stone. In another window a rough flower box, made from the unfinished lumber of a machinery crate, hung from a dirty sill. In it a few pathetic artificial flowers braved the winter wind, covered with soot that floated down from a thousand smokestacks that towered over the city.

I had gotten as far as St. Edward Street and paused in front of the Walt Whitman Library next to P.S. 67. Across the street was a huge apartment building, twelve stories high and a block long. Its six hundred windows faced the street, each one representing some miserable state of humanity shivering behind the panes. In one window hung a tattered drape, once bright with color, now faded and torn from the effects of its environment. Most windows were void of shades or drapes, staring like the naked eyes of a frozen corpse out onto the street below.

I turned and retraced my steps back toward Washington Park. What's wrong with these people here in this filthy place? I thought. Why do they live like this? No yards. No grass. No open fields. No trees. I didn't know that once you moved into one of these concrete cages you became its prisoner. There's no leaving the asphalt jungle.

That afternoon I walked back down the street. I had noticed what looked like a carnival with rides and sideshows in the playground behind the St. Michael-St. Edwards Catholic Church at the corner of Auburn and St. Edwards Streets. I arrived at 4 p.m. and the music from the carnival was blaring out into the street. I still had a little money left over from the robbery and the thought of a carnival tingled my blood. At the gate I noticed a group of kids standing around an Italian organ grinder. They were wearing black jackets with a crimson double M stitched on the back. The music from the organ grinder was almost drowned out by the noise the kids were making as they clapped their hands and jitterbugged in the middle of the sidewalk.

In the center of the group was a dark-haired, fair-skinned boy about my own age. His handsome face was wreathed in a grin as he kicked his feet against the sidewalk in a fast bebop. Hands on hips, he spun around in time to the music. Suddenly, his black eyes met mine. He came to an abrupt halt, and the grin on his face was instantly replaced with a hard cold look.

"Hey, baby, what you doing this territory? This Mau Mau turf. We don't want no squares hanging around here."

I looked back at him and realized that the other boys with the black jackets had formed a quiet little circle around us. The handsome boy with the steel cold eyes walked up to me and pushed me with his chest, smirking. "What click you belong to, man?"

"I don't belong to no click," I replied. "I come down here to ride on the carnival. That a crime or something?"

A boy in the crowd stepped forward. "Hey man, you know what this is?" he said, brandishing an open knife. "This is a blade, baby. It'll cut your gut. How you like to get smart with me? I ain't as tender as Israel."

The boy referred to as Israel motioned the other boy back and continued, "You see, a square can get killed in a hurry. Maybe I kill you. Now, if you wanna live you better beat it."

I was angry, and felt in my pocket for my own switchblade. But I realized that the odds were too great for me. I didn't want to be a chicken, but knew there would be another time for me to show my courage. I nodded my head and turned back down the street toward Washington Park and my apartment. Behind me, I could hear the gang laughing and hooting. "That's tellin 'im, Israel baby. That little S.O.B. learned his lesson this time. It'll be a cold day in hell before he sticks his nose back around here again."

I was mad and frustrated. Going under the elevated tracks on Myrtle, I walked into the park area and sat down on a bench. I didn't notice that a young kid, maybe thirteen years old, had been following me. I turned and looked at him. He grinned and sat down on the bench beside me. "Gave you a rough time, didn't they?" he said.

"Watcha mean?" I asked. "I coulda took any one of them but didn't see no sense in fighting all of them at once."

"Man, these gangs are tough around here," he said, reaching into his shirt pocket and pulling out a homemade cigarette. "They'll kill you if you don't run with 'em."

He lit the cigarette and noticed I was watching him. "You smoke pot?" he asked. I shook my head although I knew what he was talking about.

"Howja like to try one? I got an extra. Man, it's cool."

"Sure," I said. I'd backed off once this afternoon and didn't want to back off again.

He fished around in his shirt pocket and pulled out a bent, crumpled cigarette. It was twisted shut on both ends and stained along the side where he had licked the paper to make it stick.

"You gotta puff it," the boy said. "If you don't, it goes out."

He lit it for me and I began to puff on it.

"No," the kid laughed, "like this."

He took a long drag on the cigarette and slowly inhaled the smoke into his lungs. "Man, that's good. If all you do is puff, it burns up and you don't get nothing out of it. Inhale, man!"

I inhaled. It had a strange sweet taste and a strong odor.

"What's it do?" I asked, beginning to feel the dizzy effects of the weed.

"Man, it sends you," the boy answered. "It makes you laugh a lot. Makes you feel like you're the best dancer, best lover, best fighter. All those guys back there at the carnival had been smoking pot. Didn't you see how their eyes were red? You can tell if they're high on grass if their eyes shine."

"Where you get this stuff?" I asked.

"Oh, it's easy. We got a hundred pushers here in the neighborhood. Most any of the big guys can get it for you. They get it from bigger connections. Cuba. Mexico. Me? My old man raises it in the back yard. We got a bunch of weeds in our back yard. No one ever goes back there and my old man planted some of the seeds in the weeds and we raise our own. It ain't as good as some of the other stuff, but it don't cost us anything."

"How much does it cost if you buy it from a pusher?" I asked, trying to learn the vocabulary and a little embarrassed that a thirteen-year-old kid knew more about it than I.

"Some of it sells for a dollar a stick. Sometimes you can get it for seventy-five cents a stick. But it's best to buy a can. You know, like a Prince Albert can. That way you can make your own for about forty cents. You have to be careful, though. Some of the guys cheat you. They'll mix oregano in with the pot and you won't get pure stuff. Always check it out before you pay for it 'cause they'll cheat you for sure."

I had finished the cigarette and stretched my feet out in front of me and put my head on the back of the bench. I didn't seem to notice the cold wind as much and the dizziness had departed, leaving me feeling like I was floating on a dreamy cloud.

I turned my head so I could see the boy. He was sitting on the bench with his head in his hands. "I thought this stuff was supposed to make you happy. How come you're not laughing?"

"Man, what I got to laugh about?" he said. "My old man's a drunk. Only he's not really my old man. He just moved in with my mother last year. I don't even know who my real old man is. And this man, he beats up on my maw all the time. Last week I tried to pull him off her and he hit me in the face with a bottle and broke off two my teeth. I threw a clock at him and hit him in the back. Then my Maw, my own Maw, called me a S.O.B. and told me to get out . . . that I had no reason to hurt her man. Now I'm living in the street just waiting until I can kill him. I don't run with no gangs. I don't run with nobody. I'm just waiting until that bum gets alone and I'm gonna kill him. I don't even love my mother no more. What I got to laugh about?"

He never raised his head while he talked. "This the same man who grows the marijuana in the back yard?" I asked.

"Yeah. He's a pusher too. Man, just wait 'til I catch him alone. I'm gonna push him – push a knife through him." He looked up, his face strained and tired, like the face of an old monkey rather than a thirteen-year-old boy. "What about your old man, he a drunk too?"

"Naw, I'm lucky. I don't even have an old man or old woman," I lied. "I'm on my own."

The kid looked up. "Yeah, me too now, I guess." Then, brightening, he said, "Well, see you around. Watch out for them gangs. They'll kill you if they catch you on the street at night."

"Hey, what about these gangs? How many are there?"

"Hundreds," he said. "Man, there's so many of 'em you can't begin to count 'em."

"What do they do?"

"Fight, man, what else? Either they're going out and fighting some other gang or they're staying home defending their turf against some invading gang. When they ain't fighting each other, they're fighting the police. They use everything they can find to fight with. They carry knives, clubs, pistols, zip guns, brass knucks, rifles, sawed-off shotguns, bayonets, baseball bats, broken bottles, gasoline bombs, bricks, rocks, bicycle chains . . . man you name it, they use it to kill you with. They even file the tips of their umbrellas, put spikes on their shoes, and some of the dago gangs carry straight razors and put razor blades between their fingers in their fist. You hang around here long and you'll find out. That's why I don't join with 'em. I just hang out in the alleys and in the dark streets and keep away from 'em. You'll learn, though, just stick around and you'll learn."

He got up and sauntered back through the park, disappearing in the twilight. I headed back to 54 Ft. Greene Place. It was already dark.

4

Baptized with Blood

Several weeks later I left my apartment about 8 p.m. and I walked down to Papa John's on the corner of Lafayette. A young Puerto Rican named Tico was leaning against the side of the building smoking a cigarette. I had met him once or twice and understood he was a knife expert.

He looked up and said, "Hey Nicky, would you like to go 'gig'? I want you to meet Carlos, President of the gang."

I had heard of gigs but never attended one, so I readily accepted his invitation and followed him down a side street and into a basement entrance under a flight of stairs in an apartment building.

I had trouble adjusting my eyes to the dim light. A single pole lamp burned in the corner. Some light came in from the windows and a little came in around the door from the street lights outside.

As I moved into the room I could see dim figures clinging to each other, swaying to the sound of soft music. Their heads drooped across each other's shoulders, as their feet moved in unison to the slow music. One of the boys clutched a wine bottle behind his girl's back and staggered as he wrapped his arm around her neck and took a long swig out of the bottle.

Several boys were sitting at a small table playing cards and smoking what I later found out were reefers – marijuana. A bottle of wine sat in the middle of the table.

On the far side of the room, away from the lamp, two couples were lying on a mat. One couple was seemingly asleep in each other's arms. The other was engaged in heavy love play. As I watched they got to their feet, arms around each other and mouths glued together in a passionate kiss, and stumbled through a side door.

Tico looked at me and winked. "There's a bed in there. We keep it so they can shack up when they want to."

A stack of pulp paper magazines with pictures of naked and semi-naked women was on the floor at my feet.

"So this is a gig," I thought.

Tico grabbed my arm and pulled me into the room. "Hey, everybody. This is my friend. How about making him feel welcome."

A blonde girl stepped out of the shadows near the door and took me by the arm. She had on a tight black sweater, a crimson skirt, and was barefooted. I put my arm around her waist and said, "Hey, baby, you wanna dance with me?"

"What's your name?" she said. Before I could answer, Tico spoke up, "His name is Nicky. He's my friend and he's a damn good fighter. He may want to join us."

The girl slid around in front of me and snuggled her body up close to mine. "Okay, Nicky, if you're such a good fighter let's see how good a dancer you are." Gliding out into the floor, I could feel her thighs rub against mine as we shuffled in step to the music.

Her motions began to excite me. She was warm and I could feel every movement of her body as she clung tightly to me. I slipped my hand under her sweater along her back and pressed her close to me.

"Ummmmm," I heard her groan. That's all it took for me and I moved my hand around under her arm.

Suddenly, she put both hands against my chest and gave me a violent shove backward. "Cut it out! What do you think you're doing?" she bit out. "Don't get fresh with me. I belong to Jose and he'd cut you to pieces if I told him you tried to feel me."

She could tell from the expression on my face I was confused. Her face broke into a grin and she reached out and pulled me back close to her. She put her lips close to my ear, "After all, this is only the first time. Don't be in such a rush. If I like you, I'll let you have it all."

We danced a while longer and then stopped to watch a couple of boys playing "chicken" with a knife. One of the boys was standing against the wall and the other was throwing a knife at his feet. The object was to get the knife as close as possible without hitting him. If the boy flinched, he was "chicken."

I caught myself hoping he would hit him. The thought of blood excited me. Even as I stood there, I began to laugh at myself hoping he would slip and stab the boy.

The blonde with the black sweater pulled me by the arm, "Come with me. I want you to meet someone important."

I followed her into a side room. A tall lanky Puerto Rican was slouched on a chair with his legs propped on a small table in front of him. A girl was sitting astraddle his lap, leaning over him as he blew smoke through her hair and laughed.

"Hey!" he shouted to us. "Ain't you got no manners? Don't you know you're supposed to ask my permission before you come in like that? You might catch me doing something I don't want nobody to see." He laughed and reached around and patted the girl's hips with both hands.

Looking at me he said, "Who's this punk?" The blonde said, "This is my friend, Nicky. Tico brought him. Tico says he's a good fighter."

The tall lanky boy shoved the girl off his lap and looked hard at me. Then he grinned and stuck out his hand. "Slip me some skin, Nicky. Me, I'm Carlos. President of the Mau Maus."

I gently laid my hand against his and pulled it back, sliding my palm along his in the gang's fashion of handshaking.

I had heard of the Mau Maus. They had named themselves for the bloodthirsty savages in Africa. I had seen them in the streets with their black leather jackets with the crimson double M stitched on the back. They wore fancy alpine hats many of which were decorated with wooden matches. Most of them carried canes and they wore sharp pointed shoes that could kick a man to death in a matter of seconds.

Carlos nodded toward the corner of the room and I recognized the boy I had seen at the carnival. "That's Israel. He's Vice President of the Mau Maus." Israel's face was expressionless as he stared at me. His deep black eyes boring holes into my soul and making me feel uncomfortable.

I found out later that the president and the vice president are nearly always together. They protect each other in case one is attacked.

"How old you, Nicky?" Carlos asked.

"Sixteen," I answered.

"You know about fighting?"

"Sure," I said.

"You willing to fight anyone, even police?"

"Sure," I replied again.

"Hey, you ever stab anyone?"

"No," I replied truthfully, but regretfully.

"Anyone ever tried to stab you?"

"Yes," I answered.

"Yeah?" Carlos said, showing renewed interest. "What you do to the guy?"

"Nothing," I replied. "But I will. I'm just waiting to catch him again and when I do, I'll kill him."

Israel interrupted. "Listen, man, you want to join our gang you do as we do. We're the toughest. Even the police scared of us. But we don't want no chickens. You want to join and you no chicken, fine. But if you chicken, we cut you open and kill you."

I knew Israel was telling the truth. I already had heard stories of young boys who had been killed by their own gangs because they ratted on a fellow gang member.

Carlos spoke up, "Two things, man. If you join the Mau Maus, it's forever. No one ever quits. Second, if you're caught by the cops and squeal, we'll get you. Either we get you when you get out of jail, or we go in the jail and get you. But we'll get you."

Israel showed a faint grin on his handsome face. "How about it, baby, you still think you want to join?"

"Give me three days," I said. "If I join your gang, I want to go all the way."

"Okay, baby," Carlos said. "You have three days to think it over. And at the end of that time, you come back here. Let me know what you decide." He was still sitting in the same slouched position with his legs stretched out in front of him. He had pulled his girl back over to him and had his left hand under her skirt and around her hips.

I turned to leave and Carlos said, "Hey, Nicky, I forgot to tell you. If you tell anyone . . . anyone . . . where we are, I'll kill you before you have a chance to turn around. Got it?"

"Got it," I said. And I knew he meant it.

Outside on the street, I quizzed Tico. "What do you think, Tico? You think I ought to join the Mau Maus?"

Tico just shrugged his shoulders. "It's a good deal, man. If you join 'em, they take care of you. If you don't join 'em, they're liable to kill you for not joining. You ain't got much choice now. Besides, you're gonna have to join one of the gangs to stay alive around here."

"What about Carlos?" I asked. "What kind of guy is he?"

"He's okay. He don't say much but when he does, everyone listens. He's in charge and they all know it."

"Is it true that the president gets his choice of the girls?" I asked.

"That's right," said Tico. "We have about seventy-five girls in our gang and the president gets his pick. A different one each day if he wants it that way. Man, they like it. You know, it's big stuff to go with the president. They fight to see who gets to play up to him. And that's not all. The gang takes care of the president. He gets the first take out of what we steal – usually enough to pay his room and buy his food and clothes. It's a pretty good deal, being president."

"Hey, Tico. If you're so good with a knife, how come you're not president?"

"Not me, man. The president don't get to fight too much. He has to stay back and plan things. Me, I like to fight. I don't want to be president."

That's what I like too, I thought. I like to fight.

Tico headed back to Papa John's and I turned toward 54 Ft. Greene Place. I could feel the blood tingling in my veins as I imagined what was ahead. The gigs, the girls. But most of all, the fights. I wouldn't have to fight by myself any more. I could hurt as much as I wanted to and not have to be hurt back. My heart began to beat faster. Maybe I'll get a chance to really stab someone. I could almost visualize the blood flowing across my hands and dripping down on the street. I made swinging motions with my hands as I walked, pretending I had a knife and jabbing and slashing at imaginary figures in the dark. I had told Carlos I'd let him know in three days. But I had already made up my mind. All I wanted was for someone to give me a switchblade and a gun.

Two nights later, I was back at the gig. I walked in and Carlos met me at the door. "Hey, Nicky, you're just in time. We got another boy who wants to join the Mau Maus. You want to watch the initiation?"

I had no idea what an initiation was but wanted to watch. Carlos continued, "But maybe you came to tell us you don't want to join, eh?"

"No," I countered. "I came to tell you I'm ready to join. I want to fight. I think I'm just as tough as anyone else and a better fighter than most of these other guys."

"Good," said Carlos. "You can watch and then it'll be your turn. We have two ways to find out if you're chicken. Either you stand still while five of our toughest guys beat you up, or you stand against the wall waiting for the knife. If you run from either, we don't let you join the gang. This kid says he's tough. Let's see how tough he really is. Then we'll see if you're that tough."

I looked across the room and saw the other boy. He was about thirteen years old with pimples on his face and a long shock of black hair that fell down over his eyes. He was small and skinny and his arms hung stiffly by his sides. He was wearing a white, long-sleeved shirt that was soiled on the front and pulled out around his belt. I thought I had seen this little pimply faced kid at school, but wasn't sure since he was younger than I.

There were about forty boys and girls eagerly awaiting the show. Carlos was in charge. He told everyone to clear the floor and they all lined up around the walls. The young boy was told to stand with his back against a bare wall. Carlos stood in front of him with an open switchblade in his hand. The silver blade glistened in the dim light.

"I'm gonna turn and walk twenty steps toward that other wall," he said. "You stand right where you are. You say you're a tough kid. Well, we're gonna find out just how tough. When I get to twenty, I'm gonna turn and throw this knife. If you flinch or duck, you're chicken. If you don't, even if the knife sticks you, you're a tough kid and you can join the Mau Maus. Got it?"

The small boy nodded.

"Now, one other thing," said Carlos, holding the knife in the face of the youngster. "If you turn chicken while I'm walking away counting, all you got to do is holler. But you better not ever stick your nose around here any more. If you do, we'll cut those big ears off and make you eat 'em and then dig your belly button out with a beer opener and let you bleed to death."

The boys and girls started to laugh and clap. "Go, man, go!" they shouted at Carlos.

Carlos turned his back to the boy and started slowly across the room. He held the long glimmering knife by the point of the blade, his arm in front of him bent at the elbow, the knife in front of his face.

"One . . . two . . . three . . . " The crowd began to shout and jeer. "Get him, Carlos! Stick it through his eye! Make him bleed, baby, make him bleed!"

The young boy was cowering against the wall, much like a mouse trapped by a tiger. He was trying desperately to be brave. His arms were rigid at his sides, his hands balled into tiny fists with his knuckles showing white against the skin. His face was drained of color and his eyes were wide with fright.

"Eleven . . . twelve . . . thirteen . . . " Carlos counted loudly as he paced off the distance. The tension mounted as the boys and girls jeered and cried out for blood.

"Nineteen . . . twenty." Slowly Carlos turned and pulled his right hand back toward his ear, holding the knife by the tip of its needle sharp blade. The crowd of kids was wild in their frenzy calling for blood. Just as he snapped the knife forward, the little boy bent over, throwing his arms around his head screaming, "No! No!" The knife thudded into the wall just inches from where his head had been.

"Chicken! . . . chicken! . . . chicken!" the crowd roared.

Carlos was angry. The corners of his mouth grew tight and his eyes narrowed. "Grab him," he hissed. Two boys moved from each side of the room and grabbed the cowering child by his arms and slammed him back against the wall.

Carlos moved across the room and stood in front of the shaking form. "Chicken!" he spat out. "Chicken! I knew you were a coward from the first time I saw you. I oughta kill you."

Again the kids in the room picked up the theme. "Kill him! Kill the dirty chicken!"

"You know what we do to chickens?" said Carlos. The boy looked up at him trying to move his mouth but no sound was coming out.

"I'll tell you what we do to chickens," said Carlos. "We clip their wings so they can't fly no more."

He snatched the knife out of the wall. "Stretch him out!" he said.

Before the boy could move, the two boys yanked his arms straight out from his body, spread eagle. Moving so fast you could hardly follow his hand, Carlos brought the knife up in a fast vicious thrust and jabbed it almost to the hilt into the child's armpit. The boy jerked and screamed in pain. The blood gushed out and quickly flooded his white shirt with a crimson red.

Pulling the knife out of the boy's flesh, he flipped it into his other hand. "See man," he leered, viciously thrusting the knife upward again into the other armpit, "I'm left-handed too."

The two boys turned loose and the child collapsed to the floor, his arms across his chest, his hands clutching pitifully at his punctured flesh. He was screaming and gagging, rolling on the floor. His shirt was almost completely covered with bright red blood.

"Get him out of here," snapped Carlos. Two boys came forward and yanked him to his feet. The boy threw back his head and screamed out in agony as they jerked his arms. Carlos clapped his hand across his mouth and the screaming stopped. The boy's eyes, wide with horror, peered across the top of the hand.

"Go home, chicken! If I hear you scream one more time or if you squeal on us, I'll cut your tongue out too. Got it?" As he spoke, he held up the switchblade, the silver blade dripping blood down over the white mother-of-pearl handle. "Got it?" he repeated.

The child nodded.

The boys pulled him across the floor and out onto the sidewalk. The gang of kids in the room shouted as he left, "Go home, chicken!"

Carlos turned. "Who's next?" he said . . . looking straight at me. The crowd grew quiet.

I suddenly realized I wasn't afraid. Matter of fact, I had become so wrapped up in the stabbing and pain that I was enjoying it. The sight of all that blood gave me a wild, savage, exhilarating feeling. I was envious of Carlos. But now it was my turn.

I remembered Carlos' statement that I had a choice of initiations. Common sense told me that Carlos was still mad. If I let him throw his knife at me, he would try to stab me on purpose. It seemed the wiser of the two moves to choose the other method.

"We got another chicken?" Carlos teased.

I stepped out into the middle of the room and looked around. One of the girls, a tall slim girl with tight black slacks shouted, "What's wrong, baby, you scared or something? We got some blood left over if you don't have any." The crowd hooted and shouted in laughter. And she was right. The floor beside the wall where the other boy had been was covered with a sticky puddle of blood.

I said, "Not me. I ain't scared. Try me out, baby. Where's your boys who want to slug me?"

I was trying to put up a good front, but deep inside I was scared. I knew I was going to get hurt. I realized that these people played for keeps. But I would rather die than be chicken. So I said, "I'm ready."

Carlos barked out five names. "Johnny!" And a short, stocky boy stepped out of the crowd and stood in front of me. He was twice my size with a deeply lined forehead and almost no neck at all. His head seemed to rest right in between his shoulders. He walked to the center of the room and cracked his knuckles with a loud popping sound.

I tried to picture my 120 pounds against his 200 pounds. He just looked blankly at me, like an ape. Waiting for the command to attack.

"Mattie!" Another boy stepped out. This one was nearer my size but his arms were long, much longer than mine. He danced into the center of the room flicking his hands out and back like a boxer. He held his chin close to his chest looking out of the tops of his eyes. He circled the room, fists flicking forward with lightning speed. The girls whistled and sighed as he kept up his shadow boxing, blowing and snorting through his nose as he swung and did short jabs.

"Jose!" A third boy joined the group. He had a deep scar on his left cheek running from below his eye to the tip of his chin. He began taking his shirt off and flexing his muscles. He was built like a weight lifter. He circled me – looking at me from all angles.

"Owl!" A roar went up from the other kids in the room. Owl was obviously a favorite. I learned later they called him Owl because he could see as well at night as in the daytime. They used him on the front line in the rumbles so he could spot the enemy gangs as they approached. He had big wide eyes and a hooked nose that obviously had been broken time and time again. One ear was half gone where he had been hit with a board that had a long nail in it. It had happened during a rumble in a school yard and the nail had snagged his ear and ripped more than half of it away. Owl was a short fat kid with the meanest look I had ever seen.

"Paco!" I never did see Paco. I heard him call out behind me, "Hey, Nicky." I turned to look and he hit me in the back just above the belt line with his fist. The pain was excruciating. I felt like he had ruptured my kidney. I tried to gasp for breath but he hit me again. As I straightened up and put my hands behind my back to grasp the hurt, one of the other boys hit me in the stomach so hard I lost my breath. I could sense myself beginning to pass out from the pain when someone hit me in the face and I heard the bone of my nose crumble under the blow.

I never had a chance to hit back. I felt myself falling. I sensed someone grabbing hold of my long hair. My body collapsed to the floor but my head was being held up by my hair. Someone kicked me in the face with a grimy shoe and I could feel the sand grind into my cheek and lips. I was being kicked all over and whoever was holding my hair was hitting me on the side of the head.

Then the lights went out and I remembered nothing else.

Sometime later, I was aware that someone was shoving me around and slapping my face. I heard someone say, "Hey, wake up."

I tried to focus my eyes but could see nothing but the ceiling. I wiped my hand across my face and could feel blood on my skin. I was covered with it. I looked up and saw the face of the one they called Owl. The blood made me go crazy. I lashed out and hit him in the mouth. Suddenly, all my energy came back. I was lying on my back in that big puddle of sticky blood, spinning round and round kicking everyone in sight, cursing, screaming, striking out with my hands and feet.

Someone grabbed my feet and pinned me to the floor until the fury wore off. Israel bent over me laughing.

"You're our kind, Nick. Man, we can use you. You may be a lot of things, but you're not chicken. That's for sure. Here." He pressed something into my hand.

It was a .32 revolver. "You're a Mau Mau, Nicky. A Mau Mau."

5

Rumble in the Streets

Israel and I became almost inseparable from the beginning.
Three nights later he came by the apartment to tell me there
was going to be a "rumble" with the Bishops. At last, I
thought, a chance to use my revolver – a chance to fight.
I could feel the hair rising on the back of my neck as Israel
described the plan.

The Mau Maus were to gather in Washington Park near
De Kalb. We were to be there by 9 p.m. Our War Councilor
had already met with the War Councilor from the Bishops, a
Negro gang, and arranged the time and place. 10 p.m. in the
playground behind P.S. 67.

Israel said, "Bring your revolver. All the other guys have
their weapons. Some of the guys have made their own zip
guns and Hector has a sawed off shotgun. We'll teach those
Bishops a lesson. If we have to kill, we kill. But if we go
down, we go down fighting. We're the Mau Maus. The
people. Them African Mau Maus drink blood, man, and
we're just like 'em."

The gang was already gathering at 8:30 when I arrived in the
park. They had hidden their weapons in the trees and tall
grass fearing the police might come by. But tonight there
were no police and Israel and Carlos were giving orders.
By 10 p.m. there were more than a hundred boys milling
around the park. Some of them had guns. Most had knives.
A few had baseball bats, sticks with nails in the ends, or
handmade clubs. Others had bicycle chains which made a
vicious weapon when swung at a boy's head. Carlos had a
two-foot bayonet and Hector had his sawed off shotgun.

61

Some of the boys were to go down two blocks and cut in
behind the school ground on Park Avenue to cut off the
Bishops' escape. They were to wait until they heard the
fight in progress and then attack from the rear flank. The
rest of us were to come in from the St. Edward Street side
of the school and try to force the Bishops to retreat where
our rear guard would cut them off.

We moved out silently, picking up our weapons from their
hiding places as we went. Tico was beside me grinning.
"What about it Nicky, you scared?"

"Man, no! This is what I've been waiting for," I said,
pulling open my jacket so he could see my revolver.

"How many bullets you got in that thing?" he asked.

"It's full, baby. Five of 'em."

"Boy," said Tico, giving a low whistle, "not bad. You
oughta get one of those black bastards tonight for sure. Me?
I'll stick to my blade."

We broke into small groups in order to sneak past the
Housing Police Station on the corner of Auburn and St.
Edward Streets. We reformed in front of the school and
Carlos gave us the attack signal.

We charged around the building into the playground. The
Bishops were waiting for us. "Yeah! Yeah! Kill 'em! Get
'em" we shouted as we swarmed into the school ground and
ran across the open space that separated the two gangs.

I broke into the front of the group, pulling my gun out of
my belt. Israel swerved to one side, swinging his baseball
bat. Kids were milling all around me, screaming and cursing
and slashing out at each other. There must have been 200
kids in the playground but it was dark and difficult to tell
the gangs apart. I saw Hector running across a basketball
court and someone ran straight into him with a garbage lid.
Hector fell backward, his shotgun going off at the same time
with a loud roar.

A negro boy near him fell forward, blood running from a
wound in his head. I ran by him and kicked at his body. He
felt like a sack of grain.

Suddenly, I was shoved from behind and went sprawling
on the hard asphalt of the basketball court. I put my hands
out to break the fall and felt the skin grind off the heel

of my hand. I turned to see who pushed me and ducked just as a baseball bat smashed into the pavement beside my head. I heard the bat splinter as it hit. A direct blow would have killed me.

A great cry went up from the Mau Maus as the rest of our gang attacked from the rear flank. "Burn 'em, baby, burn 'em!" I stumbled to my feet as the Bishops, now in confusion, started to run toward the alleys that exited on St. Edward. Israel was beside me shouting, "Shoot that one there, Nicky, shoot him."

He was pointing at a small boy who was trying to get away but had been hurt and was half running, half limping as he fell behind the fleeing Bishops. I pointed my gun at the staggering figure and pulled the trigger. The gun went off but he kept running. I grabbed the gun with both hands and pulled the trigger once more.

"You got 'im, man, you got 'im." The small boy was falling forward from the impact of the bullet in his hip. He was still crawling when Israel grabbed my arm and shouted, "Let's blow, baby, here come the cops." We could hear the police whistles and shouts in front of the school as the cops began rounding up the Bishops who were pouring out the alley trying to get away. We ran in the opposite direction, scattering across the back of the school ground. I glanced back as I clambered over a chain link fence. In the dim light, I could see three boys lying still on the ground and several others sitting up holding wounds. The whole battle hadn't lasted longer than ten minutes.

We ran for about six or seven blocks until we were so winded we had to stop. Carlos and two other boys caught up with us and we jumped into a drainage ditch behind a service station.

Israel was out of breath but was laughing so hard he almost gagged. "Did you see that crazy Nicky?" he panted out between laughs. "Man, he thought it was a cowboy movie and he was shooting his gun in the air."

The others were gasping for breath and laughing too. I joined in. We lay on our backs in the ditch laughing until we thought our sides would split. Israel caught his breath and pointing his index fingers up choked out, "Bang! Bang!

Bang!" and broke into gales of laughter again. The rest of us held our stomachs and rolled over in the ditch giggling and laughing.

I felt good. I had seen blood run. I had shot someone, maybe killed him. And we had gotten away. I had never sensed this feeling of belonging that I felt in the ditch with those boys. It was almost as if we were a family and for the first time in my life I felt like I was wanted.

Israel reached over and put his arm around my shoulders. "You're alright Nicky. I've been looking for someone like you for a long time. We're the same kind – both of us are nuts."

We broke into laughter again but deep inside I felt it was better to be nuts and be wanted, than to be normal and always on your own.

"Hey, how about something to drink?" Carlos said, still fired up from the excitement. "Who's got the money?"

We were all broke.

I spoke up, "I'll get us some money."

"Whatcha gonna do, rob someone?" Israel asked.

"That's right, baby. Wanna come along?"

Israel punched my arm with his fist, "You're okay Nicky baby. Man, you ain't got no heart, no feelings at all. All you want to do is fight. Let's go, man, we're with you."

I glanced at Carlos who was supposed to be the leader. He was on his feet ready to follow. This was my first indication that the other boys would follow the one who was the meanest, the most bloodthirsty, the most courageous.

We got up from the ditch and ran across the street to the shadows of an alley. On the corner the lights burned in an all-night eating joint. I led the way into the store.

There were three people in the luncheonette. Two of them, a man and a woman, were behind the counter. An old man had just gotten up from his stool at the counter and was paying for his meal. I walked up to him and pushed him back against the counter. He turned in surprise and fear, his mouth trembling, as I clicked open the blade of my knife and jabbed it gently into his stomach.

"Com'on, old man. Give it here," I said, motioning with my head toward the bills he had in his hand.

The man behind the counter started toward the pay phone on the wall. Israel flicked open his switchblade and grabbed the man by his upper apron. Pulling him hard across the counter he said, "Hey, man, you wanna die? Huh?" I heard the woman gasp and put her hand over her mouth to muffle a scream. Israel pushed the man backward into the donut case and snatched the phone off the hook. "You wanna call the fuzz, big man?" he sneered. "Okay, here!" he smirked as he ripped the receiver off the wall and tossed it at the man. "Call 'em!" The befuddled man caught it and stood holding it by the dangling cord.

"Hurry up, old man. I can't wait all night," I snarled. He brought his shaking hand up in front of me and I snatched the bills from his fingers. "That all?" I asked. He tried to answer but no sound came from his shaking lips. His eyes began to roll backward in their sockets and saliva drooled from the side of his mouth as he made funny little groans.

"Let's get out of here," one of the other boys said. Carlos hit the key on the cash register and scooped out all the bills as we backed out the door. The old man slumped to the floor, holding his chest with both hands and making funny clucking noises with his mouth.

"Hey wait," Israel said, as he grabbed a handful of change from the cash register. Nickels and dimes bounced off the hard floor. Israel was laughing. "Never leave a joint without leaving a tip," he snickered. We all laughed. The man and woman were still huddled at the far end of the counter and the old man was kneeling on the floor, bending over from the waist.

I picked up a heavy sugar container and smashed it through the plate glass window.

"Man, you're crazy," Carlos shouted as we started to run down the street. "That'll bring every cop in Brooklyn. Let's get out of here." The old man fell forward on his face and we ran down the dark street toward home, laughing and shouting.

Two months later Carlos was busted by the police and got six months. We had a big gang meeting that night in the auditorium at P.S. 67. Nobody's supposed to go in the school after hours, but we made a deal with Firpo, the Chaplains' vice president, whose old man was the caretaker at the school. He let us use the school auditorium at night for gang meetings because he was afraid of his son. That night we promoted Israel to president and I was the unanimous choice for vice president.

After the gang meeting, we had a gig in the basement of the school. A lot of the debs were there and one of the boys introduced me to his sister, Lydia, who lived across the street from the school. We stayed a long time at the school that night, smoking pot, drinking cheap wine, and sitting on the inside stairwell necking while some of the others danced to a phonograph. The stairwell was encased with a heavy iron mesh wire and couples would go up into the darkness for sex activity.

I pulled Lydia by the hand, "Let's get out of here." As we walked out the door she snuggled up against me, "I'm yours forever, Nicky. Anytime you want me, I'm yours."

We walked down to Washington Park but there was no place we could have any privacy. Finally, I boosted Lydia over the chain link fence and she fell, laughing, in the weeds on the other side. I followed her over and we lay in the tall weeds in each other's arms. She was giggling as I fondled her but I suddenly had the impression that someone was watching us. I glanced up at the building right across the street and could see the faces of a dozen girls in the nurses' home as they peered down upon us. It was as though we were making love on the stage in an opera house.

I started to get up and Lydia said, "What's wrong?"

"Look up there," I whispered. "The whole damn city is watching us."

"Who cares?" Lydia giggled and pulled me down.

We returned to the park many times after that, completely oblivious to the curious faces in the window or to the other couples who might be lying in the weeds near by.

The next four months were filled with fights, robberies, and gang activities. I was picked up by the police four times but they never could prove anything against me. Each time I got off with a warning.

The gang members liked and respected me. I was afraid of nothing and would just as soon fight in broad daylight as under the cover of darkness.

One afternoon one of the Mau Maus told me that Lydia had squealed on me to an Apache. My temper flared and I said I was going to kill Lydia. I went back to my apartment to get my gun. One of the boys told Lydia's brother and he ran to warn her. When I got to her apartment, I talked to Luis, her older brother. He told me one of the Apaches had caught Lydia on the street the night before and slapped her around, trying to find out where I lived so he could come to kill me.

I left the apartment and went to Israel's apartment. We went looking for the Apache Luis had told us about. We found him down at the corner of Lafayette and Ft. Greene in front of Harry's Meat House. Six other Mau Maus gathered around in a small circle. I knocked the boy to the ground and hit him with a metal pipe. He was begging me not to kill him. The gang was laughing and I took my time and hit him again and again until he was covered with blood. The bystanders ran as the beating continued. Finally, he could hold his arms up no longer to ward off the blows and I viciously smashed the pipe across his shoulders and kept hitting him until he lay unconscious in a pool of blood.

"You greasy chump! That'll teach you to slap my girl around." We broke and ran. I was anxious to tell Lydia what I had done to defend her honor, even though an hour before I had been ready to kill her.

As the summer wore on the street fights got worse. The heat in the apartments was unbearable and we would stay out on the streets most of the night. Scarcely a night went by without some kind of gang activity.

None of our gang had cars. If we wanted to go someplace, we rode the subway or stole a car. I couldn't drive but one night Mannie Durango came by and said, "Let's steal a car and go for a ride."

"You got one in mind?" I asked.

"Yeah man, right around the block. It's a beaut and some jerk's left the keys in it."

I went with him and there it was, sitting in front of an apartment building. Mannie was right, it was a beaut. It was a Chevrolet convertible with the top down. We jumped in and Mannie got behind the wheel. I slumped down in the seat and smoked a cigarette, flipping the ashes over the door like a sophisticated rich man. Mannie was turning the wheel back and forth and making noises with his mouth like tires squealing and a racing car engine.

"Rrruummmmmm! RruuUUmmmmmm! Rrooowrrrrr!" I began to laugh.

"Hey Mannie, can you really drive this car?"

"Sure, man, just watch this."

He turned the key that was hanging in the ignition and the car roared to life. He pulled the gear shift into reverse and slammed his foot on the accelerator smashing into a parked delivery truck. We could hear the tinkle of broken glass.

"Hey, man," I laughed, "you real good driver. Boy you really know how to handle this thing. Let's see you go forward."

Mannie slammed the lever into drive and I braced myself as he gunned the car forward into the back of another car. Again, there was a loud crash and we could hear the tinkle of broken glass.

We were both laughing so hard we didn't notice a man running out of the apartment shouting at us.

"Get the hell out of my car you dirty Spics," he shouted, trying to pull me out of the seat. Mannie threw the car in reverse and knocked the man off balance dragging him backward. I picked up a coke bottle off the front seat and smashed it across his hand as he clung desperately to the door. He screamed out in pain. Mannie threw the car in forward and we hurtled out into the street. I was still slouched in the seat laughing. I tossed the coke bottle on the sidewalk and heard it break as we sped away.

Mannie couldn't drive. He squealed around the corner and headed up the wrong side of Park Avenue. We narrowly missed two cars and another car pulled up on the sidewalk, horn blowing, trying to miss a head-on collision. Both of us were laughing and hollering. Mannie ran through a service station and turned down a side street.

"Let's burn this car," Mannie said.

"No man! This is a beautiful car. Let's keep it. Com'on, let's show it off to the girls."

But Mannie couldn't turn it around and finally smashed it into the back of a truck at a stop light. We jumped out and ran down the sidewalk leaving the badly dented car crumpled under the back of the truck.

Mannie was my kind of guy. Little did I know what horror lay in store for him.

Each day was full of frenzied criminal activity. The nights were even worse. One night Tony and four other guys grabbed a woman on her way home and dragged her into the park where all five of them went with her twice. Tony tried to choke her to death with his belt. She later identified him and he was sent to prison for twelve years.

Two weeks later, sixteen of us caught an Italian boy walking through Mau Mau turf. We surrounded him and knocked him to the ground. I stood over him teasing him with my knife, flicking at his adam's apple and poking at the buttons on his shirt. Cursing me, he slapped the knife out of my hand and before I could move Tico grabbed it and slashed him across the face. The boy screamed as Tico ripped his shirt off and slashed a huge "M" on his back. "Man, that'll teach you not to come into Mau Mau turf," he said. We ran, leaving him bleeding on the sidewalk.

Every day the newspapers carried stories of killings in the front yards, on the subways, in the back streets, in the halls of the apartment buildings, in the alleys. Every night there was a rumble.

The school officials at Brooklyn Tech put heavy gauge wire screens over all the doors and windows at the school. Every window, even those five stories above the street, were covered with wire mesh.

Many of the shop owners were buying police dogs and chaining them inside their stores at night.

The gangs were becoming more organized and new gangs were being formed. Three new gangs sprung up in our area. The Scorpions, the Viceroys, and the Quentos.

We soon found out that New York City law prohibited a

policeman from searching a girl. Therefore, we let the girls carry our guns and knives until we needed them. If a cop stopped to search us, the girls would stand back and shout, "Hey, you dirty cop. Leave him alone. He have nothing. He clean. Why not come squeeze me and then I have you put in your own jail. Hey, cop, you wanna put your hands on me? Com'on."

We learned how to make zip guns that would fire a .22 caliber bullet by using a car radio antenna and the workings from a door latch. Occasionally, these guns would explode in a boy's hand or backfire and blind him. But we were turning them out in great quantity and selling them to other gang members – knowing they would use them against us if they ever had a chance.

On July 4th that summer, all the gangs got together at Coney Island. The newspapers estimated that more than 8,000 teenage gang members barged into Coney Island. None of them paid. They just pushed past the gate and no one dared say anything. The same was true with riding the subways.

On August 1st, Israel was picked up by the police. When he got out of jail, he told us things were real hot for him and he wanted to take a back seat until things cooled off. We agreed and the gang elected me president and told Israel he would serve as vice president until the heat was off. I had been in the gang six months when I took over.

It didn't take me long to realize that the Mau Maus were highly feared and that I had gained quite a reputation as a bloodthirsty hood. I gloried in the recognition.

One night we all went to a big dance that was sponsored by the St. Edward-St. Michael church center. The church was making an attempt to get the kids off the streets and had opened a canteen down the street from the police station for weekend dances. Every Friday night they would have a big band and all the gang members would come to the center to dance. They stood around outside and drank beer and cheap wine. The week before we had gotten drunk and when the priests tried to get us to quiet down, we beat them up and spit on them. The police had come and chased us all away. Seldom a Friday night went by that the canteen dance didn't turn into a riot.

On this particular night, I went with Mannie and Paco. We were all drinking heavily and smoking marijuana. I spotted a cute blonde girl and danced several times with her. She told me her brother was in trouble with the Phantom Lords. They were going to kill him.

"Where's your brother?" I asked. "Nobody gonna hurt him if I say not. Let me talk to him."

She took me to one side of the room and introduced me to her brother. He told me that the Phantom Lords over on Bedford Avenue wanted to kill him for dating one of their debs. The boy was staggering drunk and scared.

"I tell you what," I said. "Your sister's nice chick. I think I'd like to take her out some. And since I like her, I'll take care of you too."

I had already made a date with the girl to take her to the movies. I told her that she would have to do anything I wanted her to since I was the President of the Mau Maus. She was scared and said she would go with me but she didn't want any of the other guys to handle her. We kissed and I told her that as long as she went with me I'd take care of her.

We looked up just as three Phantom Lords came through the door. They were dressed in loud coats and checkered pants with long key chains. One of the boys, swinging his key chain, sauntered over and winked at the blonde. She backed off and I put my arm around her. "Hey baby," he sneered, "how about going out with me? My brother's got a car outside and we can have the back seat all to ourselves."

"You wanna get killed," I snarled.

"Big man," the Phantom Lord laughed, "we already making plans to kill your drunk friend and we might just kill you too, you punk."

Mannie gave the boy a Bronx cheer – a razz. The boy jerked his head around. "Who did that?"

Mannie began to laugh but I sensed trouble and said, "Nobody." I started to back away, but the boy swung at Mannie and knocked him down. Besides Israel, Mannie was my closest friend. No one was going to hit him and get away with it. I swung and hit the boy a vicious blow in the back, just over his kidneys. He grasped his back with both hands and screamed in agony.

Mannie scrambled to his feet and drew his knife. I fumbled for mine as the other boys in the room formed a semi-circle and moved toward us. There were too many for us to fight and we backed toward the door. When we got to the stairs, a big boy lunged at me with his knife. He missed but the knife sliced through my jacket. As he stumbled past I hit him in the back of the head and kicked him down the concrete steps. Two others jumped at me. Mannie pulled my coat and we started to run. "Let's go," I shouted. "I'm going after the Mau Maus and we're gonna burn this place."

The boys glanced at each other. They didn't know I was a Mau Mau since I was dressed in a suit and tie that night. They began to back into the room and Mannie and I turned and left.

The next day I called Mannie and Paco. We were going after Santo, the Phantom Lord who had threatened the blonde's brother. Mannie and I had been drinking and were almost drunk. We walked to the Candy Store on 3rd Street and I spotted some Phantom Lords. "Which one of you guys is Santo?" I asked. One of the boys glanced in the direction of a tall kinky headed guy. I said, "Hey baby, what's your name? Santo Claus?"

Mannie laughed and the boy looked up and called me a S.O.B.

"Hey, baby," I said, "you just goofed. You know who the Mau Maus are?"

"Yeah, I've heard of 'em. They know better than to hang around here, though."

"Today they hang around, baby. These are the Mau Maus. My name is Nicky. I'm their president. You're always gonna remember that name baby."

The owner of the store reached for the telephone. I put my hand in my pocket and pressed my finger against the lining like I had a gun hidden inside. "You!" I shouted. "Put that down!"

The others were scared and backed off. I walked up to Santo and slapped him twice in the face. I still had my other hand in my pocket. "Maybe you remember me now, baby."

He flinched and I hit him in the stomach. "Com'on," I said

to Paco. "Let's get out of here. These kids are scared." We turned and started out and I spat over my shoulder. "Next time tell your mommy to put your diaper on before she lets you out. You're still a baby." We laughed at each other and walked out.

When we got on the street, Mannie put his hand in his jacket pocket and pointed his finger through the cloth. "Bang! Bang! You're dead!" he said. We laughed and sauntered down the street.

That night Israel came by and said the Phantom Lords were getting ready for a big rumble because of the fight at the Candy Store.

Israel and I stopped by for Mannie and headed into Phantom Lord turf to surprise them ahead of time. When we got near the Brooklyn Bridge, we split up. Israel and Mannie went around the block and I walked straight down the street. Moments later, I heard Israel yell and I went dashing around the building. They had surprised one of the Phantom Lords by himself and had him on the sidewalk begging for mercy.

"Take his pants off," I commanded. The boys unbuckled his belt and pulled off his pants. They threw them in the gutter and then ripped his shorts off.

"On your feet, freak, and start running." We watched him as he ran terrified down the street. We were laughing and calling him names.

"Com'on," said Israel, "none of them bums are around here. Let's go back home." We started back when suddenly we were surrounded by a gang of twelve or fifteen Phantom Lords. It was an ambush. I recognized some members of a Jewish gang with them. A guy came at me with a knife and I hit him with a pipe. Another slashed at me and I spun and hit him in the side of the head with the pipe.

Then I felt an explosion in the back of my head and I was on the sidewalk. My head felt like it was going to roll off. I tried to look up but someone kicked me in the face with a shoe that had cleats on it. Someone else kicked me in the small of the back. I tried to get up and was slugged above the eye with a pipe. I knew they would kill me if I couldn't get away but I couldn't get up. I fell back on the sidewalk on my stomach and felt the boy with the cleats jump on the back of my legs and then stomp on my hips. His cleats were razor sharp. I could feel the sharp steel ripping through my thin trousers and gouging out the flesh on my hips and buttocks. I fainted from the pain.

The next thing I remember was Israel and Mannie dragging me along a back alley. I knew I was hurt bad because I couldn't use my legs. "Com'on. Hurry up," they kept saying. "Those bastards will be back any minute. We gotta get away."

I passed out from the pain again and when I awoke, I was on the floor in my apartment. They had dragged me all the way home and up the three flights of steps to my room. They helped me crawl into bed and I passed out again. The hot sun was streaming through my window when I awoke and crawled out of bed. I was so stiff I could hardly move. The lower part of my body was covered with dried blood. I tried to take my pants off but the cloth stuck to my skin and I felt I was tearing the skin off. I staggered down a flight of steps to the public bath and stood under the shower with my clothes on until the blood softened and I could peel them off. My back and hips were a mass of deep cuts and horrible bruises. I staggered back up the steps naked, remembering the boy running down the street with his pants off.

Boy, I thought, if he could see me now.

I crept into my room and spent the rest of the day nursing my cuts. Being President of the Mau Maus was okay but at times it could be murder. This time it almost was.

6

Hell Burners

That fall my brother Louis, who lived in the Bronx, came to my apartment to plead with me to come live with him. He had read about my trouble with the police in the New York papers. "Nicky, you're playing with life and it's a dangerous game. You're going to get killed." He said he and his wife had talked it over and they wanted me to come to their apartment. I just laughed at him.

"How come you want me come live with you?" I asked. "Nobody else wants me, how come you decided you want me?"

"That's not so, Nicky," Louis answered. "We all want you. Frank, Gene, all of us want you. But you've got to be willing to settle down."

"Listen," I said, "nobody wants me. You're just a fake. Not you, not Frank, not Gene, not Papa or Mama . . . "

"Now hold on," Louis interrupted, "Papa and Mama they love you."

"Yeah? Then how come they sent me away from home? How you answer that smart boy?"

"They sent you away because they couldn't handle you. You're like a wild man . . . like you're running from something all the time."

"Yeah? Well maybe I'm running from you punks. Listen, you know how many times Papa ever sat down and talked to me? Once. Only one time did he ever sit down and talk to me. And then he told me a story about a stupid bird. Once! That's all. Man, don't tell me he love me. He didn't have time for no one but himself."

Louis got up and paced the floor. "Nicky, can't you listen to reason?"

"Why should I go to your place? You'd make me go back to school just like Frank. Here I've got it made. I've got 200 boys who do what I tell them and seventy-five girls who go with me anytime I ask them. They give me all the money I need. They help pay my rent. Even the police are scared of me. Why should I come home with you? The gang's my family. That's all I need."

Louis sat on the side of the bed long into the night trying to tell me that one day all this would change. He said that if I didn't get killed or put in prison, one day I was going to have to get a job and would need an education. I told him to forget it. I had a good thing going and wasn't about to back out.

Alone in my room the next afternoon the fear, which I had so expertly hidden, swallowed me up. I lay back on the bed and drank wine until I was so drugged and dizzy I couldn't sit up. That night I slept in my clothes but I was not prepared for what I experienced. Nightmares! Horrible, blood-curdling nightmares! I dreamed of Papa. I dreamed he was chained in a cave. He had teeth like a wolf and his body was covered with mangy hair. He was barking pitifully and I wanted to get close to him and pat him but was afraid he would snap at me.

Then there were the birds. Louis' face kept coming and going in front of me as he rode off on the back of a bird, soaring free into the heavens. Then I would be engulfed by millions of swirling birds, ripping at my flesh and pecking at my eyes. Every time I'd break free from them I'd see Louis flying like a speck in the sky on the back of a bird, winging his way to some unknown freedom.

I woke up screaming, "I'm not afraid. I'm not afraid." But when I dozed back to sleep I'd see Papa chained in the blackness and the birds would swarm in and attack me.

The effect continued. For more than two years I was afraid to go to sleep. Every time I would doze off the horrible dreams would reappear. I remembered Papa and wished he would come to New York and cast the demons out of me. I was possessed with guilt and fear, and at night would lie in my bed fighting sleep and saying over and over, "No good. No good. No way out. No way out." Only the gang activity kept me from going completely insane.

* * *

The Mau Maus had become a part of my life. Even though we were strong enough to stand alone, occasionally we would form an alliance with another gang. In the winter of 1955 the Hell Burners, from Williamsburg, approached us to form an alliance.

It was almost dark and several of us had gathered in the playground at P.S. 67 to discuss an upcoming rumble with the Bishops. I looked up and saw three boys appear out of the shadows and walk toward us. Immediately we were on guard. One of the Mau Maus slipped into the shadows and started around the three who were almost to us.

I shouted out, "Hey, what you guys want?"

One of them spoke up. "We're looking for Nicky, leader of the Mau Maus."

I knew this could be a trick. "Yeah, what you want with Nicky?"

"Man, listen, this ain't no trick. We're in trouble and we need to talk to Nicky."

I was still suspicious. "What kind of trouble?" I asked.

"My name's Willie the Butch," the boy said, close enough now that I could see him. "I'm leader of the Hell Burners. We need help."

I was pretty sure of him now. "What kind of help?"

"You hear what the Phantom Lords did to Ike?" He gestured with his head at the boy on his right.

I had heard. It had been in all the papers. Ike was fourteen years old and lived on Keap Street. He had been playing with two other kids when a gang of Phantom Lords attacked them. The other kids got away, but they pinned Ike against a fence. When he tried to fight back, they overpowered him and dragged him into a basement across the street. There, according to the newspaper account, they tied his hands together in front of him and slapped and kicked him until he was unconscious. Then they poured lighter fluid over his hands and set him afire. He staggered out on the street where he collapsed and was found by a passing patrol car.

I took a quick look at the boy Willie the Butch introduced as Ike. His hands and arms were in bandages and his face was badly bruised.

Willie continued, "You're the only guys who can help us.

We want to be brother clubs. Everyone's afraid of the Mau Maus, and we need your help to rumble against the Phantom Lords. If we don't avenge Ike, we'll be chicken."

The other gangs knew of my reputation and the reputation of the Mau Mau gang. This wasn't the first time someone had come to us for help. And we were glad to give it because it gave us an excuse to fight.

"What if I don't help you?"

"Then we'll lose our turf to the Phantom Lords. Last night they came into our turf and burned our candy store."

"They burned your candy store? Well, baby, I'm gonna burn them. All of 'em. Tomorrow night I'll be in Hell Burner turf and we'll make plans on killing those dudes."

The next night I left my apartment after dark and walked into Williamsburg. On the way, I picked up ten members of my gang. As we walked into their turf we could sense the tension in the air. The Hell Burners were scared and had taken to the roof tops. Suddenly, we were bombarded with stones and bottles. Fortunately, their aim was bad and we quickly ducked into the door of an apartment building to escape the barrage of rocks and glass hurtling down from the upper levels.

I told the other boys to stay put and I went up through the apartments to the top floor. There I found a ladder leading to the ceiling with a trap door to the roof.

Easing the door open, I could see the boys on the front side of the roof leaning over the edge looking toward the street below. I quietly slipped through the trap door and hid behind an air ventilator pipe.

Sneaking up behind two of them I tapped them on the shoulder. "Aughhhhhhhh!" they screamed. Both of them almost fell off the roof. They looked back at me with eyes wide, hands gripping the side of the parapet and mouths open in fear.

"W-w-w-whoooooo you?" they stuttered.

I couldn't help but grin. "Hey, baby, I'm Nicky. Who you? An owl or something?"

"W-w-w-hoooo Nicky?" one of them stammered out.

"Come on, baby, I'm the leader of the Mau Maus. We've come to help you guys unless you kill us first. Where's your leader? Where's Willie the Butch?"

Willie was on another roof. They took me to him. About fifteen of the Hell Burners crowded around as the rest of the Mau Maus came up and joined us.

Willie told me how they were trying to ward off the invasion of the Phantom Lords, but so far had been unsuccessful. Everything was quiet tonight, but they never knew when the gang would appear in the street and rip them to pieces. The police knew there was a gang war going on but there wasn't anything they could do to stop it.

Willie had a revolver in his hand, but from what I could understand, none of the other boys had guns.

I listened and then began to map the strategy for the rumble. The gang grew quiet as I talked. "The reason you're losing is you're on the defensive. You're letting them come here and you're having to defend your own turf. Man, the way to rumble is to go to them."

I paused for effect, then continued. "And no guns."

There was a stir in the crowd. "No guns? How can you handle a rumble without guns?"

"We'll use silent weapons." I reached into my coat and pulled out a two-foot bayonet, complete with scabbard. I slipped it out of the scabbard and slashed it through the air. I could hear low whistles from the crowd of boys standing around.

I had won their respect and approval. They were listening to me now, anxious to see how I was going to lead them.

I turned back to Willie. "I want five of your toughest boys. We'll take five of ours. And tomorrow night we'll go into Phantom Lord territory and talk to their leaders: They don't want the Mau Maus after them. I'll tell them we're brother clubs and if they don't let you alone, they'll have to fight us, too. If they disagree, we'll burn their candy store just to let them know we mean business. Whataya say?"

"Yea, yea, baby," the gang began to clamor. "Let's burn those bastards. Let's rip 'em good. Yeah, let's show 'em baby."

The next afternoon I came with five of our boys and we met at the candy store on White Street in Hell Burner territory. The store had been fixed up since the gang fight several nights before. Five of the Hell Burners, including Willie the

Butch, met us there. I talked to the manager and told him
we were sorry the Phantom Lords had torn up his store and
we were going to make sure it never happened again. Then
I asked him to hold my bayonet until we returned.

It was about 5 p.m. and a light rain was falling in the cool
twilight. We left the store and walked across town toward
3rd Street into Phantom Lord turf. There were five of them
in the candy store. They saw us coming but couldn't escape
because we had the door blocked.

We were all standing with our hands in our coat pockets
like we had guns. I walked up to the boys who were now
on their feet standing behind their table. Cursing, I asked,
"Where's your leader?"

A mean looking kid with dark glasses spoke up, "Freddy's
our leader."

"Which one of you is Freddy?"

A boy about eighteen with rough complexion and kinky
black hair stepped out and said, "I'm Freddy, who the
hell are you?"

I still had my hands in my pockets, with the collar of the
raincoat pulled up around the back of my neck. "I'm Nicky,
President of the Mau Maus. You heard of the Mau Maus?
This is Willie the Butch, leader of the Hell Burners. We're
brother clubs now. We want to call off the fighting."

"Okay, man," said Freddy. "Come on over here and let's
talk about it."

We stepped to one side to talk but one of the Phantom
Lords cursed Willie. Before I could move, Willie pulled
his hand out of his pocket and flicked open a switchblade.
Instead of backing off, the boy jabbed his umbrella toward
Willie. The metal tip, filed to a needle sharp point, slashed
through his raincoat grazing his ribs. Immediately, one of
the Hell Burners grabbed a heavy sugar container off the
counter and threw it at the boy with the umbrella, hitting
him on the shoulder and knocking him down.

Freddy began to shout, "Hey! Cool it!" But no one heard
him, as the boys surged toward each other. Freddy turned
to me, "Make 'em stop."

"Man, you make 'em stop. Your boys started it."

Just then someone hit me in the back of the head. I heard

broken glass tinkle as a bottle smashed against a mirror behind the counter.

Outside a squad car screeched to a stop in the middle of the street, red lights blinking. Two uniformed policemen leaped out, leaving the doors of the car wide open as they ran toward the candy store with billy clubs in their hands.

The other boys had seen them at the same time. As if by a given signal, we all poured out of the door and scattered between the cars. A policeman was right behind me but I turned over a big garbage can in the middle of the sidewalk, slowing him up enough to get away down an alley.

But the stage was set for an all-out rumble.

The next night more than a hundred Mau Maus gathered at the candy store in Hell Burner turf. Willie the Butch was there with more than fifty of his boys and we marched together down the middle of the street toward the candy store in Phantom Lord turf.

Charlie Cortez, one of the Mau Maus, had been high on heroin for the last week and tonight was in a mood for fighting. When we got to the candy store, he snatched the door open and grabbed one of the Phantom Lords who tried to break and run. He slashed at him with his knife but missed and shoved him backward toward me.

I was laughing. This was my kind of odds – about 150 to fifteen. I swung at the stumbling boy with a heavy lead pipe with a huge joint on one end. He screamed in pain as the pipe smashed across his shoulder. As he crumpled to the sidewalk, I hit him again, this time on the back of the head. He dropped heavily on the concrete as the blood seeped through a deep gash.

"Come on," someone screamed, "let's burn this whole turf." The boys scattered. Some of them headed into the candy store and the others surged into a pool hall next door. I got caught in the wave and was carried into the candy store. I still had my pipe in my hand and was swinging out at everything. The windows had already been broken and I could see the manager of the store huddling underneath the counter trying to protect himself. The boys had gone wild. They were tearing up everything. Someone turned over the juke box and I was on top of it with my pipe, smashing it to pieces. Others were behind the counter ripping the cabinets off the walls, breaking glasses and dishes. Someone cleaned out the cash register and then two of the boys heaved it through the broken plate glass window.

I ran into the street, my face covered with blood from a piece of flying glass. I was running up and down the street smashing my pipe against car windshields.

About fifty boys were inside the pool hall. They had turned over all the pool tables and broken the cue sticks. Now they were back out on the street throwing pool balls at all the shops across the street.

A gang of boys had stopped a car in the middle of the street and were climbing all over it, jumping up and down on the hood and the roof until it was bent beyond shape. Everyone was laughing and shouting and destroying.

Sirens wailed as police cars converged from both ends of the street. Ordinarily, this would act as a signal for the boys to break and run. But the riot fever had taken control and we no longer cared.

A squad car worked its way to the middle of the block but the patrolmen were unable to get their doors open as the boys surged around the car, pummeling it with broken bottles, bricks and clubs as they smashed out the headlights and shattered the windows. The policemen, trapped inside, tried to call out on their radio for help, but we clambered onto the top of the car and snatched the antenna off. One of the boys kicked at the siren until it came loose and fell in the street.

More police cars screeched to a halt at the end of the block. It was bedlam. More than 150 boys were fighting, shouting, overturning cars, breaking glass. Policemen waded into the seething, screaming mob slashing out with their billy clubs. I saw Charlie struggling with two cops in the center of the street. I ran to help him but heard gunfire and knew it was time to beat it.

We scattered in all directions. Some of the boys ran down the streets and through the alleys. Others took off into the apartments, up the steps and onto the roof tops. In a matter of minutes the mob scene had cleared and there was nothing left but a block full of destruction. Not a car had gone undamaged. The candy store was completely demolished. So was the pool hall. All the windows had been broken in the bar across the street and most of the whiskey stolen out of the showcase. Someone had opened a car door, slashed the seats and then set the stuffing on fire. The police were trying to put out the fire but the car was still burning as we left.

Everyone escaped except Charlie Cortez and three Hell Burners. Gang law stated that if you were caught you had to bear the rap yourself. If you began to "sing" or "rat out" you would be punished by the gang. Or, if you were in prison, they would punish your family. Charlie was sentenced to three years and the others received sentences also.

But the Phantom Lords never came back into Hell Burner territory again.

7

Lucifer's Child

As the second summer approached it seemed the entire ghetto was aflame with hate and violence. The gangs had retrenched during the winter and emerged in the spring with strongly organized forces. All that winter we had been making zip guns, stealing firearms, and storing up munitions. I had gained a reputation as the most feared gang leader in Brooklyn. I had been arrested eighteen times and once that winter had spent thirty days in jail awaiting trial. But they never could make the charges stick.

As warm weather came we began to act like crazy wild people. The Dragons had been having a running battle with the Viceroys. On May 1st, Mingo, President of the Chaplains, walked into a candy store carrying a sawed off shotgun in his arm.

"Hey, baby," he said, pointing the shotgun across his arm at a boy sitting in a booth, "you Sawgrass?"

"Yeah man, that's me. What you gonna do about it?"

Mingo didn't answer. He just pulled the shotgun up into position and pointed it at his head. "Hey, fella," Sawgrass grinned weakly getting to his feet and backing up. "Don't point that thing at me. It might go off."

Mingo was high on heroin and just looked at him blankly as he pulled the trigger. The blast struck him just above the nose and blew the top of his head off. The rest of his body fell twitching on the floor. Blood, bone and pellets were smashed against the far side of the wall.

Mingo turned and walked out of the candy store. When the police caught up with him, he was walking down the street, the shotgun dangling from a limp hand. They shouted at him to stop. Instead, he turned and pointed the shotgun at the cops. They opened fire on him and he fell to the street riddled with bullets.

But inside everyone of us was a Mingo. It was as though the whole city were crazy.

That summer we declared war on the police. We wrote a letter to the cops at 88th Precinct and to the Housing Police. We told them we were declaring war on them and from that time on any cop who came into our turf would be killed as the enemy.

The police doubled their patrols, and often three men would walk the beat together. This didn't slow us down. We would gather on the roof tops and throw bricks, bottles, and garbage cans at them. When they stepped out to see who was throwing things, we would open fire. Our aim was very bad and our home-made zip guns were very inaccurate except in close fighting. Our fondest dream was to kill a cop.

One of our favorite tricks was to throw the gasoline bomb. We'd steal the gas from parked cars at night and store it in soda and wine bottles. We'd make a wick with a rag, light it and burst it on the side of a building or on a police car. It would explode in a mass of flames.

Sometimes this backfired. One afternoon Dan Brunson, a member of our gang, lit a gasoline bomb to throw at the police station. The wick burned too fast and the bomb exploded in his face. Before anyone could get to him he was covered with flaming gasoline. The cops rushed out and beat out the flames with their hands. One of them was badly burned while smothering the fire. They rushed Dan to the hospital but the doctors said it would be years before he could ever be normal again.

We eased off on our fighting the following week, but soon it resumed even more furiously.

Holidays were favorite times for the gangs to rumble. Easter, Memorial Day, and July 4th most of the 285 gangs in the city would assemble at Coney Island. Everyone wore his best clothes and tried to show off, which resulted in vicious and often fatal fights. That July 4th the Bishops killed Larry Stein, one of our guys. He was only thirteen years old and five of them beat him to death with bicycle chains and then buried his body in the sand under the boardwalk. He wasn't found for almost a week.

When we got the news nearly 200 of us met in the basement of the school for a revenge meeting. The room was charged with hatred. Half the guys were drunk and wanted to go out that night and burn the Bishops' apartment houses and set fire to the Bedford Avenue section of Brooklyn. However, I was able to maintain order and we agreed to attend Larry's funeral the next afternoon and then meet again tomorrow night to make plans for a rumble.

The next afternoon we gathered at the cemetery for the burial. Two cars pulled up and a small group of mourners got out. I recognized Larry's mother and father and his four brothers. The Mau Maus had been hanging back in the cemetery and when the funeral party arrived we all moved forward – more than 200 boys and girls, most of us wearing our black jackets with the red double M on the back.

I stepped out to speak to Mrs. Stein. She saw me coming and began to scream. "Get them out of here! Get them out of here! Monsters. Witches." She turned and started to stagger back to the car but fainted and fell to the grass. Her husband knelt over her and the little brothers stood in stark horror looking at our gang as it moved out of the tombs to stand around the grave.

Mr. Stein looked up at me and cursed, "You're responsible for this. If it weren't for you and your filthy gang Larry would be alive today." He started toward me with hatred spitting from his eyes, but the funeral director grabbed him and pulled him back.

"Please wait on the other side of the grave," the funeral director said to me. "Give us a chance, won't you?"

I obliged and we dropped back beyond the grave while they revived Mrs. Stein and proceeded with the service.

That night we had our second meeting. This time nothing was going to stop us. We'd learned that afternoon that the GGIs had killed one of the Bishops and they were to have the funeral the next day. The boys wanted to bust up the funeral by throwing firebombs from the buildings. The intense gang loyalty in avenging this fallen gang member was astounding. They were seething with hatred and finally could not contain it any longer. It was Mannie who shouted that he was heading to the funeral parlor where the Bishop's body was awaiting burial. "Let's go burn that creepy place," he shouted. "If we wait until tomorrow it'll be too late. Let's go now."

"Yeah, yeah, yeah, let's go," they shouted in chorus. More than fifteen of them converged on the little negro funeral parlor, overturned caskets and slashed the curtains with their knives.

The service was held the next day under heavy police guard, but we felt avenged.

The rumbles in the streets were exceeded only by the nightmare of violence that seethed in my own heart. I was an animal, without conscience, morals, reason, or any sense of right and wrong. The gang supported me from their nightly robberies and Frank helped me some. But I preferred to make it on my own.

In the Spring of 1957 Frank came by and said that Mama and Papa were coming for a visit from Puerto Rico. He wanted me to come to his apartment the next night to see them. I refused. I had no need of them. They had rejected me and now I wanted nothing to do with them.

The next evening Frank brought Papa to my room. He said Mama refused to come since I did not want to see her.

Papa stood at the door a long time and looked at me as I sat on the side of my bed.

"Frank has told me about you," he said, his voice rising as he spoke until he was almost shouting when he finished. "He says you're a gang leader and the police are after you. This true?"

I didn't answer him but turned to Frank, who was standing beside him and snarled, "What the hell you been telling him? I told you I didn't want to see none of them."

"I told him the truth, Nicky," Frank said calmly, "maybe it's about time you faced the truth yourself."

"He has a demon," Papa said, staring at me without blinking his eyes. "He is possessed. I must release him."

I looked at Papa and laughed nervously. "Last year I thought I had a demon. But even the demons are afraid of me now."

Papa walked across the room and placed a heavy hand on my shoulder. He pushed me down until I had to kneel on the floor. He towered above me, his huge hands binding me like chains.

"I sense five evil spirits in him," Papa said. He motioned Frank to grab hold of my arms and hold them over my head. I struggled to get loose but they were too strong for me. "Five demons!" Papa chanted, "this is why he is delinquent! Today we shall cure him."

Clasping his hands on top of my head he exerted great pressure as he pressed down and twisted his hands, like he was trying to screw the top off a jar.

"Out! Out!" he screamed, "I command you to leave." Papa was speaking to the demon in my mind.

Then he took both hands and slapped me hard on the sides of the head, slapping my ears again and again. I could hear him screaming for the demons to come out of my ears.

Frank was holding my arms above my head as Papa put both his huge hands around my throat and began to choke me. "There's a demon in his tongue. Out demon, out." Then he shouted, "There it is. I see it coming out."

"His heart is black, too," he said, and hit me in the chest with his fist several times until I thought my ribs would cave in.

Finally, he grabbed my hips and pulled me to my feet, slapping his hand over my groin and commanding the evil spirits to leave my loins.

He released me and Frank backed away saying, "He has done you a great favor, Nicky. You've been very evil but he has made you clean."

Papa was standing in the middle of the room shaking like a leaf. I cursed and stormed out the door and ran down the stairs to the street. Two hours later I found a sailor sleeping off a drunk on a bench in Washington Park. I rolled him and took his wallet. If Papa had cast any demons out of me, it didn't take them very long to get back in. I was still Lucifer's child.

The nightmares grew worse. Papa's appearance seemed to intensify my fear of the future. Night after night I lay in my bed screaming as I awoke from one recurring nightmare after another. I redoubled my frenzied fighting trying to cover up the consuming fear within.

That summer our fights with the police became even more intense. Every night we were on the roof tops waiting for the cops to come by below. We would drop sand bags, throw bottles and rocks – but we needed guns, rifles in particular. And these cost money.

I had an idea for an easy setup for a robbery. I had noticed that every Saturday at 3 a.m. a man drove up to one of the apartments in a big black Cadillac. The guys watched him a lot and we had a lot of jokes about him. We knew he was from Jersey and that he always waited until Mario Silvario left for work. We figured he was sleeping with Mario's wife.

One night some of the guys dared Albert and me to spy on them. So we climbed out on the fire escape and watched him go to bed with Mrs. Silvario.

Every Saturday at 3 a.m. it was the same thing. He'd park his Cadillac, lock the doors and go up the stairs to Mario's apartment.

I told Mannie what an easy job I thought it would be and he agreed. We asked Willie the Butch to bring his revolver and meet us at 2 a.m.

When we got to the apartment, Willie was already there checking his revolver. He had taken all the bullets out and set them up in a line on the steps. Seeing us walk up he reloaded and stuck it in his belt.

Our plan was for Willie and Mannie to wait behind the building. When the man got out of his car, I was going to walk up to him and ask him a question. Then Willie and Mannie would come out and Willie would hold the gun on him while we searched him and took his money.

The clock on the big building in Flatbush at the corner of Houston chimed 3 a.m. and Willie wanted to check the gun again. This time he went back behind the building and came back in a few minutes whispering it was all set.

About 3:15 a.m. the Cadillac turned the corner and stopped in front of the building. Willie and Mannie crouched in the shadows and I pulled my raincoat around me and walked out onto the sidewalk. The man got out of his car. He was a big fellow, about forty years old with an expensive coat and hat. He carefully locked his car and started toward the building. The streets were empty. Only the cars on the nearby thoroughfare broke the silence.

He saw me coming and stepped up his pace. "Hey, sir," I said, "I'm lost. Could you tell me the way to Lafayette Avenue?"

The man drew back and looked in all directions. "Beat it, kid," he said, "I don't want any trouble."

"Hey, man, all I want to know is the way to Lafayette Avenue." I grinned and put my hand in my raincoat pocket like I had a gun pointing at him.

"Help! Robbers!!" he screamed backing off toward his car.

I pushed myself up against him, "Shut up, or I'll kill you."

He gasped and looked at me in disbelief. Then he started to shout, "Somebody help me! Help!"

Just then Willie threw his arm around the man's neck from behind and jabbed the barrel of the gun into the side of his face. "Make another sound and I'll kill you," Willie hissed.

The man stood frozen as Mannie and I began to frisk him.

In his coat pocket I found the biggest roll of bills I'd ever seen. They were rolled together with a rubber band around them. I guess he was taking it to Mario's wife.

"Hey, look, Willie. How about this? This guy's rich. Man, look at all this money."

I backed off laughing. We'd struck it rich. I was bebopping in the street and began to make fun of him. "Hey, man, if I let you sleep with my old lady will you give me some money every week?"

Mannie got in on the act and started to unbuckle the man's belt. "How about it, man? You won't mind if we take your pants off so all the ladies can see how handsome you are?"

The man clenched his teeth and started to moan. "Hey, man, we're doing you a favor," Mannie said. "Come on, let's get these pants down like a good little boy."

He pulled the buckle loose and the man started to scream again, "Help! Hel . . . "

But I jumped forward and slapped my hand over his mouth. He viciously sunk his teeth into the heel of my palm. I jerked back shouting, "Shoot 'im, Willie! Burn 'im! He bit me."

Willie stepped back and with both hands pointed the revolver at the man's back and pulled the trigger. I heard the pin snap forward but nothing happened.

I hit the man as hard as I could in the stomach with my good hand. He bent forward and I hit him on the side of the head with my other hand but it hurt so badly I thought I was going to faint. I moved to one side circling him, "Shoot 'im, Willie. Let 'im have it."

Willie pulled the trigger again. Still nothing happened. He kept trying but it wouldn't go off.

I grabbed the gun from Willie and hit the man in the face. There was the crunching sound of metal against bone. The flesh opened up and I glimpsed the stark white of his cheekbone, framed by scarlet red. He was trying to scream when I hit him again, on top of the head. He crumpled into the gutter, one hand dangling into the open drain along the curb.

We didn't wait. Lights were coming on in the apartment windows and we could hear somebody shouting. We ran down the street and cut into an alley that led behind the school. I was pulling my raincoat off as I ran and stuffed it into a garbage can.

We separated at the next street. I ran back to my street and up the stairs to my room. Once inside, I locked the door and stood in the darkness panting and laughing. This was the life.

I turned on the light and looked at my hand. I could see the man's teeth marks in the heel of my palm. I washed it out with some wine and wrapped my handkerchief around it.

I turned off the light and flopped on my bed. The police sirens wailed in the distance and I laughed to myself. "What a bundle," I thought as I felt in my pocket for the roll of bills.

God! It wasn't there! I jumped to my feet frantically searching all my pockets. Suddenly, it hit me. I had stuck it in my raincoat pocket when the fight began. Oh, no! I had stuffed the raincoat in the trash can. And the gun! Willie's gun was gone too. I must have dropped it after I'd hit the man.

I couldn't go back down there now. The place would be crawling with cops. I'd have to wait until morning, but the garbage man would have come by then and the coat and money would be gone.

I fell back on the bed and pounded the mattress with my fist. All that trouble, and nothing to show for it.

8

The Laugh of Satan

During the two-year period I had been leader of the Mau
Maus seventeen people had been killed. I had been arrested
more times than I could remember. We lived – all of us in the
gangs – as though there were no law. Nothing was sacred,
except our loyalty to each other – especially the bond of
loyalty that I felt toward Israel and Mannie.

One night Israel sneaked up to my room in the middle of
the night and threw a pigeon through the door. He stood
outside and laughed as he heard my frightened screams.
When he opened the door and flipped on the light I was
under the bed. I tried to cover up my fear by laughing
as he threw the pigeon out the window. But after he left,
I lay trembling on the bed, the sound of flapping wings
ringing in my ears. When I finally drifted into a fitful slum-
ber I dreamt of falling. I awoke thinking I had heard the
laugh of Satan.

The next morning Israel returned to tell me Mannie had been
stabbed and was in the hospital.

"Whatsamatter, Nicky?" he said, after he had finished
telling me about the stabbing. "How come you're acting
like this?"

My stomach was tied in a knot and I could feel the blood
draining from my face. Mannie and Israel were the only
friends I had. Now suddenly I felt some of my security
slipping away as Israel told me how close Mannie had come
to being killed.

I shook my head, "I'm okay. Just mad. I'll get in to see
him and we'll find out who did it and burn him good."

That afternoon I tried to get in the hospital but there were two uniformed policemen at the door. I climbed up the fire escape and pecked on the window until Mannie unlocked it from the other side. He was weak and barely able to crawl back into bed.

"Who did it, baby?" I asked. "No one's gonna stab you and get away with it."

"It was the Bishops. They caught me by myself and got me twice, once in the leg and once in the side."

"Which one?" I asked. "Do you know which one did it?"

"Yeah. It was that guy that they call Joe. He's their new vice president. He act like a big shot all the time. When he run away he said they coming back to kill me. That's why the cops are out there."

"Well, just you get well, baby. And when you get out we'll get that dirty nigger."

I crawled back down the fire escape and that night met with Israel and Homer Belanchi, our war councilor, to make plans for revenge. We decided on a kidnapping.

The next day Homer stole a car. We hid it behind an old warehouse for two weeks until Mannie was out of hospital.

It was the week before Christmas 1957, when we made our move. Homer drove the car and we picked up Mannie. He was still limping on a cane. Augie, Paco and I were in the back seat. We cruised down St. Edward Street past the Catholic Center. There was a Christmas dance at the Center that night and two uniformed policemen were standing guard at the door. We didn't see any Bishops hanging around so we drove down to the candy store and parked across the street. It was almost 11 p.m. and we told Mannie to wait in the car.

We crossed the street and walked into the candy store. There were several Bishops in the store and I said, "Hey you guys, we're looking for our friend the Vice President of the Bishops. We heard he wants to make peace and we came to talk to him about it. Is he around?"

One of the Bishops said, "You mean Joe? Yeah, he's back there in the corner kissing his girl."

We sauntered back to where Joe was sitting on the floor beside his girl. He looked up and Augie said, "Man, we are the people. The Mau Maus. We've come for you."

Joe tried to climb to his feet but Augie put his foot against his shoulder and pushed him back down. Both of us had pistols in our pockets and he could see we had them pointed at him.

He began to scream. Augie pulled his gun and pointed it at the other boys in the store. "Don't move. Any of you. First one to move is a dead man."

The owner looked like he was going to panic. "We ain't gonna do anything to you, Pops," Augie said. "Just hold still and we'll be outta here in a minute."

I spoke to Joe, who was still sitting on the floor beside the terrified girl. "Hey, Punk, you got two choices. Either you go with us now or we kill you where you sit. You want a minute to think about it?"

The boy started to stammer something and I said, "Good, glad you thought it over." I jerked him to his feet and we walked out the door while Israel held his gun on the other boys in the store.

"You tell the Bishops we'll bring him back after we teach him a lesson about stabbing a Mau Mau," Augie said. We closed the door behind us and forced him to run across the street where we piled into the car. He sat in the back between Augie and me while we held our guns on him. Homer started the car and we drove to an abandoned building near the Manhattan Bridge.

We took him inside and tied him to a chair with a gag in his mouth.

"Maybe we kill you fast. Maybe we just let you stay here the rest of your life," I sneered at him. Augie spat in his face and we walked out, bolting the door behind us. It was midnight.

We didn't go back for two nights. When we did we took twenty-five of the Mau Maus with us. Joe was lying on his side still tied to the chair. He had tried to escape but was too tightly bound. We sat him upright and flipped on the light. He had been two full days without water or food. The building was freezing. He blinked in fear and horror as we stood around him.

I called Mannie to come and stand before him. "Mannie, is this the boy who stabbed you and threatened to kill you?"

Mannie limped up on his cane. "That's him. He's the one."

I pulled the gag off his mouth. His lips and tongue were puffed and cracked. His throat was dry and he made grating, gasping noises as he tried to talk.

"See, he admits he's the one," I said laughing.

Augie grabbed his long hair and pulled his head backward. Mannie flicked the ash off his cigarette and held it close to the boy's throat. Joe's eyes were wild with fear and Mannie laughed as he gently touched the glowing coal against the tender skin. He screamed out in pain and Mannie pulled it away.

"Again," Augie said to Mannie. "He stabbed you twice."

This time Mannie slowly ground the cigarette out on the boy's mouth, deliberately forcing it between his clenched cracked lips. The boy's chin quivered slightly as he ran his parched tongue across the angry red blisters in a feeble attempt to get rid of the ash and shreds of tobacco which clung to them.

"Now, boys, it's your turn," Augie said.

Each boy in the room lit a cigarette and moved toward him while Augie grabbed his hair again and held his head backward. He screamed with fear, his throat making only funny grating noises like sandpaper scraped over screen wire. The boys pressed in on him, each one grinding his cigarette out against his face and neck. He screamed over and over until he fainted from the pain.

We untied him and he slumped to the floor in the dirt and cobwebs. Cursing loudly the boys kicked him with their pointed shoes, breaking his ribs and jaw. We then dumped him in the back of the car and drove to the candy store in Bishop turf. Augie wrote a note and pinned it to his back: "Nobody hurts a Mau Mau and gets away with it." We drove slowly by the store and rolled his unconscious body into the street. Then we roared away.

Christmas Day I met Mannie in Gino's. We were sitting on a stool at the counter smoking cigarettes and laughing about the week before.

I looked up and saw five of the Bishops crossing the street. I glanced around and even though we were in the heart of

Mau Mau turf, we were alone. I poked Mannie, "Bishops, man. Let's blow this place."

But it was too late. They saw us duck behind the counter to leave by the side door. We had a head start and burst out the door and across the street into an alley. We were running as fast as we could but in his weakened condition, Mannie was falling behind. When we rounded the corner of the alley and out into the street – they met us head on.

I put my head down and ran right through them. They were surprised at my daring and not prepared for the attack. I hit one of them in the stomach with my head and he fell backward to the sidewalk, skidding along on the seat of his pants. I put my hand on the hood of a parked car and vaulted over it into the street. A delivery truck rumbled down the street and harshly blew his horn as I sped toward safety. I hoped Mannie had taken advantage of my attack and was following.

Suddenly, I realized Mannie hadn't caught up. I glanced back. None of the Bishops were following me. I stopped running and stepped back out in the street to see what had happened. Back at the mouth of the alley I saw all five of them had Mannie crouched against the wall hitting him with their fists and kicking him in the stomach and groin.

I saw a quick flash of light and knew it was the reflection of the sun on a knife blade. I ran back fumbling for my knife and shouting, "Bastards! You filthy pigs! Leave him alone. I gonna kill you."

But it was too late. I saw the boy with the knife pull his arm back and with an underhand gesture jab the knife toward Mannie's ribs with great force. Mannie gasped and I saw him jerk upright. He remained erect against the wall for a short moment, and then started to collapse face first toward the concrete. As he fell, the boy with the knife viciously plunged it once more into his chest.

I had paused at the curb. I didn't believe they would try to kill him. Now I was like a wild man. I rushed into the mob slashing with my knife and swinging with my fist. They scattered and ran in both directions down the street. Mannie was left lying on the sidewalk, blood running out of his mouth and nose and a puddle beginning to form where it seeped out from under his leather jacket.

He was lying on his stomach with his face turned sharply at the neck looking up at me with terror-filled eyes. He tried to speak but when he opened his mouth nothing came out but little bubbles of blood.

I knelt and turned him over on his back. I picked up his head and nestled him in my lap, cuddling his head against my leather jacket. His blood stained my pants and was warm and sticky on my hands.

He kept trying to say something. His eyes were wide with terror. But when he opened his lips to talk, all I could hear was a gurgle in his lungs. He kept blowing little blood bubbles with his lips.

"Mannie, Mannie," I screamed. "Don't die, Mannie. Don't die, Mannie."

He opened his mouth once, ever so slightly, and the sound of escaping air came out. It sounded like the soft hiss of a tire as it settles flat against the street. His head rolled in my arms and I felt his chest collapse under his jacket.

I stared at his unblinking eyes. He was dead!

"Mannie! Mannie! Mannie!" I was screaming at the top of my lungs, my own voice filled with the stark horror of the reality I had just experienced.

I heard voices down the street. A woman screamed, "Hey, what's going on down there?"

I couldn't stay. With my police record they would try to blame me. There was nothing else I could do now. The voices grew louder. I scrambled to my feet. Mannie's limp body dropped heavily back on the sidewalk. The hollow sound of his head cracking against the hard concrete echoed with every step as I raced down the back alley and out onto the next street. In my mind I could picture Mannie lying there on the sidewalk, his face turned up at me with those terrified eyes glazed open in death. I was scared.

I ran all the way to my apartment. I slammed the door behind me and grabbed my revolver out of the closet. My breath came in great gulps as I sat trembling on the side of the bed with my pistol aimed at the closed door. I was petrified with fear.

I had never seen death so close up – at least not face to face. He was my friend. One minute he was laughing and talking. The next he was lying on the street with blood bubbling out his mouth. . . . I couldn't cope with this. I had thought I was brave – unafraid of anything. But death was too much for me. I began to get sick at my stomach. Great waves of nausea swept over me and I gagged over and over. I wanted to cry, but didn't know how.

I jumped to my feet and ran against the wall. "I'm not afraid! I'm not afraid!" I screamed over and over.

I was like a man possessed with demons. I looked at my hands. I could see the dried blood against my skin and under my fingernails. Again the image flashed through my mind of his cracked lips and glazed eyes.

I began to hit my head against the wall, screaming, "Nobody can hurt me! Nobody can hurt me. Nobody . . . "

In exhaustion, I fell to the floor and gasped for breath. Fear! Stark, terrifying, indefensible, unconquerable fear! It was like a nightmare come true. I rolled over and over on the floor hugging my chest with both arms and moaning and screaming. The walls of the room seemed to close in toward me and the ceiling moved upward, stretching out until it was ten miles away. I lay in the bottom of the tiny rectangle looking up at the door and window which were thousands of feet above me. I was cramped and caught in the bottom of what was like a square soda straw that was ten miles high with no way of escape.

Then, from above, a thick oozy black cloud appeared and began to settle down the straw toward me. I was suffocating. I opened my mouth to scream but nothing came out but bubbles of blood. I was clawing at the walls trying to escape, trying to climb out. But my neck kept flopping over to one side and I could sense my head hitting the floor with a sound like Mannie's when it struck the concrete as he rolled out of my lap.

The black cloud descended and I lay on my back with hands and feet extended upward trying to ward it off. It was the cloud of death—death—death – and it was coming after me. I could hear the soft hiss of air escaping from my deflating lungs. I gagged and tried to scream, but only more bubbles and then that low gurgle I had heard in Mannie's chest as the blood gushed through his lungs and up into his throat. I heard it in my own chest. Suddenly, the black cloud was upon me and I heard a hollow laugh echoing back up the sides of that square straw where I lay. Over and over it echoed. DEATH . . . Death . . . Death . . . It was the laugh of Satan.

When I awoke it was morning. The sun was trying to peek into my dirty window. I was still on the floor, cramped, sore and cold. The first thing I noticed were my hands, still covered with dried caked blood.

9

Into the Pit

Three days before Easter four of us were on the corner of Auburn and St. Edward in front of St. Edward-St. Michael Church. We knew that the priests collected a lot of money during the Easter week special services and we were making plans to break into the church.

A policeman came out of the Housing Precinct Station across the street and saw us leaning up against the iron spike fence around the church. He crossed the street and said, "Get out of here, you Puerto Rican pigs." We just stood there with our arms draped across the top of the fence and looked at him with blank stares.

He said it again. "You Spics, I said clear out of here." The other boys scattered but I held my ground. The cop glared at me, "I said move, you dirty Spic, move." He drew back his billy club as if to hit me.

I spat on him. He swung at me with his club and I ducked as it smashed into the fence. I charged into him and he grabbed me around the neck. He was twice as big as I, but I was going to kill him if I could. I was reaching for my knife when I felt him unbuckle his holster and reach for his revolver. He was calling for help at the same time.

I quickly backed away and put my hands up. "I surrender! I surrender!"

Police poured out the door of the Housing Precinct and rushed across the street. They grabbed hold of me and dragged me back across the street, up the steps and into the station.

The cop who had struggled with me slapped my face hard. I could taste the blood from my lips.

"You're a big man with a gun, but inside you're a coward just like all the rest of these filthy cops," I said.

He hit me again and I pretended to faint and fell to the floor.

"Get up, you dirty pig. This time we're going to send you away for good."

As they dragged me into the other room I heard the desk sergeant mutter, "That kid must be out of his mind. Man, they ought to put him away for good before he kills somebody."

I had been picked up by the police many times before, but they never had been able to hold me. No one would ever testify against me because they knew when I got out I would kill them, or the Mau Maus would kill them for me.

This time they took me across town and put me in a cell. The jailer pushed me as I went into the cell and I turned and charged at him with both fists. He pulled me out in the corridor and another cop held me while he beat me with his fists.

"The only way to handle these S.O.B.'s is to beat the hell out of 'em," he said. "They're all a bunch of stinking, filthy pigs. We got a jail full of niggers, wops, and spics. You're just like all the rest and if you get out of line, we'll make you wish you were dead."

They pushed me back into the cell and I lay on the hard floor cursing them. "Okay, punk," the turnkey said as he closed the cell door, "Why don't you get up and jitterbug for us now? Not so tough are you?" I bit my lips and didn't reply. But I knew I would kill him when I got out.

The next day the jailer came back to my cell. When he opened the door, I charged him again knocking him back across the corridor. He slapped me in the head with his keys. I felt the blood running from a cut over my eye.

"Go ahead, hit me," I screamed. "But one day I'm gonna come to your house and kill your wife and children. Just you wait and see."

I was only being booked on a minor offense of resisting arrest and failing to obey an officer. But I was making it worse. The jailer knocked me back in the cell and locked the door.

"Alright, Spic, you can stay there and rot!"

* * *

My hearing came up the following week. I was handcuffed and marched into the courtroom. I sat in a chair while the policeman began reading off the charges.

The judge, a stern-faced man in his fifties with rimless glasses, said, "Wait a minute, haven't I had this boy before in this court?"

"Yes, your honor," the policeman answered, "this is his third appearance in this court. Besides this, he has twenty-one arrests in his record and has been charged with everything from robbery to assault with intent to kill."

The judge turned and looked at me.

"How old are you, young man?"

I slouched down in my chair and looked at the floor.

"Stand up when I speak to you!" the judge snapped.

I stood to my feet and looked at him.

"I said, how old are you?" he repeated firmly.

"Eighteen," I answered.

"You're eighteen and you've been arrested twenty-one times and have been in this court three times. Why aren't your parents with you?"

"They're in Puerto Rico," I answered.

"Who do you live with?"

"With nobody. I don't need nobody. I live with myself."

"How long have you lived by yourself?"

"Ever since I came to New York three years ago."

"Your honor," the officer interrupted, "he's no good. He's the President of the Mau Maus. He's the heart of all the trouble we've had in the housing project. I've never seen a kid as mean and vicious as this one. He's like an animal and the only thing to do with a mad dog is to pen him up. I'd like to recommend, your honor, that you put him in prison until he's twenty-one. Maybe by then we can restore some order in Ft. Greene."

The judge turned and looked at the officer. "You say he's like an animal, eh? A mad dog, you say."

"That's right, your honor. And if you turned him loose he'd kill someone before dark."

"Yes, I believe you're right," the judge said, looking back at me. "But I think we need at least to try to find out what makes him like an animal. Why is he so vicious? Why does he want to hate and steal and fight and kill? We have hundreds just like him coming through our courts every day and I think the state has something of an obligation to try to salvage some of these boys – not just lock them up for the rest of their lives. And I believe, that deep down in the heart of this vicious 'mad dog' there's a soul that can be saved."

He turned to the officer, "Do you think we ought to try?"

"I don't know, your honor," said the policeman. "These kids have killed three officers in the last two years and we've had almost fifty murders down there since I've been on that beat. The only thing they respond to is force. And I know if you turn him loose we'll just have to lock him back up again – only the next time it will probably be for murder."

The judge glanced down at the sheet of paper in front of him.

"Cruz, is it? Come up here Nicky Cruz and stand before the bench."

I got up and walked to the front of the courtroom. I could feel my knees beginning to shake.

The judge leaned over the desk and looked straight at me.

"Nicky, I've got a boy just about your age. He goes to school. He lives in a good house in a nice neighborhood. He doesn't get into trouble. He plays baseball on the school team and makes good grades. He's not a mad dog like you are. And the reason he isn't a mad dog is because he has someone to love him. Obviously, you don't have anyone to love you – and you don't love anyone either. You don't have the capacity to love. You're sick, Nicky, and I want to know why. I want to know what it is that makes you hate so much. You're not normal like other boys. The officer is right. You're an animal. You live like an animal and you act like an animal. I ought to treat you like an animal, but I'm going to find out why you're so abnormal. I'm going to put you under the custody of our court psychologist, Dr. John Goodman. I'm not qualified to determine whether or not you're psychotic. He will examine you and make the final decision."

I nodded. I didn't know whether he was going to turn me loose or keep me in jail, but I did understand that he wasn't going to send me to prison, at least not right then.

"One more thing, Nicky," the judge said, "if you get into any more trouble, if I get a single complaint about you, if you misbehave at all, then I'm going to assume that you are entirely incapable of understanding directions and responding to responsibility and I will send you immediately to Elmira to the work farm. Understand?"

"Yes, sir," I answered. And I was surprised at myself. It was the first time I had ever said "sir" to any man. But it just seemed the right thing to do in this case.

The next morning the court psychologist, Dr. John Goodman, came to my cell. He was a big man with premature gray temples and a deep scar on his face. His shirt collar was frayed and his shoes unshined.

"I've been assigned to review your case," he said, sitting down on my bunk and crossing his legs. "This means we'll have to spend some time together."

"Sure, big man, anything you say."

"Listen, punk, I talk to twenty kids a day like you. You smart your mouth off at me and you'll wish you hadn't."

I was taken aback by his abrupt manner but sneered arrogantly, "You talk mighty big for a headshrinker. Maybe you like to have a visit from the Mau Maus one of these nights."

Before I could move the doctor had hold of the front of my shirt and almost lifted me off the floor. "Let me tell you something, squirt. I spent four years in the gangs and three years in the Marines before going to college. See this scar?" He twisted his head so I could see the deep scar running from the point of his cheekbone into his collar. "I got that in the gangs, but not until I had almost killed six other punks with a baseball bat. Now if you want to play rough, you've got the right man."

He shoved me backward and I stumbled against the cot and sat down.

I spat on the floor, but said no more.

His voice returned to its matter-of-fact tone as he said, "Tomorrow morning I have to make a trip up to Bear Mountain. You can ride along and we'll talk."

* * *

All the next day I was under the informal examination of the psychologist. We drove out of the city into upper New York state. It was my first trip out of the asphalt jungle since I had landed from Puerto Rico three years before. I felt a tinge of excitement but remained sullen and arrogant when he asked me questions.

After a brief stop at the clinic he took me by the zoo in the public park. We walked down the path in front of the cages. I stopped and looked at the wild animals pacing back and forth behind bars.

"Do you like zoos, Nicky?" he asked.

"I hate 'em," I answered, turning away from the cages and walking back down the path.

"Oh? Why's that?"

"I hate them stinking animals. Always pacing. Always wanting out."

We sat on a park bench and talked. Dr. John pulled some notebooks out of his brief case and asked me to draw some pictures. Horses. Cows. Houses. I drew a picture of a house with a huge door in the front.

"Why did you put such a big door on the house?" he asked.

"So the stupid headshrinker can get in," I answered.

"I won't accept that. Give me another answer."

"Alright, so I can get out in a hurry in case someone's chasing me."

"Most people draw doors to get in."

"Not me, I'm trying to get out."

"Now draw me a picture of a tree," he said.

I drew a tree. Then I thought it wasn't right to have a tree without a bird, so I drew a bird in the top of the tree.

Dr. Goodman looked at the picture and said, "Do you like birds, Nicky?"

"I hate 'em."

"It seems to me you hate everything."

"Yeah. Maybe I do. But I hate birds most of all."

"Why?" he asked, "because they're free?"

In the distance I could hear the dark rumbling of thunder.

This man was beginning to scare me with his questions. I took my pencil and bored a hole through the picture of the bird. "So, forget about the bird. I just killed him."

"You think you can get rid of everything you're afraid of by killing them, don't you?"

"Who the hell do you think you are, you stupid quack?" I screamed. "You think you can get me to draw a stupid picture and ask me some dumb questions and know all about me? I ain't afraid of nobody. Everybody's afraid of me. Just ask the Bishops, they'll tell you about me. There ain't no gang in New York that wants to rumble with the Mau Maus. I ain't afraid of nobody." My voice had reached a fever pitch as I stood to my feet in front of him.

Dr. Goodman kept making notes in his pad. "Sit down, Nicky," he said, glancing up, "you don't have to impress me."

"Listen, man, you keep picking on me and you'll wind up a dead man."

The rumbling on the horizon grew louder as I stood shaking in front of him. Dr. Goodman looked up at me and started to say something, but rain drops began to splatter on the path beside us. He shook his head. "We'd better go before we get wet," he said.

We slammed the car doors just as the first huge drops of heavy rain splashed on the windshield. Dr. John sat silently for a long time before starting the car and pulling out on the road. "I don't know, Nicky," he said, "I just don't know."

The trip back was misery. The rain was pelting the car without mercy. Dr. John drove silently. I was lost in thought. I hated going back to the city. I dreaded the thought of going back to jail. I couldn't stand to be caged like a wild animal.

The rain quit but the sun had already gone down as we drove past the hundreds of blocks of towering, grimy apartments. I felt like I was sinking into a pit. I wanted to get out and run. But instead of turning toward the jail, Dr. John slowed down and turned on Lafayette toward the Ft. Greene project.

"Ain't you taking me to jail?" I asked, puzzled.

"No, I have the prerogative of locking you up or turning you loose. I don't think jail will do you any good."

"Yeah man, now you're on my beam," I grinned.

"No, you don't understand what I mean. I don't think anything will do you any good."

"What do you mean, Doc, you think I'm hopeless?" I laughed.

He pulled his car up at the corner of Lafayette and Ft. Greene Place. "That's exactly right, Nicky. I've worked with kids like you for years. I used to live in the ghetto. But I've never seen a kid as hard, cold and savage as you. You haven't responded to a thing I've said. You hate everyone and you're afraid of anyone that threatens your security."

I opened the door and got out. "Well, you can go to hell, Doc. I don't need you or nobody."

"Nicky," he said, as I started to walk away from the car. "I'll give it to you straight. You're doomed. There's no hope for you. And unless you change you're on a one way street to jail, the electric chair, and hell."

"Yeah? Well, I'll see you there," I said.

"Where?" he said.

"In hell, man," I said laughing.

He shook his head and drove off into the night. I tried to keep laughing but the sound died in my throat.

I stood on the street corner with my hands in the pockets of my raincoat. It was 7 p.m. and the streets were full of nameless faces with hurrying legs . . . moving, moving, moving. I felt like a leaf on the sea of humanity, being blown in every direction by my own senseless passions. I looked at the people. Everyone was moving. Some were running. It was May but the wind was cold. It whipped my legs and made me cold inside.

The words of the psychologist kept running through my mind like a stuck record, "You're on a one-way street to jail, the electric chair, and hell."

I had never looked at myself before. Not really. Oh, I liked to look at myself in the mirror. I had always been a clean boy, which is a bit unusual for most Puerto Ricans in my section. Unlike most of the guys in the gang, I took pride in the way I dressed. I liked to wear a tie and colored shirt. I always tried to keep my slacks pressed and used lots of lotion on my face. I never did like to smoke too much because it made my breath smell bad.

But inside I suddenly felt dirty. The Nicky I saw in the mirror wasn't the real Nicky. And the Nicky I was looking at now was dirty . . . filthy . . . lost.

The juke box in Papa John's was blaring forth with a loud bebop tune. The traffic in the street was bumper-to-bumper. Horns were blowing, whistles shrilling, people shouting. I looked at their blank nameless faces. No one was smiling. Everyone was in a hurry. Some of the creeps were drunk. Most of the goofeys in front of the bar were hopped up. This was the real Brooklyn. This was the real Nicky.

I started up the street toward my room on Ft. Greene. The newspapers were whipping against the iron fence and the iron grates in front of the stores. There were broken bottles and empty beer cans along the sidewalk. The smell of greasy food drifted down the street and made me sick at my stomach. The sidewalks shook beneath my feet as the subways rattled and faded into the dark unknown.

I caught up with an old wretch of a woman. I say "old" but from the rear I couldn't tell her age. She was short, shorter than I. And she had a black scarf pulled tight around her head. Her reddish yellow hair that had been dyed and dyed some more, stuck out around the edges. She had on an old Navy peajacket that was about six sizes too large for her. Her scrawny legs covered with black slacks stuck out like toothpicks below the hemline of the peajacket. She had on men's shoes without any socks.

I hated her. She symbolized all the dirt and filth in my life. I reached in my pocket for my blade. I wasn't kidding this time. I kept wondering to myself how hard I would have to shove it to get the blade to go through the hard felt of the peajacket and into her back. It gave me a warm sticky feeling inside to imagine the blood dripping out from under the edge of the jacket and puddling on the street.

Just then a small dog came running down the street toward us and swerved to miss her. She turned and stared at him with empty ageless eyes. I recognized her as one of the burned out whores who used to live on my block. From the look on her face, the droopy eyelids, and the blank stare in her eyes, I could tell she was high.

I turned loose of the blade, my mind now back on myself, and started to pass her. As I did, I saw her vacant eyes watching a bright red balloon as it bounced before the wind down the middle of the street.

A balloon. My first instinct was to dash into the street and step on it. I hated it. Damn, I hated it! It was free.

Suddenly, a huge wave of compassion swept over me. I identified with that stupid bouncing balloon. It's a strange thing that the first time I was to feel pity in all my life it was to be for an inanimate object being blown before the wind, going nowhere.

So, instead of stepping into the street and stomping on it, I passed the old woman by and speeded up to keep up with the balloon as it bounced and rolled down the dirty street.

It seemed to be strangely out of place in that filthy setting. All around it were papers and trash being blown by the cold wind also. On the sidewalk were the broken wine bottles and crushed beer cans. Towering up on each side were the dark dismal concrete and stone walls of the inescapable prison where I lived. And here, in the midst of all this was a free, red balloon, being blown before the invisible forces of the winds of nature.

What was it about that stupid balloon that interested me? I quickened my pace to keep up with it. I found myself hoping it wouldn't hit a piece of broken glass and explode. And yet knowing it could not possibly last. It was too delicate. It was too clean. It was too tender and pure to continue to exist in the midst of all this hell.

I held my breath each time it bounced in the air and came back down in the street. Waiting for that final, irrevocable explosion. And yet it continued on its merry course in the middle of the street. I kept thinking, "Maybe it will make it. Maybe it can get all the way down the block and be blown free into the park. Maybe it has a chance after all."

I was almost praying for it. But then the dejection returned as I thought of the park. That stinking, stupid park. What if it does make it to the park? What then? There's nothing for it there. It will bounce against that rusty fence and explode. Or even if it makes it over the fence and gets inside, it will fall on some of those stickers in the grass and weeds and be gone.

"Or," I thought to myself, "even if somebody picks it up, all they'll do is carry it to their filthy apartment and it will be imprisoned the rest of its life. There is no hope. No hope for it – or for me."

Suddenly, without warning, a police van rolled down the street. Before I could break away from my chain of thought it was on top of the balloon and I heard the pitiful "pop" as the van mercilessly ground it into the pavement. The van was gone – down the street and around the block. It didn't even know what it had done, and even had it known it wouldn't have cared. I wanted to run after the van and shout, "You dirty coppers. Don't you care?" I wanted to kill them for crushing me into the street.

But the life was gone out of me. I stood on the curb and looked into the dark street but there was no sign of the balloon. It had been ground into the trash and rubble in the middle of Ft. Greene and had become like all the other dirt in Brooklyn.

I turned back to my steps and sat down. The old whore shuffled on down the street into the darkness. The wind still whistled and the papers and trash kept blowing down the street and sticking on the fence around the park. Another subway rattled by underneath and rumbled into the darkness. I was afraid. Me, Nicky. I was afraid. I was shaking not with the cold, but from the inside out. I put my head in my hands and thought, "It's useless. I'm doomed. It's just like Dr. John said. There's no hope for Nicky except jail, the electric chair, and hell."

After that I didn't seem to care any more. I turned the presidency of the gang back over to Israel. I was in the pit as deep as I could get. There was no hope any more. I might as well become like all the others in the ghetto and turn to the needle. And I was tired of running. What was it the judge said I needed? Love! But where can you find love in the pit?

10

The Encounter

It was a hot Friday afternoon in July, 1958. Israel, Lydia, and I were sitting on the steps in front of my apartment when some of the kids came running down the street. "Hey, what's going on?" I shouted at them.

"There's a circus down at the school," one of the kids shouted back.

Excitement in Brooklyn is sparse and far between. This is one of the reasons that we had to provide our own excitement in the form of fights, narcotics, and sex. Anything was better than the boredom of sitting around. So we headed across the park toward the school on St. Edward Street.

When we arrived a large crowd had formed in front of P.S. 67. We elbowed our way through the crowd, pushing the little kids to the ground so we could see what was taking place.

A man was standing on the fireplug blowing "Onward Christian Soldiers" on a trumpet. He kept playing the same song over and over again. Next to him, standing on the sidewalk, was another man. The skinniest, weakest, puniest looking man I had ever seen. Above them fluttered an American flag on a stick.

The trumpet player finally stopped and the crowd began to shout at him. Almost a hundred boys and girls had gathered, blocking the street and sidewalk.

The skinny man had a piano stool that he had gotten out of the school. He climbed up on it and opened a black book. We began to shout and holler at him. He stood there with his head bowed and we could see that he was afraid. The shouting became louder. The crowd was packed in tight and I was standing with an arm around Lydia. She was giggling as I tried to reach around her shoulder and feel under her sweater.

Suddenly, I realized that everything had grown quiet. I shifted my attention from Lydia and looked up at the man on the piano bench. He was standing with his head bowed, his black book open in his hands in front of him. An eerie feeling swept over me, like I used to have back home when my father practised his witchcraft. Everything got strangely quiet, even the cars on Park Avenue, just half a block away, didn't seem to be making any noise. It was an unearthly quiet. I was afraid.

The old fear that I hadn't felt since joining the Mau Maus suddenly swept over me. It was the fear I had battled in court in front of the judge. It was the fear I felt the night I walked home after my day with the court psychologist. Each time I had been able to push it aside, to run from it. But now, it crept into my heart and body and I could feel it grabbing hold of my very soul. I wanted to break and run but everybody else was listening – waiting.

Suddenly, the skinny man raised his head and in a voice so faint you could hardly hear him, he began to read from the black book . . . "For God so loved the world that He gave His only begotten son, that whosoever believeth in Him, should not perish, but have everlasting life."

I was shaking with fear. This guy had to be some kind of priest or witch or something. He was talking about love. I knew about "love". I was an expert. I reached over and pinched Lydia's hip. She looked at me. "Listen to him, Nicky." I scowled and turned my head back toward the skinny man. He said something about asking for a miracle to happen. I didn't know what a miracle was, but everyone else was listening and I didn't want to be different.

He had finished speaking and was standing up there waiting for something to happen. Then, he said he wanted to talk to the presidents and vice presidents of the gangs. I began to sense that this man was dangerous. He was invading our world and I didn't want any strangers intruding.

He continued, "If you're so big and tough, you wouldn't be afraid of coming up here and shaking hands with a skinny preacher, would you?"

There was a stir in the crowd. Someone called out from the rear, "Hey, Buckboard, whatsamatter, you scared?" He was referring to Buckboard, the president of the Chaplains, our brother gang.

I heard a movement in the rear of the crowd and looked up and there came Buckboard along with Stagecoach and two other Negro members of the gang. They were walking toward the skinny preacher, who had now gotten down off the stool and was standing to meet them.

I grew more nervous. I didn't like this at all. I glanced around but everyone seemed to be smiling and were opening up for Buckboard and Stagecoach to come through.

They shook hands and then the preacher and the trumpet player took Buckboard and Stagecoach and the other two boys over to the doorway of the school. They stood there talking and I walked away from Lydia and got close to Israel. "What're they doing?" I asked him. Israel didn't answer. He had a funny look on his face.

Suddenly, I saw the whole bunch of them get on their knees right there in the street. Buckboard and Stagecoach had taken off their hats and were holding them in their hands and kneeling down on the sidewalk.

When they got up, they started walking back toward the crowd. I shouted at Buckboard, "Hey, Buckboard, you got religion now?" Buckboard was a big boy, about 6'2" and weighed close to 200 pounds. He turned and looked at me in a way I had never seen him look before. His face was serious, dead serious. His eyes pierced deep into mine and I understood what he meant, even though I didn't understand what had happened to him. He said with his eyes, "You better lay off, Nicky, this ain't no time for fooling around."

Suddenly, someone yelled at me. "Hey, Nicky, you gonna let those niggers show you up? You afraid to go up, too?"

Israel punched me and nodded his head in the direction of the two men. "Come on, Nicky, let's go." I could see that he was serious and I pulled back. There was something sinister about this whole thing . . . something dangerous and deceptive. It smacked of something I was deathly afraid of.

The crowd began to hoot and shout. "Hey, look at our leader. He's afraid of the skinny preacher."

Israel pulled at my jacket. "Come on, Nicky, let's go." I had no choice but to go forward and stand in front of the two men.

Israel shook hands with the two men. I was still afraid, hanging back. The skinny man walked over to me and stuck out his hand. "Nicky, my name is David Wilkerson. I'm a preacher from Pennsylvania."

I just stared at him and said, "Go to hell, preacher."

"You don't like me, Nicky," he said, "but I feel different about you. I love you. And not only that, I've come to tell you about Jesus who loves you, too."

I felt like a trapped animal about to be caged. Behind me was the crowd. In front of me was the smiling face of this skinny man talking about love. No one loved me. No one ever had. As I stood there my mind raced back to that time so many years ago when I had heard my mother say, "I don't love you, Nicky." I thought, "If your own mother doesn't love you then no one loves you – or ever will."

The preacher just stood there, smiling, with his hand stuck out. I always prided myself on not being afraid. But I was afraid. Deeply afraid that this man was going to put me in a cage. He was going to take away my friends. He was going to upset everything and because of this I hated him.

"You come near me, Preacher, and I'll kill you," I said, shrinking back toward the protection of the crowd. I was afraid, and I didn't know how to deal with it.

The fear overwhelmed me. I was close to panic. I snarled at him and turned and walked back through the crowd. "This man's a Communist, boys," I shouted. "Leave him alone. He's a Communist."

I didn't know what a Communist was, but I knew it was something everyone was supposed to be against. I was running, and I knew it. But I couldn't fight this kind of approach. If he had come at me with a knife, I would have fought him. If he had come begging and pleading, I would have laughed at him and kicked him in the teeth. But he came saying, "I love you." And I had never come up against this kind of approach before.

I barged through the crowd with my head up and chest out. I reached out and grabbed Lydia by the arm and pulled her away with me and we started up St. Edward, away from the school.

Some of the boys followed and we went down into the basement and I turned the phonograph on as loud as it would play. I was trying to drown out the sound of those words "Jesus loves you." Why would something like that bug me so badly? I danced a while with Lydia and drank a half bottle of cheap wine and smoked a pack of cigarettes. Chain smoking – lighting one from the tip of the other. Lydia could sense I was nervous. "Nicky, maybe you ought to talk to the preacher. Being a Christian may not be as bad as you think." I stared at her and she dropped her head.

I was miserable. And afraid. Suddenly, there was a commotion at the door and I looked up and saw the skinny preacher walk in. He seemed so out of place, with his nice suit and white shirt and neat tie, walking into this filthy basement room. He asked one of the boys, "Where's Nicky?"

The boy pointed across the room where I was sitting with my head in my hands, cigarette dangling out of my mouth.

Wilkerson walked across the room like the place belonged to him. He had a big smile on his face. He stuck out his hand again and said, "Nicky, I just wanted to shake hands with you and . . . " Before he could finish, I slapped him in the face – hard. He tried to force his grin but it was obvious that I had made an impression on him. He held his ground and the fear once again welled up inside me so that I was sick to my stomach. I did the only thing I knew to retaliate. I spat on him.

"Nicky, they spit on Jesus, too, and he prayed, 'Father forgive them, for they know not what they do'." I screamed at him, cursing. "Get the hell out of here!" and I pushed him backwards toward the door.

"Nicky, before I leave let me tell you just one thing. Jesus loves you."

"Get out, you crazy priest. You don't know what you're talking about. I'll give you twenty-four hours to get off my turf or I'll kill you."

Wilkerson backed out the door, still smiling. "Remember, Nicky, Jesus loves you." It was more than I could take. I reached down and picked up the empty wine bottle and smashed it to the floor. I had never felt so frustrated, so desperate, so completely undone.

I stomped out the door, my pride welling up inside of me. I was aware that all the other guys knew that this guy had really gotten under my skin. The only way I knew to fool them was to act tough. If I showed my true emotions, for even a moment, I felt I would lose all respect from the gang.

"That stupid, crazy witch," I said, "if he comes back here, I'll set him on fire." I slammed the door shut behind me and stood on the sidewalk looking after him as he walked briskly away. "Cocky," I thought. Yet, I knew deep inside there was something real about this strange man.

I turned and walked in the other direction. Stopping by the pool parlor, I ordered a rack of balls and tried to concentrate on the tip of my pool cue. But all I could hear in my mind was the voice of that skinny preacher and the words, "Jesus loves you."

"I don't care," I thought, "he ain't going to scare me. Nobody's gonna scare me."

I scratched the next two shots and threw the stick on the table. "Jesus loves you," the words rang over and over in my ears. I told the boys that I was sick and I crept back to my apartment.

I was afraid that I really was sick. I had never gone to my room this early. It was 10:30 and I always waited until 3 or 4 a.m. before coming to bed. I closed the door behind me and locked it. I was shaking as I crossed the room and turned on the little lamp on the table beside my bed. I took my gun out of the closet and put two bullets in the magazine and laid it on the table beside my bed. I kicked off my shoes and changed clothes. Laying my pack of cigarettes on the table, I lay back on the bed and looked at the ceiling. I could hear those words of David Wilkerson over and over, "Jesus loves you, Nicky, Jesus loves you."

I reached up and flipped off the light and lit a cigarette.
I was chain smoking again. I couldn't rest. I twisted one
way and then another. I couldn't sleep. The hours went
by. I finally got up and turned on the light and looked at
my watch. 5 a.m. I had turned on the bed all night long.

Getting up, I dressed and put my gun back in the closet. I
took my cigarettes and walked down the two flights of stairs
and opened the front door of the apartment. The sky was
just beginning to turn gray in the distance. I could hear the
sounds of the great city as it yawned and stretched to life.

I sat on the front steps with my head in my hands. "Jesus
loves you . . . Jesus loves you . . . Jesus loves you."

I heard a car pull up in front of the apartment and heard
the door slam shut. A hand clapped me on the shoulder. I
lifted my weary head and saw the skinny preacher standing
in front of me. He was still smiling and he said, "Hi, Nicky.
Do you remember what I told you last night? I just wanted
to come by and tell you again. Nicky, Jesus loves you."

I jumped to my feet and made a motion for him. Wilkerson
had obviously wised up and he jumped back out of my reach.
I stood there snarling at him like an animal preparing to leap.
Wilkerson looked me straight in the eye and said, "You could
kill me, Nicky. You could cut me in a thousand pieces and lay
them out on the street. But every piece would cry out, Jesus
loves you. And you'll never be able to run from that."

I tried to stare him down, but he kept talking. "Nicky,
I'm not scared of you. You talk tough but inside you're just
like all the rest of us. You're afraid. You're sick of your sin.
You're lonely. But Jesus loves you."

Something clicked. How did he know that I was lonely?
I didn't know what he was talking about when he said sin.
I was afraid to admit my fear. But how did he know I was
lonely? The gang was always with me. I had any of the girls
I wanted. People were afraid of me – they would see me
coming and move off the sidewalk and into the street. I had
been the leader of the gang. How could anyone think I was
lonely? And yet I was. And now this preacher knew it.

I tried to get smart. "You believe you're going to change
me just like that?" I said, snapping my fingers. "You think
I'm going to hear you and pick up a Bible and walk around

like a preacher and people are going to start saying Nicky Cruz – angel – saint?" But I realized that he meant business. That he was sincere.

"Nicky, you didn't sleep much last night, did you?" Again, I was amazed. How did he know that I hadn't slept?

Wilkerson continued, "I didn't sleep much last night either, Nicky. I stayed awake most of the night praying for you. But before I did, I talked to some of your boys. They tell me that no one can get close to you. They are all afraid of you. But Nicky, I've come to tell you that somebody does care. Jesus cares. He loves you." And then he looked me straight in the face, "One day, soon, Nicky, God's Spirit is going to deal with you. One day, Nicky, you are going to stop running and come running to Him."

I said no more. I got to my feet and turned my back on him and walked back into the apartment, shutting the door behind me. I climbed the steps to my room and sat on the side of the bed looking out the window. His car was already gone when I looked down. In the east, the sky was beginning to turn a rosy hue. The huge building across the street that housed Brooklyn Tech blocked my view of the horizon. But suddenly, like catching a whiff of the sea when you're still miles up the river, I had a feeling there was more to life than this. More than these towering concrete buildings – these prison walls of glass and stone.

I thought of his words, "One day you will stop running, and come running to Him." I didn't even know who He was. But I thought, sitting there on the side of my bed looking out over the trash-filled street with the sound of the trucks grinding and roaring down the thoroughfare, that He must be something like the sun rising out of the ocean on a cloudless day. Or maybe something like the morning star that still hung in the dawning sky. Maybe . . . Someday . . .

The time was closer than I knew.

In the days ahead I couldn't escape my encounter with the man that represented God. It was Israel that bugged me constantly about him. Every time I saw him he said something about God.

"Damn it, Israel, if you don't shut up about that God stuff I'm gonna kill you."

But Israel kept talking about it and I suspected he was seeing Wilkerson on the side. But I didn't like it. I sensed this was one man who could possibly destroy our gang. Now that Mannie was gone only Israel was left. And even he seemed to be drifting in another direction. His constant references to Wilkerson and his constant desire to force me to talk drove me to the brink of despair.

I could take no more. The night before July 4th when all the gangs were supposed to converge on Coney Island, Israel spent the night with me. He talked long into the night trying to convince me to stay away from Coney Island the next night and go talk to Wilkerson instead. I put my hands over my ears trying to drown out his constant chatter. Eventually, he dropped off to sleep. I lay in bed staring at the dark ceiling, the fear almost consuming me. I had to stop it. I had to shut Israel up. I couldn't stand to hear any more about Wilkerson.

I reached under my mattress and closed my hand on the wooden handle of the icepick I had hidden there. I could hear Israel breathing deeply in the bed next to me. The more I thought about him bugging me about God the more it infuriated me.

I could stand it no more. "This will teach you to bug me," I screamed as I snatched the icepick from under the mattress and plunged it toward Israel's back.

The screaming aroused him and he jerked upright in the bed just as the icepick plunged deep into the mattress behind him.

I pulled it out and tried to swing it again shouting, "I told you to shut up about God. Why didn't you shut up? Why? Why? Why?"

Israel grabbed me and we grappled, rolling off the bed onto the floor as I stabbed blindly at him.

He shoved me backward and fell on top of me, straddling my chest with his body, holding my hands over my head against the floor.

"Why couldn't you shut up?" I kept screaming.

"What's wrong with you?" Israel was yelling, trying to hold me down. "You're crazy. It's me. Your friend. What's wrong with you?"

Suddenly I realized he was crying as he yelled and struggled with me. Tears were streaming down his face. "Nicky. Nicky. Stop. I'm your friend. Don't make me hurt you. Please stop. I'm your friend. I love you."

He had said it. It swept over me like he had poured icewater in my face. He had said it just like Wilkerson had said it. I relaxed my grip on the icepick and he snatched it out of my hand. I had never seen him cry before. Why was he crying?

He held the icepick poised over my face. His hand was gripping it so tightly I could see the white of his knuckles in the dim light. He was shaking as his muscles tensed. For a moment I thought he was going to stab me in the head with it, then he viciously slung it across the room. He was still crying as he released me and threw himself on his bed.

I rolled over, frustrated, confused and exhausted. What was wrong with me? I'd just tried to kill my best friend!

I ran from the room and up the steps to the rooftop. Outside it was dark and sultry. I made my way across the roof to the place where old man Gonzales kept his pigeons in a cage. I pried the cage open and grabbed a bird. The others fluttered and flapped and flew off into the night.

I held the pigeon tightly against my bare chest and made my way to the air ventilator and sat down.

Birds! I hated them. So free. God I hated those who were free. Wilkerson was free. Israel was approaching freedom. I could sense it. This bird was free but I was trapped in my cage of hate and fear.

I felt my fingers tighten around the bird's head, stretching it away from his body. "I'm not afraid."

The bird gave a small pitiful squeak and I felt his body quiver as the bones in his neck separated. "See, Mama, I'm not afraid."

I went out of control. I twisted his neck back and forth until I felt the skin and bones separate and with a vicious yank

I ripped his head from his body. The warm blood squirted into my hands, dripping on my knees and onto the tarred rooftop. I held the gory head in my hand and looked at it crying, "Now, you're not free. No one is free."

Slinging the head off the roof top, I smashed the still quivering body against the roof. At last, that damned bird was dead, never to haunt my dreams again.

I stayed on the roof top, intermittently sleeping and waking. Each time I'd sleep the nightmare would recur, more horrible than ever before. At dawn I returned to my room. Israel was gone.

I spent most of the next day looking for him. I finally found him sitting alone in the basement room where we held our gigs. All the others had gone to Coney Island.

"Hey man, I'm sorry about last night," I began.

"Forget it," Israel said with a weak grin.

"No baby, I'm sorry. That's not like me. Something's wrong with me."

Israel got up and faked a punch at my jaw. "Sure, baby. You're just like me, nuts."

I spent the rest of the afternoon with him. It was the first time in three years I missed Coney Island on July 4th.

During the second week of July, 1958, Israel came by and told me about Wilkerson's big meeting over at St. Nicholas Arena. In fact, Wilkerson had been down and talked to Israel, inviting the Mau Maus to the meeting. There was to be a special bus for us in front of P.S. 67, and they were going to have special seats reserved for us at the front of the auditorium. Israel had told Wilkerson that he'd make sure the Mau Maus were there.

I shook my head and started to get up from the steps and walk back inside. I wanted nothing to do with it. The waves of fear started over me again and I choked up so tight I had trouble speaking.

"Hey man," Israel called as I started to turn away, "You ain't chicken are you?"

Israel had hit me at the only chink in my armor – in my only tender place. I turned back at him, "Nicky ain't afraid of no-one . . . that skinny preacher . . . you . . . not even God."

Israel just stood there with a little smile playing across his handsome face. "Sounds to me like you're scared of something. How come you don't want to go?"

I remembered Buckboard and Stagecoach kneeling there on the sidewalk in front of the school. I knew that if it could happen to them . . . The only thing I knew to do was run — keep running. But to run now, in the face of Israel's challenge, would make it seem like I was afraid. Really afraid.

"What time that bus supposed to be there?" I asked.

"7 p.m.," Israel answered. "The meeting starts at 7:30. You gonna come?"

"Yeah man! You think I'm chicken or something? Let's get the whole gang and go over there and burn that joint good."

Israel nodded and walked off down the street, swinging his hips and jitterbugging. I turned and climbed the steps to my room, three floors above the sidewalk. I felt sick.

I locked the door behind me and flopped on my back on the bed. I reached for a reefer. Maybe this would help. I was out, so I smoked a regular cigarette.

Thoughts flooded my mind like water rushing through a flood gate at the tide basin. I was scared. The cigarette shook and the ashes fell off onto my shirt and tumbled down onto the dirty bed sheets. I was scared to get on that bus. I hated to leave my own turf. The thought of having to travel away from the little plot of familiar territory put terror into my heart. I was afraid if I found myself in a large crowd of people I would be swallowed up and become a blob — a nothing. I knew that once I got to the arena I would have to do something to call attention to myself.

But most of all, I was afraid of what I had seen out there on the street that day. I was afraid that someone or something bigger and more powerful than I would force me to my knees in front of people and that I would cry. I was desperately afraid of tears. Tears were the ultimate sign of weakness, failure, softness, and childishness. I hadn't cried since I was eight years old. Something made Israel cry. Not me — ever.

Yet, if I didn't go, I would be branded a chicken by Israel and the rest of the gang. I had no choice.

It was hot that July night when we scrambled on board the bus. There were a couple of men dressed in suits and ties who were supposed to keep order. They might as well have stayed at home. The noise on the bus was deafening.

I felt better once I was with my crowd. It was the loneliness of my room that depressed me. But on the bus it was different. More than fifty Mau Maus crowded onto the bus. The harried men tried to keep order but finally gave up and let us take over. The gang was pulling at each other, shouting obscenities, opening windows, smoking, drinking wine, pulling the bell cord, and shouting for the bus to get under way.

When we arrived at the arena, we opened the emergency doors and some even crawled out the windows. There were several teenage girls standing around in front of the arena with tight shorts and brief halters. Cries such as, "Hey baby, how about a piece?" and "Come on in with me, chick, we're heading for a real gig," punctuated the night. Some of the girls joined us as we marched in.

Israel and I led the parade into the arena. An usher tried to stop us at the inner door. Inside, we could see people turning around and looking at us as we stormed into the foyer.

"Hey man, let us in," Israel said. "We are the People. The Mau Maus. The Priest himself invited me. We got reserved seats."

Down front, a member of the Chaplains saw us and stood up and shouted, "Hey, Nicky, baby. Come on down. These seats are for you." We pushed by the startled and helpless usher and swaggered into the arena.

We were dressed in our Mau Mau uniforms. None of us removed our black hats. We paraded down the aisle, tapping loudly with our canes and shouting and whistling to the crowd.

Looking out over the crowd, I could see members of rival gangs. There were Bishops, GGIs, as well as some of the Phantom Lords from the Bedford Avenue Park. The arena was almost full and it had all the makings of a full scale rumble. This might not be so bad after all.

The din of noise was deafening. We took our seats and joined in, whistling and shouting and tapping our canes against the floor.

To one side, a girl started playing the organ. A young Puerto Rican kid stood up and clasped his hands to his chest and threw back his head. "Oh Jeee—sus," he shouted. "Save my big, black soul." And he collapsed into his chair amid howls and gales of laughter from the gangs.

Several boys and girls stood up near the organ and went into the fish, the girls shaking their hips at double beat to the time of the music and the boys jitterbugging around them. Applause and shouts of approval greeted their performances. Things were beginning to get out of hand.

Suddenly, a girl walked out on the stage. She walked to the center and stood behind the microphone, her hands clasped in front of her, waiting for the noise to subside.

It grew louder. "Hey, baby, wiggle it a little bit," someone shouted. "How about a date, honey?" A lanky kid I had never seen before stood up and closed his eyes and held out his arms and said in an Al Jolsen accent, "Maaa-mmy!" The crowd increased its clapping and whistling.

The girl began to sing. Even from our vantage point in the third row, it was impossible to hear her over the din of the crowd. As she sang, several boys and girls got up on the seats and began gyrating and dancing. The girls in their short shorts and brief halters and the boys with their black Mau Mau jackets, pointed shoes, and pointed alpine hats covered with matches and decorated in front with a silver star.

The girl finished her song and glanced nervously toward the wings. We began to cheer and clap and call for another song. However, she walked off the stage and suddenly the skinny preacher stepped forward.

I hadn't seen him since that early morning encounter several weeks before. My heart skipped a beat and the fear came flooding back. It was like a dark foreboding cloud that settled on every aspect of my personality. Israel was on his feet. "Hey, Davie! Here I am. See, I told you I'd come. And look who's here," he said, pointing to me.

I knew I had to do something or I was going to crack from the fear. I jumped to my feet and shouted, "Hey Preach . . . whatcha gonna do . . . convert us or something?"

The Mau Maus joined in the laughter and I sat back down, feeling better. They still recognized me. Despite the fact that

I was petrified with fear, and had relinquished the presidency to Israel: I was still their leader and they still laughed at my jokes. I was back in control of the situation.

Wilkerson began to speak: "This is the last night of our city wide youth crusade. Tonight, we're going to do something different. I'm going to ask my friends, the Mau Maus, to receive the offering."

Pandemonium broke loose. Gang members all over the auditorium knew our reputation. For the Mau Maus to take up the offering was like asking Jack the Ripper to baby-sit. The people began to laugh and shout.

But I was on my feet in a second. I'd been waiting for some opportunity to show off, to draw attention to myself in a big way. This was it. I couldn't believe that the preacher would call on us, but if he wanted us to do it, we'd really do it.

I pointed at five others, including Israel. "You, you, you . . . let's go." The six of us walked to the front and lined up in front of the stage. Behind us things got quiet – deathly quiet.

Wilkerson bent down and handed each one of us a big ice cream carton. "Now," he said, "I want you to line up here in front of the platform. The organ will play and I'm going to ask the people to come forward and give their offering. When it is finished, I want you to come around behind that curtain and up onto the stage. I'll wait here until you bring me the offering."

It was too good to be true. There was no doubt in anyone's mind what we would do. Anyone who didn't take advantage of a situation like this was a fool.

The offering was large. The aisles were full of people who were coming to the front. Many of the adults put in large bills and others put in checks. If we were going to receive the offering, I was determined to make it a good one. Some of the gang members came forward, jitterbugging and dancing down the aisles and either pretended to put in money or tried to take some out of the cartons. When this happened, I'd put my hand in my pocket like I was going for my knife and say, "Hey, wait a minute, baby. You forgot to put anything in."

They would begin to laugh until they saw I was serious. "Man, the priest said give . . . you gonna give or do I have to get my boys to cut it out of you?"

Nearly everyone made some kind of a contribution.

When all had come forward, I motioned with my head and we all marched out the right side of the auditorium through the drapes that hung along the wall. Right above our heads was a huge red-lettered sign that said, "EXIT". It was noticeable to everyone and as we disappeared behind the curtain, the laughter began. It was low at first, just a few snickers. Then, we could hear it rising to a crescendo until the whole auditorium was engulfed in gales of laughter at the poor preacher who had been duped by the Mau Maus.

We gathered behind the curtain. The boys looked at me expectantly, waiting for me to tell them what to do. I could talk to them with my eyes. They were looking for a sign, for a flick of my eyes toward the exit that would say, "Let's run. Let's take this money and bug out of here."

But something inside me was tugging in the other direction. The preacher had singled me out and had shown confidence in me. I could do what was expected of me by the crowd, or I could do what he trusted me to do. The preacher's trust ignited a spark inside of me. Instead of flicking my eyes toward the exit door, I shook my head "no." "Come on," I said. "Let's take the loot to the skinny priest."

The boys couldn't believe me, but they had to do what I told them to do. There were two boys ahead of me as we started up the steps behind the platform. One of them reached into the ice cream bucket and took out a $20 bill and stuffed it into the pocket of his jacket.

"Hey, you! What the hell you think you're doing? Put that money back. That belongs to the priest."

The boys turned and looked at me in unbelief. "Hey, Nicky. Don't get so excited. Look at all this dough. No one'll know. Come on! There's plenty for all of us and him too."

I reached in my pocket and in a deft movement pulled out my knife. Flicking the switchblade open I said, "Man, this gonna be your cemetery unless you put it back."

There was no more argument. He humbly returned the wadded bill to the bucket. "Wait a minute, we're not finished," I said. "How much money you have in your pocket, bright boy?"

"Aw, Nicky, come on," he stuttered. "That's my money. My mother gave it to me to buy some slacks."

"How much?" I asked again, pointing the gleaming tip of the knife at his adam's apple.

He flushed and reached in and pulled out two $10s and a $5. I said, "In the bucket."

"Man, you crazy or something. My old woman'll skin me alive if I lose this." He was almost screaming.

"Well, I'll tell you something, bright boy. I'm gonna skin you alive right here if you don't. In the bucket!"

He looked at me again in disbelief. The knife convinced him I meant business. He wadded it up and threw it in the bucket.

"Now, let's go," I said.

We walked single file out onto the stage. A lot of kids began to boo. They thought we had made a fool out of the preacher and were sorry we hadn't ducked out the door as they would have done. But it gave a warm, satisfying feeling to know I had done something right. Something honorable. For the first time in all my life I had done right because I wanted to do right. I liked the feeling.

"Here, Priest!" I said, "this is yours." I was nervous standing there in front of the crowd. But as I handed him the money the room grew quiet again.

Wilkerson took the cartons from us and looked me straight in the eye. "Thank you, Nicky. I knew I could count on you." We turned and filed back to our seats. The auditorium was quiet enough to hear a pin drop.

Wilkerson began to preach.

He spoke for about fifteen minutes. Everyone was quiet but I didn't hear a single word. I kept remembering that warm feeling I had when I handed him the money. Inside, I was reproaching myself for not having taken off with the loot. But something had come alive inside of me and I could feel it growing. It was a feeling of goodness – of nobleness – of righteousness. A feeling I had never experienced before.

I was interrupted in my chain of thought by a disturbance behind me. Wilkerson had reached a point in his sermon telling us we ought to love one another. He was saying that the Puerto Rican ought to love the Italian and the Italian ought to love the Negro and the Negro ought to love the Whites and we all ought to love one another.

Augie stood up behind me. "Hey Preach. You some kind of a nut or something. You want me to love them Dagos? You're crazy! Looky here." And he pulled up his shirt and pointed to a huge crimson scar on his side. "Two months ago one of them filthy Guineas put a bullet in me. You think I can forget that? I'll kill that S.O.B. if I see him again."

"Yeah," a boy from the Italian section jumped to his feet and ripped open his shirt. "See this?" He pointed to a jagged scar around his shoulder and down onto his chest. "One of them nigger gangs cut me with a razor. I'll love them alright – with a lead pipe."

A colored boy in the back stood up and with venom in his voice hollered, "Hey, Guinea, you wanta try it now?"

The room was suddenly charged with hatred. A colored boy from the Chaplains got up, turning over chairs. He was trying to work his way out from the row of chairs heading toward the Phantom Lord section. I could sense a rumble.

A newspaper photographer ran down the aisle with his camera. Stopping at the front, he turned and began to take pictures.

Israel spoke quickly to three of the boys at the end of the row. "Get him!" They jumped to their feet and struggled with the photographer. One of the boys managed to snatch his camera out of his hands and threw it to the floor. As the photographer bent to pick it up, a boy from across the aisle kicked it down the aisle toward the front of the room. The photographer scrambled after it on his hands and knees. Just as he reached out his hand for it, another boy kicked it away from him toward the far wall. The photographer was on his feet running after the camera, but before he could get to it, another boy kicked it hard and it slid across the tile floor and smashed into the concrete wall, broken and useless.

All of us were on our feet. The room was charged with hatred. I was looking for a way out into the aisle. A full scale riot was building.

Suddenly I had a compelling urge to look at Wilkerson. He was standing calmly on the stage. His head bowed. His hands clasped tightly in front of his chest. His knuckles showed white against the skin. I could see his lips moving. I knew he was praying.

Something clutched at my heart. I stopped and looked at myself. All around me the bedlam continued but I was looking inward. Here was this skinny man, unafraid, in the midst of all this danger. Where did he get his power? Why wasn't he afraid like all the rest of us? I felt shame. Embarrassment. Guilt.

The only thing I knew about God at all was what I had learned from seeing this man. I thought about my one other exposure to God. When I was a child my parents had taken me to church. It was full of people. The priest mumbled and the people chanted back at him. It was a miserable hour. Nothing seemed to apply to me. I never went back.

I slumped down in my chair. All around me the pandemonium continued. Israel was standing up looking backward. He was shouting, "Hey! Cool it! Let's hear what the preacher has to say."

The Mau Maus sat down. Israel continued to shout for quiet. The noise died. Like a fog moving in from the sea the silence swept toward the back of the room and then up into the balconies. Again, that deathly hush hung over the arena.

Something was happening to me. I was remembering. I remembered my childhood. I remembered the hate for my mother. I remembered the first days in New York when I ran like a wild animal set free from a cage. It was as though I were sitting in a movie and my actions were flashing in front of my eyes. I saw the girls . . . the lust . . . the sex. I saw the stabbings . . . the hurt . . . the hatred. It was almost more than I could stand. I was completely oblivious to what was going on around me. All I could do was remember. And the more I remembered the greater the feelings of guilt and shame. I was afraid to open my eyes for fear someone would be able to look inside and see what I was seeing. It was repulsive.

Wilkerson was speaking again. He said something about repenting for your sin. I was under the influence of a power a million times stronger than any drug. I was not responsible for my movements, actions, or words. It was as though I had been caught in a wild torrent of a rampaging river. I was powerless to resist. I didn't understand what was taking place within me. I only knew the fear was gone.

Beside me I heard Israel blow his nose. Behind me I heard people crying. Something was sweeping through that massive arena like the wind moving through the tops of the trees. Even the curtains on the side of the auditorium began to move and rustle as if stirred by a mysterious breath.

Wilkerson was speaking again. "He's here! He's in this room. He's come especially for you. If you want your life changed, now is the time." Then he shouted with authority: "Stand up! Those who will receive Jesus Christ and be changed – stand up! Come forward!"

I felt Israel stand to his feet. "Boys, I'm going up. Who's with me?"

I was on my feet. I turned to the gang and waved them on with my hand. "Let's go." There was a spontaneous movement out of the chairs and toward the front. More than twenty-five of the Mau Maus responded. Behind us about thirty boys from other gangs followed our example.

We stood around the bottom of the stage looking up at Wilkerson. He dismissed the service and told us to follow him to the back rooms for counseling.

Israel was in front of me, his head bowed, his handkerchief to his face. We went through the door and into a hallway that led to the dressing rooms.

Several of the gang members were standing around in the hallway giggling. "Hey, Nicky, what's the matter, baby, you got religion?" I looked up and one of the girls stepped forward in front of us. She pulled her halter up and exposed her bare breast for us to see. "You go in there, honey, and you can kiss this goodbye."

I realize now they were jealous. They felt we were going to share our love with God and they wanted it all for themselves. This was all they knew about love. It was all I knew about love. But at the moment it made no difference. I pushed her away spitting on the floor and said, "You make me sick." Nothing else mattered at the moment except the fact that I wanted to be a follower of Jesus Christ — whoever He was.

A man talked to us about the Christian way of life. Then Wilkerson came in. "All right, fellows," he said, "kneel down right here on the floor."

I thought he was crazy. I never had knelt down in front of anyone. But an invisible force pressed down on me. I felt my knees buckling. I couldn't remain erect. It was as though a giant hand were pushing me downward until my knees hit the floor.

The touch of the hard floor brought me back to reality. It was summer. It was time for the rumbles. I opened my eyes and thought to myself. "What're you doing here?" Israel was beside me, weeping loudly. In the midst of all this tension I giggled.

"Hey, Israel, you're bugging me with that crying." Israel looked up and smiled through the tears. But as we looked at each other I had a strange sensation. I felt the tears welling up in my eyes and suddenly they spilled over the sides and dripped down my cheeks. I was crying. For the first time since I cried my heart out under the house in Puerto Rico — I was crying.

Israel and I were both on our knees, side by side, with tears streaming down our faces, yet laughing at the same time. It was an indescribably exotic feeling.

Tears and laughter. I was happy, yet I was crying. Something was taking place in my life that I had absolutely no control over . . . and I was happy about it.

Suddenly I felt Wilkerson's hand on my head. He was praying — praying for me. The tears flowed more freely as I bowed my head and the shame and repentance and the wonderful joy of salvation mixed their ingredients in my soul.

"Go on, Nicky," Wilkerson said, "Go ahead and cry. Pour it out to God. Call on Him."

I opened my mouth but the words that came out were not mine. "O God, if you love me, come into my life. I'm tired of running. Come into my life and change me. Please change me."

That's all it was. But I felt myself being picked up and swept heavenward.

Marijuana! Sex! Blood! All the sadistic, immoral thrills of a million lifetimes put together could not begin to equal what I felt. I was literally baptized with love.

After the emotional crisis passed, Wilkerson quoted some Scripture to us. "If any man be in Christ, he is a new creature: old things are passed away; behold all things are become new." (II Cor. 5:17).

It made sense. For the first time in my life it made sense. I had become new. I was Nicky and yet I was not Nicky. The old way of life had disappeared. It was as though I had died to the old way – and yet I was alive in a new kind of way.

Happiness. Joy. Gladness. Release. Relief. Freedom. Wonderful, wonderful freedom.

I had stopped running.

All my fear was gone. All my anxieties were gone. All my hatred was gone. I was in love with God . . . with Jesus Christ . . . and with those around me. I even loved myself. The hatred I'd had for myself had turned to love. I suddenly realized that the reason I had treated myself in such a shoddy way was I didn't really love myself as God intended for me to love myself.

Israel and I embraced, the tears running down our faces and wetting each other's shirts. I loved him. He was my brother.

Wilkerson had stepped out but was now back in the room. I loved him, too. That skinny, grinning preacher I had spat on just a few weeks before – I loved him.

"Nicky, Israel," he said, "I want to give you a Bible. I have other Bibles for the Mau Maus, too. Come with me and I'll get them for you."

We followed him to another room. There in boxes on the floor were copies of the black book. He bent over and picked up a pocket sized edition of the New Testament and started to pass it to us. "Hey, Davie," I asked, "what about these big books? Could we have the big ones? We want everyone to know we're Christians now."

Wilkerson looked surprised. The "big books" were just that. They were giant sized editions of the Bible. But the boys wanted them and he was willing to give them to us.

"Man," Israel said, grinning at me, "How about that? A twenty-five-pound Bible!" It felt like it, too. But the weight of it was small in comparison to the weight that had been lifted from my heart that night as the sin was removed and the love flowed in.

Late that night I climbed my steps to my room as a new person. It was a little after 11 p.m. which was early for me – but I was anxious to get back to my room. There was no more need to run. The streets had no appeal to me. I had no more need to be recognized as the gang leader. I had no more fear of the night.

I went to my closet and took off my Mau Mau jacket and shoes and put them in a bag. "No more," I thought to myself. "No longer will I need these." I reached up to the shelf and took down my revolver. By force of habit I started to put the shells in the magazine so I could sleep with the gun on my night stand. But suddenly I remembered. Jesus loves me. He will protect me. I took the bullets and placed them back in the small box and put the gun back on the shelf. In the morning I would turn it in to the police.

I walked by the mirror. I couldn't believe what I saw. There was a light coming from my face I had never seen before. I smiled at myself. "Hey, Nicky. Look how handsome you are. Too bad you have to give up all the girls now that you are so handsome." I broke out laughing at the irony of it all. But I was happy. The burden of fear was gone. I could laugh.

I knelt beside the bed and threw my head back. "Jesus . . . " Nothing else came out. "Jesus . . . " And finally the words came. "Thank you, Jesus . . . thank you."

That night, for the first time in my memory, I put my head on my pillow and slept nine beautiful hours. No tossing on the bed. No fear of sounds outside my room. The nightmares were gone.

11

Out of the Wilderness

Early the next morning I was out on the street rounding up the guys who had gone forward the night before. I told them to bring their guns and bullets and meet me in Washington Park. We were going to march on the police station.

Going back to my room I stuck my revolver in my belt and picking up my big Bible I started back to Washington Park to meet the others.

Walking down Ft. Greene Place I came face to face with an old Italian woman I had seen before. In the past she had crossed the street when she saw me coming. This time I held up my big black book that said, "Holy Bible" on the cover in gold letters as I approached.

She stared at the Bible, "Where'd you steal that Bible?"

I grinned, "I didn't steal it. A preacher gave it to me."

She shook her head, "Don't you know you shouldn't lie about sacred things? God will punish you for this."

"I'm not lying. And God is not going to punish me because he has forgiven me. I'm heading to the police station now to give them my gun." I pulled back my shirt so she could see the gun stuck in my belt.

Her eyes moved slowly from the gun to the Bible and lingered in disbelief. "Hallelujah!" she screamed as her face broke into a wreath of smiles. Throwing up her arms she shouted again, "Hallelujah!"

I grinned and ran past her toward Washington Park.

About twenty-five of the Mau Maus were there. Israel had them organized and we marched down St. Edward to the Housing Police Station on the corner of Auburn Street.

We didn't stop to think what it must have looked like

to the police. Twenty-five of the toughest gang members in Brooklyn were marching down the middle of the street carrying an arsenal of weapons and ammunition. I have thanked the Lord many times that they didn't see us until we were at the door. Had they seen us a block away they would have barricaded the doors and probably shot us down in the street.

When we walked in the Desk Sergeant jumped to his feet and reached for his pistol. "What's going on here? What're you guys up to?"

"Hey, easy man," Israel said. "We ain't coming to cause no trouble. We come to turn in our guns."

"You've what?" the sergeant shouted. "What the hell is going on here anyway?" He turned and shouted over his shoulder, "Lieutenant, you better get in here right away."

The lieutenant appeared at the door, "What are these kids doing here?" he asked the sergeant. "What's this all about?"

Israel turned to the lieutenant, "We've all given our hearts to God and now we want to give our guns to the police."

"Yeah," one of the guys chimed in, "maybe you can use them to shoot the bad kids with."

We all laughed and the lieutenant turned to the sergeant. "Is this on the level? Better get some of the guys to check outside. We might be in for an ambush or something."

I stepped up. "Hey, Lieutenant, looky here." I held up my Bible. "The preacher gave us these Bibles last night after we all turned our hearts over to Christ. We're not gonna be gang members any longer. Now, we're Christians."

"What preacher?" the lieutenant asked.

"Man, Davie Wilkerson. That skinny preacher who's been hanging around talking to all the gangs. We had a big meeting over at St. Nicholas Arena last night and we all came to God. If you don't believe us, call him."

The lieutenant turned to the sergeant. "You got that preacher's number?"

"Yes sir, he's staying with a Mrs. Ortez."

"Call him and tell him to get over here as quick as he can. We may be in for big trouble. If this is something he's stirred up, I'll have him in jail so fast it'll make his head swim."

The sergeant placed the call and handed the phone to the lieutenant. "Reverend Wilkerson? You better get down here right away. I've got a room full of Mau Maus and I don't know what's going on." There was a pause and then the lieutenant hung up. "He's on his way. But before he gets here I want your guns – all of them."

"Sure, General," Israel said, "that's what we came down here for." Then turning to the gang he said, "Alright you guys. Bring your guns up here and lay them on the counter. Leave your bullets too."

The policemen couldn't believe their eyes. By this time four other cops had come in and they stood there in unbelief while the stack of pistols, zip guns, and homemade rifles grew higher.

When we finished the lieutenant just shook his head. Turning to Israel he said, "Alright. Now suppose you tell me what's really going on."

Israel again related what had taken place at St. Nicholas Arena. He told him we had become Christians and that we were going to live a different kind of life. He then asked the lieutenant if he would autograph his Bible.

This seemed like a great idea and all of us crowded around asking the cops to autograph our Bibles.

Just then David pushed through the door. He took one look at all of us and walked straight up the lieutenant. The lieutenant asked all the other officers to come into the room.

"Reverend," he said, "I want to shake your hand." Wilkerson glanced around with a quizzical look on his face but stuck out his hand while the policeman pumped it firmly.

"How did you do it?" he asked. "These boys declare war on us and have given us nothing but trouble for years. Then this morning they all troop in here and you know what they want?"

Wilkerson shook his head.

"They want us to autograph their Bibles!"

Wilkerson was speechless. "You asked these policemen to what?" he stammered.

I opened my Bible and showed him the lieutenant's autograph on the flyleaf. "Well, praise the Lord!" David said.

"See, Lieutenant, God is at work here in Ft. Greene!"

We all stepped out on the street and left the sergeant shaking his head in wonder at the pile of guns stacked on the counter in front of him.

We clamored around Wilkerson. Israel spoke up, "Hey, Davie, I been reading my Bible most of the night. Look! I'm in the Bible. Here's my name all over the place. See? Israel. That's me. I'm famous."

Several weeks later Reverend Arce, the minister at a Spanish Church called Iglesia de Dios Juan 3:16 (Church of God John 3:16) came by my apartment. Israel was there. We had been spending a lot of time together reading our Bibles and walking around praying out loud. Reverend Arce wanted us to come to his church the next night and give our testimonies. It was a Wednesday night service and he promised to come by and pick us up.

It was the first real church service I had ever been in. We sang for almost an hour. Israel and I were on the platform and the church building was packed full. Reverend Arce preached a full length sermon and then called on me to give my testimony.

After I finished speaking, I sat on the front row and listened to Israel.

It was the first time I had heard him speak in public. He stood behind the pulpit, his handsome face radiating the love of Christ. In his gentle voice he began to tell of the events which led up to his conversion. Even though we had been together daily during the past few weeks, tonight I witnessed in him a depth of feeling and expression I had never seen before. His words took me back to that night in St. Nicholas Arena when Israel had so willingly responded to the Gospel. I thought of my own attitude toward Davie. I had hated him – God knows how I hated him! How could I have been so wrong? All he wanted to do was let God love me through him – instead, I had spat on him, cursed him, wanted to kill him.

Israel's mention of David's name snapped me back to reality.

"I was still testing Wilkerson's sincerity," Israel was

saying, relating his feelings after that first street meeting when he had heard Davie preach.

"One afternoon Wilkerson came by and asked me to take him to meet some of the other gang leaders. He wanted to invite them to the meetings he was having at St. Nicholas Arena.

"We went down into Brooklyn together and I pointed out Little Jo-Jo, who was President of the Coney Island Dragons, one of the largest street gangs in the city. I just pointed him out. I didn't want him to know I set him up for Davie since they were big enemies of the Mau Maus.

"I told Davie I'd walk home. As he walked up to Little Jo-Jo, I ducked behind some apartment steps to listen. Jo-Jo looked him over real good and then spat on his shoes. This is the highest sign of contempt you can give a fellow. Jo-Jo didn't say a word, he just spat on Davie's shoes. Then he turned away and sat down on the steps.

"Jo-Jo didn't have a home. Matter of fact, he didn't have much of anything. He slept in the park in warm weather and when it rained or got cold he slept in the subway. Jo-Jo was a real bum. He stole clothes out of those big welfare boxes on the corner and wore 'em 'til they were just rags. Then he'd steal some more.

"That day he had on a pair of old sloppy canvas shoes with his toes stickin' out and some big old droopy pants like belonged to a fat man.

"I figured if Wilkerson was a phony it would show up when he met Jo-Jo. Jo-Jo could spot a phony. If Wilkerson wasn't for real, Jo-Jo would stick him with his shiv.

"He looked up at Wilkerson and said, 'Get lost, rich man. You don't belong around here. You come to New York and talk big about God changing people. You get shiny new shoes and new pants and we ain't got nothing. My old lady kicked me out 'cause there are ten kids in our hole and no money. Man, I know your type. You down here slummin' like them rich folks who ride the bus through the Bowery. Well, you better get lost 'fore someone runs a shiv in your belly.'

"I could tell that something was getting hold of Davie's heart. Maybe he knew Jo-Jo was telling the truth. He told me later it was because he remembered something about some General Booth who had said, 'It is impossible to comfort men's hearts with the love of God when their feet are perishing with cold.' Maybe I don't quote that just right, but anyhow Davie said that's what flashed through his mind. And you know what he did? He sat down on those steps – right there on that street – and pulled his shoes off and handed them to Jo-Jo.

"Old Jo-Jo, he just looked up at Davie and said, 'What you trying to prove preacher? That you got a heart or something? I ain't gonna put your stinkin' shoes on.'

"But Davie talked right back to him. 'Man,' he said, 'you been griping about shoes. Now put 'em on or quit your belly-achin'.'

"Jo-Jo said, 'I ain't never had no new shoes.'

"And Wilkerson just kept at him, 'Put 'em on,' he said.

"So Jo-Jo put on Davie's shoes. As he did Davie started walking down the street toward his car. I kinda crouched back in behind the steps while Jo-Jo chased Davie down the street. Old Davie was in his socks and had to walk two blocks to the car with all the folks laughin' at him. That's when I saw he was for real."

Israel paused in his testimony, choking back tears. "Nothing Davie had said had gotten through to me. But this guy was no phony. He lived what he preached. I knew then I couldn't resist the kind of power that could make a man do something like that for someone like Jo-Jo."

Following the service I made my way slowly through the crowd still overwhelmed with the church service and the power of the presence of God in me as I spoke. I kept thinking that maybe God wanted me to preach. Could this be His way of speaking to me? I didn't know, but I felt I needed time to think about it.

The people were still milling around the vestibule and standing out front on the sidewalk. I was still shaking hands when I walked out the front door. Just then two cars across the street roared to life. I heard a woman scream. Glancing in that direction I saw gun barrels sticking out the windows and recognized some of the Bishops. They began shooting wildly in my direction as the cars jerked away from the curb. People were falling down in front of the church and running

wildly back into the building trying to escape the fusillade
of shots. I ducked behind a door as bullets smacked into the
stone beside me. The cars sped off into the night.

As the excitement died down an old man walked up beside
me and put his arm around my shoulder, "Son, don't get
discouraged. Jesus Himself was tempted in the wilderness
following his baptism. You should feel honored that Satan
has singled you out for persecution. I predict you will do
great things for God if you persevere." He patted me on the
shoulder and disappeared into the crowd.

I didn't know what "persevere" meant, but I wanted to do
great things for God. I wasn't too sure that I was honored
because Satan had sent the Bishops around to try to kill
me, though.

Things seemed to have quieted down and I went back out
to start the long walk home. Reverend Arce had driven Israel
home but I wanted to walk. I needed to think. Mr. Delgado
who had been working with David Wilkerson, asked me to
come home and spend the night with him. He was a kind,
gentle, well-dressed man. I thought he must be very wealthy.
I was ashamed of my poor manners and clothes and declined
his offer. He gave me a dollar bill and told me that if I ever
needed money to let him know.

I thanked him and started back to the apartment. Crossing
Vanderbilt Avenue, I spotted Loca standing in front of her
apartment. "Hey, Nicky, where you been all this time?
Someone said you dropped out of the gang. Is that right?"

I told her it was.

"Hey, baby, we miss you. Things just aren't the same
without you around. How come you don't come back?"

Suddenly, someone locked their arms around me from
behind. "Hey, you really do want me back, don't you?"
thinking it was one of our gang. Loca's face was frozen with
terror. I hoisted my head and recognized Joe, the Apache
we had kidnapped and burned.

I was struggling to get loose when I saw the knife in his
right hand. He held me from behind with his left hand around
my neck while he swung the blade over my shoulder toward
my heart. I threw my right hand up to ward off the eight-inch
blade and it stabbed me in the hand between my ring finger

and little finger, going all the way through my hand and barely grazing my chest.

I spun around and he slashed at me again. "I'm gonna kill you this time," he cursed. "You think you can get away from me by hiding behind a church, then baby you're wrong. I'm gonna do the world a favor and kill a chicken who's turned square."

I shouted at Loca, "Get out of here! This guy's crazy!"

He moved toward me and jabbed the knife at my stomach. I jumped back and snatched a radio aerial off a parked car. Now the odds were even. In my hand, the aerial was as deadly as his switchblade.

I circled the boy, slashing the air with the metal rod. I was back in my own element now. I felt confident I could kill him. I thought ahead, knowing from experience what his next move would be. When he lunged at me with his knife, I would dance back and catch him off balance. I could blind him with a back-handed swing and paralyze or kill him with the second blow.

I held the antenna in my left hand, my right hand dripping with blood, held in front of me to ward off his knife.

"Com'on, baby," I whispered. "Try it once more. Just once more. It'll be your last."

The boy's eyes were narrowed with hate. I knew I'd have to kill him because nothing else would stop him.

He started toward me and I stepped back as the knife whizzed by my stomach. Now! He was off balance. I brought the antenna back to whip it across his unprotected face.

Suddenly, it felt as though the hand of God grabbed my arm. "Turn the other cheek." The voice was so real it was audible. I looked on this Apache not as the enemy, but as a person. I felt sorry for him standing there in the night spitting curse words with hate written on his face. I could picture myself just a few weeks before standing in the dark street trying to kill an enemy.

I prayed. For the first time, I prayed for myself. "God, help me."

The Apache regained his balance and looked up at me. "What you say?"

I said it again, "God, help me." He stopped and stared at me.

Loca ran up thrusting the neck of a broken whiskey bottle into my hand. "Slit him open, Nicky."

The boy started to run. "Throw it at him, Nicky, throw it!"

I pulled back my arm but instead of throwing the bottle at the fleeing Apache, I threw it against the side of the building.

Then I took my handkerchief and wrapped it around my badly bleeding hand. The blood soaked through and Loca ran up the steps to her room and brought me a bath towel to absorb the bleeding. She wanted to walk me home but I told her I could make it and started down the sidewalk.

I was afraid to go to the hospital, but I knew I needed help. I was getting weak from loss of blood. I would have to cross Washington Park from Fulton Place to get to Cumberland Hospital. I figured I'd better go before I bled to death. Standing on the corner of De Kalb by the Fire Station, I waited for the light to change. But my eyes began to roll and I knew I had to get across the street before I fainted.

I staggered out into the middle of the traffic. Just then I heard a shout and one of the Mau Maus came running out in the street to help me. It was Tarzan, a real nut who wore a huge Mexican hat.

"What you trying to do, Nicky, commit suicide?" He thought I was crazy because I had given my heart to God.

"Man, I'm hurt. Hurt bad. Help me get to Israel's apartment, will you?"

Tarzan walked with me to Israel's apartment and we climbed the five flights of stairs to his room. It was midnight when I rapped on the door.

Israel's mother opened the door and invited me in. She could see I was hurt. Israel came out of the other room. He looked at me and started to laugh. "Man, what happened to you?"

"I got stuck by an Apache."

"Hey, baby, I didn't think this could ever happen to you."

Israel's mother interrupted and insisted that I go to the hospital. Israel and Tarzan both helped me down the stairs and to the emergency room at the nearby hospital. Tarzan agreed to take my wallet with the one dollar in it and tell my brother Frank what happened to me. Israel waited until the doctor examined my hand. Tendons had been cut and they were going to have to put me to sleep to operate. Israel looked serious when they wheeled me out. "Don't worry, baby, we'll get the guy who did it."

I wanted to tell him that we didn't need to get revenge any more. God would take care of that. But the door closed softly behind me.

Early the next morning Israel was in my room. I was still groggy from the anesthesia but I could tell there had been a change about him. I finally got my eyes open and saw that he had completely shaved his head.

"Hey, baldie, what's up?" I mumbled.

Israel had the old look back on his face. "Man, first they almost shoot us in front of the church and now they stab you. This Jesus business is for the birds. That guy had no right to treat you that way. I'm gonna get him for you."

I was coming to my senses and raised up in the bed. "Hey, man, you can't do that. I could've gotten him myself last night but I left it in God's hands. If you go back to the street you'll never come back. Remember what Davie said about putting your hand to the plow . . . Man, you stick with me and leave the fighting alone."

I struggled to sit up and noticed that Lydia and Loretta had come in with Israel.

I fell back on the bed still weak from the loss of blood and the surgery. My entire arm was in a big cast from the tips of my fingers to my elbow.

Loretta was a cute black-haired Italian girl I had dated on several occasions. She spoke up. "Nicky, Israel's right. Those guys will come in the hospital and kill you if you don't come back to the gang. Let's make it like old times again, okay? You get well and come on back to the Mau Maus. We'll be waiting for you."

I turned and looked at Lydia. "Is that the way you feel too?" I asked.

She hung her head. "Nicky, there's something I've got to tell you. I'm ashamed to bring it up now when I should have done it a long time ago. I've been a Christian for two years now."

"What?" I stared at her in unbelief. "You mean to tell me you've been a Christian all this time and never did tell me. How can you be a Christian and do all the things you've done? Think about what we've done together. Don't tell me you're a Christian. Christians don't act like that. They aren't ashamed of God. I don't believe you."

Lydia bit her bottom lip and tears came to her eyes as she twisted the sheet with her hands. "I'm ashamed, Nicky. I was scared to tell you about Christ. I was afraid that if I told you I was a Christian you wouldn't want me any more."

Israel walked over to the side of the bed. "Hey, com'on, Nicky. You're just upset. You'll feel better later on. Loretta and I think you ought to come back to the gang. I don't know about Lydia. But you think about it and don't worry. I'll talk to some of the guys and we'll get that guy who did this to you."

I turned away from them. Loretta came over and kissed me on the side of the face. I felt hot tears on my cheek as Lydia bent low to kiss me. "I'm sorry, Nicky. Forgive me, please."

I said nothing and she kissed me and ran out. I heard the door close behind them.

After they left I could almost feel the presence of Satan in the room. He was speaking to me through Israel and Loretta. He was preparing me through my disappointment over Lydia. "Nicky," he whispered. "You're a fool. They are right. Go on back to the gang. Remember the good times. Remember the satisfaction of getting revenge. Remember how sweet it was to be in the arms of a beautiful girl. You've let your gang down, Nicky, but it's not too late to go back."

As he was tempting me the nurse came in with my dinner tray. I could still hear his whisper. "Last night was the first time in your life you never fought back. What a coward you are. Big brave Nicky Cruz, crying there in St. Nicholas. Running from an Apache and letting him get away. Sissy. Square. Coward."

"Mr. Cruz?" It was the nurse speaking as she stood beside

my bed. "If you'll turn over I'll fix your dinner tray."

I jerked up in bed and slapped at the tray knocking it from her hands and onto the floor. "Get the hell out of here!"

I wanted to say more but nothing else came out. All the old curse words had disappeared. I couldn't even think of them at the time. I just sat there with my mouth open and suddenly the tears flooded my eyes and ran down my face like waterfalls. "I'm sorry. I'm sorry," I sobbed out. "Please call a minister. Call Reverend Arce."

The nurse quietly picked up the dishes and patted me on the shoulder. "I'll call him now. You lie down and rest."

I lay back on my pillow and sobbed. In a short time Reverend Arce arrived and prayed with me. As he prayed I felt release from the spirit that had possessed me. He told me he was going to send Mr. Delgado up to see me in the morning and he would see I was taken care of.

That night after the nurse had helped me change my pajama top, I knelt beside the bed in the hospital room. During the afternoon they had moved someone into the other bed in the room but I thought he was asleep. I began to pray out loud, which was the only way I knew how to pray. I didn't know you could "pray to yourself." I thought you had to pray "to God" and the only way I knew how to pray was to talk to Him – out loud. So I began to pray.

I asked God to forgive the boy who had stabbed me and to protect him from harm until he could learn about Jesus. I asked God to forgive me for the way I had acted toward Lydia and for slapping the tray out of the nurse's hand. I told Him I would go anywhere and do anything He wanted me to do. I reminded Him I wasn't afraid to die but asked him to let me live long enough to one day tell Mama and Papa about Jesus.

I was on my knees for a long time before I crawled back into bed and went to sleep.

The next morning I was dressing to leave the hospital when the man in the next bed whispered and motioned for me to step closer. He was an old man with a tube in his throat. He was shaking and very pale and could barely speak above a whisper.

"I was awake last night," he whispered.

I was embarrassed and grinned foolishly.

"Thank you," he said. "Thank you for your prayer."

"But I wasn't praying for you," I confessed. "I thought you were asleep. I was praying for myself."

The old man reached over and grabbed my one good hand with his cold, clammy fingers. His grip was very weak but I could feel him squeezing. "Oh, no, you're wrong. You were praying for me. And I prayed too. For the first time in many, many years, I prayed. I, too, want to do what Jesus wants me to do. Thank you."

Big tears rolled down his drawn hollow cheeks as he spoke. I said, "God bless you, my friend," and walked out. I had never tried to minister to anyone else in all my life. I didn't know how even now. But I had a strong warm feeling that God's Spirit had ministered through me. And I was glad.

Mr. Delgado met me in the lobby. He had paid my bill and ushered me out to his car. "I called David Wilkerson last night," he said. "He's in Elmira conducting a series of meetings. He wants me to bring you and Israel up there tomorrow."

"Davie mentioned it the last time I saw him," I said. "But Israel has gone back to the gang. I don't think he'll go."

"I'll go see him tonight," Mr. Delgado said. "But today I want you to stay at my house where you'll be safe. We'll leave early in the morning and drive to Elmira."

It seemed ironic that I would be going to Elmira to be with Davie. This was where the police wanted to send me, but for a very different reason. I spent the rest of the day praying for Israel, that he wouldn't go back to the gang but would come with me to Elmira.

The next morning we got up early and drove through the city toward Brooklyn and the Ft. Greene project. Mr. Delgado said that Israel had agreed to go with us and was supposed to meet us on the corner of Myrtle and De Kalb at 7 a.m. When we got there Israel was not there. I began to feel sick at my stomach. We circled the block but didn't see him. Mr. Delgado said we were in a hurry but we'd ride by his apartment on St. Edward Street across from P.S. 67 and see if we could find him. We drove by but didn't see any

trace of him. Mr. Delgado kept looking at his watch and said
we would have to go on.

"Can't we circle the block just one more time," I said,
"maybe we've missed him."

"Look, Nicky," he said, "I know you love Israel and
you're fearful he'll go back to the gang. But he's got to
learn to stand on his own two feet sometime. He said he'd
meet us at 7 a.m. and he's not here. We'll circle the block
one more time but it's a six-hour drive up to Elmira and
David is expecting you at 2 p.m."

We drove down the street one more time and then headed
through the Bronx to pick up Jeff Morales. Jeff was a Puerto
Rican boy who wanted to go into the ministry. David had
asked Mr. Delgado to bring him up for the night to interpret
for me when I spoke in the church.

As we pulled away from the city, I felt a sense of relief.
I leaned back in the seat and sighed. The weight was lifted.
But in my heart there was a deep sadness because we were
leaving Israel behind and I had an ominous feeling of doom
and despair about his future. I didn't know it then, but it
would be six years before I would see him again.

That night David introduced me to the people in Elmira
and I gave my testimony. David had told me to start at
the beginning and tell my story just as it happened. I was
hazy on the details and couldn't remember much of what
had taken place. I was quickly realizing that not only had
God taken many of the old desires away from me, He had
wiped many of the memories out of my mind. But I told the
story the best I could. Many times I would get ahead of my
interpreter and Jeff would have to say, "Slow down, Nicky,
give me a chance to talk." The people laughed and cried and
when the invitation was given, many of them came to the
altar to give their hearts to Christ. The feeling that God was
calling me to a special ministry grew stronger as I saw Him
at work in my life.

The next day I had a chance to talk with David for a long
time. He asked me if I were serious about going into the
ministry. I told him I didn't know anything about it and
couldn't speak understandable English, but I felt God had

His hand on my heart and was leading me in that direction. David said he would do everything possible to arrange for me to go to school.

School! I hadn't been in school for three years and then I had been kicked out. "Davie, I can't go back to school. The principal told me if I ever came back he'd turn me over to the cops."

David laughed. "Not that school, Nicky. Bible school. How would you like to go to California?"

"Where?"

"California, on the west coast."

"Is that near Manhattan?" I asked.

Wilkerson burst out laughing. "Oh, Nicky, Nicky. The Lord has got a lot of work to do in you. But I think He's just powerful enough to do it. You just wait and see. Great things are going to happen through your ministry. I believe it."

I shook my head. I'd heard the Manhattan cops were just as tough as the cops in Brooklyn. If I were going to school, I'd sure hope it'd be someplace out of the city of New York.

Davie wanted me to remain in Elmira while he wrote the Bible school which I later found out was in La Puente, California, outside Los Angeles. The school was a three-year Bible School for boys and girls who wanted to prepare for the ministry but couldn't afford to go to college. Of course, I hadn't completed high school but David was writing an air mail letter asking them to accept me anyway. He said he was making no bones about my past career but was telling them of my dreams and ambitions and asking them to accept me on probation even though I had only been a Christian a few weeks.

But things were not so good in Elmira. Someone had spread a rumor that I was still a gang leader and was trying to form a gang up there. David was upset over the matter and knew it could mean trouble. I was staying with him at night but was afraid people would criticize David. We agreed to pray about it.

That night David talked to me about the Baptism in the Spirit. I listened intently but didn't understand what he was trying to get over to me. He read passages of scripture from the book of Acts, I Corinthians, Ephesians. He explained that after a person is saved God wants to fill him with His power. He explained about the conversion of Saul in Acts 9; that three days after Saul was converted, he received the Baptism in the Holy Spirit and was filled with new power.

"That is what you need, Nicky," David said. "God wants to fill you with power and give you special gifts."

"What kind of gifts you mean?" I asked him.

He opened his Bible to I Corinthians 12:8-10 and explained about the nine gifts of the Spirit. "These are given to those who are Baptized in the Holy Spirit. You may not receive all of them, but you will receive some of them. We Pentecostals believe that everyone who is baptized in the Spirit speaks in tongues.

"You mean I'll be able to speak in English without even studying?" I asked, amazed.

David started to say more but closed his Bible. "The Lord told the apostles to 'tarry' and they would receive power. I don't want to rush this with you, Nicky. We'll wait on the Lord and He will Baptize you when you are ready to receive it. In the meantime, we've got a problem on our hands and we've got to pray about it."

He flipped off the light and I said, "If he gives me another tongue I hope it's Italian. I know the cutest Italian girl you've ever seen and I sure would . . . " I was interrupted by Wilkerson's pillow as it sailed across the room and smashed me in the face.

"To sleep, Nicky. Tomorrow is almost here and half the town thinks you're still a gang leader. If He gives you another tongue it had better be something these people up here can understand when you tell them you're really not a murderer."

The next morning David had a worried look on his face when he came back from the morning meeting. "Things aren't too good, Nicky. We're going to have to get you away from here before tonight and I don't know where I can send you unless it's back to New York."

"Do you think the Lord heard our prayers last night?" I asked.

David looked shocked. "Well, of course I do. That's why I pray, because I believe He hears me."

"Did you pray God would take care of me?"

"You know I did."

"Then how come you're so anxious?"

David stood and looked for a minute, "Come on, let's go get a late breakfast. I'm starved, aren't you?"

At 2 p.m. that afternoon the phone rang in the motel room. It was the pastor of the church were David was preaching. There was a woman in his office who wanted to talk to the two of us. David said we'd be right over.

We walked in and the pastor introduced us to a Mrs. Johnson who had driven 200 miles from her home in upstate New York. She was seventy-two years old and said that last night the Holy Spirit had spoken to her. She had read about me in the papers and said the Holy Spirit had told her I was in trouble and she was to come after me.

I looked at David and big tears were running down his face. "Your name may be Mrs. Johnson, but I think it is really Mrs. Ananias."

She looked at David with a strange look. "I don't understand."

The pastor interrupted. "He's referring to the Ananias mentioned in Acts 9 whom the Holy Spirit touched and sent to minister to Paul."

Mrs. Johnson smiled. "I only know that the Lord gave me directions to come pick up this young boy and take him home with me."

David told me to get ready to drive back with her. He told me he should have an answer back from La Puente in a few days and he would send for me as soon as he did. I didn't want to go, but after hearing what had happened the night before and seeing what was happening now, I was afraid to stay.

Two weeks later I got a call from David. He was elated. The people at the Bible Institute had written back and were so intrigued over the prospects of my coming they agreed to waive all the requirements and take me as a regular student.

He told me to catch a bus back to New York. I'd leave for California the following day.

This time I didn't mind the ride back to New York. I remembered the ride with Dr. John and my depressed feeling of dropping back into the pit. But the pit was gone. This time I was on my way out of the wilderness.

I was to have a five-hour wait in the bus station before David could meet me. I had agreed to wait in the lobby to keep out of trouble. However, trouble had a way of tracking me down. It came in the form of ten Viceroys who formed a silent circle around me as I sat reading a magazine.

"Hey, look at pretty boy," one of them said, making reference to my suit and tie. "Hey, Dude, you're outta your territory. Don't you know this Viceroy turf?"

Suddenly, one of the boys spoke up. "Hey, you guys know who this is? This that jerk from the Mau Maus who turned preacher."

Another one walked up to me and stuck his finger against my face. "Hey, preacher, can I touch you? Maybe some your holy-roly rub off on me."

I slapped his hand away from my face. "You wanna die?" I snarled, the old Nicky breaking through. "Well, just touch me one more time and you're a dead man."

"Hey," the boy jumped back in mock surprise. "Listen to him. He looks like a preacher but he talks like a—," and he used a filthy name.

Before he could move, I sprang to my feet and sank my fist into his stomach. As he bent over from the blow, I hit him on the back of the head with my fist. He fell unconscious to the floor. The other boys were too surprised to move. The people in the bus station were scattering and hiding behind the benches. I backed out the door. "You guys try anything and I'll have everyone of you killed. I'm going after the Mau Maus. I'll be back in an hour and we'll kill every one of you Viceroys."

They knew I meant it and they knew the Mau Maus were twice as vicious and powerful as they were. They looked at each other and backed toward the other door, dragging their limp companion with them.

"I'll be back," I shouted. "You guys better be on the move

because you're as good as dead right now."

I ran out the door toward a nearby subway entrance. But on the way down the block I passed a Spanish church. Something in me slowed me down and then turned me around. I walked slowly up the steps into the open building. Maybe I should pray first, I thought. Then I'll go after the Mau Maus.

But once inside the church I forgot about the Mau Maus – and the Viceroys. I began to think about Jesus. And then about my new life ahead. I knelt at the altar and the minutes passed like seconds and I finally felt a tap on the shoulder. I looked around. It was Wilkerson.

"I figured when I didn't find you in the bus station you'd be here," he said.

"Naturally," I answered. "Where did you think I'd be, back with the gang?" He laughed as we walked toward his car.

12

School Daze

The Bible Institute in La Puente, California, is small and unpretentious. It is located on a small tract of land just out of town. Most of the seventy students enrolled in the school were Spanish speaking and most of them came from modest circumstances.

Steve Morales and I arrived by plane from New York. The school was different – more different from anything I had ever experienced. The rules were very strict and the schedule very disciplined. The school was highly regimented with classes held Tuesday through Saturday. Most of the students lived in barracks type dormitories on the campus.

It took several months for me to get accustomed to the Institute. I had always had my own way, but at the Institute everything was done by a bell from the time we got up at 6 a.m. until lights out at 9:30 p.m. There was virtually no free time and we were required to spend more than two hours a day in prayer besides the six hours in class. My biggest problem was not being able to talk to the girls. This was strictly forbidden and the only time we could converse was a few stolen moments before and after class or while washing dishes during our regular KP duty.

However, it was the philosophy of the school to teach discipline and obedience. And even though this was very difficult for me, it was just the kind of training I needed. Anything less strict would have allowed me too much freedom.

The meals were filling but far from appetizing. Our usual breakfast was hot mush and toast, but once a week we had an egg. This type diet, however, was a definite part of our training, since most of us would be Spanish ministers in poor sections of the nation and would be forced to live on very meager substance.

The teachers were very patient with me. I didn't know how to act and felt my insecurity keenly. I tried to make up for it by acting smart and showing off.

I remember one morning during the third month of school we were standing while the teacher led us in a lengthy opening prayer. I had been eyeing this cute black-haired, very pious Mexican girl in front of me for some weeks but hadn't been able to attract her attention. In the middle of the prayer I gently slipped the chair away from her desk thinking she'd surely notice me now. At the "amen" we all sat down. She noticed me all right! She turned around from her awkward position on the floor and looked up at me with eyes that were spitting fire. I was overcome with laughter as I reached down to help her up. She glared at me and scrambled to her feet unassisted. She never said a word and somehow it wasn't funny anymore. As she swung her chair back into position, she deliberately jabbed the sharp leg into my shin. I don't think anything has ever hurt as much. I could feel the blood draining from my face and thought I was going to faint. Everyone in the class laughed. I finally regained control of myself and looked up at her. She glared back at me with eyes that could burn a hole through an armored tank. I smiled weakly but felt like I was going to throw up. She turned around and sat rigidly at her desk facing the teacher.

The professor cleared his throat and said, "Now that we have finished with the morning devotion we shall begin. Mr. Cruz will be the first one to recite for us this morning."

I looked at him with a weak, blank look. "Mr. Cruz!" he said, "You have prepared your recitation have you not?" I tried to say something but my leg was hurting so badly I couldn't talk.

"Mr. Cruz, you know the penalty for failing to have your lesson ready. I know that you have great difficulty with the language and that you have not disciplined your mind to think in academic terms. We are all trying to be patient with you but unless you co-operate I have no choice but to give you a zero and flunk you in this course. I ask you once more, do you have your material ready?"

I nodded and got to my feet. My mind was completely blank. I hobbled around to the front of the room and faced the class. I looked down at the pretty girl with the dark eyes. She smiled very sweetly and opened her notebook so I could see page after page of neatly written notes on the very material I was supposed to recite. I looked at the teacher and said faintly, "Excuse me." I ran out of the room toward the dormitory.

I had made a complete fool of myself. I thought I could act smart and everyone would laugh at me like they had in the gangs. But these people were different. They tolerated me because they felt sorry for me. I was a misfit. An outcast.

I sat down on the side of my bed and wrote David Wilkerson a long letter. I told him it was tough out here and I had made a mistake in coming. I was sorry I had let him down but was afraid I was going to embarrass him if I stayed in school. I asked him to send me a plane ticket home. I put a special delivery stamp on it and mailed it to Wilkerson's home in Pennsylvania.

His reply arrived a week later. I eagerly tore open the envelope to find a short note.

> "Dear Nicky:
>   Glad to hear you are doing so well. Love God and flee Satan.
>   Sorry we have no money in the budget right now. I will write you later when we get some money. Your friend, David."

I was sick, upset, and frustrated. This time I wrote Mr. Delgado a special delivery letter. I knew he had money but was afraid to tell him I was having such a rough time at school. I told him my family in Puerto Rico needed money and I had to come home to get a job and help them. I hadn't heard from my family in a year, but this seemed the only story I could tell and get away with it.

* * *

A week later I received a special delivery letter from Delgado.

"Dear Nicky:
So glad to hear from you. I have sent money to your family so you can stay in school. God bless you."

That night I went to talk to Dean Lopez. I told him the problems I was having. I was rebelling against all authority. The day before it had been my turn to mop the auditorium and I had thrown the mop on the floor and told them I had come to California to go to school, not work like a slave. I still walked like a jitterbug. I knew I shouldn't even think like the old Nicky used to think – but I couldn't help it. When the other guys in the dorm tried to pray for me, I shook them off and told them they were too good for me. I was a crook. A gangster. They were all saints. They wanted to pray for me and put hands on me, but I refused to let them get close to me. I wept bitter tears as I sat in his little office and cried out for help.

Dean Lopez was a small, bronze-skinned man. He listened and nodded his head and finally reached for his battered Bible which was hidden under a huge stack of ungraded test papers.

"Nicky, you must get involved with the Holy Spirit. You have been saved and you want to follow Jesus, but you are never going to have any real victory in your life until you receive the Baptism in the Holy Spirit."

I sat and listened as Dean Lopez spoke to me from his open Bible of the marvelous victory that could be mine if I would receive God's Spirit.

"In Acts 1," he said, "the apostles were in your situation, Nicky. They had been saved but they had no inner power. They were depending on the physical presence of the person of Jesus Christ to give them power. As long as they could be close to Him they were filled with power. But when they were separated from Him they were powerless. Only one time in the Gospels do we find record of Jesus healing anyone without being in their presence. This was in the case of the centurion's servant. But even then, the centurion had to come to Jesus in order for his faith to be fulfilled. In Matthew it is recorded that Jesus commissioned the twelve disciples and gave them power against unclean spirits, to cast them out, and to heal all kinds of disease. But even with His commission, they still did not have the necessary power to follow through. Evidence of this is found later in the same book when a man brought his son to Jesus for healing, saying he had brought him to the disciples and they were powerless to cure him."

I listened intently as the dean's fingers flipped with expert knowledge through the pages of the well-used Bible. "In the Garden of Gethsemane Jesus withdrew from his disciples to pray. But as soon as He was out of their sight they became powerless. He had asked them to stay awake and watch for the soldiers, but instead they went to sleep."

I thought to myself, "That's me. I know what He wants me to do but I don't have the power to do it. I love Him and want to serve Him, but am powerless."

The dean kept talking caressing his Bible with his hands like he was touching the finger tips of a dear old friend. His eyes glistened with moisture as he talked of his precious Lord. "Then you remember later that night when Peter was standing outside the palace. When they took his Lord away he lost his power. He became a spiritual coward. And that night even a servant girl called his bluff and caused Peter to curse his Savior and deny he ever knew Him."

Lopez caught his breath in a sharp gasp and huge tears formed in his eyes and dropped on the yellowed pages of the open Bible. "Oh, Nicky, that's so like all of us. How tragic! How terribly tragic, that in His hour of need He had to stand alone. Would to God I had been there to stand with Him . . . to die with Him. And yet, Nicky, I fear I would have been just like Peter, for the Holy Spirit had not yet come and depending on my own strength, I, too, would have deserted Him."

He had to stop talking as his voice choked up. He pulled his handkerchief from his pocket and blew his nose loudly.

He reopened his Bible to Acts and continued. "Nicky, do you remember what happened after the crucifixion?"

I shook my head. I knew very little about the Bible.

"The disciples all gave up. That's what happened. They said that it was all over and they were going to go back to their fishing boats. The only power they had was the power that came from the physical presence of Jesus in whom the Spirit of God lived. But after the resurrection Jesus told the disciples to return to Jerusalem and to wait until they received a new power . . . the promised power of the Holy Spirit.

"The last promise Jesus gave His followers was they would receive power. Look here in Acts 1:8." He held the Bible across the desk so I could read it with him. " 'But ye shall receive power, after that the Holy Ghost is come upon you: and ye shall be witnesses unto me both in Jerusalem, and in all Judea, and in Samaria, and unto the uttermost part of the earth.'

"You see, Nicky, this is not a command to go witness. It is a promise that you will receive power. And when the apostles received the power, they could not help but become witnesses. They received the power in the Baptism of the Holy Spirit. The Spirit had returned from Heaven in a mighty and magnificent way and had filled every one of those apostles with the same power that had filled Jesus."

I squirmed in my chair. "If He is sending His Spirit," I said, "why hasn't He sent Him to me?"

"Oh, He has," the dean answered, now back up on his feet and walking to and fro beside his little desk, "He has! You just haven't received Him yet."

"Sent Him. Received Him. What's the difference?"

"The Spirit of God is in you, Nicky. He came into your life that night in St. Nicholas Arena. 'No man can say that Jesus is the Lord, but by the Holy Ghost.' It was the Spirit who convicted you of your sin. It was the Spirit who gave you the power to accept Jesus as your lord. It is the Spirit who has opened the doors for you to be at school. But you have not let Him fill you completely."

"How do I do this?" I asked honestly. "I've tried to purify my life by getting rid of all my sins. I've fasted and prayed, but nothing has happened."

He smiled, "It's not anything you do, Nicky. You simply receive Him."

I shook my head. I was still puzzled.

Dean Lopez took his Bible once again and expertly flipped it open to the book of Acts. "Let me tell you about a man named Saul. He was going to a 'big rumble' in Damascus and was struck down by the Spirit of Christ. Three days later he was Baptized in the Spirit and began to preach. This time the power came through the laying on of hands."

"Is that the way I get it?" I asked. "Can someone lay their hands on me and I will be baptized in the Holy Spirit?"

"It could come that way," Dean Lopez answered. "Or you may receive it when you are all by yourself. But once it happens your life will never be the same."

He paused, then looking me straight in the eye said, "The world needs your voice, Nicky. There are hundreds of thousands of young people all over America who still live where you lived – and in the same manner you lived. They are caught in the clutches of fear, hate, and sin. They need a strong prophetic voice that will rise up out of the slum and ghetto and point them to Christ who is the way out of their misery. They will not hear the eloquent pulpiteers of the day. They will not listen to the seminary and Bible school teachers. They will not hear the social workers. They will not hear the professional evangelists. They will not attend the large churches and would not be welcome even if they did. They need a prophet out of their own ranks, Nicky. And from this hour, I am praying you will be that prophet. You speak their language. You have lived where they live. You are like them. You have hated like they hate. Feared like they fear. And now God has touched your life and called you out of the gutter so you may call others to follow in the Way of the Cross."

There was a long period of sacred silence. I heard him speak again. "Nicky, do you want me to pray for you to receive the Holy Spirit?"

I thought a long time, then answered, "No, I feel this is something I must receive myself. If I am to stand alone then I must receive it alone. I believe He will fill me when He is ready . . . for I am ready now."

Dean Lopez looked down and smiled, "You are wise, young Nicky. These words could have come only from

God's Spirit. The time is fast approaching when your life shall change completely. I shall pray for you as you pray for yourself."

I glanced at the clock on the wall. I had been with him four hours. It was 2 a.m.

The next five nights were spent in agonizing prayer in the chapel. My days were filled with class activity but at night I'd go to the chapel to plead with God to Baptize me in His Holy Spirit. I didn't know how to pray except out loud and I got louder and louder. I would kneel at the altar and cry out to God, "Baptize me, baptize me, baptize me!" But nothing happened. It was as though the room were a box with no outlets and my prayers could not ascend to Heaven. Night after night I went to the chapel and knelt and hit the altar rail with my fists and screamed, "Baptize me, God, please baptize me that I might have the power of Jesus." I even tried to mouth words in an unknown tongue, but nothing came out.

Friday night, after a week of fruitless praying four and five hours a night I was about to break under the strain. At midnight I left the chapel and was walking slowly across the campus when I heard a man screaming behind the class building. I dashed around the corner and ran head on into Roberto, a former junkie. "Hey, Roberto! Roberto! What's the matter?"

He threw his arms in the air and shouted, "Praise God! Praise God! Praise God!"

"What's happened? Why are you so happy?"

"I've been Baptized in the Spirit. Tonight, just a few minutes ago, I was praying and God touched my life and filled me with joy and happiness. I can't stop. I've got to go. I've got to tell the world. Praise God, Nicky, praise His wonderful name!" He broke away and ran across the campus, leaping in the air and shouting, "Hallelujah! Praise God!"

"Hey, wait a minute," I shouted after him. "Roberto! Roberto! Where did you receive the Baptism? Where were you when it happened?"

He turned and breathlessly pointed toward the classroom building. "In the classroom. In the big classroom. I was at the front on my knees and he filled me with fire. Hallelujah! Praise God!"

I waited to hear no more. I was off across the campus in a mad dash heading for the classroom. If He touched Roberto maybe He is still there and He will touch me too. I skidded through the door of the building and bounded down the hall to the big classroom. Screeching to a stop at the door, I peered in. It was dark and quiet.

Slowly I entered the dark empty room and felt my way through the chairs and desks to the front. I knelt beside the desk where the pretty dark-eyed girl had flopped so unceremoniously on the floor when I had pulled the chair from under her. I had no time to reconstruct the event in my mind as I put my hands together in traditional style and turned my face toward the ceiling.

Then in a loud voice I cried out, "God, it's me, Nicky! I'm here, too. Baptize me!" I waited expectantly. Nothing happened.

Maybe I'm speaking to the wrong person, I thought. I'll try again. "Jesus," I screamed at the top of my voice. "It's me, Nicky Cruz, down here in the classroom in La Puente. I'm waiting to be baptized in your Spirit. Let me receive the Baptism." The expectancy was so strong I was almost lifted off the floor. My mouth was open ready to speak in tongues. My legs were tense under me ready to leap and run like Roberto did. But nothing happened. Nothing. Silence. The floor grew hard and my knees began to hurt and I slowly stood up and dejectedly walked back across the dark campus to my dormitory.

The smell of night-blooming jasmine was in the air. The grass was wet under my feet from the early dew. In the bushes I heard the lone cry of a whippoorwill and someplace in the distance I heard the deep bellow of a night diesel pulling its cargo up from the valley. The moon slipped behind a dark cloud like a seductive lady withdrawing into her apartment and closing the door. The smell of the jasmine and gardenias wafted on the cool night air and the street lights blinked as the wind tossed the palm fronds across their shafts of light. I was alone in God's paradise.

I slipped quietly into the dorm and felt my way to my bunk. I lay back on my bed with my hands under my head and stared into the darkness. I could hear the soft breathing of the other boys. "God!" I sobbed. And I felt the hot tears come to my eyes and run down into my ears and onto the pillow. "I've been asking for a week and you've let me down. I'm no good. I know why you haven't filled me. I'm not good enough. I act like a jackass around all the other people. I don't even know how to hold my knife and fork. I can't read very well and I can't think fast enough to keep up. All I know is the gang. I'm so out of place here and I'm so dirty and sinful. I want to be good. But I can't be good without your Spirit and you won't give Him to me because I'm not good enough."

The image of my old room at 54 Ft. Greene Place flashed through my mind and I shuddered uncontrollably. "I don't want to go back, God, but I just can't make it here. All these boys and girls are so pious and holy and I'm so filthy and sinful. I know when I'm out of place. I'm going back tomorrow."

I turned over and fell into a troubled sleep.

After class the following day, I went back to my dormitory to pack my things. I had made up my mind to sneak off campus and begin the long journey home – hitchhiking. It was useless to remain here.

That evening as I sat on my bunk my thoughts were interrupted by one of the off-campus students.

"Ah, Nicky! Just the one I wanted to see."

I thought to myself, "And you're just the one I didn't want to see."

"Nicky," he continued with a joyful sound about him. "We're having a Bible study and service down at the little mission on Guava Boulevard. I want you to come with me."

I shook my head. "Not tonight, Gene. I'm tired and have a lot of studying to do. Ask one of the other boys."

"But there are no other boys around," he said as he slapped me on the back of the shoulder, "and besides, the Spirit has told me to come after you."

"Humph, the Spirit, eh? Well, the Spirit has told me to stay here and get some rest since I've been so busy talking to Him all week. Now go away and let me rest." I lay down and turned my back to him.

"I will not leave unless you come with me," he said stubbornly. And he sat down on the foot of my bed and crossed his legs.

I was exasperated. This guy was crazy. Couldn't he tell I didn't want to go?

"All right," I sighed, "I'll go with you. But don't be surprised if I fall asleep in the church service."

"Let's go," Gene said gleefully, pulling at my arm. "We're late now and I'm supposed to preach."

I had decided I'd go with him and sneak out after the service and hitchhike out of town. I stuck my toothbrush and a few other necessities in my pocket and figured I could leave the rest of the stuff here. It wasn't worth much anyway.

We arrived at the little mission about 7:30 p.m. It was brown adobe with stucco inside. The crude wooden slat benches were filled with sincere, simple Mexican people. "At least I'm among good company," I thought. "Yet even these people are better than I. At least they're here because they want to be here. I'm here because I was forced."

Gene preached about fifteen minutes and then gave the altar call. I was sitting on the back row beside a grizzled man who smelled strongly of dirt and sweat. His clothes were grimy as if he had just come in from one of the farms and hadn't washed up. As Gene prayed the old man next to me began to weep. "Jesus, Jesus, Jesus," he whispered over and over. "Thank you, Jesus. Oh, thank you, Jesus."

Something moved in my soul. It was as though someone had turned on a faucet, slowly at first. Then I began to fill up. "Thank you, Jesus," the old farmer next to me prayed, "thank you."

"Oh God!" I sobbed out. "Oh Jesus, Jesus, Jesus." I was clenching my teeth and trying to hold it in but the dam had burst and I was running down the aisle toward the front, stumbling and staggering until I fell at the crudely splintered altar rail and cried uncontrollably.

I felt Gene's hand on my head. "Nicky," I could barely make out his words over my sobs. "Nicky, God was not going to let you run away tonight. His Spirit came to me an hour ago and sent me to your dormitory to get you and bring you to this meeting. I knew you were going to run away. He sent me to stop you."

How did he know? No one knew. No one but God.

"God sent me to you, Nicky. All the boys and the teachers have been praying for you at school. We feel that God has placed His hand on you in a marvelous and wonderful way. We feel He is about to move you out into a great and awesome ministry. We love you. We love you. We love you."

The tears were coming like rivers. I wanted to talk but could say nothing. I felt him step across the unpainted altar rail, put his arm around my shoulders and kneel beside me. "Can I pray for you, Nicky? Can I pray that Christ will baptize you in His Holy Spirit?"

I tried to answer but the crying grew worse. I nodded my head and made some funny sounds which he interpreted to be an affirmative answer.

I was unaware of his praying. I don't even know whether he prayed or not. Suddenly, I opened my mouth and from it came the most beautiful sounds I've ever heard. I felt a great cleansing from within, as though my body had been purged from the bottoms of my feet to the top of my head. The language I was praising God with was not English or Spanish. It was an unknown tongue. I had no idea what I was saying but I knew it was praise to the most Holy God in words that I could never form myself.

Time had no meaning and the hardness of the unfinished two by eight that I was kneeling on seemed to make no difference. I was praising God the way I had always wanted to, and I was never going to stop.

It seemed like only moments later that I felt Gene shake my shoulder. "Nicky, it's time to go. We've got to get back to school."

"No, this is good," I heard myself say, "let me stay here forever."

"Nicky!" he was insistent, "we've got to go. You can finish when we get back but we've got to get back to the school."

I looked up. The church was empty except for the two of us. "Hey, where is everybody?"

"Man, it's 11 p.m. They've been gone for over an hour."

"You mean I've been praying for two hours?" I couldn't believe it.

"Thank you, Jesus! Thank you!" I shouted as we ran for the car.

Gene let me out in front of the dorm and drove off. I ran inside and turned on the light. I was singing, "Holy, Holy, Holy, Lord God Almighty," at the top of my voice.

"Hey, what's going on? What's wrong with you?" they began shouting. "Turn that light off. What kind of a crazy nut are you anyway? Turn the light off!"

"Shut up," I shouted. "Tonight I celebrate. You don't know what has happened to me but I do and tonight I sing . . . 'Sunshine, Sunshine in my soul today . . . ' " A barrage of pillows came at me from all over the room. "Turn the light out!" But I knew a light had been turned on in my soul that would never be turned out. It would burn forever.

That night I dreamed again, for the first time since I had been saved. In my dream I stood on the hill top near Las Piedras in Puerto Rico, where I had stood many times before in my nightmare. Looking up in the sky I saw the familiar form of a bird. I shuddered in my sleep and tried to rouse myself. O God, don't let them start again. Please! But the bird grew nearer. Only this time it was not the legless bird or even a pigeon. It was a dove, settling gently on my head. The dream faded and I lapsed into a deep, satisfying sleep.

13

Where Angels Fear to Tread

The days that followed were filled with joy and victory. The first change I noticed was in my conduct. I wasn't a jitterbug any longer. I stood at attention during the prayers, praying with the leader. Instead of acting smart I began to show consideration to others, especially the girl who sat in front of me with the beautiful dark eyes.

I found her name was Gloria. The day I shared my testimony with the class she came up to me and shook my hand in a dignified, lady-like way, "God bless you, Nicky. I've been praying for you."

I had a feeling she probably had been praying I would "drop dead." But I knew she was genuinely happy God had touched me. It showed in her beautiful smile and deep dark eyes that twinkled like the stars at midnight.

The next week I got up enough courage to ask her to go with me to a mission service we were holding at a little church near the campus. She smiled and her dimples winked as she nodded "yes."

During the year we attended many church services together. Although we were always with a group of people, I learned a great deal about her. She was born in Arizona. Her father was Italian and her mother Mexican. They had moved to California when she was five and her parents had opened a bar in Oakland. During her senior year in high school she had been saved and decided to enter Bible School. Her pastor, Reverend Sixto Sanchez, suggested she write the Bible Institute. They accepted her and she entered school in the fall of that year.

As the school year drew to a close I sensed Gloria was

going through some deep inner turmoil. The regimentation of the school was telling on her. At the close of the year she told me she didn't believe she could take it another year and wouldn't be back. I was disappointed but made her promise to write me.

That first summer I remained in Los Angeles. Some friends took me in and gave me a place to stay. But I missed Gloria deeply. When school started in the fall, I was grateful to find a waiting letter. She had kept her promise.

She told me, in part, of the motivations that caused her to leave school. "My experiences were different from yours, Nicky," she wrote. "Even though Mom and Dad ran a bar, I had been raised in a good moral atmosphere. When I was saved, I went to extremes with my life. I was taught that it was sinful to copy any of the patterns of the world. I took off all my makeup, refused to wear a bathing suit, and didn't even wear jewelry. Everything about me was negative. Then when I got to school, it was even worse. I was about to crack up. I wanted to tell you but we never had any time alone. I hope you understand and will keep praying for me. But I won't be back to school . . . "

The second year at Bible school moved fast. My grades improved and the other students were beginning to accept me. I had several opportunities to preach at street services and to give my testimony in some of the nearby churches.

In April, I got a letter from David Wilkerson. He was still living in Pennsylvania but wanted me to return to New York that summer and work with the gangs in Brooklyn. He had made plans to rent an apartment on Clinton Avenue between Fulton and Gates and had secured commitments from Thurman Faison and Luis Delgado to serve with me if I would come. Money was short but they would furnish us a place to stay and pay us each $7 a week.

That night after study hour I went to the Dean's office and called David collect. The phone rang a long time and finally a drowsy voice answered. He grunted he would accept the charges.

"Hey, Davie, it's me, Nicky. Have you finished supper?"

"Nicky, have you any idea what time it is?"

"Sure, baby, it's 10 p.m."

"Nicky . . . " there was just the slightest hint of exasperation in the voice, "it may be 10 p.m. in California, but it's 1 a.m. here and Gwen and I have been asleep for two hours. And now you've wakened the baby too."

"But Davie, I just wanted to give you the good news." I could hear the child screaming in the background.

"What can be so good that it wouldn't wait until morning, Nicky?"

"This won't wait, Davie. I'm coming to New York to work with you this summer. God has told me He wants me to come."

"That's wonderful, Nicky. It really is. I'm thrilled. So is Gwen and so is the baby. I'll be sending you a plane ticket. Good night."

I stayed awake all night making plans for my return to New York.

The trip home helped me see just how much I had changed. It was as though my whole life had been toned up – had come alive. As we began our descent to Idlewild Airport in New York, my heart tingled with memories and excitement. I spotted the silhouette of the Empire State Building on the horizon, and then the Brooklyn Bridge. I never realized how massive the city was as it sprawled out for hundreds of square miles. My heart overflowed with love and compassion for the millions of people below who were trapped in the asphalt jungle of sin and despair. My eyes blurred with tears as we circled the city. I was sad yet happy – afraid yet anxious. I was home.

David met me at the airport and we embraced and wept unashamedly. Putting his arm around my shoulder he led me to the car, bubbling over with excitement about his new dream.

I listened as he talked of his plans for the future; of his new Teen Challenge. But he could see something was troubling me and finally slowed down enough to ask what it was.

"Davie, what have you heard from Israel? Where is he? Is he okay?"

David hung his head and finally looked up at me with somber eyes. "No, Nicky, everything is not okay. I didn't say anything about it in my letters because I was afraid it would discourage you. I guess I might as well tell you now so you can begin to pray with me about it."

We sat in the hot car in the airport parking lot while David told me of Israel.

"Israel is in prison, Nicky. He was involved in a murder in December after you left for school. He's been in prison ever since."

My pulse quickened and I felt a cold sweat in the palms of my hands. I took a deep breath. "Tell me all you know, Davie, I've got to hear it."

"I didn't hear about it until it was all over and he had been shipped to prison in Elmira. I drove up to New York to see Israel's mother. She cried when she talked to me and told me there had been a big change in Israel's life after he accepted Christ, but then after the disappointment he returned to the gang."

"What disappointment?" I asked.

"Don't you know?"

"You mean about me getting stabbed? He said he was going to get the guy who did it."

"No, it was something deeper than that. His mother told me that the day you got out of the hospital Mr. Delgado came by the apartment and asked him to go with you to meet me in Elmira the next day. Israel got excited about it and said he'd go. She got him up the next morning at 4 a.m., ironed his clothes and packed his suitcase. He walked over to Flatbush Avenue and waited from 6 a.m. until 9 a.m. Somehow he missed you. He went back to the apartment, threw his suitcase on the floor and told his mother that all Christians were a bunch of fakes. That night he went back to the gang."

I could feel the tears coming to my eyes as I turned to David. "We looked for him. We looked all over for him. I wanted to stay and look some more but Mr. Delgado said we had to go. Oh, David, if only we had known. If only we had looked a little harder and a little longer maybe he would be in school with me now."

David blew his nose and continued. "After he went back to the gang, he and four others shot a kid from the South

Street Angels in front of the Penny Arcade. He died on the spot. Israel pled guilty to murder in the second degree and was sentenced to five years in the state penitentiary. He's there now."

There was a long pause and I finally asked David if he had seen or heard from him since he went to prison.

"I wrote him but found he could not write back. He could only write his immediate family. Even his correspondence courses had to be sent through the prison chaplain. I prayed for him all that next summer and finally made a trip up to Elmira just to see him. They were getting ready to transfer him to the work camp at Comstock and would only let me see him for a few minutes. He was doing alright, I guess, but he still has more than three years to serve."

We sat in silence for a long time and I finally said, "I think we ought to pray for Israel."

David bent over the steering wheel and began to pray out loud. I turned around in the seat and got on my knees on the floorboard with my elbows resting on the seat. We spent almost fifteen minutes praying there in the parking lot. When we finished David said, "We've done all we can for Israel right now, Nicky, but there is a city full of others just like him that we can still salvage for Jesus Christ. Are you ready to go to work?"

"Let's go," I said, but I knew my work would never be finished until I was able to free Israel. David started the car and pulled out into the heavy New York traffic. I was on fire for the Lord. "I want to visit my old gang members tomorrow," I said nonchalantly. "I want to tell them about Jesus."

David cocked his head to one side as he pulled off the highway and braked to a stop at a red light. Looking over at me he said, "I'd go slow about that if I were you, Nicky. A lot has happened since you've been away. You remember when you became a Christian? They almost killed you. I'd be careful. There's enough to do without getting tangled up with the Mau Maus right now. Only fools walk in where angels fear to tread."

The stop light changed and we pulled off, swinging wide to pass a bus. "I may be a fool, Davie, but this time I'm a fool for

Jesus' sake. He will go with me and will protect me. Angels may fear to tread in Mau Mau turf, but I go with Jesus."

David grinned and nodded his head as he turned into Clinton Avenue. Pulling to a stop in front of an apartment building he said, "He's your guide, Nicky. Not me. You do what He tells you and you'll witness nothing but victory. Come on, I want you to meet Thurman and Luis."

The next day was the big day. I had stayed awake most of the night praying. I put on my suit and flashy tie, tucked my new leather Bible under my arm and started across town to the Ft. Greene project. I was on my way to see the Mau Maus.

The city hadn't changed much. A few of the older buildings had been condemned and boarded up, but everything else was just as I had left it two years before. But I was different. I had gained weight and cut my hair, but the big difference was inside. I was a new Nicky.

As I crossed Washington Park my heart began to beat faster. I was looking for the Mau Maus; yet, for the first time I was worried about how I would greet them – and what they would say when they saw me. How would I introduce myself? I wasn't scared, I just wanted wisdom to handle the situation for the glory of God.

As I came out of the park I spotted a gang of Mau Maus leaning up against the side of a building. David's words flashed through my mind, "only fools walk in where angels fear to tread," but I breathed a prayer out loud to the Holy Spirit to go with me, and walked up to the loitering gang.

There were about thirteen boys in the crowd. I spotted Willie Cortez and slapping him on the back I said, "Hey, Willie, baby . . . "

He turned and stared at me. "Don't tell me you Nicky?"

"Yeah, man, I'm Nicky."

"Man, you look like a saint or something."

"Cool it, baby. I've just come in from California. Things are going well for me. I'm a Christian and going to school."

He grabbed me by the shoulders and turned me around several times, looking at my clothes and my features. "Man, Nicky, I can't believe it. I can't believe it."

Then turning to the other gang members who were staring

curiously he said, "Hey, you guys, take off your hats. This is Nicky. He used to be our president. He was a big jitterbug. He made history with the Mau Maus. He was the toughest of 'em all."

The boys took off their hats. Willie Cortez was the only one in the group I recognized. Most of these kids were younger, much younger. But they were impressed. They had heard of me and crowded around sticking out their hands.

I put my arm around Willie's shoulder and grinned at him. "Hey, Willie, let's take a walk through the park. I want to talk to you."

We walked off from the group and into Washington Park. Willie was walking slowly beside me with his hands in his pockets, shuffling his shoes on the concrete. "Willie," I broke the silence, "I want to tell you what Christ has done to my life."

Willie didn't lift his head but kept on walking as I talked. I told him how I'd felt as a member of the gang two years ago and how I had given my heart to Christ. I told him of the way God had led me out of the wilderness of the concrete jungle to a place where I was now a creative human being.

Willie interrupted, and I could tell his voice was shaking. "Hey, Nicky, lay off, will ya? You make me feel bad. When you talk something happens inside my chest. Something has changed you. You're not the same old Nicky. You scare me."

"You're right, Willie, something has changed me. The blood of Christ changed me and washed me clean. I'm a different man. No longer am I afraid. No longer do I hate. Now I love. And I love you, Willie. And I want to tell you that Jesus loves you too."

We reached a bench and I motioned for Willie to sit down. He sat and looked up at me. "Nicky, tell me more about God."

For the first time in my life I realized how important it is to talk to my friends about Christ. I could see the loneliness in his face; the ignorance – the fear. He was just as I had been two years before. But now I wanted to tell him the way out.

I sat down beside him and opened my Bible to the passages

I had marked in red pencil. Tediously I read the passages in the Bible concerning man's sin. As I read, "for the wages of sin is death," Willie looked up at me with fear in his face.

"What you mean, Nicky? If I'm a sinner and God is going to kill me for sinning, then what can I do? I mean, man, I've gotta do something. What can I do?" His eyes were wild with excitement as he jumped to his feet.

"Sit down, Willie, I'm not finished. Let me show you the rest of it. God loves you. He does not want you to go to hell. He loves you so much He sent His only Son to pay the price of your sin. He sent Jesus to die for you that you can have eternal life. And Willie, if you will accept Him; if you will confess Him, He will save you."

Willie slumped back down on the bench, a look of desperation on his face. I sat looking at him, my eyes filling up with tears. I squeezed them shut and began to pray but the tears pushed through my tightly shut lids and ran down my cheeks. When I opened my eyes, Willie was crying too.

"Willie, do you know what it means to repent?"

He shook his head.

"It means to change. To turn around. Willie, if you don't mind, I want you to do something. It might hurt your pride. But I'm going to pray for you. Will you kneel down?"

I had no idea Willie would respond. People were walking up and down the sidewalk right in front of the bench where we were sitting, but Willie nodded his head and without hesitation knelt on the sidewalk. Looking up he said, "Nicky, if God can change you, He can change me too. Will you pray for me now?"

I put my hands on Willie's head and began to pray. I felt his body shaking under my hands and heard him sobbing. He began to pray. We were both praying out loud – very loud. Through my tears I cried out, "God! Touch Willie! Touch my friend Willie. Save him. Let him be a leader to lead others to You."

Willie was praying in a loud tortured voice. "Jesus . . . Jesus . . . Help me! Help me!" He was gulping for air as he wept and cried out, "Oh Jesus, help me!"

We remained in the park for the rest of the afternoon. At dusk Willie returned to his apartment promising to bring the rest of the gang to my place the next night. I stood and watched him walk off into the summer dusk. Even from behind you could notice the difference. Something had flowed through me to Willie Cortez. I don't think I walked back to Clinton Avenue that evening . . . I floated . . . praising God with every breath. I remembered running through the big field in front of our house in Puerto Rico, flapping my arms and trying to fly like a bird. Tonight I raised my head and breathed deep. At last, I was airborne.

I spent the rest of the summer with the gang doing street preaching and personal work. I fasted religiously, going without food, from 6 a.m. on Wednesday until 6 a.m. on Thursday. I found when I fasted and spent the time in prayer, things happened in my life. I had also been writing Gloria and just lately her letters were taking on a warm friendly tone as if she enjoyed writing me. Her plans for the coming year were still indefinite and I spent much time praying for her.

Two weeks before I was to return to school one of the Christian businessmen on David's advisory board stopped by with a check. He said the men wanted to give me something extra for the work I had done and suggested I use it for a plane ticket to Puerto Rico to visit my parents before going back to school. It was the thrill of my life.

I arrived in San Juan late Monday afternoon and caught a bus to Las Piedras.

It was almost dark when I got off the bus and started through town toward the familiar path that led up the grassy hill to the white frame house on top of the knoll. A hundred thousand memories flooded through my heart and mind. Someone shouted, "It's Nicky. It's Nicky Cruz!" and I saw a man running ahead of me up the hill to tell Mama and Papa I was home. Seconds later the door burst open and four of the younger boys came flying down the hill. I hadn't seen them in five years but recognized them as my brothers. Behind them, skirt flying in the wind, came my mother. I dropped my suitcase and ran up the hill to meet them. We collided in a flurry of happy screams, tears, and hugs. The boys scrambled over me, knocking me to the ground in a happy wrestling match. Mama was on her knees hugging my neck and smothering me with kisses.

Regaining my composure I saw that two of the younger boys had run after my suitcase and were lugging it up the path toward the house. I looked up toward the house and there standing straight and tall, was the powerful solitary figure of Papa looking down the path toward me. I started toward him slowly. He remained steadfast, erect, watching me. Then I began to run and he started slowly down the steps toward me until he, too, broke into a run and met me in front of the house. Grasping me in his big bearlike arms he swung me off the ground and hugged me close to his chest. "Welcome home, little bird, welcome home."

Frank had written Mama and Papa that my life had changed and I was in school in California. The word had gotten around that I had become a Christian and many of the church people in Las Piedras came to the house that night to see me. They told me that others wanted to come but were afraid to come to the "Witch's House." They believed Papa could speak to the dead and in their superstition they were afraid to come near the house. However, they wanted to have a service in the home of one of the Christians and asked me to preach and give my testimony. I told them I would conduct the service but it would be in my home. They looked at each other and the leader of the group said, "But, Nicky, many of our people are afraid of the demons. They are afraid of your Papa."

I told them I'd take care of things here and tomorrow night we would have a big Christian service in my home.

Later that evening when Papa heard what we had planned, he objected violently. "I will not have it. There will be no Christian service in this house. Those people will ruin my business. If we hold a Christian service the others will never come around . . . will be ruined as a spiritualist. I forbid it."

Mama argued with him. "Can't you see how the Lord has changed your son? There must be something to this. The last time you saw him he was like an animal. Now he is a preacher, a Christian minister. We will have the service and you will attend."

Mama seldom argued with Papa, but when she did she always got her way. She got it this time. The next night the house was packed with people from the village as well as several preachers who had driven in from nearby towns. It was steamy hot as I stood at the front of the room and shared my testimony. I went into great detail of the devil's hold over me and how I had been loosed from his power by the power of Christ. The people were very vocal while I preached, murmuring approval and sometimes shouting and clapping in glee as I described various events in my life.

At the close of the service I asked them to bow their heads. Then, inviting those who would accept Christ as their personal Saviour to step forward and kneel, I closed my eyes and prayed silently.

There was a commotion and I could sense that some were coming forward. I heard them weeping as they knelt in front of me. I maintained my position with my eyes closed and my face raised to heaven. I could feel the perspiration pouring off my face, down my back, and dripping off my legs. I was soaked with sweat from the heat I had generated while preaching. But I felt God was working and I continued to pray.

Then I heard a woman on the floor in front of me begin to pray. I recognized the voice and opened my eyes in joyous unbelief. There, kneeling in front of me with her face buried in her skirt, was my mother and two of my younger brothers. I fell to the floor in front of her and threw my arms around her sobbing figure.

"Oh, Nicky, my son, my son, I believe in Him too. I want Him as Master of my life. I am sick to death of demons and evil spirits and I want this Jesus to be my Saviour." Then she began to pray, and I listened to the same voice that had once sent me to my bedroom and later under the house in wild hysterics crying I hate you . . . I now heard that voice crying out to God for salvation, and great sobs shook my body as she prayed for forgiveness. "Please, dear God, forgive me for having failed my son. Forgive me for driving him away from home. Forgive me for my own sin and for not having believed in you. I do believe. I now believe in you. Save me, oh God, save me!"

I opened my arms and encompassed my two younger brothers, one fifteen and the other sixteen, and we huddled together on the floor praying and praising God.

Eventually, I stood and looked at the crowd. Many others had come and were kneeling on the floor praying and weeping. I went from one to the other laying my hands on their heads and praying for them. Finally, I stopped and looked at the back of the room. There against the far wall stood the solitary figure of Papa, towering tall and erect above the bowed heads. Our eyes locked in a long stare and his chin quivered visibly. Tears filled his eyes – but he turned and abruptly walked out of the room.

Papa never did make an open profession of faith. But his life noticeably softened from that time on. And after that night there was never another spiritualist service held in the Cruz home. I returned to New York two days later and one of the native pastors baptized my mother and two brothers in water baptism the following week.

I had less than a week in New York before leaving for California and my last year of school. The night before I was to leave there was a big youth rally at Iglesia de Dios Juan 3:16. We made a big effort to get the Mau Maus to attend. I had become friends with Steve, their new president, and he said if I was going to be there he would make sure the gang came to the service.

I was standing in the vestibule before the service started examining the old bullet holes from two years back when the Mau Maus began to arrive. More than eighty-five of them showed up. The little church was crowded to capacity. As they came in I shouted at them. "Hey, man, this is God's turf. Take off your hats." They obeyed willingly. One fellow was standing in the far corner of the vestibule with one of the debs. He shouted, "Hey, Nicky, can I hug my girl over here?"

I shouted back, "Yeah, man, go ahead but no kissing and no making out." The rest of the gang roared in laughter and went on in the auditorium.

At the close of the service, the pastor asked me to share my testimony. I turned and looked at the boys. I knew that I was leaving the next day for California and a sudden chill ran up my spine. Some of these boys would be dead or in prison when I returned. I preached. I preached as a dying man to dying men. I forgot about emotional restraints and poured my heart out. We had already been in the church two hours and I preached another forty-five minutes. No one moved. When I finished, the tears were streaming down my face and I pled with them to commit their lives to God. Thirteen of the boys came forward and knelt at the altar. If only Israel were here . . .

One of the boys who came forward was my old friend, Hurricane Hector. I remembered the time I had initiated him into the gang and the time we'd had a "fair fight" and he had run when he saw I was going to kill him for stealing my alarm clock. Now, Hurricane was kneeling at the altar.

After the service I walked back toward Ft. Greene with Hurricane. He was the war councilor for the Mau Maus. Since I had been instrumental in getting him to join the Mau Maus, I felt a deep burden for him. I asked him where he lived.

"I'm staying in an abandoned apartment."

"Man, how come you're not still living with your folks?" I asked.

"They threw me out. They're ashamed of me. You remember, I was one of those guys who came forward that night at St. Nicholas Arena with you and Israel. Several weeks later I talked my folks into going to church with me and they were converted. We all got active in the church and I was working with young people. I had dropped out of the gang and everything just like you and Israel. But the church was too strict. I wanted to have parties for the young people and they didn't believe in parties. I finally got discouraged and dropped out."

It was the same old story. He had met with the Mau Maus later and they talked him into coming back to the gang, just like they tried to talk me into it. They told him that Christians were squares, punks, sissies and that the gang was the only group that had the real answers to life. They literally evangelized him back into the gang.

A series of arrests followed. His parents tried to talk to him but he was bull-headed and they finally became so exasperated with him they told him he was going to have to leave unless he could abide by their rules. He chose to leave and had been living in an old condemned building.

"Sometimes I go hungry," he said, "but I would rather starve than ask my old man for anything. He's a real square. All he wants to do is go to church and read his Bible. I used to be like that but now I'm back where I belong, with the Mau Maus."

We had reached his apartment building. The windows were all boarded up and he told me he had a place behind where he could pry up a board and sneak in. He slept on a pad on the floor.

"Hurricane, how come you came down tonight?" I asked him, referring to the fact he answered the altar call.

"I came down because inside I want to be right, Nicky. I want to follow God. But I can't find the right answers. Each time I turn to Him and then turn away things get harder. I wish you were back in the gang, Nicky. Maybe I could get back to Christ if you were here."

We sat on the curb and talked into the small hours of the morning. I heard the clock in the tower chime 4 a.m., "Hurricane, I feel the Spirit of God telling me to say this to you. The clock just chimed 4 a.m. It's late. But if you will give your heart to Jesus, He'll take you back. It's late, but not too late. You feel guilty, but God will forgive you. Won't you come to Jesus now?"

Hector put his head in his hands and began to cry. But he kept shaking his head and saying, "I can't, I can't. I want to do it. But I know if I do, I'll go right back to the gang tomorrow. I can't do it. I just can't."

I told him, "Hector, you won't live another year if you don't come to Christ now. You'll be dead this time next year. They'll kill you." My heart was overflowing with words that were not mine as I prophesied to him.

Hector just shook his head. "If it happens, it happens, Nicky, and I can't do anything about it."

We were sitting on the curbstone on Lafayette Avenue. I asked him if I could pray for him. He shrugged his shoulders. "It won't do no good, Nicky, I know it."

I stood in the gutter and put my hands on his head and

prayed that God would soften his hard heart so he would return to Christ. When I finished, I shook hands with him. "Hurricane, I hope to see you when I get back. But I have a strong feeling that unless you turn back to Christ, I'll never see you again."

The next afternoon I left for California. I didn't know at that time just how accurate my prophecy was.

14

Gloria!

The summer in New York transformed my life, my thinking, my point of view. I returned to California determined to preach.

But I didn't discover the greatest blessing until I returned to the campus at La Puente. Gloria had returned to school. I didn't realize just how much I had missed her until I saw her again.

But the situation at school was still impossible. Everything seemed designed to keep us apart. The regulations were just the same as they had been two years before when we faced this same frustration. Conversation at the tables was limited to "pass the salt" and hawk-eyed professors watched our every move on the campus. Even though I hated KP, I began volunteering for extra duty washing dishes just to be near Gloria. The noisy kitchen was anything but private, but I found that we could carry on a semi-private conversation as long as we were both bent over the sink – I with my arms buried up to my elbows in hot soapy water and Gloria handling the rinsing and draining.

As the months flew by I realized I was falling in love with her. My grades continued to improve and I developed an appetite like a horse, due in part, I'm sure, to all the extra exercise I was getting at the dish washing sink. But I was frustrated because I couldn't express my love. Every time we had a few minutes alone someone would interrupt us. I tried to get to the classroom early, but invariably some of the other students would wander in just about the time I tried to get serious with Gloria. The frustration was driving me crazy.

And even with my Spanish ancestry, I found it almost impossible to work myself into a romantic mood over a sinkful of greasy dishes in a kitchen of hymn-singing students.

One Thursday night I received permission to walk into town. I stopped at the first phone booth and called Gloria's dormitory number. When the counselor answered, I put my handkerchief over the receiver and in a low bass voice asked for Miss Steffani. There was a pause and I heard the counselor whispering to Gloria, "I think it's your father."

Gloria giggled when she heard me stammering on the other end of the phone. I was frustrated, I was desperate. "I need to be with you," I mumbled.

"Nicky, what are you trying to say?" Gloria whispered, remembering she was supposed to be talking to her father.

I stuttered and stammered but the proper words wouldn't come. All my associations with girls had been on the gang level, and I really didn't know how to talk to one as pure and sweet as Gloria. "I think if I could see you face to face I could tell you better," I said. "Maybe I better go back to my room and stop bothering you."

"Nickieeee!" I heard her scream, "don't you dare hang up on me." I could hear the other girls in the room giggling. Gloria, though, was determined to force it out of me.

"Sshhhh, they'll know it's me," I said.

"I don't care who knows it. Now tell me what you're trying to say."

I groped for words and finally said, "I'm thinking it would be nice if you'd go around with me this year at school." I had said it. It had actually come out. I stood with choked breath waiting for her reaction.

"Go around with you? What does that mean, go around with you?" Gloria was shouting again and this time I could hear the girls laughing out loud.

"Just that," I said highly embarrassed. I could feel the color rising in my cheeks even though I was standing in a phone booth a half mile away from her. "I just thought I'd ask you to go around with me."

Gloria was whispering again, "You mean you want me to be your girl?"

"Yes, that's what I mean," I said, still blushing and trying to scrooch down inside the phone booth.

I could tell she had her mouth right up against the receiver as she breathed into the phone, "Oh yes, Nicky, that would be wonderful. I have felt God was leading us together for a purpose. I'll write you a long note and slip it to you at breakfast tomorrow."

After I hung up I stood in the booth a long time. It was a warm night but I was drenched with cold sweat and my hands were shaking like leaves on a willow.

I learned later that after Gloria hung up, the counselor looked up and with a stern frowning voice said, "Gloria, why would your father call this time of night and ask you to go around with him?"

One of the girls spoke up between giggles and said, "Because her father's name is Nicky."

Gloria blushed through her dark complexion as the whole room broke into gales of laughter. It's not often a girl receives an invitation from a man of her dreams to "go around with him" while forty girls listen in. The counselor was indignant and gave them three minutes to get ready for bed. But Gloria spent half the night with her head under her pillow with only the soft light from the street as illumination, writing me her first love letter. It was totally illegible, but was the most cherished letter I'd ever received.

Several weeks later I was approached by one of our teachers, Esteben Castillo, to assist him in beginning a mission work in San Gabriel near the school. He said he had enlisted seven other students to work with him on the weekends. He had discovered a little church building that had been closed and deserted. The students were to go on Saturday and knock on every door in the surrounding neighborhood to invite the people to services at the mission. The students would help clean up the little building and teach in a Sunday School and Professor Castillo would preach and be the pastor.

I was honored by the invitation and especially thrilled when he winked and told me he had also asked Gloria to serve on the committee with me. "You are a very wise teacher, Señor Esteben," I smiled back. "I think we can do a great work for the Lord with this excellent committee you have selected."

"Perhaps after you finish with the Lord's work, there will be a little time for other important things," he grinned.

I could see that word had already gotten around that Gloria had agreed to go around with me . . . I mean, be my girl. I was deeply thankful for this wise and understanding teacher who helped provide a way for our love to develop and blossom in the natural, God-intended manner.

Every Saturday for the next month we worked at the little mission building and went door to door inviting people to the Sunday services. Finally, the opportunity came for Gloria and me to spend the day together. We had seen each other constantly but always in the presence of others. But today, for the first time, we were going to have three glorious uninterrupted hours alone. Gloria had packed a picnic lunch and after a full morning of inviting people to the services, we went into a small park to eat and talk.

We both began at once – and then giggled at each other in our embarrassment. "You first, Nicky. Let me listen," Gloria said.

The minutes turned into hours as we sat and talked. I had been so anxious to share my life with her – all the little details. I talked on endlessly and she sat with rapt attention, her back against the trunk of a large tree. I suddenly realized that I was doing all the talking and she was doing all the listening.

"I'm sorry, Gloria, but there is so much on my heart and I want you to know it all . . . all the good and all the bad. I want to share every moment of my past with you. Forgive me for doing all the talking. Now you talk. Tell me what's on your heart."

She began slowly at first, but then the words came easier and she poured out her heart to me. She trailed off and grew silent. "What is it, Gloria? Go on."

"I've grown cold, Nicky. I realized it when I came back to school and saw the change in you. You're different. You're not silly nor insecure any more like you used to be. You have grown, matured and you are deeply spiritual. I see in you a life that has been yielded to the Lord. And Nicky . . . " and her eyes filled with tears. "I-I-I want that for myself. I want the peace. The assurance. The confidence that you have in your life. I have gone dry spiritually. Even though God healed me and led me back to school, I am still spiritually cold. I try to pray but nothing happens. I am empty. Dead. I want what I see in you."

She dropped her head in her hands. I moved over and put my arm awkwardly around her shoulders as we sat under the spreading tree. She turned to me and buried her head in my chest. Both my arms encircled her sobbing form and I smoothed her hair with my hand. Gloria turned her tear stained face toward mine and our lips met in a long lingering kiss of love.

"I love you, Nicky." The words slipped from her moist lips into my ear. "I love you with all my heart."

We did not move from our sitting positions for a long time, but clung tightly together like two vines embracing as they reach for the heavens.

"Gloria, I want to marry you. I've known it for a long time. I want to live the rest of my life with you. I have nothing to offer. I've sinned deeply but God has forgiven me. And if you can find it in your heart to forgive me also, I want you to be my wife."

I felt her arms tighten around my waist as she buried her head deep into my shoulder. "Oh yes, my darling. Oh yes. If God will allow it, I will be yours forever."

She raised her head and our lips met in another kiss. I leaned backward pulling her down beside me. We lay on the grass, arms around each other in a deep embrace.

I felt a burning, prickling sensation in my legs. God was close but the past was still inside me. The thought flashed through my mind that this was one of God's most beautiful creatures. Was I about to contaminate her with sinful desires? The burning sensation moved up my legs. It was becoming more acute.

Suddenly, I bolted upright pushing her backward as she rolled in the grass. "Nicky!" she screamed. "What's wrong?"

"Ants!!" I hollered. "Millions of 'em! They're all over me!"

I began to run, slapping furiously at my legs and kicking my shoes off. It was hopeless. My socks were covered with thousands of little red crawling demons. I could feel them all the way up to my knees and climbing higher. No amount of slapping seemed to stop their relentless attack and forward movement. Gloria was staring at me with wild unbelief as I ran in circles slapping and scratching.

"Turn around! Turn around!" I shouted. "Look the other way! Quick!" She turned her back and looked out over the park. I frantically fumbled with my belt buckle and snatched the belt loose.

"Nicky . . . " she began and turned back around.

"Turn around! Don't look!" I screamed. She realized what I was doing and obediently turned her back.

It took a long time to brush them all off. Some of them had tried to dig in under the skin. I had to beat my pants against a tree to knock all of them off. Finally, I was able to tell Gloria it was safe to turn back around.

We walked back to the school. Or rather, she walked and I hobbled. I tried to keep from getting mad because she was laughing. But for the life of me I couldn't see a single funny thing about it.

I left her in front of the girl's dormitory and made a bee line for my dorm and the shower. Standing under the cold water and rubbing soap into the red welts that covered my legs I thanked God for Gloria – and for the protecting power of His Spirit. "God," I spoke into the cascading water that gushed out of the shower head, "I know she's for me. These ants prove it. I praise your name for showing me and pray that you won't ever have to show me again."

The next night, Sunday, I was scheduled to preach at the San Gabriel Mission. I felt the Spirit of God upon me as I shared my testimony with the small group of humble people who had come to the service. At the close of the service I gave the invitation. I saw Gloria as she slipped out of her seat at the back of the little room and walked forward. Our eyes locked in an embrace as she knelt at the altar and then bowed her head in prayer. I knelt beside her while Señor Castillo put his hands on us and prayed. I felt Gloria's hand grip my elbow as the Spirit of God filled her heart. The hand of God was upon us both.

At Christmas I went home with her to Oakland. She had arranged for me to stay with friends since her parents were still not sympathetic to her education at the Institute. Her pastor, Reverend Sanchez, lined up a speaking engagement at a small Spanish-speaking church, Mission Bethania. I spent the days with Gloria and preached at night. Nothing could have made me happier.

In the Spring of my final year I received another letter from David. He was buying a big old house on Clinton Avenue to open a center for teenagers and dope addicts. He was inviting me to return to New York after graduation and work at Teen Challenge.

I talked it over with Gloria. It seemed as though the Lord were forcing His plans upon us. We had thought we would wait another year until Gloria finished school before being married. But now doors were opening and it seemed that God wanted me to return to New York. Yet, I knew I couldn't return without her.

I wrote David and told him I would have to pray about it. I also told him that Gloria and I wanted to get married. Wilkerson wrote back saying he would wait for my answer and that Gloria would be welcome too.

We decided on a November wedding and one month later we arrived in New York to accept Wilkerson's offer and began our work at Teen Challenge.

The huge old three-storey mansion at 416 Clinton was in the heart of an old residential section of Brooklyn just a few blocks from the Ft. Greene project. That summer college students had come in and helped clean up the house and start the ministry. David had secured the services of a young couple to live in the big house as supervisors. They had arranged for Gloria and me to live in a tiny garage apartment at the rear of the big house.

It was very small and crude. The shower was next door in the main center and the only bed was a couch, but to us it was heaven. We had nothing and needed nothing. We had each other and we had a burning desire to serve God at any cost. When David apologized for our poor cramped accommodation, I reminded him it was no sacrifice to serve Jesus – only an honor.

Just before Christmas I made my visit back into Mau Mau turf. My heart had been burdened over Hurricane Hector and I wanted to find him and work with him personally now that I was back in Brooklyn to stay. I found a group of Mau Maus at the candy store and asked them, "Where's Hurricane?"

The fellows looked at each other and one of them said, "Talk to Steve, our president, he'll tell you what's happened."

I was afraid of the truth but went to Steve's apartment. "What happened to Hector?" I asked him after we exchanged greetings.

Steve shook his head and stared at the wall. "Let's go downstairs and I'll tell you. I don't want my old lady to hear."

We walked down the stairs and stood just inside the door to escape the cold wind while Steve told me the story.

"After he talked to you that night before you went back to California, he became very restless. He was impatient. I've never seen him that way. We had a big rumble with the Apaches and he was like a wild man, trying to kill everyone who got in his way, even the Mau Maus. Then, three months later, he got it."

"How did it happen?" I asked, the depression bubbling up into my heart and lungs and causing my breath to come in shallow gasps. "Who did it?"

"Hurricane, Gilbert, two other guys and me went to kill an Apache. He lived by himself on the fifth floor of an apartment. We found out later we had the wrong guy. But Hurricane was determined to kill this guy and we went with him to help. Hurricane had a revolver. We knocked on this guy's door. It was dark. But this guy was smart. Cracking the door he peeked out and saw Hurricane with his revolver. He jumped out into the hall and swung at the light bulb with a two-foot bayonet. It was one of them bulbs that hang down from the ceiling and he smashed it. We couldn't see nothing. He was like a crazy man, swinging and jabbing with that bayonet. Hurricane shot his gun three times and then we heard a big scream, 'He kill me! He kill me!' We didn't know who it was and thought Hurricane had killed the Apache. We all beat it down the steps – five flights of 'em, and out into the street."

Steve turned and looked back up the steps of his own apartment to see if anyone was trying to listen. "When we got to the street we saw Hurricane wasn't with us. Gilbert ran back up the steps and found Hurricane standing up against the wall with that bayonet stuck all the way through him. Gilbert said it was poking out his back. The Apache had run back in his room and locked the door. Hector was scared and was crying. He was leaning up against the wall with that big knife poked all the way through his gut begging Gilbert to keep him from dying. He said he was scared to die. He cried something about the clock striking and then he fell down in the hallway on top of the knife and died."

My throat was dry and my tongue felt like it had cotton stuck on it. I stuttered, "Why did you leave him there?"

"Because we were all scared. We panicked. We'd never seen death like that. All the guys scattered and ran. The cops came but there was no proof and they let the Apache go. It shook us up pretty good."

I turned to leave when Steve asked me, "Nicky, what do you think he meant about the clock striking?"

I shook my head. "I dunno. I'll see you later."

I was in a daze as I walked back toward Clinton Avenue. With each step I could hear the clock on the tower at Flatbush Avenue chime and could hear my voice saying to Hurricane Hector, "It's late, Hector, but not too late. But if you don't give your heart to Christ I'll never see you again."

"Dear God," I whispered, "please don't let me ever walk away from another of my friends without trying a little harder."

My beginning salary was $10 a week plus room and board. Since the little garage apartment had no kitchen facilities, we ate all our meals over at the big house. Gloria and I both loved hot Spanish food. But at the center they had to eat very stable foods, so we squandered most of our $10 each week on Spanish food. This was our one extra pleasure in life.

We began our work in the streets. Wilkerson had written a little tract which we called the "Chicken Tract". It had a message to teenagers challenging them to accept Christ and not be "chicken". We passed these things out by the thousands on the streets of Brooklyn and Harlem.

It was immediately evident that our major work was going to be with the dope addicts. Many of the gang members who before had been satisfied to smoke marijuana and drink wine had graduated to heroin.

Our method was a brazen one. We'd walk up to groups of kids standing on the street corners and start conversation.

"Hey, baby, you want to kick your habit?"

Almost invariably they would answer, "Yeah man, but how?"

"Come to Teen Challenge over on Clinton. We'll pray for you. We believe God answers prayer. You can kick the habit through the power of God." We'd give them a copy of the chicken tract.

"Yeah, man, is that so? Well, maybe I'll call you or come by someday." It was slow to begin with. Most of my time was spent just standing around on the street corners talking. The addicts don't work. They get their money by stealing, robbing, mugging and purse snatching. They break into apartments and steal the furniture and sell it. They pick pockets. They steal clothes off the lines, milk off the doorsteps, anything to pick up enough money to feed their habit. All through Williamsburg there are little gangs of eight to ten persons standing on the corners planning robberies or trying to figure out how to get rid of stolen property.

By Christmas I had my first convert at the Center.

His name was Pedro and he was a Mau Mau. He was a big tall colored boy who had been living with a married woman. One day the woman's husband confronted him in a bar and Pedro slashed him with a knife. The husband was a member of the Scorpions, an across-town gang, and Pedro heard the gang was coming after him. I found him one night and listened to his story and offered him refuge at Teen Challenge. He willingly accepted. Three days after moving into the Center he accepted Christ and gave his heart to the Lord.

For the next three months we lived, breathed, and ate Pedro. Gloria and I spent our first Christmas as husband and wife in our small two-room apartment with Pedro as our guest. He ate every meal with us. He went with us every place we went. On weekends we'd ride the subway to various churches to attend services. Pedro always went with us.

One night in March I came to bed late as usual. Gloria had already crawled into our sofa-bed in the front room. I thought she was asleep and undressed quietly to keep from waking her. Slipping into bed I gently put my arm around her shoulders when I realized she was crying. I could feel her body shaking and sobbing under my arm.

"Hey, baby, what's the matter?"

That was all it took and the tears came in huge sobs. I lay beside her rubbing her back and comforting her until she calmed down enough to talk. "What is it, Gloria? Don't you feel good or something?"

"It's not that, Nicky. You don't understand and you never will."

"Understand what?" I was confused by her hostile attitude.

"That leech!" Gloria spat out the word. "That leech, Pedro! Can't he understand I want to spend some time with you alone. We've only been married four months and he has to go with us every place we go. He'd probably take a bath with us except there's only room for one in the bathroom."

"Hey, com'on," I soothed, "this doesn't sound like my Gloria. You oughta feel proud. He's our first convert. You oughta be praising the Lord."

"But, Nicky, I don't want to share you all the time. I married you and you're my husband and at least I ought to be able to spend some time with you without that grinning Pedro hanging around all the time saying, 'Praise the Lord.' "

"You're not serious about that are you, Gloria?"

"I've never been more serious about anything. One of us has to go. Either you're married to me or you can go sleep with Pedro. I mean it. But you can't have us both."

"Aw, listen, darling. If we send him back on the street, he'll go right back to the gang or the Scorpions will kill him. We've got to keep him here."

"Well, if he goes back to the gang then there's something wrong with your God. What kind of God did Pedro give himself to, anyway? A God who will turn loose of him the first time he gets into trouble? I don't believe that. I believe that if a man has had a conversion experience, God is big enough to keep him forever. And if we're going to have to play nursemaid to every one of these fellows you're inviting in here then I'm getting out." Gloria's voice reached a fever pitch as she talked.

"But, Gloria, he's my first convert."

"Maybe that's what's wrong with you and him too. He's *your* convert. Maybe if he was the Lord's convert you wouldn't have to be so worried about him going back to the gang."

"Well, maybe you're right. But we still have to give him a place to stay. And remember, Gloria, the Lord has called me to this work and you agreed to go with me."

"But Nicky, I just don't want to have to share you all the time."

I cuddled her close to me. "You don't have to share me now. And tomorrow I'll talk to Pedro and see if he can't find something to do instead of hanging around us all the time. Okay?"

"Okay," she mumbled as she put her head against my shoulder and snuggled close.

Sonny arrived the last day of April – along with a prediction of a May snow. He was the first addict I worked with.

I walked into the chapel that night and noticed a pale-faced boy sitting in the far corner. I could tell he was an addict and went to him and sat down beside him. Putting my arm around his shoulders I began to talk frankly to him. He kept his head bowed and his eyes staring at the floor while I spoke. "I know you're an addict . . . a junkie. I can tell you've been hooked many years and that you can't break the habit. You think no one cares. You think no one can help you. Let me tell you God cares. He can help you."

The boy raised his head and gave me a blank stare. Finally, he told me his name was Sonny. I found out later he had been raised in a religious home, but had run away and been in jail countless times for addiction and theft. He'd had to kick the habit "cold turkey" in jail several times, but he was hopelessly hooked.

Sonny was a compulsive addict, who had a unique way of getting money to feed his habit. His buddy would run down the street and snatch a woman's purse and when she began to scream, Sonny would run up saying, "Don't scream, lady. I know that thief. I'll get your purse back. Just wait here and I'll be back in a minute." The woman would stop screaming for the police and stand waiting while Sonny darted off down the street to join his friend and divide the spoils.

Kneeling beside him in the chapel, I said, "I want to pray for you. You need Jesus in your life." I felt a surge of compassion race through my heart and began to cry as I prayed. "God, help this man. He's dying. You're the only one who can help him. He needs hope, love. Please help him."

When I finished Sonny said, "I have to go home."

"I'll take you home."

"No," he said with a look of panic on his face. "You can't do that."

I knew he was scheming so he could get out and get a shot. "Then we'll keep you here," I said.

"No," he said again. "I have to go to court in the morning. They're going to sentence me to jail. I don't even know why I'm here."

"You're here because God sent you," I said. "God is using me to help you. Stay with us here at the Center tonight and I'll go to court with you in the morning." He insisted on going home and I promised I'd pick him up at 8 a.m.

Early the next morning I went with him to court. On our way up the courthouse steps I told him, "Sonny, I'm going to pray God will cause the judge to postpone your trial for two months so you can break the habit and find Christ. After that, he might let you off altogether."

Sonny sneered, "Fat chance. That stinkin' judge never postpones anything. He'll have me in jail before noon. Just you wait and see."

I paused on the steps of the courthouse and began to pray out loud, "God, I ask you in Jesus' name to send your Holy Spirit to touch that judge and have him postpone Sonny's case so Sonny can become a Christian. I thank you for answering my prayer. Amen."

Sonny looked at me like I was crazy. I tugged at his arm, "Com'on, let's go hear the judge say he's going to postpone your case."

We entered the courtroom and Sonny reported to the bailiff at the front of the room. He then took his seat with the other defendants while I sat in the back.

The judge heard three cases and sentenced the boys to long jail terms. The third boy to be tried began to scream when the judge passed sentence on him. He scrambled up on the table and tried to get to the judge, screaming he was going to kill him. Everyone in the courtroom jumped to their feet while the police knocked the boy down and handcuffed him. As they dragged him out the side door screaming and kicking, the judge mopped his brow saying, "Next case." Sonny stood nervously while the judge thumbed through his file. Glancing up over his glasses he said, "For some reason your pre-trial investigation is not complete. I want you to report back in sixty days."

Sonny turned and looked at me with eyes full of disbelief. I smiled and motioned him to come with me. We had a difficult task ahead and needed to get started.

Coming off heroin "cold turkey" is one of the most agonizing experiences imaginable. I prepared a room for Sonny on the third floor of the center. I knew it would take constant supervision so I warned Gloria that I was going to spend the next three days with Sonny. I set up a phonograph with religious records and determined to sit beside him in that room until he had screamed it out.

The first day he was restless, pacing the floor and talking rapidly. That night he began to shake. I sat with him through the night as he had hideous sieges of chills, shaking until his teeth clattered and the whole room vibrated. At times he'd break loose from me and run for the door, but I had it locked and he couldn't break through.

At dawn the second day his shaking subsided and I managed to get him downstairs for a little breakfast. I suggested we take a walk around the block and he no sooner got outside than he began to throw up. He bent low over the sidewalk, holding his stomach and retching. I pulled him upright but he broke away and staggered into the street where he collapsed. I dragged him back to the gutter and held his head in my lap until the seizures passed and he regained his strength. Then we returned to our room on the third floor to wait and pray.

As the night approached he screamed out, "Nicky, I can't make it. I'm too far gone. I've got to have a shot."

"No, Sonny, we're going to come through this together. God will give you the strength to make it."

"I don't want the strength to make it. I want a shot. I've got to have it. Please, please, please, Nicky. Don't keep me here. For God's sake let me go. Let me go."

"No, Sonny, for God's sake I will not let you go. You are precious to Him. He wants to use you but He cannot do it as long as this demon has possession of you. For God's sake, I'll keep you here until you're whole again."

I sat with him through the long night as he broke into cold sweats and heaved until I thought his stomach would turn inside out. I bathed his head with wet towels, turned the phonograph up loud, and sang to him with Bev Shea and the Statesmen Quartet.

The next day I was dead on my feet. Once again I tried to get food down him but it came right back up. I sat beside his bed and prayed until sundown.

He fell into a fitful sleep, moaning and twitching. Twice he bolted up in bed and tried to get to the door. The last time I had to tackle him and drag him back to bed.

About midnight, sitting in the chair beside his bed, I felt the black cloud of sleep descending on me. I tried to fight it off but I had been forty-two hours without sleep. I knew if I went to sleep now he might sneak out and never come back. We were close to victory, but I couldn't fight it any longer and felt my chin touch my chest. "Maybe if I close my eyes for a moment . . ."

I awoke with a start. The eerie glow from the street lights reflected in the large bare room on the third floor of the building. I didn't think I had been asleep more than a few seconds but something inside warned me I had slept far longer. I glanced at Sonny's bed. It was empty. The covers were ruffled and thrown back. He was gone!

My heart leaped into my throat. I jumped to my feet and started for the door when I spotted him kneeling on the floor beside the window. A wave of relief swept over me as I walked slowly to the window and knelt on the bare hardwood floor beside him. A light spring snow was falling and reflecting in the street lights on the sidewalk. The street and sidewalk were blended together in a pure white carpet and the tree branches outside the window with their tiny delicate buds just beginning to peep out, were sparkling with the soft white snow. Each tender flake glistened individually as it floated by the street light, reminding me of a scene that might appear on the front of a Christmas card.

Sonny said, "It's beautiful. It's indescribable. I have never seen anything so beautiful, have you?"

I was staring at him. His eyes were clear and his voice steady. There was a radiance about his face; his tongue was no longer thick nor his speech slurred.

He smiled at me, "God is good, Nicky. He is wonderful. Tonight He has delivered me from a fate worse than hell itself. He has released me from bondage."

I looked out the window at the delicate picture of pure beauty before me and whispered, "Thank you, Lord, thank you." And I heard Sonny murmur, "Thank you."

For the first time I left Sonny alone and walked through the new snow back to the apartment. I was bareheaded and the frosty snow that fell so gently stuck in my hair and puffed softly under my feet as I walked up the outside wooden steps.

I knocked softly and Gloria unlatched the door. "What time is it?" she said drowsily.

"About 3 a.m.," I answered. We stood in the door and I held her close to me while we watched the soft gentle snow drift silently to earth covering the dark and ugly with a beautiful blanket of pure innocence.

"Sonny has come to Christ," I said. "A new life has been born into the Kingdom."

"Thank you, Jesus," Gloria said softly. There was a long pause as we stood just inside the door and watched the panorama of beauty before us. Then I felt Gloria's arm tighten around my waist. "Sonny is not the only new life that has come into existence. I haven't had time to tell you, you've been so busy these last three days, but there is a new life in me, too, Nicky. We're going to have a baby."

I caught her up and crushed her against my chest in love and joy. "Oh, Gloria, I love you! I love you so much!" Very gently I bent over and slipped my arm under the back of her knees and slowly lifted her into my arms. I kicked the door and it clicked shut, plunging the room into total darkness. I carried her to the sofa and tenderly lowered her onto the bed. Sitting down beside her I gently laid my head against her soft tummy, cuddling as close as possible to the new life inside. She took both her hands and stroked my face and head. The exhaustion took over and I fell into a deep peaceful sleep.

Following his conversion, Sonny introduced us to the dark underworld of the big city and showed us the world of the addicts, the prostitutes, and hardened criminals.

Gloria and I spent many hours on the streets handing out tracts and our numbers increased at the Center. We had very few teenagers however. Most were adults. We opened the third floor to house the women. Gloria helped with the girls and I worked with the men, although as the director, I was in charge of both groups.

David had moved to a home on Staten Island and was coming in each day when he was in town to supervise the work at the Center. We purchased a small nine-passenger bus and Gloria and one of the boys went out twice a week to pick up gang members and bring them to the Center for services.

Pedro left to take an apartment in Jersey but Sonny stayed until September when he left for La Puente and the Bible Institute. That same summer the apartment on the second floor of the Center became vacant and Gloria and I moved into 416 Clinton. The men's dormitory room was at the rear of the second floor. Downstairs we had our office, kitchen, and dining hall, and a big room we used for a chapel. I hoped that since we had relocated to the big building it would help ease Gloria's tension. Yet, having to live in the same house with forty narcotic addicts does not lend itself to a life of calm and ease.

The tension continued. Gloria and I had very few private moments since I was spending every waking hour with the addicts. In the fall of 1962 I had to make an emergency trip home to Puerto Rico. Mama had sent a cablegram to Frank. Papa was dead. Frank, Gene and I took our wives and flew to Puerto Rico where I conducted my father's funeral service. I had returned as a Christian minister and even though Papa never openly accepted Christ as God's Son, I buried him with the assurance that there had been a change in his life and that God, in His loving mercy, would be able to judge him according to his heart. The "Great One" was dead — but the memories of a Papa I had learned to love lived on in my heart.

Alicia Ann was born in January 1963. She helped fill a void in Gloria's lonely life since she now had someone with whom to share her love during the long days. I yearned to spend time with them, but my driving desire to minister to the junkies kept me away from dawn 'til midnight. I warned her not to let anyone else hold the baby, for even though I loved the addicts I knew that minds severely damaged by drugs were capable of anything.

But I never knew how many nights Gloria cried herself to sleep in the loneliness of our apartment. She must have been God's choice for my life. No other woman would have been able to stand the strain.

15

Excursion into Hell

I had been out of town for a couple of days and when I returned, Gloria told me about Maria. Twenty-eight years old, she had come in off the street half frozen, suffering acute withdrawal symptoms from heroin, and at the edge of death. Gloria asked me to remember her especially that night as I preached in the little chapel.

After the services, Gloria brought Maria into my office. She stammered out the words as we talked, still suffering from her withdrawal.

"Tonight," she said, "I had the strangest feeling that I wanted to turn loose of my worthless life. As you preached I had this feeling that I really wanted to die to this wretched life of mine. And yet, for the first time in all my life, I want to live. I can't understand it."

I explained to her that she was experiencing what the Bible calls "repentance." "Maria, you cannot receive the love of God until you are willing to die to yourself. Tell me, do you want to die to the old way of life? Do you want the life of drugs and prostitution to be put to death, buried, and forever forgotten?"

"Oh yes, yes, yes," she sobbed. "I'm willing to do anything to escape it."

"Are you willing to die to self?" I probed.

"Yes," she answered, choking back the tears, "even that."

"Then let me tell you about a love so wonderful, so beautiful, so magnificent that it can take even a person like you and make them clean and pure. Let me tell you about Jesus." And for the next ten minutes I talked to her about God's perfect love that was poured out to us in Jesus Christ.

She buried her face in her hands and sobbed. I walked over to her and put my hand on her shoulder. "Maria, let's kneel here and pray . . . " and before I could finish my sentence, Maria was on the floor on her knees. I could feel the dam burst. Maria had been born again to a new life in Jesus Christ.

A month later Maria stopped by my office. The drug urge was tearing her apart and she wanted to leave the Center Her boy friend, Johnny, had already given in to the call of the drug, and had left the Center some days before in the middle of the night.

I got up and closed the door behind her. "Maria," I said, "nothing else in all my life is as important as your future. Let's talk about what has happened in your life."

She was ready. She went back to the time she was nineteen and had graduated from high school. I let her talk.

"It was Johnny who taught me how to smoke marijuana. My girl friends had told me about their experiences with marijuana. They said it was okay as long as you didn't go on to something stronger. Johnny always seemed to have a supply of reefers and I thought it was a lot of fun."

Maria paused as if remembering those first days as she began her descent into hell, and I thought how typical she was of the dozens of addicts who were coming to the Center. Ninety percent of them started with a stick of pot and then graduated to dope. I knew what was coming but felt she needed to express it. "Tell me about it, Maria, what was the effect?" She relaxed in her chair, her eyes half closed, as she told me her story.

"I felt my troubles would just float away," she answered. "One time I felt myself floating miles and miles above the earth. Then I began to come apart. My fingers left my hands and floated off into space. My hands left my wrists. My arms and legs left my body. I came into a million pieces and floated off on a soft breeze."

She paused again, recollecting. "But the pot wasn't enough. All it did was whet my desire for something stronger. I was mentally hooked.

"Johnny gave me my first 'fix'. He had been talking about it for several weeks. One afternoon I had been crying all day.

Nothing had gone right and Johnny came in with the needle and spoon. I knew what he was going to do, but he seemed so confident that it would help me, I let him go ahead. I didn't know about drug addiction then. But he assured me I'd be all right.

"He pulled the belt tight around my arm above my elbow until the vein stood out like a big mound under my skin. He emptied the white, sugar-like contents of the little envelope into a spoon. Adding water with an eye dropper, he held a match under the spoon until the liquid boiled. Once again he used the eye dropper and sucked the now dissolved heroin back into the dropper. Then, with expert knowledge, he jabbed the vein with the end of the hypodermic needle. Then, carefully with the eye dropper, he squeezed the potent liquid into the open end of the hypodermic. Laying the dropper aside he worked the needle up and down in my arm until the liquid disappeared in the vein. I felt nothing as he withdrew the needle. I didn't know it then, but I had just become a 'mainliner.'

" 'Johnny, I'm getting sick,' I said.

" 'Naw, you're all right baby,' he said, 'just take it easy and pretty soon you'll be floating. Johnny promises and I don't ever go back on my promises, do I?'

"But I couldn't hear him. I began to heave and before I could move I had vomited on the floor. I fell back across the bed and began to shake and perspire. Johnny sat there beside me and held my hand. Soon I relaxed and a warm, fluid feeling swept over me. I thought I was rising up toward the ceiling and above me I could see Johnny's smiling face. He bent over me and whispered, 'How's it doing, baby?'

" 'Swell,' I whispered, 'Man, that's getting good.' I had begun my excursion to hell.

"I didn't have another fix for about a week. This time when Johnny suggested it I was ready. The next one came three days later. After that, Johnny didn't have to suggest it to me, I was asking for it. I didn't know it at the time, but I was addicted . . . hooked.

"The following week Johnny came home and I was beginning to shake. I asked him for a fix.

" 'Now listen, baby, I love you and all that, but this stuff costs money, you know.'

" 'I know it, Johnny, but I need a fix.'

"Johnny smiled, 'I can't do it, baby. Man, you're beginning to cost me.'

" 'Please Johnny,' I pleaded with him, 'don't tease me. Can't you see I need a fix?'

"Johnny started toward the door. 'Not today. Just sweat it out. I ain't got the time or the money.'

" 'Johnny!' I was screaming. 'Don't leave me. For God's sake don't leave.' But he was gone and I heard the key turn in the lock.

"I tried to get hold of myself but I couldn't do anything. I walked to the window and saw Johnny down at the end of the block talking to a couple of the girls. I knew who they were. They worked for Johnny. He referred to them as part of his 'stable.' They were prostitutes who bought his stuff on the money they made at their trade. Johnny always kept them supplied and they would pass the stuff along to their customers for a commission.

"I stood there at the window and watched him as he reached into his coat pocket and slipped one of the girls a small white envelope. I knew it was the stuff. I watched Johnny give away the precious heroin and could hardly stand it. Why should he give it to her and not let me have it? God, I needed it.

"Suddenly, I heard myself screaming. 'Johnny! Johnny!' I was screaming out the window at the top of my voice. He looked up and then started back toward the apartment. When he came in, I was across the bed sobbing and shaking. I had lost all control of myself.

"He closed the door behind him. I sat up on the bed and tried to talk, but before I could say anything he came to me and I felt the back of his hand as it smashed across my mouth.

" 'What the hell are you trying to do?' he screamed. 'You trying to get me picked up or something?'

" 'Johnny, please. Help me. I need a fix. I saw you give the stuff to those girls. Why don't you give it to me? Please?' I had reached a stage of complete desperation. I was shaking and sobbing at the same time. I could taste the blood as it ran down the side of my mouth but I didn't care. All I wanted was that needle.

"Johnny grinned. 'Now listen, baby, you're different from those sluts down there on the street. You got class. But this stuff ain't free. It costs – plenty. Those girls down there work for theirs. What're you doing for yours? Huh?'

" 'I'll work, Johnny. I'll do anything. Anything. Just give me that needle.'

" 'I don't know,' said Johnny. 'You got too much class to be working out there on the street.'

" 'Johnny, I'll do anything. Just tell me.' I could feel the floor coming up toward me as I sank to his feet and put my arms around his knees and legs to keep from falling on my face.

" 'You mean you're willing to hustle for me on the street?' He paused and then continued with enthusiasm. 'You can do it, baby, I know you can if you want to. Man, you can out-do those other chicks ten to one. The guys would come flocking to you and between us we could make a real killing. How about it? I'd be making money and could buy you as much H as you wanted – you'd never have to go through this again. What about it? Is that what you want?'

" 'Yes, Johnny, yes, yes, yes. Just give me a shot.'

"Johnny walked over to the stove and turned on the burner. He pulled out his spoon and sprinkled a little bit of the white powder into the bottom and held it over the flame. Filling the needle, he walked over to where I was crouched on the floor.

" 'Man, baby, this is the beginning of heaven for both of us. With you on my side we can reach the moon.' I felt the needle penetrate the vein. The shaking stopped almost immediately – within seconds. Johnny helped me up and onto the bed where I sank into a deep sleep. But Johnny was wrong. It wasn't the beginning of heaven. It was the beginning of a long, horrible nightmare that would last for eight terrifying years. Not heaven – But hell.

"Hell is a bottomless pit, where you keep on falling, going down, down, never reaching bottom. In the fall into drug addiction there is no place to stop and catch on. There is no way to arrest the descent. I was on my way down.

"Johnny couldn't use me unless I was addicted. But when I became a slave to drugs, I also became his slave. I had to do what he wanted . . . and he wanted me to prostitute for him to bring in the money. He kept me supplied, but I could see that things weren't quite the heaven he said they would be.

"For one thing, I soon learned Johnny also had another woman. I knew he didn't want to marry me, but never thought he was keeping another woman. I found out about it the hard way.

"Things had been a little slow the night before and I had gotten up and gone down the street the next afternoon to do a little shopping. I liked to get out and forget what I was and pretend I was just like all the other people. I was standing at the corner of Hicks and Atlantic waiting for the light to change when I felt a hand on my shoulder that spun me completely around.

"'You're Maria, ain't you?' She was a dark woman with long black hair that flowed down across her shoulders. Her eyes were spitting fire. Before I could answer her she said, 'Yeah, you're the one. I've seen you before. You're the one messing with my man. I'll teach you, you cheap whore.'

"I tried to back away from her but she slapped me in the face. The light had changed and people were milling all around but I wasn't going to be pushed around by anyone, not like this. I reached out and snatched her hair and pushed her backwards at the same time.

"She screamed like a wild woman. 'You dirty slut. Sleeping with my man. I'm gonna kill you.' She was crazy. She swung at me with her purse and I ducked. I pushed my body against her and she fell backward against the rail around the entrance to the subway. I heard her gasp for air as her backbone slammed into the hard iron pipe.

"I took her head in my hands and pushed her backwards over the pipe and down toward the black steps that led to the subway below. I was trying to get my fingernails into her eyes where I knew I could hurt her. Suddenly, she sank her teeth into the side of my hand. I could feel the flesh tear as I ripped my hand out of her mouth screaming with pain.

"As I backed up someone grabbed me from behind and the crowd moved in between us. The man who grabbed me whirled me around and pushed me out into the street where I stumbled and fell. The crowd was still milling around the other woman and I darted across the street and down the sidewalk on the other side.

"I never looked back, but ran to the apartment, soaked my hand and got the girl across the hall to bandage it. That night I was back on the street . . . I never saw her again.

"I didn't feel any more obligations to Johnny, though. I knew I could get a fix from one of a dozen guys, all who would be glad to have me working for them. So it became a long nightmare. I lived with one man after another. All were drug addicts. I sold my body and they went out and stole.

"I learned to work in partnership with some of the other girls. We'd rent a room for the night. Then we'd go out on the street and wait. Some of the men were regular customers. Most were complete strangers. Niggers, wops, Orientals, Puerto Ricans, whites . . . their money was all the same color.

"Some nights I'd draw a complete blank. Others, I'd get as many as nine or ten during the evening. That was a good night. But by then, it was costing me almost $40 a day just to keep in fixes, and that meant I had to get at least five customers a night to keep going.

"It was sheer hell. When I could sleep during the day I'd wake up screaming from horrible dreams. I was imprisoned in my own body and I was my own jailor. There was no escape from that fear, dirtiness, and ugliness of sin.

"I was afraid of drunks. Some were perverts and sadists. Several of the girls had been tortured into unnatural acts. One girl got in with a guy one night who got his kicks out of beating a girl with a belt. He was half drunk and by the time they got to the room, he was almost crazy with excitement. He made her undress and then took her bra and tied her hands to the doorknob and beat her across the stomach and breasts with his belt until she passed out from screaming.

"I preferred to use the room I'd rented. On some occasions the man might want me to go to his apartment or to a hotel room. Some of them were businessmen in town for trips or conventions. But I was afraid to go to a man's room. Terrible things happened and some of the girls never came back.

"Some of the men were afraid to go to my room, afraid they'd get rolled. They'd want me to go with them in their car.

"After a couple of bad experiences, I put a stop to this.

"One man let me out clear over on the other side of town, and it took me all night to get back home on the subway. The other man took me out on a lonely road. He was drunk and demanded his money back. When I refused he put a pistol to my head and pulled the trigger. The gun misfired and I ran, but it was my last time to go in someone's car.

"The guys on the street weren't the only ones to give me trouble. I was in constant trouble with the police, too. I was in jail eleven times over the eight years of my addiction. The longest sentence was six months. I was picked up for everything. Shop lifting. Drug addiction. Petty theft. Vagrancy. And yes, prostitution.

"I hated the jails. My first time in jail I cried and cried. I promised myself I'd never do anything to get picked up again. But four months later, I was back. Ten times I was back.

"The police were constantly bugging me. One cop would come around every couple of days while I was on the street and try to get me to go with him. But I knew there wasn't any money in it, so I never did.

"But the heroin was tearing me apart. I remember my first overdose. I was still working and had moved back in with mother. I had left Johnny. Mother was working in a factory and I was in an office. I told mother I needed some new clothes for my job and begged her into getting a loan at the bank.

"I came home from work early one afternoon and got the money out of the bureau. Going down into Harlem where the pusher lived, I bought the stuff and put it inside my bra. Then I went down a couple of blocks to a basement where some junkies I knew lived. I was desperate. Shaky. I loaded the needle from a bottle cap and shot myself in the vein. I knew at the time something was wrong. I got dizzy and fainted. I can remember someone playing around with me, trying to get me to my feet. I think they got scared when I didn't respond. Someone ripped my bra off, got the rest of the H, and then pulled me out of the basement leaving me crumpled on the sidewalk.

"When I woke up I was in Bellevue. The police had found me and taken me to the hospital. Someone had rolled me. All my money was gone. There were three cops standing around my bed, all of them asking me questions at the same time. I told them I had been drinking and someone had put something in my liquor. But they knew. And they had the doctor mark an "OD" on my record for "overdose". That was the first of three.

"The last one almost killed me.

"I had been drinking in my room. The combination of cheap wine and the overdose of heroin knocked me out.

"I fell asleep on the bed and my cigarette fell in my hair. I can remember the strange feeling. I dreamed that the hand of God reached down and shook me . . . and kept shaking me. I can remember saying, 'Damn it, God, leave me alone. Stop that shaking.' But the shaking didn't stop. And I woke up.

"I knew something was wrong, but I felt nothing. I could smell something putrid – the smell of burned meat. I tried to get up but fell on the floor. Crawling to the mirror I pulled myself up and looked. The face I saw wasn't mine. I was bald. All my hair had burned off. My face was a mass of blisters and charred flesh. Both ears were almost completely burned off. The smoke, like smoke from burned toast, curled up from both my ears. Both hands were burned and blistered where subconsciously I had tried to beat out the fire.

"I began to scream. A man across the hall heard my hysterical screaming and knowing I was a junkie came and pounded on the door.

"I stumbled to the door and grasped the knob trying to open it, but the flesh on my palms stuck to the metal when I turned the knob. The flesh slipped off my hands and I couldn't twist the knob.

"Somehow, he got the door open from the other side. He wanted to take me to the hospital but I refused. I collapsed back on the bed and asked him to take me to my friend Inez's apartment. He did. I spent the night there.

"But the burns were second and third degree and the pain became unbearable. I was scared of the hospital. I had been there before. Knowing I was hooked, I realized if I went to the hospital, I'd have to kick the habit and come off cold turkey. I didn't think I could stand it. I would die. And I was afraid of dying.

"But the next day, Inez forced me to go to the hospital. She didn't have to force much. I knew I was going to die unless I did. I was there a month and a half while the burns healed.

"After I was released, I went back to the street. I took my first shot forty-five minutes after walking out the door of the hospital and that night I was back on the beat. Only it was harder now because of the scars and burns. No one wanted me. My clothes were covered with cigarette burns and coffee stains. My flesh was dirty and smelled. Sometimes I would walk down the street gagging. And the addiction was driving me insane.

"A Spanish fellow named Rene used to talk to me on the streets. He had been a pusher but had gotten tangled up with Teen Challenge and had kicked the habit. He had become a Christian and for the last several months had been after me to come here and kick it also.

"One cold night in March, I was desperately craving a fix. I stumbled down the block and around the corner to 416 Clinton and collapsed on the stairway next to the desk.

"Mario was at the desk that night. He called Gloria. She gently picked me up and I leaned on her as we walked through the side door in front of the desk and into the chapel.

"'Kneel down, Maria,' she said. 'Kneel down and pray.'

"I was in a stupor and thought I was dying. But if it took this to stay alive, I'd do it. I knelt on the floor behind one of the benches but before I could get my head down, I began to vomit. I vomited all down the front of my blouse and on the floor. I began to cry and shake and collapsed in a heap on the floor, with both hands in front of me in my own vomit.

"I looked up and the other girls in the room had come around me. I recognized some of them that I had seen in jail, but they were different. They all looked like angels, floating on air across the chairs and tables coming slowly toward me. They were smiling. There was a shine on their faces. Their eyes sparkled, not from pot or H, but from an inward light that shone down on me.

"I was in a daze and it seemed like my head was spinning round and round.

"Gloria was there beside me and I was aware that she was kneeling in my vomit. I turned my head to try to cry but could only heave.

"The girls gathered around me and I could hear them praying. Gloria stood to her feet and I could feel her hands on my head. A power, an electric, spiritual power came flooding through my body, almost picking me up off the floor as it flowed through her delicate hands into my burned out body.

"I heard music. Some of the girls were singing. I shuddered and threw up again.

" 'Please, can't I go to bed?' I stammered.

"I felt strong arms under my armpits as one of the girls picked me up and almost carried me up the stairs. I heard water running and could feel them pulling at my clothes. I was too sick to care. I thought they were going to drown me. I thought maybe they were all a bunch of queers and were going to kill me. I didn't care.

"They gently put me under the shower and washed me off. It was the first time in months I had been clean all over and it helped. They helped me dry off and put a clean slip on me and led me to a bunk bed in a large room that was filled with other bunks.

" 'Can I have a smoke?' I asked one of the girls. Gloria said, 'Sorry, Maria, we don't smoke here. But here's some candy. Try it. I think it will help.'

"I collapsed across the bed and began to shake. They took turns rubbing my back. Every time I'd ask for a smoke Gloria would pop another piece of candy in my mouth.

"They sat with me for two days and two nights. During the night, I'd wake up trembling and see Gloria there beside my bed, reading her Bible or praying out loud. I was never alone.

"It was on the third night that Gloria said, 'Maria, I want you to come downstairs to the chapel service.' I was weak.

So weak. But I came down to the chapel and sat in the back of the room.

"That was the night you were speaking. And it was that night that I came into this office and knelt here and cried out my heart to the Lord."

Maria stopped talking. Her head was bowed forward, her eyes staring at the Bible resting on top of my desk.

"Maria," I whispered gently, "didn't the Lord hear that cry?"

She looked up, "Oh yes, Nicky. I've never doubted that. But when the pull of the drugs gets so strong, I want to give in." A tear ran down her cheek. "Just keep praying for me. With God's help I'll make it now."

16

With Christ in Harlem

David was on the road most of the time, recruiting summer workers and raising money for the center. As time went on, he had less and less personal contact with the addicts themselves and found himself in the role of an administrator – a role which I felt he did not want to assume but which was thrust on him by circumstances.

The majority of our field work was done in the street meetings and in personal street corner encounters. Almost every afternoon we set up our platform and loudspeaker in some ghetto section of the city.

One afternoon Mario and I took a small group in our passenger bus into the heart of Spanish Harlem. We were handing out tracts, trying to round up a crowd for a street service, but meeting with little success.

Mario said to me, "I'm gonna get us a crowd."

"Not this afternoon," I said. "No one cares. We might as well pack up and go home."

"No," Mario said. "We're gonna get a crowd. You and the others start putting up the speakers. In less than an hour we're gonna have the biggest street meeting we've ever had."

"Man, how do you think you're gonna have a meeting without any people? They're just not interested today."

"Never mind. Just let me handle it," Mario said. Smiling shyly he hurried down the street and around the corner.

We started putting up the equipment. It was strictly a faith venture. I felt like Noah building his ark on the top of a dry mountain. But we hammered away, trusting God to provide the showers.

He did. Fifteen minutes later we had finished and I was back on the corner handing out tracts when I saw a huge mob of boys running down the street toward me. They were waving sticks and baseball bats and yelling at the top of their voices. I turned and started back to the platform when I saw another mob of kids coming from the other direction, shouting and waving sticks. "I gotta get out of here," I thought. "These kids are going to rumble." But it was too late! I was surrounded by the screaming, elbowing gangs. I kept waiting for them to start slugging.

Suddenly I saw Mario running down an alley in the middle of the block shouting up the fire escapes: "Hey, everybody, the leader of the vicious Mau Mau gang from Brooklyn is going to speak in fifty minutes. Come hear him. Come hear the great Nicky Cruz, the most dangerous man in Brooklyn. Come prepared. He's a killer and still dangerous."

The kids were pouring from the apartments, down the fire escapes, and running toward me. They were flocking by me shouting, "Where's Nicky? I want to see him. Where's the leader of the Mau Maus?"

Mario came up, grinning from ear to ear. "See, I told you I'd get a crowd."

We looked around. He'd gotten a crowd all right. There must have been 300 kids milling around in the middle of the street.

I shook my head. "I just hope you don't get us all killed. Man, these kids are mean."

Mario was still grinning and puffing from running. "Come on, Preacher. Your congregation's waiting."

With perspiration running down his face, he crawled up to the mike and held out his hands for silence. The kids listened as he spoke, much like a carnival barker getting an audience keyed up for the sideshow.

"Ladies and gentlemen. Today is the big day. The leader of the vicious and famous Mau Maus is going to speak to you . . . the most dangerous man in New York. He's feared by young and old alike. Only he's not the leader any more. He's the ex-leader. And this afternoon he's gonna tell you why he's no longer with the gang and why he's running with Jesus. I now give you the one and only, NICKY CRUZ, ex-leader of the Mau Maus."

He was shouting when he finished and I jumped to the platform behind the mike. The kids in the crowd began to shout and clap. I stood there on the platform grinning and waving my hand while they applauded. Many of them recognized me or had read about me in the paper. About 200 adults had gathered at the back of the crowd. Two police cars pulled up, one on each side of the mob.

I held out my arms and the shouting, whistling and applauding grew quieter. In a moment the crowd was silent.

I felt strongly anointed by the Holy Spirit as I began to preach. The words came freely and without strain. "I used to be the leader of the Mau Maus. I can see you've heard of my reputation." Once more the crowd broke into spontaneous applause. I held out my arms and they quieted down.

"This afternoon I want to tell you why I'm the *ex*-leader of the Mau Maus. I'm the *ex*-leader because Jesus changed my heart! One day, in a street meeting just like this, I listened to a preacher tell me of someone who could change my life. He told me Jesus loves me. I didn't even know who Jesus was. And I knew *no*body loved me. But Davie Wilkerson told me Jesus loves me. And my life is now changed. I gave myself to God and He gave me new life. I used to be just like you. I was running in the streets. Sleeping on rooftops. I had been kicked out of school for fighting. The police were looking for me and I'd been arrested many times and put in jail. I was afraid. But then Jesus changed my life. He gave me something to live for. He gave me hope. He gave me new purpose in life. No longer am I smoking pot and fighting and killing. No longer do I lie awake at night afraid. No longer do I have nightmares. Now people speak to me when I pass by. The police respect me. I'm married and have a little baby. But most of all, I'm happy and am no longer running."

The crowd was hushed and attentive. I finished my message and gave an altar call.

Twenty-two responded to the invitation and knelt down at the front of the crowd while I prayed.

I finished praying and looked up. The policemen had left their cars and were standing with their hats in their hands and their heads bowed. I turned my face toward the sky. The sun was shining in Harlem.

* * *

Spanish Harlem became a favorite place for us to hold street meetings. We seemed to be able to draw bigger crowds and the need for the Gospel was more apparent than any other place we preached. I kept reminding our team that "where sin abounded, grace did much more abound."

Gloria had a hard time accepting Spanish Harlem. She couldn't get used to the smell. She tried not to act snobbish, but some of the open markets were almost more than she could stomach. It was even hard for me to get used to the flies that swarmed over the meats, fruits and vegetables.

And then, added to this, was the odor of the addicts. They seem to ooze a foul odor. And when grouped together, especially during the heat of the summer, the smell is almost repulsive.

We learned much during those first months of street preaching. We learned that the ones who had the most success were the ones who had come off the streets and could present a first-hand testimony of the changing, transforming power of Jesus Christ. I was not as successful in preaching to dope addicts as some of the addicts themselves. We found they made our best preachers. Their honest, sincere bumbling testimonies made a terrific impact on other addicts. More and more we began to carry them with us into the streets to do our preaching. However, this too raised problems.

Many times at the street preaching services the addicts on the street would try to tempt and tease our men and women. They'd light up a pot stick in front of them and deliberately blow the smoke in their faces. I've even seen a man pull out a needle and package of heroin and wave it in the face of one of our addicts saying, "Hey, baby, don't you miss this? Man, this is living. You gotta try it." The temptation was almost overpowering, but these lives were protected by a shield of God's strength.

I found Maria, in particular, to be unashamed to stand before a crowd of her former associates, prostitutes and junkies, and testify to the grace of God. Her simple testimony often moved the crowds to tears as she told of a God who is a close personal friend. Who, in the form of His Son

Jesus Christ, walks the hard streets of the city touching people in their sin and making them whole. Most of them had never been exposed to a God like this. The God they had heard of, if they had heard of one at all, was a God of judgment who curses sin and whips people into line like a policeman. Or perhaps they identify God with the cold, formal, mumbo-jumbo churches they had seen.

One day a former gang member, a young negro boy who had been on heroin, was testifying concerning his childhood. He told of having to leave home at the age of thirteen because the apartment was too crowded. He spoke of different men who lived with his mother. He told of sleeping on the rooftops and in the subways. He testified of having to scrounge food for himself, begging and stealing. He had no home at all and would use the rooftops or the alleys for a latrine. He was living like a wild animal in the streets.

As he talked, an old woman in the back of the crowd began to weep. She became almost hysterical in her weeping and I went around behind the crowd to minister to her. After her weeping subsided, she told me this boy could have been her son. She had five boys to leave home and live just like that in the streets of the city. Her guilt was more than she could bear. We gathered around her and prayed for her. She threw her head back and looked toward the Heavens, crying out for God to forgive her and protect her sons, wherever they were. She found her peace with God that afternoon, but the damage to her boys had already been done. And in thousands of other cases the damage was still being done. We felt like we were trying to dry up the ocean by dipping at the surf with a teaspoon. However, we knew that God did not expect us to win the world – just to testify and be faithful. And that was our goal.

Late one Thursday evening we set up a street meeting in the corner of a school yard in Spanish Harlem. It was a hot summer night and a large crowd had gathered to listen to the peppy Spanish choruses and fast Gospel music that blared from our loudspeakers.

The crowd was restless and jumpy. As the music moved into a faster tempo some of our girls and boys stood in front of the mike and began to sing, clapping their hands to the fast songs. To one side, though, I noticed a disturbance. A group of "little people" were dancing to the music. There were about five or six of them jitterbugging in the street, wiggling their hips and kicking their feet. Some of the audience was distracted and had begun to urge them on, laughing and clapping with them. I left my position and walked around to them.

"Hey, you kids. How come you're dancing here? This is Jesus' turf."

One of them said, "That man over there paid us to dance. See, he gave us a dime." They pointed to a slim young man, about twenty-eight years old, who was standing on the edge of the crowd. I walked over to talk to him. He saw me coming and began to jitterbug to the music himself.

I tried to talk to him. He kept dancing up and down, kicking his feet and shaking his hips saying, "Man, that's tough music, cha-cha-cha."

He spun around in the street and slapped his hands against his thighs. Shaking his hips and throwing his head back like a wild man he chanted, "Be-bop, cha-cha-cha . . . dum-de-dum-dum . . . swingin', man, swingin'."

I finally broke through to him, "Hey man, I want to ask you something."

He kept right on dancing to the time of the music, "Yeah, Daddio, whatcha want? . . . whatcha want? . . . be-bop, de-dum-dum . . . whatcha want?"

I said, "Did you give those kids money to make them dance and break up our meeting?" My patience was beginning to wear a little thin.

Whirling around he said, "That's right, man, you got the right daddy this time. I'm your man . . . da-da-de-da" . . . He was smacking his lips and kicking his feet high in front of his face as he whirled.

I thought he was crazy. "Why?" I shouted at him. "Man, what's wrong with you anyway?"

"Because we don't like you. We don't like Christians. No. No. No. We don't like Christians. Da-da-dum-de-dum."

I was exasperated. "Well, man," I said, balling up my fists and starting toward him, "we're gonna finish this service and you're gonna shut up or I'll bust you against that building and shut you up for good."

He could see I was serious, but he couldn't shut off his mischief quite that fast. He clapped his hand over his mouth in an obvious move and then stared back over his hand in mock terror. But he stopped dancing and he shut up.

I went back to the microphone and preached that evening about my experiences growing up in New York. I testified about the dirt, poverty, shame and sin that had been in my life. Then I preached about the sin of parents who allow their children to grow up in such sin. I begged them to set a good example for their children.

People began to take off their hats as I spoke. This is one of the best signs of reverence and respect. I noticed tears in the eyes of many of the people and the appearance of scattered handkerchiefs. I knew that the power of Christ was moving in a special way, but didn't realize the impact that He was to have in the moments to follow.

As I spoke I noticed an old man, an obvious wino, standing in the middle of all those people weeping. A young girl close to the front buried her head in her hands and knelt in the street, her bare knees against the hard, dirty pavement. One of our girl workers left the group and knelt beside her, praying with her. I continued to preach.

It was obvious that the power of God's Spirit was at this meeting. As I finished preaching and gave the altar call I noticed an addict on the edge of the crowd in great agony of spirit. He reached into his shirt pocket and pulled out several "bags" and threw them into the street at his feet. He began to scream, stomping on the little white envelopes. "I curse you, you filthy powder. You've ruined my life. You've driven my wife away. You've killed my children. You've sent my soul to hell. I curse you! I curse you!"

He collapsed to the pavement on his knees, weeping and rocking back and forth with his face in his hands. One of our male staff members hurried to his side. Two other of our addicts gathered around him, one with his hand on his head and the other kneeling, all of them praying out loud as he cried out for forgiveness.

Eight or nine addicts came to the front of the crowd and knelt in the street in front of the microphone. I went from one to the other, laying my hands on their heads and praying for them, completely oblivious to the sound of the heavy traffic and the stares of curious onlookers.

After the service we counseled with those who had come and told them about the Center. We invited them to come and live with us while they kicked the habit. There were always some who would come with us right then. Others would be hesitant and refuse. Some would come around a week or so later and ask to be admitted.

As the crowd departed, we gathered up our equipment and started to load it in the bus. One of the little kids who had been dancing in the street began pulling on my coat sleeve. I asked him what he wanted and he said that the "dancing man" wanted to talk to me. I asked him where the man was and he pointed across the street to a dark alley.

It was already night and I had no desire to walk into a dark alley where a crazy man was hiding. I told the kid to tell the man I would be glad to talk to him – out here under the street lights.

The kid went back and in a few minutes he returned. We had almost finished disassembling our equipment. He shook his head and said the man needed to see me but he was too embarrassed to come out in the light.

I started to tell the kid, "no dice." But suddenly I remembered David Wilkerson coming to me in the basement room where I had gone to hide after that first street service. I remember how he walked in unafraid and said, "Nicky, Jesus loves you." It was this fearlessness and compassion that led me to accept Christ as my Saviour.

So, looking into the black sky I told the Lord that if He wanted me to talk to this wild "dancing man," I would go. But I was going in His Spirit and not in my own might and power and I was expecting Him to go before me – especially into that dark alley.

I made my way across the street and stopped at the entrance to the alley. It was like the entrance to a tomb. I whispered a prayer, "Lord, I sure hope you've gotten here ahead of me," and in I went. I felt my way down the masonry walls into the darkness.

Then, I heard the muffled sound of a man sobbing. I moved forward and in the dim light could see him crouched on his haunches in the midst of a group of stinking garbage cans. His head was between his legs and his body was racked with convulsive sobs. I moved forward and knelt beside him. The rank odor from the garbage cans was overpowering. But here was human need, and the desire to help was even stronger than the stench from the alley.

"Help me. Please help me," he sobbed out. "I read about you in the papers. I heard that you had been converted and had been to Bible school. Please help me."

I couldn't believe that this was the same man who only minutes before had been dancing and singing in the street, trying to break up our meeting.

"Will God forgive me? Tell me, have I slipped too far? Will He forgive me? Please help me."

I told him God would forgive. I knew. He had forgiven me. I asked him about himself. He poured out his story as I knelt there in the filth of the alley beside him.

He had once felt that God was calling him into the ministry. He had given up his job and attended a Bible School to study for the ministry. Returning to New York, however, he met a woman who seduced him away from his wife. His wife and two children begged him not to leave them. They reminded him of his vows to God and his marriage vows. But he was a man possessed with a demon and left his wife and moved in with the other woman. Then two months later she left him, telling him she was tired of him and he wasn't any fun any more. He had gone to pieces and was now smoking pot and taking pills. I asked him what kind of pills and he said he was taking Bombitas (Desoxyn), Nembies, Tuinal, and Seconal (barbiturates). He felt he was losing his mind.

"I was trying to drive you away," he moaned. "That's why I acted like I did out on the street and in the school yard. I was afraid. I was afraid of God and afraid to face Him. I want to come back to God. I want to go back to my wife

and children but don't know how. Will you pray for me?"
He raised his head and I saw eyes full of pathos and guilt,
pleading for help.

I helped him to his feet and we walked out of the alley
and across the street to the bus. Six of us got in the bus.
He sat in one of the middle seats with his head bent over
on the back of the seat in front of him. We began to pray
with him, all of us praying audibly. He was praying also.
Suddenly I was aware that he was quoting Scripture. From
out of his memory and his training at Bible School poured
forth the words of the 51st Psalm – the Psalm that King
David prayed after he committed adultery with Bathsheba
and sent her husband into battle to be killed. Never have
I felt the power of God so close as I did when this former
minister, who had become a servant of Satan, received the
Spirit of Christ and cried out his prayer of confession and
request for forgiveness in the words of the Holy Scripture.

> Have mercy upon me, O God, according to thy loving-
> kindness: according unto the multitude of thy tender
> mercies blot out my transgressions.
> Wash me thoroughly from mine iniquity, and cleanse
> me from my sin.
> For I acknowledge my transgressions: and my sin is
> ever before me.
> Against thee, and thee only have I sinned, and done
> this evil in thy sight: that thou mightest be justified
> when thou speakest, and be clear when thou judgest.
> Behold, I was shapen in iniquity, and in sin did my
> mother conceive me.
> Behold, thou desirest truth in the inward parts, and in
> the hidden part thou shalt make me to know wisdom.
> Purge me with hyssop, and I shall be clean! wash me,
> and I shall be whiter than snow.
> Make me to hear joy and gladness, that the bones
> which thou hast broken may rejoice.
> Hide thy face from my sins, and blot out all mine
> iniquities.
> Create in me a clean heart, O God, and renew a right
> spirit within me.

Cast me not away from thy presence; and take not thy
   Holy Spirit from me.
Restore unto me the joy of thy salvation; and uphold
   me with thy free spirit.
Then will I teach transgressors thy ways; and sinners
   shall be converted unto thee.
Deliver me from blood guiltiness, O God, thou God of
   my salvation; and my tongue shall sing aloud of thy
   righteousness.

He finished praying. The bus was quiet. Then Gloria spoke
up in a soft, beautiful voice, finishing the words of the Psalm.
"The sacrifices of God are a broken spirit: a broken and
contrite heart, O God, thou wilt not despise."

We all arose from our knees. He was wiping his face with
his handkerchief and blowing his nose. The rest of us were
blowing and sniffing too.

He turned to me. "I gave my last dime to those crazy kids
to dance in the street. Could you give me a quarter to call
my wife and catch a subway. I'm going home."

I've made it a practice never to give junkies or winos
money. I know that almost without exception it will go
for dope or booze. But this was the exception. I reached
in my pocket and pulled out my last dollar bill. He took it
and hugged me around the neck, his face still wet from tears.
Then he went to the others and hugged each of them too.

"You'll be hearing from me," he said. "I'll be back."

He was back. Two days later he brought his wife and
two children by the center to introduce them. There was a
radiance in his face that could never be produced by drugs
or pills. It was the light of God.

17

Through the Valley of the Shadow

It is almost impossible to put forty drug addicts under one roof without having problems – especially when they're supervised by green inexperienced personnel. The only thing that kept the organization of Teen Challenge from exploding was the Holy Spirit. We were sitting on a powder keg and anyone of us could light the fuse on some psychopathic mind and blow us all into oblivion. Our only hope was to stay as close to God as possible.

It was difficult to tell those who were genuine from those who were counterfeit, for most of these men and women were professional con artists. They made their living telling lies. But we trusted them as far as we could.

I was a stickler for discipline and soon learned most of them didn't resent it if it were just and reasonable. In fact, they relished it because it gave them a firm base of operation – a solid sense of belonging. However, I knew all of them didn't feel this way.

David agreed with my philosophy. But the distasteful responsibility of having to constantly reprimand the offenders began to weigh heavily upon me. Many times I had to get out of bed in the middle of the night to quell a disturbance and sometimes even dismiss someone for an infraction of the rules.

Most of the major decisions were left up to me and we had to add additional staff members, most of them just out of college. I became keenly aware of my lack of formal training and sensed my own insecurity. I knew little or nothing about administrative procedures and even less about the psychological aspects of interpersonal relations necessary to maintain communication and rapport with my fellow staff members. I could sense jealousy on the part of some of those working under me and became aware of a gradual breakdown in relationships.

When David would stop by the Center, I'd try to explain that I had problems too big to handle, but he'd always come back at me with, "You can handle it, Nicky. I have great confidence in your ability."

But the problems continued to stack up like dark clouds on the horizon before a storm.

In the fall I flew with Davie to Pittsburgh to speak in Kathryn Kuhlman's city-wide crusade. Miss Kuhlman has one of the world's greatest Spirit-filled ministries. Her work through the Kathryn Kuhlman Foundation reaches all parts of the globe. She had visited Teen Challenge and had taken a personal interest in my work. I had shown her around the city and taken her into the ghetto. "I thank God for lifting you out of these slums," she had said to me. "If you ever have a problem too big to handle, call me."

I thought I might try to talk to her while I was in Pittsburgh because the burden on my heart was becoming heavier. However, I got caught up in the bigness of her program. That night, speaking through my friend Jeff Morales who had come along to interpret, I shared my testimony with several thousand people in the great auditorium. After the service we had dinner in a small restaurant but I never had the opportunity to speak to Miss Kuhlman alone. So I left Pittsburgh even more frustrated over my inability to handle my own personal problems.

By January 1964, we had grown too large to keep the women on the third floor at 416 Clinton. We made arrangements to secure a house across the street for the women's quarters. I was aware of conspiracies behind my back with some of the junkies I had been forced to discipline. Besides this, we had taken several lesbians into the Center who were giving us considerable trouble. I was constantly afraid one of them might try to seduce some of the inexperienced college girls who had been brought in to work as counselors.

Handling addicts was like trying to beat out a forest fire

with a wet towel. Every time I got one little situation under control another would break out. I found myself getting personally involved and when a junkie returned to the world, I began to take it personally.

Gloria warned me about trying to bear all the burden alone, but the responsibility fell heavy on my shoulders.

Then Quetta came to the Center. She was a "male" lesbian and at one time had been "married" to another girl. She wore men's clothes, pants, jacket, even men's shoes and underwear. She was in her early thirties with very fair skin and pitch black hair cut like a man. She was a thin, willowy, attractive girl with an outgoing personality.

Quetta was one of the biggest narcotic pushers in the city. For years she had run a "shooting gallery" in her apartment. Men and women had come not only to buy heroin, but to participate in sexual immorality. She supplied all that was needed – needles, cookers, heroin, pills, and for those with unnatural desires – men and women. It was a messy situation.

When the police raided Quetta's apartment they picked up twelve persons including some professional prostitutes and uncovered ten "outfits" (spoon, needle, and eyedropper). They literally demolished the apartment, ripping out the walls and tearing up the floor until they discovered her cache of drugs worth thousands of dollars.

Quetta came to the center while on probation. I explained the rules to her and told her she was to dress in women's clothing and let her hair grow. Furthermore, she was never to be alone with one of the other junkies unless a woman staff member was present. She was too sick to disagree and seemed thankful to be out of jail. In less than a week she made a profession of faith and gave every outward evidence of being converted.

I soon realized, however, that even conversions can be counterfeit. Even though we used Quetta to testify in many of the street meetings, I felt there was something false about her.

Two weeks later one of the girl counselors came to me early one morning. She was white as a sheet and shaking like a leaf. "What's wrong, Diane? Come in and sit down."

Diane was our newest staff member, a country girl from Nebraska who had just recently graduated from Bible College. "I don't know how to tell you, Nicky," she said. "It's Quetta and Lilly."

Lilly was one of the junkies who had come into the center just a week before. She had been attending the services but hadn't made any commitment to the Lord. I felt my mouth go dry. "What about them?" I said.

Diane blushed and hung her head. "They were in the kitchen together last night about midnight. I walked in on them, and Nicky, they were . . . were . . . ," Her voice trailed off in shame and embarrassment. "I haven't been able to sleep all night. What can we do?"

I got up from my chair and paced back and forth around the desk. "Go back to the building and tell them I want to see them in my office immediately," I choked out. "This place is dedicated to the Lord. We can't have any of this type of thing going on."

Diane left and I sat at my desk with my head in my hands, praying desperately for wisdom. Where had I failed? We had let Quetta testify for the Center. The newspapers had carried her story and given much publicity. She had even spoken in churches about the change in her life.

I waited more than an hour and then started out the door to see what was keeping them. Diane met me on the steps. "They left. Both of them. They got scared and said they were leaving. We couldn't stop them."

I turned and walked slowly back to the Center. I took the defeat personally – and hard. For three days Gloria prayed with me and talked to me as I sulked over my seeming inability to reach these addicts with the true message.

"Nicky, even Jesus had failures among his followers," she said. "Remember all those who have been faithful and successful. Remember Sonny who is in Bible School studying to be a minister. Think of Maria and the wonderful change in her life. Remember what God has done for you. Have you forgotten your own salvation experience? How can you doubt God and grow discouraged over these isolated failures?"

Gloria was right, but I was unable to pull myself out of

my despondency. As the summer wore on the burden of guilt grew greater. I felt I was a total failure. Communications had broken down between me and most of the other staff members. David still believed in me, but I was acutely and painfully aware of the constant failures in the Center. The tension grew greater. Gloria kept trying to pull me out of my defeated attitude, but I was entirely negative in everything I did.

The only bright spot was the arrival of Jimmy Baez. Jimmy had been hooked on narcotics for eight years. He wandered into the Center asking for medicine, thinking it was a hospital.

"We have no medicine here but Jesus," I told him.

He thought I was crazy. "Man, I thought this was a clinic. You're a bunch of kooks." He looked wildly around trying to get out of my office.

"Sit down, Jimmy. I want to talk to you. Christ can change you."

"No one can change me," Jimmy mumbled. "I've tried and can't leave it alone."

I got up from my desk and walked over to him. Placing my hands on his head I began to pray. I felt him shudder and he fell to his knees, calling out to God. From that night on he never wanted another shot of heroin.

"See," Gloria said, when I told her about Jimmy's conversion, "God is showing you He can still use you. How can you continue to doubt Him? Why not be positive? It's been several months since you went out for the street services at night. Get to work for God and you'll feel the leadership of the Holy Spirit like you used to."

I took her advice and agreed to lead the street services the last week in August. The first night out we set up our platform in Brooklyn and I began to preach. It was a hot sultry night but the crowd was large and attentive. I preached hard and felt good about my message. As I neared the end of my sermon I gave the altar call.

Suddenly, I glanced up and on the far back edge of the crowd I saw him. His face was unmistakable. It was Israel. All these years. I had been praying, searching, inquiring . . . and suddenly there he was, a face in the crowd.

My heart leaped. Perhaps God had sent him back. I felt

the old fire pour into my heart as I gave the invitation.
He seemed to be listening intently, stretching his neck to
hear my words. The portable organ began to play and the
girls' trio broke into song. I saw Israel turn and start to
walk away.

Jumping down from the platform I elbowed my way furiously through the crowd, trying to reach him before he
disappeared in the mob of people.

"Israel! Israel!" I shouted after him. "Wait! Wait!"

He paused and turned around. It had been six years since
I'd seen him. He was heavier and more mature. But his
handsome face was like chiseled marble and his eyes were
deep and sad.

I threw my arms around him and tried to pull him back toward the crowd. He resisted and stood unmovable. "Israel,"
I screamed bubbling with joy. "Is it really you?" I jumped
back and held his shoulders at arm's length looking him over.
"Where have you been? Where are you living? What are you
doing? Tell me everything. Why haven't you called me? I've
looked all over New York for you. This is the greatest day
of my life."

His eyes were distant and cold, his manner strange and
withdrawn.

"I've got to go, Nicky. It's been good to see you again."

"Got to go? I haven't seen you in six years. You've been
in my daily prayers. You're coming home with me." I began
to tug at his arm but he shook his head and pulled his arm
away from me. I could feel the strong muscles rippling
under his skin.

"Someday, Nicky. Not now." He shrugged me off and
started to walk away.

"Hey, wait a minute. What's wrong with you? You're my
best friend. You can't just walk away."

He turned and froze me in one spot with a chilly stare
from those steel gray unflinching eyes. "Later, Nicky!" he
spat out. He turned sharply and walked down the sidewalk
into the darkness.

I stood and called out to him in despair. But he never
turned around. He just kept walking into the darkness from
whence he came.

I returned to the Center a broken man. I dejectedly made my way up the narrow stairs to the third floor and shut the door behind me in one of the attic rooms. "God," I cried out in an agonized voice, "what have I done? Israel's lost and it's my fault. Forgive me." I dropped to the floor and fell into a period of uncontrollable crying. I beat my hands against the wall in utter despair. But I received no answer. For two hours I remained in the hot attic room, exhausting myself physically, emotionally, and spiritually.

I knew I was going to leave the Center. I felt my ministry was finished. I was a failure in everything I tried to do. Everyone I touched went bad. Quetta. Lilly. Now Israel. It was hopeless for me to stay on and fight the mounting battles that I couldn't overcome. It was hopeless for me even to remain in the ministry. I was finished. Whipped. Beaten. I pulled myself to my feet and stood looking out the small attic window at the dark sky. "God, I'm beat. I've been wrong. I've been trusting in myself and not in you. If this is the reason you've let this thing come to pass, I am willing to confess my terrible sin. Humble me. Kill me if you must. But, dear God, don't throw me on the scrap heap."

The sobs came again and shook my body. I stood in the door looking back. The room was silent. I didn't know whether He heard me or not. But at that moment it made little difference. I had done all I knew to do.

I went back down the steps to my apartment. Gloria had put the baby to bed and was clearing the remnants of her late supper from the table. I closed the door and walked toward the chair. Before I could sit she was in front of me. Her arms encircled my waist as she drew me close. She knew nothing of what had taken place in the street or the upper room, but because we were one flesh, she could sense I had been wounded. And she was beside me to hold my failing spirit and give strength in time of need.

I crushed her to me and buried my face in her shoulder as the tears began again. For a long time we stood there, pressed tightly against each other, my body racked with sobs. At last the crying passed and I pulled her face up with my hands and looked deep into her eyes. They were filled with tears, like deep fountains with water springing up from the pure earth beneath. But she was not crying. She was smiling, ever so faintly. And the love that flowed from her heart overflowed in her eyes as the tears spilled out over the edges and ran in little rivulets down her light bronze cheeks.

I held her face tightly in my hands. She was beautiful. More beautiful than ever before. She smiled and then her lips parted as she reached for me in a soft lingering kiss. I could taste the salt from my own tears and the moist warmth of her mouth against mine.

"It's over, Gloria. I'm finished. I'm going to leave. Maybe I've grown proud. Maybe I've sinned. I don't know, but I know the spirit has departed from me. I'm like Samson going out to fight the Philistines without the power of God. I'm a failure. I ruin everything I touch."

"What is it, Nicky?" her voice was soft and gentle. "What has happened?"

"Tonight I saw Israel. For the first time in six years I saw my dearest friend. He turned his back on me. It's my fault he's like he is. Had I not left him alone in the city six years ago, he would be working beside me today. Instead, he spent five years in prison and tonight is lost. God doesn't care any more."

"Nicky, that is almost blasphemy," Gloria said, her voice still soft. "You cannot blame yourself for what happened to Israel. You were just a scared kid that morning you drove out of town. It wasn't your fault you missed Israel. It's wrong to blame yourself. And how can you dare say God doesn't care any more? He does care. He cared enough to save you."

"You don't understand," I said, shaking my head. "Ever since Davie told me Israel went back to the gang I have blamed myself. I have carried the burden of guilt on my heart. Tonight I saw him, and he turned his back on me. He wouldn't even speak to me. If only you could have seen the cold hardness in his face."

"But, Nicky, you can't give up now, just when God is beginning to work . . . "

"Tomorrow I'm going to resign," I interrupted. "I don't belong here. I don't belong in the ministry. I'm not good enough. If I stay, the whole Teen Challenge will be destroyed. I'm like Jonah. Maybe I'm still running from God and don't know it. They need to throw me overboard so a fish can eat me up. If they don't get rid of me the whole ship will sink."

"Nicky, that's crazy talk. Satan is causing you to say that," Gloria said, on the verge of tears.

I pulled away. "Satan is in me all right. But I'm still going to resign."

"Nicky, the least you can do is talk to Davie first."

"I've tried, a hundred times. But he's always too busy. He thinks I can handle things. Well, I can't take it any more. I'm a misfit and it's time for me to admit it to myself. I'm a failure . . . a failure."

After we went to bed Gloria slipped her arm around my head and rubbed the back of my neck. "Nicky, before you resign will you promise me one thing? Will you call Kathryn Kuhlman and talk to her?"

I nodded my head in agreement. My pillow was wet with tears as I heard Gloria whisper, "Nicky, God will take care of us."

I buried my head in my pillow, praying that God would never let the sun come up on another day in my life.

In those days of darkness and indecision a single bright star appeared in the form of this tall dignified lady who seemed to exude the very presence of the Holy Spirit. Just talking with Miss Kuhlman on the phone the next morning seemed to help. She insisted I come to Pittsburgh at her expense before making my final decision.

The next afternoon I flew to Pittsburgh. I was surprised she didn't try to talk me into staying at Teen Challenge. Instead, she said, "Perhaps God is leading you into a different ministry, Nicky. Perhaps He is leading you through the valley of the shadow in order to bring you out into the sunshine on the other side. Just keep your eyes on Jesus. Don't become bitter or discouraged. God has placed His hand on you, He will not desert you. Remember, Nicky, when we go through the valley, He goes with us."

We prayed together and she prayed if it were God's will

for me to leave Teen Challenge that He keep the cloud of discouragement close around me. If He wanted me to stay, that He lift the cloud so I could feel free to remain in New York.

I flew back to the city the next morning, thankful for the friendship and confidence of this gracious and dynamic Christian.

That night, after the baby was in bed, I sat at the kitchen table and talked again to Gloria. I just wanted out. We would start all over, maybe in California. Gloria said she would follow me wherever I went. Her great love and confidence gave me a new strength. Before I went to bed I took a piece of paper and a stub of a pencil and wrote out my resignation.

It was a miserable weekend. Monday morning when David arrived at the Center, I handed him the resignation and waited while he read it.

He hung his head. "Am I the one who has failed you, Nicky?" he asked softly. "Have I been in such a hurry I haven't been here to help you when you needed me? Come into the office and talk to me."

I silently followed him down the hall and into the office. He closed the door behind us and looked at me with a deeply grieved face. "Nicky, I don't know what's behind this. But I know I'm to blame for much of it. I have been chastizing myself daily for not spending more time with you. But I've been on the go so much raising money for the Center. I haven't even been able to spend time with my family. The burden has rested heavy on my shoulders. So before we talk I want to ask you to forgive me for having failed you. Will you forgive me, Nicky?"

I hung my head and nodded it silently. David sighed deeply and collapsed into a chair. "Talk to me, Nicky."

"It's too late to talk, Davie. I've been trying to talk to you. I feel this is what I have to do."

"But why, Nicky, why? What has caused this sudden decision?"

"It's not sudden, Davie. It's been coming for a long time." And then I poured my heart out to him.

"Nicky," David said, his piercing eyes looking straight at

me. "All of us go through these periods of depression. I have let people down and have been let down by people. I have wanted to throw in the towel many times. Often I have found myself with Elijah under the juniper bush crying, 'It is enough, O Lord, take away my life.' But, Nicky, you have walked where angels fear to tread. I just can't see you running from these little defeats."

"They aren't little to me, Davie. My mind is already made up. I'm sorry."

The next day I put Gloria and Alicia on a plane for Oakland and two days later I flew to Houston to keep my last scheduled speaking engagement. It was August 1964. I had been at Teen Challenge two years and nine months.

In Houston I was ashamed to tell the people that I had resigned from Teen Challenge. But my preaching was cold and ineffectual. I was anxious to get on to California and be with Gloria.

Flying across the nation I slowly became aware that I was no longer flying on an expense account. We had saved very little money and the plane tickets and moving expenses would just about drain us. I was scared. Insecure. Frightened.

I remembered the times people had tried to press cash into my hand when I was speaking in rallies and conferences. I would thank them and ask them to write out a check to Teen Challenge. I wanted nothing for myself. My whole life had been wrapped up in the Center. It seemed ironic that even in Houston I had continued to tell the people to make out the checks to Teen Challenge, knowing I barely had enough money to live on for the next few days.

Gloria met me at the airport. She had rented a small apartment. We were broke and depressed. I had given God almost six years of my life and I felt He had turned His back on me. I'd quit, leave the ministry, and start from the bottom in some other field. The sun sank into the Pacific Ocean and my whole world plunged into blackness.

I had no idea which way to turn. I found myself withdrawing from everything. I didn't even want to go to church with Gloria, preferring to just sit around the house staring at the walls. Gloria tried to pray with me but I felt hopeless and shrugged her off, telling her she could pray but I was empty.

Within weeks word got around I was back in California. Invitations to speak in churches began to pour in. I soon got tired of telling them "no" and trying to make up some kind of excuse. I finally told Gloria not to take any more long distance calls and not to answer the letters that came in the daily mail.

But we were getting desperate financially. We had used up all our savings and Gloria had been unable to get a job.

As a last resort I accepted an invitation to preach in a youth crusade. I was spiritually cold. For the first time in my life I went into the pulpit without praying. Sitting on the platform I was amazed at how hard and cold I was. I was shocked at my mercenary attitude. Yet I was desperate. If God had let me down like I felt He had in New York, then I felt no obligation to seek His blessing in preaching. If they'd pay me, I'd take it. It was as simple as that.

But it was not quite that simple with God. Obviously, He had far bigger plans than for me just to draw a paycheck for preaching. Preaching to Him is sacred business – and He has promised, "My word . . . shall not return to me empty."

When I gave the invitation something happened. First, a young teenage boy stepped out from the crowd and came forward, kneeling at the altar. Then another came from the far side of the auditorium. Then more streamed forward until the aisles were full of young people coming to the altar rail and kneeling to commit their lives to Jesus Christ. The crowd was so great at the front of the church that many had to stand behind those kneeling at the crowded rail. In the back of the church I saw people falling to their knees and crying out to God. Still they came. I had never been in a service when the Spirit of God swept through a congregation with such power.

God was trying to say something to me, not in whispers, but in thundering tones. He was telling me He was still on His throne. He was reminding me that even though I had let Him down, He was not going to let me down. He was telling me in unmistakable terms He was not through with my life . . . that He still had use for me, even when I was unwilling to be used.

I felt my knees shaking and tried to hold on to the back of the pulpit. Suddenly, my eyes were full of tears as I, the preacher of the night, stumbled forward and knelt at the back side of the altar rail. There, with heart overflowing with repentance, I poured out my soul to God in recommitment.

Following the service Gloria and I sat in the car in the church parking lot. We had planned to go out and eat and then take a drive. Instead, we agreed to go home.

As we entered the door, I fell to my knees. Gloria was beside me and we both wept and cried out to God. And I knew. I knew there was more. I knew that all things do work together for good to them that love God. I looked up through the tears and suddenly realized He was beside me. I could feel His presence. I could almost hear Him say, "Yea, though I walk through the valley of the shadow of death I will fear no evil, for thou art with me. Thy rod and thy staff they comfort me . . . "

We had been through the valley of the shadow. But His grace had brought us through and now the sunlight of tomorrow glistened on the distant mountain peaks signifying the dawning of a new day.

18

Walkin' in Jesus' Turf

The big break came just before Christmas when I received
an invitation from a layman's group known as the "Full
Gospel Business Men's Fellowship International." It was
through this group of dedicated businessmen that speaking
invitations from high schools and colleges began to pour in.
During 1965 I traveled to most of the major cities across
the nation. My crusade rallies, many of them sponsored
by churches of all denominations, were having wonderful
success and I spoke to crowds up to ten thousand.

I thanked God daily for His goodness. But I was still
restless and had a deep yearning in my heart. I couldn't
seem to put my finger on the problem but I was becoming
more restless every day.

Then I met Dan Malachuk, a tall, extroverted businessman
from New Jersey who unknowingly brought my problem
to the surface. He casually mentioned one night that he
understood my original desire was to work with the "little
people." I didn't respond to his question but neither could
I get it out of my mind.

I remembered my own childhood. If only someone had
cared enough to lead me to Christ as a child then maybe—

I talked it over with Gloria. God was using my testimony in
large crusades, but every time I saw an article in the newspaper about children arrested for sniffing glue or smoking
marijuana, my heart ached. We kept praying that God would
provide a way for us to reach these children.

A few months later Dan helped arrange a four-day crusade
in Seattle. All this time I had been speaking through my

interpreter, Jeff Morales. Jeff had moved to California in order to travel with me to the large rallies where the audiences had trouble with my accent. But just a half hour before I was to leave for the airport Jeff called.

"Nicky, I'm in bed with pneumonia. The doctor refuses to let me go. You're going to have to be on your own."

Standing on the platform before a battery of microphones and TV cameras I surveyed the huge crowd. Could they understand me with my Puerto Rican accent? Would they laugh at my poor grammar? Nervously I cleared my throat and opened my mouth to speak. No words – only a garbled mumble. I cleared my throat and something came out that sounded like "uuuggghhhllkfg."

The crowd fidgeted nervously but politely. It was hopeless. I was too used to having Jeff stand beside me. I bowed my head and asked for power. "Dear Lord, if you can give me an unknown tongue to praise your name, then I'm trusting you to give me a known tongue to tell these kids about you."

I raised my head and started to speak. The words were perfect and flowed from my mouth with supernatural power. Jeff had been replaced by Jesus and from that moment on I knew as long as I was speaking for Him I would never need an interpreter.

After the final service Dan stopped by my hotel room.

"Nicky, God is blessing in a marvelous way. They took a love offering of $3,000 for you to use in your ministry."

"Dan, I can't take that money."

"Nicky," Dan said as he made himself at home sprawling on the couch and kicking off his shoes, "the money is not for you. It's for God's work through you."

"And I can use it any way I feel God wants?" I asked.

"That's right," Dan said.

"Then I'll use it for the little people. I want to start a Center to minister to them."

"Wonderful," Dan exploded, straightening up on the sofa, "call it Outreach for Youth."

Outreach for Youth it was. I returned to California with the $3,000 determined to open a Center where I could take the little people off the street and win them to Christ.

We set up our Center in Fresno at 221 N. Broadway. We applied for our official California charter and I hung out a sign on the front porch, "Outreach for Youth, Nicky Cruz, Director".

Right away I started combing the streets. My first day out I found an eleven-year-old boy sitting in a doorway. I sat down beside him and asked his name.

He looked at me out of the corner of his eyes and finally said, "Ruben, watcha wanna know fer?"

"I dunno," I slurred back, "you just looked kinda lonesome and I thought I'd talk to you."

He willingly told me his father was a junkie. He'd been sniffing glue just the day before. He was a sixth grade dropout at school. I listened and then told him I was opening a center for kids like him and asked if he'd like to come live with me.

"You mean you want me to come?"

"Sure," I said, "but we'll have to talk to your daddy first."

"Hell," the eleven-year-old boy answered, "my old man'll be glad to get rid of me. The one you gotta clear it with is my probation officer."

The probation officer was delighted and that night Ruben moved in with us.

Within the next several weeks we picked up two more kids. We enrolled them all in school and held daily Bible studies at the Center. Ruben gave us a great deal of trouble at first, but at the end of the second week he made a profession of faith during one of the Bible studies. The next afternoon when he came from school he went straight to his room and began to study. Gloria winked at me. "What more evidence could you want that his conversion was sincere?" she said. I needed none. Deep inside I felt good. The restlessness was disappearing.

As the days went by we began getting calls from distraught mothers who said their children were completely out of hand and begging us to take them in. In a matter of weeks we were full and still getting calls. Gloria and I spent much time in prayer asking God to direct us.

Early one morning, after only a couple of hours of sleep, the phone rang. I fumbled for the receiver. It was Dan

Smith, an active member of the Full Gospel Business Men's chapter in Fresno.

"Nicky, God is leading in a mysterious way. Several of us have been praying about the work you are doing. God has laid it on my heart to help you form a Board of Directors. I have talked with Earl Draper, an accountant, with Reverend Paul Evans, and H. J. Keener, manager of a local TV station. We are willing to work with you if you want us."

It was another answer to prayer as this small group of business and professional people rallied behind the Center to help give direction.

Later that same month Dave Carter joined our staff to work with the boys. I had known Dave, a tall, quiet Negro, when he was a gang leader in New York. He had gone to Bible School after his conversion and since he had no family connections was able to spend many hours counseling individually with the love-starved boys. We also had two young Mexican girls, Frances Ramirez and Angie Sedillos, join us to add the woman's touch and help with the secretarial work.

The final member of the staff was someone very special to me. It was Jimmy Baez. Jimmy had just graduated from Bible School and married a quiet, soft-spoken girl. He was coming to work as our Supervisor, but to me he was more than that. He was walking proof of the changing, transforming power of Jesus Christ. It was difficult to imagine this scholarly looking young man with handsome face and dark rimmed glasses was the same frail emaciated lad who had crawled into Teen Challenge shaking from withdrawal of heroin and begging for drugs.

With our hearts filled with faith in God and our hands busy with the "little people" we moved forward. God was blessing and I didn't think I could hold any more of His marvelous surprises. But for those who love God there is no limit to the surprises of tomorrow.

That Fall, Dan Malachuk arranged for me to return to New York for a series of speaking engagements. After meeting me at the airport we drove back into town past mile after mile of slum apartments. I sat slumped in the front seat of Dan's car and watched the ghetto flash by. Something kept tugging at my heart. I was no longer a part of the ghetto but it was still a part of me. I began to wonder about old friends and gang members – especially Israel. "Jesus," I prayed, "please give me one more chance to witness to him."

After the meeting that night Dan followed to my hotel room. The phone was ringing when we entered.

I answered and there was a long silence on the other end before I heard a weak but familiar voice say, "Nicky, it's me. Israel."

"Israel!" I shouted. "Praise God! My prayer is answered. Where are you?"

"I'm home, Nicky, in the Bronx. I just read in the paper you were in town and called your brother, Frank. He said I could catch you at the hotel."

I started to say something else but he interrupted me. "Nicky, I-I-I was wondering if I might be able to see you while you're in town. Just to talk over old times."

I could hardly believe my ears. I turned to Dan. "It's Israel. He wants to see me."

"Ask him to meet us at the hotel tomorrow night for dinner," Dan said. The long awaited reunion was set for 6 p.m. the next evening.

I prayed for him all that night asking God to give me the right words to touch his heart for Christ.

Dan and I paced the hotel lobby from 5.30 until 7 p.m. He hadn't shown up. My heart was in my throat as I remembered that early morning nine years before when we had missed him the first time.

Suddenly I saw him. His handsome features, deep set eyes, wavy hair. Nothing had changed. I couldn't speak as the tears came to my eyes. "Nicky," he choked out as he grasped my hand, "I can't believe it." Suddenly we were laughing and talking at the same time, completely oblivious to the human traffic all around us.

Long moments later he pulled away and said, "Nicky, I want you to meet my wife, Rosa."

Beside him was a short, sweet little Puerto Rican girl with a grin that spread all the way across her beautiful face. I reached down to take her hand but she grabbed me around the neck and kissed me solidly on the cheek.

"It like I know you," she winked and said with broken English. "I been living with you all this time. Israel talk about you much these three years."

We started downstairs to the Hay Market Room for dinner. Israel and Rosa hung back and I could sense something was bothering them. "Hey, Israel, what's the matter, baby? Dan is paying for it. Come on."

Israel gave me an embarrassed look and finally pulled me to one side. "Nicky, I don't belong in such a fancy place. I've never been to a swanky joint like this. I don't know what to do."

I put my arm around his shoulder. "I don't know what to do either," I said. "Just order the most expensive thing and let the 'Jolly Green Giant' pay for it," I grinned, pointing at Dan.

After dinner we took the elevator to my room on the fourteenth floor. Israel was relaxed and seemed his old self as he told us of his home in the ghetto.

"It isn't the most pleasant place to live," he said. "We have to keep our dishes in the refrigerator to keep the roaches off. But it could be worse. Downstairs the rats come in out of the alley and bite the kids while they sleep."

Israel paused and reflected. "It's like you're chained down there," he said. "You can't get away. It's a bad place to raise the kids. Last week three little girls in my building, all around nine years old, were raped in the back alley. We don't dare let the children out on the street and I'm sick of it. I want out. But . . . "

His voice trailed off and he got up from his chair and walked to the window looking out toward the glimmering tower on the Empire State Building. "But you gotta live someplace, and any place else the rent's too high. But maybe next year . . . maybe next year we can move to a nicer place. I haven't done too badly. I started out as a dishwasher and have worked my way up to a clerk on Wall Street."

"But after you make it, what then?" I interrupted.

Israel turned and looked at me with a puzzled stare. "What did you say?" he asked.

I knew the time had come to dig deeper into the past. "Israel, tell me what went wrong."

He walked back to the couch where Rosa was sitting and sat nervously beside her. "I don't mind talking about it. I guess I need to. I've never even told Rosa. You remember that morning after you got out of the hospital when you and that man were going to meet me?"

I nodded. The memory was painful.

"I waited out there for three hours. I felt like a fool. I was sick of Christians and that night I went back to the gang."

I interrupted. "Israel, I'm sorry. We looked for you . . . "

He shook his head. "Who cares? It was a long time ago. Maybe things would have been different had I gone with you. Who knows?"

He paused and then began again. "After that we got in this trouble with the South Street Angels. This guy came in our turf and we told him we didn't want no jigs around. He got smart and we hit him. He ran and five of us chased him into South Street turf and caught him at the Penny Arcade. We dragged him outside and started fighting with him. The next thing I know one of our guys had this gun in his hand and was shooting. Paco started holding his belly and mocking saying, "Oh, I'm shot! I'm shot! All our guys were laughing."

"Then the jig fell to the ground. He really was shot. He was a dead man. I could see the hole in his head."

Israel paused. The only sound was the muffled roar of the traffic on the street far below.

"We ran. Four of us got caught. The other guy got away. The guy who pulled the trigger got twenty years. The rest of us got five to twenty."

He stopped talking and hung his head. "It was five years of hell."

Regaining his composure he continued. "I had to get a 'fix' to get out of prison."

"What do you mean, a 'fix'?" Dan interrupted.

"My Parole Board said I would be released when I could prove to them I had a job waiting for me. They said I'd have to go back to my old home. I didn't want to go back to Brooklyn. I wanted to start out all over again but they said I had to go back home. So I got a 'fix' through this

junkie who was in there with me. He knew a man who had
a dress factory in Brooklyn and this man told my mother if
she'd pay him $50 he'd promise me a job. She gave him the
money and he wrote a letter saying I had a job when I got
out of prison. It was the only way I could get a job. Man,
who wants an ex-con working for him?"

"But did you get the job?" Dan asked.

"Naw," Israel said. "I told you it was a 'fix'. There wasn't
any job. This was just a way to get out of jail.

"So I came out and went to the employment agency and
lied to them about my past. You think they'd have hired me
if I told them I just got out of prison the day before? I got a
job as a dishwasher and then a dozen other jobs. I've been
lying ever since. You've got to lie to get a job. If my boss
now knew I was an ex-con he'd fire me, even though I've
been out of prison four years and done a good job. So, I lie.
Everyone does."

"Didn't your parole officer help you?" Dan asked.

"Yeah, that was one guy who really tried. But what could
he do? He had a hundred other guys to help too. No, it was
up to me and I've made it this far on my own."

The room grew quiet. Rosa had been sitting quietly beside
Israel all this time. She had never heard him speak of this
part of his life.

I said, "Israel, do you remember that time we went looking
for the Phantom Lords and ran into an ambush?"

Israel nodded, "I remember."

"You saved my life that night, Israel. Tonight I want to
return that favor. Tonight I want to tell you something that
will save your life."

Rosa reached over and ran her arm through his. They both
turned and looked at me expectantly.

"Israel, you're my dearest friend. You can tell there's been
a change in my life. The old Nicky is dead. The person you
see tonight is not really Nicky at all. It's Jesus Christ living
in me. Do you remember that night at St. Nicholas Arena
when we gave our hearts to the Lord?"

Israel nodded, his eyes dropping toward the floor.

"God came into your heart that night, Israel I know it.
God made a bargain with you. And He is still keeping

His end of that bargain. He has not turned loose of you, Israel. You've been running all these years, but He still has hold of you."

I reached for my Bible. "In the Old Testament there's a story of a man called Jacob. He, too, was running from God. Then one night, just like tonight, he had a rumble with an angel. The angel won and Jacob surrendered to God. And that night God changed his name. No Jacob any more – but Israel. And Israel means 'one who walks with God'."

I closed my Bible and paused before continuing. Israel's eyes were wet with tears and Rosa was clutching his arm. "I have laid awake at night for years praying for you – thinking how wonderful it would be to have you working beside me – not like we used to do – but in God's work. Israel, tonight I want you to become one who walks with God. I want you to step out and start walkin' in Jesus' turf."

Israel looked up, his eyes full of tears. He turned and looked at Rosa. She was puzzled and spoke to him in Spanish. I had been talking in English and realized Rosa had not understood all I said. She asked him what I wanted. Israel told her I wanted them to give their hearts to Christ. He talked rapidly in Spanish, telling her his desire to return to God – like Jacob of old to go back. He asked her if she would come with him.

She smiled and her eyes sparkled as she nodded.

"Praise God!" I shouted. "Kneel down beside this sofa while I pray."

Israel and Rosa knelt beside the sofa. Dan slipped from his chair and knelt on the other side of the room. I put my hands on their heads and began to pray, first in English, and then in Spanish, slipping back and forth between the two languages. I felt the Spirit of God flowing through my heart and down my arms and fingertips into their lives. I prayed, asking God to forgive them and bless them and receive them into the fullness of His Kingdom.

It was a lengthy prayer. When I finished I heard Israel begin to pray. Slowly at first, then with intensity as he cried out, "Lord, forgive me. Forgive me. Forgive me." Then his prayer changed and I could feel the new strength shudder through his body as he began saying, "Lord, I thank you."

Rosa joined in, "Thank you, God, thank you."

Dan put Israel and Rosa in a cab and paid their fare back to their apartment in the Bronx. "Nicky," he said, wiping his eyes as they drove away, "this has been the greatest night of my life and I feel God is going to send Israel to California to work with you."

I nodded. Maybe so. God always has a way of taking care of things.

Epilogue

It was a late Spring afternoon as Nicky and Gloria lounged on the front steps of the Center at 221 N. Broadway watching Ralphie and Karl cutting the grass in the deepening twilight. It was almost time for the street meeting in the ghetto. In the backyard you could hear the happy sounds of Dave Carter and Jimmy Baez laughing at Allen, Joey, and Kirk playing croquet. Supper was over and inside Francie and Angie supervised the other boys in the nightly clean-up. Alicia and little Laura, now sixteen months old, played happily in the fresh mown grass.

Gloria sat on a lower step gazing affectionately and thoughtfully at her dark-skinned husband as he leaned against the post, eyes half closed as if lost in a dream world. She reached up and placed her hand on his knee.

"Honey, what's wrong? What are you thinking?"

"What do you mean?" he asked drowsily, reluctant to turn loose of his thoughts.

"I mean, what are you dreaming about now? Are you still running? We have the Center for the little people. Israel and Rosa are living in Fresno and serving the Lord. Sonny is pastoring a big church in L.A. Jimmy is working with you and Maria is serving God in New York. Next week you fly to Sweden and Denmark to preach. Why are you still dreaming? What more could you ask from God?"

Nicky straightened up and looked deep into the inquiring eyes of his companion. His voice had a faraway sound as he said, "It's not what I ask of God, sweetheart, but what He's asking of me. We are only scratching the surface with our ministry."

There was a long pause. Only the sounds of the happy activity echoed around the house. "But Nicky," Gloria said, still gazing intently at him, "it's not just your task. It's the task of all Christians – everywhere."

"I know that," he said. "I keep thinking about all those big churches in the inner city that are sitting empty during the week. Wouldn't it be wonderful if those unused classrooms could be turned into dormitories filled with hundreds of unloved children and teenagers from the slums? Each church could become its own Center manned by volunteers . . . "

"Nicky," Gloria interrupted, squeezing his knee, "you're too much of a dreamer. Do you think those church people are going to turn their beautiful buildings into dormitories for lost and homeless kids? Those church people want to help, but they want someone else to do it for them. They fuss now if a drunk interrupts a worship service. Think what they would say if they came to church some Sunday morning and found their sacred temples desecrated with beds and cots and a bunch of former junkies and glue-sniffers in the spick and span halls. No, Nicky, you're a dreamer. These people don't want to get their hands dirty. They rebel against having their carpets stained with dirt from bare feet."

Nicky shook his head. "You're right, of course. I keep wondering what Jesus would do. Would He get His hands dirty?"

He paused and looked past her toward the distant mountains, reflecting. "You remember last year when we drove out to Point Loma on the bay in San Diego? Remember that huge lighthouse? For years it's guided ships into the harbor. But now times have changed. I read just last week that there is too much smog and they've had to build a new lighthouse down near the water so the light can shine under the smog."

Gloria listened intently.

"This is what's happened today. The church still stands with its light shining high. But few can see it because times have changed and there is much smog. A new light is needed to shine near the ground – down where the people are. It is not enough for me to be a keeper of the lighthouse, I must be a bearer of the light as well. No, I'm not running any more. I just want to be where the action is."

"I know," Gloria said, her voice reflecting her deep pride and understanding. "And that's what I want for you. But you may have to go it alone. You know that, don't you?"

"Not alone," Nicky said, reaching down and placing his hand over hers. "I'll be walking in Jesus' turf."

The sound of the boys laughing in the back yard grew louder as they finished their game and headed inside. Karl and Ralphie had picked up their Bibles and were sitting on the curb in front of the house.

Nicky lowered his head and glanced at Gloria out of the top of his eyes. "I got a call this afternoon from a mother in Pasadena." He paused for an expected reaction. Gloria just waited for him to continue. "Her twelve-year-old boy had been picked up by the police for peddling marijuana. Her husband wants to put him in prison." Nicky stopped talking and his voice trailed off. "But we don't have any room and we're out of money."

They sat in silence. Nicky watched a small sparrow hopping up and down in the grass. His eyes filled with tears as he thought of the unknown child . . . so typical of thousands of others . . . hungry for love . . . willing to risk jail just to get some attention . . . looking for something real . . . looking for Jesus Christ and not knowing it.

Gloria interrupted his thoughts. "Nicky," she said softly, her fingers entwining with his, "What are you going to do?"

Nicky grinned and looked her in the face saying, "I'm going to do what Jesus would have me do. I'm going to get involved."

"Oh Nicky, Nicky," Gloria said as she threw her arms around his legs. "I love you! There's always room for one more. And God *will* provide."

Jimmy backed the bus out of the driveway. The boys scrambled aboard for the street service in the ghetto. Nicky pulled Gloria to her feet, " 'Vamanos!' Let's run. It's time to do Jesus' work."

*   *   *

I was about to make a broadcast in the radio studio down the hall from my office, when in walked Nicky Cruz. Glancing around to make sure no one else was present, he closed the door and stood silently before me, shoulders hunched, his hands thrust deep into his pockets. His face was nearly expressionless, although as I studied him, there were the tell-tale signs of a man fighting to control his emotions.

"Here," he said tersely, his hands coming slowly out of his pockets. For a moment I hardly knew whether to be alarmed or relaxed!

Then, on the table in front of me, Nicky began assembling the strangest assortment of objects I had ever seen. He identified them as he laid them down: a zip gun, a brutal looking pair of iron knuckles, a bone-handled switchblade, two lead weights ingeniously taped on the end of a leather thong, and "the works" – a hypodermic needle, dropper and bottle-cap cooker, the indispensable tools of the addict.

"These were the tools of the trade," Nicky said, his eyes shining with resolve. He looked down at the table, touching each object lightly as if in farewell. "I've lived by them. My life depended on them. But now I don't need them anymore. I give them to Him."

He'd have literally put them into the Lord Jesus' nail-scarred hands, if it had been possible. He was giving them to me as a sort of trusteeship. And now it was *my* turn to register emotion.

I still have the bizarre collection, and now and then I get it out to remind myself of the Nicky Cruz who used to be . . . and of the God whose mercy and grace has made him what he is today.

Kathryn Kuhlman
Pittsburgh, Pennsylvania

The Hiding Place

Corrie ten Boom with
John and Elizabeth Sherrill

Preface

When we were doing the research for *God's Smuggler*, a name kept cropping up: Corrie ten Boom. This Dutch lady —in her mid-seventies when we first began to hear of her —was Brother Andrew's favorite traveling companion. Brother Andrew is a missionary behind the Iron Curtain; his fascinating stories about her in Vietnam, where she had earned that most honorable title "Double-old Grandmother"—and in a dozen other Communist countries— came to mind so often that we finally had to hold up our hands to stop his flow of reminiscence. "We could never fit her into the book," we said. "She sounds like a book in herself." It's the sort of thing you say. Not meaning anything.

It was in May, 1968, that we attended a church service in Germany. A man was speaking about his experiences in a Nazi concentration camp. His face told the story more eloquently than his words: pain-haunted eyes, shaking hands that could not forget. He was followed at the lectern by a white-haired woman, broad of frame and sensible of shoe, with a face that radiated love, peace, joy. But—the story that these two people were relating was the same! She too had been in a concentration camp, seen the same savagery, suffered the same losses. His response was easy to understand. But hers?

We stayed behind to talk with her. And as we did, we realized that we were meeting Andrew's Corrie. Cornelia ten Boom's worldwide ministry of comfort and counsel had begun there in the concentration camp where she had found, as the prophet Isaiah promised, "a hiding place from the wind, a covert from the tempest . . . the shadow of a great rock in a weary land."

On subsequent visits we got to know this amazing woman

well. Together we visited the crooked little Dutch house—
one room wide—where till her fifties she lived the uneventful life of a spinster watchmaker, little dreaming as she cared for her older sister and their elderly father that a world of high adventure lay just around the corner. We went to the garden in south Holland where young Corrie gave her heart away forever. To the big brick house in Haarlem where Pickwick served real coffee in the middle of the war. . . .

And all the while we had the extraordinary feeling that we were not looking into the past but into the future. As though these people and places were speaking to us not about things that had already happened but about the world that lay ahead of us in the 1970s. Already we found ourselves actually putting into practice how-to's we learned from her about:

- handling separation
- getting along with less
- security in the midst of insecurity
- forgiveness
- how God can use weakness
- dealing with difficult people
- facing death
- how to love your enemies
- what to do when evil wins

We commented to her about the practicalness of everything she recalled, how her memories seemed to throw a spotlight on problems and decisions we faced here and now. "But," she said, "this is what the past is for! Every experience God gives us, every person He puts in our lives is the perfect preparation for the future that only He can see."

Every experience, every person. . . . Father, who did the finest watch repairs in Holland and then forgot to send the bill. Mama, whose body became a prison, but whose spirit soared free. Betsie, who could make a party out of three potatoes and some twice-used tea leaves. As we looked into the twinkling blue eyes of this undefeatable woman, we wished that these people were part of our own lives.

And then, of course, we realized that they could be. . . .

John and Elizabeth Sherrill

July, 1971
Chappaqua, New York

CHAPTER ONE

The One Hundredth Birthday Party

I jumped out of bed that morning with one question in my mind—sun or fog? Usually it was fog in January in Holland, dank, chill, and gray. But occasionally—on a rare and magic day—a white winter sun broke through. I leaned as far as I could from the single window in my bedroom: it was always hard to see the sky from the Beje. Blank brick walls looked back at me, the backs of other ancient buildings in this crowded center of old Haarlem. But up there where my neck craned to see, above the crazy roofs and crooked chimneys, was a square of pale pearl sky. It was going to be a sunny day for the party!

I attempted a little waltz as I took my new dress from the tipsy old wardrobe against the wall. Father's bedroom was directly under mine but at seventy-seven he slept soundly. That was one advantage to growing old, I thought, as I worked my arms into the sleeves and surveyed the effect in the mirror on the wardrobe door. Although some Dutch women in 1937 were wearing their skirts knee-length, mine was still a cautious three inches above my shoes.

You're not growing younger yourself, I reminded my reflection. Maybe it was the new dress that made me look more critically at myself than usual: forty-five years old, unmarried, waistline long since vanished.

My sister Betsie, though seven years older than I, still had that slender grace that made people turn and look after her in the street. Heaven knows it wasn't her clothes; our little watch shop had never made much money. But when Betsie put on a dress something wonderful happened to it.

On me—until Betsie caught up with them—hems sagged, stockings tore, and collars twisted. But today, I thought, standing back from the mirror as far as I could in the small room, the effect of dark maroon was very smart.

Far below me down on the street, the doorbell rang. Callers? Before 7:00 in the morning? I opened my bedroom door and plunged down the steep twisting stairway. These stairs were an afterthought in this curious old house. Actually it was two houses. The one in front was a typical tiny old-Haarlem structure, three stories high, two rooms deep, and only one room wide. At some unknown point in its long history its rear wall had been knocked through to join it with the even thinner, steeper house in back of it—which had only three rooms, one on top of the other—and this narrow corkscrew staircase squeezed between the two.

Quick as I was, Betsie was at the door ahead of me. An enormous spray of flowers filled the doorway. As Betsie took them, a small delivery boy appeared. "Nice day for the party, Miss," he said, trying to peer past the flowers as though coffee and cake might already be set out. He would be coming to the party later, as indeed, it seemed, would all of Haarlem.

Betsie and I searched the bouquet for the card. "Pickwick!" we shouted together.

Pickwick was an enormously wealthy customer who not only bought the very finest watches but often came upstairs to the family part of the house above the shop. His real name was Herman Sluring; Pickwick was the name Betsie and I used between ourselves because he looked so incredibly like the illustrator's drawing in our copy of Dickens. Herman Sluring was without doubt the ugliest man in Haarlem. Short, immensely fat, head bald as a Holland cheese, he was so wall-eyed that you were never quite sure whether he was looking at you or someone else—and as kind and generous as he was fearsome to look at.

The flowers had come to the side door, the door the family used, opening onto a tiny alleyway, and Betsie and I carried them from the little hall into the shop. First was the workroom where watches and clocks were repaired. There was the high bench over which Father had bent for so many years, doing the delicate, painstaking work that was known as the finest in Holland. And there in the center of the room was my bench, and next to mine Hans the apprentice's, and against the wall old Christoffels'.

Beyond the workroom was the customers' part of the

shop with its glass case full of watches. All the wall clocks were striking 7:00 as Betsie and I carried the flowers in and looked for the most artistic spot to put them. Ever since childhood I had loved to step into this room where a hundred ticking voices welcomed me. It was still dark inside because the shutters had not been drawn back from the windows on the street. I unlocked the street door and stepped out into the Barteljorisstraat. The other shops up and down the narrow street were shuttered and silent: the optician's next door, the dress shop, the baker's, Weil's Furriers across the street.

I folded back our shutters and stood for a minute admiring the window display that Betsie and I had at last agreed upon. This window was always a great source of debate between us, I wanting to display as much of our stock as could be squeezed onto the shelf, and Betsie maintaining that two or three beautiful watches, with perhaps a piece of silk or satin swirled beneath, was more elegant and more inviting. But this time the window satisfied us both: it held a collection of clocks and pocketwatches all at least a hundred years old, borrowed for the occasion from friends and antique dealers all over the city. For today was the shop's one hundredth birthday. It was on this day in January 1837 that Father's father had placed in this window a sign: TEN BOOM. WATCHES.

For the last ten minutes, with a heavenly disregard for the precisions of passing time, the church bells of Haarlem had been pealing out 7:00 o'clock, and now half a block away in the town square, the great bell of St. Bavo's solemnly donged seven times. I lingered in the street to count them, though it was cold in the January dawn. Of course everyone in Haarlem had radios now, but I could remember when the life of the city had run on St. Bavo time, and only trainmen and others who needed to know the exact hour had come here to read the "astronomical clock." Father would take the train to Amsterdam each week to bring back the time from the Naval Observatory and it was a source of pride to him that the astronomical clock was never more than two seconds off in the seven days. There it stood now, as I stepped back into the shop, still tall and gleaming on its concrete block, but shorn now of eminence.

The doorbell on the alley was ringing again; more

flowers. So it went on for an hour, large bouquets and small ones, elaborate set pieces and home-grown plants in clay pots. For although the party was for the shop, the affection of a city was for Father. "Haarlem's Grand Old Man" they called him and they were setting about to prove it. When the shop and the workroom would not hold another bouquet, Betsie and I started carrying them upstairs to the two rooms above the shop. Though it was twenty years since her death, these were still "Tante Jans's rooms." Tante Jans was Mother's older sister and her presence lingered in the massive dark furniture she had left behind her. Betsie set down a pot of greenhouse-grown tulips and stepped back with a little cry of pleasure.

"Corrie, just look how much brighter!"

Poor Betsie. The Beje was so closed in by the houses around that the window plants she started each spring never grew tall enough to bloom.

At 7:45 Hans, the apprentice, arrived and at 8:00 Toos, our saleslady-bookkeeper. Toos was a sour-faced, scowling individual whose ill-temper had made it impossible for her to keep a job until—ten years ago—she had come to work for Father. Father's gentle courtesy had disarmed and mellowed her and, though she would have died sooner than admit it, she loved him as fiercely as she disliked the rest of the world. We left Hans and Toos to answer the doorbell and went upstairs to get breakfast.

Only three places at the table, I thought, as I set out the plates. The dining room was in the house at the rear, five steps higher than the shop but lower than Tante Jans's rooms. To me this room with its single window looking into the alley was the heart of the home. This table, with a blanket thrown over it, had made me a tent or a pirate's cove when I was small. I'd done my homework here as a schoolchild. Here Mama read aloud from Dickens on winter evenings while the coal whistled in the brick hearth and cast a red glow over the tile proclaiming, "Jesus is Victor."

We used only a corner of the table now, Father, Betsie and I, but to me the rest of the family was always there. There was Mama's chair, and the three aunts' places over there (not only Tante Jans but Mama's other two sisters had also lived with us). Next to me had sat my other sister,

Nollie, and Willem, the only boy in the family, there beside Father.

Nollie and Willem had had homes of their own many years now, and Mama and the aunts were dead, but still I seemed to see them here. Of course their chairs hadn't stayed empty long. Father could never bear a house without children and whenever he heard of a child in need of a home a new face would appear at the table. Somehow, out of his watch shop that never made money he fed and dressed and cared for eleven more children after his own four were grown. But now these, too, had grown up and married or gone off to work, and so I laid three plates on the table.

Betsie brought the coffee in from the tiny kitchen, which was little more than a closet off the dining room, and took bread from the drawer in the sideboard. She was setting them on the table when we heard Father's step coming down the staircase. He went a little slowly now on the winding stairs; but still as punctual as one of his own watches, he entered the dining room, as he had every morning since I could remember, at 8:10.

"Father!" I said kissing him and savoring the aroma of cigars that always clung to his long beard, "a sunny day for the party!"

Father's hair and beard were now as white as the best tablecloth Betsie had laid for this special day. But his blue eyes behind the thick round spectacles were as mild and merry as ever, and he gazed from one of us to the other with frank delight.

"Corrie, dear! My dear Betsie! How gay and lovely you both look!"

He bowed his head as he sat down, said the blessing over bread, and then went on eagerly, "Your mother—how she would have loved these new styles and seeing you both looking so pretty!"

Betsie and I looked hard into our coffee to keep from laughing. These "new styles" were the despair of our young nieces, who were always trying to get us into brighter colors, shorter skirts, and lower necklines. But conservative though we were, it was true that Mama had never had anything even as bright as my deep maroon dress or Betsie's dark blue one. In Mama's day married women—and unmarried ones "of a certain age"—wore black from the chin to the ground.

I had never seen Mama and the aunts in any other color.

"How Mama would have loved everything about today!" Betsie said. "Remember how she loved 'occasions'?"

Mama could have coffee on the stove and a cake in the oven as fast as most people could say, "best wishes." And since she knew almost everyone in Haarlem, especially the poor, sick and neglected, there was almost no day in the year that was not for somebody, as she would say with eyes shining, "a very special occasion!"

And so we sat over our coffee, as one should on anniversaries, and looked back—back to the time when Mama was alive, and beyond. Back to the time when Father was a small boy growing up in this same house. "I was born right in this room," he said, as though he had not told us a hundred times. "Only of course it wasn't the dining room then, but a bedroom. And the bed was in a kind of cupboard set into the wall with no windows and no light or air of any kind. I was the first baby who lived. I don't know how many there were before me, but they all died. Mother had tuberculosis you see, and they didn't know about contaminated air or keeping babies away from sick people."

It was a day for memories. A day for calling up the past. How could we have guessed as we sat there—two middle-aged spinsters and an old man—that in place of memories we were about to be given adventure such as we had never dreamed of? Adventure and anguish, horror and heaven were just around the corner, and we did not know.

Oh Father! Betsie! If I had known would I have gone ahead? Could I have done the things I did?

But how could I know? How could I imagine this white-haired man, called Opa—Grandfather—by all the children of Haarlem, how could I imagine this man thrown by strangers into a grave without a name?

And Betsie, with her high lace collar and her gift for making beauty all around her, how could I picture this dearest person on earth to me standing naked before a roomful of men? In that room on that day, such thoughts were not even thinkable.

Father stood up and took the big brass-hinged Bible from its shelf as Toos and Hans rapped on the door and came in. Scripture reading at 8:30 each morning for all who were in the house was another of the fixed points around which life in the Beje revolved. Father opened the big volume and Betsie and I held our breaths. Surely, today of all days, when there was still so much to do, it would not be a whole chapter! But he was turning to the Gospel of Luke where we'd left off yesterday—such long chapters in Luke too. With his finger at the place, Father looked up.

"Where is Christoffels?" he said.

Christoffels was the third and only other employe in the shop, a bent, wizened little man who looked older than Father though actually he was ten years younger. I remembered the day six or seven years earlier when he had first come into the shop, so ragged and woebegone that I'd assumed that he was one of the beggars who had the Beje marked as a sure meal. I was about to send him up to the kitchen where Betsie kept a pot of soup simmering when he announced with great dignity that he was considering permanent employment and was offering his services first to us.

It turned out that Christoffels belonged to an almost vanished trade, the itinerant clockmender who trudged on foot throughout the land, regulating and repairing the tall pendulum clocks that were the pride of every Dutch farmhouse. But if I was surprised at the grand manner of this shabby little man I was even more astonished when Father hired him on the spot.

"They're the finest clockmen anywhere," he told me later, "these wandering clocksmiths. There's not a repair job they haven't handled with just the tools in their sack."

And so it had proved through the years as people from all over Haarlem brought their clocks to him. What he did with his wages we never knew; he had remained as tattered and threadbare as ever. Father hinted as much as he dared—for next to his shabbiness Christoffels' most notable quality was his pride—and then gave it up.

And now, for the first time ever, Christoffels was late.

Father polished his glasses with his napkin and started to read, his deep voice lingering lovingly over the words. He had reached the bottom of the pages when we heard Christoffels' shuffling steps on the stairs. The door opened and all of us gasped. Christoffels was resplendent in a new black suit, new checkered vest, a snowy white shirt, flowered tie, and stiff starched collar. I tore my eyes from the spectacle as swiftly as I could, for Christoffels' expression forbade us to notice anything out of the ordinary.

"Christoffels, my dear associate," Father murmured in his formal, old-fashioned way, "what joy to see you on this —er—auspicious day." And hastily he resumed his Bible reading.

Before he reached the end of the chapter the doorbells were ringing, both the shop bell on the street and the family bell in the alley. Betsie ran to make more coffee and put her taartjes in the oven while Toos and I hurried to the doors. It seemed that everyone in Haarlem wanted to be first to shake Father's hand. Before long a steady stream of guests was winding up the narrow staircase to Tante Jans's rooms where he sat almost lost in a thicket of flowers. I was helping one of the older guests up the steep stairs when Betsie seized my arm.

"Corrie! We're going to need Nollie's cups right away! How can we—?"

"I'll go get them!"

Our sister Nollie and her husband were coming that afternoon as soon as their six children got home from school. I dashed down the stairs, took my coat and my bicycle from inside the alley door, and was wheeling it over the threshold when Betsie's voice reached me, soft but firm.

"Corrie, your new dress!"

And so I whirled back up the stairs to my room, changed into my oldest skirt and set out over the bumpy brick streets. I always loved to bike to Nollie's house. She and her husband lived about a mile and a half from the Beje, outside the cramped old center of the city. The streets there were broader and straighter; even the sky seemed bigger. Across the town square I pedaled, over the canal on the Grote Hout bridge and along the Wagenweg, reveling in the thin winter sunshine. Nollie lived on Bos en Hoven Straat, a block of identical attached houses with white curtains and potted plants in the windows.

How could I foresee as I zipped around the corner, that one summer day, when the hyacinths in the commercial bulb flats nearby were ripe and brown, I would brake my bicycle here and stand with my heart thudding in my throat, daring to go no closer for fear of what was taking place behind Nollie's starched curtains?

Today I careened onto the sidewalk and burst through the door with never a knock. "Nollie, the Beje's jammed already! You ought to see! We need the cups right now!"

Nollie came out of the kitchen, her round pretty face flushed with baking. "They're all packed by the door. Oh I wish I could go back with you—but I've got batches of cookies still to bake and I promised Flip and the children I'd wait for them."

"You're—all coming, aren't you?"

"Yes, Corrie, Peter will be there." Nollie was loading the cups into the bicycle bags. As a dutiful aunt I tried to love all my nieces and nephews equally. But Peter . . . well, was Peter. At thirteen he was a musical prodigy and a rascal and the pride of my life.

"He's even written a special song in honor of the day," Nollie said. "Here now, you'll have to carry this bagful in your hand, so be careful."

The Beje was more crowded than ever when I got back, the alley so jammed with bicycles I had to leave mine at the corner. The mayor of Haarlem was there in his tailcoat and gold watch chain. And the postman and the trolley motorman and half a dozen policemen from the Haarlem Police Headquarters just around the corner.

After lunch the children started coming and, as children always did, they went straight to Father. The older ones sat on the floor around him, the smallest ones climbed into his lap. For in addition to his twinkling eyes and long cigar-sweet beard, Father ticked. Watches lying on a shelf run differently from watches carried about, and so Father always wore the ones he was regulating. His suit jackets had four huge inside pockets, each fitted with hooks for a dozen watches, so that wherever he went the hum of hundreds of little wheels went gaily with him. Now with a child on each knee and ten more crowded close, he drew from another pocket his heavy cross-shaped winding key, each of the four ends shaped for a different size clock. With a flick of his finger he made it spin, gleaming, glinting. . . .

Betsie stopped in the doorway with a tray of cakes. "He doesn't know there's anyone else in the room," she said.

I was carrying a stack of soiled plates down the stairs when a little shriek below told me that Pickwick had arrived. We used to forget, we who loved him, what a shock the first sight of him could be to a stranger. I hurried down to the door, introduced him hastily to the wife of an Amsterdam wholesaler, and got him upstairs. He sank his ponderous bulk into a chair beside Father, fixed one eye on me, the other on the ceiling, and said, "Five lumps, please."

Poor Pickwick! He loved children as much as Father did, but while children took to Father on sight, Pickwick had to win them. He had one trick, though, that never failed. I brought him his cup of coffee, thick with sugar, and watched him look around in mock consternation. "But my dear Cornelia!" he cried. "There's no table to set it on!" He glanced out of one wide-set eye to make sure the children were watching. "Well, it's a lucky thing I brought my own!" And with that he set cup and saucer on his own protruding paunch. I had never known a child who could resist it; soon a respectful circle had gathered round him.

A little later Nollie and her family arrived. "Tante Corrie!" Peter greeted me innocently. "You don't *look* one hundred years old!" And before I could swat him he was sitting at Tante Jans's upright piano filling the old house with melody. People called out requests—popular songs, selections from Bach chorales, hymns—and soon the whole room was joining in the choruses.

How many of us were there, that happy afternoon, who were soon to meet under very different circumstances! Peter, the policemen, dear ugly Pickwick, all of us were there except my brother Willem and his family. I wondered why they should be so late. Willem and his wife and children lived in the town of Hilversum, thirty miles away: still, they should have been here by now.

Suddenly the music stopped and Peter from his perch on the piano bench hissed across the room, "Opa! Here's the competition!"

I glanced out the window. Turning into the alley were Mr. and Mrs. Kan, owners of the other watch shop on the street. By Haarlem standards they were newcomers, having opened their store only in 1910 and so been on the Barteljorisstraat a mere twenty-seven years. But since they sold a good many more watches than we did, I considered Peter's comment factual enough.

Father, however, was distressed. "Not competitors, Peter!" he said reprovingly. "Colleagues!" And lifting children quickly off his knees, he got up and hurried to the head of the stairs to greet the Kans.

Father treated Mr. Kan's frequent visits to the shop below as social calls from a cherished friend. "Can't you see what he's doing?" I would rage after Mr. Kan had gone. "He's finding out how much we're charging so he can undersell us!" Mr. Kan's display window always featured in bold figures prices exactly five guilders below our own.

And Father's face would light up with a kind of pleased surprise as it always did on those rare occasions when he thought about the business side of watchmaking. "But Corrie, people will save money when they buy from him!" And then he would always add, "I wonder how he does it."

Father was as innocent of business know-how as his father had been before him. He would work for days on a difficult repair problem and then forget to send a bill. The more rare and expensive a watch, the less he was able to think of it in terms of money. "A man should pay for the privilege of working on such a watch!" he would say.

As for merchandising methods, for the first eighty years of the shop's history the shutters on the streets had been closed each evening promptly at 6:00. It was not until I myself had come into the business twenty years ago that I had noticed the throngs of strollers crowding the narrow sidewalks each evening and had seen how the other stores kept their windows lighted and open. When I pointed this out to Father he was as delighted as though I had made a profound discovery. "And if people see the watches it might make them want to buy one! Corrie, my dear, how very clever you are!"

Mr. Kan was making his way toward me now, full of cake and compliments. Guilty for the jealous thoughts I harbored I took advantage of the crowd and made my escape downstairs. The workroom and shop were even more crowded with well-wishers than the upstairs rooms. Hans was passing cakes in the back room, as was Toos in the front, wearing the nearest thing to a smile that her perpetually down-drawn lips would permit. As for Christoffels, he had simply and astonishingly expanded. It was impossible to recognize that stooped and shabby little man in the glorious figure at the door, greeting newcomers with a formal welcome fol-

lowed by a relentless tour of the shop. Quite obviously it
was the greatest day of his life.

All through the short winter afternoon they kept coming,
the people who counted themselves Father's friends. Young
and old, poor and rich, scholarly gentlemen and illiterate
servant girls—only to Father did it seem that they were all
alike. That was Father's secret: not that he overlooked
the differences in people; that he didn't know they were
there.

And still Willem was not here. I said goodbye to some
guests at the door and stood for a moment gazing up and
down the Barteljorisstraat. Although it was only 4:00 in
the afternoon the lights in the shops were coming on against
the January dusk. I still had a great deal of little-sister
worship for this big brother, five years older than I, an
ordained minister and the only ten Boom who had ever been
to college. Willem saw things, I felt. He knew what was
going on in the world.

Oftentimes, indeed, I wished that Willem did not see quite
so well, for much that he saw was frightening. A full ten
years ago, way back in 1927, Willem had written in his
doctoral thesis, done in Germany, that a terrible evil was
taking root in that land. Right at the university, he said,
seeds were being planted of a contempt for human life such
as the world had never seen. The few who had read his paper
had laughed.

Now of course, well, people weren't laughing about Germany. Most of the good clocks came from there, and
recently several firms with whom we had dealt for years
were simply and mysteriously "out of business." Willem
believed it was part of a deliberate and large-scale move
against Jews; every one of the closed businesses was Jewish.
As head of the Dutch Reformed Church's program to
reach Jews, Willem kept in touch with these things.

Dear Willem, I thought, as I stepped back inside and
closed the door, he was about as good a salesman of the
church as Father was of watches. If he'd converted a single
Jew in twenty years I hadn't heard about it. Willem didn't
try to change people, just to serve them. He had scrimped
and saved enough money to build a home for elderly Jews
in Hilversum—for the elderly of all faiths, in fact, for
Willem was against any system of segregation. But in the

last few months the home had been deluged with younger arrivals—all Jews and all from Germany. Willem and his family had given up their own living quarters and were sleeping in a corridor. And still the frightened, homeless people kept coming, and with them tales of a mounting madness.

I went up to the kitchen where Nollie had just brewed a fresh pot of coffee, picked it up, and continued with it upstairs to Tante Jans's rooms. "What does he want?" I asked a group of men gathered around the cake table as I set down the pot. "This man in Germany, does he want war?" I knew it was poor talk for a party, but somehow thoughts of Willem always set my mind on hard subjects.

A chill of silence fell over the table and spread swiftly around the room.

"What does it matter?" a voice broke into it. "Let the big countries fight it out. It won't affect us."

"That's right!" from a watch salesman. "The Germans let us alone in the Great War. It's to their advantage to keep us neutral."

"Easy for you to talk," cried a man from whom we bought clock parts. "Your stock comes from Switzerland. What about us? What do I do if Germany goes to war? A war could put me out of business!"

And at that moment Willem entered the room. Behind him came Tine, his wife, and their four children. But every eye in the room had settled on the figure whose arm Willem held in his. It was a Jew in his early thirties in the typical broad-brimmed black hat and long black coat. What glued every eye to this man was his face. It had been burned. In front of his right ear dangled a gray and frizzled ringlet, like the hair of a very old man. The rest of his beard was gone, leaving only a raw and gaping wound.

"This is Herr Gutlieber," Willem announced in German. "He just arrived in Hilversum this morning. Herr Gutlieber, my father."

"He got out of Germany on a milk truck," Willem told us rapidly in Dutch. "They stopped him on a streetcorner— teen-aged boys in Munich—set fire to his beard."

Father had risen from his chair and was eagerly shaking the new-comer's hand. I brought him a cup of coffee and a plate of Nollie's cookies. How grateful I was now for

Father's insistence that his children speak German and English almost as soon as Dutch.

Herr Gutlieber sat down stiffly on the edge of a chair and fixed his eyes on the cup in his lap. I pulled up a chair beside him and talked some nonsense about the unusual January weather. And around us conversation began again, a hum of party talk rising and falling.

"Hoodlums!" I heard the watch salesman say. "Young hooligans! It's the same in every country. The police'll catch up with 'em—you'll see. Germany's a civilized country."

And so the shadow fell across us that winter afternoon in 1937, but it rested lightly. Nobody dreamed that this tiny cloud would grow until it blocked out the sky. And nobody dreamed that in this darkness each of us would be called to play a role: Father and Betsie and Mr. Kan and Willem— even the funny old Beje with its unmatching floor levels and ancient angles.

In the evening after the last guest had gone I climbed the stairs to my room thinking only of the past. On my bed lay the new maroon dress; I had forgotten to put it back on. "I never did care about clothes," I thought. "Even when I was young...."

Childhood scenes rushed back at me out of the night, strangely close and urgent. Today I know that such memories are the key not to the past, but to the future. I know that the experiences of our lives, when we let God use them, become the mysterious and perfect preparation for the work He will give us to do.

I didn't know it then—nor, indeed, that there was any new future to prepare for in a life as humdrum and predictable as mine. I only knew as I lay in my bed at the top of the house that certain moments from long ago stood out in focus against the blur of years. Oddly sharp and near they were, as though they were not yet finished, as though they had something more to say....

CHAPTER TWO

Full Table

It was 1898 and I was six years old. Betsie stood me in front of the wardrobe mirror and gave me a lecture.

"Just look at your shoes! You've missed every other button. And those old torn stockings your very first day at school? See how nice Nollie looks!"

Nollie and I shared this bedroom at the top of the Beje. I looked at my eight-year-old sister: sure enough, her high-buttoned shoes were neatly fastened. Reluctantly I pulled off mine while Betsie rummaged in the wardrobe.

At thirteen, Betsie seemed almost an adult to me. Of course Betsie had always seemed older because she couldn't run and roughhouse the way other children did. Betsie had been born with pernicious anemia. And so while the rest of us played tag or bowl-the-hoop or had skate races down frozen canals in winter, Betsie sat and did dull grown-up things like embroidery. But Nollie played as hard as anyone and wasn't much older than I and it didn't seem fair that she should always do everything right.

"Betsie," she was saying earnestly, "I'm *not* going to wear that great ugly hat to school just because Tante Jans paid for it. Last year it was that ugly gray one—and this year's is even worse!"

Betsie looked at her sympathetically. "Well, but . . . you can't go to school without a hat. And you know we can't afford another one."

"We don't have to!"

With an anxious glance at the door, Nollie dropped to her knees, reached beneath the single bed which was all our tiny room would hold, and drew out a little round hat box. Inside nestled the smallest hat I had ever seen. It was of fur, with a blue satin ribbon for under the chin.

"Oh, the darling thing!" Betsie lifted it reverently from the box and held it up to the patch of light that struggled into the room over the surrounding rooftops. "Where did you ever—"

"Mrs. van Dyver gave it to me." The van Dyvers owned the millinery shop two doors down. "She saw me looking at it and later she brought it here, after Tante Jans picked out ...*that*."

Nollie pointed to the top of the wardrobe. A deep-rimmed brown bonnet with a cluster of lavender velvet roses proclaimed in every line the personage who had picked it out. Tante Jans, Mama's older sister, had moved in with us when her husband died to spend, as she put it, "what few days remain to me," though she was still only in her early forties.

Her coming had greatly complicated life in the old house —already crowded by the earlier arrivals of Mama's other two sisters, Tante Bep and Tante Anna—since along with Tante Jans had come quantities of furniture, all of it too large for the little rooms at the Beje.

For her own use Tante Jans took the two second-story rooms of the front house, directly over the watch shop and workroom. In the first room she wrote the flaming Christian tracts for which she was known all over Holland, and in the second received the well-to-do ladies who supported this work, Tante Jans believed that our welfare in the hereafter depended on how much we could accomplish here on earth. For sleep she partitioned off a cubicle from her writing room just large enough to hold a bed. Death, she often said, was waiting to snatch her from her work, and so she kept her hours of repose as brief and businesslike as possible.

I could not remember life in the Beje before Tante Jans's arrival, nor whose these two rooms had been before. Above them was a narrow attic beneath the steep, sloping roof of the first house. For as long as I could recall, this space had been divided into four truly miniature rooms. The first one, looking out over the Barteljorisstraat—and the only one with a real window—was Tante Bep's. Behind it, strung like railroad compartments off a narrow aisle, were Tante Anna's, Betsie's, and our brother Willem's. Five steps up from these rooms, in the second house behind, was Nollie's and my small room, beneath ours Mama's and Father's room, and beneath theirs the dining room with the kitchen tacked like an afterthought to the side of it.

If Tante Jans's share in this crowded house was remarkably large, it never seemed so to any of us living there. The world just naturally made place for Tante Jans. All day long the horse-drawn trolley clopped and clanged past our house to stop at the Grote Markt, the central town square half a block away. At least that was where it stopped for other people. When Tante Jans wished to go somewhere she stationed herself on the sidewalk directly in front of the watch-shop door and as the horses thundered close, held up a single gloved finger. It looked to me more possible to stop the sun in the sky than to halt the charge of that trolley before its appointed place. But it stopped for Tante Jans, brakes squealing, horses nearly falling over one another, and the driver tipped his tall hat as she swept aboard.

And this was the commanding eye past which Nollie had to get the little fur hat. Tante Jans had bought most of the clothing for us three girls since coming to live with us, but her gifts had a price. To Tante Jans, the clothes in fashion when she was young represented God's final say on human apparel; all change since then came from the style-book of the devil. Indeed, one of her best-known pamphlets exposed him as the inventor of the mutton sleeve and the bicycle skirt.

"I know!" I said now as the buttonhook in Betsie's swift fingers sped up my shoes, "you could fit the fur hat right inside the bonnet! Then when you get outside, take the bonnet off!"

"Corrie!" Nollie was genuinely shocked. "That wouldn't be honest!" And with a baleful glance at the big brown hat she picked up the little fur one and started after Betsie round the stairs down to breakfast.

I picked up my own hat—the despised gray one from last year—and trailed after them, one hand clinging to the center post. Let Tante Jans see the silly hat then. I didn't care. I never could understand all the fuss over clothes.

What I did understand, what was awful and alarming, was that this was the day I was to start school. To leave this old house above the watch shop, leave Mama and Father and the aunts, in fact leave behind everything that was certain and well-loved. I gripped the post so tight that my palm squeaked as I circled around. The elementary school was only a block and a half away, it was true, and Nollie had gone there two years without difficulty. But Nollie was different from me; she was pretty and well-behaved and always had her handkerchief.

And then, as I rounded the final curve, the solution came to me, so clear and simple that I laughed out loud. I just wouldn't go to school! I'd stay here and help Tante Anna with the cooking and Mama would teach me to read and I'd never go into that strange ugly building at all. Relief and comfort flooded me and I took the last three steps in a bound.

"Shhh!" Betsie and Nollie were waiting for me outside the dining room door. "For heaven's sake, Corrie, don't do anything to get Tante Jans started wrong," Betsie said. "I'm sure," she added doubtfully, "that Father and Mama and Tante Anna will like Nollie's hat."

"Tante Bep won't," I said.

"She never likes anything," Nollie said, "so she doesn't count."

Tante Bep, with her perpetual, disapproving scowl, was the oldest of the aunts and the one we children liked least. For thirty years she had worked as a governess in wealthy families and she continually compared our behavior with that of the young ladies and gentlemen she was used to.

Betsie pointed to the Frisian clock on the stairwall, and with a finger on her lips silently opened the dining room door. It was 8:12: breakfast had already begun.

"Two minutes late!" cried Willem triumphantly.

"The Waller children were never late," said Tante Bep.

"But they're here!" said Father. "And the room is brighter!"

The three of us hardly heard: Tante Jans's chair was empty.

"Is Tante Jans staying in bed today?" asked Betsie hopefully as we hung our hats on their pegs.

"She's making herself a tonic in the kitchen," said Mama. She leaned forward to pour our coffee and lowered her voice. "We must all be specially considerate of dear Jans today. This is the day her husband's sister died some years ago—or was it his cousin?"

"I thought it was his aunt," said Tante Anna.

"It was a cousin and it was a mercy," said Tante Bep.

"At any rate," Mama hurried on, "you know how these anniversaries upset dear Jans, so we must all try to make it up to her."

Betsie cut three slices from the round loaf of bread while I looked around the table trying to decide which adult would be most enthusiastic about my decision to stay at home. Father, I knew, put an almost religious importance on education. He himself had had to stop school early to go to work in the watch shop, and though he had gone on to teach himself history, theology, and literature in five languages, he always regretted the missed schooling. He would want me to go—and whatever Father wanted, Mama wanted too.

Tante Anna then? She'd often told me she couldn't manage without me to run errands up and down the steep stairs. Since Mama was not strong, Tante Anna did most of the heavy housework for our family of nine. She was the youngest of the four sisters, with a spirit as generous as Mama's own. There was a myth in our family, firmly believed in by all, that Tante Anna received wages for this work—and indeed every Saturday Father faithfully paid her one guilder. But by Wednesday when the greengrocer came he often had to ask for it back, and she always had it, unspent and waiting. Yes, she would be my ally in this business.

"Tante Anna," I began, "I've been thinking about you working so hard all day when I'm in school and—"

A deep dramatic intake of breath made us all look up. Tante Jans was standing in the kitchen doorway, a tumbler of thick brown liquid in her hand. When she had filled her chest with air she closed her eyes, lifted the glass to her lips and drained it down. Then with a sigh she let out the breath, set the glass on the sideboard and sat down.

"And yet," she said, as though we had been discussing the subject, "what do doctors know? Dr. Blinker prescribed this tonic—but what can medicine really do? What good does anything do when one's Day arrives?"

I glanced round the table; no one was smiling. Tante Jans's preoccupation with death might have been funny, but it wasn't. Young as I was I knew that fear is never funny.

"And yet, Jans," Father remonstrated gently, "medicine has prolonged many a life."

"It didn't help Zusje! And she had the finest doctors in Rotterdam. It was this very day when she was taken—and she was no older than I am now, and got up and dressed for breakfast that day, just as I have."

She was launching into a minute-by-minute account of Zusje's final day when her eyes lit on the peg from which dangled Nollie's new hat.

"A fur muff?" she demanded, each word bristling with suspicion. "At this time of year!"

"It isn't a muff, Tante Jans," said Nollie in a small voice.

"And is it possible to learn what it is?"

"It's a hat, Tante Jans," Betsie answered for her, "a surprise from Mrs. van Dyver. Wasn't it nice of—"

"Oh no. Nollie's hat has a brim, as a well-brought-up girl's should. I know. I bought—and paid—for it myself."

There were flames in Tante Jans's eyes, tears in Nollie's when Mama came to the rescue. "I'm not at *all* sure this cheese is fresh!" She sniffed at the big pot of yellow cheese in the center of the table and pushed it across to Father. "What do you think, Casper?"

Father, who was incapable of practicing deceit or even recognizing it, took a long and earnest sniff. "I'm sure it's perfectly fine, my dear! Fresh as the day it came. Mr. Steerwijk's cheese is always——" Catching Mama's look he stared from her to Jans in confusion. "Oh—er—ah, Jans—ah, what do you think?"

Tante Jans seized the pot and glared into it with righteous zeal. If there was one subject which engaged her energies even more completely than modern clothing it was spoiled food. At last, almost reluctantly it seemed to me, she approve the cheese, but the hat was forgotten. She had plunged into the sad story of an acquaintance "my very age" who had died after eating a questionable fish, when the shop people arrived and Father took down the heavy Bible from its shelf.

There were only two employes in the watch shop in 1898, the clock man and Father's young apprentice-errand boy. When Mama had poured their coffee, Father put on his rimless spectacles and began to read:

"Thy word is a lamp unto my feet, and a light unto
my path. . . . Thou art my hiding place and my
shield: I hope in thy word...."

What kind of hiding place, I wondered idly as I watched
Father's brown beard rise and fall with the words. What
was there to hide from?

It was a long, long psalm; beside me Nollie began to
squirm. When at last Father closed the big volume, she,
Willem, and Betsie were on their feet in an instant and
snatching up their hats. Next minute they had raced down
the last five stairs and out the alley door.

More slowly the two shopworkers got up and followed
them down the stairs to the shop's rear entrance. Only then
did the five adults notice me still seated at the table.

"Corrie!" cried Mama. "Have you forgotten you're a big
girl now? Today you go to school too! Hurry, or you must
cross the street alone!"

"I'm not going."

There was a short, startled silence, broken by everybody
at once.

"When I was a girl—" Tante Jans began.

"Mrs. Waller's children—" from Tante Bep.

But Father's deep voice drowned them out. "Of course
she's not going alone! Nollie was excited today and forgot
to wait, that's all. Corrie is going with me."

And with that he took my hat from its peg, wrapped my
hand in his and led me from the room. My hand in Father's!
That meant the windmill on the Spaarne, or swans on the
canal. But this time he was taking me where I didn't want
to go! There was a railing along the bottom five steps: I
grabbed it with my free hand and held on. Skilled watchmaker's fingers closed over mine and gently unwound them.
Howling and struggling I was led away from the world I
knew into a bigger, stranger, harder one....

Mondays, Father took the train to Amsterdam to get the
time from the Naval Observatory. Now that I had started
school it was only in the summer that I could go with him.
I would race downstairs to the shop, scrubbed, buttoned,
and pronounced passable by Betsie. Father would be giving
last-minute instructions to the apprentice. "Mrs. Staal will

be in this morning to pick up her watch. This clock goes to
the Bakker's in Bloemendaal."

And then we would be off to the station, hand in hand, I
lengthening my strides and he shortening his to keep in step.
The train trip to Amsterdam took only half an hour, but it
was a wonderful ride. First the close-wedged buildings of
old Haarlem gave way to separate houses with little plots of
land around them. The spaces between houses grew wider.
And then we were in the country, the flat Dutch farmland
stretching to the horizon, ruler-straight canals sweeping past
the window. At last, Amsterdam, even bigger than Haarlem,
with its bewilderment of strange streets and canals.

Father always arrived a couple of hours before the time
signal in order to visit the wholesalers who supplied him
with watches and parts. Many of these were Jews, and these
were the visits we both liked best. After the briefest possible
discussion of business, Father would draw a small Bible
from his traveling case; the wholesaler, whose beard would
be even longer and fuller than Father's, would snatch a book
or a scroll out of a drawer, clap a prayer cap onto his head;
and the two of them would be off, arguing, comparing, inter-
rupting, contradicting—reveling in each other's company.

And then, just when I had decided that this time I had
really been forgotten, the wholesaler would look up, catch
sight of me as though for the first time, and strike his
forehead with the heel of his hand.

"A guest! A guest in my gates and I have offered her no
refreshment!" And springing up he would rummage under
shelves and into cupboards and before long I would be
holding on my lap a plate of the most delicious treats in the
world—honey cakes and date cakes and a kind of confection
of nuts, fruits, and sugar. Desserts were rare in the Beje,
sticky delights like these unknown.

By five minutes before noon we were always back at the
train station, standing at a point on the platform from which
we had a good view of the tower of the Naval Observatory.
On the top of the tower where it could be seen by all the
ships in the harbor was a tall shaft with two movable arms.
At the stroke of 12:00 noon each day the arms dropped.
Father would stand at his vantage point on the platform
almost on tiptoe with the joy of precision, holding his pocket
watch and a pad and pencil. There! Four seconds fast.

Within an hour the "astronomical clock" in the shop in Haarlem would be accurate to the second.

On the train trip home we no longer gazed out the window. Instead we talked—about different things as the years passed. Betsie's graduation from secondary school in spite of the months missed with illness. Whether Willem, when he graduated, would get the scholarship that would let him go on to the university. Betsie starting work as Father's bookkeeper in the shop.

Oftentimes I would use the trip home to bring up things that were troubling me, since anything I asked at home was promptly answered by the aunts. Once—I must have been ten or eleven—I asked Father about a poem we had read at school the winter before. One line had described "a young man whose face was not shadowed by sexsin." I had been far too shy to ask the teacher what it meant, and Mama had blushed scarlet when I consulted her. In those days just after the turn of the century sex was never discussed, even at home.

So the line had stuck in my head. "Sex," I was pretty sure, meant whether you were a boy or a girl, and "sin" made Tante Jans very angry, but what the two together meant I could not imagine. And so, seated next to Father in the train compartment, I suddenly asked, "Father, what is sexsin?"

He turned to look at me, as he always did when answering a question, but to my surprise he said nothing. At last he stood up, lifted his traveling case from the rack over our heads, and set it on the floor.

"Will you carry it off the train, Corrie?" he said.

I stood up and tugged at it. It was crammed with the watches and spare parts he had purchased that morning.

"It's too heavy," I said.

"Yes," he said. "And it would be a pretty poor father who would ask his little girl to carry such a load. It's the same way, Corrie, with knowledge. Some knowledge is too heavy for children. When you are older and stronger you can bear it. For now you must trust me to carry it for you."

And I was satisfied. More than satisfied—wonderfully at peace. There were answers to this and all my hard questions —for now I was content to leave them in my father's keeping.

Evenings at the Beje there was always company and music. Guests would bring their flutes or violins and, as each member of the family sang or played an instrument, we made quite an orchestra gathered around the upright piano in Tante Jans's front room.

The only evenings when we did not make our own music was when there was a concert in town. We could not afford tickets but there was a stage door at the side of the concert hall through which sounds came clearly. There in the alley outside this door we and scores of other Haarlem music lovers followed every note. Mama and Betsie were not strong enough to stand so many hours, but some of us from the Beje would be there, in rain and snow and frost, and while from inside we would hear coughs and stirrings, there was never a rustle in the listeners at the door.

Best of all was when there were concerts at the cathedral, because a relative was sexton there. Just inside his small private entrance a wooden bench ran along the wall. Here we sat, our backs chilled by the ancient stone, our ears and hearts warmed by the music.

The great golden organ was one that Mozart had played, and some of its notes seemed to come from heaven itself. Indeed, I was sure that heaven was like St. Bavo's, and probably about the same size. Hell, I knew, was a hot place, so heaven must be like this cold, dank, holy building, where smoke rose like incense from the footwarmers of the paying customers. In heaven, I fervently believed, everybody had footwarmers. Even in the summer the chill never left the marble grave slabs on the floor. But when the organist touched the keys we scarcely noticed—and when he played Bach, not at all.

I was following Mama and Nollie up a dark, straight flight of stairs where cobwebs clutched at our hair and mice scuttled away ahead of us. The building was less than a block from the Beje, and probably a century newer, but here was no Tante Anna to wax and scrub.

We were going to see one of the many poor families in the neighborhood whom Mama had adopted. It never occurred to any of us children that we ourselves were poor; "the poor" were people you took baskets to. Mama was always cooking up nourishing broths and porridges for forgotten old men and pale young mothers—on days, that is, when she herself was strong enough to stand at the stove.

The night before, a baby had died, and with a basket of her own fresh bread Mama was making the prescribed call on the family. She toiled painfully up the railless stairs, stopping often for breath. At the top a door opened into a single room that was obviously cooking, eating, and sleeping quarters all at once. There were already many visitors, most of them standing for lack of chairs. Mama went at once to the young mother, but I stood frozen on the threshhold. Just to the right of the door, so still in the homemade crib, was the baby.

It was strange that a society which hid the facts of sex from children made no effort to shield them from death. I stood staring at the tiny unmoving form with my heart thudding strangely against my ribs. Nollie, always braver than I, stretched out her hand and touched the ivory-white cheek. I longed to do it too, but hung back, afraid. For a while curiosity and terror struggled in me. At last I put one finger on the small curled hand.

It was cold.

Cold as we walked back to the Beje, cold as I washed for supper, cold even in the snug gas-lit dining room. Between me and each familiar face around the table crept those small icy fingers. For all Tante Jans's talk about it, death had been only a word. Now I knew that it could really happen—if to the baby, then to Mama, to Father, to Betsie!

Still shivering with that cold, I followed Nollie up to our room and crept into bed beside her. At last we heard Father's footsteps winding up the stairs. It was the best moment in every day, when he came up to tuck us in. We never fell asleep until he had arranged the blankets in his special way and laid his hand for a moment on each head. Then we tried not to move even a toe.

But that night as he stepped through the door I burst into tears. "I need you!" I sobbed. "You can't die! You can't!"

Beside me on the bed Nollie sat up. "We went to see Mrs. Hoog," she explained. "Corrie didn't eat her supper or anything."

Father sat down on the edge of the narrow bed. "Corrie," he began gently, "when you and I go to Amsterdam—when do I give you your ticket?"

I sniffed a few times, considering this.

"Why, just before we get on the train."

"Exactly. And our wise Father in heaven knows when we're going to need things, too. Don't run out ahead of Him, Corrie. When the time comes that some of us will have to die, you will look into your heart and find the strength you need—just in time."

CHAPTER THREE

Karel

I first met Karel at one of the "occasions" for which Mama was famous. Afterward I never could remember whether it was a birthday, a wedding anniversary, a new baby—Mama could make a party out of anything. Willem introduced him as a friend from Leiden and he shook hands with us one by one. I took that long strong hand, looked up into those deep brown eyes and fell irretrievably in love.

As soon as everyone had coffee I sat down just to gaze at him. He seemed quite unaware of me, but that was only natural. I was a child of fourteen, while he and Willem were already university men, sprouting straggly beards and breathing out cigar smoke with their conversation.

It was enough, I felt, to be in the same room with Karel. As for being unnoticed, I was thoroughly used to that. Nollie was the one boys noticed, though like so many pretty girls, she seemed not to care. When a boy asked for a lock of her hair—the standard method in those days of declaring passion—she would pull a few strands from the ancient gray carpet in our bedroom, tie them with a sentimental blue ribbon, and make me the messenger. The carpet was quite threadbare by now, the school full of broken hearts.

I, on the other hand, fell in love with each boy in my class in turn, in a kind of hopeless, regular rhythm. But since I was not pretty, and far too bashful to express my feelings, a whole generation of boys was growing up unaware of the girl in seat thirty-two.

Karel, though, I thought as I watched him spooning sugar into his cup, was different. I was going to love Karel forever.

It was two years before I saw Karel again. That was the winter, 1908, that Nollie and I made a trip to the university at Leiden to pay Willem a visit. Willem's sparsely furnished room was on the fourth floor of a private home. He gathered both Nollie and me into a bear-hug and then ran to the window.

"Here," he said, taking in from the sill a cream bun he had been keeping cold there. "I bought this for you. You'd better eat it quick before my starving friends arrive."

We sat on the edge of Willem's bed gulping down the precious bun; I suspected that to buy it Willem had had to go without lunch. A second later the door slammed open and in burst four of his friends—tall, deep-voiced young men in coats with twice-turned collars and threadbare cuffs. Among them was Karel.

I swallowed the last bite of cream bun, wiped my hands on the back of my skirt and stood up. Willem introduced Nollie and me around. But when he came to Karel, Karel interrupted.

"We know each other already." He bowed ever so slightly. "Do you remember? We met at a party at your home." I glanced from Karel to Nollie—but no, he was looking straight at me. My heart poured out a rapturous reply, but my mouth was still filled with the sticky remains of bun and it never reached my lips. Soon the young men were seated at our feet on the floor, all talking eagerly and at once.

Perched beside me on the bed, Nollie joined in as naturally as though visiting a university was an everyday event for us. For one thing, she looked the part: at eighteen she was already in long skirts, while I was acutely conscious of the six inches of thick black school-girl stockings between the hem of my dress and the top of my shoes.

Also, Nollie had things to talk about: the year before she had started Normal School. She didn't really want to be a teacher, but in those days universities did not offer scholarships to girls and Normal Schools were inexpensive. And so she chatted easily and knowledgeably about things of interest to students—this new theory of relativity by a man called Einstein, and whether Admiral Peary would really reach the North Pole.

"And you, Corrie. Will you go on to be a teacher, too?"

Sitting on the floor at my feet, Karel was smiling at me. I felt a blush rise beneath my high collar.

"Next year, I mean," he persisted. "This is your final year in secondary school, isn't it?"

"Yes. I mean—no. I'll stay home with Mama and Tante Anna."

It came out so short and flat. Why did I say so little when I wanted to say so very much? ...

That spring I finished school and took over the work of the household. It had always been planned that I would do this, but now there was an added reason. Tante Bep had tuberculosis.

The disease was regarded as incurable: the only known treatment was rest at a sanatorium and that was only for the rich. And so for many months Tante Bep lay in her little closet of a room, coughing away her life.

To keep down the risk of infection, only Tante Anna went in or out. Around the clock she nursed her older sister, many nights getting no sleep at all, and so the cooking and washing and cleaning for the family fell to me. I loved the work, and except for Tante Bep would have been completely happy. But over everything lay her shadow: not only the illness, but her whole disgruntled and disappointed life.

Often I would catch a glimpse inside when I handed in a tray or Tante Anna passed one out. There were the few pathetic mementos of thirty years in other people's homes. Perfume bottles—empty many years—because well-bred families always gave the governess perfume for Christmas. Some faded Daguerrotypes of children who by now must have children and grandchildren of their own. Then the door would shut. But I would linger in that narrow passage under the eaves, yearning to say something, to heal something. Wanting to love her better.

I spoke once about my feelings to Mama. She too was more and more often in bed. Always before when pain from the gallstones had got too bad she'd had an operation. But a small stroke after the last one made further surgery impossible, and many days, making up a tray for Tante Bep, I carried one upstairs to Mama also.

This time when I brought in her lunch she was writing letters. When Mama wasn't supplying the neighborhood with caps and baby dresses from her flying needles, she was composing cheery messages for shut-ins all over Haarlem. The fact that she herself had been shut-in much of her life never seemed to occur to her. "Here's a poor man, Corrie," she cried as I came in, "who's been cooped up in a single room for three years. Just think, shut away from the sky!"

I glanced out Mama's single window at the brick wall three feet away. "Mama," I said as I set the tray on the bed and sat down beside it, "can't we do something for Tante Bep? I mean, isn't it sad that she has to spend her last days here where she hates it, instead of where she was so happy? The Wallers' or someplace?"

Mama laid down her pen and looked at me. "Corrie," she said at last, "Bep has been just as happy here with us— no more and no less—than she was anywhere else."

I stared at her, not understanding.

"Do you know when she started praising the Wallers so highly?" Mama went on. "The day she left them. As long as she was there, she had nothing but complaints. The Wallers couldn't compare with the van Hooks where she'd been before. But at the van Hooks she'd actually been miserable. Happiness isn't something that depends on our surroundings, Corrie. It's something we make inside our-selves."

Tante Bep's death affected her sisters in characteristic fashion. Mama and Tante Anna redoubled their cooking and sewing for the needy in the neighborhood, as though realizing how brief was anyone's lifetime of service. As for Tante Jans, her own particular specter moved very close. "My own sister," she would exclaim at odd moments of the day. "Why, it might as well have been me!"

A year or so after Tante Bep's death, a new doctor took over Dr. Blinker's house calls. The new man's name was Jan van Veen and with him came his young sister and nurse, Tine van Veen. With him also came a new gadget for taking blood pressure. We had no idea what this meant but everyone in the household submitted to having the strip of cloth wrapped around his arm and air pumped into it.

Tante Jans, who loved medical paraphernalia of every kind, took a tremendous fancy to the new doctor and from then on consulted him as often as her finances would per-mit. And so it was Dr. van Veen, a couple of years later, who first discovered that Tante Jans had diabetes.

In those days this was a death sentence as surely as tuber-culosis had been. For days the household was numb with the shock of it. After all these years of fearing even the idea, here was the dread thing itself. Tante Jans went straight to bed on hearing the news.

But inaction went poorly with her vigorous personality and one morning to everyone's surprise she appeared for breakfast in the dining room precisely at 8:10, with the announcement that doctors were often wrong. "All these tests and tubes," said Tante Jans, who believed in them implicitly, "what do they really prove?"

And from then on she threw herself more forcefully than ever into writing, speaking, forming clubs, and launching projects. Holland in 1914, like the rest of Europe, was mobilizing for war, and the streets of Haarlem were suddenly filled with young men in uniform. From her windows overlooking the Barteljorisstraat, Tante Jans watched them idling by, gazing aimlessly into the shop windows, most of them young, penniless, and lonesome. And she conceived the idea of a soldiers' center.

It was a novel idea for its day and Tante Jans threw all the passion of her nature into it. The horse-drawn trolley on the Barteljorisstraat had recently been replaced with a big new electric one. But it still squealed to a stop, spitting sparks from rails and wire, when Tante Jans stood imperiously before the Beje. She would sweep aboard, her long black skirts in one hand, in the other a list of the well-to-do ladies who were about to become patronesses of the new venture. Only those of us who knew her best were aware, beneath all the activity, of the monstrous fear which drove her on.

And meanwhile her disease posed financial problems. Each week a fresh test had to be made to determine the sugar-content of her blood, and this was a complicated and expensive process requiring either Dr. van Veen or his sister to come to the house.

At last Tine van Veen taught me to run the weekly test myself. There were several steps involved, the most crucial being to heat the final compound to exactly the right temperature. It was hard to make the old coal-burning range in our dark kitchen do anything very precisely, but I finally learned how and from then on each Friday mixed the chemicals and conducted the test myself. If the mixture remained clear when heated, all was well. It was only if it turned black that I was to notify Dr. van Veen.

It was that spring that Willem came home for his final holiday before ordination. He had graduated from the university two years before and was now in his last months of theological school. One warm evening during his visit we were all sitting around the dining room table. Father with thirty watches spread out before him was marking in a little notebook in his precise, beautiful script: "two seconds lost," "five seconds gained," while Willem read aloud from a history of the Dutch Reformation.

All at once the bell in the alley rang. Outside the dining room window a mirror faced the alley door so that we could see who was there before going down to open it. I glanced into it and sprang up from the table.

"Corrie!" said Betsie reprovingly. "Your skirt!"

I could never remember that I was wearing long skirts now, and Betsie spent many evenings mending the rips I put in them when I moved too fast. Now I took all five steps in a bound. For at the door, a bouquet of daffodils in her hands, was Tine van Veen. Whether it was the soft spring night that put it in my mind, or Willem's dramatic, pulpit-trained voice, I suddenly knew that the meeting of these two people had to be a very special moment.

"For your mother, Corrie," Tine said, holding out the flowers as I opened the door. "I hope she's—"

"No, no, you carry the flowers. You look beautiful with them!" And without even taking her coat I pushed the startled girl up the stairs ahead of me.

I prodded her through the dining room door, almost treading on her heels to see Willem's reaction. I knew exactly how it would be. My life was lived just then in romantic novels; I borrowed them from the library in English, Dutch, and German, often reading ones I liked in all three languages, and I had played this scene where hero meets heroine a thousand times.

Willem rose slowly to his feet, his eyes never leaving Tine's. Father stood up too. "Miss van Veen," Father said in his old-fashioned manner, "allow me to present to you our son, Willem. Willem, this is the young lady of whose talent and kindness you have heard us speak."

I doubt if either one heard the introduction. They were staring at each other as though there were not another soul in the room or in the world.

Willem and Tine were married two months after his ordination. During all the weeks of getting ready, one thought stood out in my mind: Karel will be there. The wedding day dawned cool and sparkling. My eyes picked Karel immediately from the crowd in front of the church, dressed in top hat and tails as were all the male guests, but incomparably the handsomest there.

As for me, I felt that a transformation had taken place since he had seen me last. The difference between my twenty-one years and his twenty-six was not, after all, as big as it had once been.

But more than that, I felt—no, not beautiful. Even on such a romantic day as this I could not persuade myself of that. I knew that my jaw was too square, my legs too long, my hands too large. But I earnestly believed—and all the books agreed—that I would look beautiful to the man who loved me.

Betsie had done my hair that morning, laboring for an hour with the curling iron until it was piled high on my head —and so far, for a wonder, it had stayed. She'd made my silk dress too, as she'd made one for each of the women in the family, working by lamplight in the evenings because the shop was open six days a week and she would not sew on Sundays.

Now looking around me I decided that our homemade outfits were as stylish as any there. Nobody would guess, I thought as the gentle press toward the door began, that Father had given up his cigars and Tante Jans the coal fire in her rooms in order to buy the silk that swished so elegantly with us now.

"Corrie?"

In front of me stood Karel, tall black hat in his hands, his eyes searching my face as though he were not quite sure.

"Yes, it's me!" I said laughing up at him. It's me, Karel, and it's you, and it's the moment I've been dreaming of!

"But you're so—so grown up. Forgive me, Corrie, of course you are! It's just that I've always thought of you as the little girl with the enormous blue eyes." He stared at me a little longer and then added softly, "And now the little girl is a lady, and a lovely one."

Suddenly the organ music swelling from the open door was for us, the arm he offered me was the moon, and my gloved hand resting upon it the only thing that kept me from soaring right over the peaked rooftops of Haarlem.

It was a windy, rainy Friday morning in January when my eyes told me what at first my brain refused to grasp. The liquid in the glass beaker on the kitchen stove was a muddy, sullen black.

I leaned against the old wooden sink and shut my eyes. "Please God, let me have made a mistake!" I went over in my mind the different steps, looked at the vials of chemicals, the measuring spoons. No. All just the same as I'd always done.

It was this wretched room then—it was always dark in this little cupboard of a kitchen. With a pot holder I snatched up the beaker and ran to the window in the dining room.

Black. Black as fear itself.

Still clutching the beaker I pounded down the five steps and through the rear door of the shop. Father, his jeweler's glass in his eye, was bent over the shoulder of the newest apprentice, deftly selecting an infinitesimal part from the array before them on the workbench.

I looked through the glass in the door to the shop, but Betsie, behind her little cashier's desk, was talking to a customer. Not a customer, I corrected myself, a nuisance—I knew the woman. She came here for advice on watches and then bought them at that new place, Kan's, across the street. Neither Father nor Betsie seemed to care that this was happening more and more.

As the woman left I burst through the door with the telltale beaker.

"Betsie!" I cried. "Oh Betsie, it's black! How are we going to tell her? What are we going to do?"

Betsie came swiftly from behind the desk and put her arms around me. Behind me Father came into the shop. His eyes traveled from the beaker to Betsie to me.

"And you did it exactly right, Corrie? In every detail?"

"I'm afraid so, Father."

"And I am sure of it, my dear. But we must have the doctor's verdict too."

"I'll take it at once," I said.

And so I poured the ugly liquid into a small bottle and ran with it over the slippery, rain-washed streets of Haarlem.

There was a new nurse at Dr. van Veen's and I spent a miserable, silent half-hour in the waiting room. At last his patient left and Dr. van Veen took the bottle into his small laboratory.

"There is no mistake, Corrie," he said as he emerged. "Your aunt has three weeks at the very most."

We held a family conference in the watch shop when I got back: Mama, Tante Anna, Father, Betsie, and me (Nollie did not get home from her teaching job until evening). We agreed that Tante Jans must know at once.

"We will tell her together," Father decided, "though I will speak the necessary words. And perhaps," he said, his face brightening, "perhaps she will take heart from all she has accomplished. She puts great store on accomplishment, Jans does, and who knows but that she is right!"

And so the little procession filed up the steps to Tante Jans's rooms. "Come in," she called to Father's knock, and added as she always did, "and close the door before I catch my death of drafts."

She was sitting at her round mahogany table, working on yet another appeal for her soldiers' center. As she saw the number of people entering the room, she laid down her pen. She looked from one face to another, until she came to mine and gave a little gasp of comprehension. This was Friday morning, and I had not yet come up with the results of the test.

"My dear sister-in-law," Father began gently, "there is a joyous journey which each of God's children sooner or later set out on. And, Jans, some must go to their Father empty-handed, but you will run to Him with hands full!"

"All your clubs . . .," Tante Anna ventured.

"Your writings . . .," Mama added.

"The funds you've raised . . .," said Betsie.

"Your talks . . .," I began.

But our well-meant words were useless. In front of us the proud face crumpled; Tante Jans put her hands over her eyes and began to cry. "Empty, empty!" she choked at last through her tears. "How can we bring anything to God? What does He care for our little tricks and trinkets?"

And then as we listened in disbelief she lowered her hands and with tears still coursing down her face whispered, "Dear Jesus, I thank You that we must come with empty hands. I thank You that You have done all—all—on the Cross, and that all we need in life or death is to be sure of this."

Mama threw her arms around her and they clung together. But I stood rooted to the spot, knowing that I had seen a mystery.

It was Father's train ticket, given at the moment itself.

With a flourish of her handkerchief and a forceful clearing of her nose, Tante Jans let us know that the moment for sentiment had passed.

"If I had a moment's privacy," she said, "I might get some work accomplished."

She glanced at Father, and into those stern eyes crept the nearest thing to a twinkle I had ever seen. "Not that the work matters, Casper. Not that it matters at all. But," she dismissed us crisply, "I'm not going to leave an untidy desk behind for someone else to clean up."

It was four months after Tante Jans's funeral that the long-awaited invitation came to Willem's First Sermon. After less than a year as assistant to a minister in Uithuizen, he had been given a church of his own in Brabant, the beautiful rural southern part of Holland. And in the Dutch Reformed Church, a minister's first sermon in his first church was the most solemn, joyous, emotional occasion that an unemotional people could conceive. Family and friends would come from great distances and stay for days.

From his own assistant pastorate Karel wrote that he would be there and looked forward to seeing us all again. I endowed that word "all" with special meaning and pressed dresses and packed trunks in a delirium of anticipation.

It was one of Mama's bad times. She huddled in the corner of our train compartment, the hand that gripped Father's whitening at the knuckles each time the train lurched or swayed. But while the rest of us gazed out at long rows of poplars in their bright June green, Mama's eyes never left the sky. What to us was a trip through the country, to her was a feast of clouds and light and infinite blue distances.

Both the village of Made and the congregation of Willem's church had declined in recent years. But the church building itself, dating back to better days, was large, and so was Willem and Tine's house across the street. Indeed by Beje standards it was enormous; for the first few nights the ceiling seemed so far overhead that I could not sleep. Uncles and cousins and friends arrived each day, but no matter how many people moved in, the rooms always looked to me half empty.

Three days after we got there I answered the front door knocker and there stood Karel, coal dus' from the train trip still speckling his shoulders. He tossed his brown carpetbag past me into the hall, seized my hand, and drew me out into the June sunshine. "It's a lovely day in the country, Corrie!" he cried. "Come walking!"

From then on it seemed taken for granted that Karel and I would go walking each day. Each time we wandered a little farther down the country lanes that wound in every direction away from the village, the dirt beneath our feet so different from the brick streets of Haarlem. It was hard to believe, at such moments, that the rest of Europe was locked in the bloodiest war in history. Even across the ocean the madness seemed to be spreading: the papers said America would enter.

Here in neutral Holland one sunlit June day followed another. Only a few people—like Willem—insisted that the war was Holland's tragedy too. His first sermon was on this theme. Europe and the world were changing, he said: no matter which side won, a way of life was gone forever. I looked around at his congregation of sturdy villagers and farmers and saw that they did not care for such ideas.

After the sermon, friends and more distant family started home. But Karel lingered on. Our walks lasted longer. Often we talked about Karel's future, and suddenly we were speaking not about what Karel was going to do, but about what *we* were going to do. We imagined that we had a huge old manse like this one to decorate, and rejoiced to discover that we had the same ideas about furniture, flowers, even the same favorite colors. Only about children did we disagree: Karel wanted four, while I held out stubbornly for six.

And all this while the word "marriage" was never spoken.

One day when Karel was in the village, Willem came out of the kitchen with two cups of coffee in his hands. Tine with a cup of her own was just behind him.

"Corrie," Willem said, handing me the coffee and speaking as though with effort, "has Karel led you to believe that he is—"

"Serious?" Tine finished the sentence for him.

The hateful blush that I could never control set my cheeks burning. "I . . . no . . . we . . . why?"

Willem's face reddened too. "Because, Corrie, this is something that can never be. You don't know Karel's family. They've wanted one thing since he was a small child. They've sacrificed for it, planned for it, built their whole lives around it. Karel is to . . . 'marry well' is the way I think they put it."

The big barren parlor seemed suddenly emptier still. "But —what about what Karel wants? He's not a small child now!"

Willem fixed his sober, deep-set eyes on mine. "He will do it, Corrie. I don't say he wants it. To him it's just a fact of life like any other. When we'd talk about girls we liked— at the university—he'd always say at the end, 'Of course I could never marry her. It would kill my mother."

The hot coffee scalded my mouth but I gulped it down and made my escape to the garden. I hated that gloomy old house and sometimes I almost hated Willem for always seeing the dark, hard side of things. Here in the garden it was different. There wasn't a bush, hardly a flower, that Karel and I hadn't looked at together, that didn't have a bit of our feeling for each other still clinging to it. Willem might know more than I did about theology and war and politics —but when it came to romance! Things like money, social prestige, family expectations, why, in the books they vanished like rainclouds, every time. . . .

Karel left Made a week or so later, and his last words made my heart soar. Only months afterward did I remember how strangely he spoke them, the urgency, almost desperation in his voice. We were standing in the driveway of the manse waiting for the horse and cart which Made still regarded as the only dependable conveyance when there was a train to be caught. We had said goodbye after breakfast and if part of me was disappointed that he still had not proposed, another part of me was content just to be beside him. Now suddenly in the driveway he seized both my hands.

"Corrie, write to me!" he said, but not gaily. Pleadingly. "Write me about the Beje! I want to know everything. I want every detail of that ugly, beautiful, crumbling old house! Write about your father, Corrie! Write how he forgets to send the bills. Oh Corrie, it's the happiest home in Holland!"

And so it was, indeed, when Father, Mama, Betsie, Nollie, Tante Anna, and I returned. It had always been a happy place, but now each little event seemed to glow because I could share it with Karel. Every meal I cooked was an offering to him, each shining pot a poem, every sweep of the broom an act of love.

His letters did not come as often as mine went singing to him, but I put this down to his work. The minister he was assisting, he wrote, had turned the parish calling over to him: it was a wealthy congregation and large contributors expected frequent and unhurried visits from the clergy.

As time went by his letters came more seldom. I made up for it with mine and went humming my way through the summer and fall. One glorious, nippy November day when all of Holland was singing with me, the doorbell rang. I was washing the lunch dishes in the kitchen, but I ran through the dining room and down the steps before the rest of the family could stir.

I flung open the alley door and there was Karel.

Beside him was a young woman.

She stood smiling at me. I took in the hat with its sweeping feather, the ermine collar, the white-gloved hand resting on his arm. Then a blur seemed to move over the scene, for Karel was saying, "Corrie, I want you to meet my fiancée."

I must have said something. I must have led them up to Tante Jans's front room that we now used as a parlor. I only recall how my family came to the rescue, talking, shaking hands, taking coats, finding chairs, so that I would not have to do or say anything. Mama broke even her own record for making coffee. Tante Anna passed cakes. Betsie engaged the young woman in a discussion of winter fashions and Father pinned Karel in a corner with questions of the most international and impersonal nature. What did he make of the news that President Wilson was sending American troops to France?

Somehow the half-hour passed. Somehow I managed to shake her hand, then Karel's hand, and to wish them every happiness. Betsie took them down to the door. Before it clicked shut I was fleeing up the stairs to my own room at the top of the house where the tears could come.

How long I lay on my bed sobbing for the one love of my life I do not know. Later, I heard Father's footsteps coming up the stairs. For a moment I was a little girl again waiting for him to tuck the blankets tight. But this was a hurt that no blanket could shut out, and suddenly I was afraid of what Father would say. Afraid he would say, "There'll be someone else soon," and that forever afterward this untruth would lie between us. For in some deep part of me I knew already that there would not—soon or ever—be anyone else.

The sweet cigar-smell came into the room with Father. And of course he did not say the false, idle words.

"Corrie," he began instead, "do you know what hurts so very much? It's love. Love is the strongest force in the world, and when it is blocked that means pain.

"There are two things we can do when this happens. We can kill the love so that it stops hurting. But then of course part of us dies, too. Or, Corrie, we can ask God to open up another route for that love to travel.

"God loves Karel—even more than you do—and if you ask Him, He will give you His love for this man, a love nothing can prevent, nothing destroy. Whenever we cannot love in the old, human way, Corrie, God can give us the perfect way."

I did not know, as I listened to Father's footsteps winding back down the stairs, that he had given me more than the key to this hard moment. I did not know that he had put into my hands the secret that would open far darker rooms than this—places where there was not, on a human level, anything to love at all.

I was still in kindergarten in these matters of love. My task just then was to give up my feeling for Karel without giving up the joy and wonder that had grown with it. And so, that very hour, lying there on my bed, I whispered the enormous prayer:

"Lord, I give to You the way I feel about Karel, my thoughts about our future—oh, You know! Everything! Give me Your way of seeing Karel instead. Help me to love him that way. That much."

And even as I said the words I fell asleep.

CHAPTER FOUR

The Watch Shop

I was standing on a chair washing the big window in the dining room, waving now and then to passersby in the alley, while in the kitchen Mama peeled potatoes for lunch. It was 1918; the dreadful war was finally over: even in the way people walked you could sense a new hope in the air.

It wasn't like Mama, I thought, to let the water keep running that way; she never wasted anything.

"Corrie."

Her voice was low, almost a whisper.

"Yes, Mama?"

"Corrie," she said again.

And then I heard the water spilling out of the sink onto the floor. I jumped down from the chair and ran into the kitchen. Mama stood with her hand on the faucet, staring strangely at me while the water splashed from the sink over her feet.

"What is it, Mama!" I cried, reaching for the faucet. I pried her fingers loose, shut off the water, and drew her away from the puddle on the floor.

"Corrie," she said again.

"Mama, you're ill! We've got to get you to bed!"

"Corrie."

I put an arm beneath her shoulder and guided her through the dining room and up the stairs. At my cry Tante Anna came running down them and caught Mama's other arm. Together we got her onto her bed and then I raced down to the shop for Father and Betsie.

For an hour the four of us watched the effect of the cerebral hemorrhage spread slowly over her body. The paralysis seemed to affect her hands first, traveling from them along her arms and then down into her legs. Dr. van

Veen, for whom the apprentice had gone running, could do no more than we.

Mama's consciousness was the last thing to go, her eyes remaining open and alert, looking lovingly at each one of us until very slowly they closed and we were sure she was gone forever. Dr. van Veen, however, said that this was only a coma, very deep, from which she could slip either into death or back to life.

For two months Mama lay unconscious on that bed, the five of us, with Nollie on the evening shift, taking turns at her side. And then one morning, as unexpectedly as the stroke had come, her eyes opened and she looked around her. Eventually she regained the use of her arms and legs enough to be able to move about with assistance, though her hands would never again hold her crochet hook or knitting needles.

We moved her out of the tiny bedroom facing the brick wall, down to Tante Jans's front room where she could watch the busy life of the Barteljorisstraat. Her mind, it was soon clear, was as active as ever, but the power of speech did not return—with the exception of three words. Mama could say "yes," "no," and—perhaps because it was the last one she had pronounced—"Corrie." And so Mama called everybody "Corrie."

To communicate, she and I invented a little game, something like Twenty Questions. "Corrie," she would say.

" What is it, Mama? You're thinking of someone!"

"Yes."

"Someone in the family."

"No."

"Somebody you saw on the street?"

"Yes."

"Was it an old friend."

"Yes."

"A man?"

"No."

A woman Mama had known for a long time. "Mama, I'll bet it's somebody's birthday!" And I would call out names until I heard her delighted, "Yes!" Then I would write a little note saying that Mama had seen the person and wished her a happy birthday. At the close I always put the pen in her stiffened fingers so she could sign it. An angular scrawl was all that was left of her beautiful curling signature, but it was soon recognized and loved all over Haarlem.

It was astonishing, really, the quality of life she was able to lead in that crippled body, and watching her during the three years of her paralysis, I made another discovery about love.

Mama's love had always been the kind that acted itself out with soup pot and sewing basket. But now that these things were taken away, the love seemed as whole as before. She sat in her chair at the window and loved us. She loved the people she saw in the street—and beyond: her love took in the city, the land of Holland, the world. And so I learned that love is larger than the walls which shut it in.

More and more often, Nollie's conversation at the dinner table had been about a young fellow teacher at the school where she taught, Flip van Woerden. By the time Mr. van Woerden paid the formal call on Father, Father had rehearsed and polished his little speech of blessing a dozen times.

The night before the wedding, as Betsie and I lifted her into bed, Mama suddenly burst into tears. With Twenty Questions we discovered that no, she was not unhappy about the marriage; yes, she liked Flip very much. It was that the solemn mother-daughter talk promised over the years for this night, the entire sex education which our taciturn society provided, was now not possible.

In the end, that night, it was Tante Anna who mounted the stairs to Nollie's room, eyes wide and cheeks aflame. Years before, Nollie had moved from our room at the top of the stairs down to Tante Bep's little nook, and there she and Tante Anna were closeted for the prescribed half-hour. There could have been no one in all Holland less informed about marriage than Tante Anna, but this was ritual: the older woman counseling the younger one down through the centuries—one could no more have got married without it than one could have dispensed with the ring.

Nollie was radiant, the following day, in her long white dress. But it was Mama I could not take my eyes off. Dressed in black as always, she was nevertheless suddenly young and girlish, eyes sparkling with joy at this greatest Occasion the ten Booms had ever held. Betsie and I took her into the church early and I was sure that most of the van Woerden family and friends never dreamed that the gracious and smiling lady in the first pew could neither walk alone nor speak.

It was not until Nollie and Flip came down the aisle together that I thought for the very first time of my own dreams of such a moment with Karel. I glanced at Betsie, sitting so tall and lovely on the other side of Mama. Betsie had always known that, because of her health, she could not have children, and for that reason had decided long ago never to marry. Now I was twenty-seven, Betsie in her mid-thirties, and I knew that this was the way it was going to be: Betsie and I the unmarried daughters living at home in the Beje.

It was a happy thought, not a sad one. And that was the moment when I knew for sure that God had accepted the faltering gift of my emotions made four years ago. For with the thought of Karel—all shining round with love as thoughts of him had been since I was fourteen—came not the slightest trace of hurt. "Bless Karel, Lord Jesus," I murmured under my breath. "And bless her. Keep them close to one another and to You." And that was a prayer, I knew for sure, that could not have sprung unaided from Corrie ten Boom.

But the great miracle of the day came later. To close the service we had chosen Mama's favorite hymn, "Fairest Lord Jesus." And now as I stood singing it I heard, behind me in the pew, Mama's voice singing too. Word after word, verse after verse, she joined in, Mama who could not speak four words, singing the beautiful lines without a stammer. Her voice, which had been so high and clear was hoarse and cracked, but to me it was the voice of an angel.

All the way through she sang, while I stared straight ahead, not daring to turn around for fear of breaking the spell. When at last everyone sat down, Mama's eyes, Betsie's, and mine were brimming with tears.

At first we hoped it was the beginning of Mama's recovery. But the words she had sung she was not able to say, nor did she ever sing again. It had been an isolated moment, a gift to us from God, His own very special wedding present. Four weeks later, asleep with a smile on her lips, Mama slipped away from us forever.

It was in late November that year that a common cold made a big difference. Betsie began to sniff and sneeze and Father decided that she must not sit behind the cashier's table where the shop door let in the raw winter air.

But Christmas was coming, the shop's busiest time: with Betsie bundled up in bed, I took to running down to the shop as often as I could to wait on customers and wrap packages and save Father clambering up and down from his tall workbench a dozen times an hour.

Tante Anna insisted she could cook and look after Betsie. And so I settled in behind Betsie's table, writing down sales and repair charges, recording cash spent for parts and supplies, and leafing through past records in growing disbelief.

But—there was no system here anywhere! No way to tell whether a bill had been paid or not, whether the price we were asking was high or low, no way in fact to tell if we were making money or losing it.

I hurried down the street to the bookseller one wintry afternoon, bought a whole new set of ledgers, and started in to impose method on madness. Many nights after the door was locked and the shutters closed I sat on in the flickering gaslight, poring over old inventories and wholesalers' statements.

Or I would question Father. "How much did you charge Mr. Hoek for that repair work last month?"

Father would look at me blankly. "Why . . . ah . . . my dear . . . I can't really . . ."

"It was a Vacheron, Father, an old one. You had to send all the way to Switzerland for the parts and here's their bill and—"

His face lit up. "Of course I remember! A beautiful watch, Corrie! A joy to work on. Very old, only he'd let dust get into it. A fine watch must be kept clean, my dear!"

"But how much did you charge, Father?"

I developed a system of billing and, increasingly, my columns of figures began to correspond to actual transactions. And increasingly, I discovered that I loved it. I had always felt happy in this little shop with its tiny voices and shelves of small shining faces. But now I discovered that I liked the business side of it too, liked catalogues and stock listings, liked the whole busy, energetic world of trade.

Every now and then when I remembered that Betsie's cold

had settled in her chest and threatened, as hers always did, to turn into pneumonia, I would reproach myself for being anything but distressed at the present arrangement. And at night when I would hear the hard, racking cough from her bedroom below I would pray with all my heart for her to be better at once.

And then one evening two days before Christmas, when I had closed up the shop for the night and was locking the hallway door, Betsie came bursting in from the alley with her arms full of flowers. Her eyes when she saw me there were like a guilty child's.

"For Christmas, Corrie!" she pleaded. "We have to have flowers for Christmas!"

"Betsie ten Boom!" I exploded. "How long has this been going on? No wonder you're not getting better!"

"I've stayed in bed most of the time, honestly—" she stopped while great coughs shook her. "I've only got up for really important things."

I put her to bed and then prowled the rooms with new-opened eyes, looking for Betsie's "important things." How little I had really noticed about the house! Betsie had wrought changes everywhere. I marched back up to her room and confronted her with the evidence. "Was it important, Betsie, to rearrange all the dishes in the corner cupboard?"

She looked up at me and her face went red. "Yes, it was," she said defiantly. "You just put them in any old way."

"And the door to Tante Jans's rooms? Someone's been using paint remover on it, and sandpaper too—and that's hard work!"

"But there's beautiful wood underneath. I just know it! For years I've wanted to get that old varnish off and see. Oh Corrie," she said, her voice suddenly small and contrite, "I know it's horrid and selfish of me when you've had to be in the shop day after day. And I will take better care of myself so you won't have to do it much longer; but, oh, it's been so glorious being here all day, pretending I was in charge, you know, planning what I'd do. . . ."

And so it was out. We had divided the work backwards. It was astonishing, once we'd made the swap, how well everything went. The house had been clean under my care; under Betsie's it glowed. She saw beauty in wood, in pattern, in color, and helped us to see it too. The small food budget which had barely survived my visits to the butcher and disappeared altogether at the bakery, stretched under Betsie's management to include all kinds of delicious things that had never been on our table before. "Just wait till you see what's for dessert this noon!" she'd tell us at the breakfast table, and all morning in the shop the question would shimmer in the back of our minds.

The soup kettle and the coffee pot on the back of the stove, which I never seemed to find time for, were simmering again the first week Betsie took over, and soon a stream of postmen and police, derelict old men and shivering young errand boys were pausing inside our alley door to stamp their feet and cup their hands around hot mugs, just as they'd done when Mama was in charge.

And meanwhile, in the shop, I was finding a joy in work that I'd never dreamed of. I soon knew that I wanted to do more than wait on customers and keep the accounts. I wanted to learn watch repair itself.

Father eagerly took on the job of teaching me. I eventually learned the moving and stationary parts, the chemistry of oils and solutions, tool and grindwheel and magnifying techniques. But Father's patience, his almost mystic rapport with the harmonies of watchworks, these were not things that could be taught.

Wristwatches had become fashionable and I enrolled in a school which specialized in this kind of work. Three years after Mama's death I became the first licensed woman watchmaker in Holland.

And so was established the pattern our lives were to follow for over twenty years. When Father had put the Bible back on its shelf after breakfast he and I would go down the stairs to the shop while Betsie stirred the soup pot and plotted magic with three potatoes and a pound of mutton. With my eye on income-and-outlay the shop was doing better and soon we were able to hire a saleslady to preside over the front room while Father and I worked in back.

There was a constant procession through this little back room. Sometimes it was a customer; most often it was simply a visitor—from a laborer with wooden klompen on his feet to a fleet owner—all bringing their problems to Father. Quite unabashedly, in the sight of customers in the front room and the employes working with us, he would bow his head and pray for the answer.

He prayed over the work, too. There weren't many repair problems he hadn't encountered. But occasionally one would come along that baffled even him. And then I would hear him say: "Lord, You turn the wheels of the galaxies. You know what makes the planets spin and You know what makes this watch run. . . ."

The specifics of the prayer were always different, for Father—who loved science—was an avid reader of a dozen university journals. Through the years he took his stopped watches to "the One who set the atoms dancing," or "Who keeps the great currents circling through the sea." The answers to these prayers seemed often to come in the middle of the night: many mornings I would climb onto my stool to find the watch that we had left in a hundred despairing pieces fitted together and ticking merrily.

One thing in the shop I never learned to do as well as Betsie, and that was to care about each person who stepped through the door. Often when a customer entered I would slip out the rear door and up to Betsie in the kitchen. "Betsie! Who is the woman with the Alpina lapel-watch on a blue velvet band—stout, around fifty?"

"That's Mrs. van den Keukel. Her brother came back from Indonesia with malaria and she's been nursing him. Corrie," as I sped back down the stairs, "ask her how Mrs. Rinker's baby is!"

And Mrs. van den Keukel, leaving the shop a few minutes later would comment mistakenly to her husband, "That Corrie ten Boom is just like her sister!"

Even before Tante Anna's death in the late 1920s, the empty beds in the Beje were beginning to fill up with the succession of foster children who for over ten years kept the old walls ringing with laughter and Betsie busy letting down hems and pants cuffs.

And meanwhile Willem and Nollie were having families —Willem and Tine four children, Nollie and Flip six. Willem had long since left the parish ministry, where his habit of speaking the hard truth had made a succession of congregations unhappy, and had started his nursing home in Hilversum, thirty miles from Haarlem.

Nollie's family we saw more often, as their school—of which Flip was now principal—was right in Haarlem. It was a rare day when one or another of their six was not at the Beje to visit Opa at his workbench or peer into Tante Betsie's mixing bowl or race up and down the winding stairs with the foster children.

Indeed it was at the Beje that we first discovered young Peter's musical gift. It happened around our radio. We had first heard this modern wonder at a friend's house. "A whole orchestra," we kept repeating to each other—somehow that seemed especially difficult to produce inside a box. We began to put pennies aside toward a radio of our own.

Long before the sum was raised Father came down with the hepatitis that almost cost his life: during the long stay in the hospital his beard turned snow white. The day he returned home—a week after his seventieth birthday—a little committee paid us a visit. They represented shopkeepers, street sweepers, a factory owner, a canal bargeman—all people who had realized during Father's illness what he meant to them. They had pooled their resources and bought him a radio.

It was a large table model with an ornate shell-shaped speaker and it brought us many years of joy. Every Sunday Betsie would scour the papers, British, French, and German as well as our own, since the radio brought in stations from all over Europe, and plan the week's program of concerts and recitals.

It was one Sunday afternoon when Nollie and her family were visiting that Peter suddenly spoke up in the middle of a Brahms concerto.

"It's funny they put a bad piano on the radio."

"Sshhh," said Nollie, but, "What do you mean, Peter?" asked Father.

"One of the notes is wrong."

The rest of us exchanged glances: what could an eight-year-old know? But Father led the boy to Tante Jans's old upright. "Which note, Peter?"

Peter struck the keys up the scale till he reached B above middle C. "This one," he said.

And then everyone in the room heard it too: the B on the concert grand was flat.

I spent the rest of the afternoon sitting beside Peter on

the piano bench giving him simple musical quizzes, uncovering a phenomenal musical memory and perfect pitch. Peter became my music student until—in about six months—he had learnt everything I knew and went on to more expert teachers.

The radio brought another change to our lives, one that Father at first resisted. Every hour, over the BBC, we could hear the striking hours of Big Ben. And with his stopwatch in his hand corrected to the astronomical clock in the shop, Father conceded that the first stroke of the English clock time after time coincided with the hour.

Father remained, however, mistrustful of this English time. He knew several Englishmen—and they were invariably late. As soon as he was strong enough to travel by train again, he resumed his weekly trips to Amsterdam to get Naval Observatory time.

But as the months passed and Big Ben and the Observatory continued in perfect agreement, he went less regularly, and finally not at all. The astronomical clock in any case was so jarred and jiggled by the constant rattle of automobile traffic in the narrow street outside that it was no longer the precision instrument it had been. The ultimate ignominy came the day Father set the astronomical clock by the radio.

In spite of this and other changes, life for the three of us —Father, Betsie, and me—stayed essentially the same. Our foster children grew up and went away to jobs or to marry, but they were often in the house for visits. The Hundredth Anniversary came and went; the following day Father and I were back at our workbenches as always.

Even the people we passed on our daily walks were perfectly predictable. Though it was years now since his illness, Father still walked unsteadily and I still went with him on his daily stroll through the downtown streets. We took our walk always at the same time, after the midday dinner and before the shop reopened at two, and always over the same route. And since other Haarlemers were just as regular in their habits, we knew exactly whom we would meet.

Many of those we nodded to were old friends or customers, others we knew only from this daily encounter—the woman sweeping her steps on Koning Straat, the man who read the *World Shipping News* at the trolley stop on the Grote Markt. And our favorite, the man we called The Bull-

dog. This was not only because we never saw him without
two large bulldogs on the end of a leash but because, with
his wrinkled, jowly face and short bowlegs he looked exactly
like one of his own pets. His obvious affection for the
animals was what touched us: as they went along he constantly muttered and fussed at them. Father and The Bulldog always tipped their hats to one another ceremoniously
as we passed.

And while Haarlem and the rest of Holland strolled and
bowed and swept its steps, the neighbor on our east geared
for war. We knew what was happening—there was no way
to keep from knowing. Often in the evening, turning the dial
on the radio, we would pick up a voice from Germany. The
voice did not talk, or even shout. It screamed. Oddly, it was
even-tempered Betsie who reacted most strongly, hurtling
from her chair and flinging herself at the radio to shut off
the sound.

And yet, in the interludes, we forgot. Or, when Willem
was visiting and would not let us forget, or when letters to
Jewish suppliers in Germany came back marked "Address
Unknown," we still managed to believe that it was primarily
a German problem. "How long are they going to stand for
it?" we said. "They won't put up with that man for long."

Only once did the changes taking place in Germany reach
inside the little shop on the Barteljorisstraat, and that was
in the person of a young German watchmaker. Germans
frequently came to work under Father for a while, for his
reputation reached even beyond Holland. So when this tall
good-looking young man appeared with apprentice papers
from a good firm in Berlin, Father hired him without hesitation. Otto told us proudly that he belonged to the Hitler
Youth. Indeed it was a puzzle to us why he had come to
Holland, for he found nothing but fault with Dutch people
and products. "The world will see what Germans can do,"
he often said.

His first morning at work he came upstairs for coffee and
Bible reading with the other employes; after that he sat
alone down in the shop. When we asked him why, he said
that though he had not understood the Dutch words, he had
seen that Father was reading from the Old Testament which,
he informed us, was the Jews' "Book of Lies."

I was shocked, but Father was only sorrowful. "He has been taught wrong," he told me. "By watching us, seeing that we love this Book and are truthful people, he will realize his error."

It was several weeks later that Betsie opened the door from the hallway and beckoned to Father and me. Upstairs on Tante Jans's tall mahogany chair sat the lady who ran the rooming house where Otto lived. Changing the bed sheets that morning, she said, she had found something under his pillow. And she drew from her market satchel a knife with a curving ten-inch blade.

Again, Father put the best interpretation on it. "The boy is probably frightened, alone in a strange country. He probably bought it to protect himself."

It was true enough that Otto was alone. He spoke no Dutch, nor made any effort to learn, and besides Father, Betsie, and me, few people in this working-class part of the city spoke German. We repeated our invitation to join us upstairs in the evenings, but whether he did not care for our choice of radio programs, or because the evening ended as the morning began, with prayer and Bible reading, he seldom did.

In the end, Father did fire Otto—the first employe he had ever discharged in more than sixty years in business. And it was not the knife or the anti-Semitism that finally brought it about, but Otto's treatment of the old clock mender, Christoffels.

From the very first I had been baffled by his brusqueness with the old man. It wasn't anything he did—not in our presence anyway—but what he didn't do. No standing back to let the older man go first, no helping on with a coat, no picking up a dropped tool. It was hard to pin down. One Sunday when Father, Betsie, and I were having dinner at Hilversum I commented on what I had concluded was simple thoughtlessness.

Willem shook his head. "It's very deliberate," he said. "It's because Christoffels is old. The old have no value to the State. They're also harder to train in the new ways of thinking. Germany is systematically teaching disrespect for old age."

We stared at him, trying to grasp such a concept. "Surely you are mistaken, Willem!" Father said. "Otto is extremely courteous to me—unusually so. And I'm a great deal older than Christoffels."

"You're different. You're the boss. That's another part of the system: respect for authority. It is the old and the weak who are to be eliminated."

We rode the train home in stunned silence—and we starting watching Otto more closely. But how could we know, how in the Holland of 1939 could we have guessed, that it was not in the shop where we could observe him but in the streets and alleys outside that Otto was subjecting Christoffels to a very real, small persecution. "Accidental" collisions and trippings, a shove, a heel ground into a toe, were making the old clockman's journeys to and from work times of terror.

The erect and shabby little man was too proud to report any of this to us. It was not until the icy February morning that Christoffels stumbled into the dining room with a bleeding cheek and a torn coat that the truth came out. Even then, Christoffels said nothing. But running down to the street to pick up his hat, I encountered Otto surrounded by an indignant little cluster of people who had seen what happened. Rounding the corner into the alley, the young man had deliberately forced the older one into the side of the building and ground his face against the rough bricks.

Father tried to reason with Otto as he let him go, to show him why such behavior was wrong. Otto did not answer. In silence he collected the few tools he had brought with him and in silence left the shop. It was only at the door that he turned to look at us, a look of the most utter contempt I had ever seen.

CHAPTER FIVE

Invasion

The slender hands of the clock on the stair wall pointed to 9:25 as we left the dining room that night. That in itself was unusual in our orderly lives. Father was eighty years old now, and promptly at 8:45 each evening—an hour sooner than formerly—he would open the Bible, the signal for prayers, read one chapter, ask God's blessing on us through the night, and by 9:15 be climbing the stairs to his bedroom. Tonight, however, the Prime Minister was to address the nation at 9:30. One question ached through all of Holland like a long-held breath: Would there be war?

We circled up the steps to Tante Jans's rooms and Father went to warm up the big table radio. We did not so often spend the evenings up here listening to music now. England, France and Germany were at war; their stations carried mostly war reports or code messages and many frequencies were jammed. Even Dutch stations carried mostly war news, and that we could hear just as well on the small portable radio we kept now in the dining room, a gift from Pickwick the Christmas before.

This, though, was to be a major broadcast; somehow we all felt it merited the large old set with its elaborate speaker. We sat now, waiting for 9:30, tense and upright in the high-backed wooden chairs, avoiding as if by a kind of premonition the cushioned and comfortable seats.

Then the Prime Minister's voice was speaking to us, sonorous and soothing. There would be no war. He had had assurances from high sources on both sides. Holland's neutrality would be respected. It would be the Great War all over again. There was nothing to fear. Dutchmen were urged to remain calm and to—

The voice stopped. Betsie and I looked up, astonished.

Father had snapped off the set and in his blue eyes was a fire we had never seen before.

"It is wrong to give people hope when there is no hope," he said. "It is wrong to base faith upon wishes. There will be war. The Germans will attack and we will fall."

He stamped out his cigar stub in the ashtray beside the radio and with it, it seemed, the anger too, for his voice grew gentle again. "Oh, my dears, I am sorry for all Dutchmen now who do not know the power of God. For we will be beaten. But He will not." He kissed us both goodnight and in a moment we heard the steps of an old man climbing the stairs to bed.

Betsie and I sat rooted to our chairs. Father, so skilled at finding good in every situation, so slow to believe evil. If Father saw war and defeat, then there was no other possibility at all.

I sat bolt upright in my bed. What was that? There! There it was again! A brilliant flash followed a second later by an explosion which shook the bed. I scrambled over the covers to the window and leaned out. The patch of sky above the chimney tops glowed orange-red.

I felt for my bathrobe and thrust my arms through the sleeves as I whirled down the stairs. At Father's room I pressed my ear against the door. Between bomb bursts I heard the regular rhythm of his breathing.

I dived down a few more steps and into Tante Jans's rooms. Betsie had long since moved into Tante Jans's little sleeping cubicle where she would be nearer the kitchen and the doorbell. She was sitting up in the bed. I groped toward her in the darkness and we threw our arms round each other.

Together we said it aloud:

"War."

It was five hours after the Prime Minister's speech. How long we clung together, listening, I do not know. The bombing seemed mostly to be coming from the direction of the airport. At last we tiptoed uncertainly out to Tante Jans's front room. The glowing sky lit the room with a strange brilliance. The chairs, the mahogany bookcase, the old upright piano, all pulsed with an eerie light.

Betsie and I knelt down by the piano bench. For what seemed hours we prayed for our country, for the dead and injured tonight, for the Queen. And then, incredibly, Betsie began to pray for the Germans, up there in the planes, caught in the fist of the giant evil loose in Germany. I looked at my sister kneeling beside me in the light of burning Holland. "Oh Lord," I whispered, "listen to Betsie, not me, because I cannot pray for those men at all."

And it was then that I had the dream. It couldn't have been a real dream because I was not asleep. But a scene was suddenly and unreasonably in my mind. I saw the Grote Markt, half a block away, as clearly as though I were standing there, saw the town hall and St. Bavo's and the fish mart with its stair-stepped façade.

Then as I watched, a kind of odd, old farm wagon—old fashioned and out of place in the middle of a city—came lumbering across the square pulled by four enormous black horses. To my surprise I saw that I myself was sitting in the wagon. And Father too! And Betsie! There were many others, some strangers, some friends. I recognized Pickwick and Toos, Willem and young Peter. All together we were slowly being drawn across the square behind those horses. We couldn't get off the wagon, that was the terrible thing. It was taking us away—far away, I felt—but we didn't want to go. . . .

"Betsie!" I cried, jumping up, pressing my hands to my eyes. "Betsie, I've had such an awful dream!"

I felt her arm around my shoulder. "We'll go down to the kitchen where the light won't show, and we'll make a pot of coffee."

The booming of the bombs was less frequent and farther away as Betsie put on the water. Closer by was the wail of fire alarms and the beep of the hose trucks. Over coffee, standing at the stove, I told Betsie what I had seen.

"Am I imagining things because I'm frightened? But it wasn't like that! It was real. Oh Betsie, was it a kind of vision?"

Betsie's finger traced a pattern on the wooden sink worn smooth by generations of ten Booms. "I don't know," she said softly. "But if God has shown us bad times ahead, it's enough for me that He knows about them. That's why He sometimes shows us things, you know—to tell us that this too is in His hands."

For five days Holland held out against the invader. We kept the shop open, not because anyone was interested in watches, but because people wanted to see Father. Some wanted him to pray for husbands and sons stationed at the borders of the country. Others, it seemed to me, came just to see him sitting there behind his workbench as he had for sixty years and to hear in the ticking clocks a world of order and reason.

I never opened my workbench at all but joined Betsie making coffee and carrying it down. We brought down the portable radio, too, and set it up on the display case. Radio was Haarlem's eyes and ears and very pulse-rate, for after that first night, although we often heard planes overhead, the bombing never came so close again.

The first morning over the radio came instructions that ground-floor windows must be taped. Up and down the Barteljorisstraat shopowners were out on the sidewalk; there was an unaccustomed neighborhood feel as advice, rolls of adhesive, and tales of the night's terror passed from door to door. One store owner, an outspoken anti-Semite, was helping Weil the Jewish furrier put up boards where a pane of glass had shaken loose. The optician next door to us, a silent, withdrawn individual, came over and taped the top of our display window where Betsie and I could not reach.

A few nights later the radio carried the news we dreaded: the Queen had left. I had not cried the night of the invasion but I cried now, for our country was lost. In the morning the radio announced tanks advancing over the border.

And suddenly all of Haarlem was in the streets. Even Father, whose daily stroll was as predictable as his own clock chimes, broke his routine to go walking at the unheard-of hour of 10:00 A.M. It was as though we wanted to face what was coming together, the whole city united, as though each would draw strength from each other Hollander.

And so the three of us walked, jostled by the crowd, over the bridge on the Spaarne, all the way to the great wild cherry tree whose blossoms each spring formed such a white glory that it was called the Bride of Haarlem. A few faded petals clung now to the new-leafed branches, but most of the Bride's flowers had fallen, forming a wilted carpet beneath us.

A window down the street flew open.

"We've surrendered!"

The procession in the street stopped short. Each told his neighbor what we had all heard for ourselves. A boy of maybe fifteen turned to us with tears rolling down his cheeks. "I would have fought! I wouldn't ever have given up!" Father stooped down to pick up a small bruised petal from the brick pavement; tenderly he inserted it in his buttonhole.

"That is good, my son," he told the youngster. "For Holland's battle has just begun."

But during the first months of occupation, life was not so very unbearable. The hardest thing to get used to was the German uniform everywhere, German trucks and tanks in the street, German spoken in the shops. Soldiers frequently visited our store, for they were getting good wages and watches were among the first things they bought. Toward us they took a superior tone as though we were not-quite-bright children. But among themselves, as I listened to them excitedly discussing their purchases, they seemed like young men anywhere off on a holiday. Most of them selected women's watches for mothers and sweethearts back home.

Indeed, the shop never made so much money as during that first year of the war. With no new shipments coming in, people bought up everything we had in stock, even the *winkeldochters*, the "shop-daughters," merchandise that had lain around so long it seemed part of the furniture. We even sold the green marble mantle clock with the twin brass cupids.

The curfew too, at first, was no hardship for us, since it was originally set at 10:00 P.M., long after we were indoors in any case. What we did object to were the identity cards each citizen was issued. These small folders containing photograph and fingerprints had to be produced on demand. A soldier or a policeman—the Haarlem police were now under the direct control of the German Commandant—might stop a citizen at any time and ask to see his card; it had to be carried in a pouch about the neck. We were issued ration cards too, but at least that first year, the coupons represented food and merchandise actually available in the stores. Each week the newspapers announced what the current coupons could be exchanged for.

That was another thing it was hard to adjust to—newspapers that no longer carried news. Long glowing reports of the successes of the German army on its various fronts. Eulogies of German leaders, denunciations of traitors and saboteurs, appeals for the unity of the "Nordic peoples." But not news that we could trust.

And so we depended again on the radio. Early in the occupation, Haarlemers were ordered to turn in all private sets. Realizing it would look strange if our household produced none at all, we decided to turn in the portable and hide the larger, more powerful instrument in one of the many hollow spaces beneath the old twisting staircase.

Both suggestions were Peter's. He was sixteen at the time of the invasion and shared with other Dutch teenagers the restless energy of anger and impotence. Peter installed the table radio beneath a curve in the stairs just above Father's room and expertly replaced the old boards, while I carried the smaller one down to the big Vroom en Dreesman department store where the radio collection was being made. The army clerk looked at me across the counter.

"Is this the only radio you own?"

"Yes."

He consulted a list in front of him. "Ten Boom, Casper, Ten Boom, Elizabeth, at the same address. Do either of them own a radio?"

I had known from childhood that the earth opened and the heavens rained fire upon liars, but I met his gaze.

"No."

Only as I walked out of the building did I begin to tremble. Not because for the first time in my life I had told a conscious lie. But because it had been so dreadfully easy.

But we had saved our radio. Every night Betsie or I would remove the stair tread and crouch over the radio, the volume barely audible, while the other one thumped the piano in Tante Jans's room as hard as she could, to hear the news from England. And at first the news over the radio and the news in our captive press was much the same. The German offensive was everywhere victorious. Month after month the Free Dutch broadcasts could only urge us to wait, to have courage, to believe in the counter-offensive which must surely some day be mounted.

The Germans had repaired the bomb damage to the airport and were using it now as a base for air raids against England. Night after night we lay in bed listening to the growl of engines heading west. Occasionally English planes retaliated and then the German fighters might intercept them right over Haarlem.

One night I tossed for an hour while dogfights raged overhead, streaking my patch of sky with fire. At last I heard Betsie stirring in the kitchen and ran down to join her.

She was making tea. She brought it into the dining room where we had covered the windows with heavy black paper and set out the best cups. Somewhere in the night there was an explosion; the dishes in the cupboard rattled. For an hour we sipped our tea and talked, until the sound of planes died away and the sky was silent. I said goodnight to Betsie at the door to Tante Jans's rooms and groped my way up the dark stairs to my own. The fiery light was gone from the sky. I felt for my bed: there was the pillow. Then in the darkness my hand closed over something hard. Sharp too! I felt blood trickle along a finger.

It was a jagged piece of metal, ten inches long.

"Betsie!"

I raced down the stairs with the shrapnel shard in my hand. We went back to the dining room and stared at it in the light while Betsie bandaged my hand. "On your pillow," she kept saying.

"Betsie, if I hadn't heard you in the kitchen—"

But Betsie put a finger on my mouth. "Don't say it, Corrie! There are no 'if's' in God's world. And no places that are safer than other places. The center of His will is our only safety—O Corrie, let us pray that we may always know it!"

The true horror of occupation came over us only slowly. During the first year of German rule there were only minor attacks on Jews in Holland. A rock through the window of a Jewish-owned store. An ugly word scrawled on the wall of a synagogue. It was as though they were trying us, testing the temper of the country. How many Dutchmen would go along with them?

And the answer, to our shame, was many. The National Socialist Bond, the quisling organization of Holland, grew larger and bolder with each month of occupation. Some joined the NSB simply for the benefits: more food, more clothing coupons, the best jobs and housing. But others became NSBers out of conviction. Nazism was a disease to which the Dutch too were susceptible, and those with an anti-Semitic bias fell sick of it first.

On our daily walk Father and I saw the symptoms spread. A sign in a shop window: JEWS WILL NOT BE SERVED. At the entrance to a public park: NO JEWS. On the door of the library. In front of restaurants, theaters, even the concert hall whose alley we knew so much better than its seats.

A synagogue burned down and the fire trucks came. But only to keep the flames from spreading to the buildings on either side.

One noon as Father and I followed our familiar route, the sidewalks were bright with yellow stars sewn to coats and jacket fronts. Men, women, and children wore the six-pointed star with the word *Jood* ("Jew") in the center. We were surprised, as we walked, at how many of the people we had passed each day were Jews. The man who read the *World Shipping News* in the Grote Markt wore a star on his neatly pressed business suit. So did The Bulldog, his jowly face more deeply lined than ever, his voice as he fussed at his dogs, sharp with strain.

Worst were the disappearances. A watch, repaired and ready, hanging on its hook in the back of the shop, month after month. A house in Nollie's block mysteriously deserted, grass growing in the rose garden. One day Mr. Kan's shop up the street did not open. Father knocked on his door as we passed that noon, to see if someone were ill, but there was no answer. The shop remained shuttered, the windows above dark and silent for several weeks. Then, although the shop stayed closed, an NSB family moved into the apartment above.

We never knew whether these people had been spirited away by the Gestapo or gone into hiding before this could happen. Certainly public arrests, with no attempt to conceal what was happening, were becoming more frequent. One

day as Father and I were returning from our walk we found
the Grote Markt cordoned off by a double ring of police
and soldiers. A truck was parked in front of the fish mart;
into the back were climbing men, women, and children, all
wearing the yellow star. There was no reason we could see
why this particular place at this particular time had been
chosen.

"Father! Those poor people!" I cried.

The police line opened, the truck moved through. We
watched till it turned the corner.

"Those poor people," Father echoed. But to my surprise
I saw that he was looking at the soldiers now forming into
ranks to march away. "I pity the poor Germans, Corrie.
They have touched the apple of God's eye."

We talked often, Father, Betsie and I, about what we could
do if a chance should come to help some of our Jewish
friends. We knew that Willem had found hiding places at
the beginning of the occupation for the German Jews who
had been living in his house. Lately he had also moved some
of the younger Dutch Jews away from the nursing home.
"Not my old people," he would say. "Surely they will not
touch my old people."

Willem had addresses. He knew of farms in rural areas
where there were few occupying troops. Willem would be
the one to ask.

It was a drizzly November morning in 1941, a year and
a half after the invasion, as I stepped outside to fold back
the shutters, that I saw a group of four German soldiers
coming down the Barteljorisstraat. They were wearing com-
bat helmets low over their ears, rifles strapped to their
shoulders. I shrank back into the doorway and watched.
They were checking shop numbers as they walked. At Weil's
Furriers directly across the street the group stopped. One
of the soldiers unstrapped his gun and with the butt banged
on the door. He was drawing it back for another blow when
the door opened and all four pushed inside.

I dashed back through our shop and up to the dining
room where Betsie was setting out three places. "Betsie!
Hurry! Something awful is happening at Weil's!" We
reached the front door again in time to see Mr. Weil backing out of his shop, the muzzle of a gun pressed against his

stomach. When he had prodded Mr. Weil a short way down
the sidewalk, the soldier went back into the store and
slammed the door. Not an arrest, then.

Inside, we could hear glass breaking. Soldiers began
carrying out armloads of furs. A crowd was gathering in
spite of the early morning hour. Mr. Weil had not moved
from the spot on the sidewalk where the soldier had left
him.

A window over his head opened and a small shower of
clothes rained down on him—pajamas, shirts, underwear.
Slowly, mechanically, the old furrier stooped and began to
gather up his clothing. Betsie and I ran across the street to
help him.

"Your wife!" Betsie whispered urgently. "Where is Mrs.
Weil?"

The man only blinked at her.

"You must come inside!" I said, snatching socks and
handkerchiefs from the sidewalk. "Quick, with us!"

And we propelled the bewildered old man across to the
Beje. Father was in the dining room when we reached it and
greeted Mr. Weil without the slightest sign of surprise. His
natural manner seemed to relax the furrier a bit. His wife,
he said, was visiting a sister in Amsterdam.

"We must find a telephone and warn her not to come
home!" Betsie said.

Like most private telephones ours had been disconnected
early in the occupation. There were public phones at several
places in the city, but of course messages went to a public
reception center at the other end. Was it right to connect a
family in Amsterdam with the trouble here? And if Mrs.
Weil could not come home, where was she to go? Where
were the Weils to live? Certainly not with the sister where
they could so easily be traced. Father and Betsie and I exchanged glances. Almost with a single breath we said,
"Willem."

Again it was not the kind of matter that could be relayed
through the public phone system. Someone had to go, and I
was the obvious choice. Dutch trains were dirty and over-
crowded under the occupation; the trip that should have
taken under an hour took nearly three. Willem was not there
when I finally reached the big nursing home just after noon,
but Tine and their twenty-two-year-old son Kik were. I told

them what had happened on the Barteljorisstraat and gave them the Amsterdam address.

"Tell Mr. Weil to be ready as soon as it's dark," Kik said.

But it was nearly 9:00 P.M.—the new curfew hour—before Kik rapped at the alley door. Tucking Mr. Weil's clothing bundle beneath his arm, he led the man away into the night.

It was more than two weeks before I saw Kik again to ask him what had happened. He smiled at me, the broad, slow smile I had loved since he was a child.

"If you're going to work with the underground, Tante Corrie, you must learn not to ask questions."

That was all we ever learned of the Weils. But Kik's words went round and round in my head. "The underground. . . . If you're going to work with the underground." Was Kik working with this secret and illegal group? Was Willem?

We knew of course that there was an underground in Holland—or suspected it. Most cases of sabotage were not reported in our controlled press, but rumors abounded. A factory had been blown up. A train carrying political prisoners had been stopped and seven, or seventeen, or seventy, had made it away. The rumors tended to get more spectacular with each repetition. But always they featured things we believed were wrong in the sight of God? Stealing, lying, murder. Was this what God wanted in times like these? How should a Christian act when evil was in power?

It was about a month after the raid on the fur shop that Father and I, on our usual walk, saw something so very unusual that we both stopped in mid-stride. Walking toward us along the sidewalk, as so many hundreds of times before, came The Bulldog with his rolling short-legged gait. The bright yellow star had by now ceased to look extraordinary, so what—and then I knew what was wrong. The dogs. The dogs were not with him!

He passed without seeming to see us. With one accord Father and I turned around and walked after him. He turned a number of corners while we grew more and more embarrassed at following him without any real excuse. Although Father and he had tipped their hats to each other for years, we had never spoken and did not even know his name.

At last the man stopped in front of a small secondhand shop, took out a ring of keys, and let himself in. We looked through the window at the cluttered interior. Only a glance showed us that this was more than the usual hodgepodge of bric-a-brac and hollow-seated chairs. Someone who loved beautiful things had chosen everything here. "We must bring Betsie!" I said.

A little bell over the door jingled as we stepped in. Astonishing to see The Bulldog hatless and indoors, unlocking a cash drawer at the rear of the store.

"Permit an introduction, Sir," Father began. "I am Casper ten Boom and this is my daughter, Cornelia."

The Bulldog shook hands and again I noticed the deep creases in the sagging cheeks. "Harry de Vries," he said.

"Mr. de Vries, we've so often admired your—er—affection for your bulldogs. We hope they are well?"

The squat little man stared from one of us to the other. Slowly the heavy-rimmed eyes filled with tears. "Are they well?" he repeated. "I believe they are well. I hope that they are well. They are dead."

"Dead!" we said together.

"I put the medicine in their bowl with my own hands and I petted them to sleep. My babies. My little ones. If you could only have seen them eat! I waited, you know, till we had enough coupons for meat. They used to have meat all the time."

We stared at him dumbly. "Was it," I ventured at last, "was it because of the rationing?"

With a gesture of his hands the little man invited us into a small room in back of the shop and gave us chairs. "Miss ten Boom, I am a Jew. Who knows when they will come to take me away? My wife too—although she is a Gentile—is in danger because of her marriage."

The Bulldog raised his chin so high his jowls stretched taught. "It is not for ourselves we mind. We are Christians, Cato and I. When we die we will see Jesus, and this is all that matters.

"But I said to Cato, 'What about the dogs? If we are taken away who will feed them? Who will remember their water and their walk? They will wait and we will not come and they will not understand.' No! This way my mind is at ease."

"My dear friend!" Father grasped The Bulldog's hand in both of his. "Now that these dear companions may no longer walk with you, will you not do my daughter and me the great honor of accompanying us?"

But this The Bulldog would not do. "It would put you in danger," he kept saying. He did, however, accept an invitation to come to visit us. "After dark, after dark," he said.

And so one evening the following week Mr. de Vries came to the alley door of the Beje bringing his sweet, shy wife, Cato, and soon she and Harry were almost nightly visitors in Tante Jans's front room.

The Bulldog's chief delight at the Beje, after talking with Father, were the tomes of Jewish theology now housed in Tante Jans's big mahogany case. For he had become a Christian forty years earlier, without ceasing in the least to be a loyal Jew. "A completed Jew!" he would tell us smilingly. "A follower of the one perfect Jew."

The books belonged to the rabbi of Haarlem. He had brought them to Father more than a year before: "Just in case I should not be able to care for them—ah—indefinitely." He had waved a bit apologetically at the procession of small boys behind him, each staggering under the weight of several huge volumes. "My little hobby. Book collecting. And yet, old friend, books do not age as you and I do. They will speak still when we are gone, to generations we will never see. Yes, the books must survive."

The rabbi had been one of the first to vanish from Haarlem.

How often it is a small, almost unconscious event that marks a turning point. As arrests of Jews in the street became more frequent, I had begun picking up and delivering work for our Jewish customers myself so that they would not have to venture into the center of town. And so one evening in the early spring of 1942 I was in the home of a doctor and his wife. They were a very old Dutch family: the portraits on the walls could have been a textbook of Holland's history.

The Heemstras and I were talking about the things that were discussed whenever a group of people got together in those days, rationing and the news from England, when down the stairs piped a childish voice.

"Daddy! You didn't tuck us in!"

Dr. Heemstra was on his feet in an instant. With an apology to his wife and me he hurried upstairs and in a minute we heard a game of hide-and-seek going and the shrill laughter of two children.

That was all. Nothing had changed. Mrs. Heemstra continued with her recipe for stretching the tea ration with rose leaves. And yet everything was changed. For in that instant, reality broke through the numbness that had grown in me since the invasion. At any minute there might be a rap on this door. These children, this mother and father, might be ordered to the back of a truck.

Dr. Heemstra came back to the living room and the conversation rambled on. But under the words a prayer was forming in my heart.

"Lord Jesus, I offer myself for Your people. In any way. Any place. Any time."

And then an extraordinary thing happened.

Even as I prayed, that waking dream passed again before my eyes. I saw again those four black horses and the Grote Markt. As I had on the night of the invasion I scanned the passengers drawn so unwillingly behind them. Father, Betsie, Willem, myself—leaving Haarlem, leaving all that was sure and safe—going where?

CHAPTER SIX

The Secret Room

It was Sunday, May 10, 1942, exactly two years after the fall of Holland. The sunny spring skies, the flowers in the lamp-post boxes, did not at all reflect the city's mood. German soldiers wandered aimlessly through the streets, some looking as if they had not yet recovered from a hard Saturday night, some already on the lookout for girls, a few hunting for a place to worship.

Each month the occupation seemed to grow harsher, restrictions more numerous. The latest heartache for Dutchmen was an edict making it a crime to sing the "Wilhelmus," our national anthem.

Father, Betsie, and I were on our way to the Dutch Reformed church in Velsen, a small town not far from Haarlem, where Peter had won the post of organist in competition against forty older and more experienced musicians. The organ at Velsen was one of the finest in the country; though the train seemed slower each time, we went frequently.

Peter was already playing, invisible in the tall organ loft, when we squeezed into the crowded pew. That was one thing the occupation had done for Holland: churches were packed.

After hymns and prayers came the sermon, a good one today, I thought. I wished Peter would pay closer attention. He regarded sermons as interesting only to venerable relics like his mother and me. I had reached fifty that spring, to Peter the age at which life had definitely passed by. I would beg him to remember that death and ultimate issues could come for any of us at any age—especially these days—but he would reply charmingly that he was too fine a musician to die young.

The closing prayers were said. And then, electrically, the whole church sat at attention. Without preamble, every stop pulled out to full volume, Peter was playing the "Wilhelmus"!

Father, at eighty-two, was the first one on his feet. Now everyone was standing. From somewhere in back of us a voice sang out the words. Another joined in, and another. Then we were all singing together, the full voice of Holland singing her forbidden anthem. We sang at the top of our lungs, sang our oneness, our hope, our love for Queen and country. On this anniversary of defeat it seemed almost for a moment that we were victors.

Afterward we waited for Peter at the small side door of the church. It was a long time before he was free to come away with us, so many people wanted to embrace him, to shake his hand and thump his back. Clearly he was enormously pleased with himself.

But now that the moment had passed I was, as usual, angry with him. The Gestapo was certain to hear about it, perhaps already had: their eyes and ears were everywhere. I thought of Nollie, home fixing Sunday dinner for us all. I thought of Peter's brothers and sisters. And Flip—what if he lost the principalship of the school for this? And for what had Peter risked so much? Not for people's lives but for a gesture. For a moment's meaningless defiance.

At Bos en Hoven Straat, however, Peter was a hero as one by one his family made us describe again what had happened. The only members of the household who felt as I did were the two Jewish women staying at Nollie's. One of these was an elderly Austrian lady whom Willem had sent into hiding here. "Katrien," as the family had rechristened her, was posing as the van Woerdens' housemaid—although Nollie confided to me that she had yet so much as to make her own bed. Probably she did not know how, as she came from a wealthy and aristocratic family.

The other woman was a young, blonde, blue-eyed Dutch Jew with flawless false identity papers supplied by the Dutch national underground itself. The papers were so good and Annaliese looked so unlike the Nazi stereotype of a Jew, that she went freely in and out of the house, shopping and helping out at the school, giving herself out to be a friend of the family whose husband had died in the bombing of Rotterdam. Katrien and Annaliese could not understand any more than I could Peter's deliberately doing something which would attract the attention of the authorities.

I spent an anxious afternoon, tensing at the sound of every motor, for only the police, Germans and NSBers had automobiles nowadays. But the time came to go home to the Beje and still nothing had happened.

I worried two more days, then decided either Peter had not been reported or that the Gestapo had more important things to occupy them. It was Wednesday morning just as Father and I were unlocking our workbenches that Peter's little sister Cocky burst into the shop.

"Opa! Tante Corrie! They came for Peter! They took him away!"

"Who? Where?"

But she didn't know and it was three days before the family learned that he had been taken to the federal prison in Amsterdam.

It was 7:55 in the evening, just a few minutes before the new curfew hour of 8:00. Peter had been in prison for two weeks. Father and Betsie and I were seated around the dining room table, Father replacing watches in their pockets and Betsie doing needlework, our big, black, slightly-Persian cat curled contentedly in her lap. A knock on the alley door made me glance in the window mirror. There in the bright spring twilight stood a woman. She carried a small suitcase and — odd for the time of year — wore a fur coat, gloves, and a heavy veil.

I ran down and opened the door. "Can I come in?" she asked. Her voice was high-pitched in fear.

"Of course." I stepped back. The woman looked over her shoulder before moving into the little hallway.

"My name is Kleermaker. I'm a Jew."

"How do you do?" I reached out to take her bag, but she held onto it. "Won't you come upstairs?"

Father and Betsie stood up as we entered the dining room. "Mrs. Kleermaker, my father and my sister."

"I was about to make some tea!" cried Betsie. "You're just in time to join us!"

Father drew out a chair from the table and Mrs. Kleermaker sat down, still gripping the suitcase. The "tea" consisted of old leaves which had been crushed and reused so often they did little more than color the water. But Mrs. Kleermaker accepted it gratefully, plunging into the story of how her husband had been arrested some months before, her son gone into hiding. Yesterday the S.D.—the political police who worked under the Gestapo—had ordered her to close the family clothing store. She was afraid now to go back to the apartment above it. She had heard that we had befriended a man on this street. . . .

"In this household," Father said, "God's people are always welcome."

"We have four empty beds upstairs," said Betsie. "Your problem will be choosing which one to sleep in!" Then to my astonishment she added, "First though, give me a hand with the tea things."

I could hardly believe my ears. Betsie never let anyone help in her kitchen: "I'm just a fussy old maid," she'd say.

But Mrs. Kleermaker had jumped to her feet with pathetic eagerness and was already stacking plates and cups. . . .

Just two nights later the same scene was repeated. The time was again just before 8:00 on another bright May evening. Again there was a furtive knock at the side door. This time an elderly couple was standing outside.

"Come in!"

It was the same story: the same tight-clutched possessions, the same fearful glance and tentative tread. The story of neighbors arrested, the fear that tomorrow their turn would come.

That night after prayer-time the six of us faced our dilemma. "This location is too dangerous," I told our three guests. "We're half a block from the main police headquarters. And yet I don't know where else to suggest."

Clearly it was time to visit Willem again. So the next day I repeated the difficult trip to Hilversum. "Willem," I said, "we have three Jews staying right at the Beje. Can you get places for them in the country?"

Willem pressed his fingers to his eyes and I noticed suddenly how much white was in his beard. "It's getting harder," he said. "Harder every month. They're feeling the food shortage now even on the farms. I still have addresses, yes, a few. But they won't take anyone without a ration card."

"Without a ration card! But, Jews aren't issued ration cards!"

"I know." Willem turned to stare out the window. For the first time I wondered how he and Tine were feeding the elderly men and women in their care.

"I know," he repeated. "And ration cards can't be counterfeited. They're changed too often and they're too easy to spot. Identity cards are different. I know several printers who do them. Of course you need a photographer."

A photographer? Printers? What was Willem talking about? "Willem, if people need ration cards and there aren't any counterfeit ones, what do they do?"

Willem turned slowly from the window. He seemed to have forgotten me and my particular problem. "Ration cards?" He gestured vaguely. "You steal them."

I stared at this Dutch Reformed clergyman. "Then, Willem, could you steal . . . I mean . . . could you get three stolen cards?"

"No, Corrie! I'm watched! Don't you understand that? Every move I make is watched!"

He put an arm around my shoulder and went on more kindly. "Even if I can continue working for a while, it will be far better for you to develop your own sources. The less connection with me—the less connection with anyone else—the better."

Joggling home on the crowded train I turned Willem's words over and over in my mind. "Your own sources." That sounded so—so professional. How was I going to find a source of stolen ration cards? Who in the world did I know. . . .

And at that moment a name appeared in my mind.

Fred Koornstra.

Fred was the man who used to read the electric meter at the Beje. The Koornstras had a retarded daughter, now a grown woman, who attended the "church" I had been conducting for the feeble-minded for some twenty years. And now Fred had a new job working for the Food Office. Wasn't it in the department where ration books were issued?

That evening after supper I bumped over the brick streets to the Koornstra house. The tires on my faithful old bicycle had finally given out and I had joined the hundreds clattering about town on metal wheel rims. Each bump reminded me jarringly of my fifty years.

Fred, a bald man with a military bearing, came to the door

and stared at me blankly when I said I wanted to talk to him about the Sunday service. He invited me in, closed the door, and said, "Now Corrie, what is it you really came to see me about?"

("Lord," I prayed silently, "if it is not safe to confide in Fred, stop this conversation now before it is too late.")

"I must first tell you that we've had some unexpected company at the Beje. First it was a single woman, then a couple, when I got back this afternoon, another couple." I paused for just an instant. "They are Jews."

Fred's expression did not change.

"We can provide safe places for these people but they must provide something too. Ration cards."

Fred's eyes smiled. "So. Now I know why you came here."

"Fred, is there any way you can give out extra cards? More than you report?"

"None at all, Corrie. Those cards have to be accounted for a dozen ways. They're checked and double-checked."

The hope that had begun to mount in me tumbled. But Fred was frowning.

"Unless—" he began.

"Unless?"

"Unless there should be a hold-up. The Food Office in Utrecht was robbed last month—but the men were caught."

He was silent a while. "If it happened at noon," he said slowly, "when just the record clerk and I are there . . . and if they found us tied and gagged . . ." He snapped his fingers. "And I know just the man who might do it! Do you remember the—"

"Don't!" I said, remembering Willem's warning. "Don't tell me who. And don't tell me how. Just get the cards if you possibly can."

Fred stared at me a moment. "How many do you need?"

I opened my mouth to say, "Five." But the number that unexpectedly and astonishingly came out instead was, "One hundred."

When Fred opened the door to me just a week later, I gasped at the sight of him. Both eyes were a greenish purple, his lower lip cut and swollen.

"My friend took very naturally to the part," was all he would say.

But he had the cards. On the table in a brown manila envelope were one hundred passports to safety. Fred had already torn the "continuing coupon" from each one. This final coupon was presented at the Food Office the last day of each month in exchange for the next month's card. With these coupons Fred could "legally" continue to issue us one hundred cards.

We agreed that it would be risky for me to keep coming to his house each month. What if he were to come to the Beje instead, dressed in his old meterman uniform?

The meter in the Beje was in the back hall at the foot of the stairs. When I got home that afternoon I pried up the tread of the bottom step, as Peter had done higher to hide the radio, and found a hollow space inside. Peter would be proud of me I thought as I worked—and was flooded by a wave of lonesomeness for that brave and cocksure boy. But even he would have to admit, I concluded as I stepped back at last to admire the completed hideaway, that a watch-maker's hand and eye were worth something. The hinge was hidden deep in the wood, the ancient riser undisturbed. I was ridiculously pleased with it.

We had our first test of the system on July 1. Fred was to come in through the shop as he always had, carrying the cards beneath his shirt. He would come at 5:30, when Betsie would have the back hall free of callers. To my horror at 5:25 the shop door opened and in stepped a policeman.

He was a tall man with close-cropped orange-red hair whom I knew by name—Rolf van Vliet—but little else. He had come to the Hundredth Birthday Party, but so had half the force. Certainly he was not one of Betsie's "regulars" for winter morning coffee.

Rolf had brought in a watch that needed cleaning, and he seemed in a mood to talk. My throat had gone dry, but Father chatted cheerfully as he took off the back of Rolf's watch and examined it. What were we going to do? There was no way to warn Fred Koornstra. Promptly at 5:30 the door of the shop opened and in he walked, dressed in his blue workclothes. It seemed to me that his chest was too thick by a foot at least.

With magnificent aplomb Fred nodded to Father, the

policeman, and me. "Good evening." Courteous but a little bored.

He strode through the door at the rear of the shop and shut it behind him. My ears strained to hear him lift the secret lid. There! Surely Rolf must have heard it too.

The door behind us opened again. So great was Fred's control that he had not ducked out the alleyway exit, but came strolling back through the shop.

"Good evening," he said again.

"Evening."

He reached the street door and was gone. We had got away with it this time, but somehow, some way, we were going to have to work out a warning system.

For meanwhile, in the weeks since Mrs. Kleermaker's unexpected visit, a great deal had happened at the Beje. Supplied with ration cards, Mrs. Kleermaker and the elderly couple and the next arrivals and the next had found homes in safer locations. But still the hunted people kept coming, and the needs were often more complicated than ration cards and addresses. If a Jewish woman became pregnant where could she go to have her baby? If a Jew in hiding died, how could he be buried?

"Develop your own sources," Willem had said. And from the moment Fred Koornstra's name had popped into my mind, an uncanny realization had been growing in me. We were friends with half of Haarlem! We knew nurses in the maternity hospital. We knew clerks in the Records Office. We knew someone in every business and service in the city.

We didn't know, of course, the political views of all these people. But—and here I felt a strange leaping of my heart —God did! My job was simply to follow His leading one step at a time; holding every decision up to Him in prayer. I knew I was not clever or subtle or sophisticated; if the Beje was becoming a meeting place for need and supply, it was through some strategy far higher than mine.

A few nights after Fred's first "meterman" visit the alley bell rang long after curfew. I sped downstairs expecting another sad and stammering refugee. Betsie and I had already made up beds for four new overnight guests that evening: a Jewish woman and her three small children.

But to my surprise, close against the wall of the dark alley, stood Kik. "Get your bicycle," he ordered with his usual young abruptness. "And put on a sweater. I have some people I want you to meet."

"Now? After curfew?" But I knew it was useless to ask questions. Kik's bicycle was tireless too, the wheel rims swathed in cloth. He wrapped mine also to keep down the clatter, and soon we were pedalling through the blacked-out streets of Haarlem at a speed that would have scared me even in daylight.

"Put a hand on my shoulder," Kik whispered. "I know the way."

We crossed dark side streets, crested bridges, wheeled round invisible corners. At last we crossed a broad canal and I knew we had reached the fashionable suburb of Aerdenhout.

We turned into a driveway beneath shadowy trees. To my astonishment Kik picked up my bicycle and carried both his and mine up the front steps. A serving girl with starched white apron and ruffled cap opened the door. The entrance hall was jammed with bicycles.

Then I saw him. One eye smiling at me, the other at the door, his vast stomach hastening ahead of him. Pickwick!

He led Kik and me into the drawing room where, sipping coffee and chatting in small groups, was the most distinguished-looking group of men and women I had ever seen. But all my attention, that first moment, was on the inexpressibly fragrant aroma in that room. Surely, was it possible, they were drinking real coffee?

Pickwick drew me a cup from the silver urn on the sideboard. It was coffee. After two years, rich, black, pungent Dutch coffee. He poured himself a cup too, dropping in his usual five lumps of sugar as though rationing had never been invented. Another starched and ruffled maid was passing a tray heaped high with cakes.

Gobbling and gulping I trailed about the room after Pickwick, shaking the hands of the people he singled out. They were strange introductions for no names were mentioned, only, occasionally, an address, and "Ask for Mrs. Smit." When I had met my fourth Smit, Kik explained with a grin, "It's the only last name in the underground."

So this was really and truly the underground! But—where were these people from? I had never laid eyes on any of them. A second later I realized with a shiver down my spine that I was meeting the national group.

Their chief work, I gleaned from bits of conversation, was liaison work with England and the Free Dutch forces fighting elsewhere on the continent. They also maintained the underground route through which downed Allied plane crews reached the North Sea coast.

But they were instantly sympathetic with my efforts to help Haarlem's Jews. I blushed to my hair roots to hear Pickwick describe me as "the head of an operation here in this city." A hollow space under the stairs and some haphazard friendships were not an operation. The others here were obviously competent, disciplined, and professional.

But they greeted me with grave courtesy, murmuring what they had to offer as we shook hands. False identity papers. The use of a car with official government plates. Signature forgery.

In a far corner of the room Pickwick introduced me to a frail-appearing little man with a wispy goatee. "Our host informs me," the little man began formally, "that your headquarters building lacks a secret room. This is a danger for all, those you are helping as well as yourselves and those who work with you. With your permission I will pay you a visit in the coming week. . . ."

Years later I learned that he was one of the most famous architects in Europe. I knew him only as Mr. Smit.

Just before Kik and I started our dash back to the Beje, Pickwick slipped an arm through mine. "My dear, I have good news. I understand that Peter is about to be released." . . .

So he was, three days later, thinner, paler, and not a whit daunted by his two months in a concrete cell. Nollie, Tine, and Betsie used up a month's sugar ration baking cakes for his welcome-home party.

And one morning soon afterward the first customer in the shop was a small thin-bearded man named Smit. Father took his jeweler's glass from his eye. If there was one thing he loved better than making a new acquaintance, it was discovering a link with an old one.

"Smit," he said eagerly. "I know several Smits in Amsterdam. Are you by any chance related to the family who—"

"Father," I interrupted, "this is the man I told you about. He's come to, ah, inspect the house."

"A building inspector? Then you must be the Smit with offices in the Grote Hout Straat. I wonder that I haven't—"

"Father!" I pleaded, "he's not a building inspector, and his name is not Smit."

"Not Smit?"

Together Mr. Smit and I attempted to explain, but Father simply could not understand a person's being called by a name not his own. As I led Mr. Smit into the back hall we heard him musing to himself, "I once knew a Smit on Koning Straat. . . ."

Mr. Smit examined and approved the hiding place for ration cards beneath the bottom step. He also pronounced acceptable the warning system we had worked out. This was a triangle-shaped wooden sign advertising "Alpina Watches" which I had placed in the dining room window. As long as the sign was in place, it was safe to enter.

But when I showed him a cubby hole behind the corner cupboard in the dining room, he shook his head. Some ancient redesigning of the house had left a crawl space in that corner and we'd been secreting jewelry, silver coins, and other valuables there since the start of the occupation. Not only the rabbi had brought us his library but other Jewish families had brought their treasures to the Beje for safe-keeping. The space was large enough that we had believed a person could crawl in there if necessary, but Mr. Smit dismissed it without a second glance.

"First place they'd look. Don't bother to change it though. It's only silver. We're interested in saving people, not things."

He started up the narrow corkscrew stairs, and as he mounted so did his spirits. He paused in delight at the odd-placed landings, pounded on the crooked walls, and laughed aloud as the floor levels of the two old houses continued out of phase.

"What an impossibility!" he said in an awestruck voice. "What an improbable, unbelievable, unpredictable impossi-bility! Miss ten Boom, if all houses were constructed like this one, you would see before you a less worried man."

At last, at the very top of the stairs, he entered my room and gave a little cry of delight. "This is it!" he exclaimed.

"You want your hiding place as high as possible," he went on eagerly. "Gives you the best chance to reach it while the search is on below. He leaned out the window, craning his thin neck, the little faun's beard pointing this way and that.

"But . . . this is my bedroom. . . ."

Mr. Smit paid no attention. He was already measuring. He moved the heavy, wobbly old wardrobe away from the wall with surprising ease and pulled my bed into the center of the room. "This is where the false wall will go!" Excitedly he drew out a pencil and drew a line along the floor thirty inches from the back wall. He stood up and gazed at it moodily.

"That's as big as I dare," he said. "It will take a cot mattress, though. Oh yes. Easily!"

I tried again to protest, but Mr. Smit had forgotten I existed. Over the next few days he and his workmen were in and out of our house constantly. They never knocked. At each visit each man carried in something. Tools in a folded newspaper. A few bricks in a briefcase. "Wood!" he exclaimed when I ventured to wonder if a wooden wall would not be easier to build. "Wood sounds hollow. Hear it in a minute. No, no. Brick's the only thing for false walls."

After the wall was up, the plasterer came, then the carpenter, finally the painter. Six days after he had begun, Mr. Smit called Father, Betsie, and me to see.

We stood in the doorway and gaped. The smell of fresh paint was everywhere. But surely nothing in this room was newly painted! All four walls had that streaked and grimy look that old rooms got in coal-burning Haarlem. The ancient molding ran unbroken around the ceiling, chipped and peeling here and there, obviously undisturbed for a hundred and fifty years. Old water stains streaked the back wall, a wall that even I who had lived half a century in this room, could scarcely believe was not the original, but set back a precious two-and-a-half feet from the true wall of the building.

Built-in bookshelves ran along this false wall, old, sagging shelves whose blistered wood bore the same water stains as the wall behind them. Down in the far lefthand corner, beneath the bottom shelf, a sliding panel, two feet high and two wide, opened into the secret room.

Mr. Smit stooped and silently pulled this panel up. On hands and knees Betsie and I crawled into the narrow room behind it. Once inside we could stand up, sit, or even stretch out one at a time on the single mattress. A concealed vent, cunningly let into the real wall, allowed air to enter from outside.

"Keep a water jug there," said Mr. Smit, crawling in behind us. "Change the water once a week. Hardtack and vitamins keep indefinitely. Anytime there is anyone in the house whose presence is unofficial, all possessions except the clothes actually on his back must be stored in here."

Dropping to our knees again we crawled single file out into my bedroom. "Move back into this room," he told me. "Everything exactly as before."

With his fist he struck the wall above the bookshelves.

"The Gestapo could search for a year," he said. "They'll never find this one."

CHAPTER SEVEN

Eusie

Peter was home, yet he was not safe, any more than any healthy young male was safe. In Germany the munitions factories were desperate for workers. Without warning soldiers would suddenly surround a block of buildings and sweep through them, herding every male between sixteen and thirty into trucks for transport. This method of lightning search and seizure was called "the razzia," and every family with young men lived in dread of it.

Flip and Nollie had rearranged their kitchen to give them an emergency hiding place as soon as the razzias started. There was a small potato cellar beneath the kitchen floor: they enlarged the trapdoor letting into it, put a large rug on top of it and moved the kitchen table to stand on this spot.

Since Mr. Smit's work at the Beje I realized that this hole under the kitchen floor was a totally inadequate hiding place. Too low in the house for one thing, and probably as Mr. Smit would say, "the first place they'd look." However, it was not a sustained search by trained people it was intended for, but a swoop by soldiers, a place to get out of sight for half an hour. And for that, I thought, it was probably sufficient. . . .

It was Flip's birthday when the razzia came to that quiet residential street of identical attached homes. Father, Betsie, and I had come early with a quarter-pound of real English tea from Pickwick.

Nollie, Annaliese, and the two older girls were not yet back when we arrived. A shipment of men's shoes had been announced by one of the department stores and Nollie had determined to get Flip a pair "if I have to stand in line all day."

We were chatting in the kitchen with Cocky and Katrien

when all at once Peter and his older brother, Bob, raced into the room, their faces white. "Soldiers! Quick! They're two doors down and coming this way!"

They jerked the table back, snatched away the rug and tugged open the trapdoor. Bob lowered himself first, lying down flat, and Peter tumbled in on top of him. We dropped the door shut, yanked the rug over it and pulled the table back in place. With trembling hands Betsie, Cocky, and I threw a long tablecloth over it and started laying five places for tea.

There was a crash in the hall as the front door burst open and a smaller crash close by as Cocky dropped a teacup. Two uniformed Germans ran into the kitchen, rifles leveled.

"Stay where you are. Do not move."

We heard boots storming up the stairs. The soldiers glanced around disgustedly at this room filled with women and one old man. If they had looked closer at Katrien she would surely have given herself away: her face was a mask of terror. But they had other things on their minds.

"Where are your men?" the shorter soldier asked Cocky in clumsy, thick-accented Dutch.

"These are my aunts," she said, "and this is my grand-father. My father is at his school, and my mother is shopping, and—"

"I didn't ask about the whole tribe!" the man exploded in German. Then in Dutch: "Where are your brothers?"

Cocky stared at him a second, then dropped her eyes. My heart stood still. I knew how Nollie had trained her children —but surely, surely now of all times a lie was permissible!

"Do you have brothers?" the officer asked again.

"Yes," Cocky said softly. "We have three."

"How old are they?"

"Twenty-one, nineteen, and eighteen."

Upstairs we heard the sounds of doors opening and shutting, the scrape of furniture dragged from walls.

"Where are they now?" the soldier persisted.

Cocky leaned down and began gathering up the broken bits of cup. The man jerked her upright. "Where are your brothers?"

"The oldest one is at the Theological College. He doesn't get home most nights because—"

"What about the other two?"

Cocky did not miss a breath.

"Why, they're under the table."

Motioning us all away from it with his gun, the soldier seized a corner of the cloth. At a nod from him the taller man crouched with his rifle cocked. Then he flung back the cloth.

At last the pent-up tension exploded: Cocky burst into spasms of high hysterical laughter. The soldiers whirled around. Was this girl laughing at them?

"Don't take us for fools!" the short one snarled. Furiously he strode from the room and minutes later the entire squad trooped out—not, unfortunately, before the silent soldier had spied and pocketed our precious packet of tea.

It was a strange dinner party that evening, veering as it did from heartfelt thanksgiving to the nearest thing to a bitter argument our close-knit family had ever had. Nollie stuck by Cocky, insisting she would have answered the same way. "God honors truth-telling with perfect protection!"

Peter and Bob, from the viewpoint of the trapdoor, weren't so sure. And neither was I. I had never had Nollie's bravery —no, nor her faith either. But I could spot illogic. "And it isn't logical to *say* the truth and *do* a lie! What about Annaliese's false papers—and that maid's uniform on Katrien?"

" 'Set a watch, O Lord, before my mouth,' " Nollie quoted. " 'Keep the door of my lips.' Psalm One Hundred Forty-one!" she finished triumphantly.

"All right, what about the radio? I had to lie with my lips to keep that!"

"And yet whatever came from your lips, Corrie, I am sure it was spoken in love!" Father's kindly voice reproached my flushed face.

Love. How did one show it? How could God Himself show truth and love at the same time in a world like this?

By dying. The answer stood out for me sharper and chiller than it ever had before that night: the shape of a Cross etched on the history of the world.

It was getting harder and harder to find safe homes in the country for the scores of Jews who were passing through our underground station by early 1943. Even with ration cards and forged papers there were not enough places for them all. Sooner or later we knew we were going to have to start hiding people here in the city. How sad that the very first should have been the dearest of all.

It was in the middle of a busy morning in the shop when Betsie slipped through the workshop door. "Harry and Cato are here!" she said.

We were surprised. Harry had never come to the Beje in the daytime because he feared his yellow star would cause awkwardness for us. Father and I hurried behind Betsie up the stairs.

Harry de Vries related the familiar story. The visit the evening before from an NSB quisling. The announcement that the shop was confiscated. Who cared if Harry were a Christian? Any Jew can convert to avoid trouble, the NSBer said. This morning the appearance of a uniformed German to make it official: the shop was closed "in the interest of national security."

"But—if I am a security risk," said poor Harry, "surely they will not stop with taking my store."

Doubtless they would not. But just then there was absolutely no available place outside the city. In fact the only underground address we had at the moment was the home of a woman named De Boer, not four blocks from the Beje.

That afternoon I knocked on Mrs. De Boer's door. She was a dumpy woman dressed in a blue cotton smock and bedroom slippers. We supplied Mrs. De Boer with ration cards and had arranged an emergency appendectomy from there. She showed me the living quarters in her attic. Eighteen Jews were staying there, most of them in their early twenties. "They've been cooped up too long," she said. "They sing and dance and make all sorts of noise."

"If you think one more couple is too much. . . ."

"No. No . . . how can I turn them away? Bring them tonight. We'll manage."

And so Harry and Cato began their life at Mrs. De Boer's, living in one of the narrow dormers in the attic. Betsie went every day to take them some homemade bread, a bit of tea, a slice of sausage. But Betsie's main concern was not for the morale of Harry and Cato, it was for their very lives.

"They're in danger, you know," she told Father and me. "It's true that these young people are at the bursting point. This afternoon they were making such a commotion I could hear them down on the street!"

There were other concerns that bitter gray winter. Though
there was little snow, the cold came early and stayed late,
and fuel was scarce. Here and there in the parks and along
the canals trees began to disappear as people cut them down
to heat cookstoves and fireplaces.

The damp unheated rooms were hardest on the very young
and the very old. One morning Christoffels did not appear
for Bible reading in the dining room, nor later in the workshop. His landlady found him dead in his bed, the water in
his washbasin frozen solid. We buried the old clockmaker in
the splendid suit and vest he had worn to the Hundredth
Birthday Party, six years and another lifetime ago.

Spring came slowly. We celebrated my fifty-first birthday
with a little party in the de Vrieses' alcove home.

It was one week later, April 22, that Cato arrived alone
at the Beje. Inside the door she burst into tears. "Those
foolish young people went crazy! Last night eight of them
left the house. Naturally they were stopped and arrested—
the boys hadn't even bothered to cut their sideburns. The
Gestapo didn't have any trouble getting information out
of them."

The house had been raided, she said, at 4:00 that morning. Cato was released when they discovered she was not
Jewish. "But everyone else—Harry, Mrs. De Boer too—
oh what will become of them!"

For the next three days Cato was at the Haarlem police
station from early morning until curfew, pestering Dutch
and Germans alike to let her see her husband. When they
sent her away, she stepped across the street and waited
silently on the sidewalk.

Friday just before the noon closing when the shop was
crowded a policeman pushed open the street door, hesitated,
then continued back into the rear room. It was Rolf van
Vliet, the officer who had been here when our ration cards
were first delivered. He took off his cap and I noticed again
that startling orange-red hair.

"This watch is still not keeping time," Rolf said. He took
off his wristwatch, placed it on my workbench, and leaned
forward. Was he saying something? It was all I could do
to hear. "Harry de Vries will be taken to Amsterdam
tomorrow. If you want to see him, come promptly at three

this afternoon." And then, "Do you see? The second hand still hesitates at the top of the dial."

At three that afternoon Cato and I stepped through the tall double doors of the police station. The policeman on duty at the guard post was Rolf himself.

"Come with me," he said gruffly. He led us through a door and along a high-ceilinged corridor. At a locked metal gate he stopped. "Wait here," Rolf said.

Someone on the other side opened the gate and Rolf passed through. He was gone several minutes. Then the door opened again and we were face to face with Harry. Rolf stood back as Harry took Cato into his arms.

"You have only a few seconds," whispered Rolf.

They drew apart, looking into each other's eyes.

"I'm sorry," said Rolf. "He'll have to go back."

Harry kissed his wife. Then he took my hand and shook it solemnly. Tears filled our eyes. For the first time Harry spoke "I shall use this place—wherever they're taking us," he said. "It will be my witness stand for Jesus."

Rolf took Harry by the elbow.

"We will pray for you many times every day, Harry!" I cried as the gate swung shut.

An instinct which I shared with no one told me that this was the last time I would ever see our friend The Bulldog.

That night we held a meeting about Rolf: Betsie and I and the dozen or so teenage boys and girls who acted as messengers for this work. If Rolf had risked his own safety to tell us about Harry's transport, perhaps he should work with us.

"Lord Jesus," I said aloud, "this could be a danger for all of us and for Rolf too." But even with the words came a flood of assurance about this man. How long, I wondered, would we be led by this Gift of Knowledge.

I assigned one of our younger boys to follow Rolf home from work next day and learn where he lived. The older boys, the ones susceptible to the factory draft, we sent out only after dark now, and then most often dressed as girls.

The following week I visited Rolf at home. "You have no idea how much it meant to see Harry," I said when I was safe inside. "How can we repay this kindness?"

Rolf ran his hands through his bright hair. "Well, there is

a way. The cleaning woman at the jail has a teenage son and they've almost picked him up twice. She's desperate to find another place for him to live."

"Perhaps I can help," I said. "Do you think she could find that her watch needs repairing?"

The next day Toos came to the door of Tante Jans's room where I was talking with two new volunteers for our work. More and more I was leaving the watch shop to her and Father as our underground "operation" required more time. "There's a funny looking little woman downstairs," Toos said. "She says her name is Mietje. She says to tell you 'Rolf sent her.'"

I met Mietje in the dining room. The hand that I shook was ridged and leathery from years of scrubbing floors. A tuft of hair grew from her chin. "I understand," I said, "that you have a son you're very proud of."

"Oh yes!" Mietje's face lit up at the mention of him.

I took the bulky old alarm clock she had brought with her. "Come for your clock tomorrow afternoon and I'll hope to have good news."

That night we listened to our messengers' reports. The long, cruel winter had opened up places at several addresses. There was a place on a nearby tulip farm, but the farmer had decided he must be paid for the risk he was taking. We would have to provide a fee—in silver rijksdaalders, not paper money—plus an additional ration card. It didn't happen often that a "host" would require money for his services; when one did we paid gladly.

When Mietje appeared the following morning I took a small banknote from my purse and tore off a corner. "This is for your son," I said. "Tonight he is to go to the Gravenstenenbrug. There is a tree stump right next to the bridge— they cut down the tree last winter. He is to wait beside it, looking into the canal. A man will come up and ask if he has change for a bankbill. Your son is to match the missing corner, and then follow this man without asking questions."

Betsie came into the dining room as Mietje was grasping my hand in her two sandpaper ones. "I'll make it up to you! Somehow, some day, I'll find a way to repay you!"

Betsie and I exchanged smiles. How could this simple little soul help with the kind of need we faced?

And so the work grew. As each new need arose, a new answer was found, too. Through Pickwick, for example, we met the man at the central telephone exchange whose department handled orders to connect and disconnect lines. With a little rewiring and juggling of numbers, he soon had our instrument in operation.

What a day it was when the old wall phone in the rear hall jangled joyously for the first time in three years! And how we needed it! For by now there were eighty Dutchmen —elderly women and middle-aged men along with our teenagers—working in "God's underground" as we sometimes laughingly called ourselves. Most of these people never saw one another; we kept face-to-face contacts as few as possible. But all knew the Beje. It was headquarters, the center of a spreading web: the knot where all threads crossed.

But if the telephone was a boon, it was also a fresh risk— as was each added worker and connection. We set the phone's ring as low as we could and still hear it; but who might happen to be passing through the hall when it rang?

For that matter how long would curious eyes up and down the street continue to believe that one small watch shop was quite as busy as it appeared? It was true that repair work was in demand: plenty of legitimate customers still passed in and out. But there was altogether too much coming and going, especially in the early evening. The curfew was now 7:00 P.M., which in spring and summer left no night-time hours at all in which workers could move legally through the streets.

It was an hour and a half before that time on the first of June, 1943, and I was thinking of all this as I sat impatiently behind my workbench. Six workers still not back and so many loose ends to tie up before 7:00. For one thing, being the first of the month, Fred Koornstra should be arriving with the new ration cards. The hundred cards which had seemed such an extravagant request a year ago were now far too few for our needs and Fred was only one of our suppliers, some of the stolen cards coming from as far away as Delft. How long can we go on this way? I wondered. How long can we continue to count on this strange protection?

My thoughts were interrupted by the side entrance bell. Betsie and I reached it at the same instant. In the alley stood a young Jewish woman cradling a tiny blanketed bundle in her arms. Behind her I recognized an intern from the maternity hospital.

The baby, he told us in the hallway, had come prematurely. He had kept mother and child in the hospital longer than permitted already because she had nowhere else to go.

Betsie held out her arms for the baby and at that moment Fred Koornstra opened the door from the shop. He blinked a moment at seeing people in the hall, then turned with great deliberation to the meter on the wall. The young doctor, seeing what he took to be an actual meterman, turned as white as his own collar. I longed to reassure both him and Fred, but knew that the fewer of the group who knew one another the safer it was for all. The poor intern gulped a hasty goodbye while Betsie and I got mother and baby up to the dining room and closed the door on Fred and his work.

Betsie poured a bowl of the soup she had cooked for supper from a much-boiled bone. The baby began a thin high wail; I rocked it while the mother ate. Here was a new danger, a tiny fugitive too young to know the folly of making a noise. We had had many Jewish children over a night or several nights at the Beje and even the youngest had developed the uncanny silence of small hunted things. But at two weeks this one had yet to discover how unwelcoming was its world: we would need a place for them far removed from other houses.

And the very next morning into the shop walked the perfect solution. He was a clergyman friend of ours, pastor in a small town outside of Haarlem, and his home was set back from the street in a large wooded park.

"Good morning, Pastor," I said, the pieces of the puzzle falling together in my mind. "Can we help you?"

I looked at the watch he had brought in for repair. It required a very hard-to-find spare part. "But for you, Pastor, we will do our very best. And now I have something I want to confess."

The pastor's eyes clouded. "Confess?"

I drew him out the back door of the shop and up the stairs to the dining room.

"I confess that I too am searching for something." The pastor's face was now wrinkled with a frown. "Would you be willing to take a Jewish mother and her baby into your home? They will almost certainly be arrested otherwise."

Color drained from the man's face. He took a step back from me. "Miss ten Boom! I do hope you're not involved with any of this illegal concealment and undercover business. It's just not safe! Think of your father! And your sister—she's never been strong!"

On impulse I told the pastor to wait and ran upstairs. Betsie had put the newcomers in Willem's old room, the farthest from windows on the street. I asked the mother's permission to borrow the infant: the little thing weighed hardly anything in my arms.

Back in the dining room I pulled back the coverlet from the baby's face.

There was a long silence. The man bent forward, his hand in spite of himself reaching for the tiny fist curled round the blanket. For a moment I saw compassion and fear struggle in his face. Then he straightened. "No. Definitely not. We could lose our lives for that Jewish child!"

Unseen by either of us, Father had appeared in the doorway. "Give the child to me, Corrie," he said.

Father held the baby close, his white beard brushing its cheek, looking into the little face with eyes as blue and innocent as the baby's own. At last he looked up at the pastor. "You say we could lose our lives for this child. I would consider that the greatest honor that could come to my family."

The pastor turned sharply on his heels and walked out of the room.

So we had to accept a bad solution to our problem. On the edge of Haarlem was a truck farm which hid refugees for short periods of time. It was not a good location, since the Gestapo had been there already. But there was nowhere else available on short notice. Two workers took the woman and child there that afternoon.

A few weeks later we heard that the farm had been raided. When the Gestapo came to the barn where the woman was hidden, not the baby but the mother began to shriek with hysteria. She, the baby, and her protectors were all taken.

We never learned what happened to them.

Although we had a friend at the telephone exchange, we could never be sure that our line was not tapped. So we developed a system for coding our underground messages in terms of watches.

"We have a woman's watch here that needs repairing. But I can't find a mainspring. Do you know who might have one?" (We have a Jewish woman in need of a hiding place and we can't find one among our regular contacts.)

"I have a watch here with a face that's causing difficulty. One of the numbers has worked loose and it's holding back the hand. Do you know anyone who does this kind of repair work?" (We have a Jew here whose features are especially Semitic. Do you know anyone who would be willing to take an extra risk?)

"I'm sorry, but the child's watch you left with us is not repairable. Do you have the receipt?" (A Jewish child has died in one of our houses. We need a burial permit.)

One morning in the middle of June the telephone rang with this message. "We have a man's watch here that's giving us trouble. We can't find anyone to repair it. For one thing, the face is very old-fashioned. . . ."

So, a Jew whose features gave him away. This was the hardest kind of person to place. "Send the watch over and I'll see what we can do in our own shop," I said.

Promptly at 7:00 that evening the side doorbell rang. I glanced at the mirror in the window of the dining room where we were still sitting over tea of rose leaves and cherry stems. Even from the side of his head I could tell that this was our old-fashioned watch. His form, his clothes, his very stance were music-hall-comedy Jewish.

I ran down to the door. "Do come in."

The smiling slender man in his early thirties, with his protruding ears, balding head, and miniscule glasses, gave an elaborate bow. I liked him instantly.

Once the door was closed he took out a pipe. "The very first thing I must ask," he said, "is whether or not I should leave behind my good friend the pipe? Meyer Mossel and his pipe are not easily separated. But for you, kind lady, should the smell get into your drapes, I would gladly say goodbye to my friend nicotine."

I laughed. Of all the Jews who had come to our house

this was the first to enter gaily and with a question about our own comfort.

"Of course you must keep your pipe!" I said. "My father smokes a cigar—when he can get one these days."

"Ah! These days!" Meyer Mossel raised his arms and shoulders in an enormous shrug. "What do you expect, when the barbarians have overrun the camp?"

I took him up to the dining room. There were seven seated at the table, a Jewish couple waiting placement and three underground workers in addition to Father and Betsie. Meyer Mossel's eyes went straight to Father.

"But," he cried. "One of the Patriarchs!"

It was exactly the right thing to say to Father. "But," he returned with equal good humor, "a brother of the Chosen People!"

"Can you recite the One Hundred and Sixty-sixth Psalm, Opa?" Meyer said.

Father beamed. Of course there is no Psalm 166; the Psalter stops with 150. It must be a joke, and nothing could please Father better than a scriptural joke. "The Hundred and Sixty-sixth Psalm?"

"Shall I recite it for you?" Meyer asked.

Father gave a bow of assent and Meyer plunged into verse.

"But that's Psalm One Hundred!" Father interrupted. And then his face lit up. Of course! Psalm 66 started with the identical words. Meyer had asked for the One Hundredth *and* the Sixty-sixth Psalm. For the rest of the evening I could hear Father chuckling, "Psalm One Hundred and Sixty-six!"

At 8:45 Father took the old brass-bound Bible from its shelf. He opened to the reading in Jeremiah where we had left off the night before, then with sudden inspiration passed the Bible across the table to Meyer.

"I would consider it an honor if you would read for us tonight," Father said.

Lifting the Book lovingly, Meyer rose to his feet. From a pocket came a small prayer cap, and then, from deep in his throat, half-sung, half-pleaded, came the words of the ancient prophet, so feelingly and achingly that we seemed to hear the cry of the Exile itself.

Meyer Mossel, he told us afterward, had been cantor in

the synagogue in Amsterdam. For all his lightheartedness he had suffered much. Most of his family had been arrested; his wife and children were in hiding on a farm in the north which had declined to accept Meyer—"for obvious reasons," he said with a grimace at his own unmistakable features.

And gradually it dawned on all of us that this endearing man was at the Beje to stay. It was certainly not an ideal place, but for Meyer nothing could be ideal right now.

"At least," I told him one evening, "your name doesn't have to give you away too." Ever since the days when Willem was studying church history, I had remembered the fourth-century church father, Eusebius.

"I think we'll call you Eusebius," I decided. We were sitting in Tante Jans's front room with Kik and some other young men who had made us a delivery of forged travel-permits too late to get home by curfew.

Meyer leaned back and stared at the ceiling pensively. He took his pipe out of his mouth. "Eusebius Mossel," he said, tasting the words. "No, it doesn't sound quite right. Eusebius Gentile Mossel."

We all laughed. "Don't be a goose," Betsie said. "You must change both names!"

Kik looked slyly at Father. "Opa! How about Smit? That seems a popular name these days."

"It does seem so!" said Father, not catching the joke. "Extraordinarily popular!"

And Eusebius Smit it became.

Changing Meyer's name was easy—at once he became "Eusie." But getting Eusie to eat non-kosher food was something else. The problem of course was that we were grateful for food of any kind: we stood in line for hours, this third year of the occupation, to get whatever was available.

One day the paper announced that coupon number four was good for pork sausage. It was the first meat we'd had in weeks. Lovingly Betsie prepared the feast, saving every drop of fat for flavoring other foods later.

"Eusie," Betsie said as she carried the steaming casserole of pork and potatoes to the table, "the day has come."

Eusie knocked the ashes out of his pipe and considered his plight out loud. He, who had always eaten kosher, he, the oldest son of an oldest son of a respected family, in fact, he Meyer Mossel Eusebius Smit, was seriously being asked to eat pork.

Betsie placed a helping of sausage and potato before him. "Bon appetit."

The tantalizing odor reached our meat-starved palates. Eusie wet his lips with his tongue. "Of course," he said, "there's a provision for this in the Talmud." He speared the meat with his fork, bit hungrily and rolled his eyes heavenward in pure pleasure. "And I'm going to start hunting for it, too," he said, "just as soon as dinner's over."

As if Eusie's arrival had broken down a last hesitation, within a week there were three new permanent additions to the household. First there was Jop, our current apprentice, whose daily trip from his parents' home in the suburbs had twice nearly ended in seizure for the factory transport. The second time it happened his parents asked if he could stay at the Beje and we agreed. The other two were Henk, a young lawyer, and Leendert, a schoolteacher. Leendert made an especially important contribution to the secret life of the Beje. He installed our electric warning system.

By now I had learned to make the nighttime trip out to Pickwick's almost as skillfully as could Kik. One evening when I had gratefully accepted a cup of coffee, my wall-eyed friend sat me down for a lecture.

"Cornelia," he said, settling his bulk on a velvet chair too small for him, "I understand you have no alarm system in your house. This is purest folly. Also I am given to believe that you are not carrying on regular drills for your guests."

I was always amazed at how well Pickwick knew what went on at the Beje.

"You know that a raid may come any day," Pickwick continued. "I don't see how you can avoid one. Scores of people in and out—and an NSB agent living over Kan's up the street.

"Your secret room is no good to you if people can't get to it in time. I know this Leendert. He's a good man and a very passable electrician. Get him to put a buzzer in every room with a door or a window on the street. Then hold practice drills until your people can disappear into that room without a trace in less than a minute. I'll send someone to get you started."

Leendert did the electrical work that weekend. He installed a buzzer near the top of the stairs—loud enough to be heard all over the house but not outside. Then he placed buttons to sound the buzzer at every vantage point where trouble might first be spotted. One button went beneath the dining room windowsill, just below the mirror which gave onto the side door. Another went in the downstairs hall just inside that door and a third inside the front door on the Barteljorisstraat. He also put a button behind the counter in the shop and one in each workbench as well as beneath the windows in Tante Jans's rooms.

We were ready for our first trial run. The four unacknowledged members of our household were already climbing up to the secret room two times a day: in the morning to store their night clothes, bedding and toilet articles, and in the evening to put away their day things. Members of our group, too, who had to spend the night, kept raincoats, hats, anything they had brought with them, in that room. Altogether that made a good deal of traffic in and out of my small bedroom—smaller now indeed by nearly a yard. Many nights my last waking sight would be Eusie in long robe and tasseled nightcap, handing his day clothes through the secret panel.

But the purpose of the drills was to see how rapidly people could reach the room at any hour of the day or night without prior notice. A tall sallow-faced young man arrived from Pickwick one morning to teach me how to conduct the drills.

"Smit!" Father exclaimed when the man introduced himself. "Truly it's most astonishing! We've had one Smit after another here lately. Now you bear a great resemblance to. . . ."

Mr. Smit disentangled himself gently from Father's genealogical inquiries and followed me upstairs.

"Mealtimes," he said. "That's a favorite hour for a raid. Also the middle of the night." He strode from room to room pointing everywhere to evidence that more than three people lived in the house. "Watch wastebaskets and ashtrays."

He paused in a bedroom door. "If the raid comes at night they must not only take their sheets and blankets but get the mattress turned. That's the S.D.'s favorite trick—feeling for a warm spot on a bed."

Mr. Smit stayed for lunch. There were eleven of us at the table that day, including a Jewish lady who had arrived the night before and a Gentile woman and her small daughter, members of our underground, who acted as "escorts." The three of them were leaving for a farm in Brabant right after lunch.

Betsie had just passed around a stew so artfully prepared you scarcely missed the meat when, without warning, Mr. Smit leaned back in his chair and pushed the button below the window.

Above us the buzzer sounded. People sprang to their feet, snatching up glasses and plates, scrambling for the stairs, while the cat clawed halfway up the curtain in consternation. Cries of "Faster!" "Not so loud!" and "You're spilling it!" reached us as Father, Betsie, and I hastily rearranged table and chairs to look like a lunch for three in progress.

"No, leave my place," Mr. Smit instructed. "Why shouldn't you have a guest for lunch? The lady and the little girl could have stayed too."

At last we were seated again and silence reigned upstairs. The whole process had taken four minutes.

A little later we were all gathered again around the dining room table. Mr. Smit set out before him the incriminating evidence he had found: two spoons and a piece of carrot on the stairs, pipe ashes in an "unoccupied" bedroom. Everyone looked at Eusie who blushed to the tips of his large ears.

"Also those," he pointed to the hats of mother and daughter still dangling from the pegs on the dining room wall. "If you have to hide, stop and think what you arrived with. Besides which, you're all simply too slow."

The next night I sounded the alarm again and this time we shaved a minute thirty-three seconds off our run. By our fifth trial we were down to two minutes. We never did achieve Pickwick's ideal of under a minute, but with practice we learned to jump up from whatever we were doing and get those who had to hide into the secret room in seventy seconds. Father, Toos, and I worked on "stalling techniques" which we would use if the Gestapo came through the shop door; Betsie invented a similar strategy for the side door.

With these delaying tactics we hoped we could gain a life-saving seventy ticks of a second hand.

Because the drills struck so close to the fear which haunted each of our guests—never spoken, always present—we tried to keep these times from becoming altogether serious. "Like a game!" we'd tell each other: "a race to beat our own record!" One of our group owned the bakery in the next street. Early in the month I would deposit a supply of sugar coupons with him. Then when I decided it was time for a drill I would go to him for a bag of cream puffs—an inexpressible treat in those sweetless days—to be secreted in my workbench and brought out as a reward for a successful practice.

Each time the order of cream puffs was larger. For by now, in addition to the workers whom we wanted to initiate into the system, we had three more permanent boarders: Thea Dacosta, Meta Monsanto, and Mary Itallie.

Mary Itallie, at seventy-six the oldest of our guests, was also the one who posed the greatest problem. The moment Mary stepped through our door I heard the asthmatic wheezing which had made other hosts unwilling to take her in.

Since her ailment compromised the safety of the others, we took up the problem in caucus. The seven most concerned—Eusie, Jop, Henk, Leendert, Meta, Thea, and Mary herself—joined Father, Betsie, and me in Tante Jans's front room.

"There is no sense in pretending," I began. "Mary has a difficulty—especially after climbing stairs—that could put you all in danger."

In the silence that followed, Mary's labored breathing seemed especially loud.

"Can I speak?" Eusie asked.

"Of course."

"It seems to me that we're all here in your house because of some difficulty or other. We're the orphan children—the ones nobody else wanted. Any one of us is jeopardizing all the others. I vote that Mary stay."

"Good," said lawyer Henk, "let's put it to the vote."

Hands began rising but Mary was struggling to speak. "Secret ballots," she brought out at last. "No one should be embarrassed."

Henk brought a sheet of paper from the desk in the next room and tore it into nine small strips. "You too," he said, handing ballots to Betsie, Father, and me. "If we're discovered, you suffer the same as us."

He handed around pencils. "Mark 'No' if it's too great a risk, 'Yes' if you think she belongs here."

For a moment pencils scratched, then Henk collected the folded ballots. He opened them in silence, then reached over and dropped them into Mary's lap.

Nine little scraps of paper, nine times the word, "Yes."

And so our "family" was formed. Others stayed with us a day or a week, but these seven remained, the nucleus of our happy household.

That it could have been happy, at such a time and in such circumstances, was largely a tribute to Betsie. Because our guests' physical lives were so very restricted, evenings under Betsie's direction became the door to the wide world. Sometimes we had concerts, with Leendert on the violin, and Thea, a truly accomplished musician, on the piano. Or Betsie would announce "an evening of Vondel" (the Dutch Shakespeare), with each of us reading a part. One night a week she talked Eusie into giving Hebrew lessons, another night Meta taught Italian.

The evening's activity had to be kept brief because the city now had electricity only a short while each night, and candles had to be hoarded for emergencies. When the lamps flickered and dimmed we would wind back to the dining room where my bicycle was set up on its stand. One of us would climb onto it, the others taking chairs, and then while the rider pedaled furiously to make the headlight glow bright, someone would pick up the chapter from the night before. We changed cyclist and reader often as legs or voice grew tired, reading our way through histories, novels, plays.

Father always went upstairs after prayers at 9:15, but the rest of us lingered, reluctant to break the circle, sorry to see the evening end. "Oh well," Eusie would say hopefully as we started at last to our rooms, "maybe there'll be a drill tonight! I haven't had a cream puff in nearly a week. . . ."

CHAPTER EIGHT

Storm Clouds Gather

If evenings were pleasant, daytimes grew increasingly tense. We were too big; the group was too large, the web too widespread. For a year and a half now we had got away with our double lives. Ostensibly we were still an elderly watchmaker living with his two spinster daughters above his tiny shop. In actuality the Beje was the center of an underground ring that spread now to the farthest corners of Holland. Here daily came dozens of workers, reports, appeals. Sooner or later we were going to make a mistake.

It was mealtimes especially when I worried. There were so many now for every meal that we had to set the chairs diagonally around the dining room table. The cat loved this arrangement. Eusie had given him the Hebrew name "Maher Shalal Hashbaz," meaning appropriately enough, "hastening to the spoils, hurrying to the prey." With the chairs set so close M. S. Hashbaz could circle the entire table on our shoulders, purring furiously, traveling round and round.

But I was uneasy at being so many. The dining room was only five steps above street-level; a tall passerby could see right in the window. We'd hung a white curtain across it providing a kind of screen while letting in light. Still, only when the heavy blackout shades were drawn at night did I feel truly private.

At lunch one day, looking through the thin curtain I thought I saw a figure standing just outside in the alley. When I looked again a minute later it was still there. There was no reason for anyone to linger there unless he was curious about what went on in the Beje. I got up and parted the curtain an inch.

Standing a few feet away, seemingly immobilized by some

terrible emotion was old Katrien from Nollie's house!

I bolted down the stairs, threw open the door, and pulled her inside. Although the August day was hot, the old lady's hands were cold as ice. "Katrien! What are you doing here? Why were you just standing there?"

"She's gone mad?" she sobbed. "Your sister's gone mad!"

"Nollie? Oh, what's happened!"

"They came!" she said. "The S.D.! I don't know what they knew or who told them. Your sister and Annaliese were in the living room and I heard her!" The sobs broke out again. "I heard her!"

"Heard what?" I nearly screamed.

"Heard what she told them! They pointed at Annaliese and said, 'Is she a Jew?' And your sister said, 'Yes.' "

I felt my knees go weak. Annaliese, blonde, beautiful young Annaliese with the perfect papers. And she'd trusted us! Oh Nollie, Nollie, what has your rigid honesty done! "And then?" I asked.

"I don't know. I ran out the back door. She's gone mad!"

I left Katrien in the dining room, wheeled my bicycle down the stairs and bumped as fast as I could the mile and a half to Nollie's. Today the sky did not seem larger above the Wagenweg. At the corner of Bos en Hoven Straat I leaned my bike against a lamppost and stood panting, my heart throbbing in my throat. Then, as casually as I was able, I strolled up the sidewalk toward the house. Except for a car parked at the street curb directly in front, everything looked deceptively normal. I walked past. Not a sound from behind the white curtains. Nothing to distinguish this house from the replicas of it on either side.

When I got to the corner I turned around. At that moment the door opened and Nollie came out. Behind her walked a man in a brown business suit. A minute later a second man appeared, half-pulling, half supporting Annaliese. The young woman's face was white as chalk; twice before they reached the car I thought she would faint. The car doors slammed, the motor roared, and they were gone.

I pedaled back to the Beje fighting back tears of anxiety. Nollie, we soon learned, had been taken to the police station around the corner, to one of the cells in back. But Annaliese had been sent to the old Jewish theater in Amsterdam from which Jews were transported to extermination camps in Germany and Poland.

It was Mietje, stooped, care-worn little Mietje whose offer of help we had discounted, who kept us in touch with Nollie. She was in wonderful spirits, Mietje said, singing hymns and songs in her high sweet soprano.

How could she sing when she had betrayed another human being! Meitje delivered the bread that Betsie baked for Nollie each morning, and the blue sweater Nollie asked for, her favorite, with flowers embroidered over the pocket.

Mietje relayed another message from Nollie, one especially for me: "No ill will happen to Annaliese. God will not let them take her to Germany. He will not let her suffer because I obeyed Him."

Six days after Nollie's arrest, the telephone rang. Pickwick's voice was on the other end. "I wonder, my dear, if I could trouble you to deliver that watch yourself?"

A message, then, that he could not relay over the phone. I biked at once out to Aerdenhout, taking along a man's watch for safe measure.

Pickwick waited until we were in the drawing room with the door shut. "The Jewish theater in Amsterdam was broken into last night. Forty Jews were rescued. One of them —a young woman—was most insistent that Nollie know: 'Annaliese is free.'"

He fixed me with one of his wide-set eyes. "Do you understand this message?"

I nodded, too overcome with relief and joy to speak. How had Nollie known? How had she been so sure?

After ten days in the Haarlem jail, Nollie was transferred to the federal prison in Amsterdam.

Pickwick said that the German doctor in charge of the prison hospital was a humane man who occasionally arranged a medical discharge. I went at once to Amsterdam to see him. But what could I say, I wondered, as I waited in the entrance hall of his home. How could I get into the good graces of this man?

Lolling about the foyer, sniffing from time to time at my legs and hands, were three perfectly huge Doberman pinschers. I remembered the book we were reading aloud by bicycle lamp, *How to Win Friends and Influence People.*

One of the techniques advocated by Dale Carnegie was: find the man's hobby. Hobby, dogs . . . I wonder. . . .

At last the maid returned and showed me into a small sitting room. "How smart of you, Doctor!" I said in German to the grizzle-haired man on the sofa.

"Smart?"

"Yes, to bring these lovely dogs with you. They must be good company when you have to be away from your family."

The doctor's face brightened. "You like dogs then?"

About the only dogs I had ever known were Harry de Vries' bulldogs. "Bulls are my favorite. Do you like bulls?"

"People don't realize it," the doctor said eagerly, "but bulldogs are very affectionate."

For perhaps ten minutes, while I racked my brain for everything I had ever heard or read on the subject, we talked about dogs. Then abruptly the doctor stood up. "But I'm sure you haven't come here to talk about dogs. What's on your mind?"

I met his eye. "I have a sister in prison here in Amsterdam. I was wondering if . . . I don't think she's well."

The doctor smiled. "So, you aren't interested in dogs at all."

"I'm interested now," I said, smiling too. "But I'm far more interested in my sister."

"What's her name?"

"Nollie van Woerden."

The doctor went out of the room and came back with a brown notebook. "Yes. One of the recent arrivals. Tell me something about her. What is she in prison for?"

Taking a chance, I told the doctor that Nollie's crime had been hiding a Jew. I also told him that she was the mother of six children, who if left without aid could become a burden to the State. (I did not mention that the youngest of these children was now seventeen.)

"Well, we'll see." He walked to the door of the sitting room. "You must excuse me now."

I was more encouraged than at any time since Nollie's arrest as I rode the train back to Haarlem. But days, then a week, then two weeks passed and there was no further news. I went back to Amsterdam. "I've come to see how those Dobermans are," I told the doctor.

He was not amused. "You mustn't bother me. I know that you have not come to talk about dogs. You must give me time."

So there was nothing to do but wait.

It was a bright September noon when seventeen of us were squeezed around the dining room table. All of a sudden Nils, seated across from me, turned pale. Nils, one of our workers, had come to report old Katrien safely arrived at a farm north of Alkmaar. Now Nils spoke in a low normal voice.

"Do not turn around. Someone is looking over the curtain."

Over the curtain! But—that was impossible! He'd have to be ten feet high. The table fell silent.

"He's on a ladder, washing the window," Nils said.

"I didn't order the windows washed," said Betsie.

Whoever it was, we mustn't sit here in this frozen, guilty silence! Eusie had an inspiration. "Happy Birthday!" he sang. "Happy Birthday to you!" We all got the idea and joined in lustily. "Happy Birthday, dear Opa . . . ," the song was still echoing through the Beje when I went out the side door and stood next to the ladder, looking up at the man holding bucket and sponge.

"What are you doing? We didn't want the windows washed. Especially not during the party!"

The man took a piece of paper from his hip pocked and consulted it. "Isn't this Kuiper's?"

"They're across the street. But—anyhow, come in and help us celebrate." The man shook his head. He thanked me, but he had work to do. I watched him crossing the Barteljorisstraat with his ladder to Kuiper's candy store.

"Did it work?" a clamor of voices asked when I got back to the dining room. "Do you think he was spying?"

I didn't answer. I didn't know.

That was the hardest. Never knowing. And one of the biggest unknowns was my own performance under questioning. As long as I was awake I felt fairly sure of myself. But if they should come at night . . . Over and over again the group worked with me—Nils, Henk, Leendert—bursting into my room without warning, shaking me awake, hurling questions at me.

The first time it happened I was sure the real raid had come. There was a terrific pounding on my door, then the

beam of a flashlight in my eyes. "Get up! On your feet!"
I could not see the man who was speaking.

"Where are you hiding your nine Jews?"

"We have only six Jews now."

There was an awful silence. The room light came on to
show Rolf clutching his head with his hands. "Oh no. Oh
no," he kept saying. "It can't be that bad."

"Think now," said Henk just behind him. "The Gestapo
is trying to trap you. The answer is, 'What Jews! We don't
have Jews here.'"

"Can I try again?"

"Not now," said Rolf. "You're wide-awake now."

They tried again a few nights later. "The Jews you're
hiding, where do they come from?"

I sat up groggily. "I don't know. They just come to the
door."

Rolf flung his hat to the floor. "No, no, no!" he shouted.
"'What Jews! There are no Jews!' Can't you learn?"

"I'll learn," I promised. "I'll do better."

And sure enough the next time I woke a little more completely. Half a dozen shadowy forms filled the room. "Where
do you hide the ration cards?" a voice demanded.

Under the bottom stair, of course. But this time I would
not be trapped into saying so. A crafty reply occurred to me:
"In the Frisian clock on the stairwell!"

Kik sat down beside me on the bed and put an arm
around me. "That was better, Tante Corrie," he said. "You
tried, this time. But remember—you *have* no cards except
the three for you, Opa, and Tante Betsie. There *is* no underground activity here, you don't understand what they're
talking about. . . ."

Gradually, with repeated drills, I got better. Still, when
the time actually came, when they were real Gestapo agents
really trained in getting the truth from people, how would I
perform?

Willem's underground work brought him frequently to
Haarlem. There was an expression of something like despair
mingled now with the worry lines in his face. Twice soldiers
had been to the nursing home, and although he had managed
to deceive them about most of the Jews still in residence
there, one sick blind old woman had been taken away.

"Ninety-one!" Willem kept saying. "She couldn't even walk—they had to carry her to the car."

So far, Willem's position as a minister had prevented direct action against him and Tine, but he was watched, he said, more closely than ever. To provide an official reason for his visits to Haarlem he started conducting a weekly prayer fellowship at the Beje each Wednesday morning.

But Willem could do nothing routinely—especially pray —and soon the meeting was attended by dozens of Haarlemers hungry for something to believe in, this fourth year of the occupation. Most of those coming to the services had no idea of the double life of the Beje. In a way they posed a fresh danger as they passed workers and couriers from other underground groups coming and going on the narrow stairs. But in another way, we thought, it might be an advantage to have these flocks of obviously innocent people in and out. That, at least, was our hope.

We were sitting around the supper table after curfew one night, three ten Booms, the seven "permanent guests," and two Jews for whom we were seeking homes, when the shop doorbell chimed.

A customer after closing? And one bold enough to stand on the Barteljorisstraat after curfew? Taking the keys from my pocket I hurried down to the hall, unlocked the workshop door, and felt my way through the dark store. At the front door I listened a moment.

"Who's there?" I called.

"Do you remember me?"

A man's voice speaking German. "Who is it?" I asked in the same language.

"An old friend, come for a visit. Open the door!"

I fumbled with the lock and drew the door gingerly back. It was a German soldier in uniform. Before I could reach the alarm button behind the door, he had pushed his way inside. Then he took off his hat and in the October twilight I recognized the young German watchmaker whom Father had discharged four years ago.

"Otto!" I cried.

"Captain Altschuler," he corrected me. "Our positions are slightly reversed, Miss ten Boom, are they not?"

I glanced at his insignia. He was not a captain or anything

close to it, but I said nothing. He looked around the shop.

"Same stuffy little place," he said. He reached for the wall switch, but I put my hand over it.

"No ! We don't have blackout shades in the shop!"

"Well, let's go upstairs where we can talk over old times. That old clock cleaner still around?"

"Christoffels? He died in the fuel shortage last winter."

Otto shrugged. "Good riddance then! What about the pious old Bible reader?"

I was edging my way to the sales counter where another bell was located. "Father is very well, thank you."

"Well, aren't you going to invite me up to pay my respects?"

Why was he so eager to go upstairs? Had the wretched fellow come just to gloat, or did he suspect something? My finger found the button.

"What was that!" Otto whirled around suspiciously.

"What was what?"

"That sound! I heard a kind of buzzing."

"I didn't hear anything."

But Otto had started back through the workshop.

"Wait!" I shouted. "Let me get the front door locked and I'll go up with you! I—I want to see how long it takes them to recognize you."

I dawdled at the door as long as I dared: definitely his suspicions were aroused. Then I followed him through the rear door into the hall. Not a sound from the dining room or the stairs. I dashed past him up the steps and rapped on the door.

"Father! Betsie!" I cried in what I hoped was a playful voice. "I'll give you three—no, uh—six guesses who's standing here!"

"No guessing games!" Otto reached past me and flung open the door.

Father and Betsie looked up from their meal. The table was set for three, my unfinished plate on the other side. It was so perfect that even I, who had just seen twelve people eating here, could scarcely believe this was anything but an innocent old man dining with his daughters. The "Alpina" sign stood on the sideboard: they had remembered everything.

Uninvited, Otto pulled out a chair. "Well!" he crowed.

"Things happened just like I said, didn't they?"

"So it would seem," said Father mildly.

"Betsie," I said, "give Captain Altschuler some tea!"

Otto took a sip of the brew Betsie poured him and glared round the table at us. "Where did you get real tea! No one else in Holland has tea."

How stupid of me. The tea had come from Pickwick.

"If you must know," I said, "it comes from a German officer. But you mustn't ask any further questions. I tried to imply clandestine dealings with a high occupation official.

Otto lingered another fifteen minutes. And then, feeling perhaps that he had underlined his victory sufficiently, sauntered out into the empty streets.

It was only after another half-hour that we dared give the all clear to nine cramped and shaky people.

The second week in October, during a particularly hectic morning with underground problems, the secret telephone number rang downstairs in the hall. I hurried down to pick it up; only Father, Betsie, or I ever answered it.

"Well!" said a voice. "Aren't you coming to pick me up?"

It was Nollie.

"Nollie! When—How—Where are you?"

"At the train station in Amsterdam! Only I have no money for the trainfare."

"Stay right there! Oh, Nollie, we're coming!"

I biked to Bos en Hoven Straat and then with Flip and the children who happened to be at home, hurried to the Haarlem station. We saw Nollie even before our train came to a stop in Amsterdam—her bright blue sweater like a patch of blue sky in the big dark shed.

Seven weeks in prison had left her pallid-faced, but as radiantly Nollie as ever. A prison doctor, she said, had pronounced her low blood pressure a serious condition, one that might leave her permanently disabled and her six children a burden to society. Her face wrinkled in puzzlement as she said it.

Christmas, 1943, was approaching. The light snow which had fallen was the only festive quality of the season. Every family it seemed had someone in jail, in a work camp, or in hiding. For once the religious side of the holidays was uppermost in every mind.

At the Beje, we had not only Christmas to celebrate but also Hanukkah, the Jewish "Festival of Lights." Betsie found a Hanukkah candlestand among the treasures stored with us behind the dining room cupboard and set it up on the upright piano. Each night we lighted one more candle as Eusie read the story of the Maccabees. Then we would sing, haunting, melancholy desert music. We were all very Jewish those evenings.

About the fifth night of the Festival, as we were gathered round the piano, the doorbell in the alley rang. I opened it to find Mrs. Beukers, wife of the optician next door, standing in the snow. Mrs. Beukers was as round and placid as her husband was thin and worried, but tonight her plump face was twisted with anxiety.

"Do you think," she whispered, "your Jews could sing a little more softly? We can hear them right through the walls and—well, there are all kinds of people on this street. . . ."

Back in Tante Jans's rooms we considered this news in consternation. If the Beukers family knew all about our affairs, how many other people in Haarlem did too?

It wasn't long before we discovered that one who did was the chief of police himself. One dark January morning when it was trying to snow again, Toos burst into underground "headquarters" in Tante's Jans's rear room clutching a letter in her hand. The envelope bore the seal of the Haarlem police.

I tore it open. Inside, on the police chief's stationery, was a handwritten note. I read it silently, then aloud.

"You will come to my office this afternoon at three o'clock."

For twenty minutes we tried to analyze that note. Some felt it was not a prelude to arrest. Why would the police give you a chance to escape? Still, it was safest to prepare for search and imprisonment. Workers slipped out of the house, one at a time. Boarders emptied wastebaskets and picked up scraps of sewing in preparation for a quick flight to the secret room. I burned incriminating papers in the long-empty coal hearth in the dining room. The cat caught the tension in the air and sulked beneath the sideboard.

Then I took a bath, perhaps the last for months, and

packed a prison bag according to what Nollie and others had learned: a Bible, a pencil, needle and thread, soap—or what we called soap these days—toothbrush, and comb. I dressed in my warmest clothes with several sets of underwear and a second sweater beneath the top one. Just before 3:00 I hugged Father and Betsie tight, and walked through the gray slush to the Smedestraat.

The policeman on duty was an old acquaintance. He looked at the letter, then at me with a curious expression. "This way," he said.

He knocked at a door marked "Chief." The man who sat behind the desk had red-gray hair combed forward over a bald spot. A radio was playing. The chief reached over and twisted the volume knob not down but up.

"Miss ten Boom," he said. "Welcome."

"How do you do, Sir."

The chief had left his desk to shut the door behind me. "Do sit down," he said. "I know all about you, you know. About your work."

"The watchmaking you mean. You're probably thinking more about my father's work than my own."

The chief smiled. "No, I mean your 'other' work."

"Ah, then you're referring to my work with retarded children? Yes. Let me tell you about that—"

"No, Miss ten Boom," the chief lowered his voice. "I am not talking about your work with retarded children. I'm talking about still another work, and I want you to know that some of us here are in sympathy."

The chief was smiling broadly now. Tentatively I smiled back. "Now, Miss ten Boom," he went on, "I have a request."

The chief sat down on the edge of his desk and looked at me steadily. He dropped his voice until it was just audible. He was, he said, working with the underground himself. But an informer in the police department was leaking information to the Gestapo. "There's no way for us to deal with this man but to kill him."

A shudder went down my spine.

"What alternative have we?" the chief went on in a whisper. "We can't arrest him—there are no prisons except those controlled by the Germans. But if he remains at large many others will die. That is why I wondered, Miss ten Boom, if in your work *you* might know of someone who could—"

"Kill him?"

"Yes."

I leaned back. Was this all a trap to trick me into admitting the existence of a group, into naming names?

"Sir," I said at last, seeing the chief's eyes flicker impatiently, "I have always believed that it was my role to save life, not destroy it. I understand your dilemma, however, and I have a suggestion. Are you a praying man?"

"Aren't we all, these days?"

"Then let us pray together now that God will reach the heart of this man so that he does not continue to betray his countrymen."

There was a long pause. Then the chief nodded. "That I would very much like to do."

And so there in the heart of the police station, with the radio blaring out the latest news of the German advance, we prayed. We prayed that this Dutchman would come to realize his worth in the sight of God and the worth of every other human being on earth.

At the end of the prayer the chief stood up. "Thank you, Miss ten Boom." He shook my hand. "Thank you again. I know now that it was wrong to ask you."

Still clutching my prison bag, I walked through the foyer and around the corner to the Beje.

Upstairs, people crowded around wanting to know everything. But I did not tell them. Not everything—I did not want Father and Betsie to know that we had been asked to kill. It would have been an unnecessary burden for them to bear.

The episode with the chief of police should have been encouraging. Apparently we had friends in high places. As a matter of fact the news had the opposite effect upon us. Here was one more illustration of how our secret was no secret at all. All of Haarlem seemed to know what we were up to.

We knew we should stop the work, but how could we? Who would keep open the network of supplies and information on which the safety of hundreds depended? If a hideaway had to be abandoned, as happened all the time, who would coordinate the move to another address? We had to go on, but we knew that disaster could not be long in coming.

As a matter of fact, it came first to Jop, the seventeen-year-old apprentice who had sought a safe home at the Beje.

Late one afternoon near the end of January, 1944, Rolf stepped stealthily into the workshop. He glanced at Jop. I nodded: Jop was party to everything that went on in the house.

"There's an underground home in Ede that is going to be raided this evening. Do you have anyone who can go?"

But I did not. Not a single courier or escort person was at the Beje this late in the day.

"I'll go," Jop said.

I opened my mouth to protest that he was inexperienced, and liable to the factory transport himself if stopped on the street. Then I thought of the unsuspecting people at Ede. We had a wardrobe of girls' scarves and dresses upstairs. . . .

"Then quickly, boy," Rolf said. "You must leave immediately." He gave Jop the details and hurried away. In a few moments Jop reappeared, making a very pretty brunette in long coat and kerchief, a fur muff hiding his hands. Did the lad have some kind of premonition? To my astonishment he turned at the door and kissed me.

Jop was supposed to be back by the 7:00 P.M. curfew. Seven came and went. Perhaps he had been delayed and would return in the morning.

We did have a visitor early the next day but it was not Jop. I knew the minute Rolf stepped through the door that bad news was weighing him down.

"It's Jop, isn't it?"

"Yes."

"What happened?"

Rolf had learned the story from the sergeant at the night desk. When Jop got to the address in Ede the Gestapo was already there. Jop had rung the bell; the door opened. Pretending to be the owner of the house, the S.D. man had invited Jop in.

"And Corrie," Rolf said, "we must face it. The Gestapo will get information out of Jop. They have already taken him to Amsterdam. How long will he be able to hold his tongue.

Once again we considered stopping the work. Once again we discovered we could not,

That night Father and Betsie and I prayed long after the others had gone to bed. We knew that in spite of daily mounting risks we had no choice but to move forward. This was evil's hour: we could not run away from it. Perhaps only when human effort had done its best and failed, would God's power alone be free to work.

CHAPTER NINE

The Raid

At the sound of someone in my room I opened my eyes painfully. It was Eusie, carrying up his bedding and night clothes to store in the secret room. Behind him came Mary and Thea with their bundles.

I shut my eyes again. It was the morning of February 28, 1944. For two days I had been in bed with influenza. My head throbbed, my joints were on fire. Every little sound, Mary's wheeze, the scrape of the secret panel, made me want to shriek. I heard Henk and Meta come in, then Eusie's laugh as he handed the day things out to the others through the low door.

Go away all of you! Leave me alone! I bit my lip to keep from saying it.

At last they collected their clothes and belongings and trooped out, closing the door behind them. Where was Leendert? Why hadn't he come up? Then I remembered that Leendert was away for a few days setting up electrical warning systems like ours in several of our host homes. I drifted back into a feverish sleep.

The next thing I knew, Betsie was standing at the foot of the bed, a steaming cup of herb tea in her hand. "I'm sorry to wake you, Corrie. But there's a man down in the shop who insists he will talk only to you."

"Who is he?"

"He says he's from Ermelo. I've never seen him before."

I sat up shakily. "That's all right. I have to get up anyway. Tomorrow the new ration cards come."

I sipped the scalding tea, then struggled to my feet. There by the bed lay my prison bag, packed and ready as it had been since the summons from the chief of police. In fact I'd been adding to it. Besides the Bible, clothing, and toilet things, it now held vitamins, aspirins, iron pills for Betsie's anemia and much else. It had become a kind of talisman for me, a safeguard against the terrors of prison.

I got slowly into my clothes and stepped out onto the landing. The house seemed to reel around me. I crept down, clinging to the handrail. At the door to Tante Jans's rooms I was surprised to hear voices. I looked in. Of course, I'd forgotten. It was Wednesday morning, people were gathering for Willem's weekly service. I saw Nollie passing around "occupation coffee" as we called the current brew of roots and dried figs. Peter was already at the piano, as he was most weeks to provide the music. I continued down around the stairs, passing new arrivals streaming up.

As I arrived, wobble-kneed, in the shop, a small sandy-haired man sprang forward to meet me. "Miss ten Boom!"

"Yes?" There was an old Dutch expression: you can tell a man by the way he meets your eyes. This man seemed to concentrate somewhere between my nose and my chin. "Is it about a watch?" I asked.

"No, Miss ten Boom, something far more serious!" His eyes seemed to make a circle around my face. "My wife has just been arrested. We've been hiding Jews, you see. If she is questioned, all of our lives are in danger."

"I don't know how _I_ can help," I said.

"I need six hundred guilders. There's a policeman at the station in Ermelo who can be bribed for that amount. I'm a poor man—and I've been told you have certain contacts."

"Contacts?"

"Miss ten Boom! It's a matter of life and death! If I don't get it right away she'll be taken to Amsterdam and then it will be too late."

Something about the man's behavior made me hesitate. And yet how could I risk being wrong? "Come back in half an hour. I'll have the money," I said.

For the first time the man's eyes met mine.

"I'll never forget this," he said.

The amount was more than we had at the Beje so I sent Toos to the bank with instructions to hand the man the money, but not to volunteer any information.

Then I struggled back up the stairs. Where ten minutes earlier I'd been burning with fever, now I was shaking with cold. I stopped at Tante Jans's rooms just long enough to take a briefcase of papers from the desk. Then with apologies to Willem and the others I continued to my room. I undressed again, refilled the vaporizer where it was hissing on its small spirit-stove, and climbed back·into bed. For a while I tried to concentrate on the names and addresses in the briefcase. Five cards needed this month in Zandvoort. None in Overveen. We would need eighteen in. . . . The flu roared behind my eyes, the papers swam in front of me. The briefcase slipped from my hand and I was asleep.

In my fevered dream a buzzer kept ringing. On and on it went. Why wouldn't it stop? Feet were running, voices whispering, "Hurry! Hurry!"

I sat bolt upright. People were running past my bed. I turned just in time to see Thea's heels disappear through the low door. Meta was behind her, then Henk.

But—I hadn't planned a drill for today! Who in the world—unless—unless it wasn't a drill. Eusie dashed past me, white-faced, his pipe rattling in the ashtray that he carried in shaking hands.

And at last it penetrated my numbed brain that the emergency had come. One, two, three people already in the secret room; four as Eusie's black shoes and scarlet socks disappeared. But Mary—where was Mary? The old woman appeared in the bedroom door, mouth open, gasping for air. I sprang from my bed and half-pulled, half-shoved her across the room.

I was sliding the secret panel down behind her when a slim white-haired man burst into the room. I recognized him from Pickwick's, someone high in the national Resistance. I'd no idea he was in the house. He dived after Mary. Five, six. Yes, that was right with Leendert away.

The man's legs vanished and I dropped the panel down and leapt back into bed. Below I heard doors slamming, heavy footsteps on the stairs. But it was another sound that turned my blood to water: the strangling, grating rasp of Mary's breathing.

"Lord Jesus!" I prayed. "You have the power to heal! Heal Mary now!"

And then my eye fell on the briefcase, stuffed with names and addresses. I snatched it up, yanked up the sliding door again, flung the case inside, shoved the door down and pushed my prison bag up against it. I had just reached the bed again when the bedroom door flew open.

"What's your name?"

I sat up slowly and—I hoped—sleepily.

"What?"

"Your name!"

"Cornelia ten Boom." The man was tall and heavy-set with a strange, pale face. He wore an ordinary blue business suit. He turned and shouted down the stairs, "We've got one more up here, Willemse."

He turned back to me. "Get up! Get dressed!"

As I crawled out from under the covers, the man took a slip of paper from his pocket and consulted it. "So you're the ring leader!" He looked at me with new interest. "Tell me now, where are you hiding the Jews?"

"I don't know what you're talking about."

The man laughed. "And you don't know anything about and underground ring, either. We'll see about that!"

He had not taken his eyes off me, so I began to pull on my clothes over my pajamas, ears straining for a sound from the secret room.

"Let me see your papers!"

I pulled out the little sack that I wore around my neck. When I took out my identification folder, a roll of bills fell out with it. The man stooped, snatched up the money from the floor, and stuffed it into his pocket. Then he took my papers and looked at them. For a moment the room was silent. Mary Itallie's wheeze—why wasn't I hearing it?

The man threw the papers back at me. "Hurry up!"

But he was not in half the hurry I was to get away from that room. I buttoned my sweater all wrong in my haste and stuffed my feet into my shoes without bothering to tie them. Then I was about to reach for my prison bag.

Wait.

It stood where I had shoved it in my panic: directly in front of the secret panel. If I were to reach down under the shelf to get it now, with this man watching my every move, might not his attention be attracted to the last place on earth I wanted him to look?

It was the hardest thing I had ever done to turn and walk out of that room, leaving the bag behind.

I stumbled down the stairs, my knees shaking as much

from fear as from flu. A uniformed soldier was stationed in front of Tante Jans's rooms; the door was shut. I wondered if the prayer meeting had ended, if Willem and Nollie and Peter had got away. Or were they all still in there? How many innocent people might be involved?

The man behind me gave me a little push and I hurried on down the stairs to the dining room. Father, Betsie, and Toos were sitting on chairs pulled back against the wall. Beside them sat three underground workers who must have arrived since I had gone upstairs. On the floor beneath the window, broken in three pieces, lay the "Alpina" sign. Someone had managed to knock it from the sill.

A second Gestapo agent in plain clothes was pawing eagerly through a pile of silver rijksdaalders and jewelry heaped on the dining room table. It was the cache from the space behind the corner cupboard: it had been indeed the first place they looked.

"Here's the other one listed at the address," said the man who had brought me down. "My information says she's the leader of the whole outfit."

The man at the table, the one called Willemse, glanced at me, then turned back to the loot in front of him. "You know what to do, Kapteyn."

Kapteyn seized me by the elbow and shoved me ahead of him down the remaining five steps and into the rear of the shop. Another soldier in uniform stood guard just inside this door. Kapteyn prodded me through to the front room and pushed me against the wall.

"Where are the Jews?"

"There aren't any Jews here."

The man struck me hard across the face.

"Where do you hide the ration cards?"

"I don't know what you're—"

Kapteyn hit me again. I staggered up against the astronomical clock. Before I could recover he slapped me again, then again, and again, stinging blows that jerked my head backward.

"Where are the Jews?"

Another blow.

"Where is your secret room?"

I tasted blood in my mouth. My head spun, my ears rang

—I was losing consciousness. "Lord Jesus," I cried out, "protect me!"

Kapteyn's hand stopped in midair.

"If you say that name again I'll kill you!"

But instead his arm slowly dropped to his side. "If you won't talk, the skinny one will."

I stumbled ahead of him up the stairs. He pushed me into one of the chairs against the dining room wall. Through a blur I saw him lead Betsie from the room.

Above us hammer blows and splintering wood showed where a squad of trained searchers was probing for the secret room. Then down in the alley the doorbell rang. But the sign! Didn't they see the "Alpina" sign was gone and— I glanced at the window and caught my breath. There on the sill, the broken pieces fitted carefully together, sat the wooden triangle.

Too late I looked up to see Willemse staring intently at me. "I thought so!" he said. "It was a signal, wasn't it?"

He ran down the stairs. Above us the hammering and the tramp of boots had stopped. I heard the alley door open and Willemse's voice, smooth and ingratiating.

"Come in, won't you?"

"Have you heard!" A woman's voice. "They've got Oom Herman!"

Pickwick? Not Pickwick!

"Oh?" I heard Willemse say. "Who was with him?" He pumped her as hard as he could, then placed her under arrest. Blinking with fright and confusion, the woman was seated with us along the wall. I recognized her only as a person who occasionally took messages for us about the city. I stared in anguish at the sign in the window announcing to the world that all was as usual at the Beje. Our home had been turned into a trap: how many more would fall into it before this day was over? And Pickwick! Had they really caught Pickwick!

Kapteyn appeared with Betsie in the dining room door. Her lips were swollen and puffy, a bruise was darkening on her cheek. She half fell into the chair next to mine.

"Oh Betsie! He hurt you!"

"Yes." She dabbed at the blood on her mouth. "I feel so sorry for him."

Kapteyn whirled, his white face even paler. "Prisoners

will remain silent!" he shrieked. Two men were clumping
down the stairs and into the dining room carrying something
between them. They had discovered the old radio beneath
the stairs.

"Law-abiding citizens, are you?" Kapteyn went on.
"You! The old man there. I see you believe in the Bible."
He jerked his thumb at the well-worn book on its shelf.
"Tell me, what does it say in there about obeying the
government?"

" 'Fear God,' " Father quoted, and on his lips in that room
the words came as blessing and reassurance ." 'Fear God
and honor the Queen.' "

Kapteyn stared at him. "It doesn't say that. The Bible
doesn't say that."

"No," Father admitted. "It says, 'Fear God, honor the
King.' But in our case, that is the Queen."

"It's not King or Queen!" roared Kapteyn. "We're the
legal government now, and you're all lawbreakers!"

The doorbell rang again. Again there were the questions
and the arrest. The young man—one of our workers—had
barely been assigned a chair when again the bell sounded.
It seemed to me that we had never had so many callers: the
dining room was getting crowded. I felt sorriest for those
who had come simply on social visits. An elderly retired
missionary was brought in, jaw quivering with fear. At least,
from the banging and thumping above, they had not yet
discovered the secret room.

A new sound made me jump. The phone down in the hall
was ringing.

"That's a telephone!" cried Willemse.

He glared around the room, then grabbing me by the
wrist yanked me down the stairs behind him. He thrust the
receiver up against my ear but kept his own hand on it.

"Answer!" he said with his lips.

"This is the ten Boom residence and shop," I said as
stiffly as I dared.

But the person on the other end did not catch the strange-
ness. "Miss ten Boom, you're in terrible danger! They've
arrested Herman Sluring! They know everything! You've
got to be careful!" On and on the woman's voice babbled,
the man at my side hearing everything.

She had scarcely hung up when the phone rang again. A

man's voice, and again the message. "Oom Herman's been taken to the police station. That means they're on to everything. . . ."

At last, the third time I repeated my formal and untypical little greeting, there was a click at the other end. Willemse snatched the earpiece from my hand.

"Hello! Hello!" he shouted. He jiggled the cradle on the wall. The line had gone dead. He shoved me back up the stairs and into my chair again. "Our friends wised up," he told Kapteyn. "But I heard enough."

Apparently Betsie had received permission to leave her chair: she was slicing bread at the sideboard. I was surprised to realize it was already lunchtime. Betsie passed the bread around the room but I shook my head. The fever was raging again. My throat ached and my head throbbed.

A man appeared in the doorway. "We've searched the whole place, Willemse," he said. "If there's a secret room here, the devil himself built it."

Willemse looked from Betsie to Father to me. "There's a secret room," he said quietly. "And people are using it or they would have admitted it. All right. We'll set a guard around the house till they've turned to mummies."

In the hush of horror which followed there was a gentle pressure on my knees. Maher Shalal Hashbaz had jumped up into my lap to rub against me. I stroked the shining black fur. What would become of him now? I would not let myself think about the six people upstairs.

It had been half an hour since the doorbell had last rung. Whoever had caught my message over the phone must have spread the alarm. Word was out: no one else would walk into the trap at the Beje.

Apparently Willemse had come to the same conclusion because abruptly he ordered us on our feet and down to the hallway with our coats and hats. Father, Betsie, and me he held in the dining room till last. In front of us down the stairs came the people from Tante Jans's rooms. I held my breath scanning them. Apparently most of those at the prayer service had left before the raid. But by no means all. Here came Nollie, behind her, Peter. Last in the line came Willem.

The whole family then. Father, all four of his children, one grandchild. Kapteyn gave me a shove.

"Get moving."

Father took his tall hat from the wall peg. Outside the dining room door he paused to pull up the weights on the old Frisian clock.

"We mustn't let the clock run down," he said.

Father! Did you really think we would be back home when next the chain ran out?

The snow had gone from the streets; puddles of dirty water stood in the gutters as we marched through the alley and into the Smedestraat. The walk took only a minute, but by the time we got inside the double doors of the police station I was shaking with cold. I looked anxiously around the foyer for Rolf and the others we knew, but saw no one. A contingent of German soldiers seemed to be supplementing the regular police force.

We were herded along a corridor and through the heavy metal door where I had last seen Harry de Vries. At the end of this hall was a large room that had obviously been a gymnasium. Windows high in the walls were covered with wire mesh; rings and basketball hoops were roped to the ceiling. Now a desk stood in the center of the room with a German officer seated behind it. Tumbling mats had been spread out to cover part of the floor and I collapsed onto one of them.

For two hours the officer took down names, addresses, and other statistics. I counted those who had been arrested with us: thirty-five people from the raid on the Beje.

People from previous arrests were sitting or lying about on the mats too, some of them faces we knew. I looked for Pickwick but he was not among them. One of them, a fellow watchmaker who often came to the Beje on business, seemed especially distressed at what had happened to us. He came and sat down beside Father and me.

At last the officer left. For the first time since the alarm buzzer sounded we could talk among ourselves. I struggled to sit up. "Quick!" I croaked. "We've got to agree on what to say! Most of us can simply tell the truth but—" My voice died in my throat. It seemed to my flu-addled brain that Peter was giving me the most ferocious frown I had ever seen.

"But if they learn that Uncle Willem was teaching this morning from the Old Testament, it could make trouble for him," Peter finished for me.

He jerked his head to one side and I clambered unsteadily to my feet. "Tante Corrie!" he hissed when we were on the other side of the room. "That man, the watchmaker! He's a Gestapo plant." He patted my head as though I were a sick child. "Lie down again, Tante Corrie. Just for heaven's sake don't do any talking."

I was waked by the heavy door of the gym slamming open. In strode Rolf.

"Let's have it quiet in here!" he shouted. He leaned close to Willem and said something I could not hear. "Toilets are out back," he continued in a loud voice. "You can go one at a time under escort."

Willem sat down beside me. "He says we can flush incriminating documents if we shred them fine enough." I fumbled through my coat pockets. There were several scraps of paper and a billfold containing a few paper rijksdaalders. I went over each item, trying to think how I could explain it in a court process. Beside the row of outdoor toilets was a basin with a tin cup on a chain. Gratefully I took a long drink—the first since the tea Betsie had brought me that morning.

Towards evening a policeman carried into the gym a large basket of fresh hot rolls. I could not swallow mine. Only the water tasted good to me, though I grew embarrassed at asking again and again to be taken outside.

When I got back the last time, a group had gathered around Father for evening prayers. Every day of my life had ended like this: that deep steady voice, that sure and eager confiding of us all to the care of God. The Bible lay at home on its shelf, but much of it was stored in his heart. His blue eyes seemed to be seeing beyond the locked and crowded room, beyond Haarlem, beyond earth itself, as he quoted from memory: "Thou art my hiding place and my shield: I hope in thy word. . . . Hold thou me up, and I shall be safe. . . ."

None of us slept much. Each time someone left the room he had to step over a dozen others. At last light crept through the high, screened windows at the top of the room. The police again brought rolls. As the long morning wore on I dozed with my back up against the wall; the worst pain now seemed to be in my chest. It was noon when soldiers entered the room and ordered us on our feet. Hastily we struggled into our coats and filed again through the cold corridors.

In the Smedestraat a wall of people pressed against police barricades set across the street. As Betsie and I stepped out with Father between us, a murmur of horror greeted the sight of "Haarlem's Grand Old Man" being led to prison. In front of the door stood a green city bus with soldiers occupying the rear seats. People were climbing aboard while friends and relatives in the crowd wept or simply stared. Betsie and I gripped Father's arms to start down the steps. Then we froze. Stumbling past us between two soldiers, hatless and coatless, came Pickwick. The top of his bald head was a welter of bruises, dried blood clung to the stubble on his chin. He did not look up as he was hauled onto the bus.

Father, Betsie, and I squeezed into a double seat near the front. Through the window I caught a glimpse of Tine standing in the crowd. It was one of those radiant winter days when the air seemed to shimmer with light. The bus shuddered and started up. Police cleared a path and we inched forward. I gazed hungrily out the window, holding onto Haarlem with my eyes. Now we were crossing the Grote Markt, the walls of the great cathedral glowing a thousand shades of gray in the crystal light. In a strange way it seemed to me that I had lived through this moment before.

Then I recalled.

The vision. The night of the invasion. I had seen it all. Willem, Nollie, Pickwick, Peter—all of us here—drawn against our wills across this square. It had all been in the dream—all of us leaving Haarlem, unable to turn back. Going where?

CHAPTER TEN

Scheveningen

Outside Haarlem the bus took the south road, paralleling the sea. On our right rose the low sandy hills of the dune country, soldiers silhouetted on the ridges. Clearly we were not being taken to Amsterdam.

A two-hour drive brought us instead into the streets of The Hague. The bus stopped in front of a new, functional building; word was whispered back that this was Gestapo headquarters for all of Holland. We were marched—all but Pickwick, who seemed unable to rise out of his seat—into a large room where the endless process of taking down names, addresses, and occupations began all over again.

On the other side of the high counter running the length of the room I was startled to see both Willemse and Kapteyn. As each of the prisoners from Haarlem reached the desk, one or the other would lean forward and speak to a man seated at a typewriter and there would be a clatter of sound from the machine.

Suddenly the chief interrogator's eye fell on Father. "That old man!" he cried. "Did he have to be arrested? You, old man!"

Willem led Father up to the desk. The Gestapo chief leaned forward. "I'd like to send you home, old fellow," he said. "I'll take your word that you won't cause any more trouble."

I could not see Father's face, only the erect carriage of his shoulders and the halo of white hair above them. But I heard his answer.

"If I go home today," he said evenly and clearly, "tomorrow I will open my door again to any man in need who knocks."

The amiability drained from the other man's face. "Get

back in line!" he shouted. "*Schnell!* This court will tolerate no more delays!"

But delays seemed all that this court existed for. As we inched along the counter there were endless repetitions of questions, endless consulting of papers, endless coming and going of officials. Outside the windows the short winter day was fading. We had not eaten since the rolls and water at dawn.

Ahead of me in line, Betsie answered, "Unmarried," for the twentieth time that day.

"Number of children?" droned the interrogator.

"I'm unmarried," Betsie repeated.

The man did not even look up from his papers. "Number of children?" he snapped.

"No children," said Betsie resignedly.

Toward nightfall a stout little man wearing the yellow star was led past us to the far end of the room. A sound of scuffling made us all look up. The wretched man was attempting to hold onto something clutched in his hands.

"It's mine!" he kept shouting. "You can't take it! You can't take my purse!"

What madness possessed him? What good did he imagine money would do him now? But he continued to struggle, to the obvious glee of the men around him.

"Here Jew!" I heard one of them say. He lifted his booted foot and kicked the small man in the back of his knees. "This is how we take things from a Jew."

It made so much noise. That was all I could think as they continued to kick him. I clutched the counter to keep from falling myself as the sounds continued. Wildly, unreasonably, I hated the man being kicked, hated him for being so helpless and so hurt. At last I heard them drag him out.

Then all at once I was standing in front of the chief questioner. I looked up and met Kapteyn's eyes, just behind him.

"This woman was the ringleader," he said.

Through the turmoil inside me I realized it was important for the other man to believe him. "What Mr. Kapteyn says is true," I said. "These others—they know nothing about it. It was all my—"

"Name?" the interrogator inquired imperturbably.

"Cornelia ten Boom, and I'm the—"

"Age?"

"Fifty-two. The rest of these people had nothing to do—"

"Occupation?"

"But I've told you a dozen times!" I burst out in desperation.

"Occupation?" he repeated.

It was dark night when we were marched at last out of the building. The green bus was gone. Instead we made out the bulk of a large canvas-roofed army truck. Two soldiers had to lift Father over the tailgate. There was no sign of Pickwick. Father, Betsie, and I found places to sit on a narrow bench that ran around the sides.

The truck had no springs and bounced roughly over the bomb-pitted streets of The Hague. I slipped my arm behind Father's back to keep him from striking the edge. Willem, standing near the back, whispered back what he could see of the blacked-out city. We had left the downtown section and seemed to be headed west toward the suburb of Scheveningen. That was our destination then, the federal penitentiary named after this seaside town.

The truck jerked to a halt; we heard a screech of iron. We bumped forward a few feet and stopped again. Behind us massive gates clanged shut.

We climbed down to find ourselves in an enormous courtyard surrounded by a high brick wall. The truck had backed up to a long low building; soldiers prodded us inside. I blinked in the white glare of bright ceiling lights.

"Nasen gegen Mauer!"—"Noses to the wall!"

I felt a shove from behind and found myself staring at cracked plaster. I turned my eyes as far as I could, first left and then right. There was Willem. Two places away from him, Betsie. Next to me on the other side was Toos. All like me standing with their faces to the wall. Where was Father?

There was an endless wait while the scars on the wall before my eyes became faces, landscapes, animal shapes. Then somewhere to the right a door opened.

"Women prisoners follow me!"

The matron's voice sounded as metallic as the squealing door. As I stepped away from the wall I glanced swiftly round the room for Father. There he was—a few feet out from the wall, seated in a straight-backed chair. One of the guards must have brought it for him.

Already the matron was starting down the long corridor

that I could see through the door. But I hung back, gazing desperately at Father, Willem, Peter, all our brave underground workers.

"Father!" I cried suddenly. "God be with you!"

His head turned toward me. The harsh overhead light flashed from his glasses.

"And with you, my daughters," he said.

I turned and followed the others. Behind me the door slammed closed. And with you! And with you! Oh Father, when will I see you next?

Betsie's hand slipped around mine. A strip of coconut-palm matting ran down the center of the wide hall. We stepped onto it off the damp concrete.

"Prisoners walk to the side." It was the bored voice of the guard behind us. "Prisoners must not step on the matting."

Guiltily we stepped off the privileged path.

Ahead of us in the corridor was a desk, behind it a woman in uniform. As each prisoner reached this point she gave her name for the thousandth time that day and placed on the desk whatever she was wearing of value. Nollie, Betsie, and I unstrapped our beautiful wristwatches. As I handed mine to the officer, she pointed to the simple gold ring that had belonged to Mama. I wriggled it from my finger and laid it on the desk along with my wallet and paper guilders.

The procession down the corridor continued. The walls on both sides of us were lined with narrow metal doors. Now the column of women halted: the matron was fitting a key into one of them. We heard the thud of a bolt drawn back, the screech of hinges. The matron consulted a list in her hand, then called the name of a lady I didn't even know, one of those who had been at Willem's prayer meeting.

Was it possible that that had been only yesterday? Was this only Thursday night? Already the events at the Beje seemed part of another lifetime. The door banged shut; the column moved on. Another door unlocked, another human being closed behind it. No two from Haarlem in the same cell.

Among the very first names read from the list was Betsie's. She stepped through the door; before she could turn or say goodbye, it had closed. Two cells farther on, Nollie left me. The clang of those two doors rang in my ears as the slow march continued.

Now the corridor branched and we turned left. Then

right, then left again, an endless world of steel and concrete.
"Ten Boom, Cornelia."

Another door rasped open. The cell was deep and narrow, scarcely wider than the door. A woman lay on the single cot, three others on straw ticks on the floor. "Give this one the cot," the matron said. "She's sick."

And indeed, even as the door slammed behind me a spasm of coughing seized my chest and throat.

"We don't want a sick woman in here!" someone shouted. They were stumbling to their feet, backing as far from me as the narrow cubicle would allow.

"I'm . . . I'm so very sorry—" I began, but another voice interrupted me.

"Don't be. It isn't your fault. Come on, Frau Mikes, give her the cot." The young woman turned to me. "Let me hang up your hat and coat."

Gratefully I handed her my hat, which she added to a row of clothes hanging from hooks along one wall. But I kept my coat wrapped tight around me. The cot had been vacated and I moved shakily toward it, trying not to sneeze or breathe as I squeezed past my cellmates. I sank down on the narrow bed, then went into a fresh paroxysm of coughs as a cloud of choking black dust rose from the filthy straw mattress. At last the attack passed and I lay down. The sour straw smell filled my nostrils. I felt each slat of wood through the thin pallet.

"I will never be able to sleep on such a bed," I thought, and the next thing I knew it was morning and there was a clattering at the door. "Food call," my cellmates told me. I struggled to my feet. A square of metal had dropped open in the door, forming a small shelf. Onto this someone in the hall was placing tin plates filled with a steaming gruel.

"There's a new one here!" the woman called Frau Mikes called through the aperture. "We get five portions!" Another tin plate was slammed onto the shelf. "If you're not hungry," Frau Mikes added, "I'll help you with it."

I picked up my plate, stared at the watery gray porridge and handed it silently to her. In a little while the plates were collected and the pass-through in the door slammed shut.

Later in the morning a key grated in the lock, the bolt banged, and the door opened long enough for the sanitary bucket to be passed out. The wash basin was also emptied and returned with clean water. The women picked up their straw pallets from the floor and piled them in a corner, raising a fresh storm of dust which started me coughing helplessly again.

Then a prison boredom—which I soon learned to fear above all else—settled over the cell. At first I attempted to relieve it by talking with the others, but though they were as courteous as people can be who are living literally on top of one another, they turned aside my questions and I never learned much about them.

The young woman who had spoken kindly to me the night before, I did discover, was a baroness, only seventeen years old. This young girl paced constantly, from morning until the overhead light bulb went off at night, six steps to the door, six steps back, dodging those sitting on the floor, back and forth like an animal in a cage.

Frau Mikes turned out to be an Austrian woman who had worked as a charwoman in an office building. She often cried for her canary. "Poor little thing! What will become of him! They'll never think to feed him."

This would start me thinking of our cat. Had Maher Shalal Hashbaz made his escape into the street—or was he starving inside the sealed house? I would picture him prowling among the chairlegs in the dining room, missing the shoulders he loved to walk on. I tried not to let my mind venture higher in the house, not to let it climb the stairs to see if Thea, Mary, Eusie—no! I could do nothing for them here in this cell. God knew they were there.

One of my cellmates had spent three years here in Scheveningen. She could hear the rattle of the meal cart long before the rest of us and tell by the footstep who was passing in the corridor. "That's the trusty from medical supply. Someone's sick." . . . "This is the fourth time someone in 316 has gone for a hearing."

Her world consisted of this cubicle and the corridor outside—and soon I began to see the wisdom of this narrowed vision, and why prisoners instinctively shied away from questions about their larger lives. For the first days of my imprisonment I stayed in a frenzy of anxiety about Father, Betsie, Willem, Pickwick. Was Father able to eat this food? Was Betsie's blanket as thin as this one?

But these thoughts led to such despair that I soon learned not to give in to them. In an effort to fix my mind on something I asked Frau Mikes to teach me the card game that she played hour after hour. She had made the cards herself with the squares of toilet paper that were issued two a day to each prisoner; all day she sat on a corner of the cot endlessly laying them out in front of her and gathering them up again.

I was a slow learner, since no cards of any kind had been played at the Beje. Now as I began to grasp the solitaire game I wondered what Father's resistance to them had been — surely nothing could be more innocent than this succession of shapes called clubs, spades, diamonds. . . .

But as the days passed I began to discover a subtle danger. When the cards went well my spirits rose. It was an omen: someone from Haarlem had been released! But if I lost. . . . Maybe someone was ill. The people in the secret room had been found. . . .

At last I had to stop playing. In any case I was finding it hard to sit up so long. Increasingly I was spending the days as I did the nights, tossing on the thin straw pallet trying in vain to find a position in which all aches at once were eased. My head throbbed continually, pain shot up and down my arms, my cough brought up blood.

I was thrashing feverishly on the cot one morning when the cell door opened and there stood the steel-voiced matron I had seen the night I entered the cell two weeks before.

"Ten Boom, Cornelia."

I struggled to my feet.

"Bring your hat and your coat and come with me."

I looked around at the others for a hint as to what was happening. "You're going to the outside," our prison expert said. "When you take your hat you always go outside."

My coat I was wearing already, but I took my hat from its hook and stepped out into the corridor. The matron relocked the door then set off so rapidly that my heart hammered as I trotted after her, careful to stay off the precious matting. I stared yearningly at the locked doors on either side of us; I could not remember behind which ones my sisters had disappeared.

At last we stepped out into the broad, high-walled courtyard. Sky! For the first time in two weeks, blue sky! How high the clouds were, how inexpressibly white and clean. I remembered suddenly how much sky had meant to Mama.

"Quick!" snapped the matron.

I hurried to the shiny black automobile beside which she was standing. She opened the rear door and I got in. Two others were already in the back seat, a soldier and a woman with a gaunt gray face. In front next to the driver slumped a desperately ill-looking man whose head lolled strangely on the seat back. As the car started up the woman beside me lifted a blood-stained towel to her mouth and coughed into it. I understood: the three of us were ill. Perhaps we were going to a hospital!

The massive prison gate opened and we were in the outside world, spinning along broad city streets. I stared in wonderment through the window. People walking, looking in store windows, stopping to talk with friends. Had I truly been as free as that only two weeks ago?

The car parked before an office building; it took both the soldier and the driver to get the sick man up three flights of stairs. We entered a waiting room jammed with people and sat down under the watchful eyes of the soldier. When nearly an hour had passed I asked permission to use the lavatory. The soldier spoke to the trim white-uniformed nurse behind the reception desk.

"This way," she said crisply. She took me down a short hall, stepped into the bathroom with me and shut the door. "Quick! Is there any way I can help?"

I blinked at her. "Yes. Oh yes! A Bible! Could you get me a Bible? And—a needle and thread! And a toothbrush! And soap!"

She bit her lip doubtfully. "So many patients today—and the soldier—but I'll do what I can." And she was gone.

But her kindness shone in the little room as brightly as the gleaming white tiles and shiny faucets. My heart soared as I scrubbed the grime off my neck and face.

A man's voice at the door: "Come on! You've been in there long enough!"

Hastily I rinsed off the soap and followed the soldier back to the waiting room. The nurse was back at her desk, coolly efficient as before; she did not look up. After another long wait my name was called. The doctor asked me to cough, took my temperature and blood pressure, applied his stethoscope, and announced that I had pleurisy with effusion, pre-tubercular.

He wrote something on a sheet of paper. Then with one hand on the doorknob he laid the other for an instant on my shoulder. "I hope," he said in a low voice, "that I am doing you a favor with this diagnosis."

In the waiting room the soldier was on his feet ready for me. As I crossed the room the nurse rose briskly from her desk and swished past me. In my hand I felt a small knobby something wrapped in paper.

I slid it into my coat pocket as I followed the soldier down the stairs. The other woman was already back in the car; the sick man did not reappear. All during the return ride my hand kept straying to the object in my pocket, stroking it, tracing the outline. "Oh Lord, it's so small, but still it could be—let it be a Bible!"

The high walls loomed ahead, the gate rang shut behind us. At last, at the end of the long echoing corridors, I reached my cell and drew the package from my pocket. My cellmates crowded round me as I unwrapped the newspaper with trembling hands. Even the baroness stopped her pacing to watch.

As two bars of precious prewar soap appeared, Frau Mikes clapped her hand over her mouth to suppress her yelp of triumph. No toothbrush or needle but—unheard-of wealth—a whole packet of safety pins! And, most wonderful of all, not indeed a whole Bible, but in four small booklets, the four Gospels.

I shared the soap and pins among the five of us but, though I offered to divide the books as well, they refused. "They catch you with those," the knowledgeable one said, "and it's double sentence and *kalte kost* as well." *Kalte kost* —the bread ration alone without the daily plate of hot food —was the punishment constantly held over our heads. If we made too much noise we'd have *kalte kost*. If we were slow with the bucket it would be *kalte kost*. But even *kalte kost* would be a small price to pay, I thought as I stretched my aching body on the foul straw, for the precious books I clutched between my hands.

It was two evenings later, near the time when the light bulb usually flickered off, that the cell door banged open and a guard strode in.

"Ten Boom, Cornelia," she snapped. "Get your things."

I stared at her, an insane hope rising in me. "You mean—"

"Silence! No talking!"

It did not take long to gather my "things": my hat and an undervest that was drying after a vain attempt to get it clean in the much-used basin water. My coat with the precious contents of its pockets had never yet been off my back. Why such strict silence, I wondered. Why should I not be allowed even a goodbye to my cellmates? Would it be so very wrong for a guard to smile now and then, or give a few words of explanation?

I said farewell to the others with my eyes and followed the stiff-backed woman into the hall. She paused to lock the door, then marched off down the corridor. But—the wrong way! We were not heading toward the outside entrance at all, but deeper into the maze of prison passageways.

Still without a word she halted in front of another door and opened it with a key. I stepped inside. The door clanged behind me. The bolt slammed shut.

The cell was identical with the one I had just left, six steps long, two wide, a single cot at the back. But this one was empty. As the guard's footsteps died away down the corridor I leaned against the cold metal of the door. Alone. Alone behind these walls. . . .

I must not let my thoughts run wildly; I must be very mature and very practical. Six steps. Sit down on the cot. This one reeked even worse than the other: the straw seemed to be fermenting. I reached for the blanket: someone had been sick on it. I thrust it away but it was too late. I dashed for the bucket near the door and leaned weakly over it.

At that moment the light bulb in the ceiling went out. I groped back to the cot and huddled there in the dark, setting my teeth against the stink of the bedding, wrapping my coat tighter about me. The cell was bitter cold, wind hammered against the wall. This must be near the outside edge of the prison: the wind had never shrieked so in the other one.

What had I done to be separated from people this way? Had they discovered the conversation with the nurse at the doctor's office? Or perhaps some of the prisoners from Haarlem had been interrogated and the truth about our group was known. Maybe my sentence was solitary confinement for years and years. . . .

In the morning my fever was worse. I could not stand even long enough to get my food from the shelf in the door and after an hour or so the plate was taken away untouched.

Toward evening the pass-through dropped open again and the hunk of coarse prison bread appeared. By now I was desperate for food but less able to walk than ever. Whoever was in the hall must have seen the problem. A hand picked up the bread and hurled it toward me. It landed on the floor beside the cot where I clawed for it and gnawed it greedily.

For several days while the fever raged my supper was delivered in this manner. Mornings the door squealed open and a woman in a blue smock carried the plate of hot gruel to the cot. I was as starved for the sight of a human face as for the food and tried in a hoarse croak to start a conversation. But the woman, obviously a fellow prisoner, would only shake her head with a fearful glance toward the hall.

The door also opened once a day to let in the trusty from Medical Supply with a dose of some stinging yellow liquid from a very dirty bottle. The first time he entered the cell I clutched at his sleeve. "Please!" I rasped. "Have you seen an eighty-four-year-old man—white hair, a long beard? Casper ten Boom! You must have taken medicine to him!"

The man tugged loose. "I don't know! I don't know anything!"

The cell door slammed back against the wall, framing the guard. "Solitary prisoners are not permitted to talk! If you say another word to one of the work-duty prisoners it will be *kalte kost* for the duration of your sentence!" And the door banged behind the two of them.

This same trusty was also charged with recording my temperature each time he came. I had to take off my shirt and place the thermometer between my arm and the side of my body. It did not look to me like an accurate system: sure enough, by the end of the week an irritable voice called through the food slot, "Get up and get the food yourself! Your fever's gone—you won't be waited on again!"

I felt sure that the fever had not gone, but there was nothing for it but to creep, trembling, to the door for my plate. When I had replaced it I would lie down again on the smelly straw, steeling myself for the bawling out I knew would come. "Look at the great lady, back in bed again! Are you going to lie there all day long?" Why lying down was such a crime I could never understand. Nor indeed what one was supposed to accomplish if one got up. . . .

Thoughts, now that I was alone, were a bigger problem than ever. I could no longer even pray for family and friends by name, so great was the fear and longing wrapped round each one. "Those I love, Lord," I would say. "You know them. You see them. Oh—bless them all!"

Thoughts were enemies. That prison bag . . . how many times I opened it in my mind and pawed through all the things I had left behind. A fresh blouse. Aspirin, a whole bottle of them. Toothpaste with a kind of pepperminty taste, and—

Then I would catch myself. How ridiculous, such thoughts! If I had it to do again would I really put these little personal comforts ahead of human lives? Of course not. But in the dark nights, as the wind howled and the fever pulsed, I would draw that bag out of some dark corner of my mind and root through it once again. A towel to lay on this scratchy straw. An aspirin . . .

In only one way was this new cell an improvement over the first one. It had a window. Seven iron bars ran across it, four bars up and down. It was high in the wall, much too high to look out of, but through those twenty-eight squares I could see the sky.

All day I kept my eyes fixed on that bit of heaven. Sometimes clouds moved across the squares, white or pink or edged with gold, and when the wind was from the west I could hear the sea. Best of all, for nearly an hour each day, gradually lengthening as the spring sun rose higher, a shaft of checkered light streamed into the dark little room. As the weather turned warmer and I grew stronger I would stand up to catch the sunshine on my face and chest, moving along the wall with the moving light, climbing at last onto the cot to stand on tiptoe in the final rays.

As my health returned, I was able to use my eyes longer. I had been sustaining myself from my Scriptures a verse at a time; now like a starving man I gulped entire Gospels at a reading, seeing whole the magnificent drama of salvation.

And as I did, an incredible thought prickled the back of my neck. Was it possible that this—all of this that seemed so wasteful and so needless—this war, Scheveningen prison, this very cell, none of it was unforeseen or accidental? Could it be part of the pattern first revealed in the Gospels? Hadn't

Jesus—and here my reading became intent indeed—hadn't Jesus been defeated as utterly and unarguably as our little group and our small plans had been?

But . . . if the Gospels were truly the pattern of God's activity, then defeat was only the beginning. I would look around at the bare little cell and wonder what conceivable victory could come from a place like this.

The prison expert in the first cell had taught me to make a kind of knife by rubbing a corset stay against the rough cement floor. It seemed to me strangely important not to lose track of time. And so with a sharp-honed stay I scratched a calendar on the wall behind the cot. As each long featureless day crawled to a close, I checked off another square. I also started a record of special dates beneath the calendar:

February 28, 1944   Arrest
February 29, 1944   Transport to Scheveningen
March 16, 1944   Beginning of Solitary

And now a new date:

April 15, 1944   My Birthday in Prison

A birthday had to mean a party, but I searched in vain for a single cheerful object. At least in the other cell there had been bright bits of clothing: the baroness' red hat, Frau Mikes' yellow blouse. How I regretted now my own lack of taste in clothes.

At least I would have a song at my party! I chose one about the Bride of Haarlem tree—she would be in full bloom now. The child's song brought it all close: the bursting branches, the petals raining like snow on the brick sidewalk—

"Quiet in there!" A volley of blows sounded on my iron door. "Solitary prisoners are to keep silent!"

I sat on the cot, opened the Gospel of John, and read until the ache in my heart went away.

Two days after my birthday I was taken for the first time to the big, echoing shower room. A grim-faced guard marched beside me, her scowl forbidding me to take pleasure in the expedition. But nothing could dim the wonder of stepping into that wide corridor after so many weeks of close confinement.

At the door to the shower room several women were waiting. Even in the strict silence this human closeness was joy and strength. I scanned the faces of those coming out, but neither Betsie nor Nollie was there, nor anyone else from Haarlem. And yet, I thought, they are all my sisters. How rich is anyone who can simply see human faces!

The shower too was glorious: warm clean water over my festering skin, streams of water through my matted hair. I went back to my cell with a new resolve: the next time I was permitted a shower I would take with me three of my Gospels. Solitary was teaching me that it was not possible to be rich alone.

And I was not alone much longer: into my solitary cell came a small busy black ant. I had almost put my foot where he was one morning as I carried my bucket to the door when I realized the honor being done me. I crouched down and admired the marvelous design of legs and body. I apologized for my size and promised I would not so thoughtlessly stride about again.

After a while he disappeared through a crack in the floor. But when my evening piece of bread appeared on the door shelf, I scattered some crumbs and to my joy he popped out almost at once. He picked up a heroic piece, struggled down the hole with it and came back for more. It was the beginning of a relationship.

Now in addition to the daily visit of the sun I had the company of this brave and handsome guest—in fact soon of a whole small committee. If I was washing out clothes in the basin or sharpening the point of my homemade knife when the ants appeared, I stopped at once to give them my full attention. It would have been unthinkable to squander two activities on the same bit of time!

One evening as I was crossing another long, long day from the calendar scratched on my wall, I heard shouts far down the corridor. They were answered closer by. Now noisy voices came from every direction. How unusual for the prisoners to be making a racket! Where were the guards?

The shelf in my door had not been closed since the bread came two hours ago. I pressed my ear to it and listened but it was hard to make sense of the tumult outside. Names were being passed from cell to cell. People were singing, others pounding on their doors. The guards must all be away!

"Please! Let's be quiet!" a voice nearby pleaded. "Let's use this time before they get back!"

"What's happening?" I cried through the open slot. "Where are the guards?"

"At the party," the same voice answered me. "It's Hitler's birthday."

Then—these must be their own names people were shouting down the corridor. This was our chance to tell where we were, to get information.

"I'm Corrie ten Boom!" I called through the food shelf. "My whole family is here somewhere! Oh, has anyone seen Casper ten Boom! Betsie ten Boom! Nollie van Woerden! Willem ten Boom!" I shouted names until I was hoarse and heard them repeated from mouth to mouth down the long corridor. I passed names too, to the right and left, as we worked out a kind of system.

After a while answers began to filter back. "Mrs. van der Elst is in Cell 228. . . ." "Pietje's arm is much better. . . ." Some of the messages I could hardly bear to relay: "The hearing was very bad: he sits in the cell without speaking." "To my husband Joost: our baby died last week. . . ."

Along with personal messages were rumors about the world outside, each more wildly optimistic than the last.

"There is a revolution in Germany!"

"The Allies have invaded Europe!"

"The war cannot last three weeks longer!"

At last some of the names I had shouted out began to return. "Betsie ten Boom is in cell 312. She says to tell you that God is good."

Oh, that was Betsie! That was every inch Betsie!

Then: "Nollie van Woerden was in cell 318, but she was released more than a month ago." Released! Oh, thank God!

Toos, too, released!

News from the men's section was longer returning, but as it did my heart leapt higher and higher:

Peter van Woerden. Released!

Herman Sluring. Released!

Willem ten Boom. Released!

As far as I could discover, every single one taken in the

raid on the Beje—with the exception of Betsie and me—had been freed. Only about Father could I discover no news at all, although I called his name over and over into the murmuring hall. No one seemed to have seen him. No one seemed to know....

It was perhaps a week later that my cell door opened and a prison trusty tossed a package wrapped in brown paper onto the floor. I picked it up, hefted it, turned it over and over. The wrapping paper had been torn open and carelessly retied, but even through the disarray I could spot Nollie's loving touch. I sat on the cot and opened it.

There, familiar and welcoming as a visit from home, was the light blue embroidered sweater. As I put it on I seemed to feel Nollie's arms circling my shoulders. Also inside the package were cookies and vitamins, needle and thread, and a bright red towel. How Nollie understood the gray color-hunger of prison! She had even wrapped the cookies in gay red cellophane.

I was biting into the first one when an inspiration came to me. I dragged the cot out from the wall to stand under the naked overhead bulb. Climbing on it I fashioned a lampshade with the paper: a cheery red glow at once suffused the bleak little room.

I was rewrapping the cookies in the brown outer paper when my eyes fell on the address written in Nollie's careful hand, slanting upward toward the postage stamp. But— Nollie's handwriting did not slant.... The stamp! Hadn't a message once come to the Beje under a stamp, penciled in the tiny square beneath? Laughing at my own overwrought imagination I moistened the paper in the basin water and worked the stamp gently free.

Words! There was definitely writing there—but so tiny I had to climb again onto the cot and hold the paper close to the shaded bulb.

"All the watches in your closet are safe."

Safe. Then—then Eusie, and Henk, and Mary, and— they'd got out of the secret room! They'd escaped! They were free!

I burst into racking sobs, then heard heavy footsteps bearing down the corridor. Hastily I jumped down from the cot and shoved it back to the wall. The pass-through clattered open.

"What's the commotion in here!"

"It's nothing. I—won't do it again."

The slot in the door snapped shut. How had they managed it? How had they got past the soldiers? Never mind, dear Lord, You were there, and that was all that mattered. . . .

The cell door opened to let in a German officer followed by the head matron herself. My eyes ran hungrily over the well-pressed uniform with its rows of brilliant-colored battle ribbons.

"Miss ten Boom," the officer began in excellent Dutch, "I have a few questions I believe you can help me with."

The matron was carrying a small stool which she leapt to set down for the officer. I stared at her. Was this obsequious creature the terrible-voiced terror of the women's wing?

The officer sat down, motioning me to take the cot. There was something in that gesture that belonged to the world outside the prison. As he took out a small notebook and began to ·read names from it I was suddenly conscious of my rumpled clothes, my long, ragged fingernails.

To my relief I honestly did not know any of the names he read—now I understood the wisdom of the ubiquitous "Mr. Smit." The officer stood up. "Will you be feeling well enough to come for your hearing soon?"

Again that ordinary human manner. "Yes—I—I hope so." The officer stepped out into the hall, the matron bobbing and scurrying after him with the stool.

It was the third of May; I was sitting on my cot sewing. Since Nollie's package had been delivered I had a wonderful new occupation: one by one I was pulling the threads from the red towel and with them embroidering bright figures on the pajamas that I had only recently stopped wearing beneath my clothes. A window with ruffled curtains. A flower with an impossible number of petals and leaves. I had just started work on the head of a cat over the right pocket when the food shelf in the door banged open and shut with a single motion.

And there on the floor of the cell lay a letter.

I dropped the pajamas and sprang forward. Nollie's writing. Why should my hand tremble as I picked it up?

The letter had been opened by the censors—held by them too: the postmark was over a week old. But it was a letter, a letter from home—the very first one! Why this sudden fear?

I unfolded the paper. "Corrie, can you be very brave?" No! No, I couldn't be brave! I forced my eyes to read on. "I have news that is very hard to write you. Father survived his arrest by only ten days. He is now with the Lord. . . ."

I stood with the paper between my hands so long that the daily shaft of sunlight entered the cell and fell upon it. Father . . . Father . . . the letter glittered in the criss-cross light as I read the rest. Nollie had no details, not how or where he had died, not even where he was buried.

Footsteps were passing on the coconut matting. I ran to the door and pressed my face to the closed pass-through. "Please! Oh please!"

The steps stopped. The shelf dropped open. "What's the matter?"

"Please! I've had bad news—oh please, don't go away!"

"Wait a minute." The footsteps retreated, then returned with a jangle of keys. The cell door opened.

"Here." The young woman handed me a pill with a glass of water. "It's a sedative."

"This letter just came," I explained. "It says that my father—it says my father has died."

The girl stared at me. "Your father!" she said in astonished tones.

I realized how very old and decrepit I must look to this young person. She stood in the doorway a while, obviously embarrassed at my tears. "Whatever happens," she said at last, "you brought it on yourself by breaking the laws!"

Dear Jesus, I whispered as the door slammed and her footsteps died away, how foolish of me to have called for human help when You are here. To think that Father sees You now, face to face! To think that he and Mama are together again, walking those bright streets. . . .

I pulled the cot from the wall and below the calendar scratched another date:

March 9, 1944   Father. Released.

CHAPTER ELEVEN

The Lieutenant

I was walking with a guard—behind and a little to the right of her so my feet would not touch the sacrosanct mat – down a corridor I had not seen before. A turn to the right, a few steps down, right again . . . what an endless labyrinth this prison was. At last we stepped out into a small interior courtyard. A drizzle of rain was falling. It was a chill raw morning in late May: after three months in prison I had been called for my first hearing.

Barred windows stared from tall buildings on three sides of the courtyard, along the fourth was a high wall and against this stood a row of small huts. So these were where the infamous interrogations took place. My breath came short and hard as I thought back to the reports I had passed on, the night of Hitler's birthday.

"Lord Jesus, You were called to a hearing too. Show me what to do."

And then I saw something. Whoever used the fourth of the huts had planted a row of tulips along the side. They were wilted now, only tall stems and yellowing leaves, but . . . "Dear Lord, let me go to hut number four!"

The guard had paused to unstrap a long military cape fastened to the shoulder of her uniform. Protected from the rain, she crunched up the gravel path. Past the first hut, the second, the third. She halted in front of the hut with the flowerbed and rapped on the door.

"*Ja! Herrein!*" called a man's voice.

The guard pushed open the door, gave a straight-armed salute and marched smartly off. The man wore a gun in a leather holster and a beribboned uniform. He removed his hat and I was staring into the face of the gentle-mannered man who had visited me in my cell.

"I am Lieutenant Rahms," he said, stepping to the door to close it behind me. "You're shivering! Here, let me get a fire going."

He filled a pot-bellied stove from a small coal scuttle, for all the world a kindly German householder entertaining a guest. What if this were all a subtle trap? This kind, human manner—perhaps he had simply found it more effective than brutality in tricking the truth from affection-starved people. "Oh Lord, let no weak gullibility on my part endanger another's life."

"I hope," the officer was saying, "we won't have many more days this spring as cold as this one." He drew out a chair for me to sit on.

Warily I accepted it. How strange after three months, to feel a chair-back behind me, chair-arms for my hands! The heat from the stove was quickly warming the little room. In spite of myself I began to relax. I ventured a timid comment about the tulips: "So tall, they must have been beautiful."

"Oh they were!" he seemed ridiculously pleased. "The best I've ever grown. At home we always have Dutch bulbs."

We talked about flowers for a while and then he said, "I would like to help you, Miss ten Boom. But you must tell me everything. I may be able to do something, but only if you do not hide anything from me."

So there it was already. All the friendliness, the kindly concern that I had half-believed in—all a device to elicit information. Well, why not? This man was a professional with a job to do. But I, too, in a small way, was a professional.

For an hour he questioned me, using every psychological trick that the young men of our group had drilled me in. In fact, I felt like a student who has crammed for a difficult exam and then is tested on only the most elementary material. It soon became clear that they believed the Beje had been a headquarters for raids on food ration offices around the country. Of all the illegal activities I had on my conscience, this was probably the one I knew least about. Other than receiving the stolen cards each month and passing them on, I knew no details of the operation. Apparently my real ignorance began to show; after a while Lieutenant Rahms stopped making notes of my hopelessly stupid answers.

"Your other activities, Miss ten Boom. What would you like to tell me about them?"

"Other activities? Oh, you mean—you want to know about my church for mentally retarded people!" And I plunged into an eager account of my efforts at preaching to the feeble-minded.

The lieutenant's eyebrows rose higher and higher. "What a waste of time and energy?" he exploded at last. "If you want converts, surely one normal person is worth all the half-wits in the world!"

I stared into the man's intelligent blue-gray eyes: true National-Socialist philosophy I thought, tulip bed or no. And then to my astonishment I heard my own voice saying boldly, "May I tell you the truth, Lieutenant Rahms?"

"This hearing, Miss ten Boom, is predicated on the assumption that you will do me that honor."

"The truth, Sir," I said, swallowing, "is that God's viewpoints is sometimes different from ours—so different that we could not even guess at it unless He had given us a Book which tells us such things."

I knew it was madness to talk this way to a Nazi officer. But he said nothing so I plunged ahead. "In the Bible I learn that God values us not for our strength or our brains but simply because He has made us. Who knows, in His eyes a half-wit may be worth more than a watchmaker. Or—a lieutenant."

Lieutenant Rahms stood up abruptly. "That will be all for today." He walked swiftly to the door. "Guard!"

I heard footsteps on the gravel path.

"The prisoner will return to her cell."

Following the guard through the long cold corridors, I knew I had made a mistake. I had said too much. I had ruined whatever chance I had that this man might take an interest in my case.

And yet the following morning it was Lieutenant Rahms himself who unlocked my cell door and escorted me to the hearing. Apparently he did not know of the regulation that forbade prisoners to step on the mat, for he indicated that I was to walk ahead of him down the center of the hall. I avoided the eyes of the guards along the route, guilty as a well-trained dog discovered on the living room sofa.

In the courtyard this time a bright sun was shining.

"Today," he said, "we will stay outside. You are pale. You are not getting enough sun."

Gratefully I followed him to the farthest corner of the little yard where the air was still and warm. We settled our backs against the wall. "I could not sleep last night," the lieutenant said, "thinking about that Book where you have read such different ideas. What else does it say in there?"

On my closed eyelids the sun glimmered and blazed. "It says," I began slowly, "that a Light has come into this world, so that we need no longer walk in the dark. Is there darkness in your life, Lieutenant?"

There was a very long silence.

"There is great darkness," he said at last. "I cannot bear the work I do here."

Then all at once he was telling me about his wife and children in Bremen, about their garden, their dogs, their summer hiking vacations. "Bremen was bombed again last week. Each morning I ask myself, are they still alive?"

"There is One Who has them always in His sight Lieutenant Rahms. Jesus is the Light the Bible shows to me, the Light that can shine even in such darkness as yours."

The man pulled the visor of his hat lower over his eyes; the skull-and-crossbones glinted in the sunlight. When he spoke it was so low I could hardly hear. "What can you know of darkness like mine. . . ."

Two more mornings the hearings continued. He had dropped all pretense of questioning me on my underground activities and seemed especially to enjoy hearing about my childhood. Mama, Father, the aunts—he wanted to hear stories about them again and again. He was incensed to learn that Father had died right here in Scheveningen; the documents on my case made no mention of it.

These documents did answer one question: the reason for solitary confinement. "Prisoner's condition contagious to others in cell." I stared at the brief typed words where Lieutenant Rahm's finger rested. I thought of the long wind-haunted nights, the scowling guards, the rule of silence. "But, if it wasn't punishment, why were they so angry with me? Why couldn't I talk?"

The lieutenant squared the edges of the papers in front of him. "A prison is like any institution, Miss ten Boom, certain rules, certain ways of doing things—"

"But I'm not contagious now! I've been better for weeks and weeks, and my own sister is so close! Lieutenant Rahms, if I could only see Betsie! If I could just talk with her a few minutes!"

He lifted his eyes from the desk and I saw anguish in them. "Miss ten Boom, it is possible that I appear to you a powerful person. I wear a uniform, I have a certain authority over those under me. But I am in prison, dear lady from Haarlem, a prison stronger than this one."

It was the fourth and final hearing, and we had come back into the small hut for the signing of the *procès-verbal*. He gathered up the completed transcript and went out with it, leaving me alone. I was sorry to say goodbye to this man who was struggling so earnestly for truth. The hardest thing for him seemed to be that Christians should suffer. "How can you believe in God now?" he'd ask. "What kind of a God would have let that old man die here in Scheveningen?"

I got up from the chair and held my hands out to the squat little stove. I did not understand either why Father had died in such a place. I did not understand a great deal.

And suddenly I was thinking of Father's own answer to hard questions: "Some knowledge is too heavy . . . you cannot bear it . . . your Father will carry it until you are able." Yes! I would tell Lieutenant Rahms about the traincase—he always liked stories about Father.

But when the lieutenant returned to the room a guard from the women's wing was with him. "Prisoner ten Boom has completed her hearings," he said, "and will return to her cell."

The young woman snapped to attention. As I stepped through the door, Lieutenant Rahms leaned forward.

"Walk slowly," he said, "in Corridor F."

Walk slowly? What did he mean? The guard strode down the long door-lined halls so swiftly that I had to trot to keep up with her. Ahead of us a prison trusty was unlocking the door to a cell. I trailed behind the guard as much as I dared, my heart thumping wildly. It would be Betsie's cell—I knew it!

Then I was abreast of the door. Betsie's back was to the corridor. I could see only the graceful upswept bun of her chestnut hair. The other women in the cell stared curiously into the corridor; her head remained bent over something in her lap. But I had seen the home Betsie had made in Scheveningen.

For unbelievably, against all logic, this cell was charming. My eyes seized only a few details as I inched reluctantly past. The straw pallets were rolled instead of piled in a heap, standing like little pillars along the walls, each with a lady's hat atop it. A headscarf had somehow been hung along the wall. The contents of several food packages were arranged on a small shelf; I could just hear Betsie saying, "The red biscuit tin here in the center!" Even the coats hanging on their hooks were part of the welcome of that room, each sleeve draped over the shoulder of the coat next to it like a row of dancing children—

"*Schneller! Aber schnell!*"

I jumped and hurried after my escort. It had been a glimpse only, two seconds at the most, but I walked through the corridors of Scheveningen with Betsie's singing spirit at my side.

All morning I heard doors opening and closing. Now keys rattled outside my own: a very young guard in a very new uniform bounded in.

"Prisoner stand at attention!" she squeaked. I stared at her wide, blinking eyes; the girl was in mortal fear of something or someone.

Then a shadow filled the doorway and the tallest woman I had ever seen stepped into the cell. Her features were classically handsome, the face and height of a goddess—but one carved in marble. Not a flicker of feeling registered in her eyes.

"No sheets here either, I see," she said in German to the guard. "See that she has two by Friday. One to be changed every two weeks."

The ice-cold eyes appraised me exactly as they had the bed. "How many showers does the prisoner get?"

The guard wet her lips. "About one a week, *Wacht-meisterin.*"

One a week! One shower a month was closer.

"She will go twice a week."

Sheets! Regular showers! Were conditions going to be better? The new head matron took two strides into the cell; she did not need the cot to reach the overhead bulb. Rip!

Off came my red-cellophane lampshade. She pointed to a box of soda crackers that had come in a second package from Nollie.

"No boxes in the cells!" cried the little guard in Dutch, as indignantly as though this had been a long-standing rule.

Not knowing what else to do I dumped the crackers out onto the cot. At the matron's unspoken command I emptied a bottle of vitamins and a sack of peppermint drops the same way.

Unlike the former head matron, who shrieked and scolded endlessly in her rusted-hinge voice, this woman worked in a terrifying silence. With a gesture she directed the guard to feel beneath the mattress. My heart wedged in my throat; my precious remaining Gospel was hidden there. The guard knelt and ran her hands the length of the cot. But whether she was too nervous to do a thorough job or whether there was a more mysterious explanation, the straightened up empty-handed.

And then they were gone.

I stood gazing numbly at the jumble of food on my cot. I thought of this woman reaching Betsie's cell, reducing it again to four walls and a prison cot. A chill wind was blowing through Scheveningen, cleaning, ordering, killing.

It was this tall, ramrod-straight woman who unlocked the door to my cell one afternoon in the second half of June and admitted Lieutenant Rahms. At the severity in his face I swallowed the greeting that had almost burst from me.

"You will come to my office," he said briefly. "The notary has come."

We might as well have been total strangers. "Notary?" I said stupidly.

"For the reading of your Father's will." He made an impatient gesture; obviously this minor matter had interrupted a busy day. "It's the law—family present when a will is opened."

Already he was heading from the cell and down the corridor. I broke into a clumsy run to keep up with the strides of the silent woman beside me. The law? What law? And since when had the German occupation government concerned itself with Dutch legal procedures? Family. Family present. . . . No, don't let yourself think of it!

At the door to the courtyard the matron turned, erect and impassive, back along the corridor. I followed Lieutenant Rahms into the dazzling early summer afternoon. He opened the door for me into the fourth hut. Before my eyes adjusted to the gloom I was drowning in Willem's embrace.

"Corrie! Corrie! Baby sister!" It was fifty years since he had called me that.

Now Nollie's arm was around me too, the other one still clinging to Betsie, as though by the strength of her grip she would hold us together forever. Betsie! Nollie! Willem! I did not know which name to cry first. Tine was in that little room too—and Flip! And another man; when I had time to look I recognized the Haarlem notary who had been called in on the watchshop's few legal consultations. We held each other at arm's length to look, we babbled questions all at once.

Betsie was thin and prison-pale. But it was Willem who shocked me. His face was gaunt, yellow, and pain-haunted. He had come home this way from Scheveningen, Tine told me. Two of the eight men crowded into his tiny cell had died of jaundice while he was there.

Willem! I could not bear to see him this way. I crooked my arm through his, standing close so that I did not have to look at him, loving the sound of his deep rolling voice. Willem did not seem aware of his own illness: his concern was all for Kik. This handsome blond son had been seized the month before while helping an American parachutist reach the North Sea. They believed he had been on one of the recent prison trains into Germany.

As for Father, they had learned a few more facts about his last days. He had apparently become ill in his cell and been taken by car to the municipal hospital in The Hague. There, no bed had been available. Father had died in a corridor, separated somehow from his records or any clue to his identity. Hospital authorities had buried the unknown old man in the paupers' cemetery. The family believed they had located the particular grave.

I glanced over at Lieutenant Rahms. He was standing with his back to us as we talked, staring down at the cold unlit stove. Swiftly I opened the package that Nollie had pressed into my hand with the first embrace. It was what my leaping heart had told me: a Bible, the entire Book in a compact volume, tucked inside a small pouch with a string for wearing around the neck as we had once carried our identity cards. I dropped it quickly over my head and down my back beneath my blouse. I couldn't even find words with which to thank her: the day before, in the shower line, I had given away my last remaining Gospel.

"We don't know all the details," Willem was saying in a low voice to Betsie, "just that after a few days the soldiers were taken off guard duty at the Beje and police stationed there instead." The fourth night, he believed, the chief had succeeded in assigning Rolf and another of our group to the same shift. They had found all the Jews well, though cramped and hungry, and seen them to new hiding places.

"And now?" I whispered. "They're all right now?"

Willem lowered his deep-sunk eyes to mine. He had never been good at concealing difficult truths. "They're all right, Corrie—all except Mary." Old Mary Itallie, he said, had been arrested one day walking down a city street. Where she had been going and why she had exposed herself this way in broad daylight, nobody knew.

"The time is up." Lieutenant Rahms left his perusal of the stove and nodded to the notary. "Proceed with the reading of the will."

It was a brief, informal document: the Beje was to be home for Betsie and me as long as we wanted it; should there ever be any money realized from the sale of house or watch shop, he knew we would recall his equal love for us all; he committed us with joy to the constant care of God.

In the silence which followed, we all suddenly bowed our heads. "Lord Jesus," Willem said, "we praise You for these moments together under the protection of this good man. How can we thank him? We have no power to do him any service. Lord, allow us to share this inheritance from our father with him as well. Take him too, and his family, into Your constant care."

Outside, a guard's footsteps sounded on the crunchy gravel walk.

CHAPTER TWELVE

Vught

"Get your things together! Get ready to evacuate! Collect all possessions in pillowcases!" The shouts of the guards echoed up and down the long corridor.

I stood in the center of my cell in a frenzy of excitement. Evacuate! Then—then something was happening! We were leaving the prison! The counter-invasion must have begun!

I snatched the pillowcase from the little wad of straw I had stuffed into it. What riches this coarse bit of muslin had been in the two weeks since it had been provided: a shield for my head from the scratch and smell of the bedding. It almost didn't matter that the promised sheets had never arrived.

With trembling hands I dropped my few belongings into it, the blue sweater, the pajamas—covered now back and front with embroidered figures—toothbrush, comb, a few remaining crackers wrapped in toilet paper. My Bible was in its pouch on my back where it remained except when I was reading it.

I put on my coat and hat and stood at the iron door clutching the pillowcase in both hands. It was still early in the morning; the tin breakfast plate had not yet been removed from the shelf in the door. Getting ready had taken no time at all.

An hour passed. I sat on the cot. Two hours. Three. It was warm in the cell this late June day. I took off my hat and coat and folded them next to me on the cot.

More time passed. I kept my eyes on the ant hole, hoping for a last visit from my small friends, but they did not appear. Probably I had frightened them by my early dashing about. I reached into the pillowcase, took one of the crackers and crumbled it about the little crack. No ants. They were staying safely hidden.

And suddenly I realized that this too was a message, a last wordless communication among neighbours. For I too had a hiding place when things were bad. Jesus was this place, the Rock cleft for me. I pressed a finger to the tiny crevice.

The afternoon sun appeared on the wall and moved slowly across the cell. And then all at once there was a clanging out in the corridor. Doors scraped. Bolts banged. "Out! *Schnell!* All out! No talking!"

I snatched up my hat and coat.

My door screeched open. "Form ranks of five—" the guard was already at the next cell.

I stepped out into the hall. It was jammed from wall to wall: I had never dreamed so many women occupied this corridor. We exchanged looks. "In-va-sion," we mouthed silently, the soundless word sweeping through the massed women like an electric charge. Surely the invasion of Holland had begun! Why else would they be emptying the prison!

Where would we be taken? Where were we headed? Not into Germany! Dear Jesus, not Germany.

The command was given and we shuffled forward down the long chill halls, each carrying a pillowcase, with her belongings forming a little bulge at the bottom. At last we emerged into the wide courtyard inside the front gate of the prison and another long wait began. But this wait was pleasant with the late afternoon sun on our backs. Far to the right I could see the columns of the men's section. But crane my neck though I would, I could not see Betsie anywhere.

At last the huge gate swung in and a convoy of gray transport buses drove through. I was herded aboard the third one. The seats had been removed, the windows painted over. The bus lurched dreadfully as it started up but we were standing too close together to fall. When the bus ground to a stop we were at a freight yard somewhere on the outskirts of the city.

Again we were formed into ranks. The guards' voices were tense and shrill. We had to keep our heads facing forward, eyes front. Behind us we could hear buses arriving, then lumbering away again. It was still light, but I knew by the ache in my stomach that it was long past suppertime.

And then, ahead and to the left of me, in the newest group

of arriving prisoners. I spotted a chestnut bun. Betsie! Somehow, some way, I was going to get to her! Now instead of wanting the day to end, I prayed that we stayed where we were until dark.

Slowly the long June day faded. Thunder rumbled and a few drops of rain fell. At last a long row of unlit coaches rolled slowly over the tracks in front of us. They banged to a stop, rolled forward a little farther, then stopped again. After a while they began backing. For an hour or more the train switched back and forth.

By the time the order came to board, it was pitch dark. The ranks of prisoners surged forward. Behind us the guards shouted and cursed: obviously they were nervous at transporting so many prisoners at one time. I wriggled and shoved to the left. Elbows and shoulders were in my way but I squirmed past. At the very steps of the train I reached out and seized Betsie's hand.

Together we climbed onto the train, together found seats in a crowded compartment, together wept tears of gratitude. The four months in Scheveningen had been our first separation in fifty-three years; it seemed to me that I could bear whatever happened with Betsie beside me.

More hours passed as the loaded train sat on the siding. For us they flew, there was so much to share. Betsie told me about each of her cellmates—and I told her about mine and the little hole into which they scrambled at any emergency. As always, Betsie had given to others everything she had. The Bible that Nollie had smuggled to her she had torn up and passed around, book by book.

It must have been 2:00 or 3:00 in the morning that the train at last began to move. We pressed our faces to the glass, but no lights showed and clouds covered the moon. The thought uppermost in every mind was: Is it Germany? At one point we made out a tower that Betsie was sure was the cathedral at Delft. An hour or more later the clack of the train changed pitch: we were crossing a trestle. But—a very long one! As the minutes passed and still we had not reached the other side Betsie and I exchanged looks. The Moerdijk Bridge! Then we were headed south. Not east into Germany, but south to Brabant. For the second time that night we wept tears of joy.

I leaned my head back against the wooden slats of the

seat and shut my eyes, reliving another train trip to Brabant.
Mama's hand had gripped Father's, then, as the train
swayed. Then, too, it was June—the June of the First
Sermon, of the garden back of the manse, of Karel. ...

I must have fallen asleep, back in that other June, for
when I opened my eyes the train had stopped. Voices were
shouting at us to move: *Schneller! Aber schnell!* An eerie
glare lit the windows. Betsie and I stumbled after the others
along the aisle and down the iron steps. We seemed to have
stopped in the middle of a wood. Floodlights mounted in
trees lit a broad rough-cleared path lined by soldiers with
leveled guns.

Spurred by the shouts of the guards Betsie and I started
up the path between the gun barrels. "*Schneller!* Close
ranks! Keep up! Five abreast!" Betsie's breath was coming
short and hard and still they yelled at us to go faster. It had
rained hard here, for there were deep puddles in the path.
Ahead of us a white-haired woman stepped to the side to
avoid one; a soldier struck her in the back with a gun butt.
I took Betsie's pillowcase along with mine, hooked my other
arm through hers and hauled her along beside me.

The nightmare march lasted a mile or more. At last we
came to a barbed-wire fence surrounding a row of wooden
barracks. There were no beds in the one we entered, only
long tables with backless benches pulled up to them. Betsie
and I collapsed onto one of these. Under my arm I could
feel the irregular flutter of her heart. We fell into an exhausted sleep, our heads on the table.

The sun was streaming through the barracks windows
when we woke up. We were thirsty and hungry: we had had
nothing to eat or drink since the early meal at Scheveningen
the morning before. But all that day no guard or any official
person appeared inside the barracks. At last, when the sun
was low in the sky, a prisoner crew arrived with a great vat
of some thick steamy substance that we gobbled ravenously.

And so began our stay in this place that, we learned, was
named Vught after the nearest small village. Unlike Scheveningen, which had been a regular Dutch prison, Vught had
been constructed by the occupation especially as a concentration camp for political prisoners. We were not yet in the
camp proper but in a kind of quarantine compound outside.
Our biggest problem was idleness, wedged together as we

were around the long rows of tables with nothing to do. We
were guarded by the same young women who had patrolled
the corridors at Scheveningen. They had been adequate
enough as long as we were behind locked doors; here they
seemed at a loss. Their only technique for maintaining discipline was to shriek obscenities and hand out punishments
to all alike. Half rations for the entire barracks. An extra roll
call at rigid attention. A ban on talking for twenty-four
hours.

Only one of our overseers never threatened or raised her
voice. This was the tall, silent head matron from Scheveningen. She appeared in Vught the third morning during the
predawn roll call and at once something like order seized
our rebellious and untidy ranks. Lines straightened, hands
were clamped to sides, whispers ceased as those cold blue
eyes swept across us.

Among ourselves we nicknamed her "The General."
During one long roll call a pregnant woman at our table
slumped to the floor, striking her head against the edge of
the bench. The General did not so much as pause in her
expressionless reading of names.

We had been in this outer camp at Vught almost two
weeks when Betsie and I along with a dozen others were
called out by name during morning roll call. When the rest
had been dismissed The General distributed typewritten
forms among us and instructed us to present them at the
administration barracks at 9:00 o'clock.

A worker on the food crew—a long-term prisoner from
the main camp—smiled encouragingly as he ladled out our
breakfast. "You're free!" he whispered. "Those pink forms
mean release!"

Betsie and I stared disbelievingly at the sheets of paper in
our hands. Free? Free to leave—free to go home? Others
crowded around, congratulating us, embracing us. The
women from Betsie's cell at Scheveningen wept unabashedly. How cruel to have to leave all these behind!

"Surely the war will be over very soon," we told them.
We emptied our pillowcases, passing out our few belongings
among those who had to stay.

Long before 9:00 we were standing in the big wooden
anteroom of Administration. At last we were summoned to
an inner office where our forms were examined, stamped,

and handed over to a guard. We followed this man down a corridor into another office. For hours the process continued as we were shuttled from one room and official to another, questioned, fingerprinted, sent on to the next post. The group of prisoners grew until there were forty or fifty of us standing in line beside a high anchor-chain fence topped with barbed wire. On the other side of the fence was a white birch woods, above our heads the blue Brabant sky. We too belonged to that wide free world.

The next barracks we entered held a row of desks with women clerks seated behind them. At one of these I was handed a brown paper envelope. I emptied it into my hand and the next moment was staring in disbelief at my Alpina watch. Mama's ring. Even my paper guilders. I had not seen these things since the night we arrived at Scheveningen. Money . . . why, that belonged to the world of shops and trolley cars. We could go to a train station with this money. Two fares to Haarlem, please. . . .

We marched along a path between twisted rolls of barbed wire and through a wide gate into a compound of low tin-roofed barracks. There were more lines, more waits, more shuffling from desk to desk, but already the camp and its procedures had become unreal to me.

Then we were standing before a high counter and a young male clerk was saying, "Leave all personal effects at the window marked 'C'."

"But they just gave them back to me!"

"Watches, purses, jewelry . . ."

Mechanically, like a machine with no will of its own, I handed watch, ring, and money through the small barred window. A uniformed woman swept them into a metal box. "Move along! Next!"

Then—were we not to be released? Outside this building a florid-faced officer formed us into a double column and marched us across a broad parade ground. At one end of it a crew of men with shaved heads and striped overalls were digging a ditch. What did it mean? What did any of it mean, this whole long day of lines and waits? Betsie's face was gray with weariness and she stumbled as we marched.

Through another fence we arrived in a yard surrounded on three sides by low concrete buildings. A young woman in a military cape was waiting for us.

"Prisoners halt!" barked the red-faced officer. "Explain to the newcomers, *Fraulein*, the function of the bunkers."

"The bunkers," the girl began in the bored voice of a museum guide, "are for the accommodation of those who fail to cooperate with camp rules. The rooms are cozy, if a bit small: about the size of a gym locker. To hasten the educational process the hands are tied above the head. . . ."

Even as the horrid recital continued, two guards came out of the bunker, carrying between them the form of a man. He was alive, for his legs were moving, but he seemed to have no conscious control over them. His eyes were sunken and rolled back in his head.

"Not everyone," the girl observed in the same detached drawl, "seems to appreciate the accommodations at the bunkers."

I seized Betsie's arm as the command to march came again, more to steady myself than her. It was Father's train-case once again. Such cruelty was too much to grasp, too much to bear. Heavenly Father, carry it for me!

We followed the officer down a wide street lined with barracks on either side and halted at one of the gray, feature-less sheds. It was the end of the long day of standing, wait-ing, hoping: we had simply arrived in the main camp at Vught.

The barracks appeared almost identical with the one we had left this morning, except that this one was furnished with bunks as well as tables and benches. And still we were not allowed to sit: there was a last wait while the matron with maddening deliberateness checked off our documents against a list.

"Betsie!" I wailed, "how long will it take?"

"Perhaps a long, long time. Perhaps many years. But what better way could there be to spend our lives?"

I turned to stare at her. "Whatever are you talking about?"

"These young women. That girl back at the bunkers. Corrie, if people can be taught to hate, they can be taught to love! We must find the way, you and I, no matter how long it takes. . . ."

She went on, almost forgetting in her excitement to keep her voice to a whisper, while I slowly took in the fact that she was talking about our guards. I glanced at the matron seated at the desk ahead of us. I saw a gray uniform and a visored hat; Betsie saw a wounded human being.

And I wondered, not for the first time, what sort of a person she was, this sister of mine . . . what kind of road she followed while I trudged beside her on the all-too-solid earth.

A few days later Betsie and I were called up for work assignments. One glance at Betsie's pallid face and fragile form, and the matron waved her contemptuously back inside the barracks where the elderly and infirm spent the day sewing prison uniforms. The women's uniform here in Vught was a blue overall with a red stripe down the side of the leg, practical and comfortable, and a welcome change after our own clothes that we had worn since the day of our arrest.

Apparently I looked strong enough for harder work; I was told to report to the Phillips factory. This "factory" turned out to be no more than another large barracks inside the camp complex. Early in the morning though it was, the tar beneath the shingled roof was beginning to bubble in the hot July sun. I followed my escort into the single large room where several hundred men and women sat at long plank tables covered with thousands of tiny radio parts. Two officers, one male, one female, were strolling the aisles between the benches while the prisoners bent to their tasks.

I was assigned a seat at a bench near the front and given the job of measuring small glass rods and arranging them in piles according to lengths. It was monotonous work. The heat from the roof pressed like a weight on my head. I longed to exchange at least names and home towns with my neighbors on either side, but the only sound in the room was the clink of metal parts and the squeak of the officers' boots. They reached the door across from where I sat.

"Production was up again last week," the male officer said in German to a tall slender man with a shaved head and a striped uniform. "You are to be commended for this increase. However we continue to receive complaints of defective wiring. Quality control must improve."

The shaved-headed man made an apologetic gesture. "If there were more food, *Herr Officier*," he murmured. "Since the cutback in rations I see a difference. They grow sleepy, they have trouble concentrating. . . ." His voice reminded me a little of Willem's, deep, cultivated, the German with only a trace of Dutch accent.

"Then you must wake them up! Make them concentrate on the penalties! If soldiers on the front can fight on half-rations, then these lazy—"

At a terrible look from the woman officer, he stopped and ran his tongue over his lips. "Ah—that is—I speak of course merely as an example. There is naturally no truth in the rumor that rations at the front are reduced. So! I—I hold you responsible!" And together they stalked from the building.

For a moment the prisoner-foreman watched them from the doorway. Slowly he raised his left hand, then dropped it with a slap to his side. The quiet room exploded. From under tables appeared writing paper, books, knitting yarn, tins of biscuits. People left their benches and joined little knots of chattering friends all over the room. Half a dozen crowded around me: Who was I? Where was I from? Did I have any news of the war?

After perhaps half an hour of visiting among the tables, the foreman reminded us that we had a day's quota to meet and people drifted back to their places. The foreman's name, I learned, was Moorman and he had been headmaster of a Roman Catholic boys' school. He himself came over to my workbench the third day I was there; he had heard that I had followed the entire assembly line through the barracks, tracing what became of my dull little piles of rods. "You're the first woman worker," he said, "who has ever shown any interest in what we are making here."

"I am very interested," I said. "I'm a watchmaker."

He stared at me with new interest. "Then I have work you will enjoy more." He took me to the opposite end of the huge shed where the final assembly of relay switches was done. It was intricate and exacting work, though not nearly so hard as watch repair, and Mr. Moorman was right. I enjoyed it and it helped make the eleven-hour workday go faster.

Not only to me but to all the Phillips workers, Mr. Moorman acted more as a kindly older brother than a crew boss. I would watch him, ceaselessly moving among his hundreds of charges, counseling, encouraging, finding a simpler job for the weary, a harder one for the restless. We had been at

Vught more than a month before I learned that his twenty-
year-old son had been shot here at the camp the week Betsie
and I arrived.

No trace of this personal tragedy showed in his care for
the rest of us. He stopped frequently at my bench, the first
weeks, more to check my frame of mind than my work. But
eventually his eyes would travel to the row of relay switches
in front of me. . . .

"Dear watch lady! Can you not remember for whom you
are working? These radios are for their fighter planes!" And
reaching across me he would yank a wire from its housing
or twist a tiny tube from an assembly.

"Now solder them back wrong. And not so fast! You're
over the day's quota and it's not yet noon."

Lunchtime would have been the best time of day if I could
have spent it with Betsie. However, Phillips workers were
not allowed to leave the factory compound until the workday ended at 6:00. Prisoners on kitchen detail lugged in
great buckets of gruel made of wheat and peas, tasteless but
nourishing. Apparently there had been a cutback in rations
recently: still the food was better and more plentiful than at
Scheveningen where there had been no noonday meal at all.

After eating we were free for a blessed half hour to stroll
about within the Phillips compound in the fresh air and the
glorious Brabant sun. Most days I found a spot along the
fence and stretched out on the warm ground to sleep (the
days started with roll call at 5:00 A.M.). Sweet summer
smells came in the breezes from the farms around the camp;
sometimes I would dream that Karel and I were walking
hand in hand along a country lane.

At 6:00 in the evening there was another roll call, then we
marched back to our various sleeping barracks. Betsie
always stood in the doorway of ours waiting for me; each
evening it was as though a week had passed, there was so
much to tell one another.

"That Belgian boy and girl at the bench next to mine?
This noon they became engaged!"

"Mrs. Heerma—whose granddaughter was taken to Germany—today she let me pray with her."

One day Betsie's news touched us directly. "A lady from
Ermelo was transferred to the sewing detail today. When I
introduced myself, she said, 'Another one!'"

"What did she mean?"

"Corrie, do you remember, the day we were arrested, a man came to the shop? You were sick and I had to wake you up."

I remembered very well. Remembered the strange roving eyes, the uneasiness in the pit of my stomach that was more than fever.

"Apparently everyone in Ermelo knew him. He worked with the Gestapo from the first day of occupation. He reported this woman's two brothers for Resistance work, and finally herself and her husband too." When Ermelo had finally caught on to him he had come to Haarlem and teamed up with Willemse and Kapteyn. His name was Jan Vogel.

Flames of fire seemed to leap around that name in my heart. I thought of Father's final hours, alone and confused, in a hospital corridor. Of the underground work so abruptly halted. I thought of Mary Itallie arrested while walking down a street. And I knew that if Jan Vogel stood in front of me now I could kill him.

Betsie drew the little cloth bag from beneath her overalls and held it out to me, but I shook my head. Betsie kept the Bible during the day, since she had more chance to read and teach from it here than I did at the Phillips barracks. In the evenings we held a clandestine prayer meeting for as many as could crowd around our bunk.

"You lead the prayers tonight, Betsie. I have a headache."

More than a headache. All of me ached with the violence of my feelings about the man who had done us so, much harm. That night I did not sleep and the next day at my bench scarcely heard the conversation around me. By the end of the week I had worked myself into such a sickness of body and spirit that Mr. Moorman stopped at my bench to ask if something were wrong.

"Wrong? Yes, something's wrong!" And I plunged into an account of that morning. I was only too eager to tell Mr. Moorman and all Holland how Jan Vogel had betrayed his country.

What puzzled me all this time was Betsie. She had suffered everything I had and yet she seemed to carry no burden of rage. "Betsie!" I hissed one dark night when I knew that my restless tossing must be keeping her awake. Three of us now shared this single cot as the crowded camp daily received new arrivals. "Betsie, don't you feel anything about Jan Vogel? Doesn't it bother you?"

"Oh yes, Corrie! Terribly! I've felt for him ever since I knew—and pray for him whenever his name comes into my mind. How dreadfully he must be suffering."

For a long time I lay silent in the huge shadowy barracks restless with the sighs, snores, and stirrings of hundreds of women. Once again I had the feeling that this sister with whom I had spent all my life belonged somehow to another order of things. Wasn't she telling me in her gentle way that I was as guilty as Jan Vogel? Didn't he and I stand together before an all-seeing God convicted of the same sin of murder? For I had murdered him with my heart and with my tongue.

"Lord Jesus," I whispered into the lumpy ticking of the bed, "I forgive Jan Vogel as I pray that You will forgive me. I have done him great damage. Bless him now, and his family. . . ." That night for the first time since our betrayer had a name I slept deep and dreamlessly until the whistle summoned us to roll call.

The days in Vught were a baffling mixture of good and bad. Morning roll call was often cruelly long. If the smallest rule had been broken, such as a single prisoner late for evening check-in, the entire barracks would be punished by a 4:00 A.M. or even a 3:30 call and made to stand at parade attention until our backs ached and our legs cramped. But the summer air was warm and alive with birds as the day approached. Gradually, in the east, a pink-and-gold sunrise would light the immense Brabant sky as Betsie and I squeezed each other's hands in awe.

At 5:30 we had black bread and "coffee," bitter and hot, and then fell into marching columns for the various work details. I looked forward to this hike to the Phillips factory. Part of the way we walked beside a small woods, separated only by a roll of barbed wire from a glistening world of dewdrops. We also marched past a section of the men's camp, many of our group straining to identify a husband or a son among the ranks of shaved heads and striped overalls.

This was another of the paradoxes of Vught. I was endlessly, daily grateful to be again with people. But what I had not realized in solitary confinement was that to have companions meant to have their griefs as well. We all suffered with the women whose men were in this camp: the discipline in the male section was much harsher than in the women's; executions were frequent. Almost every day a salvo of shots would send the anguished whispers flying: How many this time? Who were they?

The woman next to me at the relay bench was an intense Communist woman named Floor. She and her husband had managed to get their two small children to friends before their arrest, but she worried aloud all day about them and about Mr. Floor, who had tuberculosis. He worked on the rope-making crew in the compound next to Phillips and each noon they managed to exchange a few words through the barbed wire separating the two enclosures. Although she was expecting a third child in September she would never eat her morning allotment of bread but passed it through the fence to him. She was dangerously thin, I felt, for an expectant mother, and several times I brought her a portion of my own breakfast bread. But this too was always set aside for Mr. Floor.

And yet in spite of sorrow and anxiety—and no one in that place was without both—there was laughter too in the Phillips barracks. An impersonation of the pompous, blustering second lieutenant. A game of blind-man's buff. A song passed in rounds from bench to bench until—

"Thick clouds! Thick clouds!" The signal might come from any bench which faced a window. The factory barracks was set in the center of the broad Phillips compound; there was no way a camp official could approach it without crossing this open space. In an instant every bench would be filled, the only sound the businesslike rattle of radio parts.

One morning the code words were still being relayed down the long shed when a rather hefty *Aufseherin* stepped through the door. She glanced furiously about, face flushing scarlet as she applied "thick clouds" to her appearance. She shrieked and ranted for a quarter of an hour, then deprived us of our noontime break in the open air that day. After this we adopted the more neutral signal, "fifteen."

"I've assembled fifteen dials!"

During the long hot afternoons pranks and talk died down as each one sat alone with his own thoughts. I scratched on the side of the table the number of days until September 1. There was nothing official about that date, just a chance remark by Mrs. Floor to the effect that six months was the usual prison term for ration-card offenders. Then, if that were the charge and if they included the time served at Scheveningen, September 1 would be our release date.

"Corrie," Betsie warned one evening when I announced triumphantly that August was half over, "we don't know for sure."

I had the feeling, almost, that to Betsie it didn't matter. I looked at her, sitting on our cot in the last moments before lights out, sewing up a split seam in my overalls as she'd so often sat mending under the lamplight in the dining room. Betsie by the very way she sat evoked a high-backed chair behind her and a carpet at her feet instead of this endless row of metal cots on a bare pine floor. The first week we were here she had added extra hooks to the neck of her overalls so that she could fasten the collar high around her throat and, this propriety taken care of, I had the feeling she was as content to be reading the Bible here in Vught to those who had never heard it as she'd been serving soup to hungry people in the hallway of the Beje.

As for me, I set my heart every day more firmly on September 1.

And then, all of a sudden, it looked as though we would not have to wait even this long. The Princess Irene Brigade was rumored to be in France, moving toward Belgium. The Brigade was part of the Dutch forces that had escaped to England during the Five-Day War; now it was marching to reclaim its own.

The guards were noticeably tense. Roll call was an agony. The old and the ill who were slow reaching their places were beaten mercilessly. Even the "red light commando" came in for discipline. These young women were ordinarily a favored group of prisoners. Prostitutes, mostly from Amsterdam, they were in prison not for their profession—which was extolled as a patriotic duty—but for infecting German soldiers. Ordinarily, with the male guards anyway, they had a bold, breezy manner; now even they had to form ruler-straight lines and stand hours at frozen attention.

The sound of the firing squad was heard more and more often. One lunchtime when the bell sounded to return to work, Mrs. Floor did not appear at the bench beside me. It always took a while for my eyes to readjust to the dim factory after the bright sun outside: it was only gradually that I saw the hunk of black bread still resting at her place on the bench. There had been no husband to deliver it to.

And so hanging between hope and horror we waited out the days. Rumor was all we lived on. The Brigade was across the Dutch border. The Brigade was destroyed. The Brigade had never landed. Women who had stayed away from the whispered little prayer service around our cot now crowded close, demanding signs and predictions from the Bible.

On the morning of September 1 Mrs. Floor gave birth to a baby girl. The child lived four hours.

Several days later we awoke to the sound of distant explosions. Long before the roll-call whistle the entire barracks was up and milling about in the dark between the cots. Was it bombs? Artillery fire? Surely the Brigade had reached Brabant. This very day they might be in Vught!

The scowls and threats of the guards when they arrived daunted us not at all. Everyone's mind had turned homeward, everyone talked of what she would do first. "The plants will all be dead," said Betsie, "but we'll get some cuttings from Nollie! We'll wash the windows so the sun can come in."

At the Phillips factory Mr. Moorman tried to calm us. "Those aren't bombs," he said, "and certainly not guns. That's demolition work. Germans. They're probably blowing up bridges. It means they expect an attack but not that it's here. It might not come for weeks."

This dampened us a bit, but as the blasts came closer and closer nothing could keep down hope. Now they were so near they hurt our ears.

"Drop your lower jaw!" Mr. Moorman called down the long room. "Keep your mouth open and it will save your eardrums."

We had our midday meal inside with the doors and windows closed. We'd been working again for an hour—or sitting at our benches, no one could work—when the order came to return to dormitories. With sudden urgency women embraced husbands and sweethearts who worked beside them at Phillips.

Betsie was waiting for me outside our barracks. "Corrie! Has the Brigade come? Are we free?"

"No. Not yet. I don't know. Oh, Betsie, why am I so frightened?"

The loudspeaker in the men's camp was sounding the signal for roll call. No order was given here and we drifted about aimlessly, listening we scarcely knew for what. Names were being read through the men's speaker, though it was too far away to make them out.

And suddenly an insane fear gripped the waiting women. A deathlike silence now hung over both sides of the vast camp. The loudspeaker had fallen silent. We exchanged wordless looks, we almost feared to breathe.

Then rifle fire split the air. Around us women began to weep. A second volley. A third. For two hours the executions went on. Someone counted. More than seven hundred male prisoners were killed that day.

There was little sleeping in our barracks that night and no roll call the following morning. About 6:00 A.M. we were ordered to collect our personal things. Betsie and I put our belongings into the pillowcases we had brought from Scheveningen: toothbrushes, needle and thread, a small bottle of Davitamon oil that had come in a Red Cross package, Nollie's blue sweater which was the only thing we had brought with us when we left the quarantine camp ten weeks before. I transferred the Bible in its bag from Betsie's back to my own; she was so thin it made a visible bump between her shoulders.

We were marched to a field where soldiers were passing out blankets from the backs of open trucks. As we filed past, Betsie and I drew two beautiful soft new ones; mine was white with blue stripes, Betsie's white with red stripes—obviously the property of some well-to-do family.

About noon the exodus from camp began. Through the drab streets of barracks we went, past the bunkers, through the maze of barbed-wire compounds and enclosures, and at last onto the rough dirt road through the woods down which we had stumbled that rainy night in June. Betsie hung hard to my arm; she was laboring for breath as she always did when she had to walk any distance.

"March! *Schnell!* Double-time!"

I slipped my arm beneath Betsie's shoulders and half-carried her the final quarter-mile. At last the path ended and we lined up facing the single track, over a thousand women standing toe to heel. Farther along, the men's section was also at the siding; it was impossible to identify individuals among the shaved heads glistening in the autumn sun.

At first I thought our train had not come; then I realized that these freight cars standing on the tracks were for us. Already the men were being prodded aboard, clambering up over the high sides. We could not see the engine, just this row of small, high-wheeled European boxcars stretching out of sight in both directions, machine guns mounted at intervals on the roof. Soldiers were approaching along the track, pausing at each car to haul open the heavy sliding door. In front of us a gaping black interior appeared. Women began to press forward.

Clutching our blankets and pillowcases we were swept along with the others. Betsie's chest was still heaving oddly after the rapid march. I had to boost her over the side of the train.

At first I could make out nothing in the dark car; then in a corner I saw a tall, uneven shape. It was a stack of bread, dozens of flat black loaves piled one on top of another. A long trip then. . . .

The small car was getting crowded. We were shoved against the back wall. Thirty or forty people were all that could fit in. And still the soldiers drove women over the side, cursing, jabbing with their guns. Shrieks rose from the center of the car but still the press increased. It was only when eighty women were packed inside that the door thumped shut and we heard iron bolts driven into place.

Women were sobbing and many fainted, although in the tight-wedged crowd they remained upright. Just when it seemed certain that those in the middle must suffocate or be trampled to death, we worked out a kind of system where, by half-sitting, half-lying with our legs wedged around one another like members of a sledding team, we were able to get down on the floor of the car.

"Do you know what I am thankful for?" Betsie's gentle voice startled me in that squirming madhouse. "I am thankful that Father is in heaven today!"

Father. Yes! Oh Father, how could I have wept for you?

The warm sun beat down on the motionless train, the temperature in the packed car rose, the air grew foul. Beside me someone was tugging at a nail in the ancient wood of the wall. At last it came free; with the point she set to work gouging the hole wider. Others around the sides took up the idea and in a while blessed whiffs of outside air began to circle about us.

It was hours before the train gave a sudden lurch and began to move. Almost at once it stopped again, then again crawled forward. The rest of the day and into the night it was the same, stopping, starting, slamming, jerking. Once when it was my turn at the air-hole I saw in the moonlight trainmen carrying a length of twisted rail. Tracks ahead must be destroyed. I passed the news. Maybe they would not be able to repair them. Maybe we would still be in Holland when liberation came.

Betsie's forehead was hot to my hand. The "red light" girl between whose legs I was wedged squeezed herself into an even tighter crouch so that Betsie could lie almost flat across my lap. I dozed too, from time to time, my head on the shoulder of the friendly girl behind us. Once I dreamed it was storming. I could hear the hailstones on Tante Jans's front windows. I opened my eyes. It really was hailing. I could hear it rattling against the side of the car.

Everyone was awake now and talking. Another storm of hail. And then we heard a burst of machine-gun fire from the roof of the train.

"It's bullets!" someone shouted. "They're attacking the train."

Again we heard that sound like tiny stones striking the wall, and again the machine guns answered. Had the Brigade reached us at last? The firing died away. For an hour the train sat motionless. Then slowly we crawled forward.

At dawn someone called out that we were passing through the border town of Emmerich.

We had arrived in Germany.

CHAPTER THIRTEEN

Ravensbruck

For two more incredible days and two more nights we were carried deeper and deeper into the land of our fears. Occasionally one of the loaves of bread was passed from hand to hand. But not even the most elementary provision had been made for sanitation and the air in the car was such that few could eat.

And gradually, more terrible than the crush of bodies and the filth, the single obsession was: something to drink. Two or three times when the train stopped, the door was slid open a few inches and a pail of water passed in. But we had become animals, incapable of plan or system. Those near the door got it all.

At last, the morning of the fourth day, the train stopped again and the door was opened its full width. Like infants, on hands and knees, we crawled to the opening and lowered ourselves over the side. In front of us was a smiling blue lake. On the far side, among sycamore trees, rose a white church steeple.

The stronger prisoners hauled buckets of water from the lake. We drank through cracked and swollen lips. The train was shorter; the cars carrying the men had disappeared. Only a handful of soldiers—some of them looking no older than fifteen—were there to guard a thousand women. No more were needed. We could scarcely walk, let alone resist.

After a while they got us into straggly columns and marched us off. For a mile the road followed the shore of the lake, then left it to climb a hill. I wondered if Betsie could make it to the top, but the sight of trees and sky seemed to have revived her and she supported me as much as I her. We passed a number of local people on foot and in horse-drawn wagons. The children especially seemed wonderful to me, pink-cheeked and healthy. They returned my stares with wide-eyed interest; I noticed, however, that the adults did not look at us but turned their heads away as we approached.

From the crest of the hill we saw it, like a vast scar on the green German landscape; a city of low gray barracks surrounded by concrete walls on which guard towers rose at intervals. In the very center, a square smokestack emitted a thin gray vapor into the blue sky.

"Ravensbruck!"

Like a whispered curse the word passed back through the lines. This was the notorious women's extermination camp whose name we had heard even in Haarlem. That squat concrete building, that smoke disappearing in the bright sunlight—no! I would not look at it! As Betsie and I stumbled down the hill, I felt the Bible thumping between my shoulder blades. God's good news. Was it to this world that He had spoken it?

Now we were close enough to see the skull-and-crossbones posted at intervals on the walls to warn of electrified wiring along the top. The massive iron gates swung in; we marched between them. Acres of soot-gray barracks stretched ahead of us. Just inside the wall was a row of waist-high water spigots. We charged them, thrusting hands, arms, legs, even heads, under the streams of water, washing away the stench of the boxcars. A squad of women guards in dark blue uniforms rushed at us, hauling and shouting, swinging their short, hard crops.

At last they drove us back from the faucets and herded us down an avenue between barracks. This camp appeared far grimmer than the one we had left. At least, in marches about Vught, we had caught sight of fields and woods. Here, every vista ended in the same concrete barrier; the camp was set down in a vast man-made valley rising on every side to those towering wire-topped walls.

At last we halted. In front of us a vast canvas tent-roof—no sides—covered an acre or more of straw-strewn ground. Betsie and I found a spot on the edge of this area and sank gratefully down. Instantly we were on our feet again. Lice! The straw was literally alive with them. We stood for a while, clutching blankets and pillowcases well away from the infested ground. But at last we spread our blankets over the squirming straw and sat on them.

Some of the prisoners had brought scissors from Vught: everywhere beneath the huge tent women were cutting one another's hair. A pair was passed to us. Of course we must do the same, long hair was folly in such a place. But as I cut Betsie's chestnut waves, I cried.

Toward the evening there was a commotion at one end of the tent. A line of S.S. guards was moving across it, driving women out from under the canvas. We scrambled to our feet and snatched up our blankets as they bore down on us. Perhaps a hundred yards beyond the tent the chase stopped. We stood about, uncertain what to do. Whether a new group of prisoners had arrived or what the reason was for driving us from the tent, no one knew. Women began spreading their blankets on the hard cinder ground. Slowly it dawned on Betsie and me that we were to spend the night here where we stood. We laid my blanket on the ground, stretched out side by side and pulled hers over us.

"The night is dark and I am far from home . . ." Betsie's sweet soprano was picked up by voices all around us. "Lead Thou me on. . . ."

We were waked up some time in the middle of the night by a clap of thunder and a deluge of rain. The blankets soaked through and water gathered in puddles beneath us. In the morning the field was a vast sodden swamp: hands, clothes, and faces were black from the cinder mud.

We were still wringing water from our blankets when the command came to line up for coffee. It was not coffee but a thin liquid of approximately the same color and we were grateful to get it as we shuffled double-file past the makeshift field kitchen. There was a slice of black bread for each prisoner too, then nothing more until we were given a ladle of turnip soup and a small boiled potato late in the afternoon.

In between we were kept standing at rigid attention on the soggy parade ground where we had spent the night. We were near one edge of the huge camp here, close enough to the outer wall to see the triple row of electric wires running along the top. Two entire days we spent this way, stretching out again the second night right where we stood. It did not rain again but ground and blankets were still damp. Betsie began to cough. I took Nollie's blue sweater from my pillowcase, wrapped it around her and gave her a few drops of the vitamin oil. But by morning she had agonizing intestinal cramps. Again and again throughout that second day she had to ask the impatient woman monitor at the head of our row for permission to go to the ditch that served as sanitary facility.

It was the third night as we were getting ready to lie down again under the sky when the order came to report to the processing center for new arrivals. A ten-minute march brought us to the building. We inched along a corridor into a huge reception room. And there under the harsh ceiling lights we saw a dismal sight. As each woman reached a desk where some officers sat she had to lay her blanket, pillowcase, and whatever else she carried onto a growing pile of these things. A few desks further along she had to strip off every scrap of clothes, throw them onto a second pile, and walk naked past the scrutiny of a dozen S.S. men into the shower room. Coming out of the shower she wore only a thin prison dress and a pair of shoes. Nothing more.

But Betsie needed that sweater! She needed the vitamins! Most of all, we needed our Bible. How could we live in this place without it? But how could I ever take it past so many watchful eyes without the overalls covering it?

We were almost at the first desk. I fished desperately in my pillowcase, drew out the bottle of vitamins and closed my fist around them. Reluctantly we dropped the other things on the heap that was fast becoming a mountain. "Dear God," I prayed, "You have given us this precious Book. You have kept it hidden through checkpoints and inspections. You have used it for so many—"

I felt Betsie stagger against me and looked at her in alarm. Her face was white, her lips pressed tight together. A guard was passing by; I begged him in German to show us the toilets. Without so much as a glance, he jerked his head in the direction of the shower room.

Timidly Betsie and I stepped out of line and walked to the door of the big, dank-smelling room with its row on row of overhead spigots. It was empty, waiting for the next batch of fifty naked and shivering women to be admitted.

"Please," I said to the S.S. man guarding the door, "where are the toilets?"

He did not look at me either. "Use the drainholes!" he snapped, and as we stepped inside he slammed the door behind us. We stood alone in the room where a few minutes later we would return stripped even of the clothes on our backs. Here were the prison things we were to put on, piled just inside the door. From the front and back of each otherwise ordinary dress a large "X" had been cut and replaced with cloth of another color.

And then we saw something else, stacked in the far corner, a pile of old wooden benches. They were slimy with mildew, crawling with cockroaches, but to me they seemed the furniture of heaven itself.

"The sweater! Take the sweater off!" I hissed, fumbling with the string at my neck. Betsie handed it to me and in an instant I had wrapped it around the Bible and the vitamin bottle and stuffed the precious bundle behind the benches.

And so it was that when we were herded into that room ten minutes later we were not poor, but rich. Rich in this new evidence of the care of Him who was God even of Ravensbruck.

We stood beneath the spigots as long as the flow of icy water lasted, feeling it soften our lice-eaten skin. Then we clustered dripping wet around the heap of prison dresses, holding them up, passing them about, looking for approximate fits. I found a loose long-sleeved dress for Betsie that would cover the blue sweater when she would have a chance to put it on. I squirmed into another dress for myself, then reached behind the benches and shoved the little bundle quickly inside the neck.

It made a bulge you could have seen across the Grote Markt. I flattened it out as best I could, pushing it down, tugging the sweater around my waist, but there was no real concealing it beneath the thin cotton dress. And all the while I had the incredible feeling that it didn't matter, that this was not my business, but God's. That all I had to do was walk straight ahead.

As we trooped back out through the shower room door, the S.S. men ran their hands over every prisoner, front, back, and sides. The woman ahead of me was searched three times. Behind me, Betsie was searched. No hand touched me.

At the exit door to the building was a second ordeal, a line of women guards examining each prisoner again. I slowed down as I reached them but the *Aufseherin* in charge shoved me roughly by the shoulder. "Move along! You're holding up the line!"

And so Betsie and I arrived at Barracks 8 in the small
hours of the morning, bringing not only the Bible, but a new
knowledge of the power of Him whose story it was. There
were three women already asleep in the bed assigned to us.
They made room for us as best they could but the mattress
sloped and I kept sliding to the floor. At last all five of us
lay sideways across the bed and managed to get shoulders
and elbows arranged. The blanket was a poor threadbare
affair compared with the ones we had given up, but at least
the overcrowding produced its own warmth. Betsie had put
on the blue sweater beneath her long-sleeved dress and
wedged now between me and the others, her shivering
gradually subsided and she was asleep. I lay awake a while
longer, watching a searchlight sweep the rear wall in long
regular arcs, hearing the distant calls of soldiers patrolling
the walls. . . .

Morning roll call at Ravensbruck came half an hour
earlier than at Vught. By 4:30 A.M. we had to be standing
outside in the black predawn chill, standing at parade attention in blocks of one hundred women, ten wide, ten deep.
Sometimes after hours of this we would gain the shelter of
the barracks only to hear the whistle.

"Everybody out! Fall in for roll call!"

Barracks 8 was in the quarantine compound. Next to us—
perhaps as a deliberate warning to newcomers—were
located the punishment barracks. From there, all day long
and often into the night, came the sounds of hell itself. They
were not the sounds of anger, or of any human emotion, but
of a cruelty altogether detached: blows landing in regular
rhythm, screams keeping pace. We would stand in our ten-
deep ranks with our hands trembling at our sides, longing to
jam them against our ears, to make the sounds stop.

The instant of dismissal we would mob the door of Barracks 8, stepping on each others' heels in our eagerness to
get inside, to shrink the world back to understandable
proportions.

It grew harder and harder. Even within these four walls
there was too much misery, too much seemingly pointless
suffering. Every day something else failed to make sense,
something else grew too heavy. "Will You carry this too,
Lord Jesus?"

But as the rest of the world grew stranger, one thing became increasingly clear. And that was the reason the two of us were here. Why others should suffer we were not shown. As for us, from morning until lights-out, whenever we were not in ranks for roll call, our Bible was the center of an ever-widening circle of help and hope. Like waifs clustered around a blazing fire, we gathered about it, holding out our hearts to its warmth and light. The blacker the night around us grew, the brighter and truer and more beautiful burned the word of God. "Who shall separate us from the love of Christ? Shall tribulation, or distress, or persecution, or famine, or nakedness, or peril, or sword? . . . Nay, in all these things we are more than conquerors through him that loved us."

I would look about us as Betsie read, watching the light leap from face to face. More than conquerors. . . . It was not a wish. It was a fact. We knew it, we experienced it minute by minute—poor, hated, hungry. We are more than conquerors. Not "we shall be." We are! Life in Ravensbruck took place on two separate levels, mutually impossible. One, the observable, external life, grew every day more horrible. The other, the life we lived with God, grew daily better, truth upon truth, glory upon glory.

Sometimes I would slip the Bible from its little sack with hands that shook, so mysterious had it become to me. It was new; it had just been written. I marveled sometimes that the ink was dry. I had believed the Bible always, but reading it now had nothing to do with belief. It was simply a description of the way things were—of hell and heaven, of how men act and how God acts. I had read a thousand times the story of Jesus' arrest—how soldiers had slapped Him, laughed at Him, flogged Him. Now such happenings had faces and voices.

Fridays—the recurrent humiliation of medical inspection. The hospital corridor in which we waited was unheated, and a fall chill had settled into the walls. Still we were forbidden even to wrap ourselves in our own arms, but had to maintain our erect, hands-at-sides position as we filed slowly past a phalanx of grinning guards. How there could have been any pleasure in the sight of these stick-thin legs and hunger-bloated stomachs I could not imagine. Surely there is no more wretched sight than the human body unloved and uncared for. Nor could I see the necessity for the complete undressing: when we finally reached the examining room a doctor looked down each throat, another—a dentist presumably—at our teeth, a third in between each finger. And that was all. We trooped again down the long, cold corridor and picked up our X-marked dresses at the door.

But it was one of these mornings while we were waiting, shivering, in the corridor, that yet another page in the Bible leapt into life for me.

He hung naked on the cross.

I had not known—I had not thought. . . . The paintings, the carved crucifixes showed at the least a scrap of cloth. But this, I suddenly knew, was the respect and reverence of the artist. But oh—at the time itself, on that other Friday morning—there had been no reverence. No more than I saw in the faces around us now.

I leaned toward Betsie, ahead of me in line. Her shoulder blades stood out sharp and thin beneath her blue-mottled skin.

"Betsie, they took *His* clothes too."

Ahead of me I heard a little gasp. "Oh, Corrie. And I never thanked Him. . . ."

Every day the sun rose a little later, the bite took longer to leave the air. It will be better, everyone assured everyone else, when we move into permanent barracks. We'll have a blanket apiece. A bed of our own. Each of us painted into the picture her own greatest need.

For me it was a dispensary where Betsie could get medication for her cough. "There'll be a nurse assigned to the barracks." I said it so often that I convinced myself. I was doling out a drop of the Davitamon each morning on her piece of black bread, but how much longer could the small bottle last? "Especially," I would tell her, "if you keep sharing it around every time someone sneezes."

The move to permanent quarters came the second week in October. We were marched, ten abreast, along a wide cinder avenue and then into a narrower street of barracks. Several times the column halted while numbers were read out— names were never used at Ravensbruck. At last Betsie's and mine were called: "Prisoner 66729, Prisoner 66730." We stepped out of line with a dozen or so others and stared at the long gray front of Barracks 28. Half its windows seemed to have been broken and replaced with rags. A door in the center let us into a large room where two hundred or more women bent over knitting needles. On tables between them were piles of woolen socks in army gray.

On either side doors opened into two still larger rooms— by far the largest dormitories we had yet seen. Betsie and I followed a prisoner-guide through the door at the right. Because of the broken windows the vast room was in semi-twilight. Our noses told us, first, that the place was filthy: somewhere plumbing had backed up, the bedding was soiled and rancid. Then as our eyes adjusted to the gloom we saw that there were no individual beds at all, but great square piers stacked three high, and wedged side by side and end to end with only an occasional narrow aisle slicing through.

We followed our guide single file—the aisle was not wide enough for two—fighting back the claustrophobia of these platforms rising everywhere above us. The tremendous room was nearly empty of people; they must have been out on various work crews. At last she pointed to a second tier in the center of a large block. To reach it we had to stand on the bottom level, haul ourselves up, and then crawl across three other straw-covered platforms to reach the one that we would share with—how many? The deck above us was too close to let us sit up. We lay back, struggling against the nausea that swept over us from the reeking straw. We could hear the women who had arrived with us finding their places.

Suddenly I sat up, striking my head on the cross-slats above. Something had pinched my leg.

"Fleas!" I cried. "Betsie, the place is swarming with them!"

We scrambled across the intervening platforms, heads low to avoid another bump, dropped down to the aisle, and edged our way to a patch of light.

"Here! And here another one!" I wailed. "Betsie, how can we live in such a place!"

"Show us. Show us how." It was said so matter of factly it took me a second to realize she was praying. More and more the distinction between prayer and the rest of life seemed to be vanishing for Betsie.

"Corrie!" she said excitedly. "He's given us the answer! Before we asked, as He always does! In the Bible this morning. Where was it? Read that part again!"

I glanced down the long dim aisle to make sure no guard was in sight, then drew the Bible from its pouch. "It was in First Thessalonians," I said. We were on our third complete reading of the New Testament since leaving Scheveningen. In the feeble light I turned the pages. "Here it is: 'Comfort the frightened, help the weak, be patient with everyone. See that none of you repays evil for evil, but always seek to do good to one another and to all. . . .'" It seemed written expressly to Ravensbruck.

"Go on," said Betsie. "That wasn't all."

"Oh yes: '. . . to one another and to all. Rejoice always, pray constantly, give thanks in all circumstances; for this is the will of God in Christ Jesus—'"

"That's it, Corrie! That's His answer. 'Give thanks in all circumstances!' That's what we can do. We can start right now to thank God for every single thing about this new barracks!"

I stared at her, then around me at the dark, foul-aired room.

"Such as?" I said.

"Such as being assigned here together."

I bit my lip. "Oh yes, Lord Jesus!"

"Such as what you're holding in your hands."

I looked down at the Bible. "Yes! Thank You, dear Lord, that there was no inspection when we entered here! Thank You for all the women, here in this room, who will meet You in these pages."

"Yes," said Betsie. "Thank You for the very crowding here. Since we're packed so close, that many more will hear!" She looked at me expectantly. "Corrie!" she prodded.

"Oh, all right. Thank You for the jammed, crammed, stuffed, packed, suffocating crowds."

"Thank You," Betsie went on serenely, "for the fleas and for—"

The fleas! This was too much. "Betsie, there's no way even God can make me grateful for a flea."

"'Give thanks in *all* circumstances,'" she quoted. "It doesn't say, 'in pleasant circumstances.' Fleas are part of this place where God has put us."

And so we stood between piers of bunks and gave thanks for fleas. But this time I was sure Betsie was wrong.

They started arriving soon after 6:00 o'clock, the women of Barracks 28, tired, sweat-stained, and dirty from the long forced-labor details. The building, we learned from one of our platform mates, had been designed to hold four hundred. There were now fourteen hundred quartered here with more arriving weekly as concentration camps in Poland, France, Belgium, Austria, as well as Holland were evacuated toward the center of Germany.

There were nine of us sharing our particular square, designed for four, and some grumbling as the others discovered they would have to make room for Betsie and me. Eight acrid and overflowing toilets served the entire room; to reach them we had to crawl not only over our own bedmates but over those on the other platforms between us and the closest aisle, always at the risk of adding too much weight to the already sagging slats and crashing down on the people beneath. It happened several times, that first night. From somewhere in the room would come a splintering sound, a shriek, smothered cries.

Even when the slats held, the least movement on the upper platforms sent a shower of dust and straw over the sleepers below—followed by a volley of curses. In Barracks 8 most of us had been Dutch. Here there was not even a common language and among exhausted, ill-fed people quarrels erupted constantly.

There was one raging now as the women sleeping nearest the windows slammed them shut against the cold. At once scores of voices demanded that they be raised again. Brawls were starting all up and down that side of the room; we heard scuffling, slaps, sobs.

In the dark I felt Betsie's hands clasp mine. "Lord Jesus," she said aloud, "send Your peace into this room. There has been too little praying here. The very walls know it. But where You come, Lord, the spirit of strife cannot exist...."

The change was gradual, but distinct. One by one the angry sounds let up.

"I'll make you a deal!" The voice spoke German with a strong Scandinavian accent. "You can sleep in here where it's warmer and I'll take your place by the window!"

"And add your lice to my own!" But there was a chuckle in the answer. "No thanks."

"I'll tell you what!" The third voice had a French burr. "We'll open them halfway. That way we'll be only half-frozen and you'll be only half-smothered."

A ripple of laughter widened around the room at this. I lay back on the sour straw and knew there was one more circumstance for which I could give thanks. Betsie had come to Barracks 28.

Roll call came at 4:30 A.M. here as it had in quarantine. A whistle roused us at 4:00 when, without even shaking the straw from clothes and hair, the stampede began for the ration of bread and coffee in the center room. Latecomers found none.

The count was made in the *Lagerstrasse*, the wide avenue leading to the hospital. There we joined the occupants of other barracks—some 35,000 at that time—stretching out of sight in the pale glow of the street lamps, feet growing numb on the cold cinder ground.

After roll call, work crews were called out. For weeks Betsie and I were assigned to the Siemens factory. This huge complex of mills and railroad terminals was a mile and a half from the camp. The "Siemens Brigade," several thousand of us, marched out the iron gate beneath the charged wires into a world of trees and grass and horizons. The sun rose as we skirted the little lake; the gold of the late fall fields lifted our hearts.

The work at Siemens, however, was sheer misery. Betsie and I had to push a heavy handcart to a railroad siding where we unloaded large metal plates from a boxcar and wheeled them to a receiving gate at the factory. The grueling workday lasted eleven hours. At least, at noontime we were given a boiled potato and some thin soup; those who worked inside the camp had no midday meal.

Returning to camp we could barely lift our swollen and aching legs. The soldiers patrolling us bellowed and cursed, but we could only shuffle forward inches at a step. I noticed again how the local people turned their eyes another way.

Back at the barracks we formed yet another line—would there never be an end to columns and waits?—to receive our ladle of turnip soup in the center room. Then, as quickly as we could for the press of people, Betsie and I made our way to the rear of the dormitory room where we held our worship

"service." Around our own platform area there was not
enough light to read the Bible, but back here a small light
bulb cast a wan yellow circle on the wall, and here an ever
larger group of women gathered.

They were services like no others, these times in Barracks
28. A single meeting might include a recital of the Magnifi-
cat in Latin by a group of Roman Catholics, a whispered
hymn by some Lutherans, and a sotto-voce chant by Eastern
Orthodox women. With each moment the crowd around us
would swell, packing the nearby platforms, hanging over the
edges, until the high structures groaned and swayed.

At last either Betsie or I would open the Bible. Because
only the Hollanders could understand the Dutch text we
would translate aloud in German. And then we would hear
the life-giving words passed back along the aisles in French,
Polish, Russian, Czech, back into Dutch. They were little
previews of heaven, these evenings beneath the light bulb.
I would think of Haarlem, each substantial church set behind its wrought-iron fence and its barrier of doctrine. And
I would know again that in darkness God's truth shines
most clear.

At first Betsie and I called these meetings with great
timidity. But as night after night went by and no guard ever
came near us, we grew bolder. So many now wanted to join
us that we held a second service after evening roll call. There
on the *Lagerstrasse* we were under rigid surveillance, guards
in their warm wool capes marching constantly up and down.
In was the same in the center room of the barracks: half a
dozen guards or camp police always present. Yet in the large
dormitory room there was almost no supervision at all. We
did not understand it.

Another strange thing was happening. The Davitamon
bottle was continuing to produce drops. It scarcely seemed
possible, so small a bottle, so many doses a day. Now, in
addition to Betsie, a dozen others on our pier were taking it.

My instinct was always to hoard it—Betsie was growing
so very weak! But others were ill as well. It was hard to say
no to eyes that burned with fever, hands that shook with
chill. I tried to save it for the very weakest—but even these
soon numbered fifteen, twenty, twenty-five. . . .

And still, every time I tilted the little bottle, a drop appeared at the tip of the glass stopper. It just couldn't be! I held it up to the light, trying to see how much was left, but the dark brown glass was too thick to see through.

"There was a woman in the Bible," Betsie said, "whose oil jar was never empty." She turned to it in the Book of Kings, the story of the poor widow of Zarephath who gave Elijah a room in her home: "The jar of meal wasted not, neither did the cruse of oil fail, according to the word of Jehovah which he spoke by Elijah."

Well—but—wonderful things happened all through the Bible. It was one thing to believe that such things were possible thousands of years ago, another to have it happen now, to us, this very day. And yet it happened, this day, and the next, and the next, until an awed little group of spectators stood around watching the drops fall onto the daily rations of bread.

Many nights I lay awake in the shower of straw dust from the mattress above, trying to fathom the marvel of supply lavished upon us. "Maybe," I whispered to Betsie, "only a molecule or two really gets through that little pinhole—and then in the air it expands!"

I heard her soft laughter in the dark. "Don't try too hard to explain it, Corrie. Just accept it as a surprise from a Father who loves you."

And then one day Mien pushed her way to us in the evening food line. "Look what I've got for you!"

Mien was a pretty young Dutch woman we had met in Vught. She was assigned to the hospital and often managed to bring to Barracks 28 some stolen treasure from the staff room—a sheet of newspaper to stuff in a broken window, a slice of bread left untouched on a nurse's plate. Now we peered into the small cloth sack she carried.

"Vitamins!" I cried, and then cast an apprehensive glance at a policeman nearby. "Yeast compound!" I whispered.

"Yes!" she hissed back. "There were several huge jars. I emptied each just the same amount."

We gulped the thin turnip water, marveling at our sudden riches. Back at the bunk I took the bottle from the straw. "We'll finish the drops first," I decided.

But that night, no matter how long I held it upside down, or how hard I shook it, not another drop appeared.

On the first of November a coat was issued to each prisoner. Betsie's and mine were both of Russian make, probably once trimmed with fur: threads showed where something had been torn from the collars and cuffs.

Call-ups for the Siemens factory had ceased and we speculated that it had been hit in one of the bombing raids that came within earshot almost nightly now. Betsie and I were put to work leveling some rough ground just inside the camp wall. This too was back-breaking labor. Sometimes as I bent to lift a load my heart cramped strangely; at night spasms of pain gripped my legs.

But the biggest problem was Betsie's strength. One morning after a hard night's rain we arrived to find the ground sodden and heavy. Betsie had never been able to lift much; today her shovels-ful were microscopic and she stumbled frequently as she walked to the low ground where we dumped the loads.

"Schneller!" a guard screamed at her. "Can't you go faster?"

Why must they scream, I wondered as I sank my shovel into the black muck. Why couldn't they speak like ordinary human beings? I straightened slowly, the sweat drying on my back. I was remembering where we had first heard this maniac sound. The Beje. In Tante Jans's rooms. A voice coming from the shell-shaped speaker, a scream lingering in the air even after Betsie had leapt to shut it off. . . .

"Loafer! Lazy swine!"

The guard snatched Betsie's shovel from her hands and ran from group to group of the digging crew, exhibiting the handful of dirt that was all Betsie had been able to lift.

"Look what Madame Baroness is carrying! Surely she will over-exert herself!"

The other guards and even some of the prisoners laughed. Encouraged, the guard threw herself into a parody of Betsie's faltering walk. A male guard was with our detail today and in the presence of a man the women guards were always animated.

As the laughter grew, I felt a murderous anger rise. The guard was young and well fed—was it Betsie's fault that she was old and starving? But to my astonishment, Betsie too was laughing.

"That's me all right," she admitted. "But you'd better

let me totter along with my little spoonful, or I'll have to stop altogether."

The guard's plump cheeks went crimson. "I'll decide who's to stop!" And snatching the leather crop from her belt she slashed Betsie across the chest and neck.

Without knowing I was doing it I had seized my shovel and rushed at her.

Betsie stepped in front of me before anyone had seen. "Corrie!" she pleaded, dragging my arm to my side. "Corrie! keep working!" She tugged the shovel from my hand and dug it into the mud. Contemptuously the guard tossed Betsie's shovel toward us. I picked it up, still in a daze. A red stain appeared on Betsie's collar; a welt began to swell on her neck.

Betsie saw where I was looking and laid a bird-thin hand over the whip mark. "Don't look at it, Corrie. Look at Jesus only." She drew away her hand: it was sticky with blood.

In mid-November the rains started in earnest, chill, drenching, daylong downpours that left beads of moisture even on the inside walls. The *Lagerstrasse* was never dry now; even when the rain let up, deep puddles stood in the road. We were not allowed to step around them as the ranks were formed: often we stood in water up to our ankles, and at night the barracks reeked with rotting shoe leather.

Betsie's cough began to bring up blood. We went to sick call at the hospital, but the thermometer registered only 102°, not enough to admit her to the wards. Alas for my fantasies of a nurse and a dispensary in each barracks. This large bare room in the hospital was where all the sick in the camp had to assemble, often standing outside in the rain for hours just to get through the door.

I hated the dismal place full of sick and suffering women, but we had to go back, again and again, for Betsie's condition was growing worse. She was not repelled by the room as I was. To her it was simply a setting in which to talk about Jesus—as indeed was everyplace else. Wherever she was, at work, in the food line, in the dormitory, Betsie spoke to those around her about His nearness and His yearning to come into their lives. As her body grew weaker, her faith seemed to grow bolder. And sick call was "such an important place, Corrie! Some of these people are at the very threshold of heaven!"

At last one night Betsie's fever registered over the required 104°. There was another long wait until a nurse appeared to lead her and half a dozen others into the hospital proper. I stayed with them as far as the door to the ward, then made my way slowly back to the barracks.

As usual, as I stood in the door of the dormitory, it reminded me most of an anthill. Some women were already asleep after the long workday, but most were stirring about, some waiting for a turn at the toilets, others picking lice off themselves and their neighbors. I twisted and squirmed through the crowded aisles to the rear where the prayer service was just ending. Nights when Betsie and I reported to sick call we left the Bible with Mrs. Wielmaker, a saintly Roman Catholic woman from The Hague who could render the Dutch words in German, French, Latin, or Greek. Women crowded around me, asking after Betsie. How was she? How long would she have to stay?

Lights-out blew and the scramble into the bunks began. I hoisted myself to the middle tier and crawled across those already in place. What a difference since Betsie had come to this room! Where before this had been the moment for scuffles and cursing, tonight the huge domitory buzzed with "Sorry!" "Excuse me!" And "No harm done!"

I found our section in the dark and squeezed into a spot in the middle. From the doorway a searchlight swept the room, lingering on blocks where anything stirred. Someone's elbow dug into my back, another woman's feet were two inches from my face. How was it possible, packed so close, to be so utterly and miserably alone?

CHAPTER FOURTEEN

The Blue Sweater

In the morning a cold wet mist hung over the *Lagerstrasse*. I was grateful that Betsie did not have to stand outside.

All day the blanketing fog hung over Ravensbruck, an eerie day when sound was muffled and the sun never rose. I was on potato detail, one of a crew hauling baskets of potatoes to long trenches to be covered with dirt against the freezing weather ahead. I was glad of the hard physical work that drove some of the damp from my bones and for the occasional bite of raw potato when guards were not watching.

Next day when the white pall still lay over the camp, my loneliness for Betsie became too much to bear. As soon as roll call was dismissed, I did a desperate thing. Mien had told me a way to get into the hospital without passing the guardpost inside the door. The latrine at the rear, she said, had a very large window too warped to close tight. Since no visiting was permitted in the hospital, relatives of patients often took this way of getting inside.

In the dense fog it was easy to get to the window unseen. I hoisted myself through it, then clapped my hand to my nose against the stinging odor. A row of lidless, doorless toilets stretched along one wall in the pool of their overflow. I dashed for the door, then stopped, my flesh crawling. Against this opposite wall a dozen naked corpses lay side by side on their backs. Some of the eyes were open and seemed to stare unblinkingly at the ceiling.

I was standing there, lead-footed with horror, when two men pushed through the door carrying a sheet-wrapped bundle between them. They did not even glance at me and I realized they took me for a patient. I ducked round them into the hall and stood a moment, stomach knotting with the sight I had seen. After a while I started aimlessly off to the left.

The hospital was a maze of halls and doors. Already I was not sure of the way back to the latrine. What if the potato crew left before I got back? And then a corridor looked familiar. I hurried, almost running from door to door. At last. The ward where I left Betsie! No hospital personnel was in sight: I walked eagerly down the aisles of cots looking from face to face.

"Corrie!"

Betsie was sitting up in a cot near the window. She looked stronger, eyes bright, a touch of color in her sunken cheeks. No nurse or doctor had seen her yet, she said, but the chance to lie still and stay indoors had already made a difference.

Three days afterward, Betsie returned to Barracks 28. She still had received no examination or medicine of any kind and her forehead felt feverish to my touch. But the joy of having her back outweighed my anxiety.

Best of all, as a result of her hospitalization, she was given a permanent assignment to the "knitting brigade," the women we had seen the very first day seated about the tables in the center room. This work was reserved for the weakest prisoners, and now overflowed into the dormitories as well.

Those working in the sleeping rooms received far less supervision than those at the tables, and Betsie found herself with most of the day in which to minister to those around her. She was a lightning knitter who completed her quota of socks long before noon. She kept our Bible with her and spent hours each day reading aloud from it, moving from platform to platform.

One evening I got back to the barracks late from a wood-gathering foray outside the walls. A light snow lay on the ground and it was hard to find the sticks and twigs with which a small stove was kept going in each room. Betsie was waiting for me, as always, so that we could wait through the food line together. Her eyes were twinkling.

"You're looking extraordinarily pleased with yourself," I told her.

"You know we've never understood why we had so much freedom in the big room," she said. "Well—I've found out."

That afternoon, she said, there'd been confusion in her

knitting group about sock sizes and they'd asked the supervisor to come and settle it.

"But she wouldn't. She wouldn't step through the door and neither would the guards. And you know why?"

Betsie could not keep the triumph from her voice: "Because of the fleas! That's what she said, 'That place is crawling with fleas!'"

My mind rushed back to our first hour in this place. I remembered Betsie's bowed head, remembered her thanks to God for creatures I could see no use for.

Though Betsie was now spared heavy outdoor labor, she still had to stand the twice-daily roll call. As December temperatures fell, they became true endurance tests and many did not survive. One dark morning when ice was forming a halo around each street lamp, a feeble-minded girl two rows ahead of us suddenly soiled herself. A guard rushed at her, swinging her thick leather crop while the girl shrieked in pain and terror. It was always more terrible when one of these innocent ones was beaten. Still the *Aufseherin* continued to whip her. It was the guard we had nicknamed "The Snake" because of the shiny dress she wore. I could see it now beneath her long wool cape, glittering in the light of the lamp when she raised her arm. I was grateful when the screaming girl at last lay still on the cinder street.

"Betsie," I whispered when the The Snake was far enough away, "what can we do for these people? Afterward I mean. Can't we make a home for them and care for them and love them?"

"Corrie, I pray every day that we will be allowed to do this! To show them that love is greater!"

And it wasn't until I was gathering twigs later in the morning that I realized that I had been thinking of the feeble-minded, and Betsie of their persecutors.

Several days later my entire work crew was ordered to the hospital for medical inspection. I dropped my dress onto the pile just inside the door and joined the file of naked women. Ahead of us, to my surprise, a doctor was using a stethoscope with all the deliberateness of a real examination.

"What is this for?" I whispered to the woman ahead of me.

"Transport inspection," she hissed back, not moving her head. "Munitions work."

Transport! But they couldn't! They mustn't send me away! Dear God, don't let them take me away from Betsie!

But to my terror I passed one station after another—heart, lungs, scalp, throat—and still I was in the line. Many were pulled out along the way, but those who remained looked hardly stronger. Swollen stomachs, hollow chests, spindly legs: how desperate for manpower Germany must be!

I halted before a woman in a soiled white coat. She turned me around to face a chart on the wall, her hand cold on my bare shoulder. "Read the lowest line you can."

"I—I can't seem to read any of them. (Lord forgive me!) Just the top letter. That big E." The top letter was an F.

The woman seemed to see me for the first time. "You can see better than that! Do you want to be rejected?"

At Ravensbruck, munitions transport was considered a privilege; food and living conditions in the factories were said to be far better than here in the camp.

"Oh yes, Doctor! My sister's here at Ravensbruck! She's not well! I can't leave her!'"

The doctor sat down at her table and scrawled something on a piece of paper. "Come back tomorrow to be fitted for glasses."

Catching up to the line, I unfolded the small blue slip of paper. Prisoner 66730 was instructed to report for an optical fitting at 6:30 the following morning. Six-thirty was the time the transport convoys were loaded.

And so as the huge vans rumbled down the *Lagerstrasse* the next day, I was standing in a corridor of the hospital waiting my turn at the eye clinic. The young man in charge was perhaps a qualified eye doctor, but his entire equipment consisted of a box of framed glasses, from gold-rimmed bifocals to a plastic-framed child's pair. I found none that fitted and at last was ordered back to my work detail.

But, of course, I had no work assignment, having been marked down for transport. I walked back uncertainly toward Barracks 28. I stepped into the center room. The supervisor looked up over the heads of the knitting crew.

"Number?" she said.

I gave it and she wrote it in a black-covered book. "Pick

up your yarn and a pattern sheet," she went on. "You'll have to find a place on one of the beds, there's no room here." And she turned back to the pile of finished socks on the table.

I stood blinking in the center of the room. Then grabbing a skein of the dark gray wool I dashed through the dormitory door. And thus began the closest, most joyous weeks of all the time in Ravensbruck. Side by side, in the sanctuary of God's fleas, Betsie and I ministered the word of God to all in the room. We sat by deathbeds that became doorways of heaven. We watched women who had lost everything grow rich in hope. The knitters of Barracks 28 became the praying heart of the vast diseased body that was Ravensbruck, interceding for all in the camp—guards, under Betsie's prodding, as well as prisoners. We prayed beyond the concrete walls for the healing of Germany, of Europe, of the world—as Mama had once done from the prison of a crippled body.

And as we prayed, God spoke to us about the world after the war. It was extraordinary; in this place where whistles and loudspeakers took the place of decisions, God asked us what we were going to do in the years ahead.

Betsie was always very clear about the answer for her and me. We were to have a house, a large one—much larger than the Beje—to which people who had been damaged by concentration-camp life would come until they felt ready to live again in the normal world.

"It's such a beautiful house, Corrie! The floors are all inlaid wood, with statues set in the walls and a broad staircase sweeping down. And gardens! Gardens all around it where they can plant flowers. It will do them such good, Corrie, to care for flowers!"

I would stare at Betsie in amazement as she talked about these things. She spoke always as though she were describing things that she saw—as if that wide, winding staircase and those bright gardens were the reality, this cramped and filthy barracks the dream.

But it wasn't a dream. It was really, achingly, endlessly true, and it was always during roll calls that the accumulated misery threatened to overwhelm me.

One morning three women from Barracks 28 lingered inside a few minutes to avoid the cold. All the following week the entire barracks was punished by an extra hour at attention. The lights on the *Lagerstrasse* were not even lit when we were driven from our bunks at 3:30 A.M.

It was during this preinspection lineup one morning that I saw what I had till then refused to believe. Headlights appeared at the far end of the long street, wavering over the snow. Trucks with open flat-beds in the rear were approaching, spattering slush as they passed. They pulled up at the front door of the hospital. The door opened and a nurse appeared, supporting an old woman whose legs buckled as she limped down the steps. The nurse lifted her gently onto the back of a truck. They were pouring out the door now, leaning on the arms of nurses and hospital helpers, the old, the ill. Last of all came orderlies with stretchers between them.

Our eyes took in every detail of the scene; our brains refused. We had known, of course, that when overcrowding reached a certain point, the sickest were taken to the brick building at the foot of the great square smokestack. But, that these women here in front of us—these very ones. It was not possible. Above all I could not put it together with the kindly behavior of the nurses. That one in the truck just ahead, bending solicitously, even tenderly, over her patient. . . . What was passing through her mind just now?

And all the while, it grew colder. One night during evening roll call a platoon somewhere far down the *Lagerstrasse* began a rhythmic stamping. The sound grew as others picked it up. The guards did not stop us and at last the entire street was marching in place, pounding tattered shoes against the frozen ground, driving circulation back into numb feet and legs. From now on this was the sound of roll call, the stamping of thousands of feet on the long dark street.

And as the cold increased, so did the special temptation of concentration-camp life: the temptation to think only of oneself. It took a thousand cunning forms. I quickly discovered that when I maneuvered our way toward the middle of the roll-call we had a little protection from the wind.

I knew this was self-centered: when Betsie and I stood in the center, someone else had to stand on the edge. How easy it was to give it other names! I was acting only for Betsie's sake. We were in an important ministry and must keep well.

It was colder in Poland than in Holland; these Polish women probably were not feeling the chill the way we were.

Selfishness had a life of its own. As I watched Mien's bag of yeast compound disappear I began taking it from beneath the straw only after lights-out when others would not see and ask for some. Wasn't Betsie's health more important? (You see, God, she can do so much *for* them! Remember that house, after the war!)

And even if it wasn't right—it wasn't so *very* wrong, was it? Not wrong like sadism and murder and the other monstrous evils we saw in Ravensbruck every day. Oh, this was the great ploy of Satan in that kingdom of his: to display such blatant evil that one could almost believe one's own secret sins didn't matter.

The cancer spread. The second week in December, every occupant of Barracks 28 was issued an extra blanket. The next day a large group of evacuées arrived from Czechoslovakia. One of them assigned to our platform had no blanket at all and Betsie insisted that we give her one of ours. So that evening I "lent" her a blanket. But I didn't "give" it to her. In my heart I held onto the right to that blanket.

Was it coincidence that joy and power imperceptibly drained from my ministry? My prayers took on a mechanical ring. Even Bible reading was dull and lifeless. Betsie tried to take over for me, but her cough made reading aloud impossible.

And so I struggled on with worship and teaching that had ceased to be real. Until one drizzly raw afternoon when just enough light came through the window to read by, I came to Paul's account of his "thorn in the flesh." Three times, he said, he had begged God to take away his weakness, whatever it was. And each time God had said, Rely on Me. At last Paul concluded—the words seemed to leap from the page—that his very weakness was something to give thanks for. Because now Paul knew that none of the wonders and miracles which followed his ministry could be done by his own virtues. It was all Christ's strength, never Paul's.

And there it was.

The truth blazed like sunlight in the shadows of Barracks 28. The real sin I had been committing was not that of inching toward the center of a platoon because I was cold. The real sin lay in thinking that any power to help and transform came from me. Of course it was not *my* wholeness, but Christ's that made the difference.

The short winter day was fading; I could no longer separate the words on the page. And so I closed the Bible and to that group of women clustering close I told the truth about myself—my self-centeredness, my stinginess, my lack of love. That night real joy returned to my worship.

Each roll call the wind seemed sharper. Whenever she could, Mien smuggled newspapers from the staff room at the hospital, which we placed inside our clothes. Nollie's blue sweater beneath Betsie's dress was black with newsprint.

The cold seemed to be affecting Betsie's legs. Sometimes in the morning she could not move them at all and two of us would have to carry her between us. It was not hard—she weighed no more than a child. But she could no longer stamp her feet as the rest of us did to keep the blood flowing. When we returned to the dormitory I would rub her feet and hands, but my own only picked up the chill from hers.

It was the week before Christmas that Betsie woke up unable to move either legs or arms. I shoved my way through the crowded aisles to the center room. The Snake was on duty.

"Please!" I begged. "Betsie is ill! Oh please, she's got to get to the hospital!"

"Stand at attention. State your number."

"Prisoner 66730 reporting. Please, my sister is sick!"

"All prisoners must report for the count. If she's sick she can register at sick call."

Maryke de Graaf, a Dutch woman on the tier above ours, helped me form a cradle with our arms and carry Betsie outside. The rhythmic stamping had already begun in the *Lagerstrasse*. We carried her to the hospital, then stopped. In the light of the street lamps, the sick-call line stretched to the edge of the building and out of sight around the corner. In the sooty snow alongside, three bodies lay where they had fallen.

Without a word Maryke and I turned and carried our load back to the *Lagerstrasse*. After roll call we got her back into bed. Her speech was slow and blurred, but she was trying to say something.

"A camp, Corrie—a concentration camp. But we're . . . in charge . . ." I had to bend very close to hear. The camp was in Germany. It was no longer a prison, but a home where people who had been warped by this philosophy of hate and force could come to learn another way. There were no walls, no barbed wire, and the barracks had windowboxes. "It will be so good for them . . . watching things grow. People can learn to love, from flowers. . . ."

I knew by now which people she meant. The German people. I thought of The Snake standing in the barracks door that morning. "State your number. All prisoners must report for the count."

I looked into Betsie's shrunken face. "We are to have this camp in Germany instead, Betsie? Instead of the big house in Holland?"

"Oh no!" she seemed shocked. "You know we have the house first! It's ready and waiting for us . . . such tall, tall windows! The sun is streaming in—"

A coughing fit seized her; when finally she lay still, a stain of blood blackened the straw. She dozed fitfully during the day and night that followed, waking several times with the excitement of some new detail about our work in Holland or Germany.

"The barracks are gray, Corrie, but we'll paint them green! Bright, light green, like springtime."

"We'll be together, Betsie? We're doing all this together? You're sure about that?"

"Always together, Corrie! You and I . . . always together."

When the siren blew next morning, Maryke and I again carried Betsie from the dormitory. The Snake was standing at the street door. As we started through it with our fragile burden she stepped in front of us. "Take her back to the bunks."

"I thought all pris—"

"Take her back!"

Wonderingly, we replaced Betsie on the bed. Sleet rattled against the windows. Was it possible that the atmosphere of Barracks 28 had affected even this cruel guard? As soon as roll call was dismissed I ran back to the dormitory. There, beside our bed, stood The Snake. Beside her two orderlies from the hospital were setting down a stretcher. The Snake straightened almost guiltily as I approached. "Prisoner is ready for transfer," she snapped.

I looked at the woman more closely: Had she risked fleas and lice to spare Betsie the sick-call line? She did not stop me as I started after the stretcher. Our group of knitters was just entering the big room. As we passed, a Polish friend dropped to her knees and made the sign of the Cross.

Sleet stung us as we reached the outside. I stepped close to the stretcher to form a shield for Betsie. We walked past the waiting line of sick people, through the door and into a large ward. They placed the stretcher on the floor and I leaned down to make out Betsie's words.

". . . must tell people what we have learned here. We must tell them that there is no pit so deep that He is not deeper still. They will listen to us, Corrie, because we have been here."

I stared at her wasted form. "But when will all this happen, Betsie!"

"Now. Right away. Oh, very soon! By the first of the year, Corrie, we will be out of prison!"

A nurse had caught sight of me. I backed to the door of the room and watched as they placed Betsie on a narrow cot close to the window. I ran around to the outside of the building. At last Betsie caught sight of me; we exchanged smiles and soundless words until one of the camp police shouted at me to move along.

About noontime I put down my knitting and went out to the center room. "Prisoner 66730 reporting. Request permission to visit the hospital." I stood ramrod straight.

The Snake glanced up, then scrawled out a pass. Outside it was still sleeting. I reached the door of the ward but the horrible nurse would not let me enter, even with my pass. So I went again to the window next to Betsie's cot. I waited until the nurse left the room, then tapped gently.

Betsie's eyes opened. Slowly she turned her head.

"Are you all right?" I formed with my lips.

She nodded.

"You must get a good rest," I went on.

She moved her lips in reply but I could not follow. She formed the words again. I bent my head to one side, level with hers. The blue lips opened again:

". . . so much work to do. . . ."

The Snake was off duty during the afternoon and evening and though I asked the other guards repeatedly, I did not again get permission to leave. The minute roll call was dismissed the following morning, I headed for the hospital, permission or no.

I reached the window and cupped my eyes to peer in. A nurse was standing directly between me and Betsie. I ducked out of sight, waited a minute, then looked again. A second nurse had joined the first, both now standing where I wanted to see. They stepped to the head and foot of the bed: I gazed curiously at what lay on it. It was a carving in old yellow ivory. There was no clothing on the figure; I could see each ivory rib, and the outline of the teeth through the parchment cheeks.

It took me a moment to realize it was Betsie.

The nurses had each seized two corners of the sheet. They lifted it between them and carried the bundle from the room before my heart had started to beat in my chest.

Betsie! But—she had too much to do! She could not—

Where were they taking her? Where had they gone? I turned from the window and began running along the side of the building, chest hurting me as I breathed.

Then I remembered the washroom. That window at the rear—that was where . . .

My feet carried me mechanically around to the back of the building. And there, with my hand on the windowsill, I stopped. Suppose she was there? Suppose they had laid Betsie on that floor?

I started walking again. I walked for a long time, still with that pain in my chest. And each time my feet took me back to the washroom window. I would not go in. I would not look. Betsie could not be there.

I walked some more. Strangely enough, although I passed several camp police, no one stopped or questioned me.

"Corrie!"

I turned around to see Mien running after me. "Corrie, I've looked for you everywhere! Oh, Corrie, come!"

She seized my arm and drew me toward the back of the hospital.

When I saw where she was headed I wrenched my arm free. "I know, Mien. I know already."

She didn't seem to hear. She seized me again, led me to

the washroom window, and pushed me in ahead of her. In the reeking room stood a nurse. I drew back in alarm, but Mien was behind me.

"This is the sister," Mien said to the nurse.

I turned my head to the side—I would not look at the bodies that lined the far wall. Mien put an arm around my shoulder and drew me across the room till we were standing above that heart-breaking row.

"Corrie! Do you see her!"

I raised my eyes to Betsie's face. Lord Jesus—what have You done! Oh Lord, what are You saying! What are You giving me!

For there lay Betsie, her eyes closed as if in sleep, her face full and young. The care lines, the grief lines, the deep hollows of hunger and disease were simply gone. In front of me was the Betsie of Haarlem, happy and at peace. Stronger! Freer! This was the Betsie of heaven, bursting with joy and health. Even her hair was graciously in place as if an angel had ministered to her.

At last I turned wonderingly to Mien. The nurse went silently to the door and opened it for us herself. "You can leave through the hall," she said softly.

I looked once more at the radiant face of my sister. Then Mien and I left the room together. A pile of clothes was heaped outside in the hallway; on top lay Nollie's blue sweater.

I stooped to pick it up. The sweater was threadbare and stained with newsprint, but it was a tangible link with Betsie. Mien seized my arm. "Don't touch those things! Black lice! They'll all be burned."

And so I left behind the last physical tie. It was just as well. It was better. Now what tied me to Betsie was the hope of heaven.

CHAPTER FIFTEEN

The Three Visions

The beauty of Betsie's face sustained me over the next days, as I went from one to another of the women who had loved her, describing to them her peace and her joy.

Two mornings after her death the count was off at roll call. The other barracks were dismissed, 28 remained in ranks, eyes front. The loudspeaker beeped and a voice came on: a woman was missing; the entire barracks would stand on the *Lagerstrasse* until she was found. Left, right, left, right, endlessly tramping to drive the chill from weary legs. The sun came up, a wan wintry sun that did not warm. I looked down at my feet: my legs and ankles were swelling grotesquely. By noontime there was no feeling in them. Betsie, how happy you are today! No cold, no hunger, nothing between you and the face of Jesus!

The dismissal order came in the afternoon. We learned later that the missing woman had been found dead on one of the upper platforms.

It was the following morning when over the loudspeaker during roll call came the words: "Ten Boom, Cornelia!"

For an instant I stood stupidly where I was. I had been Prisoner 66730 for so long that I almost failed to react to my name. I walked forward.

"Stand to the side!"

What was going to happen? Why had I been singled out? Had someone reported the Bible?

The roll call dragged on. From where I stood I could see almost the entire *Lagerstrasse*, tens of thousands of women stretching out of sight, their breath hanging white in the night air.

The siren blew for dismissal; the guard signaled me to follow her. I splashed through the slush, trying to keep up with the strides of her tall boots. My legs and feet were still painfully swollen from the long count the day before, my shoes were held together with bits of string.

I hobbled behind the guard into the administration barracks at the opposite end of the *Lagerstrasse* from the hospital. Several prisoners were standing in line at a large desk. An officer seated behind it stamped a paper and handed it to the woman in front of him.

"*Entlassen!*" he said.

Entlassen? Released? Was—was the woman free then? Was this—were we all—

He called a name and another prisoner stepped to the desk. A signature, a stamp:

"*Entlassen!*"

At last "Ten Boom, Cornelia," was called. I stepped to the desk, steadying myself against it. He wrote, brought down the stamp, and then I was holding it in my hand: a piece of paper with my name and birthdate on it, and across the top in large black letters: CERTIFICATE OF DISCHARGE.

Dazed, I followed the others through a door at our left. There at another desk I was handed a railway pass entitling me to transportation through Germany to the Dutch border. Outside this office a guard pointed me down a corridor into still another room. There the prisoners who had been ahead of me were tugging their dresses over their heads and lining up against the rear wall.

"Clothing over here!" a smiling prison trusty told me. "*Entlassen* physical," she explained.

I drew the Bible over my head along with the dress, rolled them together and buried the bundle at the bottom of the clothing pile. I joined the others, the wooden wall rough against my bare back. Strange how the very word "Release" had made the procedures of prison a hundred times more hateful. How often Betsie and I had stood like this. But the thought of freedom had stirred in me and the shame of this inspection was greater than all the others.

At last the doctor arrived, a freckle-faced boy in a military uniform. He glanced along the lineup with undisguised contempt. One by one we had to bend, turn around, spread our fingers. When he reached me his eyes traveled down to my feet and his lips puckered in disgust.

"Edema," he said. "Hospital."

He was gone. With one other woman who had not "passed" I scrambled back into my clothes and followed the trusty from the building. Day had broken, a sullen gray sky spitting snow. We started up the *Lagerstrasse*, past the endless streets of barracks.

"Then—we're not—aren't we to be released?"

"I imagine you will be, as soon as the swelling in your legs goes down," the trusty said. "They only release you if you're in good condition." I saw her look at the other prisoner: the woman's skin and eyes were a dull dark yellow.

Sick call stretched around the side of the hospital, but we walked straight through the door and into a ward at the rear. The room was crammed with double-decker cots. I was assigned a place on an upper bunk next to a woman whose body was covered with erupting pustules. But at least it was near a wall where I could keep my swollen legs elevated. That was what mattered now: to get the swelling down, to pass the inspection.

Whether that ray of freedom shed a new, relentless light on Ravensbruck, or whether this was truly the most savage place yet, I could not tell. The suffering was unimaginable. Around me were survivors of a prison train which had been bombed on its way here. The women were horribly mutilated and in terrible pain, but at each moan two of the nurses jeered and mimicked the sounds.

Even in the other patients I saw that stony indifference to others that was the most fatal disease of the concentration camp. I felt it spread to myself: how could one survive if one kept on feeling! The paralyzed and the unconscious kept falling out of the crowded narrow cots; that first night four women fell from upper bunks and died on the floor. It was better to narrow the mind to one's own need, not to see, not to think.

But there was no way to shut out the sounds. All night women cried out a German word I didn't know. "*Schieber!*" Over and over from rasping throats: "*Schieber!*"

Finally I realized that they were calling for bedpans. It was out of the question for most of the women in this room to make it to that filthy latrine next door. At last, reluctant to lower my legs, I climbed down from my cot and set about the chore. The gratitude of the patients was heart-wrenching. "Who are you. Why are you doing this?"—as though cruelty and callousness were the norm, ordinary decency the marvel.

As a wintry dawn crept through the windows, I realized it was Christmas Day.

I went each morning to the clinic at the front of the hospital where I could hear the tramping of feet on the *Lagerstrasse* outside. Each time the verdict was "Edema of the feet and ankles." Many of those who attended the clinic were, like myself, discharged prisoners. Some had been released months ago: their discharge papers and railway passes were ragged from opening and refolding. And—what if Betsie were still alive? Surely our prison term would have been up together. But Betsie would never, never have passed the physical. What if she were here with me? What if I were to pass the inspection and she . . .

There are no "ifs" in God's kingdom. I could hear her soft voice saying it. His timing is perfect. His will is our hiding place. Lord Jesus, keep me in Your will! Don't let me go mad by poking about outside it.

I kept looking for someone to give the Bible to. How easy it would be, back in Holland, to get another—a hundred others. There were not many Hollanders in the ward who would be able to read the Dutch text, but at last I slipped it around the neck of a grateful young woman from Utrecht.

The sixth night I spent in the ward both bedpans were suddenly and mysteriously missing. In an upper bunk on the center aisle were two Hungarian gypsies whose muttering was part of the babble of the room. I never walked past their cot because one of them had a gangrenous foot which she would thrust in the face of anyone who came near. Now someone screamed out that the gypsies had the bedpans, hidden under their blankets to save them the trip to the toilets. I went to their cot and pleaded with them—though I didn't know whether they understood German or not.

Suddenly in the dark something wet and sticky coiled round my face. The woman had taken the bandage from her foot and flung it at me. I ran sobbing down the corridor and washed and washed beneath the wall spigot in the latrine. I would never step into that aisle again! What did I care about the wretched bedpans! I couldn't bear . . .

But of course I did go back. I had learned much, in the past year, about what I could and could not bear. As the gypsies saw me heading down the aisle toward them, both bedpans clattered onto the floor.

The next morning the doctor on duty at the clinic stamped the medical approval on my discharge form. Events that had dragged so slow now moved with bewildering speed. In a dressing shed near the outer gate of the camp I was outfitted with clothes. Underthings; a woolen skirt: a truly beautiful silk blouse; sturdy, almost-new shoes; a hat, an overcoat. I was handed a form to sign stating that I had never been ill at Ravensbruck, never had an accident, and that the treatment had been good. I signed.

In another building I received a day's bread ration and food coupons for three additional days. I was also given back my watch, my Dutch money, and Mama's ring. And then I was standing with a group of ten or twelve just inside the gate.

The heavy iron doors swung open; at the heels of a woman guard we marched through. We climbed the little hill: now I could see the lake, frozen from shore to shore. The pines and the distant church steeple sparkled in the winter sun like an old-fashioned Christmas card.

I could not believe it. Perhaps we were only going to the Siemens factory; tonight we would march back to camp. But at the top of the hill we turned left, toward the center of the small town. I could feel my feet swelling in the tight new shoes, but I bit my lip and made myself stride along. I imagined the guard turning around, pointing a scornful finger: "Edema! Send her back to camp!"

At the small train station the guard turned and left us without a backward glance. Apparently we were all traveling as far as Berlin, then each pursuing her separate route home. There was a long wait on cold iron benches.

The feeling of unreality persisted. Only one thing seemed familiar, the hungry hollow in my stomach. I put off getting into my bread allowance as long as I could, but at last reached into my overcoat pocket. The packet was gone. I sprang up from the bench, looking beneath it, retracing my steps through the station. Whether I had dropped it or it had been stolen, the bread was gone, and with it the ration coupons.

At last a train pulled into the station and we crowded eagerly to it but it was for military personnel only. Late in the afternoon we were allowed aboard a mail train, only to be put off two stops farther on to make room for a food shipment. The trip became a blur. We reached the huge, bomb-gutted terminal in Berlin sometime after midnight.

It was New Year's Day, 1945. Betsie had been right: she and I were out of prison. . . .

Snow drifted down from a shattered skylight as I wandered, confused and frightened, through the cavernous station. I knew that I must find the train to Uelzen, but months of being told what to do had left me robbed of initiative. At last someone directed me to a distant platform. Each step now was agony in the stiff new shoes. When I reached the platform at last, the sign said not Uelzen but Olsztyn, a town in Poland in exactly the opposite direction. I had to cross those acres of concrete floors again.

Ahead of me an elderly man, pink-cheeked from working in the roofless station, was raking bomb rubble into a pile. When I asked him for directions he took me by the arm and led me himself to the proper platform. "I was to Holland once," he said, voice wistful with recollection. "When the wife was alive, you know. Right on the sea we stayed."

A train was standing on the track and I climbed aboard. It was hours before anyone else arrived, but I did not dare get off for fear I would not find my way back again. By the time the train started up I was dizzy for lack of food. At the first stop outside Berlin I followed the other passengers into the station café. I showed the woman behind the cash-box my Dutch guilders and told her I had lost my coupons.

"That's an old story! Get out of here before I call the police!"

The trip was endless. Many miles of track could be traveled only at a crawl. Some sections were gone altogether and there were interminable, long detours and many changes of train. Often we did not stop in a station at all, for fear of air raids, but exchanged freight and passengers in the countryside.

And all the while, out my window passed once-beautiful

Germany. Fire-blackened woods, the gaunt ribs of a church standing over a ruined village. Bremen especially brought tears to my eyes. In all that wasteland I saw one human being, an old woman poking at a heap of bricks.

In Uelzen there was a long wait between trains. It was late at night, the station was deserted. As I dozed in an empty coffee bar my head dropped forward until it rested on the small table in front of me. A blow on my ear sent me sprawling almost to the floor.

"This is not a bedroom!" the furious station agent shrieked. "You can't use our tables to sleep on!"

Trains came. Trains didn't come. I climbed on and off. And then I was standing in a line at a customs shed and the sign on the little station building said *Nieuwerschans*. As I left the building a workman in a blue cap and blue overalls stepped up to me. "Here! You won't get far on those legs! Hang onto my arm."

He spoke Dutch.

I clung to him and hobbled across some tracks to where another train was waiting, engine already puffing smoke. I was in Holland.

We jerked forward. Flat, snow-covered fields glided past the window. Home. It was still occupied Holland, German soldiers still stood at intervals along the tracks—but it was home.

The train was going only as far as Groningen, a Dutch city not far from the border. Beyond that rails were torn up and all except government travel banned. With the last of my strength I limped to a hospital near the station.

A nurse in a sparkling white uniform invited me into a little office. When I had told my story, she left the room. In a few minutes she was back with a tray of tea and rusk. "I left the butter off," she said. "You're suffering from malnutrition. You must be careful what you eat."

Tears tumbled into the hot tea as I drank. Here was someone who felt concern for me. There were no available beds in the hospital, she said, but one of the staff was away and I was to have her room. "Right now I have a hot tub running."

I followed her down gleaming corridors in a kind of happy dream. In a large bathroom clouds of steam were rising from a glistening white tub. Nothing in my life ever felt as good as that bath. I lay submerged to my chin, feeling the warm water soothe my scab-crusted skin. "Just five minutes more!" I would beg each time the nurse rapped at the door.

At last I let her hand me a nightgown and lead me to a room where a bed was turned down and waiting. Sheets. White sheets top and bottom. I could not get enough of running my hands over them. The nurse was tucking a second pillow beneath my swollen feet. I struggled to stay awake: to lie here clean and cared for was such joy I did not want to sleep through a minute of it.

I stayed in the hospital at Groningen ten days, feeling my strength return. For most meals I joined the nurses in their own dining room. The first time I saw the long table set with silverware and glasses, I drew back in alarm.

"You're having a party! Let me take a tray to my room!" I did not feel ready yet for laughter and social chatter.

The young woman beside me laughed as she pulled out a chair for me. "It's not a party! It's just supper—and skimpy enough at that."

I sat down blinking at knives, forks, tablecloth—had I once eaten like this, every day in the year? Like a savage watching his first civilized meal I copied the leisurely gestures of the others as they passed bread and cheese and unhurriedly stirred their coffee.

The ache in my heart was to get to Willem and Nollie— but how could it be done with the travel ban? Telephone service, too, was more limited than ever, but at last the girl at the hospital switchboard reached the telephone operator in Hilversum with the news of Betsie's death and my release.

In the middle of the second week, hospital authorities arranged a ride for me on a food truck headed south. We made the illegal trip at night and without headlights: the food had been diverted from a shipment headed for Germany. In the gray early morning the truck pulled up to Willem's big brick nursing home. A tall, broad-shouldered girl answered my knock, and then went dashing down the hallway with the news that I was here.

In a moment my arms were around Tine and two of my nieces. Willem arrived more slowly, limping down the corridor with the help of a cane. We held each other a long time while I told them the details of Betsie's illness and death.

"Almost," said Willem slowly, "almost I could wish to have this same news of Kik. It would be good for him to be with Betsie and Father." They had had no word of this tall blond son since his deportation to Germany. I remembered his hand on my shoulder, guiding me on our bicycles through the blacked-out streets to Pickwick's. Remembered his patient coaching: "You *have* no cards, Tante Corrie! There *are no Jews*." Kik! Are the young and brave as vulnerable as the old and slow?

I spent two weeks in Hilversum, trying to adjust to what my eyes had told me that first moment. Willem was dying. Only he seemed unaware of it as he hobbled along the halls of his home bringing comfort and counsel to the sick people in his care. They had over fifty patients at the moment, but what I could not get over was the number of young women in help: nurse's aides, kitchen helpers, secretaries. It was several days before I perceived that most of these "girls" were young men in hiding from the forced-labor conscription which had grown more ruthless than ever.

And still something in me could not rest until I got back to Haarlem. Nollie was there, of course. But it was the Beje, too, something in the house itself that called me, beckoned me, told me to come home.

The problem, again, was getting there. Willem had the use of an official car for nursing-home business, but only within a radius of Hilversum. Finally, after many relayed phone calls, he told me the trip had been arranged.

The roads were deserted as we set out; we passed only two other cars all the way to the rendezvous spot with the car from Haarlem. Ahead, pulled off onto the snow at the side of the road, we saw it, a long black limousine with official government plates and curtained rear windows. I kissed Willem goodbye and then stepped quickly, as instructed, into the rear of the limousine. Even in the curtained gloom the ungainly bulk beside me was unmistakable.

"Oom Herman!" I cried.

"My dear Cornelia." His great hand closed around both of mine. "God permits me to see you again."

I had last seen Pickwick sitting between two soldiers on the prison bus in The Hague, his poor bald head bruised and bleeding. Now here he was, waving aside my sympathy as though that had been an incident too trivial to recall.

He seemed as well informed as ever about everything that went on in Haarlem, and as the uniformed driver sped us along the empty roads, he filled me in on all the details I ached to know. All of our Jews were safe except for Mary Itallie, who had been sent to Poland following her arrest in the street. Our group was still operating, although many of the young men were in hiding.

He warned me to expect changes at the Beje. After the police guard had been removed, a series of homeless families had been housed there, although at the moment he believed the living quarters above the shop were empty. Even before the house was unsealed, loyal Toos had returned from Scheveningen and reopened the watch business. Mr. Beukers, the optician next door, had given her space in his shop from which she had taken orders to give to our repairmen in their homes.

As my eyes adjusted to the dim light I made out my friend's face more clearly. There was perhaps an extra knob or two on the misshapen head, teeth were missing—but to that vast, kindly ugliness the beating had made no real difference at all.

Now the limousine was threading the narrow streets of Haarlem. Over the bridge on the Spaarne. Across the Grote Markt in the shadow of St. Bavo's, into the Barteljorisstraat. I was out of the car almost before it stopped, running down the alley, through the side door, and into Nollie's embrace. She and her girls had been there all morning, sweeping, washing windows, airing sheets for my homecoming. Over Nollie's shoulder I saw Toos standing in the rear door to the shop, laughing and sobbing both at once. Laughing because I was home; crying because Father and Betsie, the only two people she had ever allowed herself to love, would never be.

Together we trooped through the house and shop, looking, stroking—"Remember how Betsie would set out these cups?" "Remember how Meta would scold Eusie for leaving his pipe here?" I stood on the landing outside the dining room and ran my hand over the smooth wood of the Frisian clock. I could see Father stopping here, Kapteyn at his heels. "We mustn't let the clock run down. . . ."

I opened the glass face, moved the hands to agree with my wristwatch, and slowly drew up the weights. I was home. Life, like the clock, started again: mornings repairing watches in the workshop, noons most often bumping on my tireless bicycle out to Bos en Hoven Straat.

And yet ... in a strange way, I was not home. I was still waiting, still looking for something. I spent days prowling the alleys and canal banks nearby, calling Maher Shalal Hashbaz by name. The elderly vegetable lady three stores down told me that the cat had mewed at her door the night of our arrest and she had taken him in. For months, she said, the small children of the neighborhood had banded together to bring food to "Opa's kitty." They had brought scraps from garbage pails and even tidbits from their own scanty plates smuggled past watchful mothers, and Mr. Hashbaz had remained sleek and fat.

It was mid-December, she said, when he had not appeared one night to her call, nor had she seen him since. And so I searched, but with a sinking heart: in this winter of Holland's hunger, all my searching brought not one single cat or dog to my call.

I missed more than the cat; the Beje needed people to fill its rooms. I remembered Father's words to the Gestapo chief in The Hague: "I will open my door to anyone in need. . . ." No one in the city was in greater need than its feeble-minded. Since the start of the Nazi occupation they had been sequestered by their families in back rooms, their schools and training centers shut down, hidden from a government which had decided they were not fit to live. Soon a group of them was living at the Beje. They still could not go out on the streets, but here at least they had new surroundings and a program of sorts with the time I could take from the shop.

And still my restlessness continued. I was home, I was working and busy—or was I? Often I would come to with a start at my workbench to realize that I had sat for an hour staring into space. The repairmen Toos had found—trained under Father—were excellent. I spent less and less time in the shop; whatever or whoever I was looking for was not there.

Nor upstairs. I loved the gentle people in my care, but the house itself had ceased to be home. For Betsie's sake I bought plants for every windowsill, but I forgot to water them and they died.

Maybe I missed the challenge of the underground. When the national group approached me with a request, I agreed eagerly. They had false release papers for a prisoner in the Haarlem jail. What could be simpler than to carry this document around the corner and through those familiar wooden doors.

But as the doors closed behind me my heart began to race. What if I couldn't get out? What if I was trapped?

"Yes?" A young police lieutenant with bright orange hair stepped from behind the reception desk. "You had an appointment?"

It was Rolf. Why was he being so stiff with me? Was I under arrest? Were they going to put me in a cell? "Rolf!" I said. "Don't you know me?"

He peered at me as though trying to refresh his memory. "Of course!" he said smoothly. "The lady at the watch shop! I heard you were closed down for a while."

I gaped at him. Why, Rolf knew perfectly—and then I recalled where we were. In the central foyer of the police station with half a dozen German soldiers looking on. And I had greeted one of our group by name, practically admitted a special relationship between us, when the cardinal rule of the underground was . . . I ran my tongue over my lips. How could I have been so stupid?

Rolf took the forged papers from my shaking hands and glanced through them. "These must be passed upon by the police chief and the military overcommand together," he said. "Can you return with them tomorrow afternoon at four? The chief will be in a meeting until—"

I heard no more. At the words "tomorrow afternoon" I had bolted for the door. I stood thankfully on the sidewalk until my knees stopped knocking. If I had ever needed proof that I had no boldness or cleverness of my own, I had it now. Whatever bravery, or skill I had ever shown were gifts of God—sheer loans from Him of the talent needed to do a job. And it was clear, from the absence of such skills now, that this was no longer His work for me.

I crept meekly back to the Beje. And it was at that moment, as I stepped into the alley, that I knew what it was I was looking for. It was Betsie.

It was Betsie I had missed every moment of every day since I ran to the hospital window and found that she had left Ravensbruck forever. It was Betsie I had thought to find back here in Haarlem, here in the watchshop and in the home she loved.

But she was not here. And now for the first time since her death, I remembered. "We must tell people, Corrie. We must tell them what we learned. . . ."

That very week I began to speak. If this was God's new work for me, then He would provide the courage and the words. Through the streets and suburbs of Haarlem I bumped on my bicycle rims, bringing the message that joy runs deeper than despair.

It was news that people needed to hear that cheerless spring of 1945. No Bride of Haarlem tree filled the air with fragrance; only the stump had been too big to haul off for firewood. No tulips turned fields into carpets of color: the bulbs had all been eaten. No family was without its tragedy. In churches and club rooms and private homes in those desperate days I told the truths Betsie and I had learned in Ravensbruck.

And always at these meetings, I spoke of Betsie's first vision: of a home here in Holland where those who had been hurt could learn to live again unafraid. At the close of one of these talks a slender, aristocratic lady came up to me. I knew her by sight: Mrs. Bierens de Haan whose home in the suburb of Bloemendaal was said to be one of the most beautiful in Holland. I had never seen it, only the trees at the edge of the huge park in which it was set, and so I was astonished when this elegantly dressed lady asked me if I were still living in the ancient little house on the Barteljorisstraat.

"How did you—yes, I do. But—"

"My mother often told me about it. She went there frequently to see an aunt of yours who, I believe, was in charitable work?"

In a rush it all came back. Opening the side door to let in a swish of satin and rustle of feathers. A long gown and a plumed hat brushing both sides of the narrow stairs. Then Tante Jans standing in her doorway with a look that froze in the bones the thought of bouncing a ball.

"I am a widow," Mrs. Bierens de Haan was saying, "but I have five sons in the Resistance. Four are still alive and well. The fifth we have not heard from since he was taken to Germany. As you spoke just now something in me kept saying, 'Jan will come back and in gratitude you will open your home for this vision of Betsie ten Boom.'"

It was two weeks later that a small boy delivered a scented envelope to the side door; inside in slanted purple letters was a single line, "Jan is home."

Mrs. Bierens de Haan herself met me at the entrance to her estate. Together we walked up an avenue of ancient oaks meeting above our heads. Rounding the final bend, we saw it, a fifty-six-room mansion in the center of a vast lawn. Two elderly gardeners were poking about the flowerbeds.

"We've let the gardens go," Mrs. Bierens de Haan said. "But I thought we might put them back in shape. Don't you think released prisoners might find therapy in growing things?"

I didn't answer. I was staring up at the gabled roof and the leaded windows. Such tall, tall windows. . . .

"Are there—" my throat was dry. "Are there inlaid wood floors inside, and a broad gallery around a central hall, and —bas-relief statues set along the walls?"

Mrs. Bierens de Haan looked at me in surprise. "You've been here then! I don't recall—"

"No," I said. "I heard it from—"

I stopped. How could I explain what I did not understand?

"From someone who's been here," she finished simply, not understanding my perplexity.

"Yes," I said. "From someone who's been here."

The second week in May the Allies retook Holland. The Dutch flag hung from every window and the "Wilhelmus" was played on the liberated radio day and night. The Canadian army rushed to the cities the food they had stockpiled along the borders.

In June the first of many hundreds of people arrived at the beautiful home in Bloemendaal. Silent or endlessly relating their losses, withdrawn or fiercely aggressive, every one was a damaged human being. Not all had been in concentration camps; some had spent two, three, even four years hidden in attic rooms and back closets here in Holland. One of the first of these was Mrs. Kan, widow of the watch-shop owner up the street. Mr. Kan had died at the underground address; she came to us alone, a stooped, white-haired woman who startled at every sound. Others came to Bloemendaal, scarred body and soul by bombing raids or loss of family or any of the endless dislocations of war. In 1947 we began to receive Dutch people who had been prisoners of the Japanese in Indonesia.

Though none of this was by design, it proved to be the best possible setting for those who had been imprisoned in Germany. Among themselves they tended to live and relive their special woes; in Bloemendaal they were reminded that they were not the only ones who had suffered. And for all these people alike, the key to healing turned out to be the same. Each had a hurt he had to forgive: the neighbor who had reported him, the brutal guard, the sadistic soldier.

Strangely enough, it was not the Germans or the Japanese that people had most trouble forgiving; it was their fellow Dutchmen who had sided with the enemy. I saw them frequently in the streets, NSBers with their shaved heads and furtive eyes. These former collaborators were now in pitiful condition, turned out of homes and apartments, unable to find jobs, hooted at in the streets.

At first it seemed to me that we should invite them too to Bloemendaal, to live side by side with those they had injured, to seek a new compassion on both sides. But it turned out to be too soon for people working their way back from such hurt: the two times I tried it, it ended in open fights. And so as soon as homes and schools for the feeble-minded opened again around the country I turned the Beje over to these former NSBers.

This was how it went, those years after the war, experimenting, making mistakes, learning. The doctors, psychiatrists, and nutritionists who came free of charge to any place that cared for war victims, sometimes expressed surprise at our loose-run ways. At morning and evening worship people drifted in and out, table manners were atrocious, one man took a walk into Haarlem every morning at 3:00 A.M. I could not bring myself to sound a whistle or to scold, or to consider gates or curfews.

And, sure enough, in their own time and their own way, people worked out the deep pain within them. It most often started, as Betsie had known it would, in the garden. As flowers bloomed or vegetables ripened, talk was less of the bitter past, more of tomorrow's weather. As their horizons broadened, I would tell them about the people living in the Beje, people who never had a visitor, never a piece of mail. When mention of the NSBers no longer brought on a volley of self-righteous wrath, I knew the person's healing was not far away. And the day he said, "Those people you spoke of —I wonder if they'd care for some homegrown carrots," then I knew the miracle had taken place.

I continued to speak, partly because the home in Bloemendaal ran on contributions, partly because the hunger for Betsie's story seemed to increase with time. I traveled all over Holland, to other parts of Europe, to the United States. But the place where the hunger was greatest was Germany. Germany was a land in ruins, cities of ashes and rubble, but more terrifying still, minds and hearts of ashes. Just to cross the border was to feel the great weight that hung over that land.

It was at a church service in Munich that I saw him, the former S.S. man who had stood guard at the shower room door in the processing center at Ravensbruck. He was the first of our actual jailers that I had seen since that time. And suddenly it was all there—the roomful of mocking men, the heaps of clothing, Betsie's pain-blanched face.

He came up to me as the church was emptying, beaming and bowing. "How grateful I am for your message *Fraulein*," he said. "To think that, as you say, He has washed my sins away!"

His hand was thrust out to shake mine. And I, who had preached so often to the people in Bloemendaal the need to forgive, kept my hand at my side.

Even as the angry, vengeful thoughts boiled through me, I saw the sin of them. Jesus Christ had died for this man; was I going to ask for more? Lord Jesus, I prayed, forgive me and help me to forgive him.

I tried to smile, I struggled to raise my hand. I could not. I felt nothing, not the slightest spark of warmth or charity. And so again I breathed a silent prayer. Jesus, I cannot forgive him. Give me Your forgiveness.

As I took his hand the most incredible thing happened. From my shoulder along my arm and through my hand a current seemed to pass from me to him, while into my heart sprang a love for this stranger that almost overwhelmed me.

And so I discovered that it is not on our forgiveness any more than on our goodness that the world's healing hinges, but on His. When He tells us to love our enemies, He gives, along with the command, the love itself.

It took a lot of love. The most pressing need in postwar Germany was homes; nine million people were said to be without them. They were living in rubble heaps, half-standing buildings, and abandoned army trucks. A church group invited me to speak to a hundred families living in an abandoned factory building. Sheets and blankets had been hung between the various living quarters to make a pretense of privacy. But there was no insulating the sounds: the wail of a baby, the din of radios, the angry words of a family quarrel. How could I speak to these people of the reality of God and go back to my quiet room in the church hostel outside the city? No, before I could bring a message to them, I would have to live among them.

And it was during the months that I spent in the factory that a director of a relief organization came to see me. They had heard of my rehabilitation work in Holland, he said, and they wondered—I was opening my mouth to say that I had no professional training in such things, when his next words silenced me.

"We've located a place for the work," he said. "It was a former concentration camp that's just been released by the government."

We drove to Darmstadt to look over the camp. Rolls of rusting barbed wire still surrounded it. I walked slowly up a cinder path between drab gray barracks. I pushed open a creaking door; I stepped between rows of metal cots.

"Windowboxes," I said. "We'll have them at every window. The barbed wire must come down, of course, and then we'll need paint. Green paint. Bright yellow-green, the color of things coming up new in the spring...."

Three Ways to Put This

The significance of Corrie's life is not that she is an exceptional person but, in her own words, "a very weak and ordinary one." The truths she discovered can operate in the lives of each one of us. The procedure for making this book your own is not complicated: simply substitute for the particulars of her story the specific family situation, job problem, obstacle or opportunity in which God has set you. Here are three examples of how to do this.

(1) *God governs all things, even those that appear to us senseless or cruel.* List below your own "hardest questions."

Perhaps you ask why children must suffer in war, or how a loving God could permit a typhoon. Include vexing personal questions: an illness in your family, an automobile accident, a business failure.

Now, one by one, transfer these loads from your own care to God's. "Lord, because I do not have the answers to these things I do not therefore conclude that there are no answers. You know why, Lord, and when I am strong enough—wise enough, loving enough—you will show me, too." Save the spaces below to record (1) answers and partial answers vouchsafed to the above questions (include dates) and (2) increased freedom, energy, strength discovered in coping with other problems.

_____	_____
_____	_____
_____	_____
_____	_____
_____	_____

(2) *God supplies grace for the present need;* with griefs and problems He also grants strength. But like Corrie's

Book to Work in Your Own Life

father on the weekly trip to Amsterdam, God gives us our ticket only as we board the train.

Put down 10 concerns that cause you anxiety (missed sleep? worry-filled days?)

_____   _____
_____   _____
_____   _____
_____   _____
_____   _____

Now read your list with this question: how many of these situations belong to today? In how many are you running ahead of God's supply?

(3) *God wills us to give thanks.* Our praise and gratitude in some mysterious way open the door for Him to bless us as He wishes. On the lines below write down the five things for which you are currently most grateful.

_____ Several times a day pause to
_____ thank God for these bless-
_____ ings; watch your sense of
_____ goodness and love in the
_____ world—and especially of
                       His love—grow accordingly.

On these lines, note five present situations for which you are most definitely not grateful:

_____ Now set yourself the dis-
_____ cipline of giving thanks daily
_____ for these things as well. See
_____ how God is able to use your
_____ changed attitude to change
                       facts.

Chasing
the Dragon

Jackie Pullinger with
Andrew Quicke

For my family, especially my Father

"The great dragon was hurled down – that ancient serpent called the devil or Satan, who leads the whole world astray. He was hurled to the earth, and his angels with him ... 'Now have come the salvation and the power and the kingdom of our God, and the authority of his Christ. For the accuser of our brothers ... has been hurled down ...' "

Rev. 12:9, 10

Contents

Preface

I first met Jackie Pullinger in 1968 when I went to Hong Kong to make a film for B.B.C. television. Thanks to a friend's introduction, she came to my hotel to tell me about her work in the Walled City, which was then just beginning. As I had run a youth club myself in the East End of London, I was fascinated by what she told me, and went to see the Walled City with her; it was exactly as she describes it.

Over the years we kept in touch by letter, and year by year her work developed. Those outside Hongkong who had ever heard of Jackie Pullinger were very few until the *Sunday Times* wrote about her work in 1974. There followed a question in Parliament about the status of the Walled City, articles by Reuters, U.P.I. and other international agencies, and a fifty-minutes film by the British TV company A.T.V. in 1978. Jackie was in England then to talk about the work, and I asked her if together we could write a fuller account of all that had happened. With some reluctance she agreed, and I revisited Hong Kong in 1979. Jackie did not agree with my first draft, and so she rewrote the whole book herself when she came to stay with our family in California.

Some of the names and places in the book have had to be changed to protect the characters concerned, nearly all of whom are still living in Hong Kong. Apart from that, everything happened as Jackie describes it; it is her story, but many of the events described can be verified from other sources.

My thanks are due to the many people who helped us complete the book against a tough time schedule. Among many I would mention Marjorie Witcombe and Mary Stack

in Hong Kong, who lent us their homes there, to Susan
Soloman in California, to my brother Edward and his friends
in the World Bank in Washington, where the manuscript was
completed, and most important of all to my wife Juliet who
did a magnificent job of editing and advising throughout.
There is much that we had to leave out, and we do not
describe what has been happening since 1976; those events
will have to await another book.

ANDREW QUICKE
London
April 1980

Glossary

amah	—a Chinese servant
congee	—a rice porridge often eaten for breakfast
daih lo	—Big Brother
daih ma	—Big Mother, the senior Chinese wife
daih pai dong	—street stall
for-gei	—waiter or worker
fui-goih	—repent
gong-sou	—a talk between rival Triads to attempt a settlement over gang affairs
"Hai bin do ah?"	—"Where do you come from?"
Hak Nam	—darkness—often used as a name for Hong Kong's walled city
hawh-fui	—regret
kai ma	—godmother ⎱ the terms are used to define a close relationship between
kai neui	—goddaughter ⎰ an older woman and a child she takes to be her own
kung-fu	—a type of Chinese martial art
lap-sap	—rubbish
Mama-san	—name for a woman who is in charge of various girl prostitutes or bar girls
"M'gong?"	—"Not talking?"
mintoi	—eiderdown
"Moe yeh"	—"Nothing"
pahng-jue	—lord of the hut or master of a drug den
"Pa ma fan"	—"Afraid of trouble"
pin-mun	—illegal business
Poon Siu Jeh	—"Pullinger" in Chinese

sai lo	—Little Brother
sai ma	—Little Mother, the junior Chinese wife or concubine
Seui Fong	
14 K	—names of different Triads, illegal in Hong
Ging Yu	Kong
Wo Shing Wo	
siu yeh	—a snack
tin-man-toi	—weatherman, meaning watchman
wunton	—dumplings stuffed with shrimp and pork
"Yau moe gau chor"	—"You must be off your head"
"Yauh"	—"I'm here"
"Yeh sou ngoi nei"	—"Jesus loves you"

Chapter One

The Trail of Blood

The guard spat into the alley, but nodded quite kindly and allowed me to pass. I left him there squatting in his soiled T-shirt. Having no further interest in me he removed one of his flip-flops and returned to picking his black toe nails. The entrance he was so ceremoniously guarding was almost hidden and I had to squeeze between two dark buildings as I crept into this strange Chinese "city" so feared by the people of Hong Kong.

The darkness blindfolded me for a moment, and although I knew the way well by this time, I stepped very cautiously along the narrow lane, barely wide enough for one to walk. I kept my eyes lowered on the ground for two reasons; to avoid stepping on nameless horrors, so falling into the open sewer, and to avoid presenting an upturned face to the windows above which intermittently spewed their refuse on to the street below. I clapped my hands to make the rats run, but some of them were so tame that they sat arrogantly in what they obviously regarded as their territory; it took several loud claps to shift them.

Then I saw it—a small spot of red gleaming in the filthy mud, and a little way ahead several more drops—it was certainly fresh blood. My stomach gripped into a tight knot, for I feared that I knew whose blood it was. Ah Sor had been given to me by a magistrate to look after as a son for one year. Then a Triad group nick-named *Seui Fong* came after him to slash him over some unfinished gang business. It seemed that they had found him. As I hurried on I saw glistening patches ahead and stepped past two more *tin-man-toi*—the watchmen for the Triad gangsters who controlled the Walled City. They knew me and yielded as I passed; their faces showed nothing.

I turned a corner into another street indistinguishable in its foul broken-walled buildings from the last, except that it contained the main gambling den operated by the brothers of the 14K gang. Then past the evil archways of the opium dens where there leaned more watchers nodding and dozing and seeing nothing. The gap between the hovels here was barely an arm's stretch wide, so I stepped into a doorway to avoid bumping into a crazed looking dope addict who was walking somewhere very fast.

Up the next street the patches of blood lay in clusters. I couldn't run in this stinking maze—it was too slippery and dark, but I was impatient to find the source of the blood. I dreaded it too.

I reached the main street, one of the few lit inside the Walled City. I had to walk more carefully now as I passed another gambling den, slimy outside with urine-soaked earth. The prostitutes recognized me and called from their orange boxes outside the blue film theatre. "Miss Poon, Poon Siu Jeh, will you help us?" They put out their hands, the backs scarred with needle marks—their aged faces almost without hope. Then I turned into my little alley to the room I rented and opened at night to welcome the Chinese gangsters.

Outside I found a large dark puddle. The shadowy people around looked unconcerned. "Please, what's happened?" I asked fearfully.

An old Cantonese man shook his head and muttered, "Nothing, nothing." But the others looked away. In a place controlled by Triads you keep your hands over your eyes to survive. It is safer to see nothing—not to be involved. Then a woman appeared with a broom and a bucket and swept the blood down the street until it was absorbed and obliterated. Several barefoot children, babies strapped to their backs, played as if nothing were happening.

Full of fear for Ah Sor I unlocked the iron gate—a protective feature of all Hong Kong dwellings, however poor—and went into our small club room. It was dark, damp smelling and hard to keep clean as there was no water supply for inhabitants of the Walled City. What they needed had to be carried in buckets from taps and stand pumps outside. Terrible things crawled out of the sewers and across the club room walls. I was always more afraid of the large cess-pool spiders than the gangsters, but that night as I sat alone in our room, my thoughts were on Ah Sor.

His mother had sold him as a baby to a childless opium addict who was frightened of going to hell without a son to worship his dead spirit. Thus Ah Sor grew up with a desperate sense of betrayal—longing to be loved, but unable to recognize it when offered. In fact, "Granny"—the addict's mother, loved him fondly, but as she was also a seller of heroin, her influence on his life could hardly be called refining. To counter-balance his sense of total unbelonging Ah Sor joined a Triad gang. It gave him prestige and a place where he belonged. He grew up fighting and earned his first spell in juvenile prison at the age of thirteen. Over the years I had come to know of his life and problems and tried to help him, but he continued to go in and out of prison and was as hopelessly hooked on drugs as was his addict stepfather. I felt I really loved him, but this love had not changed his life a bit, and so I sat on one of our crude handmade benches in the club and did the only thing I could—I prayed.

Five minutes later a girl burst into my room, panting. "Miss Poon, go to the hospital immediately, Elizabeth Hospital—they called for you!"

"Who is it there—is it Ah Sor?" I was so relieved that there was some news at last.

"I just have to tell you to go quickly—something about

dying," and the girl disappeared into the dingy labyrinth. She was only a message carrier who knew nothing.

I locked up and collected a couple of boys I knew on the way out. We chased back through the alleys as fast as we could and once outside the Walled City they hailed a taxi.

"Quickly, quickly, Elizabeth Hospital! Maybe our friend die!! More quickly!"

Hong Kong taxis need no encouragement to speed and our driver mentally slew the other drivers. He zigzagged in and out of the traffic lanes, driving deliberately with only one hand on the steering wheel, never slowing, but crashing on his brakes at the last moment. My hands were clenched as I was praying and thinking and racing all at the same time. "Maybe my friend die," I thought in Cantonese. What a miserable kind of half life he had had and how I longed to show him something better. If only he could know that somebody cared.

"God, please save his life—let him be saved." The driver was by now bouncing up and down in his seat with excitement and for several terrifyingly long moments he took his eyes off the road completely and swung round in his seat to observe the macho impression he was making on us. By this time we were all praying out loud. As if finding the Casualty Department were a surprise, our taxi screeched to a sudden halt and we leaped out to find Ah Sor before he died.

But it was not Ah Sor who was dying. It was Ah Tong who had left that sinister trail along the streets. I had only known Ah Tong by reputation, as one of the most depraved gang leaders, living off prostitution and using his gang followers such as Ah Sor to make collection from the brothels. Even among his own kind he was despised because he used to go to parties, seduce young girls and then sell these ruined lives into the rackets. As we waited in the passage outside his ward I learned more of the story.

Apparently the *Seui Fong* gang had hidden down a dark alley near my room armed with knives and water pipes. This was reciprocal warfare over a brother who had been wronged years previously. The target was Ah Sor. As he moved toward the street with Ah Tong and another brother he was unaware of the ambush. A knife glinted, the gang jumped and made for their victim. But Ah Tong saw them coming and threw himself in the way to protect Ah Sor. His arm was slashed until it was nearly severed before the attackers left him lying in a pool of his own blood. Ah Sor, with the other brother, ran home, fetched a *mintoi* (Chinese eiderdown) and wrapped up their protector, their gang boss. They staggered with him along the streets until they reached an exit and could take a taxi. Once having delivered their burden to the hospital, they fled. (There are police at hospitals who ask questions about gang fights and they did not want any report of this incident.)

Yet another brother relayed this story before he in turn disappeared, but the only information I could extract from the nurse was that the patient would almost certainly lose his arm, if not his life.

Sitting there on the hard hospital seat I thought over what I had heard. I grew more and more impressed with the behaviour of the man I had yet to see. All right, he was evil and lived a revolting life, but I felt he had shown a rare degree of love. Jesus said, "Greater love has no one than this, that one lay down his life for his friends."

Ah Tung had been ready to die. I rang up some friends, told them to come to the hospital and we stayed there all night praying for his life. When his family turned up they stood aghast at our totally incomprehensible behaviour. Whatever were we, good people, Christians even, doing praying for their son? To them he was bad, had left their home young, ran the streets, organized the gangs and merited only a "turning by on the other side".

At last the Sister gave us permission to enter the ward. I heard the Chinese nurses telling each other, "They're pastors, come to pray."

But dressed as I was in old jeans and a sweater I could understand their curious stares. We were hardly a conven-

tional group come to administer the last rites in the middle
of the night.

I stood by the bedside and looked at Ah Tong. He lay
desperately pale from loss of blood with drips in his un-
injured arm and a huge wad of dressing over the sutured
injury. He was deeply unconscious still. Afraid to disturb
his bandages we cautiously laid our hands on him and
prayed for him in Jesus' name. He did not immediately sit
up, though I believed he might, and as long as we were there
he did not recover consciousness. The bulletins from the
hospital each day, however, were extraordinary. It seemed
he was making amazing progress—almost miraculous? And
then to our joy and with the incredulous consent of the
medical staff, he was discharged. It was within five days of
the attack. He had made a remarkable recovery, keeping
not only his life, but also the full use of his arm.

Anyone would think that after this miracle Ah Tong
might be pleased to see one of his intercessors, but far from
it. In the following months if he ever spotted me in the dark
and dreary alleys he would run as if I were the Chief Inspector after him. He was afraid to see me. But I did get
several messages saying "thank you," from him.

"Thank me for what?" I asked the message bearer—a
yellow toothed youth with a grown-out perm.

"He believes your prayers saved his life."

The boy was sniffing and sweating and clearly in need of a
fix, but he looked at me with respect. Anything his boss
believed, he was prepared to believe, too. But if Ah Tong
believed that, why did he run from me? The illogicality of it
all puzzled me for some time. Months afterwards I found
the pathetic reason behind it all. He was an addict and he
needed a shot of heroin several times a day. All the time he
had been in hospital his girl friend, whom he had originally
raped and sold into a live sex show when she was fourteen,
had been bringing him drugs.

He knew I was a Christian and he knew that Christians
were good people, and he knew drug addicts were bad

people. So it was wrong for him to express his gratitude in person. He felt dirty—not clean enough for those good Christians.

It was several years later that Ah Tong fell across the doorstep of my little Walled City room. It was nearly the middle of the night. I do not think he had come through any conscious decision. He looked at me with devil-tormented eyes and blurted out, "Poon Siu Jeh, I'm desperate. I've tried to kick it so many times, but I can't get off drugs. Can you help me?"

"No, I can't," I said, "but I have good news for you. Jesus can. I think you should understand something about Jesus' life. Some years back you were willing to die for your brother, Ah Sor, and I've never forgotten that. You did something very wonderful."

Ah Tong's brows were drawn in concentration as he listened and his face mirrored his disappointment, hope, and puzzlement.

"What would you think about dying for someone in the other gang?" I asked.

"Tcha!" A lump of spit shot from his mouth and he looked bitterly at me. "You must be joking! Your brother is one thing, but no one dies for his enemy!"

"That is just what Jesus did. He not only died for his own gang, but for everyone in the other gangs. He was the Son of God. He never did wrong, but healed people and made them whole—and He died for His enemies—for us. If we believe in Him, He will give us His life because He loves us."

I do not think the drug-riddled mind of Ah Tong understood all of the doctrine of redemption. He was crazy for drugs and this had been a long speech, but I could see that something had happened. He was absolutely amazed at the idea that Jesus loved someone like himself. For the first time in years something—or someone, had penetrated his mean heart and he was moved.

I hurried him out of the Walled City, down to the Kowloon waterfront, across the harbour on the ferry and up to the small flat on Hong Kong island. He knew we were going to the "church" but quite what he had in mind I do not know for he looked stunned as we entered the apartment.

It was minute by Western standards and not like a church at all. He was standing in what was obviously the living/dining room which was bright and cheerfully decorated—even curtained. Everything was so clean and beautiful, and it felt like a home, not a church. But most extraordinary of all were the people, who were all smiling. There seemed to be a lot of Westerners, as well as a lot of Chinese young men and all of those he recognized. There were men he had known in jail; there were men he had fought with or against. There were men with whom he had taken drugs. But now they were all shining and happy and fat with good health. They began to tell him that they believed in Jesus and that Jesus' power had changed their lives.

'Yeow—even you here too?" he said as he greeted another friend.

"Yup, it's true, Ah Tong." (They spoke in the equivalent of Cantonese Cockney.)

"You know us—we'd never use this 'holy' talk if we didn't really believe. I mean—well, you'd expect Miss Poon and those priests to spout the Bible and all that, but they've never kicked drugs—they don't know what it's like. I got so the pain, the screaming agony was so bad that I prayed to Jesus like they told us and it worked!

"My pain went away and I felt really changed, and—well—sort of new. I got this strength like—it's called the Holy Spirit and I spoke in a new language and I didn't have any pain at all."

It was a bit incoherent but Ah Tong clearly thought, "If they can, so can I. If Jesus did it for him, He can do it for me."

He told us he would believe Jesus was God and ask Him to change his life. Then he prayed and as he did so, his desperately thin and pain-lined face softened and relaxed. He smiled.

The other one-time crooks looked at one another joyfully. Once more they were taking part in a miracle. Ah Tong had received the gift of speaking in a language he had never learned and found that praying came easily. Joy filled his eyes and as he lay on his bunk bed he grew more and more at peace. We all joined him and sat with him until he slept soundly.

Ah Tong stayed on in the house. There was no need for him to go "cold turkey", an experience that so tortures the human body that it can result in an addict's death. (The term is derived from the fact that when an addict is withdrawing from drugs without medication, as well as severe and painful symptoms there are also fits of cold shivers which cause "turkey" skin.) We gave him no medication, not even aspirin. We did not even give him cigarettes to help him in his withdrawal from heroin. Every time he began to feel a slight pang he went back to praying and using his new language. His withdrawal period was pain-free. No vomiting, no cramps, no diarrhoea, no shivers. With this miracle Ah Tong began a new life.

Chapter Two

Slow Boat to China

Immigration control boarded the ship and I stood first in the queue longing to disembark and get on with my adventure. Earlier that morning I had dressed, once again finally locked my bags ready for disembarkation, and had gone up on deck. The sight took my breath away. All the places we had passed by earlier on the voyage seemed so flat by comparison. Here was perspective. Here were mountains shimmering and fading into the mist in an Oriental painting. I found myself filled with peace and as I recognized that this was the place God had chosen, I said thank you.

So now I stood waiting and looking across the South China sea at the Pearl of the Orient, Hong Kong. Around us was the harbour separating Victoria Island and the Kowloon Peninsula. It was thronged with small craft; little fishing sampans bobbing up and down as they were sculled with peculiar skill by slant-eyed girls; lighters gaily painted in red, blue, yellow, and green hurrying to unload the freight ships anchored in the channel; and the *wallah wallahs* offloading their crew.

Ferry boats moved between outlying islands carrying shift workers, and crowding the water fronts were the ancient junks bringing food to the Colony from mainland China. They looked oddly old-fashioned for behind them, along the shoreline rose row upon row of magnificent modern skyscrapers clinging to the sides of the mountain on

Hong Kong Island right up to the peak where they disappeared into ethereal clouds.

Close at hand behind the dockyards with their warehouses strangely named "godowns" I saw glimpses of Chinese streets, their signs displayed in large characters hanging horizontally from the buildings. They looked quaint, exciting, hinting of the exotic East acclaimed by tourist guides. As I lifted my eyes I saw behind them in the distance on the Kowloon side more mountains. These were the hills of the Nine Dragons in the New Territories that stretched away to the border with Mao's China, a mere twenty miles away. Hong Kong from the water on a sunny morning looked beautiful; but it was a facade.

The immigration officer did not echo my eagerness. He took from me my completed forms stating that I was entering the Colony to work and settled down to question my replies. They did not make him happy.

"Where you live?"

"I don't actually have anywhere to live yet."

"Where your friends?"

"I haven't got any of those here yet."

"Where you work?"

"Well, no—I don't have a job either."

The young Cantonese looked at me darkly. His Hong Kong English had managed the interrogation fine so far, but my answers were not according to the book. Maybe he thought I looked a bit pathetic so he tried some supplementary questions: "Where your mother?" He was quite kind now.

"She's in England."

"Where your return ticket?"

"Oh, I haven't got one of those"—this quite blithely. It had not worried me having a one-way ticket and I could not see why he was so concerned.

Finally he brightened—we were in a place where one commodity usually solves most problems. "How much money you got?"

I felt quite pleased as I considered myself rather well-off: by dint of limiting my soft drinks on the month's journey out I had arrived with almost what I had when I boarded the ship. "About H.K. $100," (£6 in 1966) I said proudly.

"Not enough," the man snapped. "Hong Kong velly expensive place! That money not enough three days!" And he bustled off importantly in his fine peaked cap and starched shorts to find his superior. They consulted a moment, then came back at me in officialdom. "Even though you Blitish," said the Chief, "we refuse you permission to leave the ship. Wait here."

I gathered they thought I was a prostitute looking for easy earnings from U.S. troops on "rest and recreation" trips from Vietnam. A girl with no means of support, no home, no friends, no nothing, I stood watching all the other passengers land and wondering what they were going to do with me. Into my mind flashed horrible visions of their locking me up in the ship's hold and sending me back to England in disgrace. I would have to meet all my friends who would say, "Told you so! Fancy setting off round the world and leaving all the plans to God — very irresponsible!" What was I going to do? How had I landed here in the first place?

*   *   *

My Mother had only been expecting one of us and when as an end-of-war bonus she gave birth to twins, my Father was granted forty-eight hours compassionate leave. It must have been a disappointment for him, hoping for a rugby team and ending up with four girls instead. So I tried to make it up to him by behaving like a tomboy; climbing and running, boys' toys and bicycles and later a passionate interest in rugger and scrum halves.

One of my first memories is when I was four. I was leaning against the radiator in our home in Sutton, outside London, and thinking, "Is it really worth being good?" I knew there was a choice, but did it pay to be good? So I went on sitting on the radiator—it made a lovely hollow noise when you banged it—and thinking. I ended up deciding that whatever I did was bound to be found out by someone some day. There would be a reckoning.

About a year later my twin and I were sitting in Sunday School when a proper missionary came to talk to us. She was dressed up like the pictures of missionaries in Victorian children's books, complete with long dark skirt and hair pulled back in a bun. Pointing at each one of us sitting on our baby chairs she fluted, "And could God want you on the Mission Field?" I remember thinking the answer to that question cannot be "no" because, of course, God wants everyone on the Mission Field. What exactly a Mission Field was I had no idea; I had a dim picture of myself sitting at the door of a mud hut, a sort of White Queen in Africa feeling worthy. There were people like that in a missionary booklet I had seen.

I told a friend at our little Junior School that I wanted to be a missionary. It was a disastrous mistake. I soon found that everyone expected me to be better than everyone else. "But I thought you were going to be a missionary?" they would say accusingly when I was naughty. I always felt this was cheating somehow—it did not seem quite fair. So I learned very early that in England it is better to keep quiet about these things.

So I invented a series of careers to throw people off the scent—a conductor; the first woman to climb Everest; a circus performer. But occasionally I was found out, once when a school friend's mother gushed, "So, you're the one who's going to be a missionary, aren't you?" I went very pink and hoped no one would mention it again.

However, privately some things still bothered me. One day I was walking over the railway bridge with my twin sister Gilly, on our way back from meeting Nellie, our friend and the family daily help. As usual we had scrounged lime green penny lollies off her but I had hardly got past the bit where it stuck to your tongue when an awful thought appeared, "What are we doing on the earth? What is life all about?" It seemed to me that I was trapped; I could not live just how I pleased in case God was there after all and then one day I would have to explain it all to Him. This was not a happy thought.

Then there was the problem of sin. I had seen the school register and the mark you got against your name every day. Lying on the tennis lawn I looked up at the sky and imagined God was up there with a big book. It had all our names in there and every time you did something wrong you got a mark. I had a look at my column and it was terribly long. I think it went on for pages. Well, there was nothing to be done because there was a song in Sunday School about being stuck with your sins.

God has blotted them out—I'm happy and glad and free!
God has blotted them out, let's turn to Isaiah and see.

I did not understand "blotting out" so it was years later before I knew what we were singing. I thought of that big book with all my sins stretching for lines and lines and God with a piece of blotting paper carefully blotting them in. At last a solution occurred to me. Youth was in my favour and I decided, "If I never do anything wrong again, ever, ever, perhaps one day I will catch up Winston Churchill! He is the goodest person on the earth, but he is very old, so if I stop sinning now maybe we will end up about equal!"

I made a second mistake my first term at boarding school. My twin and I were sitting at the end of the table eating the compulsory piece of brown bread for tea. The head of our table was a tall girl named Mirissa; she told me off for not cutting my bread into half before eating it. I thought I would try to atone for the brown bread by making polite conversation, but, unfortunately, I chose the wrong topic. Having heard the first Billy Graham broadcast a short time previously I mentioned how impressed I had been with the evangelist.

"Mass emotion!" she drawled disdainfully and dismissed the subject. I was in such awe of the seniors that ever after in school when such matters cropped up I would sneer, "Mass emotion!"

Confirmation came round and it was our form's turn to be "done". I was rather serious about all this, feeling that I was one of the few who really believed in God. The others were only doing it for the dresses and the Confirmation Tea to which we could invite relatives and godparents. Yet my real fear was that the vicar would ask us individually what we believed, before we could get through; but I need not have worried—he never did. So that was all right. But I had to ask him a question first.

"What should I think about when the Bishop puts his hands upon my head?"

The vicar thought for a moment, "Ah—I should er . . . er —pray!" he concluded triumphantly. Gilly and I walked forward in our school-issue white dresses and knelt down. The Bishop laid hands on us—I can only remember walking back to my seat filled with joy. Actually I felt like laughing —like splitting my sides. How improper—this was a confirmation service, and this was the solemn bit. Laughing was for the tea after. I found my service sheet and covered up my face so that no one should see me smiling in the pew, and then quickly put my head down in an attitude of prayer. I had hoped to carry off the ceremony looking both reverent and graceful and there did not seem to be any connection between the service and this unseemly gladness. I was giving my life to God; I had expected nothing back.

My next move was to find the classified phone directory, look up missionary societies and take the address of the first one.

"I'm thinking of becoming a missionary," I wrote, "and I think I should start preparing now. What subjects should I take?" They responded by joining me to their postal youth fellowship. It was lovely getting extra mail at boarding school breakfast, but I had to make sure I leaned across the label on the brown envelopes so that no one would find out where my letters came from.

I worked in the holidays in Father's factory, or gave

coaching lessons or delivered letters for the Post Office at
Christmas. For several years I held the unofficial title of
"our Number 1 Post-girl of the year", and was even elected
Miss Croydon (South) 1960. My princely wage was 2s. 4½d.
per hour plus luncheon vouchers; these I exchanged at the
Post Office Canteen for Woodbine cigarettes. I was a woman
of the world!

And on to the Royal College of Music where I discovered
very quickly that musicians regard love as the food of music
and had a hard time eluding a persistent horn player. I did
have a great predilection for the brass section, however, and
spent an unfortunate amount of my time trailing them
around from pub to rehearsal to concert to pub. I sat on their
instrument cases in the train and did very little practice on
my piano or oboe.

From time to time I passed the Christian Union notice
board and got a twinge of conscience. But those Christians
looked so wet, pimply and feeble and were mostly organists
anyway. Not my scene at all. They sat in a holy huddle by
themselves in the canteen and looked unattractive, like those
awful people who came up to me and asked if I was "saved"
or "washed in the blood". I did not know what they were
talking about and did not want to either. They looked grim
—no make up and felt hats and though they assured me I
would change once I "knew Jesus" I certainly did not want
to change into one of them.

Instead I went to a series of parties where the chosen
forms of recreation were sordid or boring. "Well, what did
you come for then?" The men flung this at me when I declined the alternatives. I always went, hoping to meet the
man of my dreams and it was a long time before I realized
that he was not likely to be at such parties.

I was sitting drably on my commuter train dragging back
home from College one day when I met two old school
friends. They took one look at me and invited me to a
London flat for coffee with a fabulous man who would talk
about the Bible. So I went. He was fabulous. But so was

everyone there. I could not get over it—they looked quite normal like me! The girls were made up and one of them was talking about bikinis. The men were discussing car racing—and yet all of them were here because they wanted to study the Bible. It was the first time in my life that my toes did not curl up when someone talked to me about Jesus. I could discuss God in that flat easily.

I was upset to hear, though, about Heaven and Hell, which I had thrown out with the mass emotionalism years before. But more disturbing was hearing that no one can go to God except through Jesus. The words were not such a shock as the discovery that Jesus said them. I was constrained either to accept what Jesus said about Himself or to forget about the Christian faith. Amongst my social set the worst sin was to be narrow, but Jesus' words offered no compromise.

Reluctantly I told Him I would believe what He had said —although I did not like it much. I was converted.

My life became more full than I had believed possible. I had not entered a narrow life after all. Shortly after a man on my Suburban line leaned across the carriage and asked if I believed in God. "No," I replied, "I know Him, it's different. I know peace, I know where I'm going."

My new life also brought difficulty. After one particular Bible study the girls sat praying; thanking God for their certainty of going to Heaven. I opened my eyes and peeped at them. They were all smiling and genuinely happy. I was appalled. For if we believed that we were going to Heaven because of Jesus—surely the converse was true also, that some people would not be going. The girls sat down to eat risotto but I dashed out thinking, "How can you just sit there believing what you do? What about the people who haven't heard? Risotto!"

This resulted in my taking part in the kind of scene which I would have despised before my conversion. I found myself playing the piano for a youth squash evangelical tea party in Waddon. This was a Saturday afternoon and I should have been at the Rugger International at Twickenham yelling "shove" with the best of them. But salvation songs and sausage-sizzles in Waddon. Then I was sure my life had really taken a new direction!

Having gained my degree I was enjoying a career teaching music. I wanted to give my whole life somewhere; I was free. I was not especially in love at the time, there was nothing to stop me giving all my time in one place. The missionary idea came back.

So I wrote to Africa (that's where missionaries go to) to schools, to societies, to broadcasting companies. And they all wrote back, no—they did not want me. One group explained, "If you could teach English and Maths then we could find a place for you, but we can't afford musicians out here yet. Maybe in a few years."

Undeterred, I sought the best advice going. My idea was to get hold of the visiting speaker, or the good-looking curate, after a meeting and ask for a private audience.

"What do you think I should do with my life?" I asked earnestly of each one.

"Have you prayed about it?" they always replied. It was maddening because I had prayed about it, but God did not give me a clear answer. My Bible told me to trust and He would lead me. I used to dash down to fetch the post in the mornings thinking guidance would come that way. But the replies were always negative.

One night I had a dream in which the family were all crowded round the dining room table looking at a map of Africa. In the middle of the different coloured countries was a pink one. I leaned over to see what it was called. It said "Hong Kong". I did not really believe that, but I did not want to show up my ignorance.

"Aah," I tried to sound nonchalant, "I never knew Hong Kong was there."

"Yes, of course, it is, didn't you know?" said my Aunty Dotty in a superior tone and I did not dare argue. When I woke up I wrote to the Hong Kong government explaining that I was a qualified musician and that I would like a teaching post. They wrote back saying that applications accompanied by three named referees had to be handled through the Ministry of Overseas Development. Finally they had no jobs for musicians. Then I tried my old Missionary Society, stating that I wanted to go to Hong Kong. Impossible, they said—they did not accept would-be missionaries until the age of twenty-five, so I would have to wait.

"But I think Jesus might come back before I'm twenty-five," I said, "couldn't I go sooner? I don't mind not being called a missionary—can't I teach in one of your schools?" However, they said there was no way; I seemed to have misinterpreted my dream. I went to pray in a tiny, peaceful village church. There I saw a vision of a woman—holding out her arms beseechingly as on a refugee poster. I wondered what she wanted—she looked desperate for something. Was it Christian Aid? Oxfam?

Then words moved past like a television credit. "WHAT CAN YOU GIVE US?" What did I honestly think I could give her? If I was going to be a missionary, what was I going to give anyone? Was it my ability to play the piano and oboe? Was I to pass on the benefit of my nice English background or my education? Was I to be a channel for food, or money, or clothing? If I only gave her those things then when I went away she would be hungry again. But the woman in the picture had been hungry for a food she did not know about.

Then it came to me that what she needed was the love of Jesus; if she received that, then when I left her she would still be full and, even better, she would be able to share it with other people. I now knew what I had to do—but I still did not know where I was supposed to do it.

Not long afterwards I met a factory worker from West Croydon who had been with us on the sausage sizzle mission.

"You got any answers yet?" He knew I was praying about the future.

"No," I said apologetically.

"You wanna come to our meeting?" he said, nodding his head knowingly, "we always get answers in ours."

What kind of monopoly on God did he think he had in West Croydon? I was furious but I was also intrigued to know what was going on at his meeting, so one Tuesday night I took the bus over.

When I arrived someone told me confidentially not to be surprised if anything odd happened. Nervously I sat myself near the door—apparently they were going to use "spiritual gifts" at their meeting and I wanted to be in a good position to get away if necessary.

I was not sure what to expect and I thought maybe someone would prophesy in a loud voice, "You'll meet a man who'll give you a ticket for such and such a country on such and such a date" and that would be God's way of answering me.

The meeting was orderly and calm with normal prayers and songs. One or two present did speak in a strange language which I did not understand and others explained what they meant. But so far there was no booming voice from God talking to me.

Then it came.

It was not a great booming voice at all. Someone was speaking quite quietly and I was completely sure that it was meant for me.

"Go. Trust me, and I will lead you. I will instruct you and teach you in the way which you shall go; I will guide you with my eye." There it was, what He had been saying all along, but now it was underlined. I was sure that God had my life in hand and was about to lead me somewhere.

There was no doubt that West Croydon got answers—but they did not tell me how I could receive spiritual gifts myself. I went home to wait. God had quite clearly promised to guide me, but I still did not know where to go. I gave in my notice for all my jobs so that I would be free to leave after the Summer term and I tried to pray by my bedside a bit more.

Still no answers.

In the Easter holidays I went to help in Richard Thompson's Shoreditch parish for a week. As a minister he had known me for some time and I felt he was in a position to give counsel. I well remember the carpet in his study, for I spent a good time staring at it before plucking up courage to speak. Then I told him that God and I had reached a stalemate; He had told me clearly to go—I knew why I was to go, but He would not tell me where. So how could I go?

Richard's reply was extraordinary, "If God is telling you to go—you had better go."

"How can I—I don't know where to. All my applications have been rejected."

"Well, if you've tried all the conventional ways and missionary societies and God still is telling you to go, you had better get on the move."

I felt frustrated.

"If you had a job, a ticket, accommodation, a sick fund and a pension, you wouldn't need to trust Him," Richard continued. "Anyone can go that way whether they are Christians or not. If I were you I would go out and buy a ticket for a boat going on the longest journey you can find and pray to know where to get off."

I did not exactly hear bells but this was the first time in all those months of searching that anything made sense.

"It sounds terrific—but it must be cheating because I'd love to do that." I still had the idea that anything to do with God had to be serious. I was sure that Christians always had to take the hard way and enjoyment was no part of suffering for their faith.

But Richard Thompson told me that it was quite scriptural. Abraham was willing to leave his country and follow Jehovah to a promised land without knowing where he was going because he trusted. In the same way thousands of years later Gladys Aylward journeyed in faith to China.

"You can't lose if you put yourself completely in God's hands, you know." Richard was quite serious. "If He doesn't want you to get on the ship He is quite able to stop you—or

to make the ship go anywhere in the world." I had visions
of being storm-driven like St. Paul. I might land on a little
desert island where one person wanted to hear about Jesus.
It was an exciting proposition.

"Maybe you will go all the way round the world just to
talk to one sailor about Christ, or maybe you will go as far
as Singapore to play the piano for a week of youth meetings
and then come back."

Richard's advice was extraordinary, but completely wise.
Never at any time did he lead me to the impression that I
was to get on a ship, grow a bun and get off as a missionary
ready to do a "work". He never suggested that I had to
achieve anything at all, I had simply to follow wherever God
led. I, too, felt I could not lose on this adventure.

So I went out and after counting up my money found the
cheapest ship on the longest route passing through the most
countries on its way. It was from France to Japan—I bought
a ticket and was all set.

Of course there were my parents and friends and others
to deal with. Understandably some were sceptical. My
Father very rightly insisted that I think long and carefully on
my "slow boat to China"; what right had I to give my
religion to people in other countries when they had perfectly
good ones of their own? Each parent was content about my
trip, but worried about the other. So I prayed and one evening heard them convincing each other that it was all right.

The telephone book missionary society was less keen.
"Very irresponsible advice for a vicar to give a young
girl," they cautioned. And I suppose it would have been had
it not been the Holy Spirit who gave Richard Thompson the
words.

The day I left was one of those days when everything goes
wrong. The taxi ordered to drive us the twenty miles to
London appeared an hour late and then stuck in a traffic jam
on Vauxhall Bridge. I remember my Mother frantically
chewing white stomach pills. Gasping, I settled into the boat-
train carriage with my nightmare of luggage and one minute

to spare. Richard Thompson came running up the platform shouting, "Praise the Lord!" in a very un-English fashion, and the train pulled out.

*   *   *

The immigration officer turned back to me in annoyance. For a moment I was afraid I had come all this way to Asia merely to be repatriated. Then I remembered that morning's reading, "Behold your name is written on the palms of God's hands,"—if my name was written there then God knew all about me. So perhaps the whole purpose of the journey was that I should get arrested in Hong Kong, locked up in the ship's hold and then I could convert the jailer. I could not lose.

"Wait a minute," I said, suddenly remembering my Mother's godson, "I do know someone here. He's a policeman." The effect was dramatic; the police were highly regarded back in 1966, and anyone who knew a policeman who ranked higher than mere immigration officials, was clearly O.K. On their faces I read, "All this bother from a stupid girl who is well connected all along."

They thrust my passport at me muttering angrily that I could land on condition that I searched for work immediately. As far as they were concerned my money would not last three days in Hong Kong.

Chapter Three

They Call It Darkness

The Walled City is guarded day and night by a ceaseless army of watchers. As soon as a stranger approaches the watchers pass the word. Their flip-flops flapping, the boys run between the noodle stalls, through doorways, across narrow alleys and up staircases. Grass Sandal whispers to Red Bamboo Pole who respectfully communicates the news to Golden Paw. The leaders of the crime syndicate have colourful names, but their activities are sordid. To strangers the real business of the Walled City is invisible; doors close, shutters clang shut, joss sticks camouflage the strange pungent smell of opium.

One name for the Walled City in Chinese is "Hak Nam", in English, "darkness". As I began to know it better I learned how true this name was; the Walled City was a place of terrible darkness, both physical and spiritual. Journalists get good copy out of it; but when you meet the men and women who have to live and suffer in such a place you can be broken by compassion.

I had thought I was going to one of those Chinese walled villages in the guide books—sort of quaint, but poor. Mrs. Donnithorne had invited me to visit her nursery school and church. But she had not prepared me for what I was to see. We got a lift as far as Tung Tau Chuen Road on the edge of the city. The street was lined with countless dentists' parlours, equipped with ancient and modern drilling equipment, their windows filled with gold and silver teeth. There were teeth in bottles, teeth on velvet cushions, teeth even on the tips of big whirring fans. This was the street of the illegal dentists; illegal because none of the amateur mouth doctors is allowed to practice in Hong Kong proper.

Behind these tawdry shops rose the ramshackle sky-scrapers of the Walled City; it seemed impossible to find a way in. But the frail old lady who was my guide knew exactly where to go; we squeezed through a narrow gap between the shops and started walking down a slime covered passageway. I will never forget the smell and the darkness, a fetid smell of rotten foodstuffs, excrement, offal and general rubbish. The darkness was startling after the glaring sunlight outside. As we walked on between the houses their projecting upper storeys almost touched each other above us, so that only occasionally would the daylight penetrate in strong shafts of brightness among the shadows. I felt I was in an underground tunnel.

As we went my guide gave me a running commentary: on my right was a plastic flower factory, on my left an old prostitute who was too old and ugly to get work. So instead she employed several child prostitutes to work for her; one seemed mentally retarded, another was a child she had bought as a baby and brought up to take over the bread-earner's role when she grew too old. They had plenty of customers; in that depraved street the ownership of child prostitutes was regarded as a good source of income. "Auntie Donnie" told me to keep my head down in case someone chose to empty his chamber pot as we were passing below. Next we reached the door to the illegal dog restaurant, where the captured beasts were flayed to death to provide tender dog steaks; then the pornographic film-show house, a crowded lean-to shed.

There was legitimate business, too. Workmen carrying loads of freshly mixed cement on their heads hurried down the alleys. Women clutching huge sacks of plastic flowers staggered out from tiny workrooms where the clank of plastic pressing machines never ceased. There was no Sabbath day of rest here; five days' holiday a year was considered quite sufficient. Whole families were involved in keeping the plastic presses running day and night; for Chinese children, the duty to work all hours for their parents was paramount, when they were not studying.

How can such a place exist inside the British Crown Colony of Hong Kong? Over eighty years ago when Britain apportioned to herself not only the Chinese island of Hong Kong, but also the mainland Peninsula of Kowloon, and the Chinese territories behind it, one exception was made.

The old walled village of Kowloon was to remain under Chinese Imperial Administration, complete with its own Mandarin magistrate administering Chinese law. Later the British traders complained and the concession was unilaterally withdrawn; the Chinese magistrate died—he was never succeeded by either Chinese or British, and lawlessness inside the Walled City came to stay. It became a haven for gold smuggling, drug smuggling, illegal gambling dens and every kind of vice. The confusion over its ownership meant that the police could not enforce the law and indeed would not even enter the infamous City. Even today they go in large groups if they are hunting particular criminals, and usually the man they want effectively disappears into its sordid alleyways.

The area is large in population, small in size. A mere six acres shelters thirty thousand people or double that; no census has ever found out the true number. The housing is appalling; no building regulations can be enforced so crazy-angled apartment blocks with no sanitation, water, or lighting straddle the streets. A maze of tangled wires is graphic evidence of the fact that their electricity is tapped from the public supplies outside the Walled City. But you cannot steal sanitation, so excrement must be emptied into the stinking alleys below. At street level there are two toilets for all thirty thousand people; the "toilets" consist of two holes over overflowing crawling cesspools, one for women, one for men.

It was unlikely that a place like the Walled City would have schools and churches. But in this appalling place where children were born and brought up, Mrs. Donnithorne had found premises and begun a general primary school. The teachers were not properly qualified, but they had attended secondary school to fourth or fifth form level. The school was small, but it had morning and afternoon shifts and taught several hundred pupils. On the very first day that I visited it, Auntie Donnie asked me to teach there. Without thinking I said, "Yes," and she immediately said, "How often?" Before I had fully realized what I was letting myself in for, I had agreed to teach percussion band, singing and English conversation three afternoons a week.

I soon found the Chinese education system so miscast that very often the brightest got fed up and dropped out. The system demands that you learn all your lessons by heart. Every month, every term and every year there are exams; should a child fail annual exams then he or she had to repeat the whole of the year's lessons. It was not unusual to come across children who had taken the Primary One exam at the end of their first year no less than three times. I formed a theory that it was the bright ones who got bored with the system and jumped off the ladder while the duller ones climbed up.

Percussion band and singing are not too difficult to teach even if there is little or no conversation between you, but when it came to teaching English conversation I was a complete failure.

All their teaching is highly regimented; I would read out, "John and Mary went into the wood" and they would repeat after me in unison, "John and Mary (it came out Mairly) went into the wood" without comprehension. Traditionally understanding in Chinese education is not held to be important, but learning is considered vital, and they all learn to repeat what the teacher says like machines.

My attempts to enliven their stories by acting out what was happening were completely misunderstood; we had a

classroom riot every time. No one had ever tried to teach
them to participate in stories and dramatic ideas; the freedom that I tried to show them resulted in classroom anarchy
within a matter of minutes. So I sadly went back to reading
out sentences from the book, the sure way to maintain calm.

Once a week one of the classrooms was converted into a
church for a Sunday night service. So Miss Poon—I now
proudly had a Chinese name—played the harmonium. It
meant pedalling at fifty m.p.h. or so to produce an accom-
paniment that could be heard against the singing, otherwise,
having started on a particular note they would continue to
sing in that key quite regardless of the one I was playing in.
I usually gave in and joined them.

Mostly the worshippers were older Chinese women—
some with babies wrapped tightly to their backs, and I discovered that many of them, being illiterate, came to church
for a reading lesson. The singing leader had a sort of rehearsal before each hymn—pointing out the characters (the
written form of Chinese—one sign for each word) one by
one. They all sang loudly and enthusiastically. Then the Bible
woman gave the teaching in Cantonese; I could not understand a word of it at that stage, but felt I shared the worship.

Among the crowd of Chinese faces on my debut night, one
woman stuck out remarkably. She was an old vegetable
seller; she had a deeply lined face with her hair combed
straight back, a large circular comb stuck on her head and
only two teeth, which showed prominently since she was
always smiling. She came up and tugged me by the sleeve
enthusiastically. Beside her was her half-blind husband—so
she pulled him along, too. She chattered on, beaming at me
and tugging still. I asked someone to translate what she was
saying. It was, "See you next week—see you next week."

I wanted to tell her that I could not come every week; it
was a long journey across the harbour and through Kowloon to the Walled City for a Sunday evening. It meant that
I got back late. This was not good as I had to be up very
early the next morning to teach.

But then I found I could not possibly say all that to her.

She would only understand that I was there or I was not; so I decided that for her sake I would be there every week.

By now I had a regular job teaching in a primary school in the mornings which I held for six months, helping Auntie Donnie three afternoons a week in her primary school, playing for the Sunday service and arranging music programmes for various welfare organizations. This filled up my time. I had been offered a superb job teaching music by a prestigious boarding school at the other end of the island; they additionally offered to refund my fare out. But it was clear I could not combine my work, teaching there and in the Walled City. I do not find that I am very good at guidance but on this occasion I had been reading a verse in the Bible which said, "For he looked for a city which had foundations, whose builder and maker was God." As I read that I felt quite sure that I should carry on teaching inside the Walled City.

The second time I went into the Walled City I had this wonderful feeling inside; the thrill you get on your birthday. I found myself wondering why was I so happy? And the next time I went into the Walled City I had exactly the same sensation. This was not reasonable—of all the revolting places in the world. And yet nearly every time I was in that underground city over the next dozen years I was to feel the same joy. I had caught a glimpse of it at confirmation, and again when I had really accepted Jesus into my life—now to find it in this profane place?

*   *   *

"There's a drug addict," said Auntie Donnie as we walked down the street to her school one morning. I had no idea at that stage what being a drug addict meant. Did he jump at you, or steal your watch or throw fits? This was a pathetic looking man slowly sorting through a pile of waste. He was going through it, item by item, to see if there was anything of value for him. He seemed very ill, his face was waxy and he looked more like seventy than thirty-five.

He wore a soiled T-shirt, a pair of cotton shorts and

battered plastic sandals. Most Chinese people keep themselves meticulously clean, but Mr. Fung was filthy, his teeth were brown and broken and his finger nails disgusting. His rough crewcut, a grey shadow over his skull, was a sure sign that he had recently come out of prison. For Mr. Fung, though, prison was somewhere to sleep with regular meals, which was more comfortable than his present existence, sleeping in the streets and eating scraps collected at restaurant doors.

But food and sleep were not important. Mr. Fung lived to "chase the dragon". This Chinese way of drug-taking has a magic ritual all its own—a sort of devilish liturgy which is sacred. Once inside a drug den each addict takes a piece of silver tinfoil; on it he places the small sand-coloured grains of heroin known as "white powder". He heats the foil with a slow burning spill of screwed up toilet paper. Gradually the heroin melts into a dark brown treacle. Then he puts the outer casing of a match box into his mouth to act as a funnel through which to inhale the fumes. He keeps the pool of treacle moving from one end of the silver foil to the other following it with his mouth. This is "chasing the dragon".

Mr. Fung never "chased the dragon" in public, but in drug dens or lavatories. It was a full nine months before I actually saw it for myself. And I soon discovered that not all drug takers looked like Mr. Fung. Some are very well dressed; they regard their neat appearance as evidence that they are not enslaved to the dragon. As I was going into the City quite frequently I saw more and more of Mr. Fung. Should I learn to say "Good morning, how are you?" or "Do you have a problem?" In any case I could not understand his reply, even had he confided in me. I wondered whether I should do something about him and others like him. I hoped someone was doing something.

Prostitution was seldom concealed. The first prostitute I met used dark mauve lipstick and mauve nail varnish; a macabre combination with her thin grey face and emaciated body. She spent her whole life squatting in a street so narrow that the sewer tunnel ran by her heels. I never saw her in any other position. When she ate, she remained squatting there with her rice bowl and her chopsticks, waiting for customers.

Further down, other women sat on orange boxes and one even had a chair. It was hard to tell their ages because most of them were drug addicts too. The score marks on the backs of their hands showed that they were "mainlining", directly injecting heroin into the veins. Day after day I walked past them and could not tell whether they were asleep or awake; they nodded all day, showing the yellow of their eyes in a heroin haze.

One day I tried touching the little one. I had learnt to say, "Jesus loves you. *Yeh sou ngoi nei*," and my heart went out to her. But she cringed away from me. Looking at the expression on her face I suddenly realized that she was feeling sorry for me because I had made a mistake.

"You're a good girl and shouldn't be talking to the likes of us! You're a nice Christian, dear, maybe you don't know who we are."

She put up the barrier and I did not know how to cross it. She was embarrassed that a clean girl had made an error and touched a dirty one.

Some of the older ones were clearly involved in procuring. As the men came out of the blue film theatre these *mama-sans* would literally pull the men in and you could hear them saying, "She's very young and very cheap," as they pushed them up the wooden flight of steps. Compared with the prices charged in other places by the more glamorous Susie Wongs they were cheap indeed at HK $5 each. Not, of course, that the girls were allowed to keep all this money; most prostitutes were controlled by Triad gangs and these brothels were only allowed to operate by the gang controlling that area. The Triads also supplied the young girls.

There were two girls I saw occasionally as I taught percussion band next to their sordid room. One was a cripple and the other was mentally retarded and they were prisoners.

They never went anywhere without a *mama-san* accompanying them. They were visited up to three times an hour and I reckoned they might be dead of disease by the time they were twenty or so. They were thirteen and fourteen at that time and later an English-speaking Triad member explained how they and others like them would have been introduced to the trade.

A group of young men would hold a party and invite girls along. Some had been warned what might happen; others were innocent victims. At the party the new girls would be seduced; if they resisted they were sometimes forcibly raped. Usually each member of the gang would take his girl off with him and stay with her for a few days. When the girl was attached to him and thoroughly accustomed to sex, he signed her over to a brothel. One girl could bring in enough to support several men.

Other girls became prostitutes because their parents could not afford to feed and clothe them. One mother told me, "It wasn't really selling my daughter, you know. My husband left me, and as there were no social security payments in Hong Kong I had nothing to live on. I couldn't afford to raise my baby myself so I gave her to this woman who wanted a child and she gave me HK $100 lucky money. It was just lucky money," she repeated.

But of course, she knew what she was doing; she was selling her daughter into prostitution for at least her teenage years. After that, most former child prostitutes escaped from their owners and made careers of their own practising the only trade they knew. Child prostitutes could start their careers as early as nine years old.

Respectable people thought of the girls as the scum of the earth; but it was only the grace of God that I had been born in a different place. I tried to work out how I could reach girls like these guarded as they were. Eventually I shelved the problem by hoping one day to find a concerned man who would pay the hourly rate, but share the good news of Christ in that time. Maybe he and I could work out a plan of escape if any of the girls wanted to get out.

Chapter Four

The Youth Club

Sometimes I think that Chan Wo Sai was the real reason why I started the Youth Club. He was a most unattractive fifteen-year-old with about as many problems in life as anyone could have; personal problems, education problems, home problems, background problems and no prospects at all. I first got to know him when I was teaching English and singing on one of my three afternoons a week at Oiwah Primary School. I was teaching them "Ten Green Bottles", a less sexy song I can hardly think of, yet there was Chan Wo Sai getting really "sent" by a traditional English nursery rhyme in a language he could not speak. Chan Wo Sai was rolling his eyes and clicking his fingers; then he got up and began to slide across the classroom towards me in a sexy hip-thrusting motion like a bad Chinese movie actor. I hurriedly ordered him back to his place, and changed to another song. And as soon as class ended I went to find out where he came from. The story was both simple and sad.

Chan Wo Sai was born in the Walled City; his mother was a prostitute and his father a drunkard. They lived in a sort of cockloft; to find him I had to go down the narrow passage where the prostitutes were living, along the main street where the older women pimps spent all day waiting, and then left at the Blue Film theatre down a very muddy path to a collapsed building. Here beyond a heap of stones he lived with his whole family in half of a room which had been added on to another building. The walls were crumbling off. There were more prostitutes next door. He'd known about them for as long as he could remember; in no way was he shocked by them; they were just part of his life. Indeed he thought their activities were very funny. His horizons were limited to the brothel next door, the gambling dens down the road and the opium dens beyond. There was nowhere in the Walled City where you could go and do anything neutral, let alone take part in a constructive activity. So I tried to get to know him, to help him with his problems.

This was difficult when I could hardly speak a word of Cantonese. All I had managed to learn as yet was a few sentences. I could say, "Good morning" and "Have you eaten yet?" But that was about all. And to make life still more difficult he had a speech impediment which made conversation hard even for fluent Cantonese speakers. Our great point of contact was the drumpad I gave him; it is a sheet of rubber stuck on a wooden board on which you can practise with drum sticks, making a noiseless drum. The drumpad provided the perfect excuse for going to see him regularly. He was supposed to practise with it, but he seldom did, and in any case he had the most hopeless sense of rhythm. But he was pleased to find that someone was interested in him; this was the first time in his life that anyone had shown care for him.

As time went on I found myself constantly thinking about him and this alarmed me. My English mind had been trained to think that love for a boy must be romantic, and because I was a Christian that sort of love would eventually lead to marriage. Yet that of course was impossible, ridiculous; my mind told me that he was a very ugly unattractive boy with a hopeless background. But I really did love him and prayed for him continually. I got to the point where I could quite seriously and willingly have given my life for him.

After some time I was able to understand and was surprised by what I saw in myself. It was as if God had given special love for him and I was meant to show it, though it was not necessarily an emotion that should or could be returned. This love was for his good; it was quite different from any love for other people that I had before, where I had always wanted something in return. I had never before loved somebody entirely for his benefit without caring what he felt for me. So it was really for Chan Wo Sai that I opened a club just for young people.

Of the various groups of people in need in the Walled City, none were worse catered for than the young teenagers. At least the younger children had the chance to go to primary school; and most Chinese parents, no matter how poor, encouraged this. But the young teenagers had nothing; getting into secondary school was almost impossible for a Walled City boy, even if his parents could afford it, which was unlikely. They found work in the sweated labour plastic factories, where the hours were unlimited and the pay pitiful.

Then disheartened by the life of ceaseless work, they dropped out. Many boys, and sometimes girls, left home to find shelter in some one-room hovel slept in by lots of others, all following the same path. Soon, with nothing to do, they drifted into crime; the Triad gangs often provided the only other employment available.

My involvement with Chan Wo Sai grew up during the summer of 1967 when all China had been thrown into confusion by the activities of the Red Guards. Now the fever crossed the border into Hong Kong; trouble was skilfully stirred by local agitators. Knowing nothing about politics I remained blissfully unaware of what was going on, although there were riots all over the Colony. I did discover, however, that some of the Walled City boys were being paid to pick up stones and throw them. I felt they could just as easily be persuaded to come on a picnic. So one hot humid day in June I said to Auntie Donnie rather pompously, "I think the Lord would have me start a Youth Club." I had visions of a hand-picked team of handsome helpers from Hong Kong Island who would sweep in with a beautifully organized programme, while I sat back and applauded.

I envisaged a room open at evenings and weekends; it

would be a place where young people could play table tennis and take part in all the other normal activities available to boys and girls in a big city, and equally could be a place where they could hear about Jesus. I envisaged committee discussions, prayer meetings, programme planning, further discussion. Auntie Donnie was more practical. "Good, I've been praying for that for years. When do you start? Next week?"

We started one week later; I could count the words of Cantonese I knew. I had not got my hand-picked team and we did not have anywhere to meet. But I borrowed a room from the School on Saturday afternoons. Gordon Siu, a young Chinese I had met at the Youth Orchestra became a tower of strength, and an invaluable translator. He was realistic: unlike some of the Chinese leaders who expected a Youth Club to be a sort of extended Bible lecture, Gordon helped us hire coaches, came on picnics, and went roller skating. Soon school ended, and so none of the pupils had much to do. The prospect of the boys being caught up in the riots stimulated me to develop the activities further.

Saturday afternoons grew into a complete Summer programme with organized picnics and hikes and visits to the forestry plantations. What started that Summer became a regular programme that happened every July and August for some years after.

The first to come were the thirteen and fourteen year olds; they began to bring friends from outside. Everyone knew from the beginning that I was there because I was a Christian, and that events would start or end with a short talk. They did not like the Jesus bit at all; for them anything to do with Christianity was either full of prohibition or middle-class. They had no idea who Jesus really was. Worse, they believed that if you could not read you could not be a Christian, because being a Christian was something to do with the Big Book. Some young people told me that they could not come to the Club because "We smoke and we drink, we go to films and we gamble—and we know Christians don't do any of those things." It soon became clear that the blocks to belief were often the result of a culture gap which local Chinese Christians did nothing to overcome.

All too soon Chan Wo Sai dropped out of school. At fifteen he was one of the oldest boys in Primary fourth form and he was at least four years behind. He decided not to finish that year of schooling; a new blue film theatre had just opened in the Walled City and he got a job selling the tickets.

To the inexperienced teacher from England, dropping out of primary school seemed a terrible thing to do; I spent all Summer trying to persuade the hostile boy to go back. Eventually he humbled himself and went to see his teachers but they refused to take him back; their explanation horrified me. One said, "Well, Jackie, we were only too pleased when he left, because we could not control him. He upset not only the teachers but the whole of the class. Good riddance to him." Yet theirs was a mission school, not a profit-orientated private academy. These were Christian teachers and I had imagined that when they met once a week for prayer meetings, they prayed for the difficult and troublesome boys like Chan Wo Sai.

But the truth was that most of the teachers had barely completed secondary school themselves; they had said they were Christians just to get the job and were incapable of handling anything other than entirely docile classes. For Chan Wo Sai, his departure was effectively the end of his education—he could not go to another school without retaking the Primary Four exam.

The only alternative was to find him a vocational training school that would teach him some skill. However, he proved to be not eligible for such courses either because he was too old, or because he had not completed primary school and could not speak English. Together we trudged round schools and factories seeking further training or an apprenticeship, and in every case we were turned away. Against Chan Wo Sai the gates were shut even though he was only fifteen.

What was to happen to him? He had dropped out, and selling tickets at the blue film theatre was as far as he was ever going to go. There was nothing I could do for him except keep this Club going. Several of his drop-out friends joined the gangs. They discovered that there they had a role. If they proved themselves they were given respect and responsibility. They were given a rank and treated as someone of importance. In the gangs they found a degree of care, consideration and closeness that they certainly found nowhere else. In school and church success in exams was equated with righteousness. "Be a good boy—don't go around with bad people, but study hard and pass your exams." The school had said it. The church had said it. Their parents had said it. For the boys like Chan Wo Sai it was terribly boring to be told the same thing again and again, and they hated hearing it. In the gangs and at my Club they did not hear the sentence of failure and rejection.

The Youth Club was indeed unlike any other activity organized in the Walled City. Nobody made any money out of it; no gangsters controlled it, and years later they even sent guards to protect it from those who wanted to smash the place up. The Club went through various addresses, but inside it was always the same; a bare room with some games equipment like table tennis and darts, crude benches and a bookshelf with Christian books bought by me which no one could read.

Nicholas was another boy I got to know very well at this stage. Both his father and mother had been on charges for selling drugs and the whole family lived in one of the nastiest houses I had ever been in. Half of it was literally a pigsty for their neighbours kept a pig below. The two eldest girls were prostitutes and there always seemed to be a lot of babies around. I never found out which baby belonged to which mother. Some were Nicholas's brothers and sisters—others his nephews and nieces. They all lived in a room the size of a broom cupboard which stank.

The church members resented Nicholas because, like Chan Wo Sai, he was such a bad influence in the school. Of course they knew about the bargirl sisters and that the father was a hopeless opium addict. In their eyes the fact that I was welcoming Nicholas to our Club meant that the Christian Church got a bad name. I should not even be seen with him.

I knew what Nicholas was like. He was vile, and was always a pain; he had Triad connections right from the beginning and later graduated to becoming a heroin addict and, necessarily, a pusher. But I loved him, even if unreasonably; for Jesus had come into the world for him, which too was unreasonable.

So I made a point of befriending him and visited him at home all hours of the day for weeks and months and years. I was terribly concerned about him and grieved for him—perhaps more deeply than for any other person over the years. I found him in drug dens; and went to him when he was arrested; prayed with him in the police station and in the prison before his trial and helped him with his trial. But none of this changed him.

I learnt that any sense of "righteousness" was lacking in that place of darkness. Crime, dishonesty, and corruption were right as long as they paid. But this attitude did not stop its supporters adopting a cliché—loaded morality in my presence. They felt it was correct since I represented the Church—the Establishment.

"Isn't he a bad boy," Nicholas's mother would lecture him in front of me. "Miss Pullinger—you must teach him a good way and take him to your Church and your Youth Club." It was nauseous prating and I hated it. Then she would moan, "Can't understand why my children are bad. I had them baptized and sent them to church." This from a woman who measured grains of "white powder" into little packets for sale to junkies.

Later on, one of the younger sisters, Annie, also became a bargirl. Then incredibly she scored the ultimate by making a wonderful marriage. Her husband was a *for-gei* and a collector of rake-off money for the police. Annie was ever so pleased about marrying him because he had his own private car. Annie's mother was delighted, too; although the night clubs, ballrooms and brothels owned and run by the son-in-law's family were only low class, at least they were very successful.

One day as I was walking down the street an old man ran up to me. He had the skeleton face of an opium addict, hollow cheeked, and grey tinged from a lifetime of the sweet stuff. He was beside himself with rage, "Poon Siu Jeh—Miss Poon. You must complain to the police!"

He was an opium den owner—an important man in the Walled City. "Why should I complain?" I asked him.

"They've closed all the opium dens." He was outraged and indignant.

"I'm delighted the police have closed the opium dens," I replied, "Why do you want me to complain?"

"Because they've let the heroin dens stay open and we've all paid them the same money—it's not fair!"

No right and wrong. Just fair and unfair.

Joseph was one of the earliest Youth Club presidents. Unlike Nicholas and Chan Wo Sai he had no overt connections with vice. His father had remarried when he was six and the new wife did not like her step-children so she did not feed them. Joseph and his sister Jenny were sent out to beg with plastic bowls, or to grub through a rubbish heap for food. They were rescued by a pastor in the New Territories and sent to Mrs. Donnithorne's Mission School. Having finished primary school Joseph got himself a room and worked as a coolie whenever he could. His sister soon joined him there.

Characters such as Nicholas would drop in on him and stay the night and his room became a breeding ground for gangsters. I began to call on him regularly too. His sister, Jenny, too was in moral danger. At fifteen she was very pretty and revelled in release from her highly supervised

Christian hostel. Now she could talk all night with her brother's friends—or go out with them.

She was not at school and it was great fun. I thought that if she remained in Joseph's room, there was only one way she could go.

I could not offer them both a home as I was already sharing my Hong Kong room with another Walled City girl, Rachel. But I thought I could squeeze in Jenny, so I bullied her out of the Walled City to live with me. I found her a secondary school, bought the uniform, the books, the lunches. She was not grateful; she wanted to be back in the Walled City and caused many headaches during the next year that she lived with us.

One of our regular attenders, Christopher, lived in the Walled City in a house that could only be described as a loft. To find it you had to walk down a narrow street where no light penetrated; the houses were built so close to each other that it was like going down a tunnel. When you reached a couple of hen coops made from soft drinks crates you had found their home. It was very, very smelly. Beside the coops and up some wooden ladders you reached the living level; you had to open Christopher's door from underneath, exactly like a trap door. There was just one room over the chickens; should it catch fire everyone would be burnt to death. Escape was impossible except by lifting the door and going down the wooden ladder. The family sleeping quarters were behind a curtain; there you found a pair of wooden bunk beds, one on top of the other. Everyone slept in these two beds, everyone being six brothers and sisters, plus the parents.

The rest of the single room was taken up with huge piles of plastic objects which Christopher's mother assembled. She earned about one Hong Kong dollar a day for this work. All the children had to help her assemble these plastic parts; they began working as soon as they were three or four years old. Christopher's younger sister did not finish primary school; she was sent to work in a factory as soon as she was thirteen. She was badly paid for the sweated labour, but every dollar and cent she earned had to be given to her mother; she was not allowed to keep anything for herself. When exhausted by a ten- or twelve-hour day and a crowded bus journey, she eventually returned home, she had as many as four more hours of work ahead of her, sewing on sequins. One sweater would take her up to a week to complete; when finished it would bring another three Hong Kong dollars in wages, all of which would be kept by her mother.

When Christopher went to work all his money went to his mother too; it was an unwritten law in Chinese families that the parents were paid back by their offspring to support them; their ambition is to retire and live off their children. Christopher's mother used to say, "I bore you, I brought you up, and I sent you to school; I paid out everything for you . . . now you children should be paying me back for having had you." The Chinese children, I knew, found the process of starting work very depressing since they entered on a lifetime's debt. They got no pride from their pay packet, because they never saw any of it. Their parents got the lot. Christopher's mother saved all this money, and later on bought herself a flat outside the Walled City.

The reason why so many Chinese families are large is an economic one; parents have far bigger families than they can afford to maintain well so that they will be rich in their old age. It seemed to me that family love and solidarity were based not so much on mutual love and respect as on economic advantage.

Christopher's younger sister, Ah Lin, finally rebelled at such exploitation; she met a boy at her factory who liked her, but her mother forbade her to go out with him. She was not allowed to come to the Youth Club either because our programme was mostly recreational. Had we provided sewing lessons or English classes it would have been permitted; but enjoyment pure and simple was to be no part of her life. Instead the girl's task was to stay at home and look after the babies, or assemble plastic parts, or carry water. Eventually the drudgery was too much; Ah Lin left home aged fourteen and went to live with the boy. Her mother recaptured her, and locked her up at home, saying she was a bad girl. She was beaten for what she had done; her action had not only brought shame on the family, it was also an attack on the family earnings. And her mother continued to refuse to let her go anywhere outside the home. Treated like chattels, it was not surprising many girls made the jump into prostitution, rather than remain imprisoned at home.

My mission was to help the Walled City people to understand who Christ was. If they could not understand the words about Jesus then we Christians should show them what He was like by the way we lived. I remembered He had said, "If someone forces you to go one mile, go with him two miles." So this was the beginning of what I called "walking the extra mile". There seemed to be a lot of Christians who did not mind walking one, not many who could be bothered to walk two, and no one who wanted to walk three. Those in need that I met seemed to need a marathon.

I became even more involved with the boys, their families and their problems. It meant walking with them in a practical way so that they should see and know who Jesus was. One example of this was when one of the boys asked me to help his sister get into a secondary school. The usual process was to queue up for a day merely to obtain an admission form to take the entrance examination. If the school were Protestant and discovered that the applicant had studied in a Catholic primary school she would not get a form so the queueing would begin at another school.

The boy's family thought that the way I would help would be by going to the headmistress and saying, "Look, I'm so and so and I know so and so; can you get this girl in?" I did it the opposite way round and queued up for whole days with the ordinary people; which surprised them as this was not at all their idea of how I was supposed to help.

Oftentimes there were problems over identity cards as many who lived in the Walled City had not been registered at birth. They thought I could have a word with the authorities and a card would be issued. Instead, if asked to help, I would go with them and sit all day at the government office to help them make the correct application. I had to do all this during the holidays as by now I was teaching music full-time at an Anglo-Chinese girls' college, St. Stephen's.

For several years I had many followers who reckoned that if they hung around for long enough they might get a baptism certificate, or a document which would enable them to get to America.

Perhaps they could get an introduction to a priest needing someone to clean in a convent; or they could grab any of the side perks they thought they could get from a church. They were real "rice Christians". They began to treat me as they treated other missionaries; they thought I was an easy "touch". They were careless with my property and equipment and were continually asking to borrow money. They simply did not believe me when I told them I had not got any. The conversations were always the same and they went like this ...

"Poon Siu Jeh (my name 'Pullinger' in Chinese) I haven't got a job and I've run out of money."

"But I'm afraid I haven't got any money."

"Oh, but you must have—you're terribly rich."

"No, no, really I haven't got any money."

"Oh yes you have, because you've got a church in America like the rest of them."

"No really I haven't got a church in America, actually I come from England; but no church sent me."

At this point another jumbo jet would lurch low across the roof tops as it came in to land at Kaitak airport which was close to the Walled City. Indeed the Walled City must have been directly under the flight path because in Summer months the tourist-filled jets came over one every couple of minutes, making conversation impossible as they thundered overhead.

The plane noise died away, and our conversation continued.

"Huh, one day I expect you'll get into one of those and fly back to where you came from."

"No, there's no danger of that because I haven't got enough money to get on one," I replied honestly.

"Well, your parents can send you the money anyway—there is plenty of money where you came from—we've seen how all those English people live up the Peak."

"No," I said, "you're wrong about that—my parents haven't got any money either." There was a pause, then Ah Ping would join the conversation. Ah Ping thought more than the others; his remarks were always more to the point, more understanding and more desperate.

"Maybe you haven't got any money now, but you could always get away from here if you had to get away. We can't. There is nowhere else for us to go; we're stuck on the edge of the sea and the only escape is into it. But you Westerners—you can fly away when you want to, and then you can forget all about us."

"No, Ah Ping. I'm not planning to fly away and forget all about you."

Ah Ping could really talk when he got warmed up, and to-day he was going to say what most of them really felt. I respected his honesty, for few Chinese ever tell Westerners what they really feel about them. "You Westerners," he continued, "you come here and tell us about Jesus. You can stay for a year or two, and your conscience will feel good, and then you can go away. Your Jesus will call you to other work back home. It's true some of you can raise a lot of money on behalf of us underprivileged people. But you'll still be living in your nice houses with your refrigerators and servants and we'll still be living here. What you are doing really has nothing to do with us. You'll go home anyhow, sooner or later."

This kind of conversation took place many times; it was an indictment of those evangelists who flew into Hong Kong, sang sweet songs about the love of Jesus on stage and on Hong Kong television, then jumped back into their planes and flew away again. "Fine," said Ah Ping to me savagely one day, "fine for them, fine for us too, we wouldn't mind believing in Jesus too if we could get into a plane and fly away round the world like them. They can sing about love very nicely, but what do they know about us? They don't touch us—they know nothing."

Sometimes I tried talking to the men who guarded the gambling dens but when I told them that Jesus loved them, they just nodded. "Yeah, yeah, how nice. That means nothing to us." And of course it did not since most of them had no idea who Jesus was or what love was. I went on—preach, preach, preach about how Jesus could give them a new life, but no one seemed to understand.

Chapter Five

Light in the Darkness

Jesus did not promise running shoes in the hereafter to the lame man. He made him walk. He not only preached but demonstrated He was God. He made blind men see, deaf men hear, and dead men return to life. Some Christians claimed that these things still happened, and I certainly needed to find them.

My missionary friends could not help me much. Most of them were well over forty; many had spent their lives in China and now felt lost. They did not expect people to be converted and explained this by saying that there was a spiritual cloud hanging over China which covered Hong Kong, too. Some missionaries had all sorts of cultural hang-ups which infected me until I found myself worrying over such questions as to whether I should wear sleeveless Summer dresses, and whether it was wrong to go bathing on Sundays. I got in the ridiculous situation where I was more concerned to please these missionary friends than to find out what God wanted me to do. I did not belong to any missionary society, was not sponsored by any group at home and in reality had all the freedom anyone could want, yet I was feeling bound and ineffective.

One day I went to play the harmonium in the Chapel. There I found a Chinese couple were to take the service and as soon as I saw them I knew they had it. What "it" was I did not know—but even watching them praying I sensed a vitality, a power. Immediately I wanted to know what made them so different. After the service I made a bee-line for the couple. They spoke hardly any English and I had hardly any Chinese. Soon it was clear what they were trying to convey.

"You haven't got the Holy Spirit."

A little indignantly I replied that I had; they replied that I had not and so the futile argument continued as we walked out of the Walled City and back to my bus stop.

"Of course I have the Spirit," I thought to myself. "I couldn't believe in Jesus if I hadn't." So what were we arguing about? These people obviously had something which I needed, which I had recognized even without understanding their sermon. They called it having the Holy Spirit and I wanted to call it something else. I quit the quarrel over terminology—receiving the Spirit, being filled with the Spirit, baptism of the Spirit, the power of the Spirit, second blessing, or what have you. If God had anything more for me I wanted to receive it and I would sort out the theological terms later. So I made an appointment to go round to the young couple's flat the next day.

Their flat proved to be a one room affair exactly like thousands of flats all over the Colony. There was one table, and on it were placed a plate of oranges and a plate of wet flannels. The oranges are a traditional Chinese food for a celebration, and were for when I had "received", and the flannels were for me to cry into.

Whatever was going to happen next was obviously meant to be a very emotional experience. My heart began to bump a bit because I was not at all sure what was going to happen next. Then I sat down and they laid their hands on my head saying over and over again in pidgin English, "Now you begin speaking, now you begin speaking, now you begin speaking."

But nothing happened; they thought I was going to burst into "the gift of tongues" and it had not worked.

Some of the West Croydon group had spoken in tongues and I had heard of other friends who had received this gift, but no one had ever been willing to discuss it. The idea of a new language in which you could speak fluently and express all the thoughts of your heart to God was wonderful. But I thought that it was something that you had to be rather advanced and spiritual to get. I shut my mouth firmly. If God was going to give me this gift—then He was going to do it, not me.

"Now you begin speaking, now you begin speaking."

I was acutely embarrassed and began to get cross with them. I felt hotter and hotter and more and more uncomfortable; here I was not speaking in tongues and they were going to be so disappointed that nothing had happened. They need not have prepared the wet flannels and the oranges—they were not going to need either plate. Eventually I could not stand it any longer, so I opened my mouth to say, "Help me God," and it happened.

As soon as I made the conscious effort to open my mouth I found that I could speak freely in a language I had never learned. It was a beautiful articulate tongue, soft and coherent in that there was a clear speech pattern with modulated rise and fall. I was never in any doubt that I had received the sign that I had asked for. But there was no accompanying exultation. I had imagined being lifted up into praise and glory but it was most unemotional.

The Chinese pair were delighted that I had spoken, though a little surprised that I was not in a flood of tears. However, they cried to make up for it, and their old mother had a good weep too. I still felt extremely embarrassed and left their house as soon as I could. I was very glad that this experience had not happened to me in front of British people.

As I got to the door they said, "Oh, you can expect the other gifts of the Spirit to appear now," but I did not understand what they meant.

Every day for the next week or so I was waiting for the gift of healing or gift of prophecy to pop up. These were the only other gifts of the spirit I had heard about, though there are nine. I knew that in England two of the ministers I most respected used these gifts and they certainly were most effective in their ministry. I also knew that there was an M.P.'s wife who had the gift of healing. They followed Bible teaching carefully, so there was no doubt in my mind as to the rightness of the gifts or their usefulness but I did not know how you knew when you had got them. How do you know if you have healing?

I remained puzzled too that I was still very cool about this great spiritual event. I had read books like *They Speak in Other Tongues*, which had left me with the impression that this experience should make me walk on the mountain tops, or sit on a cloud brimming over with love. I wondered if I had not got the right thing; maybe it was all vastly over-rated anyway. I went round Hong Kong trying to find someone who would talk to me about it and no one would. Missionary friends said darkly, "Something very dangerous happened in China and there was a split between the groups." Still more to my surprise the Pentecostal churches would not talk about it. I went to their services; they still retained the noise, the hand-clapping and the repeated Amens and Hallelujahs; but the gifts of the Spirit were absent. The Pentecostal missionaries explained that they had made a pact with the Evangelicals not to discuss these things because they could not agree about them. They agreed to talk only about Jesus. But I could see the gifts were in the Bible, they came from God, so how could they be dangerous?

As months passed I began to dismiss the whole subject. This experience patently had not changed my Christian life; in fact, if anything, life became even more difficult about this time. I was still rushing round the Walled City, going to some kind of Christian meeting every night, trying with every ounce of my being to help people, but nobody seemed to have been helped. I felt cheated.

* * *

"Who do they think they are?" I thought, when I first heard about the Willans. An American couple, their young daughter Suzanne and companion Gail Castle had just arrived in Hong Kong and were going to start a prayer meeting.

"What a cheek! Hong Kong doesn't need another one. I'm already going to one of these every day of the week. Anyway, they've only just come—they should wait to see the church situation first."

It was two years since I had left England—a year since I had supposedly received the "gift of the Spirit". I felt quite an authority on prayer meetings in the Colony. But my clarinet pupil's mother—Clare Harding—urged me to go, saying that it would be charismatic. This new term described a meeting where they expected the various gifts of the Spirit —charisma—to be manifested.

"Well, I'll just go for a few weeks until I've learned all about it—then I'll go back to the other meetings," I told Clare. And so I was introduced to Rick and Jean Stone Willans.

"Do you pray in tongues, Jackie?"

I was shocked by Jean's American forthrightness. No English person would be that direct. "Well, no actually. I haven't found it that useful. I don't get anything out of it so I've stopped." It was a relief to discuss it with someone.

But Jean would not be sympathetic. "That's very rude of you," she said. "It's not a gift of emotion—it's a gift of the Spirit. You shouldn't despise the gifts God has given you. The Bible says he who prays in tongues will be built up spiritually, so never mind what you feel—do it." Then she and Rick made me promise to pray daily in my heavenly language. They insisted that the Holy Spirit was given in power to the Early Church to make them effective witnesses to the risen Christ.

Then to my horror they suggested we pray together in tongues. I was not sure if this was all right since the Bible said that people should not all speak aloud in tongues at the same time. They explained that St. Paul was referring to a public meeting where an outsider coming in would think everyone was crazy; we three would not be offending anyone, and would be praying to God in the languages He gave us.

I could not get out of it. We prayed and I felt silly saying words I did not understand. I felt hot. And then to my consternation they stopped praying while I felt impelled to continue. I knew already that this gift, although holy, is under our control; I could stop or start at will. I would have done anything not to be praying out loud in a strange language in front of strange Americans, but just as I thought I would die of self-consciousness God said to me, "Are you willing to be a fool for My sake?"

I gave in. "All right, Lord—this doesn't make sense to me, but since You invented it, it must be a good gift, so I'll go ahead in obedience and You teach me how to pray."

After we finished praying Jean said she understood what I had said, God had given her the interpretation. She translated. But it was beautiful; my heart was yearning for the Lord and calling as from the depths of a valley stream to the mountain tops for Him. I loved Him and worshipped Him and longed for Him to use me.

It was in language so much more explicit and glorious than any I could have formulated. I decided that if God helped me to pray like that when I was praying in tongues, then I would never despise this gift again. I accepted that He was helping me to pray perfectly.

Every day—as I had promised the Willans—I prayed in the language of the Spirit. Fifteen minutes by the clock. I still felt it to be an exercise. Before praying in the Spirit I said, "Lord—I don't know how to pray, or whom to pray for. Will You pray through me—and will You lead me to the people who want You." And I would begin my fifteen-minute stint.

After about six weeks I noticed something remarkable. Those I talked to about Christ believed. I could not understand it at first and wondered how my Chinese had so suddenly improved, or if I had stumbled on a splendid new evangelistic technique. But I was saying the same things as before. It was some time before I realized what had changed. This time I was talking about Jesus to people who wanted to hear. I had let God have a hand in my prayers and it produced a direct result. Instead of my deciding what I wanted to do for God and asking His blessing I was asking Him to do His will through me as I prayed in the language He gave me.

Now I found that person after person wanted to receive Jesus. I could not be proud—I could only wonder that God let me be a small part of His work. And so the emotion came. It never came while I prayed, but when I saw the results of these prayers I was literally delighted. The Bishop should have told me what to expect at my confirmation when this could have started.

I began to get to know the Willans better and they became wonderful friends and counsellors. The bonds of "Christian" conventions burst and I found once more the glorious freedom to live we have in Christ Jesus. At my conversion I had accepted that Jesus had died for me; now I began to see what miracles He was doing in the world today.

Chapter Six

The Triads

"Hai bin do ah? Where do you come from?" The slight sallow faced youth stared terrified as four members of the famed 14K Triad advanced menacingly towards him. In gang parlance they were asking him which black society he belonged to. He could not reply; he was trembling and his breath came in short gasps.

"M'gong? Not talking then?" Ah Ping, the spokesman, jeered at him and stepped closer until he was at kicking distance. There was no escape—the boy and his tormentors all knew what was coming. He was trapped down one of the Walled City alleys with the wall behind and the gangsters in front. They taunted him—teasing out his fear, advancing in ghastly slow motion. They were enjoying their captive's terror, his cringing body.

The first blow came with amazing speed and ground into the boy's ribs. Chinese boxers are skilled, their movements supple. Their *kung-fu* training effects a litheness and economy of action which is precise and lethal. The victim fell to the ground as more blows rained on his stomach, his chest, his groin. He moaned, doubled up in agony, but still he did not speak. So they drove him along the street and kicked him while he crawled and then limped away. He would not be back. He had learned what happened when you walked down enemy territory unprotected.

This made the Triads feel good. They were secure and superior in their own streets. They controlled what went on, and who was allowed through their turf. Before long I found that the room I had rented for the Youth Club was right in the middle of the 14K patch.

I had just watched the sickening scene, but I did not yet know how inevitable was this beating up according to Triad tradition.

"Why did you do that?" I demanded. "Why? What has that boy done to you?" I suddenly felt rather unwell.

Ah Ping shrugged. "Probably nothing," he conceded, but the corners of his mouth turned down disdainfully. "He could not identify himself or show his reason for being here so we got to teach him a lesson. He perhaps from our enemies the Ging Yu, and we got to let them know who's in power down here."

I was learning.

One of the former police chiefs in Hong Kong, H. W. E. Heath, wrote in 1960, "Triad activities have been noted in the official law and police reports of Hong Kong for the past one hundred and sixteen years. For the past one hundred and thirteen years special ordinances and related legislation have been created in attempts to deal with the problem. The Triad Societies are still with us." In its earliest phases the Triad Society was a Chinese secret society whose members were bound by oath to overthrow the foreign conquerors of their country and restore the ancient ruling house of China, the Ming Dynasty.

Today the historical Triad Society has degenerated into hundreds of separate Triad societies all claiming to be part of the Triad tradition, but in fact being mainly criminal gangs who use the name and rituals as covers for their own evil purposes. To join the original Triad Society it was essential to go through certain rituals. These included learning poems, handshakes, and handsigns, and shedding and drinking blood. Sacrifices were laid down; when you entered the Triad society you swore to follow your "brother" for ever; he became your *daih lo*, or big brother; you became his *sai lo*, or little brother, and you were then related forever. If you proved yourself, an aspiring Triad would ask to "follow" you and you became his big brother. Thus the Triad Society was a pyramid of relationships. Inside each gang there was a complicated hierarchy of ranks and duties. The officers had colourful names like Red Pole, White Paper Fan and Grass Sandal. At other times they were known simply by their numbers, as 489, 438, 426, and 415. Ordinary members were called "49 boys".

All over Hong Kong the Triads inspired terror, which made it easier to run protection rackets. The Walled City was the perfect place for them; they took the fullest advantage of its uncertain sovereignty. Two main gangs operated there, divided geographically by a certain street. There was tacit understanding between the groups over territory, and business. The "Ging Yu" controlled all the heroin dens, both the selling points and the smoking dens. They also ran protection rackets and controlled prostitution east of Old Man Street. Far more feared were the brothers of the 14K, which is a relative newcomer amongst the traditional Triad societies, having been formed in China in 1949. It derived its name from No. 14 Po Wah Street, Canton, where it was organized to support the Chinese Nationalistic cause and still retains strong political ties with Nationalist sympathizers. It has been reputed to have a hundred thousand members worldwide, and sixty thousand in Hong Kong alone. I understood that it controlled all opium "divans", gambling, blue films, child brothels, illegal dog restaurants, and protection rackets on the West side of the city.

It was highly decentralized, with each area gang leader looking after his particular patch. However, they could call on each other for help when needed; they all knew the main office bearers, and referred to members of related gangs as "cousins". So within a matter of minutes, a Triad could call out a dozen brothers, and within hours several hundred could be ready for a fight.

Whereas the non-Triads slipped in and out of the place praying not to be stopped, even those committed to the 14K or the Ging Yu walked abroad only in their own territory.

However, I used to pick my way over all the streets and made a point of learning every exit until I was more familiar with the place than the gangsters themselves, who were necessarily limited to one half of the City.

The Triads that I knew were certainly criminals, but to some extent they followed the old maxim that there is honour among thieves. In return for absolute obedience, the *daih lo* promised to look after his *sai lo*. If the little brother was imprisoned, then the big brother made sure that inside prison he got food, drugs, and protection. Not that all Triad members took drugs; drug taking was frowned on, because it lessened their usefulness. It was our shared concern for the addicts that later placed me at the same tea table as some of the Triad bosses.

It was no surprise when I learned that Christopher was about to be initiated into the 14K. How else could he walk on certain streets if he belonged to no gang? How else could he retaliate when wronged without a group of brothers to fight for him?

Christopher had been attending the Youth Club regularly but now carefully avoided me. Every time I tried to approach him he disappeared into the maze. He had started to gamble and was hanging around with well-known criminals. However, he had a conscience about this and he did not want to let me see what he was doing. There came the day, though, when I trapped him. We met head on when I was carrying my heavy piano accordion and this was large enough to prevent Christopher from passing me. We were in one of the tiny passages where retreat was impracticable: he was wedged in and I asked him to carry the instrument for me to the repair shop.

As we walked I talked to him in my pidgin Cantonese. I asked him, "Christopher, who do you think Jesus came into the world for?" He did not reply.

"Was it for rich or poor people?" I continued.

"That's easy—I know that one. He came for poor people." His schoolteachers would have been happy.

"But does he love good people or bad people?" I probed.

"Jesus loves good people, Miss Poon." It was a dismal catechism; he was hating this walk, this talk.

"You're wrong." Luckily as he was carrying the accordion I could wave my arms about. It helped to fill in the gaps in my vocabulary. "Do you know, if Jesus were alive today, he'd be here in the Walled City sitting on the orange boxes talking to the pimps and prostitutes down there in the mud." You are not supposed to tell Chinese people that they are wrong because they will lose face, but I was longing for him to understand. This was no time to be playing conventions. "That's where he spent a lot of his time. In the streets with well-known criminals—not waiting in a neat clean church for the nice guys to turn up."

"Why did he do that?" Christopher asked incredulously. It sounded as if he really wanted to know.

"Because," I said slowly, "that is why He came—not to save the good people, but to save the bad ones—the lost ones —those who have done wrong."

Christopher stopped suddenly—he was clearly overwhelmed by what he had heard. By this time we had walked out of the Walled City passing the street market hawking everything from plastic slippers to pressed duck. He said he wanted to hear some more so we left the accordion in the repair shop nearby and found a public bench by the traffic roundabout. I told him the story of Naaman the army commander afflicted with leprosy and finished up, "It's so simple —all you have to do is come to Jesus to be washed clean." I turned to Christopher to see if he understood.

The traffic was roaring past us; people were yelling as they always do in Hong Kong. Another plane came into land, flying a few feet over our heads as it skimmed the flyover and thundered onto the runway. Christopher heard nothing; he had his eyes shut and he seemed to be talking quietly. He was not talking to me; he was admitting to Jesus how he had failed in his life and asking Him to make him clean. Sitting by the dusty, noisy roadside he became a Christian.

There were many problems in store for him. The next Saturday he came back to the Youth Club. Bravely he stood up in front of the others and said that the week before he had not believed in Jesus; now he knew Him. The announcement was greeted at first with silence—it was so extraordinary a thing to say. Then came the jeers and taunts. Boys from bad homes did not become Christians; that was for good, educated, middle-class students. He was joking, he was mad.

Christopher was not. He now refused to carry on with his Triad initiation. He already had the book of poems, laws and ceremonial dialogue to be learnt before he could be accepted. He sent it back. To make such a stand was both very firm and very courageous; such a thing had never happened before amongst those people. His decision was a break-through for me too; now I knew that it was not true about there being a "cloud of unbelief" over Hong Kong. Jesus was alive in Hong Kong just as much as in England, and those who looked for Him could find Him.

The change in Christopher was remarkable. He worked so well at his factory that he was promoted to the rank of supervisor. Instead of gambling sessions with the Triads he now spent his time at the Youth Club and on Sundays he came to the evening service in the little Oiwah church.

As I continued praying in the Spirit in private so the results became apparent when more boys like Christopher made decisions to become Christians; we met together for Bible study and prayer anywhere we could, in the Youth Club room, in teahouses, in the streets or in my home. One day when we were praying one of them had a message in tongues.

We waited and then Christopher began to sing the interpretation. Astonishingly this beautiful song came in English which he hardly spoke. This is what he sang:

> Oh God who saves me in the darkness,
> Give me strength and the power

So I can walk in the Holy Spirit
Fight against the devil with the Bible
Talk to the sinners in the world
Make them belong to Christ.

Another boy, Bobby, had the same interpretation but in Chinese. He did not understand Christopher's English song and so did not know that what he spoke was a confirmation of God's message.

Although the Christian group was growing, not all of the Walled City boys were so clear about why I was there. Many of them came to the Youth Club for what they could get out of it. When we went on Saturday picnics or camps I did not make them pay. I paid—I paid for the coach, rubber boats, football boots, rollerskates, and I even bought them picnics. They were not grateful; they considered themselves under-privileged people and imagining I had a wealthy organization behind me they wanted to squeeze me for anything that was going. They regarded this as their right and were demanding and aggressive. Such was Ah Ping.

Over the months and years I got to know Ah Ping very well. He came to the Youth Club a lot. He was often with us on the walks and expeditions. I learned that he had been initiated into the Triads when only twelve, four years before, and already had a great reputation as a fighter who had started to collect followers (*sai lo*) of his own. One night, when he was hanging around in the street outside I came to the Youth Club room feeling very depressed and needing a kind word. He sensed that I was feeling a bit down and said, "You'd better go—you'd better leave this place, Poon Siu Jeh. You'd better go, because it's no good you working here. You should find a nice group of nice students to work with, you find some well-behaved school kids to preach to; they'll make nice Christians. We're no good—we never do what you want us to do." I listened without replying.

"Don't know why you stay here—you find us school places, and we don't go to school. You find us houses and we muck them up. You find us jobs and we lose them; we won't ever change. All we do is take—we take you for every penny you've got, and we kick you around. So why do you stick it? What's the point?"

"Well, I stick around because that's what Jesus did for me. I didn't want Jesus, but He didn't wait until I wanted Him. He didn't wait until I had promised to reform. He didn't wait until I got good. He died for me anyway. He died for me when I hated Him, and He never even told me off on the Cross; He just said He loved me and forgave me. This is the Jesus that came into the world and made dead people rise; this is the Jesus who came into the world and did miracles. This is the Jesus who only ever did good, and He died for me. They said He was the Son of God, and He loves you, too, in the same way."

Ah Ping did not answer at first; then he said, "It couldn't be—nobody would love us like that. I mean, we . . ." his voice faltered, then he continued, "I mean we have to rape and we fight, and we steal, and we stab. Nobody could love us like this."

"Well, Jesus did. He doesn't love the things you've done, but He loves you. Really it doesn't make sense; but all the wrong things that you've done He said were His. When He died on the Cross, Jesus pleaded guilty to your crimes. That's really unfair, isn't it? He said your stealing, your stabbing was His; if you give Him all the bad things you've done He'll give you His new life, His righteousness. It's sort of like giving Him your dirty clothes and getting back His clean ones."

Ah Ping was shattered. He could hardly believe there was a God like that. He sat down there on the stone steps to the street and told Jesus that although he could not understand why He loved him he was grateful; and he asked Jesus to forgive him and change him.

Ah Ping was the first gangster from the fully initiated Triads to join the Christians. When he was only fourteen a young bargirl had offered to "support" him in return for his protection. He had even sought my advice over it. Now his lifestyle changed dramatically. Each night he brought his brothers to the clubroom and asked me to tell them about Jesus. More and more known crooks turned up to shake me by the hand, or thump my arm-muscle. The few remaining straight types, the students, left the Club as they felt discriminated against. It must have been the only Christian club in Hong Kong where the good guys felt less welcome than the bad ones. However, I felt there were dozens of places all over Hong Kong where the nice boys were catered for, so I let them go. It was not for some years that we were able to bring together these two elements and break down the wall of separation between them.

Some of my friends in Hong Kong met Ah Ping and invited him to tell his story in church. "Be careful," I warned him as we came out of the Club room at midnight into the black street. "Satan doesn't like people talking about Jesus so he'll probably have a go at you before Saturday. Go straight home tonight and don't stop along the way."

"All right, all right, Miss Poon," he said nodding sweetly. As soon as I had gone he exploded. "Tchs. The Devil. Ha. What rubbish! I know these streets like the back of my hand. What, me worry?" And he wandered around instead of going home.

As if from nowhere seven men jumped out of a black alley and attacked him. They were Chiu Chow gangsters, big for Chinese, and wild fighters. There was no reason for their attack, but that did not stop it coming. Later Ah Ping told me, "As they came at me I had two thoughts. First of all, 'Huh, it's all Miss Poon's fault;' and then, 'you're supposed to pray.'" So he prayed as the wooden bats beat him unconscious into the ground.

"Didn't do you much good praying, did it?" scoffed one of the Club members when he heard the story.

"Yes, it did," retorted Ah Ping, "I'll tell you why. As soon as I began to pray, my father came down the street and when the Chiu Chows saw him, they ran away. Otherwise I would have been killed."

As it was, he was left on the ground with a gash in his back and a hole in his throat. His father summoned help from his gang brothers from the 14K. They found him and took him to a doctor who gave it as his professional opinion that his injuries were so bad that he would not be able to walk or speak for at least two weeks.

Ah Ping's brothers determined to seek revenge on his behalf. They held a council in their gang pad and discussed tactics. "O.K. The Chiu Chows made it seven to one. We will take fifty to attack them. That's reasonable." Then they took long knives and choppers from their secret arms cache and told Ah Ping, "Look, we know where one of these Chiu Chows lives. We are going to take him and his family members out of their house one by one and stab them. Right?"

Ah Ping indicated, through his injured throat, "No, I'm a Christian now and I don't want you to fight back." Then he gathered one or two Club members who were believers, found my room and asked them to pray with him.

All night they prayed for the gang who had attacked him. Ah Ping once told me that Triads were so touchy that they would threaten and even kill over trifles; once he had seen a boy wearing the same shirt as he was so he'd fought him. He had come a long way since those days; as well as praying for his enemies he also asked the other boys to lay their hands on him and pray for healing.

The next morning he was completely healed, and he could talk clearly. In fact he spoke in church just two days later. He spoke of the change in his heart, how he had given up stealing, and how he had been healed. He also mentioned that he would no longer take the devil lightly. Now he *knew* he was around.

"Blessed are the peacemakers,"—gang fights are not easy to stop. This kind of problem was one which the new converts would have to face all too often.

* * *

I remember one Sunday evening inside Oiwah church. It was not a day off for most people in the Walled City; the fact that you could actually get to church was a source of pride to these marginally more prosperous Chinese folk. As I looked up from the organ keys I could see some of the teachers from the Oiwah school, together with various hawkers, vegetable sellers and other traders. All looked solid, law-abiding decent folk, serious and respectably dressed, though most were very poor. The fact that I troubled about the young tearaways really rather appalled them. "This Westerner," they thought, "simply doesn't understand how wicked these boys are." They did not like having the boys in church with them, whereas I sat there hoping and praying that some of them would come.

All at once the little door swung open violently and the boys arrived. The sight of their Teddy boy shirts and tight trousers sent a ripple of fear through the congregation, who thought it was a raid by the Triads. And this time I too was a little surprised, because the boys were in a terrible state; normally scruffy, this time they were caked with filth and blood, having come straight to church after a terrible fight. Several of the boys had dull red abrasions on their faces. One hunched over limping from a blow to the groin. Their clothes were torn and their eyes were staring. However they sat down and stayed quiet throughout the service. As soon as it was finished I got up and hurried across to find out what had happened.

Apparently they had walked into a trap carefully set for them. As the boys entered the local public lavatory outside the Walled City to spruce up for church, a group of youths leapt out of the cubicles where they had been hiding and savagely attacked them with bats.

Several were quite badly hurt; I took them out of the Walled City, called a taxi and went off to hospital with them. That they should come and find me at church after such a terrible fight pleased me very much. Naïvely I thought it was wonderful, "Praise God, they've come to church and they've come in here—they haven't gone to their gang leaders; they've come to Christians."

I was soon to find out that the rest of the congregation saw the whole incident quite differently. They were outraged that the boys should have dared to invade their church looking and smelling so dreadfully. They did not accept that boys like that could become Christians; they expected an inward change to be followed by an outward change into shirts and ties and lace-up shoes. And they were particularly upset that I had allowed the boys to come into church immediately after partaking in violence. The elders were convinced that I was being used by a bunch of unscrupulous rascals. In their experience no one like that had ever become a Christian. And when I asked that some of the boys who had become Christians should be baptized, their answer was a straight "No". They told me very firmly that the boys should have a time of testing first. This ban on their baptisms meant that the boys could not take part in the breaking of bread ceremony either.

At first I continued to encourage the boys to come to the church, even though they were clearly not welcome. Then one day a wise older missionary, George Williamson, came to the Walled City; he watched what was going on and understood the whole situation immediately.

"Jackie," he said, "why do you make these boys come to church here?"

There was no escape; I had to give him answers. "Well, for two reasons really," I began rather hesitantly. "One reason is very negative. It's because I don't want to be criticized and I don't want everyone to think I'm doing my own thing." George smiled warmly; he knew how the older generation disapproved of women missionaries taking their own initiative.

"Secondly," I continued a little more confidently, "I think these boys need elder brothers and sisters and need the family of the church. In the same way the church needs them. It is not healthy for us to be simply a young persons' group."

I felt that George with his background would be sure to

agree with me. But he did not. "No, Jackie, your boys are not ready yet. You should look at it like this. They are like seedlings, which you wouldn't transplant too young because they'd die. At the moment the boys can't take the knocks they are getting from the established Church. It's too soon to expect them to make allowances for the attitudes of these church people. You can't expect them to have that sort of grace." I felt amazed; he was asking me to go ahead and do my own thing. He continued, "Look on them as seedlings; take them away and care for them; tend them until they have grown up. Then they will be strong enough to stand and take the knocks. And then you can plant them and they can help the church to grow up. The church in Hong Kong isn't ready for them yet."

Therefore instead of insisting that new young Christians join the church, I expanded our Bible study group; we met several times a week and were now open on Sunday mornings also. The Club room was used more and more and began to be well known among Triads even outside the Walled City as a splendid place to spend Saturday evenings. We had raucous singing sessions and ping pong. If I insisted on a prayer most of them would go outside and hoot in friendly fashion in the alley till I had got it over with. Then back they swarmed.

Without Dora Lee I could never have coped. She had been head girl at St. Stephen's school and together with other students helped me with the kind of Chinese translation I could not manage, like translating from the Bible. She was an outstanding Christian, for years giving up most of her weekends in order to help the boys understand Christ.

Dora's help was valuable in other ways; she taught me much about how Chinese people think and react. The more I understood, the more I realized how English methods for telling the world about Jesus Christ and how to follow Him did not work out as practical possibilities on the other side of the world. Worthy members of the Christian Union talk about prayer in terms of getting up early and having a "quiet time". But this sort of advice was quite impracticable for the boys I knew. They often lived in a house with ten other people; it was never quiet; no one had a bed to himself let alone a room. They slept on the bed on a rota system, some working while others rested. The idea of finding a quiet place to study their Bibles and contemplate the Almighty was a joke. But praying in a new language is essentially practical, because they could walk along any noisy Hong Kong street and no one would notice.

Many of them could not read, so my suggestions had to be workable. This I learned through a sad experience when one of the boys prayed that he desired to follow Jesus. In misguided fervour I gave him a copy of St. John's gospel, scripture notes on St. John, a booklet entitled, *Now you are a Christian* and another, *The Way Ahead*.

I did not see him for two years and felt hurt and concerned for his spiritual well-being. When I saw him again I asked why he had been avoiding me for so long. He looked embarrassed.

"I wanted to know Jesus and you gave me a library."

I re-examined some of my concepts about studying the word of God. The early Christians certainly had no Bibles; they must have learned another way. For those who could read I suggested they take a few moments from their factory benches by retreating to the toilets to read a few verses. Others found they could memorize a few lines. I tried to see all the boys I knew as often as I could, encouraging them to follow Christ's teachings. They did make progress, but there was never enough time to see everyone. My school duties curtailed my time and my inadequate Chinese meant that I found it pretty difficult to convey spiritual truths. I needed more hours to study; practising with the boys was not enough when I did not understand the complex structure of the language.

As the pressure grew worse, I began to pray about it. "Lord, I've got too much to do. I need more time to spend with these boys. And I can't do this if I have to spend much of the day teaching. You have promised to provide our daily bread; please let me know if you will provide mine without my 'earning' it."

Three days later the phone rang; it was Clare Harding, the friend who had introduced me to the Willans. She came straight to the point. "Jackie, I wanted you to know that when you leave St. Stephen's we want to offer you some money."

I was staggered; no one knew that I was even considering such a move. "But hang on a bit," I gasped in reply, "who told you I was leaving St. Stephen's anyhow? As it stands at the moment I'm not."

Clare did not hesitate, "Yes, I know you aren't leaving right now. But Neil and I have been praying together. And I wanted you to know that if you were thinking of leaving we'd like to offer you two hundred dollars a month." *

"Well, in any case if I left it wouldn't be until July at the earliest, because I must continue teaching until the end of the school year."

Clare replied, "The money can't be available until July anyway, but I just felt I had to ring and tell you now." It was mid-November.

Her call was a great encouragement. I felt that if God could tell someone, who did not know I was even considering leaving my job, to offer me a monthly cheque worth about £15, then it was nothing for Him to provide my whole living. Now ten years later I realize that this was the point where I decided to "live by faith". But at that time I had never even heard of the phrase and I would have found it hard to tell anyone about my financial needs. I knew surely that if God wanted me to do this job, He would provide, and it never worried me in the slightest as to how He would do it.

* Then £15.

Chapter Seven

Big Brother is Watching You

The telephone was ringing and ringing in my dreams; I struggled awake, clambered out of bed and lifted the receiver. It seemed to be the depths of the night; actually the time was around five a.m. Ah Ping spoke in a quick, strained voice.

"Poon Siu Jeh, you've got to come quickly. Someone has broken into the club and there is a terrible mess everywhere." He rang off.

Despite the sticky heat I shivered as I hurriedly climbed into my yesterday's clothes. I had moved by this time to the Kowloon side of Hong Kong and was sharing my apartment block with eight thousand other sardines. When I reached the street it was still asleep and deserted. No buses that early so I ran and ran.

My friend at the baker's stall was lifting a tray of hot pineapple buns out of his oven and carefully parking them on the pavement. At last I found a cab which would take me to the Walled City, and then I hurried again through the tortuous alleyways, the smells and the filth to the club room. I was ready to find a mess. The scene that greeted me was beyond my imagination. Benches, books, ping-pong bats, skateboards had been thrown around and smashed up. Far worse, the filth of the alleys had invaded our clean club. Someone had deliberately painted sewage all over the floor and walls. Ah Ping had no need to explain anything; the destruction screamed its own message.

I wanted to sit down and cry. My pride crumbled to dust. I thought these boys were my people who trusted me as a friend; we had our problems, but really everything was fine. Then they threw faeces all over my walls and they showed what they honestly thought of me, the club and its four-year life.

"All right, God. Enough is enough. I don't mind working here for ever, as long as they appreciate me. But if they don't want me or You I don't have to stay here. I can be a Christian in Kensington and do normal things like normal people: dinner parties and discussion groups, apologetics and concerts. After all I really don't want to stay down here for the rest of my life playing ping-pong. I mean, God, it's no joy for me to have a little room like this; I'm doing it for them. I'm willing to pour my life out for them, but if they don't want it they need not have it. Let's close the room up." Resentment burned at me. "They'll soon miss the club if I close it up; they'll soon see what they've done was really harming themselves."

But at the same time I also heard what Jesus had said: when people hit you you should let them hit you again; when they persecute you you should bless them. There was another insistent passage about praising God in all your troubles. I did not want to do that—I wanted to howl and wallow in self pity. I wanted my enemies to suffer too. I certainly did not feel like rejoicing or turning the other cheek.

So I spent the whole day sweeping up the place muttering tearfully, "Praise God, praise God." I hunched over the bamboo brush and swiped the floor savagely—less savagely as the day wore on and more sadly. "Praise God, praise God." I had fits of sobbing and the foundations of my world lay in ruins.

The next night I opened the club as usual. But for the first time I was frightened—not of being beaten up for God had always protected me from that. I was deeply frightened of being rejected by the boys that I loved and ministered to. I did not know who had done it and why, and I stayed there in the club trembling all over. I was lonely and vulnerable.

A youth I had never seen before leant against the club door. He jerked his head at me and spoke coolly, "Got any trouble?"

"No. No. It's fine, thank you very much," I replied hastily. "But why are you asking?" He sucked in his cheeks and thumbed his chest nonchalantly. "Got any trouble, you just let me know."

"I'm happy to hear that," I said. "But who are you, who sent you?"

"Goko sent me," he replied abruptly.

I was shaken; I knew exactly who Goko was; the leader of the whole of the Walled City Triad set-up. He was the leader of one branch of the 14K and was reputed to have several thousand little brothers in the Walled City and surrounding areas. He controlled all the opium dens and vice in the area. The fact that this stranger had even used Goko's name to me was undoubtedly a compliment. It is both a term of endearment and respect meaning, "my big brother". He was the Big Brother of the big brothers. One of the little brothers in my club had confided his name to me with awe; even ten years later gangsters were daunted that I knew his name, for it was only ever mentioned amongst themselves. Although I knew his name I'd never met him. For some years I had sent him messages but he had always refused to see me. The messages had been simple like "Jesus loves you". I could understand why Goko did not want to see me but not why he had gone to the trouble of sending me a guard for the club.

"Goko said if anyone bothers you or touches this place, we're gonna 'do' him," my protector continued. Exactly how they intended to "do" him he demonstrated rather graphically as he picked up an imaginary dagger and thrust it low into a victim's belly.

"Thank you very much, how kind of you—I'm really most grateful. Would you mind telling Goko that I'm most appreciative of his offer and I don't want to offend him but I don't accept it. Actually Jesus is looking after us," I said.

"Yau moe gau chor,"—the Cantonese expression is the equivalent of "you must be cracked". The stranger was not at all impressed with my stand; his contemptuous expression showed that he thought he was talking to a crazy Westerner. Anyone who thought that Jesus was a fit protection here in the Walled City had to be deranged.

The following evening my protector returned, and the night after that. He clocked on every night just like a night-watchman. I discovered his name was Winson, and that he was under orders to watch the club. I began to tell him about Jesus. He certainly did not want to hear what I told him, but as he was on guard duty he had to stay. After a few nights softening up he began to talk about "his friend" who had an opium problem. I soon realized that his friend was Winson himself. So I told him that opium was no problem. All you have to do with anyone who has an opium or a heroin problem or any other kind of addiction is to lock them in a room for a week. Certainly they suffer agonies during the process of coming off the drug; they may even lose their sanity, but they will lose their physical dependence. However the cure does not last; as soon as you unlock the door they go straight out to take whatever drug it is to which they are addicted, because their mind and their heart continue to crave for it with a force they can not possibly control themselves. Only Jesus, the Lord of life, can settle a man's heart inside, and take away the craving.

I told him this many times. He always stood outside the club door, lounging in proprietary fashion. He would never condescend to come in, never interfere. He watched and listened to the boys' spirited renderings of the current "in" hymn. Then one night late in the evening when the club was almost empty I said, "Now, how about you coming inside and praising God."

"Okay," he said without hesitation.

I was stunned, for by this time I knew who Winson really

was. His rank in the 14K Triad was number 426, which meant he had the special rank of fight-fixer. His job was to fix the fights, choose the weapons, the location, and the strategy. He was a very tough Triad indeed. And yet here he was standing inside my club praising God at the top of his voice. He was belting out, solo, "Give me oil in my lamp," as loudly as he could, and as he had no idea how to sing, it was an amazing noise, a wonderful burst of tuneless sound. Then he began to pray in Chinese—mercifully he had never heard anyone praying before, so it came out quite spontaneously. I have never since listened to such a joyous prayer. I kept thinking "Where did he get that from?" Although, of course, I knew.

It was an extraordinary session for next he began praising God in a new language. This was even more surprising as he had never heard about the gift from me, nor to my knowledge had he heard anyone else speaking in tongues. After about half an hour he stopped. The miracle had taken place: he and I knew that he was completely cured of his drug addiction. He had come through withdrawal as he prayed.

When his voice died away I told him, "Praise the Lord; that is wonderful. Now what you have to do next is to lead your gang to make the same discovery for themselves. You can't follow your big brother Goko any more. No man can have two Big Brothers. You have to follow Jesus or Goko. You cannot follow both." So Winson went back to his gang leader Goko to tell him and the other gang leaders that he now believed in Jesus.

It was Ah Sor, at eighteen already a seasoned jail-bird, who told me later what had happened the night of the attack on the club. One of the boys had had some troubles which he felt were all my fault. (These drop-out kids had such a problem with authority that whenever anything went wrong in their lives they blamed the nearest establishment figure.) He had come round and started yelling and throwing things at the Youth Club windows. This incited his friends to action and soon they were all on the rampage. Most of them had no idea what they were angry about; it was just mob violence.

Goko had a report within hours about this mayhem on his patch and was so displeased that he summoned the offenders to appear before him. He ordered them to return anything they had taken, and to go back to the Youth Club the next night and behave.

"Can't do that," one of them replied. "We've broken up the place; she'll never welcome us back."

"Oh yes, she will," Goko had said, "because Miss Poon is a Christian and she'll forgive you no matter how many times you offend. She'll open the door and welcome you back."

So they had come back and Goko had sent Winson to see that his orders were carried out. I felt very small when I heard what he had said. Obviously he knew how Christians were supposed to behave even though my inclination had been to do exactly the opposite.

Now that I knew Big Brother was watching I was much encouraged in the direction the club had taken. Something of Jesus had got through, unaided by social programmes and church services. Most of the hangers-on had by now disappeared, as they discovered that I was speaking the truth when I said there were no more funds apart from what I was putting in myself. There was no social advantage in being a member of our club; in fact, the reverse—most other churches quite definitely disapproved of this disorganized Youth Centre. Social workers and Youth counsellors visiting me asked what the programme was. I found this rather difficult to explain in terms of a schedule.

"Well, I open the club door at night and sometimes one person comes, sometimes fifty. I make friends with them and talk. Sometimes we sing or pray, sometimes we go on an outing. I maybe sit all night with one who has no place to sleep or share a bowl of rice with a hungry one."

Finally I hit on an impressive phrase, "I'm doing unstructured Youth work," was my reply to the social workers who nodded earnestly and decided that this was the latest sociological technique already pioneered in forward-looking countries.

I had tried regular projects but they were rarely successful, and I was frustrated in looking for helpers who would understand this. We had a football coach at one time who hired football pitches and had a weekly training session. All the boys were crazy about football and over forty signed up for the activity. Twenty of them turned up for the first practice; the next week there were ten and the third week none at all.

The coach was most discouraged and wanted to quit and teach at the Y.M.C.A. where the youngsters were really keen. I tried to make him understand what had happened. The Walled City boys lived such strange lives that they usually had no idea what day of the week it was. They slept by day and got up in the evening since most of the vice operations they were associated with happened at night time. Sometimes they stayed up for seventy-two hours at a time or slept for two days. They stayed in gang pads, opium dens or wherever they could find a floor or staircase. The idea of football coaching was most attractive but actually getting there was another matter. They did mean to go but they had absolutely no self-discipline. The third week of the course one of their brothers had got married so they all went to the wedding feast. It never occurred to them to inform me or the instructor.

Had the instructor come back the following week he would have found perhaps a couple of lads and the next week four and the third week maybe a dozen. Once they had the idea that the instructor was really concerned about them and would turn up even in a typhoon for one boy they would have given him their loyalty and their friendship; eventually he would have built up a team for life.

Many people came to me and asked to help in the club. It sounded romantic and exciting to work in the Walled City, but few stuck it more than a few weeks. If they held classes or games which were not well supported they lost heart and never returned. I needed to find Christian workers who loved the people they were working with more than the activity through which they were trying to reach them.

Like the Walled City boys I now slept by day and got up at night, at least in theory. In fact, since I had language lessons, court appearances, prison visits and other matters concerned with sorting out problems for them, it meant that I was also up by day. Every day on waking the only way I could get out of bed was by promising myself that I could come back and sleep later in the day. "I will, I really will," I would mutter as I struggled into consciousness, but I never did. Instead I learned how to cat-nap, sleeping on buses and ferries.

One night, we went to the hills for a barbecue. It was the Autumn Moon Festival and the boys had strung up paper lanterns all over the hillside. In the clear moonlight I saw a large rough-looking young tough sitting amongst us stuffing himself with pork chops, beef steaks and chicken wings. As I had bought all these myself and reckoned on sufficient for our entire coach load I was quite mad at him. But while I watched, the other boys gave him their rations and seemed mesmerized by his every word. Ah Ping whispered that this was his own *daih lo*, the leader of his particular gang and of most of those present. He was actually the real brother of Goko and was the number two in the Walled City. As more and more of his "brothers" had been attending our club, Sai Di, curious and maybe a little jealous, had decided to come to this function himself. If he chose to he had the power to run all the boys and the club itself, so there was a distinct possibility that this was a take-over bid.

"Would you mind coming for a talk?" I asked him and indicated a small patch of scrub just over the crest. He was amused at this request from a mere girl and made a great show of rising from his haunches and lumbering towards me amidst cat-calls and whistles. But when we were out of ear-shot he dropped the macho attitude and listened quite seriously when I told him that the whole reason for the club was that I wanted them to know the love of Jesus.

His reply was an indictment and a confirmation. "I know," he said, "we've been watching you. Many missionaries come to Hong Kong to help us poor people. They put us in sociological boxes and analyze us. Then they take our pictures to shock the Westerners by our living conditions. Some men get famous because they've been here. But inside the Walled City we usually get rid of them within six months." He spoke maliciously. "We find ways to discourage them until they have no heart to continue—had you been a man we would have had you beaten long ago." He added, "We couldn't care less if you have big buildings or small ones. You can be offering free rice, free schools, judo classes, or needlework to us. It doesn't matter if you have a daily programme or hymn singing once a week. These things don't touch us because the people who run them have nothing to do with us. What we want to know is if you are concerned with us. Now you have been here for four years we have decided that maybe you mean what you say."

I did not sing in front of him but my heart was bursting, there on a hump in the Chinese mountains.

* * *

Now that the "rice-Christians" had departed from our club I found that those who remained were the ones who wanted to be friends and who eventually would become interested in spiritual things. Because they could not understand why I would actually be there if I had not been "sent" by an overseas church, they began to consider seriously the possibility that Jesus was real. One day we were sitting on the benches in the clubroom when Ah Keung, known as the Walled City joker and a great friend of Ah Ping's said, "Poon Siu Jeh, we sat up for the whole night last evening discussing you and we came to one of two conclusions. Either the British government have sent you here as a spy or what you say about Jesus must be true, because there can't be any other explanation. Nobody's going to spend their life with us down here unless they have to, or unless Jesus is real."

So Ah Keung became a believer too and proved to be a most "hot-hearted" enthusiastic Christian. I began to visit him and found out his fearful background. Ah Keung was one of six sons who lived with their father in Western District on Hong Kong Island. His mother ran away after the birth of the sixth boy and went to live with a policeman. His father was a member of the powerful Wo Shing Wo Triad society who controlled that area but after his friend was murdered in a gang fight he decided to move to a new environment and chose a room in the Walled City. He worked as a *for-gei* in a gambling den doing *pin-mun* meaning that he did odd jobs in the den, including collecting bets and pawning the gamblers' watches. As this was a night job he never saw his sons during the day and they were not brought up at all. When they woke they ate their father's food, should there be any, and if not then they went to beg it from neighbours and street stalls.

As they grew older the brothers became clever confidence tricksters. None of them went to school, and, of course, they were all Triad members. The eldest three were imprisoned at the ages of thirteen, fourteen, and fifteen for selling drugs; not only did they make money this way, they also each became addicted. Later the fifth and sixth brothers were also arrested for drug related crimes and the sixth had received a sentence of six months hard labour by the time he was fourteen. Ah Keung was the only brother who was never in prison, because he became a Christian just in time.

One night he rushed into the club room panting that I had to come to his home quickly. I ran down the street after him, dodging in and out of the prostitutes and around the gambling den where Ah Keung's father worked. I had to step with care here for the entrance to Ah Keung's alleyway was very slimy. The gamblers used that alley to relieve themselves in the absence of toilets. It was eighteen inches wide

and led to a stone staircase which was crumbling and dripping with green slime. The atmosphere was evil.

Up the stairs the door was open that night. The one room
dwelling was not large enough for all six plus father to sleep,
but since two or three of them were usually in prison at any
one time, that was no great problem.

When I got there I found the eldest brother injecting himself with heroin; on the floor there lay a man with stripes and
bruises on every limb, and blood-soaked shirt and shorts.
He had been beaten up savagely. I have never been brave at
the sight of blood, as it makes me feel physically sick. Here I
was faced with the job of cleaning him up and caring for him
and my first reaction was to send him to hospital.

"We can't take him," they said in unison, "he's a gang
member. He walked across someone else's territory and they
beat him up. If we take him to hospital he'll be asked questions by the police. And then they'll find out he's a drug
addict."

I had no alternative. I had to help, so I took their bucket
of water and some filthy old bandages, went out and borrowed a shopkeeper's Mercurochrome, and began to clean
the man up. Unexpectedly I did not feel sick and faint, I was
calm and happy. Jesus had said that he came to bind up the
wounded and that is exactly what they had asked me to do.
As I washed away his blood I told the sullen man about this.
I told him about Jesus' love and how he could know Him
too. He made no response but I was sure he understood. He
came back one day two years later.

After this incident I became more involved with Ah
Keung's family. I visited those in prison, tried to help them
find jobs on their release, and found alternative homes for
some of them. One night I was walking out of the City about
two a.m. when I overheard the second brother, Sai So, giving
my telephone number to another addict.

"833179," he was saying as they ate their soup noodles at
a makeshift table in the street. "Remember that number
next time you are arrested. It doesn't matter what time of

day or night you call, Miss Poon will come. It doesn't matter whether you've done the crime you're arrested for or not, she'll come. The only thing you must do is to tell the truth. You see, she's a Christian."

As I walked home I knew that "Your labour in the Lord is not in vain". Here I was privileged enough to see the fruits of some of those labours. Some of the vilest criminals in Hong Kong now knew that Jesus' name was truth.

As well as Ah Keung's brothers most of the boys I knew were frequently arrested and sent to court. As I got to know them better I sometimes believed their claims that they were innocent because I checked their alibis myself. Of course most of them were criminals, but they were not always guilty of the crimes with which they were charged. It seemed to me quite wrong that they should either confess to crimes which they had not committed, or deny crimes in which they were involved. I discovered that they regarded the whole business of arrests as a fatalistic game. And they felt that legal proceedings, carried out in a language which they could not understand, bore little relationship to the truth.

Several times I was walking with Ah Ping outside the Walled City and he would say, "Whew, I've walked to the end of the street and I didn't get arrested." It was not that he had done anything—only that he had seen a couple of detectives who recognized him. Both the policemen and Ah Ping knew that he was fair game. If they wanted, they could stop him, search him, and ask him a few questions. Or they could take him away and pin a crime on him. It happened frequently. Boys would sign "confessions" as they knew they could not afford legal representation and a guilty plea would earn a lighter sentence than a 'not guilty' plea.

I began to plead with the boys to tell the truth and nothing but the truth in court. This led to my spending many, many hours in courts and magistracies and I shared the criminals' shame as I saw people pointing at me and saying, "There's that simple Christian sitting with those crooks." I knew the boys had done wrong things, and perhaps some of them were still involved in crime but I was always willing to go and sit with them, guilty or not as long as they spoke the truth. But the shame was awful and it helped me to understand what an amazing sacrifice Christ had made when He not only publicly associated with us sinners but took our wrong doings as His own.

One evening I received a call from Mau Jai, a nickname meaning "Little Cat". It was seven forty-five p.m. and we had a roomful of St. Stephen's girls and Walled City boys who had just been praying together in my flat.

"Johnny's just been arrested. Get to the police station quickly," he said.

"How do you know, Mau Jai?" I asked. "And where are you?"

"Can't talk here. I tell you later," he said tersely.

On the way to the police station I thought about Johnny who was one of the most repulsive-looking drug addicts I knew. He was small and desperately thin, more a skeleton than a man. "If that one can be saved—anyone can," I had said when I first saw him. He was a carpenter earning quite a good wage but using the entire lot to smoke heroin. He was a Triad too, but useless to his gang.

When I arrived at the station I asked to see Johnny, but was told that he was not there.

"He must be here—he was arrested forty-five minutes ago," I said. But the desk sergeant denied it. "Why don't you go home and we'll telephone you if he appears," he suggested patronizingly.

"I'll stay until you produce him," I said and prepared to settle down for the night.

Two minutes later they indeed produced him but I was too late. He had already confessed to a crime. He was charged with being in possession of a screwdriver with intent to break into a building a mile outside the Walled City. The time Johnny was alleged to have committed the crime was eight-fifteen p.m., but I knew this could not be true since Little Cat had phoned me half an hour before that. I went to look for him.

It transpired that Johnny and Little Cat had been taking

drugs together in one of the largest dens in the Walled City when two detectives had come in and taken Johnny off. The detectives should not have been there; this was not their beat, but they knew well where the dens were and addicts made easy pickings. The evil of the situation was that certain police far from intending to stop this ugly business actually had an arrangement with the vice bosses that they would ignore the dens in return for "tea" money.

Show raids were made but several times I heard den watchers getting the tip off from police phoning to say that they were on their way. During the Walled City's heyday of crime there was a syndicate payment from the vice and drug dealers which amounted to $100,000 daily. Although uniformed police rarely went inside apart from raiding parties I was told that several plain clothes detectives were actually running some of the illegal businesses in league with the Triads. This made it extremely difficult to sort out the good guys from the bad guys and I began to understand why the boys I knew were so muddled about right and wrong.

Johnny's family lived in a squalid flat just outside the Walled City. They were desperately poor but borrowed money and bailed him out. This was a mistake since he used the remand period of several weeks to take even more heroin until he had used up all the family money and pawned most of their belongings. I visited him and tried to persuade him to plead not guilty because he was innocent of this particular charge.

Johnny was reluctant; "I can't deny the confession I've signed. The police said they'd arrest me for something else if I did. And I need to keep in with them."

Addicts claimed they were often given heroin at the police station in return for their confessions. But Johnny had to learn to stick to the truth. I told him all about Jesus and how He always spoke the truth even though it cost Him His life. Then we prayed together and Johnny agreed that it would be right to tell the truth but said that it was too dangerous for him at that stage. He explained it all patiently. "If I do tell the truth in court that means I'm letting everyone know where the drug dens are. Worse still I'm saying that the police themselves know where they are, but that they are not doing anything about them. Both my friends and the police will want to get me for saying so in court after that."

I went on meeting him. When I say we prayed it is not strictly true. I prayed and he listened. He thought I did not understand the danger he would be in when I continued to tell him to speak the truth. On the day of the trial he had quite decided to go along with the police story and plead guilty even though I had hired a solicitor to defend him. The solicitor cost me more than a month's living expenses but I saw it as God's money which I would use in His name. Just before he went into the witness box I showed him a Bible passage telling us not to be frightened when in court, for the Holy Spirit tells us what to say.

He told me afterwards that when he stood up in court he suddenly had an overwhelming conviction that he had to tell the truth though he did not want to at all. What might have been a simple case lasting a few moments became a major battle lasting over a week. There were long cross examinations of the police evidence by our solicitor but eventually the magistrate accepted it as the correct version and found Johnny guilty. The emotional strain of the week overcame me when he pronounced the verdict and I burst into tears in court.

To see an English girl weeping for a Chinese criminal and drug addict was unusual; the prosecuting police inspector snapped his brief case shut and came up to talk to me. He asked me why I was crying. "Because he didn't do it," I sobbed, "He isn't guilty."

"Well, he's got a record as long as your arm," said the inspector kindly, "in fact he has thirteen previous convictions. I shouldn't waste your sympathy on him."

"That's not the point," I replied, "he hasn't done this one."

"Well," said the Prosecutor, "you know this is Hong

Kong justice. Even if he hasn't done this one, he's done another crime. It's fair enough in the long run."

"That's not right," I insisted, "Jesus' name is truth and we are called to tell the truth here in court."

By this time the arresting detectives and their companions had gathered around. They knew I knew they had been lying. They saw the tears streaming down my cheeks. They saw me as a fool and they laughed. They laughed and they sneered as they left the court for a celebration meal. It was difficult not to feel bitter against them.

Johnny was sent to prison and from there to a drug rehabilitation centre. He was assigned a probation officer who summoned his mother saying, "Don't let that Christian interfere with your lives—you're not Christians—you've got idols—you are idol worshippers." He was very rude and unco-operative but I continued to visit Johnny.

The final verdict was yet to come. On appeal the Chief Justice overruled his conviction and Johnny was technically free. However, he went back to drugs and later back to prison. Out of prison again he returned to drugs once more and continued this terrible cycle.

But Johnny had never forgotten what had happened in court. I often used to go and visit him as he lay slumped on the chair which served as his bed. After about two years he did believe in Jesus for himself, became a Christian, went to a Christian drug rehabilitation centre and was transformed. After graduating from there he became a male nurse in a T.B. sanitorium working on the addict's ward.

This is to anticipate a few years, but out of that court case came other good results. It was the first case when I had asked a solicitor to represent our boys, and many others followed. Each time the police won the case. "Don't think that Western women can help you," they would scoff in the interrogation room. "She has no power." But their actions belied their words. Several boys told me they had been stopped by plain clothes men who asked them, "Are you from that place? Are you from that woman's club?" When they replied yes, they were not detained. The reason was that if the police charged one of our boys when he was innocent, then they were faced by a week's trial rather than a ten-minute hearing. Although they won the cases, this was too costly in time. It was one more sign to me that I was being watched, and that in this way Jesus was preached.

Another result came thirty months later. It was Christmas time and I wanted very much to celebrate with a proper Christmas dinner for the boys, but we had no money. I thought they should have the best on Jesus' birthday so having booked the restaurant I prayed for funds. Suddenly the phone rang; it was my solicitor's office.

"We've been checking our records and we find we have to refund you a thousand dollars," said a voice.

"No, you don't," I gasped, "you don't owe me anything."

"We've been checking through Johnny Ho's case and we owe you a thousand dollars on fees."

"Surely not," I said, "that was a correct payment, in fact I know you took the case cheaply anyway."

"Our records show that there was an appeal and that is paid by legal aid."

"Yes, I know that," I said, "but the original hearing was not on legal aid. We had to pay for that. Will you please check your books very carefully because if you give me the money I shall spend it."

They checked their books and they sent me the money. So on Johnny's trial money we all had a wonderful Christmas dinner two and a half years later; God was watching over us too.

Johnny's mother was overjoyed when he became a Christian. Every time I passed the market she threw eggs and sausages at me. Not literally, but she sold these at her market stall and was so grateful that she showered gifts upon me. Another lady at a noodle stall did the same thing. I could hardly pass without a large bowl being thrust at me. Eventually I had to by-pass her particular street, for my jeans were getting too tight.

Chapter Eight

Chasing the Dragon

Emerging from the dark city one night I was in a thoughtful mood; my lifestyle was extraordinary in the sense that on no two days did I get up or sleep at the same time and I prayed a lot as I walked, for I found that I needed to talk to God all the time. That night I reiterated a heartfelt prayer of thanks.

"Thank God I'm not married. Thank God I've been left free to have time for other people's children." It would have been awful to have to phone up a husband saying, "Put on the baked beans, dear, I've been held up." I was sharing a flat with a girlfriend called Stephanie at this time and mercifully she never worried what time I came home. It was well past midnight when I climbed onto a minibus (known as a fourteen-man bus) on my way home to Jordan Road.

My prayers were interrupted by the sight of a pathetic figure; a boy of about fifteen who looked like a living skeleton. Huge hideous eye sockets were dark in a yellowish-grey face. This child-ghoul sat down in front of me and I tried to think where I had seen him before. The bus lurched and grated through the small hours while I searched my memory until I remembered when I had first seen him.

It was five years earlier when I had first begun to go to the Walled City. There was a large teahouse outside, where this small boy waited to open taxi-doors for a few cents tip. I noticed that he did not even get to keep all of this since there was an older beggar also in rags who obviously controlled the pitch. The boy looked desperately sick; clearly he was sleeping in the streets. Since I could not then speak the language I asked Chinese friends to write me notes to him offering to meet him at a particular place or clinic and get help for him. What I did not know was that he had been a drug addict since the age of ten, when his step-father threw him out of his home. He had never kept any rendezvous, but I had continued to pray for him.

So here he was again; I thanked God for bringing him back. Now I could speak Chinese, I had another chance to help him. He got off the bus in Mongkok, a busy area full of bars, ballrooms, dreary nightlife. I got off too and followed him. He was carrying a filthy red plastic toothmug which he used for begging. I tapped him on the shoulder and introduced myself suggesting that we went to eat the seasonal rice dumpling which hung from the street stalls during the Dragon Boat festival. The poor boy was terribly embarrassed. He hid his toothmug behind his back and as we proceeded to the *daih paih dong*, the street stall, he dropped it into a pile of rubbish.

He looked more and more uncomfortable as we ate; it was clearly time for his next fix. His mind as well as his body was rotted by the amount of heroin he had consumed; he understood nothing of what I was saying. There was no point in telling Ah Tsoi about Jesus for he could not concentrate for long enough to take it in. I thought that if we could find help for his addiction and his mind cleared, then I could tell him.

For the next few weeks I used to meet Ah Tsoi at all times of the day and night. He never slept in the same place, and I was frightened to lose him in case he got arrested. With track marks all down the veins on both arms he was an easy target for arrest. Worse still I discovered that he was holding people up daily to pay for his habit, while on probation, having already been in prison for drug offences. Twice I forced him to begin keeping appointments with his probation officer again.

I was obsessed with helping Ah Tsoi. The more I saw of this pathetic character the more fond of him I grew. Finally Pastor Chan agreed to take him into his Christian Drug Rehabilitation Centre and I was overjoyed. This was the answer to my prayers. We were going to change Ah Tsoi's life. As he had a little time to wait before going to the centre I began to give him money. It was not much, only five Hong Kong dollars a day. I felt a little uneasy about this but he needed that minimum amount to support his habit. If I did not give it to him he would be forced to mug and steal so I convinced myself that I was acting rightly. It was only for a few days, anyhow.

At last the day came for his departure to Pastor Chan's. I went out to the market and bought him a pair of shorts, a vest and a T-shirt, some underclothes, flip-flops and even swimming trunks because Pastor Chan's centre was by the sea. Finally I bought him a toothbrush, and flannel pyjamas, new jeans and an extra shirt. I thought this was like a mother would feel, and I felt very tender towards Ah Tsoi as I wrapped all these into a neat parcel ready for him to collect. I had asked him to come round to my flat to have a bath before he set off.

No Ah Tsoi. It was two hours after he should have arrived and there was no sign of him. Perhaps he was having a last fix somewhere. Then, just as I was wondering whether he would come at all, he arrived. He was filthy but by now there was no time to bathe. Stephanie had a camera and we wanted to take a picture of him before he went. He snarled at once, "I'm not going to be one of your film stars; no 'before and after' pictures of me. I'm not an exhibit." He went off in a very surly frame of mind, but I did see him safely into Pastor Chan's hands.

I went to bed and slept nearly twenty hours. For the first time in weeks I could sleep easily. I was exhausted, but relieved. Thank God that Ah Tsoi was someone else's problem now. Pastor Chan could teach him about Jesus and help him to grow up. Now I could go on to find the next one . . .

I was awakened by a telephone call. Ah Tsoi had run away. He could not stand the pain of withdrawal, and had tried to smoke his blanket to ease the craving. The others tried to persuade him to pray but he refused and slipped away into the night. He went on to a neighbouring village to steal blankets and money. The centre staff tried to find him to persuade him to come back but when they eventually caught up with him he refused to return. There was nothing more they could do. That was the end of the matter.

It was as if a part of me had died. I felt completely shattered and lay down on the stone floor and wept. I cried all day, unable to move off the floor. As I lay there I thought this was the end; I did not know what more I could have done. I had given Ah Tsoi everything I had. I had given him all my time, my love, my money, my food, and I had tried to tell him about Jesus. I had passed him to other Christians but it had not worked. I had failed.

I did not feel angry at God but very disappointed and perplexed by the whole episode. I could not understand why He let me get involved with Ah Tsoi in the first place if it was not going to work out. At last I gathered strength to pray. "No more of those, please God; no more drug addicts because I can't bear it. I had almost enough love for one person, and I gave him all of it. It wasn't enough and I don't think I've got any more."

Next morning I got on to a bus to go to my Chinese lesson. Hong Kong buses do not allow one the luxury of choosing a seat; I was wedged in with the other forty-odd standing passengers when, out of the corner of my eye, I saw a mentally handicapped boy; I did not want to look at him so I turned round. And there I was, facing another drug addict. I could only shut my eyes and pretend that they were not there. It would not hurt if I could not see them . . .

"God, I'm not looking because I don't want to go through all that pain again. I did believe that You would help but it didn't succeed. Why not?" I thought back to the time when walking through the Walled City I was first learning about addicts. In one street there were over a hundred openly smoking heroin; every single street seemed to have its emaciated wrecks. "It would be worth my whole life if You would use me to help just one of them," I had prayed.

Slowly as I recovered from the Ah Tsoi ordeal, I saw more clearly my mistakes in dealing with him. I had tried to give him everything I had; I had even prayed to God to save him, though in reality I was trying to save him myself. I wanted Ah Tsoi off drugs; but he was not desperate enough to want it for himself—especially when I subsidized his habit.

I had not dared to take Ah Tsoi off drugs and through withdrawal myself. (This was before I had seen Winson come off opium miraculously.) I was convinced that he needed expert care and when the expert care I fixed up did not work, I was shattered.

Later Pastor Chan took me to tea. He had bravely walked a lone path in Hong Kong by opening a farm for rehabilitating addicts in the New Territories. Without medical assistance he brought them through withdrawal. Then they continued to heal and grow strong in Christ because he gave them eighteen months of discipline with love.

Many of his graduates became church workers and counsellors in government and voluntary agencies. While the government-supported drug-centres had impressive statistics I had never met any addicts who had been through them and stayed off drugs; Pastor Chan's men were the only ones I had ever known personally who were still drug-free. He had slowly built up his programme through experience and heartbreak, so it was very comforting when he said, "Miss Pullinger, you will make a very good worker because you care."

Social workers are taught not to be involved with their cases but I knew that had I not been so close to the people concerned, I could not have stayed. Ah Tsoi's failure taught me that I was not brave or nice enough to take on such a job simply because it was a worthwhile project. I could not imagine how drug workers could tackle their depressing task without God, and I had a deep respect for them; but I knew that my own resources had run out. Despite my prayers for no more addicts, however, it was not the end of my dealings with them, merely the beginning. I found that I could care for them again with God's love.

As my acquaintance with the Triads grew it seemed as if every other one was on drugs because they were so easy to obtain and so cheap. The heroin then was undiluted with additives and extremely potent. The U.S. government warned its servicemen visiting Hong Kong on their "rest and recreation" trips from Vietnam that if they injected what seemed a normal dose they could overdose and die.

One night I visited a heroin den. It was in a large tin shed on the outskirts of the city but operated with the knowledge of the police. It was a filthy place with long low rough tables at which were seated what appeared to be effigies. I felt I had invaded a devil's banquet, a weird and silent meal. Each table was ruled over by a *pahng-jue*, a host. For fifty cents he provided the screws of toilet paper, the tinfoil and the cardboard funnels necessary for "chasing the dragon". Few Chinese addicts injected heroin, only doing so when their physical need was greater than their resources. They were afraid of overdosing—they could remember the days when each morning the corpses of dead addicts were piled by the single toilet ready for collection ...

Amongst the fifty odd bodies sucking in their horrid delight sat a boy in his early teens. His skin was pale and waxen, and his strength had died. His girl friend, who looked about fourteen, sat beside him supporting him in her arms as he inhaled his poison. It was a peculiarly intimate pose, and I was touched until I remembered that this girl had to sell her body to support her man. I looked at the others present knowing that every man there would have to pay for his habit this way unless he stole or pawned his family's belongings. It was a degrading scene, but I was fascinated and attracted. I felt the pull of the drug which every potential addict knows and which defies logic. He knows it kills, he knows it leads to addiction and depravity. He knows all the arguments with his head, but he still has to try it. And having tried once he has to continue until he is part of the mystique which drew him.

Every addict has a love-hate relationship with his drug. His mind despises it and its hold over him. His body longs for it when deprived for too long and cheats his mind into seeing it as a salvation. No one ever knows when he crosses the line from "playing" with drugs to being dependent on them. One novice vomits the first time and tries again to see whether it improves. Another feels little effect and imagines that he can take it again quite safely. He starts with a small dose but what satisfies at first is soon not enough and he needs to take more to prevent withdrawal pains. He takes bigger doses more and more often until he is arrested or dies.

I felt the pull of the drug. It was attractive. It was demonic.

*   *   *

When Winson came into the Youth Club and was set free from his opium addiction God showed me that the battle with this dragon could be won. At that moment I believed that his experience should be possible for others if they were converted and filled with God's power. Very soon after Ah Ping told me that his addicted friend wanted to come to our annual Summer camp and I welcomed him readily. Ah Ming was a powerful Triad from Hong Kong Island, a cousin to this branch of the 14K. We met on the ferry which was taking us to Lamma Island for the camp, but Ah Ming avoided shaking hands or talking to me—he was coming on his own terms.

A couple of English students, Tim and Nick, were to join us a few days later but for the first two days of the camp I had no men helpers so I prayed, "Please, God, send the right boys to the camp, and keep the wrong ones away."

Our camp site was at the top of a mountain, serene and beautiful. The only distressing factor in our one-hour walk up the hill was the thirty-pound sack of rice which I had to carry most of the way. The boys thought this was woman's work, and anyway they were there to play, not work. Years later they became more helpful and protective, but I was still very much on trial at this point.

The camp programme was very strict, with work details and bedtimes carefully arranged, but it proved difficult to effect by myself. I slept with the few girls in tents and the boys slept in an enormous dormitory; I could not go in to search their belongings or to turn out the lights. I realized that most of those thirty were Triad members and began to feel uneasy. Still, I had prayed that prayer about keeping the wrong ones out . . .

Ah Ming appeared outside the boys' dormitory and saw me sitting out there in the dark with my hurricane lamp. He had not expected that. "Hmm. I do—er—I do like looking at the stars," he improvised.

"Yes," I agreed, "so do I. They're beautiful, aren't they?"

We sat there for maybe three hours in very polite conversation. He was obviously longing to go off and take his drugs. Finally I could not sit it out any longer so I went to bed and Ah Ming went to the other side of the mountain to take his heroin.

I had prayed that God would keep the wrong ones away so I had to deduce that the boys who had come were God-sent, but taking drugs on a Christian camp was not quite what I had in mind. The missionaries had advised me that the way to build a church was to work on one boy. When he was a Christian and doing well then you could work on another one till the house was full. I had done it completely backwards, however, and was landed with a dormitory full of gangsters. Who was running whom I was not sure. I began to think that the missionaries were right.

Two days later Ah Ming was *in extremis* having run out of his drug supply. He sent a brother to me who announced that there was an urgent matter that three of them had to attend to, so they would be leaving. I intended to argue this but since the rest of us were having morning service they escaped.

I sent Nick to chase after them; he was an enormous six-footer. That he could not speak a word of Chinese was greatly to his advantage for the wily addicts had invented a very good explanation as to why their departure was imperative. Fortunately Nick could not understand them so as they continued to walk he continued to follow.

They walked over three hills. All they could hear was this Englishman repeating, "You must come back, you must come back, you must come back," and "Jesus loves you, Jesus loves you." But no way were three sick addicts going to turn round and come back. The craving for heroin was so strong that they would have climbed a hundred mountains, or even killed someone, in order to get the ferry back to their supply.

Meanwhile, back at the camp we were praying for their return.

Without knowing why they did so the three fleeing boys stopped dead. Then they lit cigarettes and began to retrace their steps. When they reappeared with Nick on top of our mountain they looked very sheepish; they could not explain this prodigal turnabout even to themselves. However, when I suggested to Ah Ming that we chat for a while he nodded as if he had been expecting this all along . . .

It was pouring with rain and we were forced to seek shelter in one of our "two-man" army tents. Poor Ah Ming did not want a lecture. He was feeling intense discomfort but he could not leave the tent because the downpour had reached monsoon intensity. "I'm sorry, Ah Ming," I began, "I know you're feeling lousy but I'd like to show you something which will help you." In the earth I drew three crosses.

"I know this sounds silly, but I want you to imagine that you could actually see all the wrong things that a man has done. We'll use this *lap-sap* (rubbish) to represent them," I continued as I collected up some bottle tops, dirt and waste paper lying around. "Now when Jesus was crucified two men were nailed on either side of Him; they were thieves, probably murderers." I placed a heap of litter on the outside crosses leaving Jesus' cross empty. "Do you know why the middle one has no *lap-sap*?" I asked Ah Ming. He looked rather bored and replied, "Yeah, Jesus never did no wrong so He got no sins on Him."

I became a story-teller, pointing to the crosses.

" 'So You're the Christ, eh?' mocked this man. 'Prove it. Call on Your henchmen to save you now. Come on then. You save Yourself and save us too while You're at it.' He was dying himself but he still had plenty of spit.

" 'You shouldn't say that,' objected that thief on the right cross; 'We done wrong—we oughta die. This man ain't done nothing,' and he turned to Jesus saying, 'Lord, remember me when You get to Your Kingdom.'

" 'Today you will be with Me together in paradise,' answered Jesus."

While I said this I lifted the heap of dirt off the right cross and placed it all on Jesus.

"You feel like throwing up now?" I noticed Ah Ming looked grey and trembly. "Well, Jesus felt like you do only even worse because as well as taking that man's sins He took all the sins and all the pains the whole world ever felt upon Himself, so that we could be free of our sin and pain."

For some time we both stared at the ground and the message drawn there. Then I said, "The thief on that side is forgiven and now can live with God, but why not the other one? Weren't they equally bad?"

"One believed and the other didn't," replied Ah Ming.

"That's all you have to do. I know you don't understand, but if you are willing to give all of your pain to Him, Jesus can take it away right now. He's God's Son and that's why He died. Are you willing?"

Ah Ming was not very willing. His eyes were running and he kept sniffing as he clutched his stomach. It was still raining outside; he was stuck in this tent in great distress. At last he could not stand it any longer.

"Suppose," he said resignedly, "suppose I—er—well, suppose I try."

It was enough.

He then prayed clearly asking Jesus to take away his pain if He were God. He asked for his wrong things to be taken away too so he could start his life again. It stopped raining.

Outside I found my English friends who joined me in the tent and we laid our hands on Ah Ming's head telling him that Jesus would give him healing and power.

When we prayed Ah Ming too received the gift of the Holy Spirit and we all prayed together for a while.

A week later when we returned from the camp Ah Ming told me how God had answered those prayers in an extraordinary way. He had gone to bed feeling confused after praying and not being at all sure what had happened. As he slept he had a strange dream. He was lying on a wooden bunk in a mountain hut. It was blowing a gale outside; through the sounds of the wind he heard a knocking at the door. As he was alone in the hut in a terrible state of drug withdrawal he did not answer it. The knocking came a second time so he went to the window to see who it was. There he saw a man carrying a candle, which he thought very odd on a rainy mountain, but being in a foul temper he went back to bed. The third time the knocking came Ah Ming thought, "Poor man, he doesn't have anywhere else to go." He went to the door and opened it, then he lay down again. The man, who seemed oddly familiar, came into the hut and over to the bunk bed where he put down the candlestick.

He asked Ah Ming to sit up and then gently put his hands on his head. The withdrawal pains disappeared; he never had any pain again. "I knew He was a healer," said Ah Ming revelling in his release from drugs.

*　　*　　*

A whistle was blowing. Early each morning Miss Poon insisted that the boys do a version of physical jerks before breakfast. They all tumbled out of bed. Ah Ping noticed that although Ah Ming had risen he was groping around on the bunk. He asked him what he was doing.

"I'm looking for the candlewax," replied Ah Ming. "I'm looking for the candlewax." The dream had been so real that he was sure that Jesus really had been there. After that he joined in the morning exercises with great vigour, surprising all his friends who knew that addicts going through withdrawal could not usually do push-ups. Later that day he was baptized in the sea. When we all returned to the mainland he looked fit and very happy.

Ah Ming did not actually do any work himself, but had a job at one of the dockyards where he used to lie in a cabin all day whilst his younger brothers fed him heroin. On his first day back at work he sat on the ferry and prayed, whilst crossing the harbour. He prayed so hard that he did not notice when his neighbouring passengers stole his flipflops as a joke. Undaunted, he carried on to work and walked through the dockyard gates shoeless. He saw, coming towards him, a gang of rival Triads armed for a fight with bottles and knives. Instinctively he picked up the nearest weapons—two heavy iron poles—and waded into the attack.

What I had not known when I prayed that God would send only the "right ones" to the camp was that Ah Ming had come to our camp especially to plan his strategy for this gang war. He had given his orders to some of his brothers at the camp, and now seeing him going into the attack they ran to various street stalls and drew out meat choppers and melon knives to be used in the battle.

Suddenly Ah Ming thought, "Help, I was praying about peace on the boat this morning. I can't fight." He dropped his poles, sat down in the road and began to pray again.

A few minutes later he looked up to see his enemies surrounding him; they were all looking down at him curiously. "What are you doing?" their leader asked.

"I'm praying. I'm a Christian now—would you like to hear about it?" They nodded, dumbfounded, so Ah Ming told them what had happened to him. They were so impressed that several came to see me later and began to attend meetings.

*   *   *

In this way our Youth Club grew bigger and bigger as those who became Christians brought their friends. I had not yet met the renowned Goko but his large chop-eating brother came in frequently to sing. Some weeks after the camp we were praying in the club room when one of the boys had a vision. Since all the boys who believed in Christ received the power of the Spirit with the gift of tongues they were not surprised when He caused wonders to happen. The vision was of us in procession walking down the street singing and dancing.

Only twelve were willing to go. The rest made excuses. "Poon Siu Jeh, we live here." As I imagined myself prancing round my parents' village in England I could sympathize.

One of our favourite songs in the club was:

> Silver and gold have I none
> But such as I have give I thee
> In the Name of Jesus Christ
> Of Nazareth, Rise up and walk.
> Walking and leaping and praising God,
> Walking and leaping and praising God,
> In the name of Jesus Christ
> Of Nazareth rise up and walk.

I took my accordion; we had one guitarist, a couple of tambourines; the rest of the twelve followed in single file. The street was too narrow for two people, but when we reached the "leaping and dancing and praising" refrain we all managed to jump around a bit.

It is the only time I can remember of that era when so many vice businesses stopped without there being a police raid. At the blue film theatre and the gambling dens the patrons rushed to the doorways to see what was happening. One of Ah Keung's brothers asleep in an illegal casino heard the singing and woke up with a start believing himself to have dropped off in our Sunday morning service. Many people had seen Christians handing out bits of paper before (the addicts used to smoke them) but never before had they witnessed singing and dancing in the streets of the Walled City.

Passing by the opium dens we came to the two largest heroin dens, where Ah Ming, who had assumed leadership of the procession, stopped and, quite unbidden, began to preach. Inside the den a tall young Chinese called Ah Mo had just finished injecting himself. He had already discovered that "Miss White" (one of the nick-names for heroin or white powder) did not keep her promises. He had hardly gained a moment of enjoyment from her; for no sooner had he taken his "fix" than he had to think about obtaining money for his next appointment with the lying lady. Ah Mo was wondering where to do his next robbery when he heard singing outside the heroin shed. Emerging from one gloom into the next he was amazed to see his friend, Ah Ming, telling the street how Jesus had changed his life.

It was obvious to Ah Mo that something very wonderful had indeed taken place, for barely three weeks previously he and Ah Ming had been squatting side by side taking heroin together in that very same den. Forgetting his projected robbery he joined the end of the procession and followed it until it wound back to the club room some thirty minutes later. There he came in and listened with wonder as the boys told him how Jesus could change him. But he shook his head and asked to speak to me privately.

"I can't be a Christian, Miss Poon. I killed my wife." And I heard the tragic tale of his rise to fame in the Triads as a muscleman. He used to throw people out of nightclubs and bars in a more glamorous district of Kowloon. Soon he was powerful enough to employ his own "bouncers" and eventually controlled a little empire. He lived with a ballroom "hostess" but he had a great macho image of himself, and enjoyed three other mistresses at the same time. When he was arrested his "hostess" visited him in prison, taking him drugs and money. She really loved him. Although he promised her to be faithful he continued to visit the others after he was released. She was so miserable that she began to take drugs too and near death was rushed to hospital to be stomach-pumped. To placate her, he hired a white wedding dress for her, morning dress for himself and they had a mock wedding picture taken in a Bridal Studio. They sent the pictures to their relations in China. But Ah Mo did not give up his lechery and so his girl overdosed a second time. The third time she overdosed she could not be saved. She died in the hospital.

Ah Mo was wracked with guilt; he lost interest in his "bouncing" business and punished himself with drugs.

As he stood before me all bones and rags it was hard to imagine that this man had inspired such a fatal passion. I told him that he could find forgiveness in Christ, his eyes grew hopeful and I caught a glimpse of the handsome man he was. He prayed to receive Jesus and left the club in a daze. Some of his cronies were in the passage outside; seeing his face they laughed, "He's got religion, he's got religion."

"But I didn't mind," Ah Mo told me later, "because my heart felt light."

I had assumed that because Winson and Ah Ming were cured miraculously of their addiction, anyone who believed in Jesus would automatically be delivered. Ah Mo was not. He continued to take drugs although I told him that this was not consistent with being a Christian.

I asked Pastor Chan to take him into his centre but he had to wait several weeks before there was a place. I puzzled why God did not save him instantly as He had saved the others.

"Praise God," Ah Mo announced when he joined our Sunday service some days later. "I haven't had to rob or steal this week to pay for my heroin habit. I've got a job."

When I discovered what that job was I found myself unable to praise God for it at all. He was employed by one of the dens as a *tin-man-toi* (weatherman). Each night from midnight until eight a.m. he sat in the street of the illegal dentists guarding one of the entrances to the Walled City. In his cigarette pack was concealed an electric plug. Should he spot a police raiding party, narcotics bureau spy or an alien Triad his duty was to fix the plug into a socket built into the crude wall. This set off an alarm bell in the various vice and drug dens so that by the time any intruder approached business had stopped and they were ready to repel invaders.

For these labours Ah Mo was paid HK$15 daily—enough for his heroin requirement but not enough for rice.

Each day I found Ah Mo and took him a little food. I had learned my lesson about not giving money. He slept in an alley behind the Kowloon City public lavatory paying HK$15 a month for this privilege to another street sleeper who was the self-appointed "king" of the street. Most days I sat and prayed with him though he was usually half asleep when I left my offering in a plastic bag.

I was thankful that the drug den watching did not continue for long. I could not justify it morally nor could I suggest an alternative. Ah Mo went to the centre, came off drugs and in one month gained twenty pounds in weight. One more dragon bit the dust.

I continued to send messages to Goko after Winson's miraculous cure. I wrote notes, sending them with various *sai lo*; I called in at gambling dens and left my name; I spoke to the lookout man outside his favourite opium den; I talked to his wife. Eventually he agreed to see me as the accumulation of messages suggested that I had an important matter to discuss. Winson was dispatched with an invitation inviting me to tea at the Fairy Restaurant outside the City. It was a Chinese cafe selling Western food and usually out of my price range. As I made my way past the street letter-writers ponderously scribing their missives, I wondered what Goko would be like. He was tall and big I knew and had been a great football player before his deterioration through opium. I had heard how he lay all day in his own den while his younger brothers fed him with opium. This dependence was in sharp contrast with the power he wielded and the dread his name inspired. He had carefully brainwashed his followers: heroin was forbidden but opium was merely the continuation of an old social custom no more harmful than drinking brandy after a meal. He was an older Triad boss and prided himself on keeping the rules such as being responsible for the funeral arrangements of a murdered gang member, and assuming financial care for his dependants.

Goko recognized me first since I was the only Westerner to enter the restaurant. He was in his mid-thirties, respectably dressed, sitting alone. He courteously gestured to me to sit down. Looking him fully in the face for the first time I could see that the opium had drawn lines of dissipation on his strong features. He seemed to have shrunk within his large frame like an old man. He smiled at me and showed teeth rotted and stained with fumes from his opium pipe. While I was with him he smoked cigarettes continuously, puffing and inhaling too frequently.

Politely the ruthless leader of corruption asked me what I would like to order. I drank coffee, he drank Horlicks, and we shared pineapple buns.

We carried on conversation-class pleasantries until I blurted, "I wish you wouldn't be so polite; please let's stop pretending. You and I have nothing in common. Why are you being so kind to me?"

Goko paused. "I believe you care about my brothers like I do." He was not using idle words: he was famous for the care he took of his followers.

"Yes, I do care about them," I agreed, "but you and I can have no union. I hate everything you stand for and I hate what you do."

It was strange but now as in future meetings the more bluntly I spoke the more Goko responded. He dropped the polite frills and began to speak straight.

"Poon Siu Jeh, you and I both understand power. I use this way;" he clenched his fist, "and you use this way," he said pointing to the heart. "You have a power which I don't have. If my brothers get hooked on drugs I have them beaten up. I don't want them on heroin and I've found I can't make them quit. But I've watched you. And I believe Jesus can." He paused to light a cigarette while I marvelled at the significance of what he had said.

"So," he continued, "I've decided to give the addicts to you."

"No," I replied quickly, "you can't do that. I know what you want to do. You want Jesus to get them off drugs and then you want them back to work and fight for you. But Christians can't serve two bosses; they have to follow either Christ or you. I believe you love your brothers, but you and I are walking different paths and can have no meeting-point. I have no intention of helping your brothers off drugs only for you to take them back. They will certainly go back to heroin if they follow you."

Goko stared down at the tablecloth covered with crumbs from the pineapple buns. He looked up slowly.

"All right, then. I give up my right to those who want to follow Jesus."

I could hardly take in what he had said. The Triads never released their members; once you became a Triad you remained a Triad for life. Even the Hong Kong law courts accepted that Triad membership was binding for ever. To try to leave was to invite savage punishment or even death. There were stories of rebellious members who had their cheeks raked or were quietly stabbed one unsuspecting night. Yet here was Goko volunteering to hand over some of his brothers. Never before had I heard of such an offer . . . he interrupted my thoughts: "I'll tell you what I'll do; I'll give you all my rotten brothers and I'll keep all the good ones for myself."

"Fine," I said, "Jesus came for the rotten ones anyhow."

So that was our strange pact and from that time onwards Goko sent me addicts to cure. When he heard what happened to Johnny he said, "I'm watching. If he lasts five years I will have to believe for myself."

Chapter Nine

Growing Pains

Winson was in difficulties. He came to me full of excitement, "Poon Siu Jeh, I have to praise the Lord. I was in the opium den last night and someone invited me to have some opium free. I did want to, but I prayed and God gave me strength so I did not take it. Instead I knelt down and sang songs about Jesus for everyone to hear."

I was furious with him. "That's not 'praise the Lord', Winson, it is tempting Him. It's not clever of you to ask for protection in a drug den—you shouldn't be there in the first place."

The problem was not easily resolved. I found out that Winson had no other place to sleep. At the time he was converted and freed from his drug addiction he was living in this opium den which was a favourite haunt of his 14K brothers.

I had told him to leave his gang and follow Jesus, but it was the same in practical terms as patting him on the back with a "Go—I wish you well; keep yourself warm and well fed," and doing nothing about his physical needs. Although they had become Christians both Winson and Ah Ping were still involved with the Triads by the very fact of living in the Walled City. They faced a dilemma when a brother was attacked. Their instinct was to defend him, as they had been raised in an atmosphere where loyalty to a brother excused violence to the point of murder. It was very hard for them to turn away from those they had grown up with and cared for. I also felt that even if they themselves no longer took an active part in crime their very presence gave tacit approval to Triad affairs.

Ah Ming likewise encountered difficulties. "Before I became a Christian I was well-known for my command. If I said 'go' my followers went; if I said 'stab' they would stab. I didn't have to think at all; I was without pity."

He reminded me of the centurion Jesus had met. "But now," Ah Ming continued, "when they come to me with grievances, I have to stop and think. I can't tell them to fight because I'm a Christian. For the first time in my life I consider the feelings of attacked victims. When my brothers see me hesitate they lose respect for me and this hurts me." Behind his fear of losing face he was growing a conscience, a sensation alien in the Triad world.

As I walked around the Walled City I kept on running into ex-addicts and Triads who had expressed a serious desire to change. Clearly they had to be removed from their evil environment, but like Winson they had no other place to live. They could not survive the constant temptations with their meagre spiritual knowledge. So I hunted for homes and Christian hostels only to find that all of them were for the respectable Chinese—tenants were required to have a job or school, two pastoral references, a month's rent in advance plus a deposit. Since none of the just-converted gangsters I knew had any one of these qualifications they were effectively excluded.

To every Westerner I knew I had at some time or another given or tried to give one of my boys to live in his house. (Chinese families never had any extra room having enough problems housing their own relations.) This was not satisfactory since he needed more watching and discipline than an English family could give. Besides most people found it a strain after a while having a gangster, albeit a converted one, living in the amah's room.

Mary Taylor burst into tears when she first saw our flat in Lung Kong Road. True, the walls were crumbling; there was a hole in the roof, night soil buckets in lieu of a lavatory, and no electricity but in my opinion it was a godsend. I really could not see why my old schoolfriend was so upset, because we had prayed about getting a place into which I could shepherd my sheep and as far as I was concerned, this was it.

I found my flat when enquiring at a street stall just outside the Walled City whether there were any apartments available in the vicinity. A very well-dressed lady who was shopping there took me straight away to this derelict place. By Chinese standards it was enormous, having over nine hundred square feet inside, and stairs leading up to a roof which had been partly covered with corrugated iron to make an extra room. She offered it to me at a very reasonable rent saying that she had kept it vacant for a year waiting for Christians to occupy it. She herself was a Buddhist.

I was so excited when I saw it that I could only see the possibilities. Mary being more pragmatic could only see its drawbacks; she may have been right for it needed an incredible amount of work to make it habitable. Walled City boys helped in the renovation by lending their skills and non-skills. It is doubtful if this method was really cheaper than employing professionals, since they were keen on soft drinks and meal breaks in exchange for their services.

On the principle that work is done more quickly if one is on the spot Mary and I moved in amongst a heap of rubble, no lights and a dubious water system, camping in one room while partitions came down and ceilings went up around us. Our greatest asset was the roof garden, once we had exchanged the heaps of old bicycle frames and bedsteads for begonias, cacti and climbing vines. These were carefully arranged so that we would not be overlooked by the mahjong school opposite which catered for off duty policemen who were very amused to see us sunbathing.

I needed to decide whether to share my house with girls or boys since so many were homeless. If I took boys into my home, which I thought rather unsuitable in my single state, it would necessarily rule out the girls, as I could not mix them. But the decision was taken for me when Ah Ping and Ah Keung had to leave the temporary home I had found for them and had nowhere else to go except back into the Walled City or Lung Kong Road.

Our new family was then joined by Joseph, the original Youth Club president. Winson left his den for us and we arranged for Ah Ming to live with friends. We were forming a Christian community and helping the boys to grow up in Christ. I felt how nice and neat it was with this one here and that one there.

However, I still had much to learn. I did far too many jobs. I cooked for the boys, fed them, clothed them, cleaned the house and got them to work or school. I was also opening the Walled City room nearly every evening and visiting vice dens and brothels whenever there was a contact. When at last I got to bed I was frequently wakened by drug addicts ringing on the door bell wanting to hear about Jesus. Prostitutes rang me from police stations, detectives appeared on the doorstep seeking information, and prison or probation officers referred cases to me since ours was one of the very few places in the colony which housed delinquent boys. I did not fancy the idea of meeting a policeman in my nightie so from that time I adopted the habit of sleeping in my clothes. I was always ready to dash out of the house in an emergency.

One such occurred when a young man phoned me at four a.m. to say that he had had an argument with his wife and she had fallen out of the top bunk in their resettlement room. He had run away in panic but would I please go to his home and check to see if she were dead or not.

Our flat became mixed after all. Another night there was a knock on the door and when I opened it there stood a little teenage girl holding a baby on one arm and an enormous suitcase on the other. Behind her crouched her younger brother and two little sisters. "Poon Siu Jeh," she whispered, "we've come to live with you."

I had first come to know these children some three years previously and had many dealings with them since. Their addicted father had not only harmed himself but caused his family dreadful suffering. The history of the Chung family was appalling. They all lived on a double bed. There was no space for anything else in the room since it was only the roof of someone else's shack, reached by a wooden staircase.

Their own roof was a plastic tarpaulin which sagged in the middle when it rained; every now and again they prodded it with a pole and emptied the rain into buckets to prevent it flooding their little room. The children learned to walk on this bed; they slept on it, cooked on it, played and did their homework on it. All five of them were painfully shy and when I went to visit the family they turned to the wall pretending that they were not there. There was nowhere else to hide.

I never saw them eat anything except white rice which was boiled to a porridge known as *congee*. This was because their miserable father spent all his earnings on heroin and never gave his family any support at all. The only income came from Mrs. Chung, a tiny little thirty-year-old, who carried water buckets for a living. She brought them from the water pumps outside the Walled City, carried them down the narrow streets on a pole, and then upstairs to people's houses. She received five cents a time for this service, but lost even that income after she got rheumatism in her legs and could no longer walk with the heavy buckets.

Although she was expecting a sixth child to be born into her foodless slum, Mrs. Chung was always smiling. She had asked to receive Jesus into her heart and she, I, and some of the Christian boys from the Youth Club often prayed together which brought her great joy. We used to take her dried bacon, salted fish and oil so that the family had more nourishment to put on the rice. Had we given her money, her husband, who came back occasionally, would have stolen it for his heroin. We took the children, who were aged from six to eleven, toys for Christmas, and we paid their school fees. Even then the children had to work in factories to keep buying the rice.

I referred this case to the Social Welfare department asking for compassionate resettlement and some kind of financial aid since I could not afford the money to support them all indefinitely. The officials in the enquiry office were unhelpful: Mrs. Chung could not read so she did not even know which floor to go to nor, since they had told her to fill in forms before she could see a social worker, had she even reached the queue which began the process of receiving help.

The next time she went I went with her and sat all day waiting to see the case worker: I suggested she classified the couple as separated, as Mr. Chung rarely came home and did not contribute to the family income anyway. I was shown brusquely out while Mrs. Chung was interviewed. When I visited the family again this poor little lady told me that she had gone back to the office to sign for aid, and that a letter would be coming. Four months later there was still no letter though she remained optimistic that it would come. Eventually I checked with the Welfare Department who looked up their files. I was told, "This family does not qualify for aid."

"If that family doesn't qualify for aid then I'm sure no one does. I've never seen anyone so poor, and they have a newborn baby," I replied. Mrs. Chung had had to walk back home from the clinic on the day she gave birth to her sixth child. "Would you please explain your assessment?" I asked.

Apparently the Welfare Authorities had asked Mrs. Chung's husband to go to the office to provide a statement about his income. He told them, "I earn HK$600 a month out of which I give my wife HK$400." This was a complete lie but it would be great loss of face for a Chinese man to admit that he could not support his family. The misinformation was carefully written down and then the Welfare Officer asked Mrs. Chung to sign her husband's statement. She did not know what it said. She thought she was signing to receive help, so she made her mark.

"Couldn't you see that he was on drugs? His word can't be trusted." I was so upset that I was aggressive.

"He told us he was completely drug free," they replied defensively.

"Don't you know what an addict looks like? That's as plain an example as I've ever seen. He has heroin staring out of his eyes." The officials, who had learned their procedures out of books, labelled me a troublemaker, but they reversed the decision and Mrs. Chung received some financial help at last.

We then helped the family to move out of the Walled City. My boys hired a lorry and we moved the double bed only to find barrels and barrels of clothes stored underneath. The family had previously been in contact with another welfare organization who had donated a dozen barrels of clothing sent from overseas for the "refugees". They were full of articles such as soiled sequinned evening dresses, but Mrs. Chung had been so keen to have possessions that she would not throw anything away. We bought one hundred and fifty hangers and strung them up in the family's new room which was otherwise completely bare. Then began the unpacking; the barrels were crawling with cockroaches. Whole nests of them had been living there for years and emerged to take up quarters in the new home. When only half the barrels had been unpacked each hanger had about three grey, crawling, mouldy items on it. There were six fat English ladies' winter coats which had rotted and stank.

There were scores of unsuitable and unwearable garments so I put great heaps of them by the trash can around the corner of the building. The next day I came back to find that the eldest girl, Ah Ling, had gone and fetched them all back — they were the only security she had.

About the time we moved into the Lung Kong flat Mrs. Chung told me with simple acceptance that she had been ordered to go out and get a job, since the Government could not support drug addicts' wives indefinitely. She told them she was not well but they refused further help. Two weeks after hearing this decree she coughed and died. She had had a cough for a long time and although it was difficult for her to get to a doctor she had visited a clinic several times. A bottle of medicine had been handed out.

I felt partly to blame for her death. I had known she had been coughing, but had never taken the trouble to accompany her to the doctor and she had not had her T.B. diagnosed. She had sought help from professionals; we had all kept her waiting; and she had died a death which might have been prevented.

After the funeral I continued to visit and support the children who were now being exploited by their father. He took the thirteen-year-old daughter away from school and sent her to work in a factory. For a pitiful wage of HK$100 a month she sewed collars on dresses; she had to give her father all the money. When the Youth Club went on outings we would take all the children with us, which was when they suggested coming to live at my house. I flatly refused this as a possibility, and told them that under the law they belonged to their father. One month after my refusal they packed all their belongings and ran away from home, to me.

They were a pathetic sight huddled in my doorway. They had complete trust that I would take them in. It did not seem very suitable; my house was already sleeping boys on the floor, but I had no option when I discovered that Ah Ling was being molested by her father. She showed me the bruises on her legs so I took her to hospital and then allocated bunks for the little ones. They were so withdrawn that it was a long time before any of them could speak to me. However, I soon discovered that our boys, themselves rejected, were really good with the children, and loved playing with the baby.

So the family in our house grew and was further augmented by constant appearances from Mrs. Chan whom I had come to know some months earlier through her son, Pin Kwong. He was a vicious addict of nineteen who had no intention of changing his ways and collected money by holding up victims at knife point in the public toilet. I often asked him about his widowed mother, but he refused to allow me to visit her saying, "She is an old idol worshipper. She won't want to hear from a Christian."

When Pin Kwong was arrested and put in prison for the fifth time I sought out his mother and found her lying on a little bed in her Walled City room. She had decided to die, because her son had been arrested yet once more. She had no husband or family and Pin Kwong was all her life. Chinese women are very proud of their sons, but he was rotten and took away any money she ever had so she had no more will to live. He had not wanted me to visit her for fear that I would discover he had been exploiting his mother for the little amount she could collect selling vegetable herbs in the market. When we found her, she had already lain there for some days without eating and was very weak. The boys went out and bought chicken essence and bones to boil for soup, and we set about restoring the elderly lady. While we fed her we told her about the Father who had given her His most precious possession, His only Son, because He loved her.

Mrs. Chan was a simple woman who had never been to school. She had never heard of Christ before, and could not follow long sentences. We laid our hands upon her and prayed out loud, asking God to teach her in a way she could comprehend. After the prayer she looked up, grinning from ear to ear, saying that when we prayed she had been healed of "sickness of the lungs" and could breathe clearly for the first time in years. It never returned.

That night she dreamed that a man in a long white robe came to her, and holding out His arms asked her to come to Him and be baptized. Since that time she was quite radiant, and when I moved into Lung Kong Road, she was delighted. We gave her a key to the new home and she pottered in and out happily cleaning everything in sight, cooking meals and introducing all her local market vendor friends, who would sell us provisions cheaply. Bestowing on me a signal honour she became my *kai ma* and I her *kai neui*, meaning godmother and goddaughter. She adored her new family and bossily clucked around us all.

Since she could not read a word I had the boys teach her Bible verses. It took her a week to learn "Jesus said, 'I am the bread of life.'" This had to be near to her heart, since she had formed a passion for the toaster and now downed marmalade sandwiches in a most un-Chinese manner.

Three years earlier than this, when Dora first started to help me in the Walled City, she had come one evening to translate for a Bible study. It was one of those times when only one of the boys turned up; the others had forgotten completely. I was feeling cross that I used up an unreasonable amount of time collecting and chasing them up for meetings. It was one of the very rare occasions when I really wished to be back in England, where Christians at least knew what day of the week it was. I did not voice these thoughts, but as we prayed God gave a message in tongues to the one boy present. Dora had an interpretation of the message.

"No one who has left house or brothers or sisters or mother or father or children or lands for me and the gospel will fail to receive a hundred times as many in this life of houses, brothers, sisters, mothers, children, and lands, and in the age to come, eternal life."

I had heard these words before but it was not until Dora's interpretation that I really listened. Hurriedly I looked up the verses in St. Mark's Gospel, to find that it did say we would receive in this life a hundred times as much as we had left. I had only ever remembered the eternal life part and that was for after death. So that evening I claimed the promise, "God, I'd like a hundred homes, a hundred brothers and sisters. A hundred mothers and children, too."

Now in the flat in Lung Kong I counted up and found that amongst the Walled City boys and students I must have at least one hundred Christian brothers and sisters. I was living in my sixth home with many others opened to me and the children were adding up. Since I had been a bit short on the mothers, Mrs. Chan appeared too. She joined a lovely church full of old ladies outside the Walled City and looked after the potential "mothers" I sent her.

More mothers in God came along. One day I was visited by a young man assisting his granny from a nearby resettlement block. She looked very frail and her head was bandaged, partially concealing an ugly gash on her temple. "I want to be baptized," she squeaked.

I was immediately suspicious. "It means nothing to be baptized if you have not believed in Jesus. If you would like to hear about Him I will be glad to tell you, but if it's the bit of paper you require I cannot help you. We do not give certificates in our church. There are many others which do and I'm sure they will be glad to help."

It turned out that having fallen down and cracked her head, this granny was afraid to die without a burial spot. There was a great shortage of these in Hong Kong and a thriving black market demanded outrageous sums. However, as a member of a Christian church, she could get a reasonable piece of consecrated real estate and this is what the old lady was after. I took her to Mrs. Chan who became friends with her and led her to Christ. The old granny had a true conversion, was baptized and died six months later with a place reserved in heaven.

I had no idea it would be so much hard work caring for the boys in my house. All the books I had ever read about criminals becoming Christians stopped short at their conversion, giving a strong impression that they lived happily ever after. Mine was a basic mistake—I thought that "If anyone is in Christ he is a new man," whereas the meaning of the text is "a new creation". Although the gangsters had become Christians they were like newborn babies and had a lot to learn. Their ignorance of normal living was appalling. Some of them such as Mau Jai (Little Cat), who had been in the drug den when Johnnie was arrested, had lived on the streets since they were five years old.

Mau Jai had not been allowed to sleep at home because

his father had two wives, and the second one, "Little Mother", was out of favour so her children were banned from the home. They had no normal childhood; deprived of this they grew up quickly in craft and cunning. Since they were used to being up all night they could not understand why they should shut their eyes at twelve p.m. They got up when they awoke and if they did not wake up in the morning that was that. If they did not feel like going to work they did not go. They associated any rules I made with prison which was the only other kind of authority they had known, and were careless in keeping them.

In Lung Kong Road boys came and went. I sometimes had the suspicion that they were running me rather than vice-versa but I did not want to admit it. For example, Ah Hung came to us on release from prison, sent by the authorities and supposedly drug free. It turned out that he took heroin the very day he was released and must have continued to take it throughout his stay with us. It was therefore not surprising that soon he lost his job as a skilled jade craftsman and disappeared from our flat. One day he turned up high on heroin to confess to having taken part in a recent robbery in which a policeman had been wounded. We persuaded him to give himself up but ten minutes later he ran away. Since he had spoken of a gun I rang the police and had six carloads of detectives screeching through the harbour tunnel and up to the flat, waving revolvers as they thought he was still there. Embarrassed, we tried to smile at crowding neighbours as if nothing unusual were happening. They all thought us extremely unfriendly not to divulge the details. A series of detectives greedily ate our meals and kept a watch on the house for twenty-four hours. One pair skipped half their night shift to find a better class of food, leaving us a night-spot telephone number where they might be reached in case of further developments.

It all turned out to be a hoax. Ah Hung appeared a day later to own up that he had not taken part in the crime. I did not believe him and so took him off to the police to confess. This was the best thing which could happen to Ah Hung because, according to information which the police later received, there was no way he could have been party to this robbery. He was jeered at for making up such a story under the influence of drink and heroin. But it was exactly what was needed to force his drug-taking into the open and bring him to the point of truly seeking help.

The Walled City boys clearly needed discipline and I was quite unable to give enough. Part of my difficulty was that I had reached the boys through being their friend and equal and it was hard to make the transition into being their teacher or pastor. I had become so involved with them that I was not firm enough: so they came in at all hours of the night and morning, left me to do all the drudgery of the housework, and were not growing up as I had hoped. Since I was out most of the night myself it was difficult to check up on what they were doing. I began to pray that God would send someone else to look after the house so that I would be free to get back on the streets.

To ease the pressure on me I asked two Chinese young Christian men to join us and to help run the house to free me for other work. This was not a success however; they wanted a salary which I could not promise; they wanted to be addressed as "teacher"; lastly they felt that any kind of manual work was beneath them since they were church workers. When I rose in the morning I asked them if they had woken up the other boys and prepared the breakfast. They replied that they were too busy having their "quiet times", that is, times for praying and reading the Bible. Their idea of the teaching role was to hold a Bible study with the boys and preach at them for one and a half hours. I discovered that this was how they had been taught to conduct Christian work—having meetings, having a title, and preaching was as much as they understood. They had not learned about Jesus washing his disciples' feet.

To help both myself and the boys I often took them to the Willans' meetings which they loved. The meetings were

always translated into Chinese so they could join in fully
and meet Christians from other countries and backgrounds.
Because of this many people prayed for us; but sadly no one
wanted to be further involved. One day Jean Willans firmly
spoke to me, "If you have to work with these boys, all right,
Jackie, but you don't have to *live* with them. At least have
somewhere where you can escape from them and regain your
strength in peace." I did not understand this attitude; in
fact I could not understand why the whole world did not
want to work in the Walled City. If someone passing through
Hong Kong said he was praying about finding work I always
thought, "You don't have to pray any longer. Can't you see
the Walled City? There it is." I did not want to be anywhere
else, yet I felt defensive about my work, exhausted but unable to escape the "maternal" obligations to my children.

Yet despite the confusion in my disorderly home I learned
that God would often use very young believers to encourage
me and the others. All those who became Christians received the power of the Spirit at the same time as they believed, just as Winson and Ah Ming had. We encouraged
them to share spiritual gifts when meeting together. So they
knew clearly that having these gifts was no cause for pride,
but a way of helping one another. One night we were praying
when one of those boys had a "prophecy"; he said that God
had given him the words to speak. "Go and pick the cab-
bages, and quickly catch the bus." It sounded a startling
message. My Cantonese still had some gaps, and it took a
few minutes' search through a dictionary before I found the
correct translation. "The harvest is ready; go out and work
to gather it in." There and then we went into the streets and
talked to the street sleepers round our alley. Impressed to
see people of his own background changed and starting a
new life, one of them prayed with us and later came off drugs
in our house.

I was also much heartened by the boys another time when
I arrived home exhausted and deeply worried about the
situation in the house. Mary had left; the two youth workers

had departed. I was feeling quite unable to manage the many converts plus a succession of boys referred by prison workers. I wondered if people in other countries could have the problems with new Christians that I did; because I certainly did not read about them.

"Please find me a nice, encouraging Bible verse," I asked the boys, feeling too tired to give them a teaching lesson. After thumbing through the Bible for some minutes the most encouraging thing any one of them could find was a very depressing text from Revelation. "Enough of that," I decided, "let's pray instead."

As we were praying I had a message in tongues and one of the boys interpreted it immediately. He had only been to school for a couple of years in his life. He could not read the Bible and he had only believed in Jesus for a few days before this event. But his interpretation was a clear, direct quotation from the Psalms:

> Those who sow in tears
> Will reap with songs of joy
> He who goes out weeping
> Carrying seed to sow
> Will return with songs of joy
> Carrying sheaves with him.
> Unless the Lord builds the house
> Its builders labour in vain.
> In vain you rise early
> And stay up late
> Toiling for food to eat—
> For he grants sleep to those he loves.
> N.I.V. (Psalms. 126, 127)

These spiritual babes through the working of the Holy Spirit were able to say exactly the right words to me at that time. Thus ministered to, I could not agree with those who considered spiritual gifts merely an optional extra. It was no wonder that St. Paul exhorted us to desire these gifts, for their purpose is to edify one another and thus glorify God.

I knew God would provide for me, but as the family in Lung Kong Road grew I was amazed to see our income grow too. Ever since I had stopped teaching full-time I found that I received all that I needed. I was able to pay for the rent, the Youth Club room and my language lessons. Sometimes a cheque would arrive in the post. Sometimes a friend would give exactly the same amount as I had been praying for. When I wanted to buy a rubber boat for a swimming expedition with the boys, a friend sent the right sum from England without knowing the need. Now while we never had enough money to pay for the next week's food or rent, we always had enough for each day. This was exhilarating for the boys who felt they had a real part in God's work when they prayed each morning for their daily bread. Sometimes an anonymous sack of rice would appear on the doorstep; on one occasion it was a coffee table.

Every Sunday after the morning meeting we invited many people to lunch with us all at Lung Kong Road. A number of guests needed the good meal so it was sad when one Sunday I had to tell the boys that we had no money for food.

"Boil the rice anyway and we'll pray for something to put on top," I said. Ten minutes before lunch a panting and sweating visitor arrived carrying tins of food and fresh bean sprouts. His Kowloon Bible class had made a collection for us on the spur of the moment and sent him with their gifts. The young man, William, enjoyed being an answer to prayer just as much as thirty of us enjoyed the huge meal only ten minutes later. It was an exciting way of life.

I committed many follies during these days, but God honoured the spirit in which I did them. One evening I had 'flu and was sitting at home feeling blurry, when in marched Geui Jai. He was a famous *kung-fu* fighter, having been the champion and renowned expert amongst the 14K Walled City brothers. He was one of the few who had received any education at all; he was clever and his English was good. He was also now a wreck of a drug addict, fallen both in status and usefulness to the gang. I often found him sleeping in the streets or staircases near my home because both his parents and his Triad brothers had kicked him out.

"Could you please lend me your typewriter, Miss Poon?" he asked me earnestly; "You see, I can get paid a little money if I help somebody with his Chinese translation and type a letter. This will give me enough money for my heroin today. So I won't have to steal it, or hold someone up."

I knew that he was hoping to quit drugs but the 'flu must have impaired my judgment. I let him take the typewriter on condition that he brought it back the same evening.

Later that night he rang up: "Miss Poon, I am sorry but I can't give it back quite yet, because I have been asked to do another job. Isn't that good? I have to type out two hundred invitations for a Lunar New Year party; please how do you spell lunar?"

This all sounded quite credible to me, until I put the phone down and had a think. How ridiculous; no one in Hong Kong types their letters two hundred times; it is so quick and easy to get them printed. Of course he had pawned it, and that was the last I would see of my typewriter.

Some of the other boys from the Walled City found out what Geui Jai had done and were very angry. They threatened to beat him up and hounded him, though I told them, "Never mind, all right, he has made a fool of me and I lost my typewriter, but so what? Jesus lost His life; a typewriter is nothing in comparison. I was willing to take the risk because I wanted to help him, and it's my fault, not his. Just forget about it." But I heard that he had to go on the run for some time, and that all the gangsters were angry with him.

Three months later God produced the first positive result. My typewriter appeared in the bookcase in my flat. I did not know how it had got there, so I questioned Ah Ping as to what happened. He finally admitted that Goko, when he heard what Geui Jai had done, had been so upset that he had sent his men after him. They found him and then demanded that he hand over the pawn-ticket. Then

Goko had gone to the pawn shop and paid his own money to redeem my typewriter. He then sent it back without a message.

Once more I sent an urgent demand to Goko for I wanted to thank him for what he had done. Once more we had a tea party. In this incongruous setting I talked to the powerful gang boss who ran illegal businesses with one hand and protected a missionary with the other.

"Thank you very much for the typewriter," I said avoiding his name for I felt that I could hardly address him as my brother, which his name implied.

"*Moe yeh, moe yeh.* It was nothing, nothing at all," he replied looking very embarrassed.

"You have touched my heart deeply," I continued, "so I would like to explain something to you."

Goko was puffing cigarettes furiously, lighting one before finishing another and then stubbing it out again after a few gasps. "Geui Jai is a bad boy—he should not have done that to you," he said.

"But you had no reason to redeem my typewriter yourself," I continued. "I am not your friend, I am against you and I have come here because I want to destroy what you stand for." Then I told him something of what Christ had done when He redeemed us with His own blood, buying back our lives with His own life while we were still His enemies. Goko listened and looked almost shy. Avoiding my eyes he paid the bill with a HK$500 note and fled. But he had listened to the story of redemption.

The second result was that Geui Jai's guilty conscience made him vulnerable. Once more during my wanderings I fell across the faded fighter sleeping on the pavements and staircases. He saw the change in Winson and Ah Ming and he was envious. His desire to be a new person grew until the day he prayed with us, went into Pastor Chan's centre and exchanged his syringe for a cross.

Those gangsters who had hounded Geui Jai could not dismiss what happened to him. He not only came off drugs but went to Bible school for some years and became a pastor.

Looking back at the experiences of those years in Lung Kong Road I have mixed emotions. It was a time of learning and of growing up: often I was in awful confusion. I find it easiest to express what I feel in the words of St. John, "A woman giving birth to a child has pain because her time has come; but when her baby is born she forgets the anguish because of her joy that a child is born into the world."

The pains of that time can be forgotten for they gave birth to many children and a partnership with the Willans. These brought me great joy.

Chapter Ten

Try Jesus

"Jean Stone Willans is a glamorous, vivacious lady. She has the gift of being able to 'speak in tongues', and she has just published the most lighthearted, entertaining book about religion that has ever been written. The book is *The Acts of the Little Green Apples* and describes the adventures of the Willans family—her husband, Rick, and daughter, Suzanne—after they came to the Far East. Mrs. Willans doesn't practise religion, she lives it. Also she seems to have established a way of communicating with God. This, she claims, is available to everyone; some people take advantage of it; some don't. The stand Jean Stone Willans takes is that if God is asking her to do His work, then He should make sure she is able to do so. Time and time again He does."

So wrote the *Hong Kong Standard* in July, 1973, describing Jean's hilarious book. I could echo its enthusiasm, for by this time Jean and Rick had become my very close friends and spiritual advisers. They taught me that God's good things were to be enjoyed, which surprised me, as I had been brought up to believe that missionaries should always have the least of everything and that it was virtuous to live in rags. The Willans had been through times of great poverty too, but certainly did not expect that God wished them to live like that forever. When they had beautiful possessions they took real pleasure in them, but were equally ready to give everything away if so directed. Maybe that is why they were such fun to be with—they had learned to be content whatever the circumstances. They were also the only people I knew with whom I could simply sit, pray all night, watch television, have a drink, play charades, or go out to a gourmet dinner—though I did know others with whom I could do one or two of those things . . .

We had discovered by this time that there was a remarkable similarity in our journeys to Hong Kong, since Jean and Rick too were called to the East through a dream and a prophecy. Their work in Hong Kong was in a completely different sphere; but meeting one of my boys changed this.

One day I was in Causeway Bay Magistracy listening to a case when I spotted David squatting in the dock. He was a friend of Ah Ming's whom I had met on the beach at Winson's baptism the previous year. David had planned to plead "not guilty" to his charges; however, when he saw me he suddenly had a pang of conscience, began to pray and pleaded "guilty". After hearing his case the judge decided to let him off and he came out of the court room in a daze. "Coffee?" I suggested as we walked out. In deference to my choice he and his colleagues by-passed the chicken's feet, entrails and other delicacies displayed in restaurant windows and joined me at a coffee-shop. David announced that he was ready to follow Jesus completely. Having seen the mess he had just emerged from in court I thought we should inform his gang boss that he would be leaving the Triads, since it would be so much better if he could make a complete break with the criminal world.

"Who is your *daih lo*, David?" I asked. He looked terrified and shifted about on his plastic seat.

"He won't want to see you."

"But what is his name?" I persisted.

"His nick-name is 'Jesus'," he said out of the side of his mouth hoping that the others sitting there had not heard him reveal all. "But he won't want to see you."

"Why don't you ask him? If you're going to be a Christian you can't follow two different leaders called Jesus. You must decide which one."

"O.K.," said David. "I'll try to find him," and he went to telephone. While we waited David's friends ate pink ice cream while I drank more cups of coffee. At last he came back looking surprised.

"He'll see you. You are to go to Block 20 of Chaiwan Resettlement Estate at midnight tonight and find the noodle stall. Someone will meet you there and take you to 'Jesus'. But you must take a hundred dollars."

"Why the hundred dollars?" I asked curiously.

"Well, nobody in Chaiwan knows you, Miss Poon," David replied. "It's not as if it were the Walled City where you are protected. Chaiwan is a very dangerous area at night and you might get mugged. If you have a hundred dollars then they will take it and leave you alone, but if you have nothing they will be angry and beat you up."

"Don't be silly," I reasoned, "I haven't got ten dollars, let alone a hundred. I'm not taking money—if I am on God's business then He will look after me. And anyway, if it would help you to understand how much God loves you then I wouldn't mind dying. I have nothing to lose."

David looked at me incredulously for a moment then said, "You're crazy! You're mad!" But he glanced at his friends and went on, "We never met anyone who would die for us before."

I arrived by minibus at eleven-thirty p.m. and spent a little time looking around Chaiwan. This enormous area at one end of Hong Kong Island consisted of resettlement blocks where tens of thousands of people were housed by the Government. Each family had one room to live, eat and sleep in, with communal toilets and showers at the end of each floor. Street level was humming with life and at night, hundreds of people sat on fold-up seats eating their *siu yeh* (bedtime snacks) at the shacks and portable noodle carts which abounded.

Midnight came; I was waiting at the Block 20 noodle stall which turned out to be down a narrow, dark corridor. Refuse had been tipped into the gutter below and there was a runnel of little grey noodles swimming past my sandals. I was absorbed in the noodle race and did not see my guide approach.

"What do you want?" The curly-haired Cantonese lolled against the wall and spoke through the cigarette stuck to his lips.

"Take me to your leader," I replied clutching my huge evangelical Bible firmly.

"Who do you want to see?" He was testing me.

"I want to see 'Jesus'."

"Why do you want to see Jesus?"

"I want to tell him about my Jesus."

This man looked amused then laughed to himself. "Are you *sure* you want to see Jesus?" He meant to sound sinister, but it all felt like part of a bad film to me.

"I'm sure."

"What do you want to talk about?"

"I want to tell him about my Jesus," I repeated.

The man changed legs, shut his eyes and with a very camp gesture thumbed himself as he grimaced — "You're talking to him." It was a very ham B movie.

"Jesus" and I sat in a cafe while I opened my big Bible and told him about my Jesus. Something happened whilst we were sitting there. He understood what I was saying. He simply understood it all. It was almost as if the Holy Spirit had come down over our formica table. "Jesus" sat there with the tears streaming down his cheeks quite oblivious of his surroundings or the pretty waitress. He prayed, asking Jesus into his life and was baptized in the Spirit in the midst of our coffee cups.

It was about three a.m. when I left Chaiwan to catch a van back to Kowloon City and my neglected flat. Just before the van left I remembered my discipleship training.

"Oh, by the way, you are supposed to tell at least one

other person that you have believed in Christ today." I sped off after having fixed an appointment with him for the next day.

When I saw him the next afternoon at a friend's apartment I hardly recognized the old "Jesus". He looked bright and keen, unlike the seedy villain of last night's movie.

"Did you tell one person that you believed last night?" I asked eagerly.

"No, I didn't," he replied. Disappointment gonged in my heart. But he continued, "I told my whole gang. We stayed up until six in the morning looking at the verses you underlined in the Bible, and now they all want to believe, too."

The prostitute kissed Jesus' feet and poured perfume on them. The demon-possessed man who was healed sat dressed and in his right mind at Jesus' feet. The woman who had been bleeding for twelve years touched His cloak and when it was discovered that her bleeding had stopped, fell at His feet trembling. There are as many descriptions of encounters with Jesus as there are Christians but no one who has not made that encounter for himself will ever understand the wonder. I wanted to jump, sing, dance, and join in the celebration which was going on in heaven in front of the angels: big bold braying brass and spiced woodwind striving with millions of desks of strings in a wonderful symphony of praise . . .

However I was still in Hong Kong very much on earth, and standing before me the clear-eyed Triad looked expectant. He had brought a *sai lo*, Sai Keung, with him, who had been there at the dawn discussion. Sai Keung did not want to discuss any more; he wanted to know how he could receive the power of Jesus like his *daih lo*; so he too received Jesus and the gift of His Spirit. I always told the boys that as they believed, Christ would give them the gift of a new tongue to help them pray—I no longer expected it to happen automatically as in Winson's case. These new believers accepted easily that if they were going to follow a powerful God it would be quite in character for Him to give them a new language to help them talk to Him. Every single one received this gift so there was no confusion about some being more spiritual than others. To avoid problems, whenever possible I avoided laying hands on a young man myself, but encouraged other Christian boys to do this so that they would know that the gift came from God Himself and that even young Christians could pray with others to receive.

Sai Keung looked radiant. He was a short stocky individual never given to long speeches but he warmly encouraged me to go back to Chaiwan the next night to talk with the others.

I went back that night and many nights afterwards. We met in the back of a photograph shop, or in the concrete park and the number of enquiries increased dramatically. We had Bible studies at noodle stores, prayer meetings in camera shops and evangelistic meetings on tenement staircases. Some of the Chaiwan gang joined the Lung Kong Road home and others joined the Willans' meetings. The work was expanding beyond the borders of the Walled City to reach people in other areas.

As was my custom I asked "Jesus" (now re-named Christian) to introduce me to his own big brother. I had the usual response.

"He won't want to talk to you. He's much too important. He controls many different areas besides Chaiwan and has hundreds of followers. If we want to speak to him we don't even know where to find him. Sometimes we don't see him for weeks. He's too busy. Forget it."

I learned that this emperor among gang leaders was named Ah Kei. I agreed that I would not try to force a meeting with him, but Christian was under instructions to pray for him and Jean and Rick also put in overtime on his behalf. We all had a feeling he was to be an important part of our ministry. I carried round sets of Bibles ready for any emergency.

The time was twelve-fifteen a.m.; the location a Chaiwan street stall, the cast Miss Poon, "Jesus" and the Chaiwan believers. The fluorescent lamps cast a hard pool of light against the blackness of the night. Ah Kei emerged from the shadows in a belligerent mood.

"Poon Siu Jeh," he challenged (though no one had introduced us) "if you can convert me I'll give you a thousand disciples." He enjoyed thus throwing down the gauntlet; indeed it was almost as if we were preparing for a duel as he stood there in his black leather gloves, sneering.

"I can't convert you, Ah Kei," I replied. It was obvious whom I was talking to by the awed reaction of our seconds. "If you believe in Jesus that is your decision. And you cannot tell your *sai los* to believe in Jesus; they will have to decide this for themselves."

We were in for a long night. Ah Kei had heard rumours of what had been happening in Chaiwan and if there was going to be a revival he wanted to control it. Sitting down at our table he ordered dishes and dishes of expensive food and drink. He scattered his largesse, conspicuously inviting all around him to eat. He would make sure we all knew how many hundreds of dollars he spent—how generous he was. He ate nothing himself and cared little if I were hungry or not; this was an exhibition.

I showed him pictures of Ah Mo looking fat and healthy now he was off drugs. Ah Kei knew him well as they used to deal together. He became rather thoughtful and after the meal invited me to accompany him alone to a secret destination where he had something to show me.

We began to walk toward the shanty town area whose vice he controlled. He was carrying his mackintosh slung over one shoulder and turned to me suddenly, "Poon Siu Jeh, do you look down on drug addicts?"

I thought that a difficult question to answer without appearing condescending, except for a Christian.

"No, I don't, Ah Kei, because they are the people Jesus came into the world for."

"Are you willing to be friends with one?" he asked, and both he and I knew to which one he was referring.

"Actually the people in the Walled City criticize me because I am more willing to be friends with an addict than with someone who thinks his life is all right," I replied.

By this time we had come to an unlighted path which led through the shanty shacks. We walked on in silence until Ah Kei stopped by the outside of a tin hut. The darkness outside gave no hint of the brilliant lighting inside, and when Ah Kei pushed through the blackout material curtain I found myself staring at dozens of surprised gamblers. The door watchers came up to us—although this was one of Ah Kei's own dens they were obviously worried by the presence of a strange Western lady at three in the morning. Ah Kei held up his hand for silence; there was a hush.

"Don't be afraid," he said, "she doesn't look down on us, she's a Christian and she's come to tell us about Jesus." He then gave me the floor and invited me to preach.

Afterwards he took me into his opium den next door. Inside the den was a terrible spectacle—there were little grey and yellow old men lying on a low platform covered with grime and slime. There were half empty cups of green tea and large spittoons filled with sordid saliva and sediment. The men lay like giant stick insects, more limbs than body, and half of them were insensible. The "weatherman" sitting at the door looked very alarmed until Ah Kei spoke. He repeated what he had said before; "Don't be afraid. She doesn't look down upon us. She's a Christian. She's come to tell us about Jesus."

All those who were actually conscious listened carefully to what I had to say and when I left I gave them a pile of my Chinese Bibles and translations of *The Cross and the Switchblade*.

To have spoken about Jesus in two of these dens was amazing itself, but now Ah Kei became a determined evangelist; he insisted that together we visit more of his empire of drug, vice, and gambling dens. We travelled from Chaiwan to Shaukiwan and then visited Lyemun, Kwun Tong, and Ngautaukok. In each place he introduced me as a Christian, and each time I was heard with respect. It was an amazing journey into vice. I scattered Chinese Bibles as I went.

In one of those dens they brought me a man doubled up with pain, whose face was contorted with suffering.

"Poon Siu Jeh, are you a doctor—are you a nurse—do you have any money—can you take him to hospital? He is in agony." They thought every Westerner was either rich or medically trained.

"No, I'm not a doctor or a nurse and I don't have any money to take him to hospital—but I tell you what I can do. I'll pray for him," I said. They sniggered at this but they agreed to find us a little room at the back where it was quiet. Then they stood around waiting curiously to see what I was going to do.

"I'll pray for him on one condition," I announced. "No one is to laugh because I'm going to talk to the living God." Complete silence.

I laid my hands on the sick man and prayed for him in Jesus' name. His stomach immediately relaxed and he got up looking surprised. He had been completely healed. Everyone else looked a bit surprised too; one of them asked, "Is this the living God—the One you've been telling us about?" They began to believe, because they saw through His works of power who Jesus was.

At the end of the evening—it was nearly morning—I gave Ah Kei a Bible and wrote in it, "To Ah Kei, my friend; I pray one day you'll be my brother." He might have laughed inwardly, "Huh—brother! Some hope," but he thanked me politely—he was still handing out favours. He had no intention of reading it and it was in fact strange that I had given him a Bible at all knowing how such men hated to read.

For the next three months I followed Ah Kei around. He had a wife and family but used to sleep wherever he found himself late at night—often on a staircase. He got so high on drugs one night that he even read two pages of *The Cross and the Switchblade*, two pages of *Run Baby Run*, and then two pages of the Bible in turn for two days. He began to confide in me and told me how much he regretted marrying so young—he already had three children under five. My sympathy was rather with his wife for having a young family and a husband who never came home.

Sometimes Ah Kei would sleep for three days at a time. At other times he would not sleep at all. During these binges he would go through a fantastic amount of money. He was being fed drugs all the time by his gang members. God told me which staircase he was sleeping on, and after a while each time I found him he had a hunted look. "Oh, it's not you again, I mean, how did you know I was here?"

Meanwhile I had armies of Christians all around Hong Kong praying for him; this had to have an effect. And so one day when I caught up with him he said, "God's been talking to me."

"What do you mean, God's been talking to you?" I asked crossly. I was annoyed because I thought he was joking.

"Yes, God has been talking to me," he insisted. "I've been reading in the Bible and it says He gives Special Grace to people like me." He almost preened himself at "Special Grace".

"What do you mean by Special Grace?" I enquired.

"It says in the Bible that if you've sinned the most you get forgiven the most." He sounded so privileged that I almost felt jealous, but he was completely serious about this discovery and was ready to ask for the Special Grace. We were in a hut next door to the gambling den he had originally taken me to. Ah Kei sat down on the floor and I sat down in the darkness too hoping I had avoided the cockroaches. We prayed together for the first time and Ah Kei asked Jesus to take his life and make him a new person. He believed that Jesus died for him, but at that point he had very little sense of sin and was still rather proud of his past.

I rushed across the harbour to Mei Foo where Jean and Rick were living. I knew they would be delighted to meet Ah Kei after praying for him so long and even more pleased that he had become a Christian.

We had a party, a grand celebration of Ah Kei's first birthday. Sarah, the Willans' Australian friend, and their daughter, Suzy, were there too and shared in our gladness. We usually prayed at parties and as Ah Kei had not yet received the gift of the Spirit we told him that God gives this power to all who follow Him. All of us sitting round began to pray together in the Spirit and when he heard this Ah Kei suddenly fell forward onto his knees with a terrible thump; afterwards he told us that when he heard the tongues he was knocked down by the awareness of his past life of robbery, drug pushing and selling girls into prostitution. As he gained this terrible sense of his own sin he felt that he could no longer sit in front of God, he had to kneel; and he began to pray in tongues. It was a near impossible sight of a Triad boss on his knees; in Chinese culture it is the most servile of positions and a gang leader lowered himself to no one.

As he continued to pray in tongues the Willans' parrot, Sydney, triumphantly extricated himself from his cage and flying across the room alighted on Ah Kei's head. For some time afterwards he was rather confused about the Holy Spirit and doves since his had been a heaven-sent parrot. That same night we took a taxi to a beach where Rick baptized Ah Kei in the sea.

During the weeks before his conversion, when I was getting to know him, Ah Kei and I sometimes settled down to read the Bible in a wooden shack at three a.m. or so. He told me that he would not believe in Jesus in a hurry because if he built a house quickly it would fall down just as fast. But the night he was baptized he began to put his life in order immediately. He went home to his wife for the first time in many months. She looked as if she would like to believe Ah Kei had changed but she had such a deep distrust of her husband that she was afraid it would all turn out a forlorn hope.

Ah Bing had married Ah Kei seven years previously. Their courtship could not have started more badly; Ah Kei met her at a party and seduced her in order to sell her as a prostitute. But he fell in love with her and decided to keep her instead, which was only temporarily to her advantage. Years of neglect then reduced this once pretty girl to a careless sloven who kept their tiny resettlement room in a filthy state.

In a way Ah Bing was right to be cynical, for when Ah Kei decided to build his Christian house it demanded too great a cost. He not only relinquished his vast illegal income and control over men, with no alternative source of cash to care for his family, but also had to face coming off opium and heroin.

He did not come off drugs and I did not know what to do about it. Some addicts who became Christians were delivered instantly, while others went to Pastor Chan's centre to withdraw where there was a greater amount of after-care. Ah Kei applied to this centre and others but was refused admittance because there was no place available. What could I say to him, "Pray, Ah Kei and you'll get off drugs miraculously?" I had seen God do this and did not understand why He did not do it every time. I could say, "Pray and perhaps you will cut down gradually." That would be compromise. I could try, "Pray and maybe God will give you money for your heroin." But surely God did not support drug habits.

I could not take Ah Kei into my house for it was already full of boys who either were supposed to have quit heroin already or had come out of prison officially drug-free. I wondered what was happening in that house sometimes— some of the residents behaved very strangely—and I certainly did not want to mix an open drug-taker with them. Instead I encouraged Ah Kei with a weak, "God will work it out," and hoped that he would get into a withdrawal centre sooner or later.

Just before Christmas I was awakened by a four-thirty a.m. telephone call. (They always seemed to choose the middle of the night.) I never liked to sound as if I had just woken up— my solution was to clear my throat and practise saying, "Good morning—good morning!" very brightly so that by the time I picked up the receiver I sounded like the bird of the dawn.

Ah Kei was in no mood for sunrise salutations. He had rung to say goodbye.

"Thank you, Poon Siu Jeh, for these past nine months of Jesus talk, your care and consideration; but my gang brothers were right all along. I can't be saved."

"Yes, you can, Ah Kei. Anything is possible with God." I meant it sincerely, but my words sounded weak to my own ears.

"It's no good. I can't be a Christian any more."

"What do you mean, you can't be a Christian?"

"I can't afford it. I've given up running the gangs, I've given up running the girls, the gambling and the drugs. Now I have nothing left to live on. I can't afford to be a Christian. Thank you very much, Miss Poon, for everything you have done; I'll never forget you but I will not be seeing you again. It just didn't work."

I tried desperately to reason with him, I dragged up every argument I could think of—I hunted around for suitable texts. We could not lose him. If I could keep him talking maybe the trouble would all go away. But Ah Kei's voice sounded harder and harder and he was impossible to reach. He was far colder than before he had become a Christian and he started to speak cruelly and bitterly. I could hear him carrying on a simultaneous argument with someone at the other end and then he said he was going out to find Ah Chuen to kill him.

"Ah Kei, you can't kill people. You're a Christian." He was long past listening to my pathetic interjections. He was high on heroin and having furiously informed me that he would shortly be forced to do a couple of robberies to raise some money, he rang off.

I stared at the phone in the gloom. I really could not believe what I had heard. I did not want to accept the fact that someone who had believed in Christ could contemplate murder. Quickly I rang up Jean and Rick. They knew that both Ah Kei and I had a talent for the dramatic but soon listened with deep concern.

"You've got to get up and pray. I think Ah Kei is going out to murder someone and he's planned a couple of robberies." There are not many people I could do that to at that time of night. The Willans prayed.

I prayed despairingly all through the Christmas celebrations. I cried all through the Christmas carols. " 'Joy to the world?" I thought tragically. "It doesn't look very joyful to me." Because I was grieved for Ah Kei I was also a little angry with God.

"Lord, I really believed You were the answer. How can it be that he knew You and then didn't want You? You didn't do everything You were supposed to either, Lord, did You? I mean, Ah Kei believed in You and others did too and look at them now. There are a load of addicts and spiritual cripples lying around the streets being a reproach to Christ. People look at them and mock, 'What a God—He started a miracle but it didn't last; it was something that came and went.' "

I hunted for any Christian who could reassure me that when Christ began a good work in someone, He would carry it to completion. I believed this was true but it certainly did not look as if God were doing His part right then.

Some days later Ah Kei turned up on my doorstep. "I don't know why I've come—I was just passing—but anyway, goodbye."

"Wait a moment," I said, "what about the robberies?"

"Well," said Ah Kei looking rather sheepish, "my wife got the pillow cases all ready, hoods for our armed robbery, slits cut in them so we could see through. The first time we got everybody together we found that one of my own gang had given the game away. So we couldn't do it. Then the second time we were sitting in the car all prepared with knives. We were ready to drive off but I just did not feel like doing a robbery that day so we didn't go."

He had also been unable to find Ah Chuen the night he

had telephoned me. I thought it was now time we did something positive about Ah Kei's future.

"Right," I said, "we are now going to see the Willans; you have got to talk to them. It's time someone was firm with you."

We left the house and on the way Ah Kei bought a gift of oranges wrapped in pink paper. He presented it to Jean and Rick and we all ate dinner together. As usual Jean was extremely hospitable but I could see she was becoming more and more annoyed at a situation where a true believer was not coming off drugs.

"Do you have any problems?" she asked him while I translated.

"Oh no, no problems," he said airily and then added, "well, just one; I'm still on heroin."

"When we were in Indonesia and had no money," Jean continued firmly, "we prayed and it simply appeared before us. If you are really serious about Jesus He will do anything you ask."

"I'm serious," nodded Ah Kei.

"Well, would you like to stay here and withdraw from heroin?" Jean asked. I was amazed; this was what I had hoped for and longed for but never dared to suggest as I knew how precious the peace of her home was to Jean. She herself had never meant to suggest it either, but concern for Ah Kei's future and the Spirit of God worked together in her to bring out an invitation which surprised her.

"I agree," said Ah Kei. He opened up his jacket, took out some red paper packets of heroin and flushed them down the lavatory bowl.

Next Ah Kei made some dramatic gestures; first we went back to his resettlement home, where he tore down the idols his mother kept and threw them out of the room. Then he reached under the bed and dragged out a box containing several weeks' supply of heroin. He washed it all down the lavatory while we watched. Finally we took him back to the Willans' flat in the Mei Foo district where he climbed into bed.

Jean called a Christian doctor and asked what to expect
from a ten-year addict with a hundred dollar-a-day habit.
The doctor said that without medication Ah Kei would
suffer agonies, accompanied by chills, fever, vomiting, diarrhoea, and intense stomach cramps. He might roll on the
floor with pain and become violent to the point of attacking
his helpers. He did not advise it—but if Jean insisted on her
course of action he would come round and administer a
substitute drug, methadone.

"We will try Jesus," said Jean refusing his offer, and so
began the experiment.

I spent three sleepless nights sitting with Ah Kei; I expected all the terrible side effects forecast, but he slept like a
baby. At the end of three days I looked haggard and un-
kempt and he looked wonderful. If, when he did wake, he
experienced any twinge of pain, we quickly urged him to
pray in tongues, and the pain miraculously disappeared.
Now we knew without a shadow of doubt that praying in the
Spirit was the answer for painless withdrawal from heroin.
Ah Kei was able to eat well too and ordered cheese sandwiches which he swallowed voraciously.

After four days Ah Kei's wife came round to see him. She
tried to persuade him to go home as he was cured. We
opposed this firmly; he still needed care and a drug-free
environment. Fortunately he was suddenly seized by withdrawal effects, sensations of terrible cold followed by feelings of tremendous heat. As Ah Kei had once before tried un-
successfully to withdraw from heroin in China, he knew how
terrible the pains could be. We all went back to praying in
the Spirit to obtain relief and as we worshipped God the
pains left him. Again God had delivered him. On the fifth
day Ah Kei knew he was free from heroin, but he still badly
wanted to smoke; he did not want to give up cigarettes. Rick
insisted that if he did not free himself from tobacco addiction
as well, then he was not free. Ah Kei was very unhappy
about this, and on the seventh day he persuaded the
Willans' Buddhist maid to give him a couple of filter-tips.
Almost immediately he felt the pains he should have felt

during his heroin withdrawal. All of us redoubled our prayer effort. And once he was willing to agree to Rick's demand the pain disappeared.

Throughout his withdrawal period and for the next few months I was commuting between my own house and Mei Foo, because the miracle of Ah Kei's healing was repeated with several of his friends. Jean took Ah Kei to the Hilton to get his hair cut; there he ran into his old friend, Wahchai, whom he had introduced into the crime rackets years earlier. He persuaded him to come back to the Willans' flat and we had an impromptu meeting. During the meeting I had a message in tongues, but there was no interpretation. As St. Paul says there has to be an interpretation every time someone has a message in tongues, we waited and waited but no one spoke. Finally Wahchai admitted that he had had an interpretation but had been afraid to speak; he could not believe that God would use him because he was still on drugs, even though he had recently been converted and received the gift of the Spirit. As he told us the interpretation of my message he began to weep uncontrollably. After that it was only a matter of sitting with him while he had a painless withdrawal from heroin; as with Ah Kei, whenever he had pains, he began to pray in the Spirit and so felt better.

At the following Thursday night prayer meeting yet another boy who had accepted Jesus asked for the power of Christ to free him from his addiction. After the prayer meeting was over I suggested that he come off drugs that very night. By this time the Willans' flat was full, so we rented a room for him in one of the apartment houses generally used as a brothel, and I sat up with him all night praying. For the next four days other boys in our group sat and prayed with him until he had completely withdrawn. We took two hourly shifts all day and night, quite confusing the proprietors of the "hotel" who were used to quite a different kind of clientele. Then when he was clear he went and spent a week in the Willans' flat to complete his rehabilitation.

Two weeks later Ah Kei decided to go off and spend a

week in China. A whole group of us went to see him off at the railway station; when he arrived at the Chinese border the Chinese security guards wanted to know who the people were who had seen him off at the Kowloon station. He replied that there was an American (Rick), an English girl (me) and his Chinese friends. "Who," they asked, "were the Westerners?"

"Ah, they are the people who told me about Jesus Christ," he replied cheerfully.

"All right, answer us this," the guards replied, "who are better, Chinese people or Westerners?"

Ah Kei replied, "Well, being Chinese I naturally think Chinese are better, but these Westerners are Christians and so they are very good. In fact, I find I like them very much." At this point the guards, who may have belonged to some kind of special security branch, revealed that they knew exactly who Ah Kei was. They knew he often tried to smuggle drugs across the border, and that he was a leader in the Triad groups.

"Why are you not trying to smuggle drugs this time?" they demanded. "Who are these Westerners; what are their names? How did you get involved with them?" The questioning was relentless.

Ah Kei was completely frank with his questioners. He explained that he was off heroin because the Westerners had told him about Jesus and had prayed with him. He explained that he had left his Triad gang and given up criminal activities.

Instead he was starting work in an office in March. The security men refused to believe him, saying that, of course, he could not have come off drugs; the Chinese opium wars had proved that no one can escape from addiction. Ah Kei insisted that he had been free from drugs for the past six weeks, and that now he believed in Jesus Christ he was a new person. The security men asked if he had achieved this result with medicine. He explained that he had used no medicines; the whole cure had been effected with Jesus and the

Bible. At this the security men bristled and said that it was impossible; clearly the Westerners were exploiting him. This was Ah Kei's cue to launch into a full scale testimony of what Christ had done for him and he talked for nearly an hour; the security men listened in quite a friendly way to the news, then allowed him to cross the border into China carrying with him his Bible. When he arrived at his village he discovered one Christian Chinese girl who did not know much about the Scriptures because she had never had a Bible. Ah Kei gave her his, and the word spread.

Once Ah Kei had become a Christian he began to tell the good news to all his family, who one by one accepted it. Ah Bing's father was so pleased to see the change in his son-in-law that he too became a Christian and was baptized with the Spirit. The dinner he gave us all to celebrate this was truly memorable; quail eggs with strips of breast of chicken; beef with mushrooms; stuffed boneless roast duck; corn soup; braised duck's feet with another type of mushroom; boneless pork fried in sweet soy sauce; steamed fish; sweet peanut soup and pastries. Afterwards the father rose to his feet and announced, "Once I was young and now I am old, but never before have I seen a bad man become a good man."

Chapter Eleven

The Houses of Stephen

Text of Testimony by Daniel, from my house in Lung Kong Road:

Before I introduce myself, I thank our Lord Jesus for rescuing me from my past and for giving me a new wonderful life in Him. My Chinese name is Ah Lam and my English name is Daniel. I don't mind which name you choose to call me by.

The reason I mentioned thanking our Lord Jesus is because I was a very bad person. I remember about ten years ago when I was just fourteen years old I left school and joined a Triad gang. The reason I joined was because I wanted to be respected, known and feared and I felt that being a Triad member would give me all this. So I dropped out from the normal way of life and began living in the underground (underworld I mean). One year later I was arrested and charged with armed robbery—I was sentenced to a Training Centre for young offenders for a period of nine months to three years.

At the time I really regretted what I did and I felt sorry and miserable. I decided then to change, to turn over a new leaf, to live a decent life as soon as I left prison. But upon my discharge, instead of living a decent life as I planned I became worse; got more deeper into crime; and went around with my old friends, back to the same places. I felt a big emptiness inside me. I wanted to forget everything and so I turned to big H (heroin).

I was heavily addicted. I tried to get off drugs a couple of times but never made it. It was by a stroke of luck—or more likely fate—that I came to know Jesus and I repented and accepted Him as my Saviour. I felt different—how can I explain it? (Words would never be able to justify my feeling.) It was as if I was released from something, as if a heavy burden was lifted from my shoulder, I felt free, wonderful. It was really a beautiful experience which I'll never forget and I can truly say I have never looked back and had cause to look back since that day. He has given me so much and I have learnt so much from Him, like patience, humbleness, love, etc. and I am learning more every day. It is a very exciting life and I thank Jesus for making all this possible.

I hope and pray you will be able to have the same experience as I have had and only then you will fully understand what my testimony is all about.

May God bless you,
Ah Lam

This was written by one of the criminals who flocked to see me or the Willans after hearing what had happened to Ah Kei. Word quickly spread along the addict grapevine that if they were willing to believe in Jesus they would receive some kind of power which enabled them to kick drugs painlessly. Addicts queued up to be admitted to Jean and Rick's house.

I tried to avoid taking them into my Lung Kong Road house. It was so near the Walled City that in thirty seconds or so a desperate addict could find an unlimited supply of heroin or opium. Also it was possible for him to jump off our roof into the next door flat, and knowing this made the junkie feel less safe in our care. In Jean and Rick's flat we gave them no option of escape. There was a secure double lock on the door, the windows were barred and there was at least one person on watch twenty-four hours of the day.

A young man brought to my house by a priest said, "I've seen what happens to addicts when they go to Miss Pullinger and I would like to try, but I'm a bit worried about the Jesus bit."

The priest replied, "Don't worry about that! Jackie won't push it." He could not have been more wrong; if we did not "push" Jesus then we had nothing to offer the junkie. He would suffer agonies through withdrawal if he could not pray. Medication only postponed pain. I had once seen six strong boys sitting on top of Little Cat when he was trying to kick drugs alone. He was a small boy, but when the need for drugs came on him he was suddenly strong enough to overthrow those six and run half-crazed.

However, we never had to face the problem of the junkies being unwilling to believe in Jesus; they did not come to us until they were ready to believe since they knew the way we worked. Their numbers grew until Jean and Rick's house was always more than full. Several times I was obliged to hire a room in a brothel, where there were washing facilities, a plentiful supply of Chinese tea and locks on the doors. There were drawbacks, too, beginning with registration . . .

Obviously we needed a place solely for the addicts to come off drugs and stay afterwards so that they could grow up as Christians. Most of them had been seriously disturbed people before they became addicted and they needed and demanded constant attention.

Involvement with Ah Kit, one of Ah Kei's relatives, brought our need for a secure house to a head. Having been off drugs for only a few days, he decided that he would like to control his own life again and left the Willans' house. All of us prayed that he would end up in a place where he could not continue his life of drugs and crime and would return to Jesus. This prayer was answered impressively—he was arrested and put behind bars. He underwent a real change of heart and genuinely repented in prison. He began to pray and talk to his cell mates about Christ as he waited for his case to come to court. He was charged with armed robbery.

At the trial, the judge commented that Ah Kit had an appalling record and well deserved a long sentence. However he heard Jean's account of Ah Kit's change of heart; and taking into account her willingness to care for him, the judge released him to our care for eighteen months.

The judge's clerk, the court officers, and prison officers looked aghast. The judge had actually done the impossible in legal terms when he released a man on such a charge. We knew differently, since two rows of us were sitting in court praying.

We took Ah Kit home to Mei Foo. On our way out we overheard the prison wardens asking one another whether it was not more powerful to have a God than a lawyer . . .

Ah Kit began very slowly to grow up as a Christian. He loved staying in the Willans' house, but he demanded twenty-four-hour attention. After a life of neglect he yearned for love—to him this was having someone talking to him all the time and being given exactly the same presents as Suzy, the Willans' daughter. Should Jean turn to talk to someone else or settle down to do her own letter writing he felt rejected. This caused such a strain on the family that Jean finally found seventeen-year-old Suzy packing her bags.

"Either the addicts go or I go," she said and meant it. She was a serious Christian but no family could survive that pressure for long.

The time had come to find a new place which had a home atmosphere, plenty of love and a twenty-four-hour surveillance by workers committed full-time to looking after the boys.

I was visiting my family in England when the Willans telegrammed the news. They had found it! Someone reading Jean's book had been so inspired that he made available a sum of money for renting a flat which was to be especially devoted to helping drug addicts who wanted to start a new life in Christ.

Society of Stephen was the name chosen by the Willans' prayer group in Hong Kong to publish literature, and later registered in the U.S.A. as a Church recognized by the State and Federal Government. As more and more criminals were being helped by the combined efforts of the Willans and myself we needed an official body through which to operate when dealing with rent laws, court cases and other official matters. So we became known throughout the addict subculture as "Stephen", and by the rest of the world as S.O.S. We called the new flat Stephen's Third House, mine having been the first and Mei Foo the second.

The first full-time worker was Diane Edwards, an American from Hawaii. She was a former Maryknoll nun who had spent five years in Hong Kong and spoke fluent Cantonese; she had been baptized in the Spirit several years before at the Willans' meetings. We sent a telegram to her in Hawaii which read, "PLEASE COME STOP HELP NEW DRUG CENTRE STOP WE LOVE YOU." Knowing that she would receive no salary but that we would share everything we had with her, Diane arrived back in Hong Kong within a week.

We began with one resident, but within a few weeks had increased to six and more were clamouring for admission. As each boy arrived the miracle was repeated: he came to Christ and came off drugs painlessly when he prayed in the language of the Spirit. Ah Kei and his family moved in to assist Diane run the house as it expanded even further . . .

By Christmas there were seventeen people in the tiny apartment with four boys sleeping on the floor. We began to pray for yet another place, a fourth house, by New Year to accommodate those waiting to come in. It was so hard to refuse them admission when we knew how simple it was to come off drugs with Jesus' power.

The Saturday meetings at the Willans' flat grew so large that they moved to a larger place on Hong Kong Island near Third House. Sometimes a hundred and fifty people including ministers, professors, priests and nuns would gather together with our Triads and ex-junkies. At the New Year's

Eve meeting we prayed a prayer of faith that God would give us the new house by the New Year and thanked Him in advance for it. We had no inkling of anywhere at that moment.

After the meeting was over at ten-thirty p.m. an English friend asked me why we were still praying and had not yet rented the new house.

"We either need the promise of some rent money, the gift of a flat or assurance from God that we should sign a lease without actually having any money," I said.

He announced, "I put the money in a special account for you two weeks ago."

So we sent a couple of boys straight out to look for places. They came back immediately having found a neighbouring flat empty and we had settled the rent with the apartment watchman by eleven-thirty p.m. All this in Hong Kong, which is surely one of the most difficult places in the world to find accommodation of any sort. We sealed the deal by seeing in the New Year with a prayer meeting in the new house. It was the most memorable watchnight service of my life.

Through praying with Ah Kei and the other addicts, I now knew that one did not have to wait until God "accidentally" delivered junkies. I saw that provided he was willing, a man could be freed through the power which Christ gave him as he prayed in the words of His Spirit. We never forced the addict to pray when going through withdrawal; it is impossible that anyone can ever be forced to pray. We simply reduced the alternatives to nil, or rather to one alternative, of suffering.

A very well-known syndicate operator from Shep Kip Mei had prayed a prayer of faith in Christ and been filled with the Spirit just before entering one of the houses, but refused to pray when his withdrawal pains started.

On the second day he packed his bags and announced that he was leaving. I refused to allow it because I believed that he had been sincere when he said that he wanted to follow Christ and come off drugs. When he rebelled it was only the heroin talking.

"You can't keep me here, you have no right," objected the Triad leader. He was not used to being crossed.

"Yes, I can," I replied. "You asked us to help you start a new life and that is what we will do. We would be selling you short if we allowed you to leave as soon as you felt pain."

"I'm leaving." He was adamant and moved purposefully toward the door where I was standing.

"You will feel much better if you pray."

"I've decided I don't want to follow Jesus after all. You can't stop me, I'm leaving."

"Well, you can choose one of four ways," I told him and counted them on my fingers. "You can knock me out and steal the keys; you can jump off the roof; you can stay here and suffer; or you can stay here and pray. But you are not leaving without my permission. You will have to step across me first."

I watched him weighing up the alternatives. A powerful man such as he did not use violence on women, it was beneath his dignity. The roof would kill him, so he stayed and sulked in his bedroom. The awful suffering drove him under his *mintoi* and finally he was so desperate that he prayed. As soon as he began the pain went and he slept peacefully. Next time he was threatened with pain he prayed. For a couple of days he was too stubborn to admit to us that it worked. When the withdrawal period was quite through he allowed himself to confess that he had prayed by himself in tongues and was now prepared to do so with other people.

Few of the junkies apart from Walled City boys had had any exposure to Christianity before coming off drugs. Far from being a hindrance this actually helped them. Now they would arrive saying, "I have heard how Ah Kei (or some other friend) has changed. He says it's Jesus who did it. I think Ah Kei is the meanest addict I know. If Jesus can change that one He can change me too."

Their faith did not depend upon any understanding of theological concepts but upon the seeing of Jesus working in others and the willingness to let Him work in their lives too. Each time they prayed they were answered and their faith grew as they were healed.

Those who explained this extraordinary spiritual happening as an example of "mind over matter" had to be ignorant of the facts. A drug addict facing withdrawal has a mind already half dead through continual drug abuse and is deeply fearful of pain. Most of our boys began to understand Jesus with their minds only after they had already experienced Him in their lives and bodies. Understanding of the Saviour, the Cross, forgiveness and redemption came some time after they had already obtained the benefits of these truths.

With four houses to run, plus the Youth Club in the Walled City and the meetings at Chaiwan we needed more and more full-time help. Doreen Cadney, an English nurse, came to assist and Gail Castle came back from the States. Several volunteers from Hong Kong and England helped for short periods and then Sarah Searcy gave up her paid job to be responsible for running the houses.

In another sense the work became easier and easier since the boys who had come off drugs themselves were very good at helping the "new boys". They happily cooked meals, did housework and had endless patience, sitting with the new arrivals encouraging them to pray and praying with them. Having recently been through withdrawal their faith was high. They were listened to with some respect when they said, "It works. Once you begin to pray the pain goes. Just ask Jesus and pray in the Spirit."

It was a balmy time. Boys arrived to get off drugs almost daily. Having seen the change in them, many "decent" people were so impressed that they began to believe too. One High Court Judge even bought our Christmas dinner after contact with boys who had become Christians.

People came to my flat at all hours with problems and went away as Christians baptized in the Spirit. We held Sunday morning meetings in Lung Kong Road which were jammed with students, Walled City boys, ex-junkies and visitors who had come to ask for healing or counsel. Sometimes I could not manage to see them all until six p.m. So I would ask the other Christians there to talk and pray with them.

For many years I had tried to do all the jobs and ministries by myself because there had been no other help available, but now we all began to share the task. Now I began to understand the meaning of the "body of Christ" for the first time as each person fulfilled a different function in the over-all work we had been called to. I found I was not indispensable after all especially in the running of the houses, which Jean managed with fairness, extraordinary spiritual discernment and a great talent for fun.

We learnt it was a long term job to turn an addict into a responsible member of society. In my Lung Kong Road experiment I had tried to get the boys jobs or a school as soon as possible. The first question asked by visitors was always, "Are they working now?" Experience gained there made us sure that even though the boys were physically fit they still had to learn much before they were ready to walk alone.

Many had been on the streets for years—their habit was to lie and con in difficult situations. We wanted to keep them very close to a Christian family with plenty of love and strict discipline until their habit was to act in a Christian way. At first we thought three months with a clear routine and teaching would be enough. Then we saw that they would need at least six months for their thinking to change —until they actually forgot their former pattern of cheating, stealing, and blackmailing. Later on we recommended a year as the minimum time to stay in the houses and we preferred two years. No boy who wanted to follow Christ was ever asked to leave and those who wanted to come off drugs were told that as they had made a free decision to follow Jesus and come into our houses, we would not permit them to leave before staying ten days. After that period, when they were completely drug-free, they had the option of leaving or staying on in the houses to learn about Jesus. We did not recommend a stay as short as ten days—indeed if we thought a boy was not completely ready to stay a year we would suggest he reconsider coming to join us. Following Christ would be a lifelong decision; and if the brand new believer did not have the basic commitment to change Christ could not change him.

Routine established itself though it was never rigid; the boys found security in this and began to settle. Once they knew we would not allow them home, back to their old district, or indeed anywhere at all unless accompanied by one of our helpers, they calmed down and began to enjoy an ordered life. Each day they prayed together and alone, went to market, cooked and did household chores. There was then a Bible study and coaching lessons in Chinese reading and English given by members of the church. Most days they played sport such as football and used the opportunity to tell others about Christ. The football pitch was next door to a Methadone Centre where addicts were provided with substitute drugs by the government. Our team of strong healthy boys was so outstanding that many addicts hanging around the centre came to hear how Christ could save them from addiction.

The people in the market noticed them too and several came up to the Saturday meetings curious to meet this Jesus who got junkies more bothered about the price of bean curd than heroin.

The donation of a rotary floor polisher and cleaner led us to form a "Stephen Cleaning Company", and teams of boys went to wax and clean flats. This provided an opportunity for spreading the gospel by shining deed as well as word. It was also an occasion to judge how well a boy would work.

There was never a better supervisor for our floor working jobs than Tony, who, dressed in neat tennis whites, watched over the other workers and ran the company like a military operation. He was used to power...

Tony and I had first met a couple of years before. I was eating shrimp dumplings in noodle soup at the Lung Kong

Road street stall. He wondered why a Westerner would be eating at a food stall especially at that time of night and with a group of notorious criminals to boot. His friend introduced us and he came up to the house where he was clearly impressed. Later he went to another church and said it made him feel good but that it was all rather like a fairy tale which he could not quite grasp. His own life had been far from a fairy tale. He was born during the Second World War in Havana, Cuba. He was the eldest son and when he was eight years old was sent by his father to China to be a helper for his childless first wife. He lived miserably with his "Big Mother" in Peking until the city fell to the Communists. "Little Mother", his real mother, wrote from Havana imploring him to return, but for a penniless eight-year-old boy without friends this was impossible. He was selected for training as a Red Guard; they thought that he would make a good spy because of his foreign looks. Eventually when he was fourteen he did escape from "Big Mother" and resourcefully travelled across China to the Hong Kong border with a friend. On the way his friend was drowned but Tony ploughed on and finally successfully crossed into Hong Kong.

When he arrived he had no money to pay for school fees so he shone shoes and picked pockets to survive. Inevitably, he met up with the Triads who trained him to robbery with violence. He began to take heroin at sixteen and soon graduated from "chasing the dragon" to injecting the drug directly into his veins. He said it became his wife, his friends, and his life. He felt no one cared about him and because of the traumatic experiences of his childhood, formed a hard shell of bitterness around him so that no one could touch or hurt him. This earned him the reputation of a "lone wolf" amongst his gang brothers. Even they feared this ruthless leader who gained so much power that he and two others formed a new branch of the 14K. They were involved in blackmail, fighting and even killing, both to survive and to maintain their supremacy in particular districts.

Ah Kei telephoned me urgently one night begging me to

look for Tony who was in desperate trouble. It was around Chinese New Year and the coldest time of year so I buttoned up tightly in order to pay a nocturnal visit to Diamond Village, the headquarters of his territory.

He was sitting in a tea house with his coat collar turned up against the cold and he was shivering. Flanking him were two henchmen, obviously addicts too judging from their gaunt bodies. But as I looked at Tony's face it was not its drug-induced degeneration which shocked me but another expression altogether.

He was going to die. He was resigned to it.

I did not know then how he intended it to occur, but it was appalling to realize that he had it planned. He began to tell me what was going on and as I listened I looked around at the congealed spittoons in the tea house. The scene was a reflection of the sordid kingdom he was preparing to relinquish.

He told a story of wars and unfinished gang business. He told a tale of coming out of jail to discover that the rival group had attempted to take over his territory. They had stolen his possessions and knowing his passion for music had taken his guitar, broken it in two and left it in the mud. It was an act which demanded retaliation and Tony knew the dreary course of events to come.

He was really weary of fighting but had no option but to plan a revenge attack. However, some vague memory of something sweeter nagged at him until he decided to appease the memory by selling his ten by six foot hut and donating the proceeds to Society of Stephen.

He was not surprised to see me in his village for he had sent for me in order to make this grand gesture. However, before I arrived the other gang had burned down his house after dragging his clothes through the dust one by one. He showed me the site and I saw the guitar strings splayed rudely over the ground.

"Miss Poon, I want to give the Church the deeds to this piece of ground," he offered.

"We don't want your land, Tony, we want your life," I replied.

"I will arrange for you to collect the documents so that you can use the land for a church," he continued.

"We don't want to build a church building, Tony, we'd like to help you build your life."

We walked down the dark path winding through the village shacks and I saw how the inhabitants watched him. He was the king of the village who had been feared and respected. They all knew of the attack and were waiting to see him take revenge. It was expected of him. He could never walk the streets again as their leader unless there were a reciprocal fight. So he had decided to kill or be killed. Either way he would end up dying and it mattered little to his tired self.

He was still muttering about the land papers when I said, "God has chosen you, Tony. Come with us." He refused so I repeated it, "He has chosen to save you. He wants you. Come with us."

I hailed a taxi and was only half in it saying, "God wants your life tonight, Tony. Come with us," when he climbed in beside me and sat down. He did not understand what he was doing but it was the last time he saw his village for several years. He never said goodbye to his gang brothers. He never went back to fetch a thing.

Up in my Lung Kong Road flat the boys were awake and ready to welcome Tony. They asked him if he too wanted to receive Jesus. He was afraid of God but kept remembering, "God has chosen you, God has chosen you," and nodded as they told him how he could be forgiven and receive a new life. Later he wrote a testimony.

They prayed for me and I accepted Jesus as my Lord and I received the baptism of the Spirit. At first I felt very cold but when I was filled with the Spirit a surprising thing happened—I felt my heart burning within me and my whole body grew warm and I wept. I had not cried since I was a child. I sat shamelessly weeping in front of everyone and I knew that I had truly been "born again".

They took me to Stephen's Third House to come off heroin. I had tried many times to come off drugs. The pain had always been greater than I could bear. The first time I went to prison I had to come off "cold turkey" and it was so terrible that I broke out of prison into barbed wire and bear the scars to this day. From that day on I always had heroin hidden on my person so that I was never caught without it. But this time it was different. My brothers in Jesus prayed for me and I also prayed in tongues and the pain disappeared. Two months later I went to live with Mr. and Mrs. Willans who run the houses. My own parents cannot be traced but Mr. and Mrs. Willans are now my parents.

I have witnessed God moving in many areas of my life since that time. I not only went with my new mother and father to China, but in 1976 I visited America and England with them and joined them in speaking in a number of churches and on radio and television. What an amazing thing for me, a former Red Pole fighter in the 14K Triad Society, an ex-convict and heroin addict, to be given a special waiver to visit the United States of America. And the Home Secretary, himself, cleared my travel to England when everyone said it was impossible.

I have since been trained in a first class hairdressing school to be a hair stylist. I work in a leading salon in Hong Kong and live with my parents in a nice apartment. It is truly astonishing and shows that my Lord Jesus is very powerful. But the greatest thing He has done for me is to change my heart and now I no longer follow sin because I follow Him.

It would have been ideal if each one of the boys could have become a special son in a family where he was cared for and loved. Tony's unusual background made him a special case however and it was wonderful to see him grow and change. He had lost his life and so found it.

The other boys in the houses were growing up too though it was sad to see some leave before we thought them ready to take on the outside world. The strongest influence over them was their parents who having ascertained that their son was drug-free, at once started whining about money and family responsibilities. For a boy with a dozen years of street habits it was too much to take on the burden of supporting a family after only a few weeks off drugs. He soon realized his need to stay really close to God's family. Some went back to drugs and then begged to come back to the house. We allowed them to do so if they seemed really serious about changing.

Siu Ming did not have parental pressures. He was an orphan and so mercifully escaped a greedy blackmailing mother. His mother had died when he was seven and he lived with his younger sister and gambling father in a small hut on a hillside. The shack was dark and infested with rats, cockroaches and snakes. The only light came from a hole in the wall covered by a board that they propped up with a stick. As with many Hong Kong families they all slept in one bed and had no kitchen, bathroom, electricity or running water. They burned oil lamps for lights and built a fire for cooking.

Siu Ming and his sister used to sit on a rock by the door of the hut waiting for their father to come home at night. If he carried something, they knew he had won and that there would be supper. If his hands were empty it meant that he had lost and they would have nothing to eat that night. They were too poor to go to school so Siu Ming sold newspapers for a living. He never learned to read or write.

At fifteen he joined a "black" or Triad Society. His father was angry and scolded him so frequently that Siu Ming left home. A year later his sister found him to tell him that their father had died. Now they had no one left and he began to take heroin in his misery. His sister pleaded with him but he was hooked and instead of listening to her he beat her. Then he left home again, this time forever.

As his newspaper selling did not bring in enough money to buy heroin Siu Ming had to rob and steal to get drugs. He was caught twice and the second time sent to a rehabilitation centre. He left there after five months and went back to drugs again. He was readmitted to the centre, came out for a holiday and was immediately arrested once more. This time he went to prison. He came out feeling bitter towards the world and went straight back to heroin.

Sui Ming's probation officer said he was without hope. He had even broken his probation order and was liable for a warrant arrest. Knowing that ordering this warrant would only begin the cycle of imprisonment again the officer decided to give Siu Ming one last chance and told him to find the Society of Stephen. He wrote my name and address in Chinese on a piece of paper and so Siu Ming set off for my house thinking he was visiting a Chinese lady. He had no idea we were anything to do with a church either, but must have been desperate for any help at all, as he bothered to cross the harbour and find Lung Kong Road.

He hid his surprise at meeting a Western woman quite well, but when I told him that Jesus really loved him, he looked undecided as to whether to accept this. Eventually he concluded, "It's either jail or Jesus," and took Jesus. Some of the former gang members living there then prayed with him and he began to speak quietly in a language he did not know. We then took him back across the harbour to Third House so that he could withdraw from heroin.

Some of the boys were smart enough to pray immediately and never had the slightest twinge. Others, like Siu Ming, waited until they were *in extremis* before learning that God did not want them to suffer at all. He refused to pray, which was understandable since his experience of praying was limited to the session in my house only a few hours earlier. He was in agony with withdrawal pains and did not know how to make a prayer even had he felt like it.

At last he said he could bear no more and in desperation agreed to pray in tongues.

He did not have to think what words to say, God's Spirit gave them. He said he felt wonderful and in ten minutes was asleep. He slept right through a day and when he awoke had a real confidence that Jesus did love him. Through this he also learned to pray in the Spirit and was freed from heroin painlessly. Although this miracle had been repeated each time with each of the boys, each one of them knew that it was specially for him.

Siu Ming was so quiet and seemed to have so little character that for the first few months he lived with us we hardly noticed him. On trips to the beach or football there was always the nightmare of counting heads hoping that none of the boys had slunk off to smoke in the toilet. He was the one we always forgot to count, he was such a nonentity. But as the year progressed he began to grow into a person who was kind, trustworthy, hardworking, and, most importantly, spiritual. He learned to read and write through the daily Bible studies and was often found praying by himself. Eventually his ministry of serving the brothers and Christ was evident; he was ordained a deacon in the church and became a helper to all the new boys who arrived.

We also had some older men living in the houses, a fact which was often obscured because we continued to refer loosely to all the inmates as "boys". Ah Lun and Mr. Wong arrived separately at Lung Kong Road but on the same day. They had both heard from other addicts about our houses and demanded to be admitted immediately. Ah Lun was running a little heroin den from his cubicle in a resettlement estate. He had been in prison eighteen times and only existed to eat and to take heroin. Mr. Wong claimed to have been a general in Chiang Kai Shek's army (this may have been true, but I met many Nationalist soldiers who all claimed the same thing and I came to suppose that it was an army composed entirely of generals). Mr. Wong also said that he had been to many different churches in Hong Kong and that ours was the first one in which Jesus was sitting.

I fobbed off the two old men. Ah Lun was almost sixty and Mr. Wong in his fifties. They did not seem suitable for mixing with our younger boys. But every day for some weeks they appeared at my stone steps waiting to be let in. I could not leave them there and deny them the opportunity to accept Christ . . . I could not send them back to heroin dens once they had accepted Christ . . .

The two old men came to live with us too and fitted in extremely well, making a more balanced family. God was adding fathers to me at last. Of course there were problems too since Ah Lun turned out to have the habits of a pack-rat and kept an enormous supply of extraneous objects under, in and on top of his bunk bed. He stored toilet paper, English books, cushions, a vast array of apparel, extra mattresses and plain junk. He also kept a supply of Jean's books for himself though he could not read a word of English. However, it made it easy when anyone in the house needed something unusual.

Mr. Wong thought himself superior to the others because of his position. He had never been a Triad. He was an army officer waiting for Taiwan to regain China. When this did not happen he turned to drugs and became as addicted as all the others. Although his rehabilitation would seem to be easier than Ah Lun's in fact he had the same basic problem as all the boys, pride. Mr. Wong used dreadful flowery Christian language which he had picked up from other churches he had visited. He was very preachy; he became self righteous and easily provoked; he was contentious and a pain in the neck.

After coming off drugs Mr. Wong thought he did not need Jesus' help any more and so stopped praying. Sarah, in charge of his house, had a way of discovering these things. So she told Mr. Wong to pray every morning and night in tongues as well as praying at least half an hour in his private devotions. His attitude immediately began to change and he remarked later, "My heart of stone is melting and God is giving me one of flesh." His style did not change.

Many of the boys were healed of other diseases when they prayed to be released from heroin. One boy had chronic asthma and T.B. when he was admitted and the others were afraid to sleep in the same room. But after two days his asthma completely disappeared and his T.B. reading was clear. We insisted he finish his course of medicine anyway. Ah Lun had an enormously enlarged liver when he arrived but he too was healed and remained normal.

As long as they were on drugs the addicts were not aware of other ailments but we soon discovered any that still remained after the withdrawal period. Teeth was the most common problem. None of us seemed to have the knack of praying for teeth so we spent a small fortune in dentists' bills and false teeth. Mr. Wong had to have every single one extracted as the heroin had rotted them so badly.

Mercifully the British army made their facilities available to use for severe cases and Mr. Wong went into the military hospital to have all his teeth out.

He grinned throughout his stay there and had no pain either which he "tried to exthplain to the British doctor was because of the Holy Thpirit". The army completed the job by donating the proceeds of their carol singing to us thereby providing the funds to buy Mr. Wong a complete new set of dazzling dentures.

This was not the first time the army had assisted the Houses of Stephen. They had helped me with my first house and often made available camp sites and coaches for outings. We found this mutually beneficial as many army friends became Christians through these contacts. If there were any who did it was certainly not the fault of the boys who would say in their enthusiastic English to a red-faced soldier, "Have you believed in Jesus yet?" and before he could formulate a polite brush off, volunteered their aid: "We will pray with you now if you like!"

One of the most hot-hearted amongst these evangelists was thirty-three-year-old Ah Fung. He did not come from the poverty-stricken background of most of our boys, but from a very monied family. He had completed several years of secondary education and considered himself a thinker. His uncle who had looked after him belonged to the socially exclusive Jockey Club and counted his members' card together with his American Social Security number and Mercedes Benz as his most prized possessions.

Despite these advantages Ah Fung was underprivileged. His father was dead, and his mother had long since disappeared. He himself was heavily addicted to heroin and needed a means to support his habit. His uncle gave him a lot of money, which only gave him greater chances to indulge his habit. Eventually even what his uncle gave him was not enough. He lied, cheated, stole or did anything else necessary to get enough money for drugs. He soon learnt that prison sentences were lighter for living off immoral earnings and turned to poncing.

When his uncle found out about his nephew's addiction he made him live at home for two months under strict supervision. Ah Fung agreed to this voluntary imprisonment but insisted that they never bother him at night; he claimed that if he was woken he could not get back to sleep again. Secure in the knowledge that he would not be disturbed, he made a dummy figure for his bed and every night slipped out of the house unnoticed. Having found his nightly fix he then slipped back into the house.

It finally dawned on the family after two months that Ah Fung was still hooked, and they threw him out. Unhappily he cheated his uncle and himself because he really did want to get off drugs. He sought professional treatment; later he made the sad claim that he had been in every drug treatment centre in Hong Kong. He even went to Taiwan and Australia in an attempt to live and work but he was still addicted.

When I met Ah Fung he had been in prison six times, was spending HK$180 a day on heroin and seemed a hopeless case. He came to my Walled City room. "Miss Pullinger, what are the procedures required for entering the Society of Stephen?" he asked. It reminded me of the old woman looking for a burial spot. "Where do I have to register, how long do I have to wait and how much does it cost?"

"Well, Ah Fung, it's not quite like that," I answered. "You see, we are not a drug treatment centre, we are a group of Christians who are concerned that your whole life should change. If you simply want to get off drugs I can recommend a centre. They will keep you for a few months and then you can leave—and go back to drugs if you like. But we don't want you at all unless you are really serious about changing and are prepared to stay at least one year."

He nodded; he would agree to anything. Some of the boys sitting in the club room told him enthusiastically about Jesus Christ, His life, His death, His resurrection. Ah Fung nodded dumbly and agreed to pray with them.

The next day we took him into Third House. He arrived tanked up, having smoked the entire "withdrawal" money which he had conned off his landlady stating that we charged. On the second day he felt the twinges which indicated he was beginning to go through withdrawal. He refused to pray and demanded to leave. His pains grew worse. He still refused to pray.

Jean and Rick were sitting down to dinner in their Kotewall Road flat when came an urgent phone call from one of the helpers who said that Ah Fung was still obstinate, shouting and struggling to escape. Rick went down to the boys' house and spoke strongly to Ah Fung as a father. He told him that whatever happened he would not be allowed to leave for eight more days and he was ashamed of his behaviour.

The voice of authority calmed Ah Fung and he prayed with Rick. When Rick laid hands on his head he said he felt a glow all over and his pains subsided. He and Rick prayed together in the Spirit until he fell asleep.

The next morning when he awoke he felt the pains coming back so he remembered what had happened the day before.

"It might work again," he thought to himself and looking round to make sure no one was watching he laid his hands upon his own head. Nothing happened. He decided to pray instead. And it was when he prayed that he was delivered.

So Ah Fung learned that it was not Rick, but Jesus who had healing hands. He stayed not only one year but two in our houses and became very helpful and responsible with the other boys. He was just one of the seventy-five boys we took in during the first twenty months. Each had his fascinating story and all without exception came off heroin without pain and trauma.

All knew the reality of a living Lord and the power of His Spirit; those who followed Him were evidence of an incredible transformation. Ah Fung himself quoted the Chinese proverb: "It is easier to alter the features of the country than to change one's disposition." He recognized a God who could move mountains.

Chapter Twelve

Entertaining Angels

They might have been twenty years old, they might be sixty even. There was no way of telling. They had given up all pretence of trying to look pretty or attractive. Their heads hung down as they squatted or propped themselves up against the wall and waited for customers.

The prostitute who had bought Maria as a baby was preparing to retire. Now she stood outside the blue film theatre urging the voyeurs to sample the juvenile delights promised upstairs or she sat by the cubicles where the young girls were contained and counted up the money.

Maria was thirteen and when her step-mother wanted her to begin work in the Walled City brothels she rebelled. It was not that she found sleeping with different men morally repugnant, but the idea of having to sleep with old men for a fee did not attract her. Having been raised in a brothel she thought it merely a way of earning a living and was indifferent to its social disadvantages. She was a very attractive perky child with beautiful clear olive skin and expressive eyes which she soon learned to use to her advantage. However, she was looking for love and attention and enjoyed flirting with the boys she met at the Youth Club during its early days. So she ran away.

Maria became a ballroom girl at a certain ballroom in Kowloon, there being little alternative for a teenage Chinese girl on her own. A ballroom girl was a much higher class of prostitute; indeed she did not think of herself as a prostitute, more as a hostess. Men paid for every dance they had with her; if a man chose to buy all her dances he could, and he would have to pay a further fee to take her home for the night. Every ballroom girl had a protector or ponce; he collected her earnings, and should the girl wish to change her man, then a transfer fee of several thousand dollars had to be paid—either by the girl or her new protector.

I did not know where she was; all I could find out was that she had run away from the Walled City, and could have gone to any of the hundreds of ballrooms or brothels throughout Hong Kong and Kowloon . . . The longer she was missing the more I worried. Eventually one Sunday afternoon after praying about her, I wandered off up the Jordan Road asking God to lead me to where she was. "Walk straight on. Do not turn to the left or to the right." It was the first occasion since I had been baptized in the Spirit that I experienced another of the spiritual gifts, the word of knowledge. I did not hear a voice or see a white cloud but I knew quite surely where God wanted me to go.

I walked ahead, crossed the main road and then understood just as clearly, "Stop here." I was standing outside a tall multi-apartment block which had many flats with windows boarded up, posing as "massage-parlours", "music halls" or "hotels". At this point completely denying the knowledge I had been given I said, "Lord, this is a silly game. I'm not playing spiritual detectives any more," and went home.

A few days later I dreamed of Maria and saw clearly the room she was living in and the man she was living with. I woke up crying for I did not know how to find her and tell her that I cared about her. The only way for me to discover her whereabouts was through the Triad network; because of their control of the vice rackets they were usually able to locate missing girls within days.

I did not need to resort to black society methods however, for a few months later Maria telephoned me herself. She said she had been trying to contact me for ages too but did not dare go back to the Walled City and did not know my new telephone number. She gave me directions on the phone and I went to visit her. It was the same block outside which I had stopped on that Sunday afternoon months earlier. It was the same room I had dreamed of except that round the walls and on the ceiling were many mirrors.

I visited her every Sunday afternoon; she told me how she loved her man, and how she was in debt to her ballroom. Ballroom girls were issued with beautiful dresses and taught to dance, but the ballroom took the cost out of their future wages. Because of these debts a ballroom girl could not leave her ballroom without paying quite a large sum; Maria was trapped. She felt one way out of the trap was to become pregnant: so she did, by her protector, but then had the baby aborted. She became pregnant a second time, and went to live with her protector's mother; after the baby was born she got a job in a factory. But her protector's family, friends, and even her protector himself looked down on her because she had been a ballroom girl. Eventually the lack of friendliness made her feel that it was not worth being a good girl working hard in a factory, so she might as well go back to the ballroom.

Her baby girl stayed with the granny; she was called Jackyan after me. I put savings into the bank for the baby's schooling, but sadly Maria and her protector spent the money on themselves, as they had no ability to think of the future.

Maria found a new protector but she still was not content, and became more and more unhappy. Every night she danced and danced; to keep going she used pep pills and when the dance hall closed she could not sleep as she was far too revved up. With the other girls she went off to the gambling dens, and the inevitable happened; she ran into debt, and was forced to borrow money from a loan shark. Many loan sharks in Hong Kong charge twenty per cent interest daily; soon she was hopelessly insolvent. The loan shark then demanded that she become a "snake", his property as a prostitute for two years, while he kept all her earnings to pay off her debts.

Maria rang me up in a panic and her voice was high with terror. To be forced to be a snake was for her the ultimate humiliation: as a ballroom girl she was independent in a way; now she was to be a prisoner to a ruthless man who would extract every penny she earned. She wanted me to produce HK$1500 to save her from this fate, but I did not even have HK$15. My greatest concern however was whether she was sincere; she had prayed to receive Christ in the past, but she had not made any serious effort to follow Him. I had no intention of paying money to a girl who was not serious about changing her life; she would soon end up in the same mess again. But clearly I had to go and see her, and I decided to take Ah Ping with me; he had been in her world and I needed his worldly discernment to know if she was exploiting me. Together we prayed about it. When I reviewed my material assets I thought of the only thing I had in the world of any financial value, which was a very precious and favourite oboe. I had played it for years in the Hong Kong Philharmonic Orchestra, and like all oboists, regarded it as a personal friend—handpicked and almost irreplaceable. Knowing nothing of my secret riches, Ah Ping had an interpretation of a message in tongues. He said "The Lord Jesus Christ gave up His most precious possession for you, even His very life. Why do you store up your treasures on earth; you should rather store up treasure in heaven?"

If Jesus had given up His life, what was an oboe in comparison? What could I say?

"All right Maria," I told her. "I will pay the money on two conditions. The first is that you let me hand over the cash in person—the second that you leave this kind of life. I'll help you find a job, a room, anything you like—but if you remain here you will soon be in trouble again."

"They will never agree to deal with you," argued Maria. "Michael is a very exacting money lender and very particular about his debts." However she had no choice and so set up a meeting in a tea-room in Jordan Road for two nights later at half past midnight.

Sadly I sold my oboe and filled a brown business envelope with fifteen $100 notes. I arrived at the restaurant and chose a central table where Maria and I drank coffee while we waited for Michael the sharp-toothed loan-shark.

Squealing tyres heralded the arrival of the collecting agents. Michael had not come himself but sent four men who slouched into the room Chicago style while their engine growled outside. They barely glanced at us, picked up the envelope and after checking the contents in the manner of a gambler checking a deck of cards walked out again without speaking.

I was very disappointed. They had played the scene too quickly. They were about to go through the door when I called out. "Hey, wait." One of them looked back, raised his eyebrows and said disdainfully, "What do you want?"

"I want to see Michael," I replied.

"What do you want to see him about then, huh?" The spokesman sounded extremely condescending.

"I have got a very important message for him."

"Well, you can give us the message."

"No," I replied. "I have to give this message to him in person."

"What is it?"

"It is a very personal message: I must tell him myself; how can I find him?"

Slightly to my surprise they gave me his telephone number; even more surprising, when I rang him up he agreed to see me. I was summoned to a skyscraper in a smart part of Kowloon; Michael's nightclub was on the twenty-first floor. It was clearly very exclusive; the doorman let me in with a golden key at least three feet long after having vetted me through a spy-hole. I was expected. Inside were thick carpets and soft lighting and everywhere there were enormous teddy bears—on the bar, on the tables, round the walls. Each table had a telephone connected with the cubicles upstairs: the members sat with their drinks downstairs, and when they wanted a girl they dialled her number. This then was the club that Maria would have had to work in, had not the money been paid. I sat at one of the downstairs tables and waited, and waited.

Various minions were sent to offer me drinks; I was assiduously attended to. Eventually Michael himself deigned to grant me my interview. He was a real smoothie; he looked very pleasant and well-groomed as he sat down opposite me. He spoke with glib eloquence about the terrible problems of living in Hong Kong, and how without this loan business he could not afford to send his eleven brothers and sisters to school. As it was, he was able to support all his family including his mother on the proceeds. Indeed he felt he actually had a service to provide to the community; when parents lost their children they often asked Michael to help, and he could usually find missing children within forty-eight hours for a fee. He knew all the clubs, bars and ballrooms and could trace them through his Triad contacts.

After completing his self-justification, he began to attack. "You are a fool. You have lost that money. You may have thought you were doing something very noble by paying for that girl but I know her and I know that she is not going to change. She is going to get back to the same thing . . . Do not think she is going to be grateful to you or change her life in any way; you have just seen the end of that money. You have been tricked into making a completely wasted gesture."

"That doesn't really matter. I'll tell you why I did it. Have you heard about Jesus?"

He had heard some of the Bible stories.

I explained, "Jesus is the One who did all those miracles. He was the one perfect man who has ever lived; He only did good, healed people and raised them from the dead, but His enemies put Him on a Cross and killed Him. He died for my sake but He did not wait till I was good before He died for me. He never said He would die for me only if I changed.

While I ignored Him He laid down His life for me and even as He was dying He still said He forgave me. That is what Jesus did for me and that is what I want Maria to understand." I stopped, uncertain if he had understood my English but aware that he was too proud to speak Chinese.

"She won't change, she will go back to her old ways; it was a wasted gesture," he repeated.

"I would rather be a fool and lose the money. After all what's losing the money? Jesus lost a life. I would rather be a fool and lose it than be a cynic and see her go to hell. Now she has a chance of a new life, whether she wants to take it or not. It is up to her now. I cannot change her life but she has the opportunity; Jesus made that opportunity."

Michael opened his mouth to reply, but no sound came. He had been struck dumb. His mouth opened and shut and his lips formed words but his throat was paralyzed by emotion. Minutes passed; still he could not speak; his eyes filled with tears. Finally he croaked, his eyes turned away, "I have nothing to say." And he was silent.

I never saw Michael again but I was joined in the lift by one of the club employees, granted permission by Michael to come after me.

"Can I talk to you?" he asked. I was surprised and a little nervous of his motives but he went on, "I want to hear about being a Christian and can you tell me where there is a place I can go?"

It was three in the morning and there was nowhere nearby where we could talk except a bar so we sat there for the rest of the night, our coffee cups on either side of an open Bible.

By this time I had started to take boys into my house and obviously could not invite Maria to share it, even if she were willing to come. We had already discovered that helping such girls was much more difficult than boys as very few of them wanted a new life.

Many had no feeling of doing wrong: they knew that society officially disapproved of their profession but felt that the stigma attached was well worth the freedom they gained.

They were free to enjoy themselves, make money and escape the drudgery and anonymity of the Chinese housewife.

Most young girls retained their illusions for some time. They loved their boyfriends romantically and willingly supported them, only realizing that they were being exploited several years later. By that time they knew no other life and discovered that they had not bought freedom at all but were captives to the game. There were no homes for retired prostitutes, no pensions either. A girl had to become hard and either attach herself to a wealthy man or trick her protector so that she could amass money for the years when she would no longer be desirable or serviceable.

Even if a girl genuinely desired to change her lifestyle, the men she supported would naturally resist and there might be as many as seven or eight of them. Some girls would have liked to leave, but were in debt to the club where they worked as well as fearing their pimps. During my visits to Maria's ballroom I met many such girls, and long before they admitted their desperation, even to themselves, they were popping pills in the girls' rest room while I chatted with them.

One evening I received a phone call at Lung Kong Road from Frederick, one of the Walled City Club boys.

"Poon Siu Jeh," he spoke very quietly. "I have a friend who has been beaten up for trying to leave the Triads. This person is desperate and has nowhere to go to escape. Can we come to your house?"

"Fine, Fred. What about tomorrow morning?" I answered. I liked the idea of the Church being sanctuary.

"Too dangerous," he said. "My friend cannot risk being seen by the gangs. We will come when it is dark."

The following evening I opened the door to receive my smuggled fugitive and saw with a shock that Fred had delivered a girl. Because of the lack of gender in Chinese speech I had naturally assumed that it was a boy running from the Triads. Actually she looked more like a bean-pole than a girl; she was emaciated and had arms and legs like stalks. Her eyes were dark and bruised. Hurriedly I let her in and tried to talk to her but she would not utter a word that evening or for some time to come. Nods and headshakes sufficed for her conversational needs. Her name was Angel.

Frederick told me that she had been employed as a prostitute by a gang in Mong Kok. This was because her mother had no room for her in their resettlement room. Several of the family were already sleeping in the passage, so the mother gave Angel to the man who asked for her, saying that she hoped they would marry. She knew he was already married but convinced herself that marriage was not out of the question and that the partnership would be economically advantageous.

It did not work out that way. Instead of the man providing for her, Angel found herself not only supporting him but four or five others. Every night she was sent to a brothel where she worked. Some of the brothels employed boys as young as fourteen to "watch" the girls. The boys sat and played cards, looked at television, or ate; they were there to make sure the girls worked proper hours and did not escape. They had no need to use force. One night Angel did not turn up for work and when she returned to the Mong Kok flat she was beaten up by her boyfriend. He told her that he would beat her to death if she did not go to work in the future.

Angel did not want to be beaten any more, neither did she want to continue this work but had nowhere to go instead. If she went home her boyfriend would find her; if she rented a room the Triads could locate her within forty-eight hours. She had no friends except other bar girls who would also be with their men. The only other person she knew was Frederick so she went to him. He had nowhere to conceal her so she came to us.

Angel looked seventeen but was actually twenty-five and rather simpleminded. After a few days she understood enough to accept that Jesus loved her, not because she would go out and earn Him money, but because He loved her as she was and forgave her. So she became a Christian and we saw some kind of animation light up her vacant eyes.

Although she had started a new life, obviously poor Angel could never be free to walk around in Hong Kong while the situation remained as it was. This was unfinished business and gang law required a settlement. There had to be a *gong-sou* or talk-out, to decide on a separation fee before Angel was officially transferred. Otherwise if she were seen in the street the gang could snatch her back, disfigure her, throw acid at her or start a gang war against us.

I arranged with Angel that we should meet her former boyfriend. I phoned him and chose the Hong Kong Hotel Coffee Shop because it had several entrances and exits so we could not be trapped. It was also public enough to prevent Angel's men from abducting her without attracting attention. I also rang the police and told them that we were having this kind of talk there and whereas obviously it did not warrant anyone coming down to make arrests it would be helpful if someone were around keeping an eye open. They kindly agreed.

One of the Lung Kong Road boys accompanied Angel and me to the hotel where we found a whole table of Triads sitting with the boyfriend.

As the discussion progressed I gradually became aware that, dotted around the coffee shop, there were several more tables occupied by their gang brothers. They watched us and directed questioning glances at Angel's boyfriend. I guessed that these dozen or more men were all there because they could only imagine that Angel had fled to another Triad. I could see that I was not making much of an impression.

I left Angel to do the talking until I realized that she was not discussing anything at all but agreeing with everything her ponce said. It was a habit of years and I could see us leaving the hotel and getting into separate taxis while she meekly went back to being a whore. I entered the conversation but the boyfriend was adamant; he would not release her. He then became quite maudlin and disgusting as he tried to convince both me and himself that he really loved and missed Angel.

"A very strange way you have of showing your love," I retorted, "sending her out to do this job and expecting her to support you; I think you are just sorry about losing your income."

"I am not willing to give her up. She is rightfully mine. She was given by her parents," he persisted.

"Angel has no chance of any kind of life with you—you cannot even marry her," I said. "She wants to break away and start a new life. She has come to believe in Jesus." It meant nothing to him and he commanded Angel to leave with him. I hung on to her arm so he could not force her. The Lung Kong Road boy hung on to her other arm and thus in unwieldy formation we walked out of the door and into a taxi. We were pulling away from the curb relieved that Angel was still with us when the boyfriend leaped at the vehicle and climbed into the front seat. He would not leave so I directed the taxi on a long detour so that he would not find out our address. I did not want him to trace Angel.

Our front seat rider swung round to glower over the back of his seat. "My boss will be extremely angry about this. He will not let Angel go. This matter must be finished. I need your phone number."

I refused to give the number and said I would contact him again and we could talk some more. At last he climbed out of the taxi and we went home.

It was all very unsatisfactory and we decided that Angel should not go to the next talk-out because they might actually snatch her back. We rang up and made an appointment to see them again. They said we could choose the place, so I chose the Diamond Cafe, just opposite our flat in Lung Kong Road. Angel's boyfriend advised that this time it should only be Angel and myself: nobody else should come; he would come by himself and he would not bring anyone else.

I did not completely trust him about this. I was also

worried about the threat of violence from a different direction, for the boys in Lung Kong Road were getting quite protective about Angel, and about me. This was just what I did not want to happen, because if there were any trouble or any violence, despite the fact that they were Christians, their instinct would be to fight, and therefore they ought not to be in such a situation. So we spent the morning looking up the stories of Gideon and Jehoshaphat in the Old Testament, where they were facing impossible odds, but did not have to fight at all; simply by praising God or by singing they got the victory. I wanted our boys to know that we did not have to fight. I was not particularly worried for myself although I would be really frightened and I would not like it if somebody wanted to kill or slash me but I would not be likely to grab a knife and stab him back. More likely I would fall to my knees, pray and die. This would be rather much to expect from the boys.

A couple of hours before the meeting was scheduled the street was beginning to fill as Angel's men were staked out at various points and up back alleys. I had the boys lined up on our roof where they could see into the cafe without being seen themselves. I said, "Your job is to pray and if you see any violence going on then you can ring the police, but you are not to rush out to defend me or anything like that." They were all ready to run into the Walled City and get Goko to send out men to fight the other gang. I had to explain forcibly, "As Christians you can't do this; you can't fight a spiritual battle this way, you're not to get involved physically." We really prayed about this, and then I went to the appointment with one boy, leaving Angel behind.

When I got to the cafe I found that Angel's boyfriend this time had not come himself, but he had sent his gang leader who also was a burly brutal figure. There were also five or six of his cohorts there, and I knew there were others outside. He was furious that I had not brought Angel: obviously they had been all ready to snatch her.

"Don't think I'm going to stand on ceremony because of

you, just because you're a Jesus lady or you have something to do with the church," he said. He did not know that I had anything to do with the Walled City so I foolishly attempted to witness by mentioning some of the boys once Goko's followers and who now were following Jesus. He leaped to the conclusion that I was something to do with the 14K.

"Right," he said, "that settles it. We're not going to stand on ceremony with you any longer." He banged on the table furiously and got up shouting until the whole cafe was terrified. "You have to produce this girl. We're not going to let you go until you do."

He ranted while I tried to tell him about Jesus but he didn't want to hear. I was stuck; I thought, "I tried to tell him about Jesus and he doesn't want to hear that, neither is he going to listen to reason about the girl. I really am cornered." I was frightened.

"Excuse me, can I make a telephone call?" I bleated and I telephoned my house which they still did not know was opposite. I spoke to Willie, an old Etonian, who was helping us for a year.

"Don't look now but outside the cafe there are two cars with men with knives in them," he said and it sounded as if he were speaking out of the side of his mouth. "They're waiting there."

I was terrified out of my mind so I whispered to Willie, "Call the police." I went back to my seat and I told them that Angel was not coming so they'd have to do the talkout with me, and that Angel wanted to follow Jesus. They could not understand what I was talking about, and I was certainly no substitute for her.

As the police cars arrived the weapon cars slid away and when the policemen came into the cafe all was tranquillity. Here were all these young men having a cup of coffee with a European girl. The young men, of course, had not got knives on them and I could hardly say to the policemen, "Look, these men are threatening me," because they were not. I went out to the lavatory at the back and there was one of the policemen there too so I said, "Excuse me but there are men with knives outside in cars."

"There's no one there, do you want me to search the cafe?" he asked helpfully.

"It's no good searching the cafe," I said. "You won't find anything."

So the police all went away again and as they went away the cars came back. I was still stuck there, not knowing what to do. The one thing that I could do in this situation was to pray, but I could not pray in English for I was in a complete blue funk. I prayed in tongues very quietly so that they could not hear.

My knees were shaking under the table and I went on praying. I had no idea what I was going to do next for this gang was getting more and more furious, and I could not see how it was going to end. Finally I got up saying, "I have to go and buy some vegetables."

Trembling violently I walked out of the cafe and as I walked out I could see men getting out of the cars which were parked close together. They were walking towards me and I did not know what would happen and was still more frightened that the Walled City boys would leap in and fight on my behalf. Mercifully a minibus was passing and although I did not know where it was going, I jumped on and got away. I went straight to the police station.

"I want to report something. I'm afraid there might be a murder." I tried to tell them about the emergency phone call and about the men with knives looking for Angel. "I'm sure they are going to go to her family's home. They don't know where I live, yet. And have no way of finding out my address. But they're going to go to her home and I know they're going to give her family members trouble." I gasped incoherently.

They all looked very bored and asked, "Where does she live?" "In Shek Kip Mei," I told them.

"Well, that's not our district." They sounded irritated. "Would you mind going to the Shek Kip Mei police station?"

"But can't you call from here," I asked them, "because I'm afraid there might be a murder."

A police inspector sitting there looked around at me and smirked. "Madam," he intoned, "people get killed every day?"

"Yes, I know they do," I said impatiently. "But I just want to tell you before it happens because I'd like to stop this one." I made such a fuss that eventually they said they would take me to Shek Kip Mei police station in one of their vehicles. I found the second police station equally unhelpful. "This should be Kowloon City business as the 999 call was made from there," they complained. "Anyway, what do you expect us to do about it?"

"Look, here is her address," I said. "Here is where her family lives. I'm pretty sure that this gang is going to go to her family and give them problems."

"We can't send someone to watch there all the time. We've got a lot of jobs to do."

"I know you can't, but could you tell the policemen on the beat to watch out for this address and to keep their eyes open."

This all took about six hours and eventually a very helpful inspector took an unofficial report, as there was no way that he could make it official since nothing had actually happened.

Twelve hours later I got a desperate phone call from one of Angel's family. I deliberately had not given them my address otherwise the gang would have got it out of them. "I'm out shopping and I can see up onto the balcony of the resettlement block," she said in a shaking voice. "There are five men sitting in my family's house and they won't leave. And there are other men sitting on the stairs with weapons, with iron bars."

I straight away rang the police. The long six-hour wrangle with them the night before proved its value, because they were already informed and they got their policemen there very quickly. Most of the men managed to escape, but they captured two or three of them. The police managed to put fear in them by implying that if they felt like it they could get this gang into a lot of trouble. Angel was never bothered again.

The strangest part of the whole story was yet to come. Angel's family told me later that they had been terrified when the gang came and sat in their house. They were questioned as to where I lived and where this church was. Mercifully they did not know and so could not tell.

"Anyway, who is this Jesus lady and who are these Christians?" asked one of the gang. "Our Angel used to be so obedient, she'd do anything we wanted before, and now she dares to resist us. Did you see that Jesus woman's eyes?" they asked Angel's family. "Because when we were sitting in that cafe we were frightened, we dared not look in her eyes because she has some kind of power." The word they used implied a supernatural power or strength. When I heard that, I really rejoiced because it had been one of the most frightening moments of my life, and I was completely out of my depth, yet they were more frightened than I was, and had not dared touch me, because they recognized a spiritual power.

Now that her freedom was secured we could not keep Angel in Lung Kong Road in the middle of boys who were trying to start a new life. Since Jean and Rick had moved to Hong Kong side to accommodate more people at the Saturday meeting, their Mei Foo house was available for the few months the lease still had to run. We decided to put Angel there together with two girls who had been referred by the courts and the girl friend of one of the addicts going through withdrawal in our houses. Sarah stayed to be the house mother and so the girls' house began.

Another of the difficulties in rehabilitating girls was that no one ever forgot their past. Somehow there was a kind of glory attached to a man's crimes; he could be forgiven and if they were not forgotten at least no one blamed him for them. For a girl however it was different: even if she became a Christian no one forgot what she had once been.

Although the lease soon expired and we were unable to continue the girls' house for long, we had learned much through this experiment. Angel who had never been to school in her life had begun to read a little. She was never molested again and later married a very nice young Christian man with a proper legal job.

It was a year later when another member of the judiciary, this time a District Court Judge, telephoned Jean and asked if she would consider taking a middle-aged woman into our houses. She had been caught at Kai Tak Airport with four and a half pounds of raw opium in her underclothes. The judge felt that this was an isolated incident in her life and though the crime actually merited several years in prison he was unwilling to pass this sentence as it seemed of no benefit to her. The probation report on her home was so discouraging that unless an alternative could be found, probation was ruled out.

Jean hurriedly told the judge that we no longer had a girls' house and could not consider mixing a female drug peddler with our boys. However, she agreed to visit the court the next day and talk to the woman.

I went with Jean to translate and when we arrived the judge, who remembered us from Ah Kit's case, cleared the court so that we could talk for as long as we liked without being disturbed. We saw a Chinese woman in her late forties sitting in the dock like a rabbit frozen with fear.

We did not want Ah Ying to think that her future depended in any way upon her response to our message as that would have provoked a weighted decision from her. Without saying where we were from or who we were, we told her about Christ and how He could take away the heaviness of sin and give her a new life with power.

She told us that she had been trying to pray in prison whilst on remand and that we were an answer to her prayers. She smiled as she realized that Jesus had forgiven her and prayed eagerly with us to receive the power of His Spirit.

Jean looked at me. I looked at her. We both shrugged

and smiled as we said in unison, "Well, we had better go in to the judge and tell him we'll take her."

Ah Ying went to live in Third House, staying in one of the helpers' rooms. She was very churchy at first and liked long flowery repetitious prayers. She was also very contentious and difficult to live with. But gradually she grew into a completely different person. It may have had something to do with the fact that she always prayed in the Spirit while she did the establishment's ironing, and some days she ironed for hours...

* * *

"God, I can't tell them about Jesus. Wouldn't it be awful if they believed." I used to hurry past some of the old prostitutes avoiding them for that reason. I was at the stage where I knew that Christ could overcome the power of drug addiction but I also knew that the new believers needed a safe strong house to grow up in. We no longer had a place for girls and had quite enough problems with the boys as it was. So what would I do with a repentant "madam"—leave her on the streets?

I could not resist speaking one night as I passed one old crone who had her pitch just near Lung Kong Road. She sat on an orange box and had no home, nowhere to sleep, nowhere for her belongings. The only way she got a bed for the night was if a man hired her, and then she could sleep the whole night in the apartment house room he rented. She had no cupboard for her clothes but kept them all in a laundry, taking out clean ones when needed and changing them for her dirty ones.

Ah King was nearly fifty and endured her prostitute's life by taking heroin. Perhaps she had been led into prostitution to make money for her heroin habit. In any case the two were now inextricably combined and she was on a hopeless course. She knew who I was as I had walked by her for years.

I began to tell her about the woman who washed Jesus'

feet with her tears and wiped them with her hair. How she was a prostitute but He, who was God's Son, liked her and spoke kindly to her. I spoke of the religious people whom He was not so keen on, and how upset they were at Jesus' manners in public, letting a soiled woman touch Him; how He had said to her, "Your sins are forgiven . . . go in peace."

Ah King listened and believed. "That's the Lord I want," she cried.

I told her how she could receive this Lord and she prayed out loud in Chinese completely naturally. The old man who was the street pimp was close to us: he was not a very high-class pimp, but one who took a few dollars from each of the elderly street women.

This coolie watched us sitting with our eyes closed praying and nearly split his sides with laughter. His howls of mirth did not put Ah King off. She sat there talking to the Lord who loved prostitutes.

"This Lord will also give you power to help you pray and this power will stay with you to teach you everything," I told her and she began to pray in a beautiful new language quietly and clearly, as the Holy Spirit taught her.

When she had prayed for ten minutes Ah King looked up with happiness flooding her face. Now came the awful moment.

I had nothing to give her. I had no house for prostitutes; my floor was already covered with boys. My purse was empty. I had not even a busfare. She continued sitting on her box.

"You know, Ah King, you don't have to look to men any more for your daily rice," I said. "Look to God."

She roared with good humoured laughter. "Do you mean to say it will fall down from heaven?"

"Maybe," I replied seriously. "If God really is God He could quite easily send you rice from heaven. You cannot live this kind of life any more."

She seemed to catch the idea. "I tell you what," she said, "next time I see you I'll tell you how it came."

I walked away leaving her on her box. I did not like doing that—it was hardly an auspicious beginning to a new life—but I decided to put her completely into God's hands.

A week later I saw her again.

"I've learned some things," she told me. "I think it is reasonable enough for God to provide my rice money but not my heroin money." That was the last time I ever saw her. When I asked the other prostitutes where she was they replied, "Oh, she does not do this any more. She has gone away. She has gone somewhere to get off drugs."

I always like to think of Ah King sitting somewhere in the best house God can provide while He rains rice down upon her.

Chapter 13

Witnesses

It was dark in the Walled City that night; only the lights of our little room blazed out bravely in the sultry gloom. Four or five boys lounged around watching a table tennis game. Into the light slipped a pathetic figure, very very young and very very thin and clearly addicted to heroin. I recognized Bibi, Winson's youngest brother, called Bibi because he was the baby of the family. He was on the run from the police; they had let him out for one day's holiday from prison and he had not gone back. I called him, sat him on a wooden bench away from the tennis table, and told him about Jesus. He seemed to begin to understand, but he did not stay more than half an hour: boys on the run can never stay long in any place. He promised me to come back again, and some days or it may have been weeks later he did come back. I told him more so that he knew enough to take the decision to follow Jesus if he chose; I warned him that he now had to make up his mind for himself. "I can't go on seeing you because I'll be breaking the law if I encourage you to visit me here. If I do not know where you live that is one thing, but if I am regularly seeing you here I will be obliged to turn you in. I will pray for you and as soon as you are ready to follow Jesus tell me and I will go with you to the police station and help you give yourself up. I will go through the whole thing with you because if you really start to pray I know you can be helped."

He did not turn himself in. Later he was arrested and

sent back to prison. I went to see him there and we talked but on his release he went back on drugs. For the next few months he dropped into the Youth Club occasionally and then I heard he had been arrested for two very serious crimes. One charge was for wounding a newspaper seller and stealing his watch; the second charge was of robbery with assault. The police claimed that they had found identity cards and property from the victims on Bibi when they arrested him. As soon as I heard the details I knew Bibi could not be guilty of at least one of the charges: he was in the club talking to me at the time that he was supposed to have been robbing the newspaper seller. I hurried to see him in prison, and discovered to my horror that he wanted to plead guilty because although he was innocent of these particular charges he had done about twenty other robberies in a completely different area of Kowloon. He said in a resigned tone, "Let's just get it over with and plead guilty."

"You can't," I insisted, "You really can't. It isn't the truth. Tell the judge you have done the other things, all right, but tell the truth."

When the case came up Bibi pleaded innocent but was found guilty in spite of my evidence, which was the only time that I have ever been a witness. In his summing up the judge said he believed that I had spoken the truth, but he thought that another witness was confused about the time of the incident. And the case was closed.

I had spent days in court praying throughout the proceedings, so inevitably the policemen and the prison officers got to know me. At the end of the trial I was walking out of the court room when the police inspector stopped me.

"How come you are involved in all this?" he asked.

"Well, I'm a Christian."

"Why are you giving evidence for the criminal then?" pressed the officer.

"I know he is a criminal; I know he is a drug addict; I know he has done many robberies, but he did not do this one: I know he didn't because I'm his alibi."

"Oh," said the policeman. "Well I'm a Christian too. Look at it my way. When these people commit crimes we know who did it but we can't always get them for it. So we charge them with what we can make stick. It's rough but fair, and society benefits," he finished.

"You may think it's fair enough to arrest someone on the wrong charge, and he may even think it's fair enough because of what he has got away with. But in the long term the effect on society is bad. There is no respect for the law or the police or truth. The criminal learns to think the way all criminals think—that getting caught is not connected with guilt or innocence; it is merely bad luck. They certainly never learn to tell the difference between right and wrong." I felt very strongly about this and I launched into the attack.

"Well at least they receive some kind of punishment for their crimes," reasoned the inspector.

"But they don't feel they are paying for the wrong that they have done," I countered. "I know men in prison for crimes they claim they have not committed: they are viciously bitter at being locked up on a false charge. The first thing they want to do when they get out is to do the crime to fit the punishment. Never mind the other ones they did before. They feel that having already served time they are owed the crime."

Surprised at my tirade the officer ended the conversation lamely. "I have never thought of it like that." He hurried away.

When he came out of prison again I met Bibi. He looked like a rat who never saw the sunlight. His face was a mauve-grey, and he had dark shadows under his eyes. He went straight back to his drug. He had promised to change, but like most addicts he was powerless; he had a celebration meal of heroin on the day of his release, though he did not plan it that way. Addicts have a favourite saying which describes their feeling on arriving in a drug den—"My heart had not decided where to go, but my feet walked themselves."

To pay for his habit Bibi found a job as a refuse collector

in the Walled City. He had to drag large rattan baskets slopping excrement through the alleys; it was the lowest form of work but it gave him a little money to begin buying his heroin: to supplement his earnings he went back to robbing people as well. Whenever he saw me he would run away. But I kept in touch by getting things on the grape vine and by walking around the streets, and I usually knew where he was living. When a television film unit came to make a film of our work we contacted Bibi and filmed him at home. The drug had eaten into his flesh and sharp-etched his bones; he shivered continuously. His family turned it into a soap opera. His mother sobbed. "Make my son good, Poon Siu Jeh, make him good. Take him into your house and make him good." His elder brother whined in chorus, "Make him good, Miss Poon, make him good."

It could not work like that of course. Bibi knew the truth, that he alone had to make the decision to change himself and no one else could make it for him. I learned that there is a time for meeting and talking, and then ultimately a time for not meeting any more. For Bibi that time had come, so I told him that we had reached the end.

"This is the last time I am coming to see you. From now on I am not going to visit you any more because you know the way to Jesus. It is up to you now. You can choose if you want to follow him or not. You know about Him and you know I care about you. It's because I care about you that I don't want to see you again. I don't want to see you in this state any more; you don't need to be. When you are ready to change, this time you must look for me."

A week later Bibi came.

"I'm ready now," he said. "I've had enough. There's no way I can get off drugs myself. My family despises me. I can't stay at home because I've got to sell drugs to buy my own; I also have to be involved in the gambling dens because I need the money. Please, please help me."

We prayed together for a long time. Bibi was filled with the Spirit and began to speak in a new language. Then he looked at me and stated, "Now you've got to take me into your house." He meant that he wanted to be admitted to Third House. I took a deep breath and said, "I'm very sorry but there's no room."

Bibi was frantic and very angry; for him the chance to get into one of the houses of Stephen was his only escape left. He shouted, "But you have to let me go there: now I'm going to follow Jesus you can't expect me to live on the streets. I'll go on taking heroin there and you can't be a Christian and go on taking heroin."

He was right of course; and I pleaded for him with the Willans and the workers in Third House, but they turned me down. "We can't take him into the house because the house is not in good order," said Sarah.

"You just have to," I argued. "That's the whole reason why we have houses: they are there so that we can take care of the boys who come to Christ, so that they can grow up into a new life. Now you won't let me bring in boys because you want a nice tidy house."

She replied firmly, "It's not helpful to anyone at all to bring a boy into a house like this if the relationships are not solid enough to support him. He must wait until the boys we already have settle down. The houses are like a family; it's important to have the relationships right inside before we take in more people." She was right too: while I was desperate to bring people into the houses as soon as they became Christians her duty was to protect the family members. If I recklessly poured people in, the whole situation would become as chaotic as it had been before we had the houses of Stephen.

When they refused to take Bibi I had to go back and tell him that there was no room. We met at Ah Wong's noodle stall in the Lung Kong Road—you could get marvellous little *wunton* dumplings and noodles there. Bibi raged at me in desperation when he heard the news and I had to answer.

"Just for a moment, Bibi, take your eyes off yourself. Forget that our house is going to save you. Just look up at the sky. It's not a very beautiful sky down in Kowloon City, but just look up and imagine the One who made all of that sky, the heavens and the earth and the sea and the birds. He's the One who makes even the things like drops in buckets. And He stretches out the heavens like a tent, and makes the mountains and the animals and the flowers. That One actually chooses that His Spirit should live in us. He chooses that His Spirit should live in us rotten as we are. Why? Because Jesus left all that glory and walked through the miserable Walled City and got beaten up and killed and died and rose again so that we could have His Spirit. Isn't it amazing that the Spirit of the God who created the whole world should actually come to live in us? Just take your eyes off our house saving you; instead imagine the wonder of our God."

I left him there at the noodle stall praying, to talk with another addict who was pressurizing me to be admitted. Half an hour later when I came back to him I found him, eyes shut, with a soft smile on his face. I called to him but he did not reply. I called more loudly but still there was no answer. At my third shout Bibi very reluctantly opened his eyes.

"What did you see?" I asked him.

He told me that he had seen Jesus, at least he thought it was Jesus, wearing a long white robe. He had been on a mountain and Jesus had come towards him with his hand held out; He said to Bibi, "Bibi, will you follow me?"

Bibi replied, "Well, yes Lord, who else?" Jesus had taken him by the hand and led him along the most beautiful path. "I can hardly describe it." Bibi searched for words in his meagre experience. "It was so beautiful. There were lovely flowers and birds and it was very sweet smelling. It was the most lovely place. We walked along this path and I heard you calling but I didn't want to come back. I heard you calling again and I still didn't want to come back."

From that time onward instead of believing that our house was going to save him now that he was a Christian, he looked up again at his Creator to do so. His peaked face was illuminated by a glow. There was room for him in our Third

House just one day later, and he stayed for two years. He became one of the best boys we had, never difficult even when he was coming off drugs, which he did without so much as a headache. He simply got up and lived normally all through the withdrawal process. Bibi's family called Jean and Rick saying that Bibi's father was ready to die, so Bibi went to see him in the hospital. When he arrived his father who had come off opium himself and become a believer said simply, "Now Jesus has made my sons good, I'm ready to go to heaven." He kissed both his sons a tender farewell; but instead of dying, he was healed as his sons prayed for him and a week later he was discharged.

Now that I was freed of the need to be a home-maker because there were several of us working together at Stephen, I could go back into the streets. So many of the addicts passed on the word that people came from areas all over the colony asking for help. A converted policeman gave me a radio bleeper so that I could be reached any time, at any place, and I found myself more and more involved in the courts and prisons where so many of the boys were shocked into facing their problems. One day I attended a trial in Causeway Bay. As I was walking out after the case I heard a cry behind me.

"Poon Siu Jeh! I've been framed! Help me, help me!"

I looked around to see the next defendant being led into the dock. He was a stranger to me. I could see the desperation of his dirt-streaked face. It was a very cool air-conditioned court room and he was standing in the cotton shorts and singlet in which he had been arrested. The boy was still gesticulating wildly to me as the magistrate came into the court room to start the case. I had no means of knowing whether he spoke the truth or not, and no right to speak in court even if I had known. However, this unimpressive boy was about to go into battle alone, as there was no legal aid offered in Magistrates' Courts at that time, I stood up with an inspiration. "Your Honour," I said, "I am not familiar with the defendant but I think it possible that he has not had reasonable access to legal representation. Could you remand this case so that enquiries can be made on his behalf."

The magistrate raised his eyebrows. This was an unusual request coming from a layman. He turned to the defendant shivering in the dock. "Do you wish to be represented?" he asked him.

"Yes," replied the boy, "But I have not been allowed to make a telephone call since my arrest and so none of my family knows that I'm here."

The magistrate remanded the case for one day and I went down to the police cells below the court to talk to the boy. In the two minutes allowed me I learned that his nickname was Sorchuen, or crazy-boy Chuen, and that he knew of me through his Chaiwan brothers.

He was shaking violently and his stale sweat was sour, his eyes were red and running, and he sniffed constantly. I had one minute left.

"Listen to me. I have no time to tell you about Jesus but if you call on His name He will hear you and save you. He is God." Immediately under the astonished gaze of the prison guard his withdrawal symptoms vanished and his face relaxed. When I saw him next day he was still dressed in the dirty shorts and singlet but his face was clear and happy.

"I really did call upon Jesus and now feel quite different," he said.

Sorchuen was found guilty of the charges laid against him and went to prison briefly. Shortly after coming out he was arrested again and this time telephoned me from the police station. I went down to see him, with an excellent young solicitor who sometimes helped us. He had been arrested on a charge of attempting to break into several cars in the Shaukiwan district. According to him this story was quite untrue. He claimed that he had actually been watching a pornographic film called "Legends of Lust" several miles away in Wanchai. After the movie finished he boarded a fourteen-man bus for Chaiwan but was stopped on the way by two detectives who asked him to alight from the van and "talk". They asked him to help them find another Triad nicknamed *Morgwai*, or Devil, and drove him in a private car to a cinema looking for the Triad. Sorchuen saw a friend there but Devil could not be located so he was taken to the police station and booked on this charge, after signing some kind of incriminatory statement in the policeman's notebook.

Nearly every time that Sorchuen was arrested he yelled "Frame". He like many other boys claimed to have been beaten up to make a confession: I discovered that a good number of them were not beaten, but they were so sure of the inevitability of the beating that they convinced themselves that it had as good as taken place and signed statements incriminating themselves. A high proportion of defended cases contained a *voir dire*, a trial within a trial, to determine whether a confession was admissable as evidence. Many a defendant was convicted solely on the strength of his "confession" in a police notebook without witnesses, exhibits, or corroborative evidence.

David the solicitor and I decided to do some investigative work. David was willing to defend Sorchuen without fee provided he was convinced of his innocence, so he wrote to the police for the registration numbers of the cars which Sorchuen allegedly tried to enter. I went looking for Devil but found that he had just been arrested too. However I found the friend in Chaiwan who had been outside the cinema when Sorchuen arrived with the detectives looking for Devil. He remembered the time and the date; it was three hours before the official time when Sorchuen was arrested in Shaukiwan. While I made these enquiries Sorchuen was still in prison on remand and had had no opportunity to contact his friend; I was convinced that he was telling the truth as their testimonies were identical.

When we got the vehicle registration numbers we took a taxi to Sheko, where lived a boy who owned one of the cars involved in the alleged crime. He worked in a button factory in Wanchai, so we chased back, located the button-holer, and asked him where he usually parked his car. "Usually," he said, "in the Shaukiwan parking lot." But on the date of the crime it had not been there. Now we had a case, now we had witnesses.

All this fuss over such a minor case was unusual and the Attorney General's department was alerted. They sent counsel to conduct the prosecution. Usually in Magistrates Courts a police inspector fulfilled this function.

During a break in the case the prosecuting counsel asked to speak with me. I had noticed him becoming more and more tetchy as the morning proceedings crawled along. He was extremely annoyed at the detailed cross examination by the defence and kept looking at his watch.

"Why are you two going to so much trouble for such a minor case?" he asked. "We should have disposed of it by now. As it is we will have to continue into the afternoon; it is such a footling matter anyway."

I knew that I should not discuss this case but I said, "Should not one present the best case possible in the interests of the defendant?"

"Yes, but why waste time on such a case at all?" he objected, very upset at spending his valuable time on a trivial affair.

"Because I believe the defendant is innocent," I said.

He looked at me astounded. "That man has a record of a dozen or so convictions! Didn't you know?"

"Yes, I know. But we are talking about today's charges. I am sure he did not commit that crime."

"Well, my dear," the barrister was patronizing—"I've been in Hong Kong for six months now . . ."

However, it was one of the few cases I was involved with where the defendant was found not guilty. But as a rider, the magistrate also handed a bouquet to the police, who he said had done an excellent job and the fact that the accused had been acquitted reflected in no way adversely on their testimony.

I was landed with Sorchuen. Praying in the cells after our first meeting had taught him that Jesus was alive but he had yet to learn that the way to be His disciple was not by going to see "Legends of Lust".

Following this case David helped with several more and helped to pull off a legal "first" in Hong Kong. It was on the occasion when two Chaiwan boys along with some others were arrested for "claiming to be members of a Triad Society". The legal point was interesting: while you cannot be arrested for being a silent Triad member you can be arrested for claiming to be one. For this reason the police needed signed confessions for the charges to hold up. The two boys had signed alleged confessions in the police station but later said that they did so under duress and that they were taught what to write. The others pleaded guilty.

M.O.T.S. (member of Triad Society) cases, as they were known, were usually rapidly dealt with, but this one became extremely complicated. Both the boys charged had become Christians a year previously; a number of us were praying that this trial would somehow glorify God. One of the issues in the case was indeed a spiritual one; to join and remain an active member of a Triad Society was a self-commitment which could not be consistent with Christianity. To take part in a Triad initiation ceremony there was also blood letting, and an invoking of spirits which the law recognized as evil by defining it as an indictable offence.

The police produced their expert witness, a 426 Redpole fighter. He got up in court and gave his evidence.

"I am a 14K office bearer. I say that according to Triad rules you are always a Triad member—for ever. You cannot leave the Triads. Even though I now spend my life giving evidence at police trials I still remain an office bearer in the 14K."

The case for the defence rested on exactly opposite assumptions. We claimed that our boys were no longer Triad members because they had renounced their Triad membership by being baptized as Christians. The boys stated in court, "Yes, we were Triad members, but we are no longer." Our solicitor produced another expert witness, a Chinese language scholar, who pointed out that when the boys' confession had been translated as saying "I am a Triad member", the translation was open to question because there is no present or past tense in Chinese. We contended that what their statement meant was "Yes, I was a Triad member; yes, I did join a Triad society, but now I am not actively involved."

Then we produced yet another expert witness, Ah Kei, who held the same rank as the police witness in the 14K Triad Society. He rose to his feet in court and said, "I too am a 426 Redpole of the 14K, but I've become a Christian. I have renounced my entire gang; these two boys here on trial were my younger brothers. Since I have given up the gang I have told the members that I no longer hold responsibility for them; if they want to follow Christ they can, or else they can go their own way."

This clinched matters for the judge. He had been forced to spend hour after hour listening to talk of baptisms and conversions, whereas usually in Triad cases the accused are speedily found guilty or not guilty. He announced to the Court: "I see no reason why a man should be branded for life; if he wants to change and become a Christian, then good."

Then the judge turned and said, "And now, Miss Pullinger, it is your responsibility to see that they continue to follow what they are supposed to have confessed. Case dismissed."

One of the reasons why there were not more acquittals was that people in Hong Kong were very unwilling to give evidence in court. There was a deep distrust of legal proceedings and a feeling that every case was rigged. Being a fervent believer in the fairness of the British judicial system I tried to persuade them that if only they spoke for themselves or their friends with complete honesty they were bound to be justified. The fact that so many cases went against them was largely due to their own apathy; they contributed to the inequities of the system they so berated.

Through attending so many court sessions I began to notice some characters who seemed to appear with remarkable regularity. There was a little granny with a long plait down her back, a total of two teeth and a beautiful deeply lined and weathered face. She held what appeared to be a shopping list, and she sat in court each morning pleading guilty to at least twenty different hawking offences all under different names. As each one was called out she would raise her hand and squeak "*Yauh*" meaning "I'm here," and then mark off on her sheet of paper the amount to be paid. I discovered that this was her career; she no longer stood laboriously in the streets hawking her goods. Instead, for a small fee, she stood in for all her market friends at court so that they could continue their little businesses.

She had a male counterpart, a delightful seventy-year-old man who squatted outside the court room playing cards with his mates. He knew exactly when to go in for his hearing, and every week he was there. The charges were read out: "Smoking opium, and being in possession of instruments for doing so". He nodded happily. "Fifty-eight previous convictions for similar offences". He went on nodding and beaming. "A hundred dollars, or fifty dollars and one day in prison". He looked as if he would explode with joy and walked out smiling broadly. I mentioned to Ah Keung who was sitting with me what bad luck it was that he always got caught.

"Oh no, it wasn't an accident," laughed Ah Keung, "he is an 'actor'. He is paid to be arrested by the drug den owners." I learned that when the den operators were informed of a police raid they closed the premises leaving behind one old addict, who was then arrested and charged. Because of his age and number of convictions he was given a minimum sentence. The den paid him a hundred and fifty dollars for this and provided free opium so he was able to indulge his habit and after paying the fine, still make a small profit. The police were pleased, the operators were pleased, the actor was delighted, and Hong Kong's arrest tally impressive.

Ah Keung's father was one of those who would have nothing to do with the courts. He asked me on one occasion to help his fifth son Ah Pooi, who had been arrested for stealing a radio from an elderly man outside the Walled City. But at the exact time he was actually inside the Walled City talking to an old woman. The woman refused to be a witness as her job was to sweep a gambling den. His father also saw two detectives take him away from there but refused to give testimony on behalf of his own son.

"*Pa mah fan*, don't want to get involved, too much trouble." Since he was involved in illegal gambling himself and the den had some arrangement with some policemen he felt that keeping good relationships was more important than vindicating Ah Pooi. Nevertheless he hoped that I would help his innocent son. I explained that since he was withholding the vital evidence there was nothing I could do. He however had an unshakable conviction that I knew the judge and merely had to wink at him in court to free the boy. Had he known the judge he would have winked . . .

It was a hard line to take. I had to be careful not to be eaten up with anger over the injustice when truth was rejected. I also had to avoid being used as a source of free legal aid by rascals who had no desire to change. In one case a young man returned from seeing a solicitor I had recommended complaining, "He is no good. He did not even teach me a story to tell in court. What a waste of money."

Yet it was not a waste of time. Many people's lives were touched through the legal cases and if there seemed to be a lack of justification in earthly courts there was a growing number of people who understood being justified in heavenly ones. A reformed criminal Suenjai was a glowing example of this. He had led a straight life for ten years working very hard to support his wife and four young children. When he was arrested and convicted for a pick-pocketing charge I was certain he could not have committed it. It was a particularly cruel blow for him to be imprisoned for a crime he had not done.

Suenjai's wife contacted me and I visited him in remand prison. He was an angry and bitter man. He wanted to talk about his re-trial: I wanted to talk about Jesus. He did not want to be preached at and was still abrasive so I prayed. Then he stopped raging and became calm. I had no Bibles with me, only a little booklet containing extracts from the Sermon on the Mount. I did not feel this was very suitable, as it did not contain much about God's love and forgiveness, or the means of salvation; it was mainly "good work" teaching. However I had nothing else so I left it for him to read.

When I next went to visit a small group in the remand centre Suenjai was sitting amongst them. I asked them, "Why did Jesus have to die?"

He answered straight off with a most academic reply. "Because it says, 'Do not think that I have come to abolish the Law or the Prophets; I have not come to abolish them but to fulfil them. I tell you the truth, until heaven and earth disappear, not the smallest letter, not the least stroke of a pen, will by any means disappear from the Law until everything is accomplished.'"

Suenjai had never been to a Christian meeting in his life and had only studied four years of primary school but he had an amazing understanding of scripture. Jesus' Sermon on the Mount led him to belief. He asked Jesus into his life and received the Holy Spirit.

Shortly before his re-trial I asked Suenjai how he would present his defence. He said that previously he had been very angry and had lots of abusive things to say; he now decided not to present a defence apart from saying "not guilty". I began to advise him differently but he stopped me short.

"It says in the Bible 'Simply let your "Yes" be "Yes" and your "No" be "No"; anything beyond this comes from the evil one .'" I said no more.

He was found guilty. Although I was convinced he had been framed and was serving fifteen months for a crime he had not done, he remained cheerful and never stopped praising God. In fact his neighbours who heard about his demeanour at the trial were so impressed that they organized a meeting in a resettlement block and asked me and some of the boys to go and tell them about this Jesus who could change a hard man's heart.

One day Suenjai told me he'd led twelve prisoners to Christ. I was a bit doubtful as I knew that his theology was only based on three chapters of Matthew, a few visits from me and his own experience: he had never read *Personal Evangelism. Four Steps into Christ* or undergone a counselling course. So I questioned him about the circumstances.

"Well," he said, "one night one of my cell-mates woke up screaming. It was as if he had been grabbed by the neck and he began to writhe on his bunk and to suffocate. I could see he was in the grip of a spirit and couldn't breathe. So I got up and said, 'Satan, in the name of Jesus, get out!'— nothing happened. So I said, 'Get out, I tell you!' I made as if to kick the spirit and it left him so he lay quite relaxed and peaceful. At that, the eleven other cell-mates got up and asked me, 'What was that? How did you do that?' 'That was Jesus,' I replied and they said they wanted to believe, too, so I told them how."

Three days after his release Suenjai's wife ran away with another man and prostituted herself. He was then supporting and looking after eight children since his widower brother was a drug addict with four children. He remained faithful in prayer and in future meetings with his wife so impressed her with his compassion and forgiveness that she came back to him eventually. His family and friends despised him for the weakness of his approach to her. His behaviour was particularly remarkable in view of the Chinese culture that demanded divorce or a savage beating for errant wives.

For some time he continued the prayer meetings in his ten by twelve foot resettlement room, inviting all the neighbours. One ex-prisoner who attended explained, "I received Christ because I saw what happened to my friend after he believed in Jesus and I couldn't not believe."

Not only did God work miracles in the hearts of criminals but on several occasions He deeply affected others involved in the trial. When Ah Kit's case had come up in court Jean, myself and several members of our group went to listen. We prayed for a long time in the Spirit before arriving, and also silently in the courtroom.

After the verdict releasing him into our care was announced, the arresting police inspector came to chat with us and was extremely friendly and interested in our work. He suggested that we lunch together so that we could continue the talk. He liked talking and it was several hours later that he at last managed to say what was important to him.

"You know I feel terribly embarrassed saying this," he confessed in his charming Scots brogue, "but when you came into court this morning I looked at you and—well—it was like those Christmas cards . . . I know you'll laugh and I feel awfully silly saying this but—well—there was a halo over your head." Ted was a big man, a Hong Kong judo champion, second row forward in the police rugby team, and obviously serious. I did not feel a bit like laughing but swallowed several times.

We invited Ted to our usual Saturday evening prayer meeting, and he came gladly. I don't think I have ever seen anyone more knocked sideways by a prayer meeting. At the end of the meeting he was sitting there gasping. Jean chatted to him and gave him a drink and some canapés. He continued sitting there silenced for a while; then he said:

"You'll never believe me but that is the strangest Saturday I have ever spent in my life. Normally I'm out with the boys every Saturday night drinking. Tonight I have watched you people really inspired by something I don't quite understand."

I was relieved to hear him so positive because during the

meeting a girl had come up and asked him bluntly whether he was saved—I was worried lest he had been put off by such a direct approach. Clearly he had not been; so we sent him home with a copy of Jean's book.

All Sunday Ted read the book. He was most upset because he could not dismiss the evidence in it. Finally he got down on his knees and prayed. Then he rang us up and asked if he could come round, because he wanted to receive the baptism of the Spirit for himself. He said, "I just couldn't sleep. I kept thinking about last night. I came to the conclusion that either you are all completely crazy, or what you said is true. I've heard for myself people speaking in tongues: I've seen for myself the way these boys' lives have changed. So I came to the conclusion that Jesus has to be true. And if He was true that affected me and I asked him into my life this morning."

The following Sunday he was baptized in the sea together with a former gang member and his wife.

The C.I.D. officer's conversion became widely known. His friends could see that his life was completely changed in big ways like his general attitude to work and in small ways like no longer swearing in the rugby scrum. One of his superintendents joked with him at a match, "No praying in tongues in the scrum, Ted; it gives you an unfair advantage." Though the superintendent was joking, there was no doubt that Ted's conversion made a big impact on the Hong Kong police.

Not long afterwards, one of his C.I.D. colleagues who was opposed to Ted's conversion said, "At least I hope you are not trying to change me."

"No," replied Ted, "I'm not trying to change you. I know you'll be all right when you repent, so there is plenty of time."

"But what if I snuff it first?" said the C.I.D. scoffer.

"Well yes, there is that," said Ted.

Chapter 14

Set the Prisoners Free

One day I received a beautifully written letter from a Taiwanese man in the remand centre. When I saw him there I found a man full of spite and venom, with a white stripe round his uniform indicating that he was dangerous. He had faked illness and tried to escape from the hospital, attacking the guards in the process. He was sharing a cell with one of the Walled City boys who had told him about me.

I told Ah Lung about Jesus. It was a great disappointment to him since he had hoped to receive advice on how to get out of prison. However after listening he said he would like to believe; I told him he should be willing to forgive his prison guards and lay aside his bitterness.

"Huh! They treat us worse than animals!" he snorted. "Don't ask me to do that. I could never love them. You asked the worst thing you could ask me." "I'm sorry, Ah Lung," I apologized. "Of course you can't forgive them until you understand that you have been forgiven yourself." I told him that whatever he had done Jesus still loved him and would forgive his sins. I then prayed and felt impressed to speak in the language of the Spirit.

Ah Lung looked up at me. He interpreted very softly, "God has spoken to me and told me that He cannot forgive me if I do not forgive others. I freely forgive my prison guards." He meant it.

Ah Lung became a model prisoner as I learned from other inmates and prison officers. He changed his plea to "guilty" in court and sat there praying which amused the interpreter and infuriated the barrister who had prepared his defence.

"But," he said, wryly, "I had to admit I had done a lot of rotten things. I was a very mean man. When I heard Jesus speaking to me it was the first time in my life I've ever admitted I was wrong."

Ah Lung spoke to a nineteen-year-old youth awaiting trial for rape who joined us when I went to the remand centre one day for a Bible study.

"I've seen my friends here in prison and I've seen a very hard and a very bitter man and I saw what happened to Ah Lung when he believed in Christ. What is it that has made this hard man change into a soft-hearted man? I want to know this Jesus." I told him that Jesus was the One that came into the world and did all those miracles; He was the Son of Almighty God and yet died for sinners.

"Do you believe He's the Son of God?" I asked.

"Oh," he said, "I don't quite understand about that." His eyes were fixed on the prison table.

"Well never mind—are you willing to believe it?"

"All right."—He kept his eyes downcast.

"Do you believe that He died for your sins?"

"I don't understand that either." He was almost cowering he was so nervous.

"It does not matter if you don't understand completely— are you willing to believe it?"

"Okay." He was willing but still did not raise his head.

"Do you believe that He rose again from the dead?"

"Oh, yes," he said immediately and looked up at last.

"How are you so sure that Jesus rose from the dead and you're not sure about the other bit?" I asked curiously.

"If Jesus didn't rise from the dead you wouldn't be here talking to me in prison."

"Well, do you want to follow Him?" I asked.

He replied in the way that many of the gangsters replied, as if to a rather irrelevant question.

"If He is the true God—of course, who else am I going to follow?"

"All right. This Jesus will give you power because He doesn't expect you to live a Christian life by following a set of rules—it's impossible. He will give you His Spirit to help you," I explained.

He began to pray as God gave him his new language there in the prison.

Two weeks later I picked up a newspaper and read that there had been a dramatic change at his trial. He had gone up to the judge and said, "My solicitor has instructed me to plead not guilty but I have to tell you that I am guilty. I have come to believe in Jesus and I am guilty of this crime." He was sentenced to nine years in prison.

When I visited him there he smiled at me. "I have such joy to know that my sins are forgiven, Miss Poon," he said.

Though his wife and his child were killed in a fire one month later he never stopped believing and sharing Jesus with others because he said, "It's such joy to know that I am forgiven—Jesus took upon Himself even such a terrible sin as rape."

He discussed with me a chapter on redemption in the Bible until it was time for me to depart. It is hard for me to say who was the more edified by the visit.

This was in direct contrast with an incident two years previously in the same prison. When I visited Daih So, Ah Keung's eldest brother, I was not allowed to use a special room so saw him in the general visit room. It was bleak, cold and damp. The prisoners were separated from the public by a cage of wire with so fine a mesh that it was difficult to see their faces. I had to peer very closely because there was also a highly reflective pane of glass which made Bible study impossible.

Daih So was only thirty but as he had been taking heroin since he was thirteen he already looked an old man. Even during his father's funeral he dribbled continuously into a spittoon and had to go out several times for drugs. He was always drooping but I liked him very much, for a pathetic innocence which hung round him. He once gave me the clearest definition of sin I have ever heard, startling in its profound simplicity. I thought he would say, "Stealing, hitting old people, or pushing dope," when I asked him "What is sin?"

"That's simple," he replied. "Sin is walking your own road."

"It's no good talking to me, Miss Poon," he said that day in prison. "I'm not going to change in here. And don't tell me to get off drugs while I'm here either, because that's impossible."

When I looked at his arms they had several lines of fresh track marks running down them. He had gone into prison "chasing the dragon" but learned to inject inside since it was more economical and easier to take.

"Don't ask me to pray! Don't!" Daih So insisted. "And if you leave a Bible here for me, I shan't read it." He turned his back on me to make further conversation impossible and called a guard to take him away.

I left feeling desolated. I went away and prayed for him. This poor man was saying he could not stop taking drugs in prison—to follow Christ would cost too much.

About six months later I was in the Walled City and a plumpish stranger ran up to me and said: "Poon Siu Jeh! It's me, Daih So."

"Daih So! you're out of prison. When did you get out? And how come you look so fit?"

"Oh, I just got out of prison a few days ago and I wanted to come and tell you that on that day when you came to visit me and told me about Jesus I didn't want to hear. I called the warder to take me out and when I got to the door I looked back and I saw you sitting there looking sad. I felt really convicted in my heart suddenly and so I asked the jailer if he would bring me back because I could see you sitting there, but when I came back there was someone else there, so I did what you told me to. I went back to my cell and I prayed and I prayed in Jesus' name and I got off drugs."

We sometimes sent people towards jail rather than helped them out. Many of the boys who came to our house of

Stephen to withdraw from drugs had committed crimes for which they had never been arrested.

We did not always insist that they resolved every incident, as they had put the past behind them. However sometimes something continued to trouble them and they needed to make settlement on a human level.

Ah Wah wanted to go to the police station and give himself up for jumping bail in August. It turned out that he had been arrested in July for possession of dangerous drugs and released on bail on the understanding that he appear in court two weeks later. Of course, being a heroin addict, he had no intention of turning up. We did not know he had jumped bail and when he said that he really wanted to change his life to become a new person in Jesus he was admitted to the houses of Stephen in November.

As the months went on and he continued praying in the Spirit and reading scripture, his conscience began to bother him. Then came his confession of his outstanding court case. Jean thought that as I had been on the unhappy side of so many cases it should be left for me to tackle as a welcome change. As I talked to Ah Wah however I thought his chances of release rather slim: it became clear that not only was he liable to be sentenced for the drug case and jumping bail—but also that when he committed his last crime he was already on a suspended jail sentence. So under the law he was bound to go back to prison. Although I was really pleased that he wanted to give himself up it seemed unlikely that we could avoid his being taken into custody. I told him to pray, and all the boys in the houses also had a huge pray-in.

Although we prayed continuously in tongues all of that Monday morning we had quite a lot of difficulty getting him arrested. We could not start the Willans' car, so waited for a taxi. One hour later still no taxi. Finally we arrived at the police station where we were kindly asked to have a cup of tea and wait. We kept saying that Ah Wah wanted to be arrested, but they were not keen and could not find the papers, so sent us out to have lunch. When we came back they fingerprinted him to see if he really was the one on their files with nine previous convictions. He looked so good that the men taking his prints thought he had come to the police station to apply for a job. When he said "no" they thought it must be that he was applying for a gun licence. He eventually persuaded them that he was giving himself up for a drug offence, and told them how Jesus had changed him. Then they asked him to teach *them* how to take fingerprints as they had less experience than he.

Eventually we were all invited into a car and driven to court, praying all the while. The magistrate asked him why he had skipped bail and he told him, "Yes, it's true that I ran away last July. I was a drug addict and I'm sorry for offending the court. But now I have believed in Jesus I know I was wrong and I have come to give myself up."

"Congratulations. You have made a very sensible decision —and I wish you every blessing in your new life. You may go."

Ah Wah had only to sign a good behaviour bond, and never at any time did anyone lay a hand on him. His relief was enormous and there was great rejoicing in our houses when he returned. We had no calf to kill but we bought ice cream to celebrate.

In many ways it was easier for the boys to be Christians inside prison than outside. They suffered mockery but they also gained respect.

Through meeting so many prisoners I learned to distinguish between *hauh-fui* (regret) and *fui-goih* (repent). Most criminals regretted being arrested but very few really repented what they had done. Until this happened there was no hope at all that they would be able to live anything but a life of crime outside.

One such habitual offender was Ah Bill who stayed in my Lung Kong Road house for only ten days before deciding he could manage his own life. But he could not cope with freedom and its choices. He wrote me a letter from prison:

H.M. Prison Stanley

Dearest Pullinger,

I have left the people in the house [of Stephen] for a long time. Please, ask after every brothers for me. I also ask after you. Hope that Jesus will help you on everything.

I have to stay here for ten more months. Then I can have my new life over again. I hope that in this time I can make my last repentance and will be accepted by the Lord, so that my dirt can be cleansed. Can you pray for me?

Last time when you came to visit me, I was transferred to Cat A because I have done something wrong in the prison. But now everything is just O.K. After this punishment, I have learnt how to be obedient. Every time you visited us and have meeting with us, and explained the Bible and really considered our condition. But I still did not give hear and broke the regulations. I was ashamed of myself.

When I first entered the prison, I came to the chapel every Sunday and I prayed in tongues every night. Some people just said some bad things against me. For example: Ha, you believe in Christ, but you still have to stay in prison. You don't need any food if you believe in Christ, do you? There are many other bad words. But I did not want to write it down. I think you can guess some. At this moment, I was very angry. But when God's miracle came in my mind, I just neglected all their words.

I have written quite long already. I am now following Jesus. Lastly, I want to talk with those new brothers. It is time that God has given us many opportunities. But have we taken these seriously? Have tried to get Him? Although I have come across many difficulties, I could get a little bit of His grace. In the past, I have wasted my time and life in a wrong way.

I would be very happy, if I can receive your letter

on next month. And I would write back to you in order
to ask some question concerning about the Bible.
  Hope you have good health.

Ah Bill

Ah Bill was one of those who found it easier to be a
Christian inside prison. Like other recidivists he actually
looked relieved when he was inside. This was not because he
liked prison; in fact he hated it. But at least inside he was
spared the necessity of making all the daily decisions like
whether he should get up and whether he should go to work.
Each time he was released he found himself less and less
able to cope with the world outside.

When Ah Kit was released into our care he told me of this
friend Kwok whom he had met in prison. He was in very
serious trouble, for although he was a twenty-year-old policeman he was also a Triad and had taken part in a gang battle.
One of the rival gang members had been killed in the fight.
No one was quite sure who had actually put in the knife but
five boys were on trial.

I found a quiet country lad, the son of a chicken farmer
from the New Territories. He was courteous, clean looking,
but drawn and thin from the worry of the remand period.
Like all Chinese his eyes were dark but his were still blacker
with a bleak despair. When I told him about Jesus dying for
him he could just about understand and he could accept that
He was God's son too. But he repeated sadly, "What hope is
there for me—I mean what future?" I prayed quickly hoping
to give the right answer.

"Did you know that the two men in the Bible that God
used more than any other men in history were murderers?"
He looked stunned while I continued, "One was called David
and the other Paul. Paul was chosen to spread the news of
God's forgiveness to more men than any other man in history. He had murdered Christians: but God showed the
whole meaning of the Gospel when He used such a man."

When he heard this Kwok's face lit up and his black eyes

shone a little. "Do you mean," he exclaimed, "that as well as being forgiven I can have work to do for God?" This idea that he could be useful so encouraged Kwok that he prayed as if his heart would burst with joy.

Two days later I saw him again. He was positively glowing as he told me, "Miss Poon, I have such peace in my heart. It is what I have been looking for all my life. I know my past is forgiven and I have hope for my future. I do not fear the results of my case any more. If I am found guilty or not guilty I do not mind. I have hope." He talked as if we might never have the chance of meeting again, packing as many words as he could into the time.

He was sentenced to death the next day. I remember watching him as the verdict was announced. He was calm. But the other youth sentenced with him looked terrified. He immediately made a show of bravado and as he passed me in the Supreme Court lifted his handcuffed hands to his neck in a dreadful gesture meant to convey hanging. He laughed.

I was not allowed to see Kwok for two years, while they were deciding whether to execute him or not. Eventually his death sentence was commuted to life imprisonment . . .

When at last I went back to see him I was nervous because I had only seen him twice and told him very little. He knew that Jesus was God's Son and loved him and died for him and he had prayed and received the power of the Holy Spirit and that was all. I thought, "Poor boy, he does not know very much. He has not had a Bible all this time; no minister has visited him and maybe he does not really remember all that much about Jesus. He has probably forgotten all that I told him."

When I went in to the special little room provided I was not quite sure what I was going to meet. But he came running into the visit room and he was still absolutely radiant. I had never before seen such pure joy on a man's face. "Oh Poon Siu Jeh, it is absolutely wonderful," he gasped. He hardly paused for breath, he was so excited.

"I have got such peace in my heart; such joy to know

my sins are forgiven. I sit in my cell, every morning and every night and I pray. I do not know what I am saying because I am speaking in that language that God has given me but I know He understands what is in my heart and I have been telling all the other prisoners about Jesus and six of them have believed too and here are their names and here are their numbers."

He thrust a list at me and later I visited them. All of them were either long term prisoners or convicted killers and one of them was the mummer who had made the hanging gesture in court. They did indeed believe. Their teacher had known little with his head but much in his heart and I never met a group of men who understood better the meaning of Jesus giving up his life for them.

I gave Kwok a Bible and he had finished the New Testament within two months. He wrote his questions on a minute two-inch square scrap of paper and there was never enough time to talk. He had read through the New Testament twice before he had time to ask, "Excuse me, Miss Poon, but what is a Gentile?" His converts grew well too and since all were baptized in the Holy Spirit they used these gifts quite freely. They had their own songs which the Spirit gave them as they prayed and they prayed for one another when they were sick.

One day I visited Kwok when I was a little tired and worried that I would not be allowed to see him and his friends again. "Don't worry about us, Poon Siu Jeh," he told me and smiled encouragingly. "We're all right here. We're praying for you." They are the freest men I know.

I received several letters from them and some of the young people in our group helped me to write return letters or wrote themselves since my written Chinese was still very poor. The English was delightful as they lifted whole phrases out of dictionaries or the Bible, or else the students translated the Chinese themselves, word by word. William was one of the students.

Dear William:

It is with much pleasure to hear from you and thanks be to the Lord Jesus Christ, for by His Wonderful name we know each other, Praise God!

In reading your letter, I was so delight to communicate with you and I want to thank you for writing me giving me so great encouragement and message in understanding the love of God—thank you! You know, Jackie uses to come and visit us in the prison every month even it is in hottest day; preaching and explaining us the Gospel. And there, we find not a word could be good enough to tell you how great is her kindness to us! We really feel deeply impressed by this—the wonderful love of God. Everytime she comes to see us, we would be very happy and there we would ask her many questions in the Bible and she would be very willingly to give us every details and explanations and that is why we never find time enough for us to be with her. Now and then I greatly believe in what the Bible says that Jesus Christ is truly died for us and I sincerely hope to do my best for Him.

It is through the power of the Holy Spirit, God gives me very many oportunately to witness to others here and many of them wish to see Jackie but I did not dare to give any answer or even tell Jackie about this, for I sense that they are asking this on purpose. I know there is nothing I can do about this and I just pray that the Holy Spirit will touch them and that they would be changed perfectly.

Now I have to close my words because it is very late at night. Please pray for us here and greets to you in His name. KWOK.

On the first occasion I had visited Ah Lung there was another white-striped Taiwanese prisoner who was on trial for bringing into Hong Kong the largest amount of heroin ever discovered on a ship. He was the second officer and he started to discuss his case with me as soon as we met.

"I'm sorry I cannot discuss court cases with you," I said. "The only reason I am allowed in here is to talk about Jesus."

"But I cannot be a Christian," said Go Hing. "Let me tell you a story." He told it in Mandarin Chinese with the odd word in English.

＊　　　＊　　　＊

Over twenty years ago there was a family who fled from mainland China and ended up as refugees in Taiwan. In this family there was a young boy, about four. He ran away from home one day with a young friend and went to play at the school house. There was a large water pool there and as he was playing with his friend, he fell in. The little boy's friend was so frightened because he knew they should not have been playing there that he ran away and did not tell anyone.

Several hours later the Headmaster got back to the school and saw to his horror and distress the body of a child floating in the water. He fished him out, but was unable to revive him. Recognizing the child, he sent for his parents and the mother arrived beside herself with grief that this beloved son of hers had died. She insisted that they take him to hospital. Of course, it was too late to save him and the doctors certified him dead but she would not believe it so she took him to another hospital where he was again certified dead. Sadly she took the body home as is the Chinese custom and dressed him in his burial clothes. She was going to sit by the body all night keeping vigil.

In the middle of the night the boy sat up, looked at his mother and said, "Why am I dressed in these clothes?" She could not believe what she was seeing. She thought it was a vision. She said, "Do you remember falling into the pool?" and the little boy said, "Yes, I remember, and I remember I was going down in the water and I opened my mouth to shout for help and the water went in and then I saw a man come."

The mother interrupted him to ask, "A man—who was he?"

"Well, he came and he held out his hand to me and he pulled me out of the water," he said.

The mother supposed that the boy had seen the Headmaster so she asked, "Do you know his name?"

"Don't you know?" replied the boy, "It's Jesus." The family had never heard Jesus' name before. They had no contact with Christians but from that time onwards the mother and the whole family became disciples of Jesus.

* * *

Go Hing told me this story very dramatically and very emotionally. Then he looked at me and asked, "Do you know how I know that story is true? I was the boy. I was brought back from death and since that time my family have been Christians. That is why I cannot be a Christian because I knew the truth and I have not followed Jesus."

"I've got very good news for you," I told Go Hing, "Jesus doesn't expect us to follow Him in our own strength, so if you are prepared to tell Him that you are sorry and ask forgiveness then He will forgive you. You can start again and He will give you the power to help you follow Him. The power is His Holy Spirit. He will give you a new language to help you talk to Him because there will be so many things in your heart that you will want to tell Him after all this time."

I could not lay hands on him under the gaze of the curious prison guard but as we prayed together he began to pray in tongues and he then began to cry.

He looked up afterwards and said, "That's the first time that I've cried since I was a boy. I feel so happy. I know Jesus is with me now."

I went back to see him some days later and told him, "You know you have to tell the truth in court. You have to tell the truth."

"I'm too frightened to tell the truth, I can't."

"You have to tell the truth. You are a Christian now."

"I can't because if I plead guilty to this case I'll be killed. According to Taiwanese law, whatever country you commit a crime in you are liable to be sentenced again in Taiwan even if you have already served a sentence. In Taiwan they still execute a man for drug peddling, armed robbery and for murder. So I can't plead guilty."

"I'm not your solicitor, I'm not giving you legal advice," I told him. "I'm just telling you that you have to speak the truth. You know Jesus saved your life and you can't go only halfway with Him."

He was found guilty and he was given twelve years in prison. I wasn't able to see him for some time but just before I went back to England, I was allowed to visit him in Stanley prison. As I looked at him through the panel he began to cry, but he was smiling.

"Because you are going, I just have to tell you this," he said. "I am known as a very hard man. I've been a seaman for many years and I'm not afraid of the great wind, and I'm not afraid of the big waves; when my father died I didn't cry; when I was arrested and I knew I would not see my wife and children again for many years, I didn't cry. There are only two occasions in my life when I've cried. One occasion was when you came to the prison before my trial and I received Jesus and His Holy Spirit, and the other occasion is today. But today I'm crying with joy because I know my sins are forgiven. There is one thing more I must tell you before you go. When you kept telling me I must tell the truth, I had no intention of doing so, but I was praying and I made a bargain with God. I said, "Okay, if she comes to see me today, I'll tell the truth this afternoon." You came, so I went and I disclosed to the police that there was as much heroin on the ship that had not yet been found as had been found. Nobody was pleased with that. Of course, my own people were furious because they had a fortune hidden away, and the police were not pleased because they were made to look foolish. The judge was very angry because the amount of

drugs was so enormous and gave me a very heavy sentence."
He smiled at me as he finished. "I have a heavy sentence
here on earth but my sins are forgiven and I go to heaven.
Better that than I have a light sentence here on earth and go
to hell."

Chapter 15

Walk in the Spirit

A delightful American sailor once took me to task about my praying in tongues. He thought I went on about it far too much. He had this gift himself, but he felt it should only be used sparingly for spiritual highs and for special occasions. I explained to him that one reason why God was able to use me was because I kept in touch through using this gift all the time. I prayed in the Spirit as I went around the Colony — in buses, on the boats, and walking along the streets, very quietly under my breath. That way it is possible to pray all the time. I offered, if he had time, to take him on a day-long tour of Hong Kong while we prayed continuously.

The next day we met up and walked down through Western District to the waterfront. The route reminded me of my first few days in Hong Kong when I began to see beneath the tourists' glamorous facade to the dirt, poverty and struggle, the ceaseless work and more work.

In one steep stepped ladder-street I passed an old man living in a cupboard five feet high, six feet long and three feet deep. He sold vegetables from his cupboard by day and climbed on top of them to sleep at night as there was nowhere else for him to live. With four and a half million people crammed into every available square foot, whole families in Hong Kong had to live in one room: this man had no family.

Further down the street I found an old lady holding out a plastic rice bowl. No one in Hong Kong had money or rooms to spare and there were no pensions either so she stayed alive by begging. There were so few old people's homes that she had not a hope of getting into one.

Walking on I saw a little girl of about five years old with a child strapped on her back, because both of her parents had to work long hours to support their children. Nobody looked after the dirty little five year old—she was looking after the baby.

Then I passed a teenage boy who paid rent for the privilege of sleeping on a four-foot shop counter. He had stopped school at the end of his primary years when he was about thirteen. He was bright and wanted to continue school but his parents took him away to work. When he got his job he gave all his money to them so that they could send all his younger brothers and sisters to school. Every time I walked past him he asked me to practise English with him to help him to get a better job.

I reached the end of the street feeling that if I spent my entire life down there I could just about get to love this street—I could just about get to love all the people and know them and their needs. But when we turned into the next street, it was a duplicate of the first and beyond that yet another. More people . . . I told the American sailor how I had prayed during the early days asking God to show me which bit of His work was mine; He had answered by sending me to the Walled City, and the miraculous events of the next dozen years. I could never have dreamed of anything so extraordinary and wonderful.

My sailor was as overwhelmed by this sight of Hong Kong as I had been. But the purpose of our day was to encourage him to walk in the Spirit so I began to pray as we went. We crossed the harbour and arrived at Jordan Road, an area I knew well as I had lived there for a while. I took him inside a building that boasted both brothels and ballrooms. It was a place where heroin addicts hung out, looking deathly sick and half-starved. We walked up the back staircase; there were various people sleeping on the stairs and we picked our way over the bodies, looking for a large tramp. I had come to find Mau Wong, the "King of the Cats"; he was much fatter than the others there because he was a "protector" for various prostitutes, and so earned quite a lot of money.

We found Mau Wong in an extremely unhappy state: he had a terrible stomach-ache and was sweating profusely and retching. He could not listen to me telling him about Jesus, so the young American and I laid hands upon him and prayed quietly in the Spirit for his healing. Very quickly his pain vanished, and a look of great surprise crossed his features. He could hardly believe what had happened to him, but he was now ready to sit down and listen. He accepted Jesus, and was baptized in the Spirit then and there. We had hardly finished praying when he got up, ran away and re-appeared bringing with him a pathetic specimen of a man with sunken cheeks. Mau Wong explained that this friend had tooth-ache; would we pray for him too? So we took him up onto the roof of the building which was flat and empty and prayed with him also. He was healed at once, then we told him who Jesus was and what Jesus had done for him. He was ready to receive Christ and His Spirit and did so straight away. Then I had a message in tongues, and Mau Wong, the "King of the Cats", was able to give the interpretation about repentance which thrilled him very much.

I was to visit Mau Wong on the back staircase several times to tell him more about Jesus; the second time I met him he gave me a knife and various equipment for smoking heroin, which he asked me to dispose of. He explained that now he was a Christian he had to earn his living in an honest way, so he had bought some shoe brushes, and was going to become a bootblack.

The young American and I left Mau Wong to continue our tour of Hong Kong; we crossed back over the harbour and took a minibus to Chaiwan. All the time I was praying aloud but quietly so that no one could hear. My sailor had thought that praying on buses was a bit much but after seeing what had happened at Jordan Road he began to join in too. The whole day we prayed without ceasing except to eat and to talk to those we met along the way.

At Chaiwan we headed for a drug den, which was quite a dangerous place for the young American to go. But they welcomed us both as if they had been waiting to hear about Jesus, and we had been anxiously expected. "Poon Siu Jeh, can I have a Bible?" asked an addict.

"How can I start a new life?" asked another.

"Am I too old to be saved?" enquired an old man. "Where can I hear about Jesus and learn doctrine?"

"There is no need to wait until you go to a meeting to hear about Christ. I'll tell you now," I said to him. I sat down and talked while a small crowd gathered and listened. The old man listened wonderingly to Bible stories and accepted Jesus like a little child. He renounced his petty fencing business and became a very regular attender of the Saturday meetings.

As we left the den we were followed by Ah Wing, a mean man who sold heroin, killing others' bodies as well as his own. He came to eat noodles with us, through no good motives at all—he just wanted a free meal. I was telling him about Jesus and he was hurrying this bit through to get to the noodles.

"Are you willing to believe that Jesus is the Son of God?" I asked him. "I'm not sure," he replied, "maybe."

I didn't think he was all that convinced but I went on to the next question.

"And do you believe that He died for you?"

"Don't understand that."

"Well never mind, are you willing?"

"All right," he mumbled.

"Are you willing to believe that He rose again from the dead?"

"Well, I suppose He must have," he acquiesced, "because I've heard of the things He is doing."

"Are you willing to follow Him?"

He answered scathingly. "Oh yes. I mean, if he is the true God, of course."

"Ah Wing, why don't you ask God if Jesus is His Son or

not? I am sure He will let you know," I suggested and began to pray quietly, motioning the American to join us.

As we prayed there at the noodle stall, Ah Wing joined in with us gently and confidently in tongues.

After a few minutes I lifted my head thinking we had done enough praying at that stall even for me. When I looked at the drug peddler I saw he was still praying, on and on and on. My sailor had moved one seat further away trying to pretend that he did not belong to us, though it was difficult for him to disown me in an area where there were no other Westerners. His attitude changed when he looked up to see the extraordinary expression on Ah Wing's face as he prayed. He had a look which was seraphic: when eventually he looked up after about twenty minutes, I asked him, "What did you see?"

"Well," he said, "when I was praying I saw what was like a picture and I think it was Jesus. He was sitting at a table, a long table; there were several other men around; I think there must have been about a dozen or so. They were passing around some bread, and then a wine cup, and drinking from it."

I explained to him the meaning, that Jesus was giving His body and His blood for us and rejoiced that God should have revealed Himself to Ah Wing through the breaking of bread.

Two more people were converted later on our walk and my American friend needed no more convincing about praying in the Spirit.

When I got back home and told Rick and Jean about Ah Wing and the others they groaned and said "Oh no! —anyone else and we'd be pleased—but yours are all addicts and where are we going to put them?"

We often had no room to house those we had brought to faith in Christ. Ever since Winson and Ah Ming I felt that I was responsible for the welfare of each believer until his life was straightened out, but each one needed so much care: most had no homes, no clothes and suffered from severe personality problems as well as drug addiction and disease.

I felt that I must go back to Chaiwan to look for Ah Wing so that I could do some "follow-up". I did not see him but found an old acquaintance, Ah Kwan, talking in a drug den with some wholesale drug peddlers. They were all being very "nice" to me, but I felt impelled to say that although Jesus loved them, and I did, too, I thought their business stank. Ah Kwan who had joined the peddlers said he would "repent" the week after because he needed three days' money first. (He lived in a wooden hut with a plastic tarpaulin for the roof, five buckets to catch the water, a tired wife of only twenty-five and four children under six. They had no income.) I told him that no one chooses when to repent, and that if he did not follow Jesus immediately and come with me, that he would be in jail within days. He was caught four hours later and sentenced to thirty months. So the word was out in Chaiwan that I was a prophet, and they began to be more careful about talking to me!

I never saw Ah Wing the drug peddler again and could not tell what happened to him afterwards. But I trusted fully that since God loved him better than I, He would definitely take care of him better than I. I had come full circle: I first believed that God would heal all addicts instantly; then I believed that they could only survive if I provided a safe environment; and then I trusted again that I could leave them completely safe in His care.

The sailor wrote to the Willans asking if he could come and help our work when he came out of the navy two years later. They replied by saying that by that time we might have five houses, fifty houses or none at all. Since none of us was called to do drug addict work but to preach Jesus we did not feel we should necessarily perpetuate the programme lest it become a burden. We would therefore be open to whichever way God moved, whether it would be into China or a dozen more flats for boys . . .

Goko's second real brother came back from Canada. He was tall and suave, dressed in an immaculate suit. We met when Johnny married a Christian nurse from the hospital where he worked. Johnny had invited the members of his old gang so that his wedding could be a witness to them.

"I have to shake you by the hand, Miss Pullinger," Goko's brother said in perfect English. "I grew up with the boys in the Walled City and I determined to study law so that I could come back and help them. But now I am back I see that there is nothing left for me to do. You have done it all. I must shake you by the hand." Quickly I disclaimed the praise, telling the brother Who had done all the work.

We walked together down the Walled City streets towards the club room. They were empty now as many illicit businesses had ceased. This was due partly to the success of the anti-corruption commission but also partly to the fact that so many of the 14K boys had become Christians. There was a local story that Sai Di, the number two in influence had telephoned a 14K cousin across the harbour and asked to borrow some brothers for a gang fight.

"Sure," replied the other leader who knew of both Goko and Sai Di's reputation, "but what about your own gang?"

"Well," replied Sai Di, "half of them are drug addicts, the other half are Christians, and they are all lousy fighters."

Goko's Canadian brother walked into the Club room and approved it. Night after night he appeared for the singing and then talked to me.

One day he asked, "What do you do for money?"

I was a bit off hand and answered tritely: "Oh God looks after us. We pray for it."

"Okay, okay—but *practically* speaking from where? It does not just fall down from heaven, does it?"

"Well, it may do," I said, and at that moment there was a knock on the door and in came an old man. He lived in a little cubicle in the Walled City, into which he could just squeeze to sleep. He handed me a grubby envelope.

"Poon Siu Jeh," he said, "I was walking along the street and somebody gave me this letter." I looked at it; it was addressed in English, 'Jackie Pullinger—Walled City'—that was all. There were few post boxes in the Walled City and it was a dangerous place to send letters anyway. No one there knows English, so how he got my letter was a mystery. I opened it up and there were one hundred American dollars from a man I had neither met nor heard of in Hawaii. I showed it to Goko's younger brother and he held up his hand as if calling a truce and said, "Enough said, point taken."

He went off home and left me to walk down the streets alone. Past the prostitutes, past the blue films, the gambling dens and drugs. Past Ah Keung's house where I had sat with him on the night his father died, watching the body and listening to the howls of the dogs as they were beaten to tender flesh for the cookpots; past the gambling dens. I passed the spot where one year previously I had witnessed the beginning of a vicious fight between two knife-wielding strangers.

"Stop. Don't fight," I had said feeling sick. Two minutes later an emissary was sent along the street to calm me down.

"We are sorry, Miss Poon," he soothed, "it won't happen again. We did not know you were here."

I walked out of the city and looked at the rubble where the Lung Kong Road house had stood and thought of Goko who now lived in the opposite building. His wife had gone missing a few months earlier after gambling away a large amount of his money in one of his dens: she was too frightened to return, knowing that he would beat her. She stole the four-year-old son of his former mistress and hid out in an apartment house. When she phoned him she said that she would return his son if he promised pardon. Goko was uncompromising. He promised no such thing and set his Triads to work tracing apartment houses, which would not take long through the Triad affiliations. His wife did not wait to be found however: terrified of her husband she drank poison and then forced the little boy to drink too, so killing them both.

I made a point of seeing Goko about once a year and when we next met for tea I offered him my sympathy. He had lost weight. He sneered at the mention of his wife but I guessed the hurt at the loss of his son. I saw the fear of being alone too, and because I wanted so much to reach him I told him I knew of his fear. He was surprised but he also longed to confide in someone.

"How do you know? I've never before told anyone I am afraid," he admitted. "I feel so lonely."

A double funeral and a luxury burial had been held, as part of keeping face before his Triad brothers. Goko told me he never confessed his emotions to another soul.

Goko and Sai Di voiced similar attitudes about Christ, although their Canadian brother believed openly.

"I'm not saying I don't believe in Jesus—I've watched those who do. But I've also watched you Christians and noticed that most of you have jobs with poor pay. I cheat, lie, and steal in order to provide for all my dependants, and I know Christians don't do these things. So I'm not going to be one because I'd want to be a real one. I understand that Jesus can provide for me but I need to be sure He can support my followers."

I have always respected the brothers' position and have prayed for them to see God as big enough to care for all their needs. Certainly neither would ever make a commitment lightly. More than once in conversation with Goko I have heard him say "O.K. If that brother wants to be a Christian, O.K. But let him follow Jesus good. I don't want him gone tomorrow and back the next day. If he is to be a Christian let him be a good one."

I left Goko's house behind me and headed back towards the houses of Stephen where those of the boys who continued to walk in the Spirit became fine and trustworthy men. Those who had known Christ but who left prematurely to follow their own desires got into trouble. One Chaiwan addict summed it all up when he applied to enter one of our houses;

"I have heard that Jesus does the same miracle for each boy who comes to your place. But whether or not you choose to continue is up to you."

Biblical References